Multicultural America

Multicultural America

AN ENCYCLOPEDIA OF THE NEWEST AMERICANS

Volume 2

Ronald H. Bayor, Editor

 GREENWOOD

AN IMPRINT OF ABC-CLIO, LLC
Santa Barbara, California • Denver, Colorado • Oxford, England

Library of Congress Cataloging-in-Publication Data

Multicultural America : an encyclopedia of the newest Americans / Ronald H. Bayor, editor.
    v. cm.
  Includes bibliographical references and index.
  ISBN 978-0-313-35786-2 (hard copy : alk. paper) — ISBN 978-0-313-35787-9
(ebook)   1. Cultural pluralism—United States—Encyclopedias. 2. Multiculturalism—United
States—Encyclopedias.   3. Immigrants—United States—Encyclopedias.   4. Ethnology—
United States—Encyclopedias.   5. Minorities—United States—Encyclopedias.   6. United
States—Ethnic relations—Encyclopedias.   7. United States—Race relations—Encyclope-
dias.   I. Bayor, Ronald H., 1944-
  E184.A1M813 2011
  305.800973—dc22   2011004677

ISBN: 978-0-313-35786-2
EISBN: 978-0-313-35787-9

15   14   13   12   11   1   2   3   4   5

This book is also available on the World Wide Web as an eBook.
Visit www.abc-clio.com for details.

Greenwood
An Imprint of ABC-CLIO, LLC

ABC-CLIO, LLC
130 Cremona Drive, P.O. Box 1911
Santa Barbara, California 93116-1911

This book is printed on acid-free paper ∞

Manufactured in the United States of America

Contents

Egyptian Immigrants

by Caroline Nagel

Introduction

There are believed to be at least two million Egyptians today who live outside the Arab Republic of Egypt, making it one of the major sources of migrant workers in the contemporary global economy. The labor of these migrant workers brings in billions of dollars to the Egyptian economy—a crucial source of foreign exchange in an economy that has struggled for decades to generate sufficient jobs for its rapidly growing population. The vast majority of Egypt's workers can be found in the Arab world, especially in oil-producing countries like Libya and Saudi Arabia. But a significant number have traveled farther afield, finding employment opportunities in the United States, Canada, Britain, and Australia. In the United States, many of these workers have settled permanently and have naturalized as American citizens. They tend to be found in the higher echelons of the labor market working in medicine, engineering, business, and other professions.

By many socioeconomic measures, Egyptian Americans can be considered a successful immigrant group. Egyptian Americans, however, face some challenges that bear upon their well-being in the United States. In addition to the difficult adjustments that most immigrants face upon moving to a new society, Egyptian Americans must also negotiate a social and political context in which Arab and Muslim identities—both of which are important to many Egyptians—are seen by some to be at odds with so-called American values. This has especially been the case since the terrorist attacks of September 11, 2001, an event that left many Muslim and Arabic-speaking immigrants feeling embattled and insecure. Since 2001, their efforts to legitimize their presence in the American tapestry and to formulate an American identity has taken on a new urgency, as it has for immigrants from Lebanon, Iraq, Palestine, and other Arabic-speaking countries.

The issue of identity among Egyptian Americans becomes very complex when we consider the diversity that exists among them. For instance, while most Egyptian Americans are Muslim, there is a significant Coptic Christian community that maintains strong ties with Egypt through the Coptic Church hierarchy. Tensions between Copts and Muslims in Egypt have carried into the U.S. context, rendering relationships between diasporic Egyptians—and hence, Egyptian American identity—problematic. At the same time, there is growing diversity among Muslim

Egyptians, with some adhering to a secularist identity that confines religious practice and identity to the private realm, and others staking their claim in public life on the basis of their Muslim identity. This essay explores these complex dynamics and the range of experiences that emerge from them.

Chronology

1805	Formation of Egyptian state virtually independent of the Ottoman Empire.
1882	Battle of Tel el-Kebir, in which Britain establishes de facto control over Egypt.
1922	Egyptian parliament unilaterally declares independence from Britain.
1952	Coup d'état by Free Officers Movement deposes British-supported King Farouk.
1956	Assumption of power by Gamal abd al-Nasir and nationalization of Suez Canal.
1967	Six Day War between Arab armies and Israel.
1971	Succession to power of Anwar Sadat, followed by the initiation of pro-Western economic and foreign policy.
1975	Codification of the Egyptian Nationality Law, granting Egyptian citizens the right to dual citizenship.
1978–1980	Eruption of violence against Copts in Upper Egypt.
1981	House arrest of Coptic Pope Shenouda III and banishment of Coptic organizations by the Sadat regime.
1981	Assassination of Anwar Sadat and succession of Hosni Mubarak.
2005	Fifth consecutive "election" of Hosni Mubarak to the Egyptian presidency.
2009	U.S. President Barack Obama gives his Muslim World speech in Cairo, seeking better relations between the Arab/Muslim world and the United States.
2011	Mass demonstrations against President Mubarak take place in Cairo, Alexandria, and other Egyptian cities following popular uprisings in Tunisia. President Mubarak forced to step down after weeks of protest, leaving the country in a fragile political state.

Background

Geography

The Arab Republic of Egypt covers an area of 390,000 square miles on the northeast corner of the African continent. It is bordered on the north by the Mediterranean Sea, on the northeast by Israel and the Palestinian-administered Gaza Strip, on the east by the Red Sea, on the south by Sudan, and on the west by Libya. Egypt is one of the most populous countries in Africa and the most populous in the Arabic-speaking world. The vast majority of the population lives within a few miles of the Nile River, which has been the lifeblood of civilization in Egypt for over 8,000 years. The great monuments of Egypt's ancient civilizations still stand along the Nile, drawing in thousands of tourists every year and contributing significantly to the Egyptian economy.

Egypt's cultural landscape bears the imprint of many non-native groups who have conquered and occupied Egypt over the centuries, including the Persians, the Greco-Macedonians of Alexander the Great, the Romans, the Byzantines, the Arabs, and the Turks. Arab Muslim rule, which lasted from the seventh century C.E. to 1250 C.E., had especially lasting legacies, including the spread of Islam and the use the Arabic language in Egypt. Today, the official language of Egypt is Arabic, and the Egyptian population is around 90 percent Muslim. Egypt is also home to al-Azhar, one of the oldest institutions of higher learning in the world and the preeminent center of Islamic scholarship.

An important element of pre-Islamic heritage, however, remains firmly grounded in Egypt in the form of the Coptic Orthodox Church, whose members constitute about 10 percent of the Egyptian population. According to church tradition, the Coptic Orthodox Church was founded in the first century C.E. by St. Mark the Evangelist, and it is considered to be one of the oldest Christian churches in the world. The Coptic Church uses a liturgical language rooted in the language spoken in ancient Egypt. Early in its history, Coptic Christians devised a modified Greek alphabet to write the language. Under Muslim rule—first Arab and then Turkish—the Copts had the status of *dhimmis,* or members of a protected religious minority group. While in certain respects they were treated as second-class citizens, they also managed to rise to positions of political and economic prominence. Overall, Copts have occupied a similar range of socioeconomic levels as their Muslim compatriots, and outside of their liturgy, Copts speak Arabic and partake in most of the same cultural practices as Muslims. But as will be described in greater detail below, relations between Muslims and Copts have deteriorated since the 1970s, and violent attacks against Copts in Egypt have encouraged the migration of thousands of Coptic Christians to the United States and Canada.

There is also a long history of Jews in Egypt, dating back to at least the 4th century B.C.E. Sephardic Jewish communities were joined in the early 20th century by

Ashkenazi Jews fleeing persecution in Europe. Like Egypt's Christians, the Jews enjoyed a relatively peaceful existence for centuries, and many achieved positions of influence and power; but they also endured discrimination and periods of persecution. Although some Egyptian Jews were involved in Egyptian nationalist movements, the creation of the state of Israel made life virtually impossible for them in Egypt after the World War II. From a population of perhaps 80,000 in the early 20th century, there are believed to be only a few hundred Jews remaining in Egypt today.

One of the most notable features of modern Egyptian society has been the exponential increase in its population. In 1800, an estimated 3 million people lived in Egypt. The size of the Egyptian population doubled between 1897 and 1947, and nearly doubled again by 1976. By 1986 the population was 50.5 million; the population today is estimated to be over 80 million people. Much of this population growth has been channeled into urban areas. In 1907, for instance, approximately 17 percent of the Egyptian population lived in cities; by 1960, this figure was 30 percent. Today, over half of Egyptians live in urban areas (Feiler 1992). With limited land and water resources available for physical expansion, Egypt's cities, and especially the capital, Cairo, are among the most densely populated urban centers in the world. While efforts have been made to improve city infrastructure, Egyptian cities are notorious for their crowded conditions and inadequate transportation networks. Egypt ranks 112th out of 177 countries according to the United Nations Human Development Index, which measures life expectancy, literacy, per capital income, and the like. Average life expectancy is 70.7 years, which is well above many countries in sub-Saharan Africa, but below that of wealthy postindustrial societies. The literacy rate is 71 percent. These general statistics, of course, mask many inequalities in Egyptian society—inequalities that have become more pronounced since the 1970s.

Egypt's contemporary economy rests on a combination of tourism, energy production (especially natural gas and hydro-electric power), manufacturing, and revenues from shipping traffic through the Suez Canal (a shipping channel connecting the Red Sea and the Mediterranean that was built in the 19th century with French capital and expertise). The country also has a strong media sector, and Egypt is a center of Arabic-language cinema, literature, and entertainment. Cotton production, while no longer the mainstay of the economy as it was in the 19th century, remains significant, and there is also a small but growing technology sector. While the economy is fairly diversified, a major problem is the inability for economic growth to keep pace with the population, leading to large-scale unemployment and underemployment. Free-market–based reforms intended to spur economic growth have, in many cases, served to exacerbate the inequalities created by this scenario. This pattern, as we will see below, has been an important factor in creating large-scale migrant outflows from Egypt.

History of Egypt

Egypt's modern history is very much tied to the broader history of the Arabic-speaking world, but also unique within it. Like much of the Arab world, it was incorporated into the Ottoman Empire in the 16th century, but it attained virtual independence within it by the early 19th century, under the modernizing leadership of Muhammed 'Ali (1805–1848). Long connected to the European economy through the production of cotton, as well as through its indebtedness to European banks, Egypt came under British colonial domination in the 1880s. By the early 20th century, anticolonial nationalist movements began to emerge among members of the educated urban classes, even as European social, political, economic, and legal norms became more deeply embedded in Egyptian society. Egypt gained formal independence from Britain in 1922, but remained under Britain's sphere of influence until 1952, when nationalist forces, led by General Gamal 'Abd al-Nasir, deposed the British-supported King Farouk (Hourani 1991).

Under Nasir, Egypt followed a path of Arab socialism—a program combining the nationalization of economic resources, state-directed economic and social development, and a stridently anti-Western political agenda aimed at nationalizing the Suez Canal and returning historic Palestine to Arab control. Nasir's ascent to power ushered in an era of industrialization, agricultural development, and urbanization in Egypt. Once a largely rural, peasant society, Egypt became more urbanized, with Cairo growing into one of the largest cities in the world through a combination of high fertility rates and rural-to-urban migration. Nasir also expanded the country's educational system, and especially its university system, with the number of university graduates almost quadrupling between 1952 and 1969. Many of these graduates found employment in the burgeoning government bureaucracy and in other economic sectors supported by the state (Ayubi 1983).

Nasir's Arab socialist agenda, however, was short-lived. Nasir's successor, Anwar Sadat, pursued a more pro-Western policy, opening up Egypt to free-market forces and foreign investment and seeking accommodation with Israel and the United States. Sadat's economic policies led to prosperity among some classes of Egyptians but also contributed to tremendous inequality. Especially negatively affected by Sadat's reforms were the growing ranks of university graduates from middle- and lower-middle-class backgrounds, who had high expectations for economic mobility, but who could not find employment in either the state or private sector.

Some of those marginalized by Sadat's economic reforms were attracted to Islamist movements. "Islamism" is a catch-all term referring to those seeking to increase the role of Islamic law and Islamic values into public, political life. In Egypt and elsewhere, Islamist movements have been accompanied by a more general upsurge of religious observance, made visible in the growing use of the headscarf by

Egyptian president Gamal 'Abd al-Nasir shakes hands with Japanese chief delegate Tatsunosuke Takasaki at the Afro-Asian Conference of 1960. (Library of Congress)

young urban women. Islamism had first appeared in Egypt in the 1920s, most notably in the form of the Muslim Brotherhood (known as the *Ikhwan* in Arabic). The early Islamists were adamantly opposed to British colonial domination of Egypt. But unlike the secular nationalists, they sought renewal of Egyptian society through a return to Islamic ways of life and the application of Islamic principles to modern economic and political systems. The Brotherhood and other Islamist groups were brutally repressed under the secularist Nasir regime of the 1950s and 1960s. Sadat, however, actively courted the Islamists, whom he viewed as an important counterweight to his left-wing Nasirist rivals.

Most Islamists are peaceful organizations working through mainstream political channels; many, moreover, have provided essential services to the swelling ranks of the urban population who lack adequate housing, transportation, and work. But some have been more extreme and militant in their beliefs and tactics. In his effort to gain the support of Islamists, Sadat tacitly approved vitriolic anti-Coptic rhetoric and even violent attacks against Coptic citizens, especially in Upper Egypt, by radicalized segments of the Islamist movement. These episodes were extremely traumatic for the Coptic community.

Sadat's policy of courting the Islamists backfired, and he was assassinated by a radical Islamist group in 1981. His successor, President Hosni Mubarak, cracked down severely on Islamist groups, whom he saw as a potential threat to his rule;

this policy led to a growing accommodation between the Egyptian state and Coptic Church leaders, who were keen to have their communities recognized as part and parcel of Egyptian society, rather than as a mere minority. Many middle-class Copts, though, continued to see the Mubarak regime, and Egyptian society in general, as a threat to the survival of the Coptic community (Sedra 1999). Copts participated *en masse* in the anti-Mubarak demonstrations in February 2011, and scenes of Christians and Muslims praying together in Cairo's Tahrir Square during the uprisings raised hopes about improved relations between Muslims and Christians in the post-Mubarak era. The destruction of a Coptic church in March 2011 and renewed clashes between Copts and Muslims, however, have dampened some of this hope.

The ongoing political turmoil in Egypt has had deleterious effects on Egyptian businesses, many of which remained closed weeks after Mubarak stepped down. Especially hard hit has been the tourism sector, which drives a significant portion of the country's economy. These problems have compounded the country's existing economic hardships, which include high levels of unemployment, inequality, and a stagnating quality of life for most Egyptians. It is unclear at this time how Egypt's evolving political situation will affect the country's economic prospects.

Causes and Waves of Migration

It is against this backdrop of urbanization, population pressures, economic precariousness, and political unrest that Egypt has become an important source of migrant workers for regional and global labor markets. Up until 1967, the Egyptian government imposed a variety of legal and bureaucratic restrictions on emigration, but labor market pressures, and the reality of increasing migration, led to the lifting of restrictions and, indeed, to new legal protections for Egyptians working abroad. The 1971 Constitution, for instance, gave Egyptians the explicit right to emigrate and to return home, and it granted public sector employees the right to return to their jobs in Egypt within two years of emigrating (thereby encouraging them to go abroad as temporary workers). In 1981, the state established the Ministry of State for Emigration Affairs, which sponsored Egyptians working abroad on contracts and provided migrant workers with various services. Other laws in the 1980s specified and expanded the rights of migrant workers and attempted to coordinate and encourage migration.

Large-scale emigration began in earnest in the early 1970s, when Egypt started to send large numbers of migrant workers to the Gulf states (especially Saudi Arabia and Kuwait), Iraq, and to neighboring Libya, whose oil wealth was fuelling ambitious development plans and creating demands for both skilled and unskilled workers. Thousands of Egyptians (as well as Palestinians, Jordanians, Yemenis, and

Moroccans) found employment working on construction projects, in the oil fields, and in professional or technical sectors, including engineering, medicine, and education (over 20,000 Egyptian school teachers, for instance, were seconded to other Arab countries to fill employment gaps in 1975–1976 alone [Wahba 2004]). From 70,000 in 1970, the number of emigrant workers from Egypt increased to 1.4 million by 1976 (Zohry and Harrell-Bond 2003). The number Egyptians working abroad peaked in 1983 at 3.28 million (Ministry of Manpower and Emigration 2003). Data from the 1980s show that migrants were drawn from a wide spectrum of society, with almost 20 percent holding university degrees but almost one-third having no education at all. Migrant workers were overwhelmingly young men from both rural and urban backgrounds. Owing to the temporary nature of labor contracts in most oil-producing states, most workers stayed abroad between two and five years (Ministry of Manpower and Emigration 2003). The earnings of these workers became a crucial source of foreign currency in Egypt. As McCormick and Wabha report, remittances to Egypt during this period "were amongst the highest in the world, peaking at $6.1 billion in the early 1990s and ranging between 5–11 percent of GDP" (2004, 3).

Starting in the early 1980s, however, the number of contracts granted to Egyptian workers in the Gulf states started to decline due to diminishing oil revenues and the consequent scaling back of construction projects. At the same time, Gulf Arab states began to replace Arab workers with Asian workers, who were generally viewed as more compliant, better trained, and cheaper. With the first Gulf War, most Egyptian workers in Iraq and Kuwait were forced to return to Egypt (Zohry and Harrell-Bond 2003). The loss of employment opportunities in the Gulf exacerbated poverty and underemployment in Egypt and exposed the country's dependence on remittances. While numbers recovered after the war (there were still approximately 2 million Egyptian workers in the Gulf in the early 1990s), Arab workers overall in 2002 constituted only about a quarter of foreign workers in the Gulf. Still, even with the replacement of Arab workers in the Gulf, Egypt has remained a major labor exporter to the oil-producing states (al Khouri 2004). Significantly, though, the proportion of skilled professionals (e.g., scientists and technical workers) in these flows to the Gulf has increased dramatically, going from around 20 percent in 1985 to 40 percent in 2000 (Ministry of Manpower and Emigration 2003). Simultaneously, there has been an increase in the migration of unskilled workers from Egypt to non-oil-producing Arab states, including Lebanon and Jordan. Much of this migration is destined for the construction sector and takes place outside of formal, legal channels (Baldwin-Edwards 2006).

Egyptian migration from the 1960s onward, therefore, has been largely a story of temporary labor flows in the Arab world. But this has not been the only story. An estimated 825,000 Egyptians have also migrated to the wealthy postindustrial world, and especially to Anglophone countries like the United States, Canada,

Australia, and Britain (Baldwin-Edwards 2006; Ministry of Manpower and Emigration 2003). In the case of the United States, Canada, and Australia, the start of Egyptian immigration corresponded with, and was enabled by, the lifting of restrictions on non-Western European immigration. In the United States, these restrictions had been put in place with the National Origins Quota Act of 1924 amidst nativist fears of unchecked eastern and southern European immigration. National origins quotas were abolished with the passage of the Immigration and Nationality Act in 1965, ushering in a new wave of large-scale immigration, most of it non-European in origin and permanent in nature.

The new immigration system gave overwhelming preference to family reunification, but 20 percent of permanent visas were set aside for those able to fill gaps in the labor market—a provision that benefited Egyptians armed with engineering and medical degrees. Egyptians also benefited in later years from the proliferation of temporary immigrant visas, many of them intended for skilled workers and researchers, and some of which were convertible to permanent visas. Both the Egyptian and American higher education systems must be recognized for their important role in the process of skilled migration. Through the 1970s, the Egyptian state sponsored, at great expense, thousands of students in overseas university programs, but an estimated 40 percent of these students did not return (Ayubi 1983). Instead, they found employment through engineering firms, research labs, hospitals, and universities in the United States (and other Anglophone countries) and applied for permanent residency and eventually citizenship. Their reasons for staying in the United States were obvious: a plethora of well-remunerated jobs matching their particular skills and, for many, better living conditions than were available in Egypt's crowded cities, where housing, in particular, had become an expensive and scarce commodity even for the middle classes (see Feiler 1992).

Although such generous subsidies for overseas university study no longer exist, Egyptian students (especially from the upper classes) continue to enroll at Anglophone universities, which are viewed as more prestigious than Egyptian institutions and which provide a foothold in the skilled labor markets of the Global North (i.e., the wealthy countries of Europe, North America, and Australasia) (Mahroom 1999). There is some suggestion that increasingly liberal skilled migration provisions in Britain, Canada, and Australia will make these countries more attractive to foreign graduate students and advanced-degree holders than the United States. The declining number of temporary U.S. visa applications by Egyptian nationals since the early 2000s seems to bear this out, yet the numbers of Egyptians applying for permanent residency in the United States remain buoyant (Department of Homeland Security 2008; for an overview of American skilled migration policies, see Papademetriou, Meissner, Rosenblum, and Sumption 2009). Unlike those finding employment in the Arab world, Egyptian migrants to the United States and other Anglophone countries tend to settle permanently owing to host society policies encouraging long-term residency and/or naturalization. Egypt's loss of large numbers of highly skilled workers raises issues about "brain drain" and the loss of key skills crucial to economic development in Egypt (Ayubi 1983). Some scholars, though, question whether the brain drain is a significant problem in light of the chronic oversupply of university graduates in Egypt (see Baldwin-Edwards 2006).

In concluding this discussion, it is important to note that not all Egyptians seeking work in the Global North are as privileged as those working in the United States and other Anglophone countries. In recent years, thousands of Egyptians and others from Arabic-speaking North Africa have been migrating illegally to Europe, taking up unskilled work regardless of their actual levels of education. Recent data from Italy, for instance, shows that 60 percent of undocumented immigrants intercepted by the police are Egyptians; in Malta, a Mediterranean country recently admitted into the European Union, this number is smaller, but still significant: 15 percent (Baldwin-Edwards 2006). These workers are increasingly vulnerable to government crackdowns on undocumented immigrants.

Demographic Profile

Size and Composition of Community

The 2000 Census reports 113,396 people born in Egypt to be living in the United States; this figure represents a very small percentage (0.4% to be exact) of the foreign-born population in the United States, which numbers over 31 million people (U.S. Census 2000). This is likely to be an underestimate of the actual number of people born in Egypt currently residing in the United States; it should be noted, in this regard, that the Egyptian statistical agency in 2000 put at 318,000 the number of "permanent migrants" from Egypt in the United States (Ministry of Manpower and Emigration 2003, 37). Despite these discrepancies in data, the U.S. Census provides a useful overview of key characteristics of the Egyptian American population. As suggested previously, the vast majority of those Egyptians who have settled in the United States have arrived since the 1960s. Table 90 details the number of Egyptians obtaining legal permanent residency between 1920 and 1999 and illustrates well the surge in Egyptian migration that began in the1960s. Table 91 shows year-by-year the number of Egyptians obtaining permanent residency in the decade of 2000–2009 against total numbers of immigrants receiving permanent residence; here we see the most significant growth yet of a permanently settled Egyptian population, with numbers increasing by almost 70,000 over the course of the decade.

Data on nonimmigrant (I-94) admissions from the U.S. Department of Homeland Security (2008) also indicate significant movement between Egypt and the United States. Non-immigrant admissions refer to those who enter into the United States on a temporary basis and for a specific reason. This can include temporary workers (such as skilled H1-B workers), students, and tourists. The peak number of I-94 admissions took place in 2001, when almost 62,000 Egyptians gained admittance in the United States. After 2001, however, numbers declined significantly, dropping to 31,447 in 2003, and never fully recovered; this decline is consistent with other Arab countries, whose citizens experienced heightened security measures in the aftermath of 9/11. (See Table 92 for more information.)

As with most other immigrant groups, the majority of Egyptians can be found in a small number of highly populated and well-established immigrant gateways, including California (25,147), New Jersey (20,079), and New York (19,907). Sizable Egyptian communities can also be found in Florida (5,787) and Virginia (4,513) (U.S. Census 2000). (See Tables 95 and 96.) The latter is especially noteworthy, as Virginia has experienced a high rate of growth in its foreign-born population only in the last 20 years. Most of the foreign born in the state are concentrated in the District of Columbia's increasingly diverse suburbs (see Friedman, Singer, Price, and Cheung 2005).

Educational and Economic Attainment

The Egyptian American population today is more educated and prosperous than the American population at large. Perhaps the most striking statistic to compare is educational attainment. According to the 2000 Census, while 24.4 percent of Americans over the age of 25 have attained a bachelor's degree or higher, 60 percent of those born in Egypt have done so; almost one-quarter, moreover, hold a graduate degree. As one might expect, median income in 1999 was approximately $8,000 more in Egyptian households than in all U.S. households; and while 12 percent of American households in 1999 earned over $100,000, 21 percent of Egyptian households did. Just over 50 percent of Egyptians are employed in management, professional, and related occupations. They are heavily overrepresented in scientific, educational, social service, and health fields.

This is not to say, however, that all Egyptian Americans are affluent professionals. Close to 14 percent work in construction, maintenance, manufacturing, and transportation occupations. Moreover, just over 11 percent of households headed by Egyptian immigrants live below the poverty line. This is much lower than the poverty rate experienced by many immigrant groups, but it is higher than the poverty rate for American families overall (around 9% in 2000). As in the population at large, single women with children are much more likely than the wider population to be living at or below the poverty line. Single female-headed households with children under 18 years old are quite rare among Egyptian immigrants—the 2000 Census lists 1,475 such households, or 2.7 percent of all Egyptian family households. But around a third of such families are living below the poverty line. So while Egyptians can be considered a success story, it is important to recognize the existence of poverty among them and, as in the American population overall, the concentrated effects of poverty among women.

Health Statistics, Issues

A review of the public health literature raises no particular health concerns with Egyptian Americans, though there has been some recognition recently of potentially high levels of hepatitis C infection in the community. The hepatitis C problem stems from public health efforts in Egypt in the 1970s to vaccinate people—especially those living in rural areas—against schistosomiasis, a water-borne parasitic disease. Many of these vaccinations were administered with used, unsterilized needles, leading to large-scale infection of the population with hepatitis C. The World Health Organization reports that approximately 20 percent of Egyptian blood donors test positive for the hepatitis C virus (this compares with a global infection rate of 3%). There are no statistics available for hepatitis C infection among Egyptian Americans, but it unlikely that infection rates are as high as they are in Egypt. Many Egyptian Americans are from middle-class, urban backgrounds; moreover, the vaccinations stopped several years ago, so recent immigrants are not as likely to be infected. Still, the rate of infection is believed to be higher than in the population at large, and steps have been taken by some Egyptian American organizations (including Coptic churches) to test members for the disease.

Adjustment and Adaptation

Family and Culture

As with all immigrant groups, the issue of cultural preservation and continuity has been an important one for Egyptians, especially as, for most of them, migration has been a permanent, rather than temporary, phenomenon. In addition to strong family life, Egyptian Americans draw on a variety of community resources to perpetuate customs and heritage. Like many contemporary immigrant groups who occupy a relatively high economic status, Egyptian Americans do not form residential clusters. There are no so-called ethnic neighborhoods or enclaves where Egyptian Americans simply reproduce Egyptian culture. But we can identify a cultural infrastructure in many large metropolitan areas—comprised of markets, restaurants, and shops selling consumer goods popular in Egypt—that sustain cultural traditions and tastes. Like Egyptian Americans themselves, these establishments tend to be dispersed in metropolitan areas and are often to be found in suburban strip malls. Many of these establishments, it must be emphasized, do not cater exclusively to Egyptians; rather, they serve multiple Arabic-speaking communities, including those from Syria, Lebanon, and Iraq, who share similar tastes in food, films, music, and other cultural forms.

Social life for Egyptians and other Arabic-speaking communities revolves largely around food, and food-based traditions are an important way that immigrant communities maintain cultural identity. Egyptians (and other Arabic-speaking communities) enjoy falafel, a fried patty made from chickpeas or fava beans and spices; *shawarma,* a sandwich made from shredded rotisseried meat; and *kushari,* a vegetarian dish of rice, lentils, chickpeas, and macaroni, which is considered the national dish of Egypt and is a favorite of Coptic Egyptians during the meatless season of Lent. Film and music are other important components of Egyptian culture. Egypt has a very rich cinematic tradition and has been the center of filmmaking in the Arab world since the early 20th century. Egyptians in the United States can access classic Egyptian films and contemporary dramas on satellite television (described below), through specialty video rental shops and, increasingly, over the Internet. Egyptian music, like Egyptian film, has produced several superstars who are well-loved throughout the Arab world. Among these is Umm Kulthum, whose recordings of classically inspired Arabic songs, dating mainly from the 1940s and 1950s, remain popular today.

In describing these important elements of Egyptian culture, we should bear in mind that "culture" is not a static entity and cultural forms are constantly changing. In Egypt itself, film and music is quite varied and reflects the influence of popular forms from the United States, Europe, and elsewhere (contemporary Egyptian music, for instance, often mixes together folk music and Western pop forms). In the immigrant context, cultural forms hold different meanings for men and women, first- and second-generation immigrants, and for different class groups and religious groups. The music and films that evoke poignant memories for some might evoke anger, disapproval, or indifference in others. Moreover, young people born and raised in the United States may find Western dramas or more hybrid forms of music coming from the Arab world or from the Arab diaspora more compelling than the classics enjoyed by their parents. So in preserving Egyptian culture, Egyptian immigrants are not simply reproducing a monolithic, unchanging entity, but are formulating particular understandings of what it means to be Egyptian; and not all versions of Egyptian-ness will be embraced by all Egyptian Americans. This theme is developed more fully in the following sections.

Families and Changing Gender Relations

Immigrants from Egypt and other Arabic-speaking countries often cite strong family bonds as a defining feature of their cultural identity. Data from the 2000 Census indicates, albeit in an abstract way, the importance of family life and the family unit to Egyptian Americans. To illustrate, about 70 percent of immigrants 15 years old and over born in Egypt are married, compared with approximately 54 percent in the population at large; fewer than 20 percent of households of those born in Egypt are non-family households, compared with almost one-third of households in the population at large. Egyptian immigrants, in other words, are more likely than the wider population to be living in a family situation.

Egyptian families, like many families in the United States, tend to be patriarchal in structure. The strength of patriarchal relations can be seen, in the first instance, in the pronounced gender imbalance among Egyptian immigrants. Whereas the American population overall is 49.1 percent male and 50.9 percent female, among Egyptian Americans, the corresponding figures are 58.6 percent and 41.4 percent. This pattern is not unique to Egyptian immigrants. Men, in general, are more likely than women to migrate as independent workers; women who do migrate tend to do so as the spouse of a primary migrant (though there are significant exceptions to this pattern) (Kofman, Philzaklea, Raghuram, and Sales 2000). The strength of the patriarchal family can also be seen in the fact that a miniscule percentage of Egyptian households (2.7%) consist of a female householder with children and no husband present. That fewer than a quarter of families with children under six have both parents in the labor force, moreover, points to the relatively low levels of labor force participation among Egyptian women (the corresponding figure in the population at large is 65%). So, too, does the fact that women's labor force participation is 18 percentage points lower than in the Egyptian population as a whole. Still, it should be recognized that close to 47 percent of Egyptian-born women living in America *do* participate in the American labor force.

Overall, there seem to be important shifts taking place in gender relationships and norms in Egyptian American communities (as there are in American society as a whole). Some scholarly discussion has brought to light the growing feminist consciousness among young, well-educated Muslim women in the West. This consciousness is linked to a wider social movement among Muslims, spearheaded by public intellectuals like Tariq Ramadan, to make Islam relevant to modern life in the West. This involves recovering what some consider a purer and more authentic version of Islam and shedding un-Islamic cultural practices and prejudices. Nadine Naber (2005) observes that many young Arab American Muslim women use of their faith to reject the racist, ethnocentric, and sexist attitudes present in their families. These women argue that Islam's message of gender equality has been obscured by *Arab* cultural practices that place women in the domestic sphere and

Gamalat Bayoumy and his wife, Mosad Mohamad, immigrated from Egypt to New York City where they earn a living as food cart vendors, July 4, 2009. (AP Photo/Verena Dobnik)

that restrict their opportunities. Their Muslim identity and their strict adherence to an Islamic lifestyle (for instance, wearing modest clothing and refraining from dating) allows them to diminish parental control and to pursue higher education and careers.

The argument that cultural practices must be distinguished from religious principles, especially when it comes to gender relations, has also been applied to the practice of female circumcision. Female circumcision—also known as female genital mutilation—has been practiced for centuries in Egypt and other parts of Africa in order to preserve girls' sexual purity. The procedure typically is done in a non-medical setting without anesthetics and often leads to infection and chronic sexual health problems. It has often been attributed to Islam, but, in fact, it is also widely practiced among Christians (conversely, the practice is unheard of in most parts of the Muslim world). The practice, which has been banned in Egypt and condemned by Muslim theologians, has come under the scrutiny of women's rights groups and lawmakers in the United States, where several cases have been reported among diverse immigrant groups (Burstyn 1995). The practice certainly exists in Egyptian American families, but most Egyptian American and Coptic Web sites are virtually silent about the practice. It is not clear whether this silence is due to communal defensiveness or because the problem is not as widespread as it is among other African immigrant groups. Overall, rates of female circumcision are higher in Ethiopia and Somalia than in Egypt; this fact, along with the high levels of education among most Egyptian immigrants, may make the practice relatively uncommon in Egyptian American communities.

Retaining a Sense of National Culture and Identity

Continued Links to Country of Origin

For many Egyptian Americans, maintaining an Egyptian cultural identity involves the fostering of direct linkages with Egypt itself. Many migration scholars have observed that immigrants' ties to their homelands are denser and more persistent today than they were in the past. One reason given for this is the increasingly active role states play in fostering linkages with émigré communities (Itzigsohn 2000). In the case of Egypt, as the state recognized the potential value of the thousands of Egyptians working abroad in the 1970s, it began to grant émigrés a number of legal protections and privileges in order to cultivate émigré ties to the homeland. One of the most important laws affecting émigrés was the Emigration and Sponsoring Egyptians Abroad Law of 1983, which granted migrants the right to dual citizenship (that is, the right to retain their Egyptian nationality upon becoming a citizen of the country of destination); this law also granted migrants exemptions from taxes and fees on remittances sent to Egyptian banks and gave migrants' investments in the Egyptian economy the same advantages as foreign direct investment (Zohry and Harrell-Bond 2003, 28–29). This law has made it feasible and attractive for Egyptian Americans to invest and to participate actively in business ventures in Egypt.

More recently, and following trends worldwide, the Egyptian state has made a more concerted effort to facilitate émigré investment in Egyptian industries. For instance, the Egyptian Ministry of Communications and Information Technology has launched an Internet portal to "create a continuous channel of cooperation and communication with Egyptian expatriates abroad" (2009). The Egyptian government uses this portal to advertise various networking events designed to bring together Egyptian émigrés working in high-technology fields, government officials working in the economic development field, and local (i.e., Canadian, British, and American) businesses for the purpose of enhancing investment in Egypt's technology sector. (It should be noted that these efforts build upon earlier ventures, organized mainly by Egyptian expatriates and international institutions, to promote the transfer of knowledge and skills from émigré scientists and scholars to Egypt.) Additionally, the Egyptian state has attempted, through its Integrated Migration Information System, created in 2001 as part of the Ministry of Manpower and Emigration, to "reinforce relationships between the Egyptian Diaspora and the home country" by strengthening ties with Egyptian nongovernmental organizations abroad and by offering forms of support (Ministry of Manpower and Emigration 2009).

The actual impact of these policies and laws is difficult to ascertain. The role of the state in fostering transnational linkages, on the one hand, should not be overestimated. Zohry and Harrell-Bond (2003), for instance, suggest that few of the government's proposals to aid migrants abroad and to offer professional training for potential migrants have ever been implemented. But, on the other hand, the state's efforts to harness the economic power of migrants undoubtedly have helped to make Egypt one of the world's largest recipients of remittances. According to data from the Central Bank of Egypt, the United States has become the single largest source of remittances to Egypt, providing over one-third of remittance dollars (cited in Ministry of Manpower and Emigration 2003, 52). Given that most Egyptian immigrants to the United States are skilled professionals who settle permanently with their families, it seems likely that at least some of these remittances are being funneled into real estate and business investments (as opposed to being used for household survival). In any event, it is clear that on a financial level, immigrants' ties with Egypt remain strong.

While economic ties are very much in evidence, the authoritarian nature of the Egyptian government has provided émigrés few opportunities to be formally engaged with the political process in Egypt. There are, however, numerous extra-governmental means through which Egyptian Americans maintain their relationship with and commitment to Egypt. Egyptian Americans, for instance, have formed community associations and nonprofit organizations for the purpose of perpetuating ties with Egypt. One example is the Egyptian American Community Foundation, a nonprofit organization based in New York City that supports philanthropic efforts in Egypt, mainly dealing with children and underprivileged groups. While these kinds of organizations are explicitly nonpolitical, they occasionally host ambassadors, consular officials, and other prominent figures in the Egyptian political establishment at conferences and community events. Egyptian American organizations are also oriented around cultural preservation, the promotion of the Arabic language, and the creation of social networks among Egyptians living in the United States. These latter goals become intertwined with conceptions of integration and assimilation in American society, themes to which we will return shortly.

Religion

Religious institutions are especially important in sustaining community life and identity, though they do so in complex ways. There are, to begin, almost 200 Coptic churches outside of Egypt, approximately half of them in the United States, and Coptic churches are to be found in 20 states and the District of Columbia. Copts are 10 percent of the population in Egypt, but they are believed to constitute a larger component of the Egyptian-origin population in the United States. Indeed, some sources claim that Copts form a majority of Egyptian Americans. This claim is

A ceremony inside St. Moses' Church, located on the grounds of St. Antony's Coptic Monastery in the Mojave Desert in southern California. St. Antony's was the first recognized Coptic monastery outside of Egypt; its first monks arrived in 1989. (Courtesy of St. Antony's Coptic Monastery

difficult to substantiate, but it is it is clear that the Coptic community in the United States is sizeable and thriving.

As in Egypt, Coptic life in the United States revolves around a liturgical calendar of holy days, feasts, and fasting periods; such events, along with the Church's unique and lengthy liturgy (which can last for several hours), serve to foster communal bonds and a sense of common identity. While maintaining ancient customs, the Coptic Church in Egypt has also modernized and revitalized itself in recent decades in order to strengthen community identity and solidarity in the face of communal tensions between Copts and Muslims. These transformations have shaped the Coptic Church in America. An important aspect of this revival has been the encouragement of extensive lay participation in Church life and the creation of an active youth ministry (see Van Doorn-Harder 2005; Smith 2005). With respect to the creation of an active youth ministry, Church activities foster the active involvement of young people in the Coptic community and their continued identification as Copts, even as their cultural frame of reference shifts to the United States. At the same time, the Church implores young people to maintain traditional values by refraining from dating, dancing, and wearing revealing clothing (see Coffman 2004), and it provides numerous opportunities (including on-line discussion forums) for young people to live their lives as Copts.

Just as the Coptic Church is an important institution for building community among Egyptian Christians, mosques and Islamic centers serve as focal points of community identity among many Egyptian Muslims. Most mosques in the United States serve multiple ethnic groups, including nonimmigrant converts, though some mosques are dominated by particular cultural or linguistic groups (for instance, Arabs, South Asians, or African Americans). In general, mosques do not house regular congregations; instead, they serve as gathering places for Muslims who wish to partake in Friday prayers. But mosques are taking on more and more community functions, similar to those found in many churches. Some Islamic centers today, in addition to housing a mosque, host scout troops, Arabic language and cultural classes, citizenship classes, and community events. At the same time, mosques are becoming important sites in which gender relations are renegotiated in an American context. In many Arab countries, for instance, Friday prayers are attended mainly by men, with women fulfilling their religious obligations at home; when women attend mosque, they are relegated to a gallery at the back of the mosque. But in some American mosques today, one can find men and women arranged side-by-side, separated by a partition, in front of the prayer leader, signifying their spiritual and social equality.

While being Muslim and attending mosque is an important aspect of identity of many Egyptian Americans, it is important to recognize the great diversity of religious practices and traditions that they follow. If for some, Islam is a complete way of life that requires regular and faithful observance of the five pillars of Islam (i.e., fasting during Ramadan, professing one's faith, praying five times a day, undertaking a pilgrimage to Mecca, and offering alms to the poor); for others, being Muslim is more of a cultural identity expressed, for instance, through avoiding pork and alcohol or taking part in the celebration of major Islamic festivals. Still others, while identifying themselves nominally as Muslims, are adamantly secular in outlook and disavow most aspects of Muslim practice and belief. Patterns of belief and practice, then, can vary a great deal, even within families. Later in this essay, we examine how different identities inform political mobilization and civic participation among Egyptian Americans.

National/Regional-Language Press and Other Media

Perhaps more influential than either the state or nonprofit organizations in terms of keeping Egyptian Americans connected with Egypt are the dozens of Arabic-language television and radio stations that are increasingly available over satellite and the Internet 24 hours a day. The Dish Network, for instance, one of the nation's largest satellite providers, offers an Arabic-language package that broadcasts dramas, films, and news from Egypt. Egyptian newspapers and magazines are also readily available over the Internet. It must be noted that Egyptian media were heavily censored by the state under the Mubarak regime, and there was limited content that challenged the state and its foreign and domestic policies. Several prominent Egyptian newscasters, however, openly broke with the government during the 2011 uprisings, and the media today appear to be operating in a much freer environment. At the same time, Al Jazeera, an international news organization based in Qatar, along with YouTube and various social media sites like Facebook and Twitter, are playing a crucial role in providing information to Egyptian communities abroad in the midst of rapidly changing political circumstances. In addition to news and entertainment outlets operating in Egypt, expatriate communities themselves provide a source of information and commentary about Egypt and the wider Arab world. Many such alternative news sources and Internet sites represent particular interest groups and organizations that were in conflict with the Egyptian state under the Mubarak regime. One such group is the Muslim Brotherhood, a moderate Islamist organization mentioned previously. Under Hosni Mubarak, the Brotherhood had been officially banned from Egyptian politics, but the organization had several legislators in the Egyptian parliament who stood as Independents. The Brotherhood has become, in many respects, a global organization, and it emphasizes the notion of a worldwide community of believers, or the *ummah*. Indeed, some scholars today see the Brotherhood and other Islamist organizations as part of a "Muslim diaspora," rather than simply as part of an Egyptian diaspora (see Mandaville [2001] for a fuller discussion of transnational Muslim society). Still, the official English Web site of the Ikhwan (www.ikhwanweb.com), based in London, clearly speaks to an important diasporic Egyptian audience and addresses many issues that are specific to Egypt. Currently, the Ikhwan Web site is focusing intensively on political events unfolding in Egypt in the aftermath of the anti-Mubarak demonstrations, including ongoing efforts to prosecute members of the Mubarak regime, to amend Egypt's constitution, and to quell violence between Muslims and Copts.

Integration and Impact on U.S. Society and Culture

Paths toward Citizenship

While Egyptian Americans maintain their linkages with Egypt through a variety of channels, they are not simply or singularly transnationals. Their lives are rooted in an American context, as well as an Egyptian context, and they, like other immigrant groups, must negotiate their membership in American society.

Part of this negotiation is the acquisition of American citizenship. Egyptian Americans, as we have seen, are a relatively privileged group who enter the United

States mainly through legal channels. They therefore have ready access to American citizenship. The U.S. census shows remarkably high rates of naturalization among Egyptian Americans. Of the 37,625 Egyptian Americans counted in the census who entered the United States before 1980, 92 percent have naturalized as citizens; over three-quarters of those entering between 1980 and 1990 have done so. The Egyptian state's acceptance of dual citizenship undoubtedly contributes to high rates of naturalization. Egyptian Americans, in other words, have nothing to lose by naturalizing as citizens, but much to gain in terms of rights and economic opportunities. Naturalization in the Egyptian American community, in this sense, can be interpreted in a variety of ways. Some Egyptians undoubtedly see an American passport as a convenience that provides access to the U.S. labor market and that grants legal protections that are nonexistent in Egypt. For many others, though, having American citizenship signifies an intention to incorporate themselves fully into the fabric of American society, even as they remain connected emotionally and materially with Egypt. How they choose to integrate, of course, is highly complex and requires an understanding of the different ways Egyptian Americans formulate public identities and position themselves in narratives of belonging in the United States.

Intergroup Relations

A first step toward understanding public identities is to recognize the inter- and intra-group relationships in which Egyptian Americans are enmeshed. Many Egyptian immigrants see themselves not only as Egyptian Americans, but also as Arab Americans, and they engage in many formal and informal interactions with other Arab-origin groups, including Palestinian, Iraqi, and Lebanese Americans. The tendency for diverse Arab-origin groups to socialize with one another reflects the cultural traditions shared by these groups—relating, for instance, to language, literature, cinema, food, and norms of hospitality and family life. Arab cultural practices, as described earlier, are sustained in part by a cultural infrastructure comprised of Arab-oriented markets, shops, restaurants, Web sites, and media outlets. At the same time, a more politically tinged pan-Arab sentiment remains salient among Arabic-speaking immigrants and their children and may, in fact, be strengthening in light of the momentous political upheavals taking place throughout the Arab world today. This pan-Arab sentiment reflects a general sense, borne of 20th-century pannationalisms, that the problems afflicting the Arab world— for example, the conflicts in Palestine and Iraq and political repression in Saudi Arabia—are shared by all Arabs.

Intergroup relationships involving Egyptian Americans also revolve around religious identities. As described above, while some mosques are dominated by a single language group (e.g., Arabs or Pakistanis), many of the large mosques and Islamic centers that have sprung up in American suburbs cater to a highly diverse group of Muslims, which include many nonimmigrant converts and African Americans. Mosques are spaces in which Egyptian Americans and other groups can think of themselves not just as Egyptian or Arab but as part of a larger Muslim community—one, indeed, that extends beyond the boundaries of the United States.

Not all relationships serve to create solidarity among Egyptian Americans or to build linkages between them and other groups. Communal tensions between Muslims and Copts in Egypt, for instance, have carried over into American society and have strained relations among Egyptian Americans. An incident in New Jersey in 2005 involving the murder of a Coptic Christian family illustrates these strains. As reported in the *New York Times*, following the murder, rumors spread that the family's father had "exchanged angry words with a Muslim on the Internet," and many in the Coptic community felt that Muslims were behind the killings (Kelley 2005). When a Muslim cleric from New York came to the family's funeral to pay his respects, he reportedly was threatened with violence and had to be escorted away by police. Police eventually charged two non-Muslim men—one of them living above the murdered family in a rented apartment—with the murder. But by this time, relationships between Copts and Muslims had been severely strained. A local interfaith coalition, involving Muslims, Hindus, Jews, and Christians, including Coptic leaders, gathered to sign a statement condemning "expressions of hate" and vowing to heal rifts between Muslims and Copts in New Jersey. The leader of a local Islamic center remarked at the time that Copts and Muslims had been working together for some years to build community solidarity, noting that "We come from the same country, from the same culture, for thousands of year, and we don't have to bemoan our problems and differences" (Kelley 2005). But despite efforts to smooth over differences, it seems that Egyptian Copts are more inclined to build a separate identity and social support system around a Coptic identity.

Forging a New American Political Identity

These diverse inter- and intra-groups relationships—between Egyptian Americans and other Arab Americans, between Muslims of different ethnic and national backgrounds, and between Copts and Egyptian Muslims—inform the ways in which Egyptian Americans negotiate their membership in the wider political sphere and position themselves as members of the American public. For some immigrants from Egypt, becoming part of American society involves adopting a hyphenated Egyptian American identity. This Egyptian American identity takes shape, in part, through organizations dedicated to community solidarity and cultural preservation. Some Egyptian American organizations, as we have seen, maintain direct ties with Egypt through philanthropic activities. Such organizations also serve to develop social networks among Egyptians in the United States and to familiarize the wider American public with cultural forms found in Egypt. Their aims, in other words, are centered on the realities of life in the United States as much as they are centered on Egypt itself. The Egyptian American Cultural Association, for instance, was founded by a group of Egyptian-born professionals in the Washington, D.C., area in the 1970s as a nonreligious, nonpolitical organization to promote interaction among Egyptian-origin people in the United States and to encourage second-generation Egyptian Americans to celebrate their cultural heritage. Their Web site (www.eacaonline.org) provides information about events throughout the Washington, D.C.—exhibitions, lectures, language classes, and weekend camps for Egyptian American children—that are intended to keep Egyptian Americans in touch with their community and heritage. The Web site also features links to Egyptian television stations, radio stations, and newspapers.

For many Egyptian Americans, the process of weaving themselves into America's multicultural fabric has involved not only creating a specifically Egyptian American associations and an Egyptian American identity, but also allying themselves with other Arab immigrant groups and mobilizing organizationally under the banner of the Arab American community. The history of Arab American organizations is a long and complex one (see Suleiman 1999); very briefly, Arab American organizations gained momentum mainly in response to on-going conflicts between Arab countries and Israel (a major ally of the United States), including the 1967 Arab-Israeli War (which ended in Arab defeat and the Israeli occupation of the West Bank) and the 1982 Israeli invasion of Lebanon. The Palestinian Intifadas, U.S. military involvements in Iraq, and the so-called War on Terror under the Bush Administration (2001–2009), combined with the growth of the Arab-origin population in the United States, have added further impetus to Arab American mobilization. Prominent Arab Americans organizations, such as Association of Arab-American University Graduates, the Arab-American Anti-Discrimination Committee, and the Arab American Institute, have always had a large contingent of Lebanese Americans (some of them the second-generation descendents of early 20th-century immigrants), but they have become increasingly diverse as the Iraqi, Palestinian, and Egyptian communities have grown in the decades after 1965. The centrality of Arab world events to Arab American political organizations suggests a strongly diasporic element to these groups. But it would be a mistake to view them entirely in diasporic terms. These organizations are very much oriented toward addressing American foreign policy in the Arab world through the American political process. At the same time, the War on Terror has created a number of purely domestic concerns among people of Arab origin in the United States. A major part of Arab American activism today involves civil rights and antidiscrimination activism, and Arab Americans have increasingly joined forces with other groups (e.g., Latinos and African Americans) to promote civil liberties and immigrant rights. Much of the discourse emanating from Arab American organizations revolves around incorporating Arab Americans into the mainstream political life and legitimizing Arab identities in America's ethnically plural society.

Not all Arab American organizations, of course, are politicized; many are oriented around cultural reproduction (though the promotion of culture is itself quite politically charged). Many Arab American organizations, like Egyptian American organizations, work to instill cultural pride and self-confidence in young, second-generation Arab Americans, who are often exposed to anti-Arab and anti-Muslim rhetoric in the media and in their local communities (see Abu El-Haj 2007). These organizations also seek to share aspects of Arab cultural life with the wider American society. Arab American organizations, for instance, often host language, cooking, and dance classes; art exhibits; and literary events that are open to the public; in some large cities, as well, Arab American groups host annual Arab cultural festivals and film festivals. There are many Arab American comedians, rappers, playwrights, poets, and novelists who articulate the Arab American experience to the wider society—an experience that revolves around an attachment to (and frustration with) the patriarchal family, a sense of personal loss vis-à-vis Palestine and Iraq, and a deep frustration with anti-Arab stereotypes.

While the Arab American community encompasses many Egyptian Americans, it is clear that some Egyptian Americans seek to negotiate American society in other ways. Coptic Christians, for instance, identify strongly with Egypt, but their social and organizational relationships with non-Coptic Egyptians Americans, let

Kareem Loutfy, a senior at Carteret High School in New Jersey, sits with his prayer rug in the living room of his home May 18, 2006. Loutfy belongs to the Egyptian American Group, an interdenominational organization of New Jersey Muslims, Arab Americans, and South Asians. (AP Photo/Mike Derer)

alone Arab Americans, seem tenuous. Most Egyptian American and Arab American organizations are explicitly and scrupulously nonreligious and nonsectarian, and there are Copts and other Christians involved in them. But interviews I have conducted with Arab American activists suggest that many Copts, like Chaldean Christians from Iraq and Maronite Christians from Lebanon, have pursued organizational solidarity apart from their Muslim compatriots as relationships between Muslims and Christians have become more contentious in countries of origin.

As alluded to earlier, the Coptic Church in North America plays a crucial role in building community life among Coptic Egyptian Americans. The Church also has an important role in presenting their community to the mainstream public. Some scholars have noted that Coptic Web sites often highlight the pre-Islamic and Pharaonic heritage of the Copts; this heritage, Botros (2006) suggests, serves to separate them from other migrants from the Muslim world, thereby giving them an elevated status. Significantly, though, official church Web sites have, up until the present time, refrained from speaking about their persecution in modern Egypt, reflecting the alliance between the Coptic hierarchy and the Mubarak regime against radical Islamists.

Lay Copts (i.e., those who are not part of the Church hierarchy) have been less inclined to keep quiet about the discrimination faced by their co-religionists in Egypt. Copts in the United States, many of whom left Egypt at the height of tensions between Copts and Muslims, opposed the accommodation between the Coptic Church hierarchy and the Mubarak regime, which it accused of supporting anti-Christian extremism, and formed lay organizations to generate opposition to the Mubarak regime among American legislators (Sedra 1999). Internet technologies have made these organizations quite effective in reaching influential political figures. One interesting example of Coptic technological savvy has been Coptic activists' use of a U.S.-based wire service, the Christian NewsWire (www.christiannewswire.com), to publicize acts of violence and oppression against Copts in Egypt. The Christian NewsWire, which circulates news releases mainly for conservative Christian groups, has posted several articles written by members of Coptic activist groups describing the victimization of Christians by the Egyptian authorities and Islamist organizations. Also notable is the Web site for the U.S. Copts Association (www.copts.com), which claims to represent "all Christians in Egypt," and which provides news clippings referring to the persecution of Christians worldwide at the hands of Islamic extremists. This activism had been criticized by the Coptic hierarchy in the United States, which reportedly forbade anti-Mubarak activists from publicizing activities or circulating petitions on Church grounds. It is not clear yet how relationships between lay organizations and the Coptic hierarchy will change in light of current political changes in Egypt, but it should be noted that Pope Shenouda III issued a letter supporting the anti-Mubarak demonstrations in 2011 and that members of the Coptic Church in Egypt are pressing for political equality in the post-Mubarak government.

Adding to the diversity of political identities and mobilizations among Egyptian Americans has been the emergence of a Muslim American identity that reflects the growing salience of Islam to young Muslims in North America and Europe. There are today several large, multiethnic Muslim organizations and Islamic centers in the United States that are projecting a modern Muslim message and identity. These organizations are not explicitly political, but they are active in national political life through their public relations work and their efforts to build relations with legislators and political leaders. As with Arab American organizations, Muslim organizations engage with civil rights and antidiscrimination groups, and many are involved in interfaith networks, as well as in dialogue and outreach efforts with non-Muslim groups. Overall, they seek a place for Muslims in America's pluralistic public sphere by actively challenging the many stereotypes of Islam that circulate in American society and by encouraging Muslims to be politically active. These organizations, and the wider movement of which they are part, are an important influence in the lives of some Egyptian Americans, and the emergence of a unique Muslim American identity adds another dimension to Egyptian Americans' incorporation into American society.

The Second and Later Generations

As we have seen, the statistics available on Egyptian Americans refer only to those born in Egypt; it is more difficult to find data specifically on second-generation Egyptian Americans in order to ascertain how they will fare, at least in socioeconomic terms, in American society. But if Egyptian Americans follow wider trends in American society, it is likely that the educational and economic status established by the first generation will carry into subsequent generations. Indeed, analyses of surveys on the Arab American population as a whole suggest that the children and grandchildren of Arab immigrants (Egyptian and otherwise) enjoy greater affluence and higher levels of education than the population at large.

The political and cultural identity of Egyptian Americans is perhaps more difficult to predict. While Egyptian American organizations have been created to keep the second generation in touch with their specific heritage and identity, it may be that larger groupings—Arab American, Muslim American—or more specific groupings, like Copts, will be more compelling to the children of Egyptian immigrants. Egyptian immigrants seem to recognize that they are in America to stay, though many savor the thought of visiting Egypt every year or even retiring in Egypt. For their children, ties with Egypt, despite the availability of Arabic-language satellite, may become increasingly tenuous, and their sense of being a member of a minority group within the United States stronger. For these young people, being part of a larger category like Arab American can be more empowering and politically meaningful than being Egyptian American. Certainly the progressive and campus politics that many of them encounter when they enter university encourage the assertion of pan-identities and coalitions between a variety of minority groups. For young Copts, however, Arab American organizations, which tend to oppose Western interventions in Arab societies and to critique anti-Muslim rhetoric, might not be so attractive. It would not be surprising if these young people seek cultural validation by distancing themselves altogether from association with the Arab-Muslim world and emphasizing their pre-Pharaonic Egyptian-ness. It may

Youth Profile

Biking across America and Working to Dispel Ignorance about Arab Americans

(Courtesy of Shareef Ghannam)

Shareef Ghannam is a student at Johns Hopkins University in Baltimore, where he is studying public health and bioethics. He is also a student activist whose involvements range from researching cancer to participating in the student-run radio station to tutoring elementary school children in Baltimore. He is deeply committed to the Araband Egyptian American communities and to the wider community of which he is a part. Shareef's viewpoints and experiences, while unique to him, provide insights into the ways that second-generation Egyptian Americans act upon their multiple identities and attachments to place.

Shareef's background is a familiar one in the Egyptian American community. His father, who was born in Cairo, and his mother, who was born in London to Egyptian parents, met while studying electrical engineering at Cairo University. They married and immigrated to the United States shortly after Shareef's oldest brother was born so that his father could attend graduate school in New York. After his father completed his Ph.D., the family eventually settled in the San Francisco Bay Area, and they remain very involved with the Egyptian American and Arab American communities.

In high school, Shareef developed an interest in cancer biology and worked as a research assistant for a year in a cancer biology lab at Lawrence Berkeley National Laboratory. In the summer before his sophomore year at Johns Hopkins, he bicycled from Baltimore to San Francisco in order to raise money for cancer research. His passion for cancer research, as one might expect, carries into his career plans: he hopes to complete a master's degree in public health, to attend medical school, and to eventually become a pediatric oncologist.

While many of his physical and intellectual energies are poured into cancer research, Shareef has strong personal attachments to his Egyptian and Arab heritage. Having grown up with the benefit of strong community ties, Shareef is concerned that his generation will allow these ties to languish. Visiting your homeland on occasion, as he puts it, is not the same as growing up in a community that actively fosters identity and heritage. This desire to strengthen community ties spurred Shareef to start the Arab Student Union at Johns Hopkins his freshman year, and his hope is to build the organization's presence on campus. There are other motivations for forming an organization for Arab students relating to the anti-Arab stereotyping that many Arab Americans face. "Even at big name universities," he states, "there is a lot of ignorance, and I'd like to change that."

Shareef's understanding of himself as an Egyptian American—as both Egyptian and American—continues to evolve through his activities and experiences. Shareef's 4,000-mile bicycle ride across America gave him the opportunity to ponder what it means to be an Egyptian American. He states that during the ride, "I came to realize that America is not all the same. All across the country, people come from very different backgrounds, but I think what makes us all uniquely American regardless of our heritage—whether Egyptian or Nebraskan—is that we can identify with something that is uniquely American, in that our origins are unimportant. I think you'd be hard-pressed to find another country in the world where this is true."

Source: Personal interview with the author, August 15, 2009.

be, however, that the revolution in Egypt, which has been supported by Coptic and Arab American organizations, may provide an opening for dialogue and interaction between different groups.

We must also consider that these various identities—Egyptian, Muslim, Arab, Coptic—will cease to be important for some, even as the Egyptian American population continues to grow. Not all immigrants or American-born Egyptian Americans will wish to be politically active or to engage with particular groups. Many live in suburban areas where their connections with other Egyptians or Arabic-speaking groups might be minimal. As an affluent group that is generally coded as white, they are in a relatively privileged position, with more flexibility than many other immigrants groups to simply blend in and to keep identities in the background. Identity can become for them purely symbolic—something to be rolled out when the occasion calls for a celebration of diversity. Of course, external events have a way of re-activating dormant identities, as was seen with second- and third-generation Lebanese Americans during Lebanon's civil war (see the final section of this chapter).

Regardless of how they choose to identify themselves, young Egyptian Americans will be required to navigate generational lines and gender expectations that are embedded in their families and communities. As noted earlier, labor force participation among female Egyptian immigrants is relatively low, but it is unclear whether these rates also apply to U.S.-born Egyptian Americans. It is also unclear at this point how particular religious trends—particularly the growing feminist

---

The EAS Café in San Francisco

The EAS Café is an Internet portal developed in 2008 by the Egyptian American Society, a San Francisco Bay Area–based organization founded in the 1970s by Egyptian expatriates. The EAS café includes numerous links to articles and news pieces of interest to the community, and it provides a discussion board that allows members to express opinions about social and political issues, to advertise their work, or to tell their story to others.

As an organization, the Egyptian American Society is explicitly nonreligious and nonpolitical, meaning that it does not represent any particular religious group or advocate a particular political agenda or party. But the EAS Café does not eschew political or religious subject matter all together. Magda Danish, the current president of the Egyptian American Society and one of the creative forces behind the EAS Café, states, "We link to articles about politics and religions all the time, but we try not to favor any publication or subject over another, and we tend to steer away from extreme opinions on both sides" (personal interview, 8/17/2009). Many of the articles posted on the EAS Café relate directly to Egypt. A perusal of the Web site in the summer of 2009 found articles on the effects of climate change on the Nile Delta, the economic disparities in Egypt, and President Mubarak's visit to the White House. On religious matters, there were articles posted on the recent arrest of Islamist political figures in Egypt, on the controversial restoration of a synagogue in Cairo's ancient Jewish quarter, and on the persecution of a convert to Christianity in Alexandria. Other articles dealt with the wider Arab world, especially with efforts to re-start Israeli-Palestinian peace talks.

While many of the links on the EAS Café relate to Egypt and the Arab world, the Web site also informs its users of Egyptian- and Arab American events taking place locally in the San Francisco Bay Area. Local Coptic churches and mosques, for instance, use the Web site to publicize events and holidays. In the summer of 2009 the Web site had advertisements for a Coptic cultural festival and an Iftar celebration marking the end of Ramadan fasting. There were also postings about the Bay Area's first annual Egyptian festival, a major Tutankhamen exhibit at a San Francisco museum, and several Arab American community events, including a "Middle Eastern comedy show" and the local premier of a film about a Palestinian immigrant family in Michigan. Regarding the importance of Arab American cultural events to Egyptian Americans, Magda Danish states, "You cannot separate Egyptian Americans from Arab Americans, particularly when culture is involved. We all have so much in common that the EAS website certainly projects all Arab American identities and addresses issues that are of interest to them, not only to Egyptian Americans."

In addition to providing information about local events, the EAS Café spotlights members of the Egyptian American community in the Bay Area. One profile describes Hala Fauzi, an Egyptian American woman who gave up her career as a Silicon Valley software engineer to pursue her love of Middle Eastern music and dance. She created her own dance troupe and studio, teaches dance at local colleges, and even hosts a semimonthly radio show, *Mezzas and Tapas* (referring to appetizers eaten in the Arab world and Spain) that showcases music from the Middle East, North Africa, and the Mediterranean basin.

Overall, EAS leaders see the EAS Café as an instrument for bringing together members of the Egyptian American community, whether Coptic, Muslim, or nonreligious. The portal is intended to be evenhanded and, indeed, "to set an example of unity and tolerance for the new generation," in the words of Magda Danish. The Web site projects an outlook that is secular, which for many Egyptian- and Arab Americans signifies not the avoidance of all discussion of religion or the pushing aside religious identities, but a rejection of divisive attitudes. Magda Danish feels that the EAS Café has succeeded in building a measure of unity among Egyptian Americans, even as wider trends in the community and in Egypt point to growing rancor. But she acknowledges that not all members of the community share the worldview of the Café's users.

For outside viewers, the EAS Café illustrates the multiple identities that exist among Egyptian Americans, and it speaks to their on-going connections to Egypt, as well as their rootedness in places of settlement. It represents the potential for new communications technologies to build community solidarity and to foster a sense of belonging that is simultaneously here and there. And finally, it provides glimpses into the activities—the festivals, exhibits, films, picnics, and networking events—through which Egyptian Americans maintain their heritage and negotiate their presence in America's multicultural society.

Source: Author's personal interview with Magda Danish, August 10, 2009.

consciousness among young Muslim women—might alter women's educational and employment status and affect familial dynamics. The 2010 Census will provide some basic answers to these questions, but in-depth qualitative research is needed to understand how these processes will influence the daily lives of Egyptian Americans.

Issues in Relations between the United States and Egypt

Relations between Egypt and the United States have been generally positive for decades, owing to Egypt's recognition of Israel in the 1970s. Under Hosni Mubarak, Egypt assumed the role of broker between the Palestinians and the Israelis, criticizing the Israeli state for its marginalizing the Palestinians but also securing for Israel the sensitive border between Egypt and Gaza. Despite being a lynchpin in America's strategy in the Middle East, however, Mubarak had come under criticism among politicians in the United States for his regime's human rights violations and alleged support for anti-Christian extremism. Relations between the two allies had also become strained due to the decision of the Bush Administration in 2003 to invade Iraq. In August 2009, President Mubarak made his first visit to Washington in five years with the intention of reinvigorating his country's relationship with the United States. Traveling with this son and presumed heir, Gamal Mubarak, President Mubarak met with President Obama to discuss Egypt's role in upcoming peace negotiations between the Israelis and Palestinians. Relations between the two leaders seemed cordial despite President Obama's much-vaunted commitment to human rights and democratization in the Arab world, which he had outlined in a speech in Cairo earlier that year. When mass protests against Mubarak began in January 2011, the Obama administration maintained its support for Mubarak, citing the importance of stability in Egypt for peace in the region, and especially for Israel's security. But the Obama administration, despite grim warnings from Israel and America's Gulf Arab allies, gradually withdrew its support for Mubarak when it became clear that the protestors would not be satisfied until Mubarak stepped down. The dramatic events in Egypt have generated a great deal of interest and concern among first- and second-generation Egyptian Americans, with some expressing their frustration at the Obama administration for its initial hesitation in supporting the protestors. How this political drama will play out—whether Islamists gain power; whether democratic freedoms are instituted; whether the Copts are included in a more equitable fashion in Egyptian society, and so on—will undoubtedly influence relationships in the Egyptian American community as much as it will influence relationships between the United States and Egypt.

Appendix I: Migration Statistics

Table 90 Persons of Egyptian nationality obtaining legal permanent residence by decade 1920–1999

Year	Number
1920–1929	1,063
1930–1939	781
1940–1949	1,613
1950–1959	1,996
1960–1969	5,581
1970–1979	23,543
1980–1989	26,744
1990–1999	44,604
2000–2009	81,564

Source: U.S. Department of Homeland Security.

Table 92 Non-immigrant admissions (I-94 only) granted to Egyptian nationals 1999–2008

Year	Number
1999	57,646
2000	60,685
2001	61,854
2002	37,475
2003	31,447
2004	32,164
2005	34,659
2006	38,115
2007	43,139
2008	47,706

Source: Department of Homeland Security.
Note: Non-immigrant admissions (I-94 only) counts those who are authorized to remain in the United States for a specified period of time; it can be granted to tourists, students, and temporary workers.

Table 91 Persons obtaining legal permanent resident status by region and country of birth: Fiscal years 2000 to 2009

Region and country of birth	2000	2001	2002	2003	2004	2005	2006	2007	2008	2009
Total	841,002	1,058,902	1,059,356	703,542	957,883	1,122,257	1,266,129	1,052,415	1,107,126	1,130,818
Egypt	4,450	5,159	4,852	3,348	5,522	7,905	10,500	9,267	8,712	8,844

Source: U.S. Department of Homeland Security. Office of Immigration Statistics. 2010. Adapted from Table 3.

Appendix II: Demographics/Census Statistics

Table 93 Sex and age of Egyptian-born population

Characteristic	Number	Percent
Total population	113,395	100.0
Male	66,490	58.6
Female	46,905	41.4
0–9 years	4,360	3.9
10–19 years	6,870	6.1
20–34 years	25,705	22.7
35–54 years	50,600	44.6
55–64 years	13,380	11.8
65–84 years	11,670	10.3
85 years and over	820	0.7

Source: Adapted from 2000 U.S. Census.

Table 94 Educational attainment, Egyptian-born population aged 25 years and older

	Number	Percent
Population 25 year and older	96,660	100.0
Less than 9th grade	3,480	3.6
9th to 12th grade, no diploma	4,395	4.5
High school graduate	13,615	14.1
Some college, no degree	11,510	11.9
Associate degree	5,960	6.2
Bachelor's degree	34,720	35.9
Graduate or professional degree	22,985	23.8
High school graduate or higher	88,785	91.6
Bachelor's degree or higher	57,705	59.7

Source: Adapted from 2000 U.S. Census.

Table 95 Five states with the largest Egyptian foreign-born populations

Area	Number	Percent
United States	113,395	100.0
California	25,147	22.2
New Jersey	20,079	17.7
New York	19,905	17.6
Florida	5,784	5.1
Virginia	4,513	4.0

Source: Adapted from 2000 U.S. Census.

Table 96 Persons obtaining legal permanent resident status during fiscal year 2009 leading states of residence region/country: Egypt

Characteristic	Total	Male	Female
Total	8,844	4,894	3,950
Arizona	60	29	31
California	1,244	643	601
Connecticut	89	49	40
Florida	379	218	161
Georgia	99	52	47
Illinois	263	136	127
Maryland	129	75	54
Massachusetts	254	139	115
Michigan	137	84	53
Minnesota	100	56	44
Nevada	38	20	18
New Jersey	1,587	853	734
New York	1,463	863	600
North Carolina	153	92	61
Ohio	182	105	77
Pennsylvania	323	181	142
Texas	369	190	179
Virginia	484	283	201
Washington	114	65	49
Other	1,377	761	616

Source: Adapted from U.S. Department of Homeland Security. Profiles on Legal Permanent Residents: 2009.

Table 97 Occupation of people born in Egypt, aged 16 years and older

	Number	Percent
Employed civilian population 16 years and over	63,760	100.00
Management, professional, and related occupations	32,320	50.7
Service occupations	7,590	11.9
Sales and office occupations	15,065	23.6
Farming, fishing, and forestry occupations	95	0.1
Construction, extraction, and maintenance occupations	2,110	3.3
Production, transportation, and material moving occupations	6,580	10.3

Source: Adapted from 2000 U.S. Census.

Appendix III: Notable Egyptian Americans

Leila Ahmed is a noted feminist scholar and author of the influential book *Women and Gender in Islam.* She currently holds the Victor S. Thomas Chair at Harvard University's Divinity School.

Farouk El-Baz is a geologist who worked with NASA on the Apollo space program in the late 1960s and early 1970s, training astronauts for lunar observation. A director of the National Air and Space Museum, Dr. El-Baz currently focuses his research on desert zones.

Pauline Kaldas is an Egyptian-born, U.S.-raised poet and short-story writer who writes about the experience of being Arab American. Her latest book, *Letters of Cairo* (2006), recounts her time as a Fulbright Scholar in Cairo.

Dalia Mogahed is the director of the Gallup Center for Muslim Studies, which led an unprecedented, representative survey of Muslims worldwide. She was appointed in 2009 to serve on President Obama's Advisory Council on Faith-Based and Neighborhood Partnerships.

Laila Shereen Sakr is a poet, activist, and avant-garde performance artist, and the co-founder of the Washington, D.C., Guerilla Poetry Insurgency. She is currently involved in building a repository of Arab digital media.

Ahmed Zewail is the 1999 recipient of the Nobel Prize in Chemistry for his work on chemical reactions using lasers. He is currently a professor at the California Institute of Technology.

Glossary

Al-Ahram: Egypt's leading newspaper, founded in 1875. Controlled by the Egyptian state, the paper has nonetheless been increasingly critical of the governing regime. It has published an English-language weekly since 1991 and is an important source of information for Egyptians living in the United States and elsewhere.

Azan (**alternatively spelled** *adhan*): The Islamic call to prayer. In Muslim-majority countries, the azan is broadcasted five times a day from a minaret, or a tower attached to a mosque. In the United States, however, local noise ordinances often require modification of the *azan*.

Copts: The Orthodox Christian community established in Egypt in the first century C.E. The term "Copt" is derived from the Greek word for Egyptian.

Iconostasis: A screen decorated with icons (ornate depictions of saints and other holy figures) used in Coptic Orthodox churches to separate the altar from the nave.

Masjid: The Arabic word for a mosque, or the place where Muslims gather for worship.

Misr: The Arabic word for Egypt.

Shawarma: An Egyptian culinary favorite made from spiced strips of lamb roasted slowly on a vertical spit. The meat is shaved and placed in soft flatbread with condiments. *Shawarma* has become popular in many U.S. and European cities due to Arab immigration.

Watan: the Arabic term used to refer to nation, homeland, or country.

References

Abu El-Haj, T. R. 2007. " 'I Was Born Here, But My Home, It's Not Here': Educating for Democratic Citizenship in an Era of Transnational Migration and Global Conflict." *Harvard Educational Review* 77 (3): 285–316.

al Khouri, R. 2004. "Characteristics and Magnitude of Arab Migration Patterns in the Mashreq: South-South Context." In *Arab Migration in a Globalized World,* 21–34. Geneva: International Organization for Migration.

Ayubi, N. 1983. "The Egyptian 'Brain Drain': A Multidimensional Problem." *International Journal of Middle East Studies* 15 (4): 431–50.

Baldwin-Edwards, M. 2006. "Between a Rock and a Hard Place: North Africa as a Region of Emigration, Immigration, and Transit Migration." *Review of African Political Economy* 33 (108): 311–24.

Botros, G. 2006. "Religious Identity as an Historical Narrative: Coptic Orthodox Immigrant Churches and the Representation of History." *Journal of Historical Sociology* 19 (2): 174–201.

Burstyn, L. 1995. "Female Circumcision Comes to America." *Atlantic Monthly* 276 (4): 28–35.

Coffman, E. 2004. "Lost in America: Arab Christians in the U.S. Have a Rich Heritage and a Shaky Future." *Christianity Today* (April): 39–42.

Feiler, G. 1992. "Housing Policy in Egypt." *Middle Eastern Studies* 28 (2): 295–312.

Friedman, S., Singer, A., Price, M., and Cheung, I. 2005. "Race, Immigrants, and Residence: A New Racial Geography of Washington, D.C." *Geographical Review* 95 (2): 210–30.

Hourani, A. 1991. *A History of the Arab Peoples*. Cambridge, MA: Belknap Press of Harvard University Press.

Itzigsohn, J. 2000. "Immigration and the Boundaries of Citizenship: The Institutions of Immigrants' Political Transnationalism." *International Migration Review* 34 (4): 1126–54.

Kelley, T. 2005. "In Jersey City, Religious Leaders Vow Healing." *New York Times,* April 21. [Online article or information; retrieved 6/6/09.] http://query.nytimes.com/gst/fullpage.html?res=980DE6DC1731F932A15757C0A9639C8B63.

Kofman, E., Phizaklea, A., Raghuram, P., and Sales, R. 2000. *Gender and International Migration in Europe: Employment, Welfare, and Politics*. New York; London: Routledge.

Mahroom, S. 1999. "Highly Skilled Globetrotters: The International Migration of Human Capital." *Proceedings of the OECD International Workshop on Science and Technology* (DSTI/STP/TIP(99)2) [Online article or information; retrieved 6/6/09.] www.oecd.org/dataoecd/35/6/2100652.pdf.

Mandaville, P. 2001. *Transnational Muslim Politics: Reimagining the Umma*. Abingdon, UK; New York: Routledge.

Ministry of Communications and Information Technology (Arab Republic of Egypt). 2009. [Online article or information; retrieved 7/25/09]. www.egyptexpats.com.

Ministry of Manpower and Emigration (Arab Republic of Egypt). 2003. Contemporary Egyptian Migration (report produced in conjunction with the International Organization for Migration). [Online article or information; retrieved 7/7/09] http://www.emigration.gov.eg/Publications/DisplayPublications.aspx

Ministry of Manpower and Emigration (Arab Republic of Egypt). 2009. [Online article or information; retrieved 7/7/2009] http://www.emigration.gov.eg.

Naber, N. 2005. "Muslims First, Arabs Second: A Strategic Politics of Race and Gender." *Muslim World* 95 (4): 479–95.

Papademetriou, D., Meissner, D., Rosenblum, M., and Sumption, M. 2009. *Aligning Temporary Visas With U.S. Labor Market Needs: The Case for a New System of Provisional Visas*. Washington, D.C.: Migration Policy Institute.

Sedra, P. 1999. "Class Cleavages and Ethnic Conflict: Coptic Christian Communities in Modern Egyptian Politics." *Islam and Christian-Muslim Relations* 10 (2): 219–35.

Smith, C. D. 2005. "The Egyptian Copts: Nationalism, Ethnicity, and Definition of Identity for a Religious Minority." In *Nationalism and Minority Identities in Islamic Societies*, edited by M. Shatzmiller, 58–84. Montreal: McGill-Queen's University Press.

Suleiman, M. 1999. *Arabs in America: Building a New Future*. Philadelphia: Temple University Press.

U.S. Census Bureau. 2000. Census 2000. [Online article or information; retrieved 6/6/2009]. www.census.gov.

U.S. Department of Homeland Security. 2008. *2008 Yearbook of Immigration Statistics* [Online article or information; retrieved 7/5/2009]. http://www.dhs.gov/files/statistics/ publications/yearbook.shtm.

Van Doorn-Harder, P. 2005. "Copts: Fully Egyptian But for a Tattoo?" In *Nationalism and Minority Identities in Islamic Societies*, edited by M. Shatzmiller, 22–57. Montreal: McGill-Queen's University Press.

Wahba, J. 2004. "Does International Migration Matter? A Study of Egyptian Return Migrants." In *Arab Migration in a Globalized World*, 179–200. Geneva: International Organization for Migration.

Zohry, A. and Harrell-Bond, B. 2003. "Contemporary Egyptian Migration: An Overview of Voluntary and Forced Migration." Working paper issued by Development Research Centre on Migration, Globalization and Poverty, University of Sussex.

Further Reading

Ahmed, L. 1993. *Women and Gender in Islam*. New Haven, CT: Yale University Press.

An excellent historical account of the status of women in Muslim societies. Written by an Egyptian American scholar, the book documents important social changes in Egypt in the 19th and 20th centuries, and helps to explain some of the views and experiences of young Muslim women today.

Arab American Institute 2009. [Online article or information; retrieved7/7/10.]. http:// www.aaiusa.org.

The Web site for one of the country's major Arab American organizations. Contains a wealth of information about Arab Americans, including analyses of census and survey data on Arab American groups conducted by James Zogby, a well-respected pollster.

Hourani, A. 1991. *A History of the Arab Peoples*. Cambridge, MA: Belknap Harvard.

An excellent overview of the history of the Arab world that situates Egypt in a wider regional perspective.

Macleod, A. E. 1993. *Accommodating Protest: Working Women and the New Veiling in Cairo*. New York: Columbia University Press.

A detailed study of the growing religiosity in contemporary Egypt and the mass adoption of Islamic clothing and headscarves by urban Egyptian women. The author argues that women today are both accommodating dominant gender norms and challenging them through their presence in public space. The author also suggests the need to be sensitive to the multiple meanings that veiling represents.

Mandaville, P. 2001. *Transnational Muslim Politics: Reimagining the Umma*. Abingdon, UK; New York: Routledge.

An interesting account of the emergence of a global Muslim consciousness, with special attention given to Muslims living in Western countries.

Suleiman, M. 1999. *Arabs in America*. Philadelphia: Temple University Press.

A collection of essays on the experiences of Arab Americans. Provides several good chapters about the racial ambivalence of Arab Americans and about the community's political mobilization.

Eritrean Immigrants

by Tricia Redeker Hepner

Introduction

Eritreans have been coming from the Horn of Africa to the United States for more than 50 years. While small numbers of Eritreans arrived in the 1960s and 1970s, often sent by the Ethiopian government to attend American universities, the majority arrived in the 1980s and early 1990s as refugees from the long war for Eritrean independence from Ethiopia. In the past decade, renewed conflict in the Horn of Africa and internal developments in Eritrea have led to renewed migration from the country. More than 36 thousand Eritrean refugees were in neighboring Ethiopia in mid-2010, and well over 100,000 remained in Sudan. In addition, an unknown number of Eritreans have made perilous journeys over great distances to try to reach North America or Europe, where they might apply for political asylum. In late 2008, the U.S. government agreed to accept up to 6,500 Eritreans residing in Shimelba refugee camp in Ethiopia, many of whom are highly educated, skilled young men and women.

Because Eritreans were considered Ethiopians until the country's independence in 1993, disaggregated data prior to 1993 is virtually nonexistent. Eritreans are a very small population overall, and little research has been done on Eritreans in the United States. As a result, much remains poorly understood with respect to basic demographic information. However, statistics published by the Department of Homeland Security in 2009 illustrating the numbers of Eritreans obtaining legal permanent resident (LPR) status from 2000 to 2009 and their leading states of residence provide some new insight. More information is also becoming available as Eritreans become more established, as researchers conduct further studies, and as more migrants arrive. Recent ethnographic work has highlighted the unique cultural characteristics of Eritrean Americans and their rich associational life, from religious institutions and community associations, to civic organizations and political parties. As a population, Eritreans remain strongly oriented towards their home country and share a well-developed national identity, which emerged out of Eritrea's three-decade struggle for independence. Second- and third-generation Eritreans have a more complex identity, which recognizes not only their Eritrean heritage but also their identities as African Americans. The experience of Eritrean Americans highlights how the sending country and government continue to be influential in the lives of individuals and their changing communities in the United States.

N

Eritrea

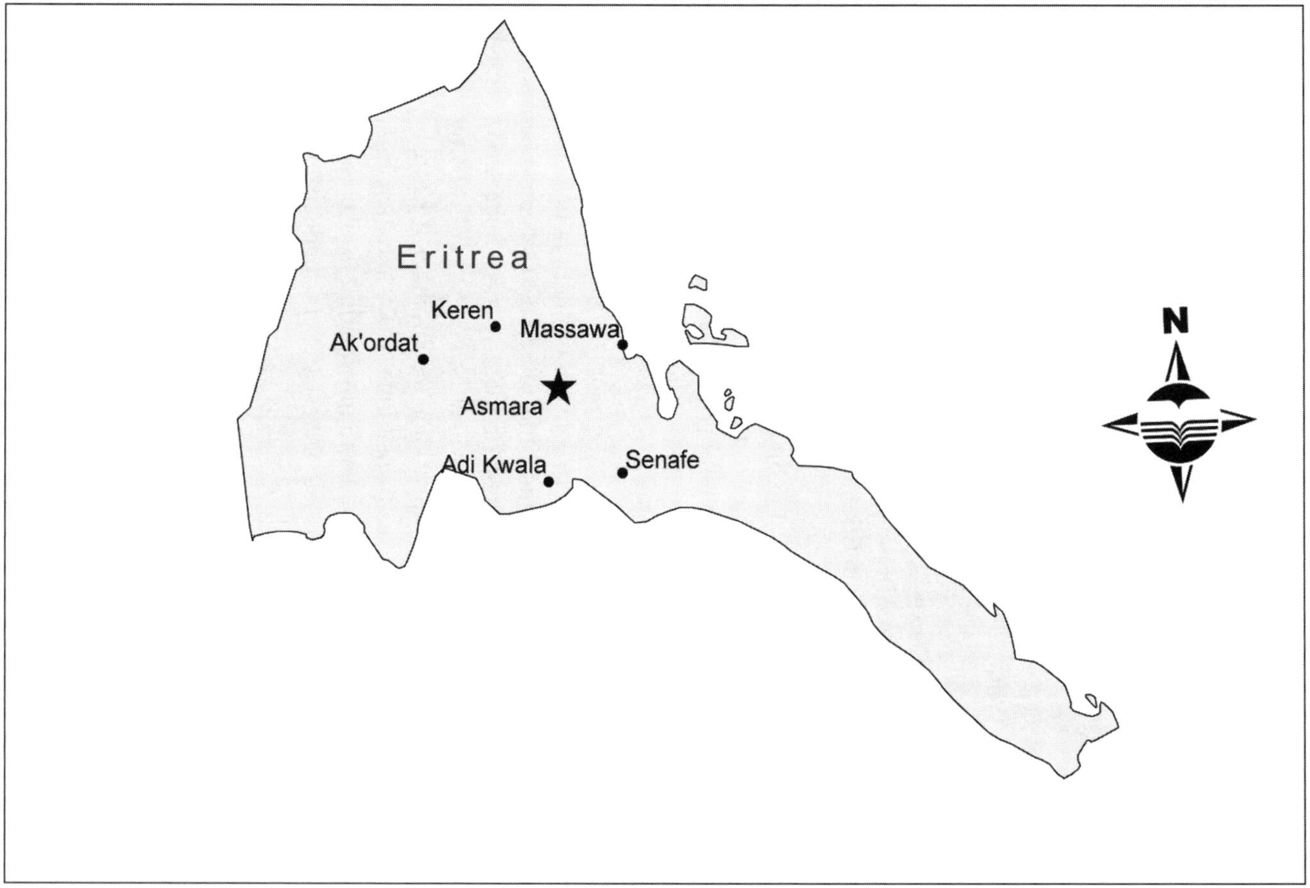

Massawa

Senafe

Keren

Asmara

Adi Kwala

Ak'ordat

Eritrean women celebrate their nation's independence, which was declared on April 27, 1993. (Corel)

Chronology

6000 B.C.E.	Earliest cave paintings in Akele Guzai and Sahel provinces.
2500–1200 B.C.E.	Egyptian and South Arabian contact with Red Sea coast.
230 B.C.E.	Port of Adulis is founded by Ptolemy.
100 C.E.	Rise of Axumite Empire.
325–360	Emperor Ezana's conversion to Orthodox Christianity.
615	Arrival of Islam with Arabian refugees.
1520–1526	Portuguese expedition to highlands.
1533–1535	Islamic expansion under Ahmed al-Ghazali.
1557–1589	Ottoman Turks control coastal areas.
1813–1885	Egyptian occupation; further expansion of Islam.
1869	Italian shipping company purchases port of Assab.
1890	Italian colony of Eritrea formally established.
1941	British occupation of Eritrea.
1952	Ethiopian-Eritrean Federation takes effect.

1961	Eritrean Liberation Front (ELF) launches armed struggle for independence from Ethiopia.
1967	Refugee flows from Eritrea begin.
1970–1972	Eritrean Peoples Liberation Front (EPLF) forms.
1972–1980	Intermittent civil war between ELF and EPLF.
1980	United States passes Refugee Act.
1981	ELF is exiled into Sudan; further refugee flows.
1981–1993	Resettlement of Eritrean refugees in the United States.
1991	EPLF liberates Eritrea.
1993	Eritrean referendum establishes the independent state; Eritrea joins the United Nations.
1998–2000	Ethiopian-Eritrean border war.
2001	Political turmoil in Eritrea.
2002	Banning of minority religions.
2002–2008	Increase in refugee flows.
2008	United States agrees to accept up to 6,500 Eritrean refugees.

Background

Geography of Eritrea

Eritrea is the newest nation-state in Africa. It gained independence from Ethiopia following a 30-year war (1961–1991). An internationally recognized national referendum was held in April 1993, in which an estimated 99.8 percent of voters in Eritrea and the worldwide diaspora cast their ballots in favor of independence. Eritrea joined the United Nations on May 28, 1993.

Situated in the northeastern region of the continent, in the Horn of Africa, Eritrea is geographically distinguished by its dramatic terrain and a regionally variable climate, with 670 miles of coastline along the Red Sea. Eritrea is bordered by Sudan to the north and west, Ethiopia to the south, and the small country of Djibouti at the southeastern tip. Beautiful, unspoiled coral reefs lie off the coast of the port city of Massawa along with hundreds of small, mostly uninhabited islands. The largest of these are the Dahlak archipelago.

Covering nearly 48,000 square miles of landmass, Eritrea is one of the smallest countries in Africa and roughly the size of the state of Pennsylvania. Historically, the country was comprised of nine provinces: Akele Guzai, Barka, Denkel, Gash-Setit,

Hamasien, Sahel, Semhar, Senhit, and Seraye. Following independence, the country was reorganized into six administrative regions: Anseba, Debub (South), Debubawi Qeyih Bahri (Southern Red Sea), Gash-Barka, Maakel (Central), and Semienawi Qeyih Bahri (Northern Red Sea). However, many people continue to refer to regions of Eritrea by their former provincial names and trace their identities through their kin groups' connections to rural lands.

Also important to Eritrea's geography are the differences in rainfall, climate, and population densities among the highland and lowland regions of the country. The highland regions, known as the *kebessa,* are an extension of the Great Rift of eastern Africa. Rising through the center of the country, the *kebessa* is mountainous and temperate, with greater rainfall, more intensive agriculture, and a higher population concentration. The capital city of Asmara, with an estimated population of 600,000, is located on the highland plateau, near the center of the country. The lowland regions to the east, south, and west, or *metahit*, are generally hot and dry, with less rainfall and a lower population density. There are many variations in climate, terrain, ecology, and livelihood as elevation changes. Along the southern Red Sea coast lies the Denkel Desert, where temperatures can rise as high as 122 degrees Fahrenheit. Eritrea's geographical diversity forms four distinct ecological zones: the coastal plain, the central highlands, the northern highlands, and the western lowlands (Killion 1998, 2).

In terms of human geography, Eritrea is similar to many other African countries in its striking linguistic and cultural diversity. An independent census has not yet been taken, but in 2008 the total population of Eritrea was estimated at about 4.5 to 5 million. Nine different ethnic groups or nationalities occupy Eritrea, and at least as many languages are spoken throughout the country. These ethno-linguistic groups and their estimated proportion of the total population of Eritrea include the Afar (3%), Bilen (5%), Hedareb (<1%), Kunama (3%), Nara (>1%), Rashaida (<1%), Saho (7%), Tigre (30%), and Tigrinya (50%) (Killion 1998, 5–6). In addition, Eritreans who were raised in Ethiopia form a unique population unto themselves, referred to as *amiche,* after a type of vehicle (AMCE) that was once imported through Eritrea and assembled in the Ethiopian capital, Addis Ababa. The major languages of Eritrea are Arabic and Tigrinya, though many people also speak Amharic (one of the major languages of Ethiopia) and some older people remember Italian (inherited from the colonial period). English is also widely used; secondary education and university has generally been provided in English, and many government offices utilize English as an international lingua franca. Because so many Eritreans migrated to other countries during the long independence war with Ethiopia, as will be discussed in detail in the following sections, it is not uncommon to hear Eritreans speaking languages like Dutch, German, Italian, Norwegian, and Swedish, especially those who were born and raised abroad.

Eritreans are divided fairly evenly among Sunni Islam and Christianity, and with some exceptions, the country remains exemplary for the peaceful coexistence between these two major religions. Islam was adopted in Eritrea in the ninth century and experienced its major growth period in the 1500s. Orthodox Christianity is the largest and oldest of the Christian traditions, having been indigenized in the fourth century C.E.; and Roman Catholicism and Swedish Evangelical Lutheranism have been present in Eritrea for hundreds of years. Other religions in Eritrea include Jehovah's Witnesses, Seventh-Day Adventists, and nondenominational evangelical or Pentecostal Christian congregations.

Eritrea's religious and cultural diversity continues to correspond to some degree to the geographical division of the country into the highland and lowland regions. Historically, Tigrinya-speaking Christians (and the minority Muslim population of the Tigrinya ethnic group, known as Jiberti) have tended to reside in the highland regions and practice sedentary farming and local trading, remaining deeply tied to their ancestral lands. Likewise, Muslims have tended to reside in the lowland regions, where they have long practiced agro-pastoralism and nomadic pastoralism and engaged in long-distance trade. While approximately 75–80 percent of Eritreans continue to reside in rural areas, urban centers like the cities of Asmara, Assab, Keren, and Massawa, are important locations for cultural integration and commerce.

History of Eritrea

The name *Eritrea* is derived from the Greek word *erythraeum,* which means "red." The region's history can be dated at least as far back as 6000 B.C.E., when early dwellers left cave paintings in Akele Guzai and Sahel. Egyptian traders launched expeditions to the coastal regions of modern-day Eritrea beginning around 2500 B.C.E., overlapping with southern Arabian contact up through 1200 B.C.E. The ancient port town of Adulis was established around 230 B.C.E., and by 100 C.E. the rise of the trading empire known as Axum encompassed the burgeoning cultural and economic networks that spanned much of contemporary Eritrea. In 325 C.E. the Axumite emperor Ezana converted to Orthodox Christianity, establishing the highland regions as a center of Orthodox culture and influence.

Beginning in the 700s, expanding Islamic empires from the north and west, such as the Beja kingdoms and the Funj dynasty of Sudan, extended their political, economic, and religious influence into Eritrea. These influences combined and competed with that of early Portuguese explorers, who arrived as early as 1520, bringing Catholicism with them. However, the Ottoman empire triumphed in establishing the greatest control over Eritrea in the 15th and 16th centuries, followed by the Egyptian occupation in the 1800s (see Killion 1998, xxiii–xxvii).

In 1869, an Italian shipping company purchased the port of Assab, which was later acquired by the Italian government in 1882. For several decades the Egyptians attempted to extend their influence from the coastal regions further into the highlands of Eritrea, which were fiercely defended by local rulers. In 1885, the Italians occupied the coastal town of Massawa, forcing the Egyptians to depart, and by 1890 the Italian colony of Eritrea was formally established.

During the colonial period, Eritrea was a settler colony for Italians as well as an agricultural plantation economy and a source of industrial development, labor, and processing of raw materials for the metropole. Under Italian rule, extensive transport and communications facilities were created to enable the colonial economy. The most famous among these is a railway system, which has undergone rehabilitation and restoration in the postindependence period. Italian architects also experimented with different styles, making Asmara one of the most unique architectural cities in the world (Denison, Ren, and Gebremedhin 2003). Although Eritrean people experienced Italian rule differently depending on where they lived (Negash 1987; Murtaza 1998), the shared experience of oppression by foreign rulers helped create the beginnings of a common sense of Eritrean national identity. The creation of colonial infrastructure, and some limited access to education, also assisted Eritreans in articulating their emerging identity as a nation.

During World War II, Italy lost its colonial holdings in Africa. Eritrea became important to the Allied forces, and especially the British and Americans, as a strategic post for monitoring communications and other political developments in the region (Wrong 2005). In 1941, the British Military Administration (BMA) began ruling Eritrea as a temporary protectorate. Eritreans took advantage of the political opportunity established under the BMA to organize their own parties, labor unions, and other voluntary associations, and these became vital for the development of early nationalism. Between 1941 and 1952, Eritreans from diverse backgrounds, both at home and in neighboring countries like Sudan, Egypt, and Syria, began participating in active political dialogue and debate about the future of their country. Some strongly favored joining Ethiopia, with which highland Eritrea especially had shared religious, cultural, and linguistic continuity for millennia. Others advocated Eritrean independence, given the transformation of the region during the colonial period and preceding occupations. In 1950 the United Nations passed a resolution that federated Eritrea with Ethiopia, with some regional autonomy for the former. The federal period was marked by increasing conflict and violence, as pro-independence nationalist factions and active civil society organizations and unions were repressed, and as Eritrea's autonomy was eroded by loyalists to the Ethiopian monarchy (Negash 1997).

In 1961, Emperor Haile Sellassie I of Ethiopia annexed Eritrea, thus disbanding the federation and attempting to re-absorb the country into the Ethiopian empire-state.

However, an armed movement for Eritrean independence, known as the Eritrean Liberation Front, or ELF, had already formed in 1960 in the lowland regions near Sudan. In 1961, following annexation, armed struggle broke out between Ethiopian forces and Eritrean rebels. The 1960s witnessed some of the first flows of refugees, as tens of thousands of lowlanders fled across the border to Sudan, and scores of highlanders who supported independence were forced into exile. Among them were early nationalist leaders like Woldeab Woldemariam and Ibrahim Sultan.

Eritrea's three-decade struggle for independence (1961–1991) remains one of the longest wars in modern African history. It has indelibly shaped Eritrean identity, postindependence developments, and the patterns of migration that led Eritreans to form a global diaspora.

From 1961 to 1970, the armed struggle for Eritrean independence was led by the ELF. In 1970, splinter factions within the ELF coalesced to form another pro-independence movement, the Eritrean Peoples Liberation Front (EPLF). In 1974, Emperor Haile Sellassie I of Ethiopia was deposed, and Ethiopia underwent its own internal revolution, leading to the rise of the Derg military regime under Colonel Mengistu Haile Mariam. In the ensuing decades, conflict wracked the Horn of Africa as the ELF and EPLF fought each other for control over the Eritrean nationalist movement, and at the same time fought against the Ethiopia Derg regime for Eritrean independence. Complicating matters was the global context of the Cold War, in which the Soviet Union backed Ethiopia militarily and politically. The struggle waged by tiny Eritrea, which lacked any superpower sponsorship or external assistance, required enormous sacrifices and commitment by Eritreans, as well as ingenuity and resourcefulness that inspired many observers (Cliffe and Davidson 1988; Connell 1997; Iyob 1995; Hepner 2009; Pateman 1993; Pool 2001).

In 1991, after 30 years of warfare, the EPLF liberated Eritrea from Ethiopian rule. Eritreans emerged from the 30-year war dramatically transformed. The differences of region, religion, culture, ethnicity, and language among Eritreans had been overlaid by a common sense of purpose and nationalist unity that enabled the population to endure "against all odds" (Connell 1997). It also entailed some transformations in traditional gender roles (Bernal 2000; Müller 2005; Wilson 1991) and a reorganization of Eritrean society, which the ELF and EPLF initiated during the war in the regions of the country they administered in the shadow of Ethiopian occupation (Connell 1997; Pool 2001).

However, some bitter legacies of the independence war lingered among Eritreans. The most significant of these was the intermittent civil war between the ELF and the EPLF (1970–1982) as both guerrilla armies vied for control over the nationalist movement. In 1981, the EPLF began driving the ELF out of Eritrea and into Sudan, where many ELF fighters, their families, and affiliated civilians became refugees. While some former ELF members rejoined the struggle with EPLF, others remained in Sudan or registered for refugee resettlement and began new lives in the United States, Canada, Europe, or Australia. In 1991, the EPLF became the Provisional Government of Eritrea, and in 1994, the Peoples Front for Democracy and Justice, or PFDJ, was formed as Eritrea's ruling (and to date, only) political party. For all intents and purposes, the PFDJ is the postindependence incarnation of the EPLF and represents the transition of Eritrea's leadership from a guerrilla movement to a government (Pool 2001).

Causes and Waves of Migration

Migration from Eritrea has largely been involuntary, the result of warfare and political conflict in the Horn of Africa. The first large-scale waves of refugees fled the lowland areas of Eritrea in the late 1960s and early 1970s as a result of the rise of the pro-independence armed struggle and the violent efforts by the Ethiopian monarchy to stamp out resistance. Between 1967 and 1975, approximately 85,000 Eritreans fled to Sudan. By the end of 1981, 419,000 Eritrean refugees were in Sudan and tens of thousands more had fled to Saudi Arabia and the Gulf States (Killion 1998, 357–58). At the war's end in 1991, an estimated 850,000 to 1 million refugees were outside Eritrea, with more than two-thirds of those in Sudan. While many of these refugees were ultimately resettled to places like the United States, Canada, Europe, and Australia, most Eritrean refugees in Sudan stayed there for the duration of the war and after independence (see Bariagaber 2006; Koehn 1991).

Overall, an estimated one-quarter to one-third of the entire population left the country in 1961–1991 due to conflict and other exacerbating factors such as famine and drought, and hundreds of thousands more were internally displaced. Despite concerted efforts undertaken by the new Eritrean government to repatriate refugees from Sudan after independence, some unofficial figures published on Eritrean Web sites indicate that in 1997 as many 550,000 Eritreans still remained in Sudan. The United Nations High Commissioner for Refugees (UNHCR) indicated that just over 300,000 refugees remained in Sudan in 1997 (see Figure 11). Both numbers contrast with the Eritrean government's figures of only 150,000 remaining in Sudan that same year, following several years of repatriation programs designed to bring refugees back to Eritrea. The discrepancies in the various figures available for Eritrean refugee populations is a persistent problem in determining the total number of Eritreans in the diaspora, as well their distribution by world region or country. While it is clear that most Eritreans in the diaspora continue to reside in neighboring countries like Sudan and Ethiopia, the exact figures continue to elude researchers. The numbers are also complicated by the fact that refugee movements are unstable; people may flee the country and then return, only to leave again. Additionally, refugee numbers are often politically contentious and subject to either artificial inflation or de-emphasis depending upon the interests of the political actors, governments, and nongovernmental organizations involved. Figure 11 shows the numbers of Eritrean refugees in Sudan from 1991 to 2009.

Migration from Eritrea slowed dramatically after independence, but less than a decade later began rising again. Two major developments in the postindependence period influenced further migration: the 1998–2000 Ethiopian-Eritrean border war, and internal political issues in Eritrea that came to a head in mid-2001.

The Ethiopian-Eritrean border war began in May 1998 after a skirmish at the border town of Badme erupted into full-scale fighting. The ensuing war claimed as many as 100,000 lives; an estimated 60,000 of those were young Eritrean men and women. Despite a peace agreement signed at Algiers in December 2000, the demarcation of the border by an international boundary commission in 2006, and the presence of a United Nations peacekeeping mission (forced to withdraw in 2008), political relations between Eritrea and Ethiopia have remained tense and volatile. In addition to the displacement of an estimated 1 million people living on both sides of the border, more than 70,000 people of Eritrean background were forcibly deported from Ethiopia to Eritrea. Some of these deportees were born and raised in Ethiopia and had never lived in Eritrea. While some remained in Eritrea following deportation, others later fled back to Ethiopia and registered with the UNHCR as refugees. Some left the refugee camps or avoided them altogether and migrated back to urban centers like Addis Ababa, the capital of Ethiopia. In August 2010, the Ethiopian government announced an out-camping policy that allows UNHCR-registered Eritrean refugees to reside where they choose in Ethiopia if they are able to provide for themselves or have a relative or friend who commits to help support them (UNHCR 2010). While UNHCR estimates that more than 60,000 Eritreans fled to Ethiopia since the 1998–2000 border war with Ethiopia, only about half of those remain in Ethiopia today (UNHCR 2010). Figure 12 shows the UNHCR's data on the numbers of Eritrean refugees in Ethiopia since 2000.

The consequences of the border war on Eritrean society have been negative. Initially, many Eritreans at home and in the diaspora responded with renewed nationalist commitment to defend the sovereignty of their country. Soon afterwards, however, critical questions about political reform and democratization were raised by members of the Eritrean government, journalists, religious leaders, university students, and Eritreans living in the diaspora. Although Eritrea's constitution was ratified in 1997, the PFDJ government, led by President Isayas Afewerki, has not implemented it. Additionally, Eritrea's first democratic elections scheduled for December 2001 were canceled, and the formation of competing political parties was banned by the only existing party, the ruling PFDJ. There were additional concerns about the fact that many people conscripted into the military and national service were being held there long after completing the required six months of combat training and 18 months of service.

In mid-2001, criticisms of the PFDJ party, and especially of President Isayas Afewerki, became visible in Eritrea's limited but lively public sphere. Fifteen members of the government authored a critical open letter wherein they called for liberal democratic reforms in the political and economic arenas. University students formed an independent union and protested mandatory summer work programs; the Catholic bishops condemned war and militarism in their 2001 pastoral letter; and the burgeoning independent media published articles and interviews related to these developments. Citing national security concerns, the government of Eritrea sent the university students to labor camps in the desert; silenced the Catholic bishops and other religious leaders; closed all private presses; and arrested most of the journalists and 11 of the government officials who had authored the open letter.

In 2002, the PFDJ then implemented a strict policy on the registration and regulation of all religious bodies. Minority Christian churches (nondenominational evangelical and Pentecostal) were shut down and pastors and laypeople were arrested for allegedly failing to comply with the registration and regulation policies. The government also forbade home-based gatherings of minority Christians and banned the possession of Bibles or the holding of prayer groups among military conscripts. Many of those arrested remain in prison several years later with little likelihood of receiving a fair hearing. Recent refugees and asylum seekers from Eritrea who have been targeted for their religious beliefs or practices describe extremely harsh conditions in detention, including the use of torture (Amnesty International 2005).

The government also asserted control over Islamic institutions, the Orthodox Church, and the Roman Catholic Church, including detaining Muslim clerics and practitioners without charge, removing the former patriarch of the Orthodox Church and placing him under house arrest, and requiring priests to enter the military. Human rights groups and the U.S. government have criticized Eritrea for violating fundamental rights to freedom of religion and conscience under the terms of international customary law and the binding international conventions the Eritrean government has signed. In 2004, the State Department designated Eritrea as a "Country of Particular Concern," under recommendation from the United States Commission on International Religious Freedom (USCIRF). Eritrea is currently ranked by international organizations like Amnesty International, Human Rights Watch, and Reporters without Borders as among the most repressive governments in the world, with the highest number of journalists imprisoned on the African continent and third in the world behind North Korea and Turkmenistan in lack of press freedom.

Forced migration from Eritrea has risen dramatically since 2000–2001, as a result of these developments. Many of those now leaving Eritrea are young men and women who were conscripted into the military for indefinite periods of time. In 2002, Eritrea ranked third among all countries with the highest net migration losses, with 13.6 people per 1,000 leaving the country annually (U.S. Agency for International Development 2004, 29).

Sudan and Ethiopia continue to be the countries of first asylum for most new Eritrean refugees. Since 2000, as many as 18,000 Eritreans have registered in Shimelba refugee camp, located in northern Ethiopia, near the disputed border. An estimated 500–800 people continue to arrive in Ethiopia each month (with some figures as high as 1,500) and at least as many are estimated to flee across the Sudanese border (Harmon-Gross 2009; Refugees International 2008). While some remain in Sudan and Ethiopia to seek protection from the UNHCR, others undertake dangerous journeys to Egypt, in hopes of arriving in Israel, or to Libya, where they might attempt to cross the Mediterranean Sea to reach Europe by way of Malta or the Italian island of Lampedusa. While en route, these refugees face harsh environmental conditions, extreme exploitation, vulnerability to trafficking, detention, rape, torture, and deportation. Many do not survive the journey, while others are forcibly returned to Eritrea, such as the more than 1,000 refugees who were deported from Egypt in 2008 (Amnesty International 2008).The primary reasons refugees give for their departure from Eritrea today are political repression, religious persecution, and forced conscription. Compounding factors include drought, severe food shortages, and general economic hardship.

Early Immigration

Among the earliest migrants were those who left the country prior to the independence war, either to seek work or education in neighboring countries, or because their political opinions made them vulnerable to violence or persecution. Other early migrants left in the 1950s and early 1960s, under the auspices of Emperor Haile Selassie's modernization programs, to become university students abroad (Balsvik 1985). Dozens of these privileged young people came to the United States, and many later became political activists on behalf of independence in Eritrea (Hepner 2009).

But most migrants from Eritrea fit the definition of a refugee as specified in the 1951 International Convention Relating to the Status of Refugees. By this definition, a refugee is anyone who crosses an international border and cannot return to his or her country of origin due to past persecution or a well-founded fear of future persecution on the basis of race, religion, nationality, political opinion, or membership in a social group. Under the 1965 Immigration Act, the United States mandated that a small percentage of all immigrants admitted could be those who fit the definition of a convention refugee. These were called "seventh-preference" immigrants, and a small number of Eritreans were admitted to the United States in the 1970s under this mandate (Koehn 1991, 151). Many of these people remained in the United States as conflict in the Horn of Africa escalated. They formed the foundations of the contemporary Eritrean diaspora and were instrumental in creating political and social organizations that supported the independence struggle in Eritrea (Hepner 2009).

Immigrant Culture/Early Issues of Assimilation and Separatism

Many of the earliest immigrants from Eritrea tended to identify as Ethiopians until around 1970, when the war of independence in Eritrea, and the nationalist movements leading it, reached a critical stage. At that point, Eritreans began separating from Ethiopians and formulating their own political and social organizations. These organizations' agendas, and Eritrean nationalist identity in the United States, also took shape in relationship to post–civil rights movements, black nationalism, and various anticolonial struggles among immigrants from colonized countries.

Later Waves of Immigration

Immigration Act of 1965 and Succeeding Legislation

While very few Eritreans arrived under the provisions of the 1965 Immigration Act, most arrived in the United States following the passage of the Refugee Act of 1980, which opened the country to refugee resettlement from nations of the global South. Tens of thousands of Eritreans then came to the United States under the auspices of the UNHCR, the United States Committee for Refugees (USCR), and other voluntary agencies that sponsor and assist refugees. However, because Eritrea was not yet an independent country, determining exactly how many Eritreans were among those categorized as Ethiopians is impossible (Koehn 1991; Woldemikael 1998). Ethnographic research on Eritreans in the United States suggests that many of the Eritreans who were resettled as refugees from Sudan in the 1980s had been affiliated with the ELF either as fighters, family members of fighters, or affiliated civilians. Others had been affiliated with the EPLF, and still others simply fled the fighting in Eritrea and were not members of any political organizations.

From the Immigration Reform and Control Act to the Present

The large-scale resettlement of Eritrean refugees ceased following independence in 1991–1993. However, migration continued through various avenues such as Family Reunification, a component of both the 1965 Immigration Act, wherein family members of resettled individuals were able to join their relatives in the United States, and also through the Diversity Visa lottery system, a component of the Immigration Reform and Control Act of 1990. Additionally, some individual Eritreans who arrived in the United States by their own means were able to seek legal status through asylum procedures or legal marriage to American citizens.

The asylum process is a domestic one in which people may remain in the United States if they have been persecuted in their home country for reasons of race, religion, nationality, political opinion, or membership in a social group, or if they fear future persecution on one or more of these grounds if they return home. According to statistics published by UNHCR, a total of 21,469 Eritreans filed for asylum in industrialized countries of the global North in 2007–2008, with an increase of 34 percent over the course of the year (United Nations High Commissioner for Refugees [UNHCR] 2009); 738 Eritreans applied for asylum in the United States in 2007 and 2008 (UNHCR 2009). Figure 13 shows the numbers of asylum applications filed by Eritreans in the United States from 1999 to 2009.

Although the numbers of asylum applications filed are important indicators of the conditions that cause migration, they nonetheless represent a small percentage of the total numbers of migrants from Eritrea in recent years. The bulk of Eritreans who have left their country and would like to come to the United States must remain in refugee camps until they are accepted and formally resettled by the UNHCR and cooperating agencies. In July 2007, the United States began receiving the first of a total of 700 Eritrean refugees of Kunama ethnicity (UNHCR 2007), and in November 2008, it was announced that the United States would accept as many as 6,500 resettled refugees from Shimelba camp in northern Ethiopia in 2009–2010 (Harmon-Gross 2009). It is uncertain whether the United States will meet this stated figure. Moreover, U.S. policies adopted in the past decade, such as the Patriot Act and related legislation, as well as the increasing rates of detention at American ports of entry, have encouraged would-be migrants to apply for protection in states with more generous asylum laws, such as Canada and the United Kingdom.

Demographic Profile

Size and Composition of Community

While the Eritrean population in the United States will continue to grow as new migrants arrive and as children are born to Eritrean parents already living in America, reliable figures remain elusive. The numbers available tend to vary considerably and represent little more than estimates. One problem is that Eritreans were counted as Ethiopians until 1993. Following independence, the Embassy of Eritrea gathered data on Eritreans in the United States for the purposes of the national referendum of 1993. Based upon those figures, the Embassy estimated the adult Eritrean population in 2003 at 30,000–40,000 (Hepner 2009, 106). However, many Eritreans did not register with the embassy for various reasons, so this number is probably low. In 2000, the U.S. Census Bureau indicated that the total Eritrean population in the United States was 17, 520—roughly half of the Eritrean Embassy's figure of seven years earlier. Again, the U.S. Census data is likely much lower than the actual numbers of

Eritreans living in America. Other estimates suggest as many as 100,000 Eritreans may live in the United States (Hepner and Conrad 2005). This high figure allows for undocumented migrants, unprocessed asylum seekers, children born in the United States who identify as ethnically Eritrean, and those who did not participate in either the Eritrean referendum or the 2000 Census. It is hoped that the 2010 Census will provide more reliable data on the total population of Eritreans in the United States.

There are also no reliable figures on the highest concentrations of Eritreans by city, state, or region. Certain cities are informally recognized as hubs for Eritrean activity, however. These include Atlanta, Georgia; Dallas, Texas; the San Francisco-Oakland Bay Area (including San Jose); and the greater Washington, D.C., area (including Virginia and Maryland). However, many other U.S. cities (including Chicago, Illinois; Columbus, Ohio; Denver, Colorado; Seattle, Washington; Minneapolis, Minnesota; Indianapolis, Indiana; Philadelphia, Pennsylvania; and Los Angeles and San Diego, California) also have Eritrean populations in the thousands. Indeed, there are Eritreans living in most if not all U.S. states, if only in very small numbers. Compared to other immigrant groups in the United States, Eritreans remain a very small population overall. These numbers and patterns of residential distribution by state are reflected in the 2009 data provided by the Department of Homeland Security on the numbers of Eritreans who obtained legal permanent resident (LPR) status in the United States from 2000 to 2009.

Eritreans in America form a close-knit community. In particular, the war for independence from Ethiopia produced an extremely strong sense of national identity and a collective commitment to supporting the state. Sacrifice, resourcefulness, courage, self-reliance, and tenacity are some of the most highly valued Eritrean characteristics, and these have served people well both in Eritrea and in the United States.

As black immigrants, Eritreans share some common experiences with other peoples of African descent, including racial discrimination and stereotyping. Many Eritrean American young people self-identify as African American while also embracing their Eritrean heritage. While some important differences among Eritreans exist based on region of origin, religion, ethnicity, language, and political opinion, Eritreans remain deeply attached to the unique cultural characteristics and historical experiences that define them as a national population. For most Eritreans, and especially those who were born in Eritrea, their lives and identities remain tightly bound to the home country. Many continue to hope that they will one day return to Eritrea permanently. More than half of all Eritreans participating in the 2000 Census reported that they were not naturalized U.S. citizens.

Because of patterns of selection in U.S. refugee resettlement procedures, most Eritreans in the United States are Christian and hail from the highland, Tigrinya-speaking regions of the country (Koehn 1991; Woldemikael 1998). While there are appreciable numbers of Muslims and people of non-Tigrinya ethnic backgrounds, the Eritrean American population is not representative of the diversity of Eritrea itself. Moreover, the historical experience of the independence war strongly

Members of the Eritrean American community march near the White House in protest of the alleged occupation by the Ethiopian military of Eritrean sovereign territories, February 13, 2006. The hundreds of peaceful protestors demanded the U.S. government enforce the Eritrean-Ethiopian ruling demarcating the border. (AP Photo/Manuel Balce Ceneta)

encouraged all Eritreans to de-emphasize their ethnic, regional, and religious identities in favor of the common national one. A positive aspect of nationalism has been a collective emphasis on unity and togetherness amid considerable crises and challenges, such as protracted war, famine, and forced migration. A negative effect has been an intense pressure to conform and a tendency to exclude or dismiss those individuals or groups who do not fit well into mainstream definitions of Eritrean identity. Subnational identities and loyalties continue to exist among Eritreans, and in recent years, there have been concerted efforts among some community leaders to draw attention to differences within the community as healthy and necessary for a tolerant, democratically oriented society. Some also view the strong form of nationalism inherited from the independence struggle as inhibiting to the development of social and political democratization in Eritrea.

Age and Family Structure

According to the 2000 U.S. Census data, the median age of Eritreans in the United States is 36 years, and the majority of the adult population (55.6%) is married. However, there is a significant percentage of households that do not constitute families as defined by the U.S. Census Bureau (30.3%) and female-headed households with no husband present (12.5%).

Educational Attainment

According to the 2000 U.S. Census data, Eritreans generally show high levels of educational attainment, with 72.2 percent completing high school, and 19.9 percent earning a college degree or higher. Ethnographic research in Eritrean American communities and anecdotal information indicates that Eritreans tend to place an extremely high premium on education, and many people born in the United States or who arrived as children have entered into the white-collar labor force as doctors, lawyers, engineers, and teachers or university professors. Many of those who arrived in the United States as adults have also attained high levels of education and entered white-collar professions, while many others, including those who came as resettled refugees, have found employment as hotel and hospitality workers, child-care givers, taxicab drivers, and restaurant staff. Because so many of the people now leaving Eritrea and seeking resettlement in the United States either through UNHCR sponsorship or domestic asylum claims are university educated (Refugees International 2008), we can expect both educational and income trajectories to increase in the coming decade.

Economic Attainment

According to 2000 U.S. Census data, the median household income of Eritreans in America is reported to be $33,284, with 20 percent of all households reporting an income range of $50,000–$74,000; and 70.8 percent of the population is in the active labor force. The major occupational sectors for Eritreans include 24.9 percent in service occupations; 23.8 percent in management, professional and related occupations; 22.2 percent in production, transportation, and material moving occupations; and 22.1 percent in educational, health, and social services.

Adjustment and Adaptation

Family, Culture, and Life-Cycle Rituals

Extended ties of kinship are of central importance to Eritreans. In some ways, Eritreans view the entire national population both in Eritrea and the diaspora as one large family. Although regional, ethnic, and religious variations exist in marking life-cycle events, Eritreans of all backgrounds and political views typically come together for all kinds of occasions. Of notable importance are traditions such as the *equb,* or informal rotating credit pool, where community members contribute sums of money to assist with expenses for funerals, weddings, baptisms, and holiday celebrations. During the *enda hazen,* or funeral wake, large numbers of people visit the grieving family and bring contributions of money or food. Weddings (*mera'a*) are enormously popular affairs and in the Orthodox Christian Tigrinya tradition especially, entail three days of events, including a religious ceremony on the first day and the *melsi,* or "homecoming" party, for the bride and groom, on the second day. During the *melsi,* the bride and groom wear elaborate capes embroidered with thick gold thread and sit on a platform above their guests, who gather to eat traditional foods like *injera* (spongy pancake bread) and *tsebhee* (meat stew) on huge round platters set on colorful baskets called *mesob,* and to drink *sewa* (mead) or *mies* (honey wine). After the meal, people dance in the unique shoulder-jerking circular fashion called *gwyla* and play the *keboro* (drum) and traditional stringed instruments like the *kraar* (lyre).

Families and Changing Gender Relations

Eritrean society is both hierarchical and patriarchal, with elder men typically holding the greatest power and prestige. Most Eritrean ethnic groups also trace descent patrilineally, or through the male line. While there are some variations among different Eritrean ethnic groups, such as the matrilineal Kunama and Nara, who trace descent through the female line (Favali and Pateman 2003), cultural norms have historically favored males over females. During the long war of independence from Ethiopia, the EPLF made considerable changes relating to gender and the family, including abolishing child betrothal, altering inheritance and land tenure practices that exclusively benefited males, and empowering women from the village to the national level. While these changes were widely lauded during the independence war (see Wilson 1991; Müller 2005), women's gains have not been retained as extensively and effectively after independence (Bernal 2000).

Elements of family and gender relations have continued to change as Eritreans have acculturated to the United States. Eritrean women have found many opportunities to excel in their educational and career choices in the United States and have enjoyed greater equity with men overall. At the same time, Eritrean American men and women often feel disquieted by what they feel is a discernible lack of respect for age and authority among American youth, and they strive to inculcate more traditional values of respect for age and authority in their children. Many Eritrean gatherings in the United States, especially those of a secular, political nature, are also overwhelmingly dominated by men with few women participating. Data on the most recent refugee movements from Eritrea also indicate that the bulk of those leaving Eritrea today are young men, which may further alter the gender, age, and family composition of Eritrean American communities.

Retaining a Sense of National Culture and Identity

Eritrean Americans have a well-developed sense of national identity and are strongly oriented towards the culture and politics of their society of origin. The government of Eritrea also makes concerted efforts to maintain linkages with its citizens living in the United States and elsewhere (Hepner 2009). Secular social and political organizations are abundant among Eritrean Americans and have been a major feature of community life for decades. During the independence war, the EPLF established chapters of the front in the United States and in other diaspora locations, where people met to discuss political issues and raise funds for the independence movement. Additionally, the EPLF set up chapters of mass organizations that were initially founded in Eritrea; these include the National Union of Women and the National Union of Eritrean Youth and Students. Many Eritreans joined these mass organizations during the war, although they also remained popular after independence. Chapters of the Eritrean Relief Association were also active throughout the diaspora. In the late 1980s and 1990s, the EPLF and then the Provisional Government of Eritrea strongly encouraged the formation of Eritrean community associations worldwide, and these continue to function throughout the United States and elsewhere. After 1994, chapters of the EPLF became chapters of the PFDJ party. Members of the PFDJ are expected by the government of Eritrea and the Eritrean Embassy in the United States to actively recruit their compatriots and to take a leading role in organizing the Eritrean diaspora overall. In addition, the government of Eritrea, via the Embassy and the PFDJ chapters, levies a 2 percent annual flat tax on all Eritrean adults living in the diaspora. While the government does not necessarily enforce the payment of taxes, failure to meet one's tax obligations can result in a lack of support or cooperation on the part of the embassy or the government of Eritrea. It has been estimated that at least 34.4 percent of Eritrea's gross national product (GNP) comes from diaspora tax payments and other remittances (Fessehatzion 2005).

Because the mass organizations and the political party chapters, as well as the community associations, were viewed as being controlled by the general administration of the Eritrean government, those Eritreans who wished to remain independent or were critical of EPLF and later PFDJ have resisted joining these organizations. In addition, because political parties and independent civil society organizations are not permitted to form in Eritrea itself, these have proliferated extensively in the diaspora. Many alternative social and political organizations have been created by Eritreans over the years, including chapters of the ELF and other parties such the Eritrean Peoples Party (EPP), the Eritrean Democratic Party (EDP), the Peoples Democratic Front for the Liberation of Eritrea (PDFLE), and others. Some of these have joined coalitions, such as the Eritrean Democratic Alliance, which has received some political and financial support from Ethiopia. Because the Eritrean and Ethiopian governments remain hostile to one another, Ethiopia has tended to support Eritrean opposition movements whose goal is regime change.

In addition to political groups, civic associations have also formed, and in recent years, these have become important platforms for articulating Eritrean concerns about democratization and human rights. These civic organizations advocate establishing democratic "rules of the game" in both Eritrea and the diaspora and do not endorse any particular political group. They also strive to address issues of immediate concern to Eritreans in the United States, such as assisting newly arriving refugees and asylum seekers, and engaging in dialogue with the U.S. government regarding its policies in the Horn of Africa. These organizations also attempt to challenge the ability of the Eritrean government to affect the U.S. diaspora through taxation and what some regard as intimidation practices, which include the photographing and videotaping of people who attend political and social events that are not endorsed by the PFDJ.

Religion

As noted earlier, Eritreans are religiously diverse and nearly evenly divided among Muslims and Christians. Most Eritreans in the United States are Christian, however, and belong to different traditions and denominations. The Eritrean Orthodox Church (Tewahdo) North American Diocese is based in Atlanta, with many satellite churches scattered throughout the United States. Since the 2006 deposing and house arrest of the Patriarch in Eritrea, *Abune* Antonios, a split has occurred among those Orthodox churches that continue to support *Abune* Antonios, and those that support the new church leadership in Eritrea. In many cities there are also Eritrean Catholic congregations and numerous nondenominational, evangelical, or Pentecostal congregations that conduct services in Tigrinya or other Eritrean languages. In cities without large Eritrean concentrations, people may attend Greek Orthodox, Roman Catholic, Lutheran, or other nondenominational churches. Eritrean Muslims tend to worship in multi-ethnic mosques, although the Eritrean Muslim Council has held an annual meeting in the United States since 2002 to discuss issues of concern and coordinate activities within their respective communities.

The most important religious holidays among Eritreans in America include *Fasika* (Orthodox Easter), *Ledet* (Christmas), *Meskel* (Day of the True Cross), *Timkat* (Day of Jesus' Baptism), Ramadan (Muslim holy month), and Eid (the final day of Ramadan).

National/Regional-Language Press and Other Media

Although the media is restricted in Eritrea and all newspapers, television stations, and radio are government owned and operated, Eritreans in the United States and other diaspora locations have developed a lively public sphere that consists of perhaps

Members of the Washington, D.C.-area Eritrean community gather to celebrate the 15th anniversary of Eritrean independence, May 28, 2006. (Marvin Joseph/The Washington Post/Getty Images)

hundreds of Web sites and several radio stations. Some print newspapers in Tigrinya and Arabic are available in the United States, but Web sites and radio tend to be most popular among Eritrean Americans. Eritreans in the United States are able to access both state-run media from Eritrea as well as independent media operated from the global diaspora. Among the most well-trafficked of all Eritrean Web sites are www. asmarino.com, www.awate.com, www.shabait.com, and www.shaebia.org, which is the official Web site of the Eritrean government. In addition to the state-run Radio Dimtsi Hafash, which Eritreans in the United States may pick up on the Internet and in some local communities, there are at least two radio stations that utilize satellite and other technologies to reach Eritrea and its diaspora communities. These include the Voice of Meselna Delina (VoMD), which is broadcasted by Eritreans living in South Africa; and Radio Assenna, which airs from the United Kingdom.

In a recent survey of Eritrean Internet usage in the diaspora, Stewart (2008) found that the Eritreans in the United States represented the majority (34.4%) of all users in the global diaspora. The demographic profile of Eritrean Internet users is largely males (82%) within the age range of 25–49, half of whom have completed a university education, and 45 percent of whom work in the professional or managerial sector. The vast majority of users reported daily Internet usage for the primary purpose of seeking news and information about Eritrea (Stewart 2008).

Celebration of National Holidays

The largest and most significant national holidays celebrated by Eritreans in America include *Ma'alti Natsinet* (Independence Day, May 24) and *Ma'alti Sema'tat* (Martyrs' Day, June 20). Other holidays, such as International Women's Day (March 8), are often celebrated by Eritreans as well. Most holiday celebrations include a party with live music, food, speeches or toasts, and collective dancing (*gwyla*).

Foodways

Eritreans are renowned for their hospitality and their generosity with food, despite a history of cyclical famine and chronic food insecurity in the Horn of Africa. Eritrean cuisine is very similar to Ethiopian cuisine: large, round, spongy pancake-like bread (*injera*) made of fermented grain (*teff,* which is native to the region, or wheat) is placed on a large round platter, over which flavorful meat and vegetarian stews are ladled and then eaten collectively by hand, using small pieces of the *injera* to scoop up the stews. Most stews are prepared using spiced butter called *tesmi* and the unique spice blend known as *berbere,* consisting of red pepper, cardamom, cloves, and other spices. The act of eating together in groups from a single large platter is important for enacting ties of social solidarity, and eating companions will sometimes feed one another a bite in a gesture of affection known as *gorsha.* For breakfast, Eritreans enjoy foods like *fool,* or cooked fava beans served with spicy green pepper, melted butter, and yogurt; and *frittata,* or scrambled eggs with diced tomatoes, onions, and spicy green pepper, which is eaten by hand with freshly baked rolls. Italian cuisine such as spaghetti, lasagna, pizza, and pastries with cappuccino, espresso, or macchiato is also very popular.

Perhaps one of the most famous of Eritrean traditions is the coffee (*boon*) ceremony. Prepared by women and girls for both everyday and special occasions, the green coffee beans are carefully roasted over a small coal fire or stove, and the fragrant smoke is wafted over the guests while incense is burned. The beans are then crushed and funneled into a clay coffee pot called *djebena.* The coffee is boiled and consumed in three separate rounds, sipped from small cups with or without sugar and milk. Popcorn, often with peanuts and raisins or simply sprinkled with sugar, is passed around with the coffee. Tea boiled with cardamom, cinnamon, and cloves (*shahi*) is also a popular drink, often enjoyed with thick, sweet bread called *hembasha.*

Music, Arts, and Entertainment

Eritreans adore the unique sounds of their cultural music, which varies from region to region, but overall reflects the twin influences of Arab and African. Drums known as *keboro* are more typically used for ritual occasions and holidays. Popular music tends to rely on synthesized beats with stringed instruments like guitars and the *kraar,* or traditional lyre, to which collective dancing known as *gwyla* is performed in a circle, with dancers jerking their shoulders to and fro, bending down low, or jumping high in the air, sometimes with great virtuosity. Features of music and dance common to Eritrea's nine different ethnic groups, each celebrated in Eritrea for their uniqueness, nonetheless come together in an interesting blend of styles. In the United States and other parts of the diaspora, these styles not only blend with one another, but sometimes with other Afrocentric influences such as reggae and hip-hop.

Eritrea has a long history of utilizing a specific artistic form that is most often exemplified in the iconography of the Orthodox Christian tradition. Beautiful stylized figures of dark-skinned people with large eyes, delicate features, and bushy hair

Mawi Asgedom

An Eritrean Refugee Is Harvard Graduate and Guide to Success

(Courtesy of Mawi Asgedom)

Mawi Asgedom came to the United States as a resettled refugee when he was a child and went on to graduate from Harvard University. Now a nationally recognized youth educator, Mawi is the founder of Mental Karate, a training organization that challenges youth to create their own inspiring journeys. He has written four books that are used in thousands of classrooms across North America and has spoken to over 500,000 students and educators. In addition to the bestselling memoir, *Of Beetles and Angels: A Boy's Remarkable Journey from a Refugee Camp to Harvard,* Mawi has written three teen-success guides, *The Code, Win the Inner Battle,* and *Nothing is Impossible.*

Mawi has hosted a yearlong teen series on PBS Chicago and many prominent media outlets have featured him including *The Oprah Winfrey Show, ESSENCE* magazine's "The 40 Most Inspiring African-Americans," and *Ebony* magazine's "30 Black Leaders Under 30."

dominate this "traditional" art form, which frequently appears in murals, triptychs, and other modes through which pictures narrate a story. In the religious context, the stories are often derived from the Bible, but this art form has also influenced contemporary artists. One such Eritrean American artist is Seattle resident Yegizaw "Yeggy" Michael, whose painting entitled "Apartment Life in Seattle" blends elements of traditional Eritrean art with modern international styles and offers a commentary on refugee and immigrant African life in the United States.

Theater and film have also enjoyed a lively audience among Eritrean Americans, who are avid consumers of television dramas, feature-length films, and music videos produced in Eritrea and marketed in the United States and other diaspora locations. Being able to enjoy artistic productions from their home country has helped Eritrean Americans feel connected to their society and culture, and exposes younger people born and raised abroad to the musical, dramatic, and artistic styles of Eritrea.

Integration and Impact on U.S. Society and Culture

Paths Toward Citizenship

Naturalization

As noted previously, U.S. Census data from 2000 indicates than less than half of all Eritreans in the United States have obtained American citizenship. This is not surprising, given the history of nationalist mobilization among Eritreans at home and abroad, and the institutionalized manner in which the EPLF and later the PFDJ exerted administrative and ideological influence in Eritrean American communities (Hepner 2009). One legacy of Eritrea's independence struggle has been the tendency for Eritreans living in the United States to remain oriented towards Eritrea. With some exceptions, first-generation migrants from Eritrea have not yet fully entered into the mainstream of American political and social life, and most remain overwhelmingly concerned with developments in Eritrea. While some efforts have been made at interfacing with the U.S. government on American policy in Eritrea and the greater Horn of Africa, especially in the past few years, the Eritrean American community does not yet comprise a unified or consistently visible ethnic lobby.

Dual Citizenship

The decision to secure American citizenship is likely affected by the policies of the Eritrean government. According to the 1992 Proclamation on Citizenship, the Eritrean government recognizes all people born to at least one Eritrean parent anywhere in the world as citizens of Eritrea, with the requisite rights and obligations (Hepner 2009, 155–56). According to the U.S. State Department, the Eritrean government does not recognize the renunciation of Eritrean citizenship. And while it does recognize dual citizenship of Eritreans residing in other countries, it reserves the right to treat all visiting Eritreans as if they were local residents, including drafting them into the military or requiring exit visas upon departure (U.S. Department of State 2008). For some Eritreans, becoming a U.S. citizen is undesirable because it suggests that one is no longer primarily committed to Eritrea. For others, U.S. citizenship represents an important declaration of autonomy or even political dissent. For still others, obtaining American citizenship is important for developing a more visible presence and forming an ethnic lobby in the United States.

Intergroup Relations

By and large, Eritrean Americans remain oriented towards their own community and concerned with intragroup dynamics and relationships. And despite a long history of warfare and conflict between Eritrea and Ethiopia, ties of kinship and culture mean that Eritreans and Ethiopians continue to interact with one another in the United States to various degrees. Some sectors of the Eritrean American community advocate for strengthening ties with other Horn of Africa populations, including Ethiopians, Somalis, and Sudanese, or developing better relationships with African Americans. Overall this has not been a dominant trend.

The Second and Later Generations

Ethnic Identity

Despite an enduring political and cultural orientation towards their country of origin, Eritreans have also forged a new American identity. This is especially true of second- and third-generation young people who were born and raised in the United States. As noted earlier, many American-born Eritreans identify simultaneously as Eritrean, American, and African American. For their Eritrean-born parents, these changing identities and the historical challenges associated with being black in America have sometimes been sources of anxiety and concern. Like many other immigrant groups, first-generation immigrants from Eritrea would like to see their children preserve their distinctive cultural identities, including language abilities and values like respect for elders and authority figures. Nevertheless, Eritrean families in the United States have had to face common problems of urban life in America, such as gang activity, drug use, teenage pregnancy, and suicide. This has been especially true in large cities like Seattle and Los Angeles.

Educational Attainment

At the same time, many Eritrean American youth have excelled in their educational and career choices, and Eritrean communities in the United States frequently organize ceremonies recognizing the achievements of their young people. As noted earlier, Eritreans place an extremely high premium on education and a strong work ethic, and children are supported and encouraged by their parents to set and achieve goals. It is not uncommon to find Eritrean American young people attending top-notch universities, such as Mawi Asgedom, who attended Harvard University.

Cultural Identification

Some Eritrean communities in the United States have utilized the existing Eritrean community associations to provide support for Eritrean youth in America, and the U.S. branch of the Eritrea-based National Union of Eritrean Youth and Students purports to do the same. But because most established Eritrean institutions in the United States have historically been mandated by the EPLF or the PFDJ in Eritrea, considerable pressures are exerted on young people to remain oriented towards Eritrea. As a result, many Eritrean American youth have felt that their needs, concerns, and cultural realities in the United States have been inadequately addressed in their ethnic community at large. In addition, many American-born youth, and even those who migrated recently from Eritrea, have had trouble relating to the concerns of their elders vis-à-vis Eritrea. It should be noted, however, that Eritreans of all ages have made considerable, if not always lasting efforts, to effectively address the specific needs of Eritrean American young people. Recently, the PFDJ party has promoted a youth wing in diaspora communities known as the YPFDJ. It remains to be seen whether this organization will serve the needs of Eritrean Americans or represent another institutional avenue through which Eritreans in America are encouraged to remain oriented towards Eritrea and the current government.

Issues in Relations between the United States and Eritrea

Since the Ethiopian-Eritrean border war of 1998–2000, relations between Eritrea and the United States have deteriorated. With the exception of the 1974–1991 era, when Ethiopia was supported by the Soviet Union, the United States has identified with Ethiopia as its primary ally in the Horn of Africa. Since relations between Eritrea and Ethiopia soured in 1998, the Eritrean government has perceived the United States as consistently favoring Ethiopia in the border dispute and in other important ways politically and economically.

Yegizaw Michael

A Successful Young Eritrean Artist

(Courtesy of Yegizaw Michael)

Yegizaw Michael, also known as Yeggy, is a successful artist whose work has been exhibited widely throughout Africa, Europe, and the United States of America. Eritrean by nationality, Yeggy was born in Addis Ababa, Ethiopia, where he grew up during the Eritrean struggle for independence. From 1987 to 1990, he attended the School of Fine Arts in Addis Ababa, before he fled to Kenya due to political unrest. In Kenya, Yeggy continued to develop and shape his unique artistic style, and in 1995 he won the "Best Artist of the Year" award. In 1997, Yeggy initiated, organized, and directed the "Artists Against AIDS" campaign in Eritrea. In 1996 and 1997 he consecutively won Eritrea's highest annual national art award, the Raimok Award. Yeggy came to the United States in 1998 as an International Artist-In-Residence, sponsored by the Africa World Press. He also did further work as a resident at Penn State University, Smith College, and the Griffis Art Center. Yeggy has created public art murals and mosaics that adorn banks, residences, restaurants, clubs, museums, and theater sets. In 2009, Yeggy's paintings were exhibited in New York City, in a show entitled *Crossings: A Visual Exploration of Crisis*. The pieces presented in the exhibition, like much of Yeggy's work, depict the challenges of migration from the Horn of Africa and of immigrant and refugee life in the United States of America. Yeggy has approached his art with a sense of purpose and a firm commitment to social justice and activism. He has organized art therapy workshops, art class for middle, high school, and community centers in his hometown of Seattle, WA. His Web site, www.yeggystudio.com, features information about his work, current and past exhibitions, and other activities and projects.

Nonetheless, Eritrea was a member of the President G. W. Bush's "Coalition of the Willing" at the start of the U.S.-led War on Terror, and in late 2002, President Isayas Afwerki engaged in dialogue with then U.S. Secretary of Defense Donald Rumsfeld regarding the potential establishment of an American military base on Eritrea's coast. (The United States ultimately decided to partner with Eritrea's smaller neighbor, Djibouti, rather than proceed in Eritrea). Thus, initial moves towards a stronger partnership between Eritrea and the United States were shunted. As the United States grew increasingly concerned with political developments in the Horn of Africa with respect to the War on Terror, Eritrea eventually emerged on the "wrong" side of the issues. In particular, U.S. intelligence sources have claimed that Eritrea has provided armaments and political support to the armed opposition in Somalia known as al-Shabab. The United States has supported the Transitional Federal Government (TFG) of Somalia, which has also been backed by Ethiopian forces, who entered Somalia at the invitation of the TFG to provide military support and help stem the growth of radical Islamist militias. Ethiopian forces began withdrawing in January 2009. Eritrea has denied allegations that it is supporting Somali militants, and has sharply condemned American interference in the Horn of Africa. Meanwhile, both the African Union and the Intergovernmental Authority on Development (IGAD) pressed the United Nations Security Council in mid-2009 for sanctions on Eritrea due to the allegations that it has armed militants in Somalia. Some observers have noted that both Ethiopia and Eritrea appear to be using Somalia as a proxy to work out their unresolved tensions over their common border; thus, a final resolution to the border issue is understood as key to resolving a host of problems in the Horn of Africa (Hepner and Fredriksson 2007). The United States's impending resettlement of possibly thousands of Eritrean refugees currently living in Ethiopia is also viewed as a foreign policy choice unfavorable to Eritrea.

Relations between the United States and Eritrea have been further embittered by the State Department's critique of Eritrea's human rights record. Both the State Department's Bureau of Democracy, Human Rights and Labor and the U.S. Commission on International Religious Freedom have issued annual reports detailing the Eritrean government's ongoing patterns of political repression, religious persecution, and abuses of military conscripts. The Eritrean government has rejected these critiques and pointed out the United States's own record of severe human rights violations in relation to the War on Terror. President Isayas Afwerki has also stated that the C.I.A. is largely to blame for encouraging refugees to flee from Eritrea, especially young people who are absconding from the military. Some leaders in the Eritrean American community have asked the Obama administration to take a stronger stand and consider instituting more sanctions on Eritrea, while supporters of the Eritrean government have called for the United States to cease interfering in the Horn of Africa and place sanctions on Ethiopia for refusing the implement the border demarcation according to the ruling of the international boundary commission in 2006.

Forecasts for the 21st Century

Eritreans in America are a dynamic, growing ethnic population in the United States. In the coming decades we can expect the Eritrean American community to continue changing, as a result of both new migration and deepening integration into American society. Since the election of Barack Obama as U.S. President in 2008, there have been renewed efforts by both the United States and Eritrea to improve their diplomatic relations, and many in the Eritrean American community are hopeful for the future.

Appendix I: Migration Statistics

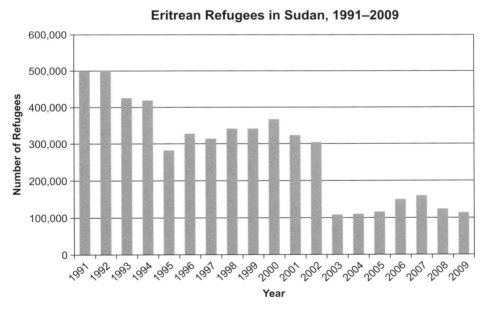

Figure 11 Eritrean refugees in Sudan, 1991–2009
Source: UNHCR Statistical Online Population Database, United Nations High Commissioner for Refugees (UNHCR), Data extracted: 14/03/2010.

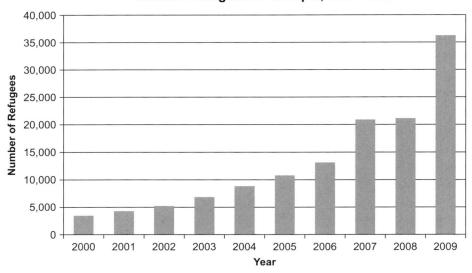

Figure 12 Eritrean refugees in Ethiopia, 2000–2009
Source: UNHCR Statistical Online Population Database, United Nations High Commissioner for Refugees (UNHCR), Data extracted: 14/03/2010.

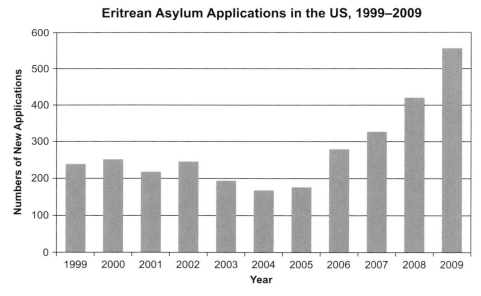

Figure 13 Eritrean asylum applications in the United States, 1999–2009
Source: UNHCR Statistical Online Population Database, United Nations High Commissioner for Refugees (UNHCR), Data extracted: 14/03/2010.

Table 98 Persons obtaining legal permanent resident status by region and country of birth: Fiscal years 2000 to 2009

Region and country of birth	2000	2001	2002	2003	2004	2005	2006	2007	2008	2009
REGION										
Total	841,002	1,058,902	1,059,356	703,542	957,883	1,122,257	1,266,129	1,052,415	1,107,126	1,130,818
Eritrea	382	540	560	556	675	796	1,593	1,081	1,270	1,928

Source: U.S. Department of Homeland Security. Office of Immigration Statistics. 2010. Adapted from Table 3.

Table 99 Persons obtaining legal permanent resident status during fiscal year 2009 by region/country of birth and selected characteristics region/country: Eritrea

Leading states of residence			
Arizona	63	49	14
California	289	163	126
Colorado	114	70	44
Florida	23	14	9
Georgia	107	61	46
Illinois	49	29	20
Maryland	118	56	62
Massachusetts	52	34	18
Michigan	12	8	4
Minnesota	70	41	29
Nevada	78	42	36
New Jersey	13	7	6
New York	23	13	10
North Carolina	46	29	17
Ohio	40	19	21
Pennsylvania	24	15	9
Texas	152	92	60
Virginia	130	69	61
Washington	169	93	76
Other	356	220	136

Source: Adapted from U.S. Department of Homeland Security. Profiles on Legal Permanent Residents: 2009.

Appendix II: Demographics/Census Statistics

Table 100 Selected demographic characteristics of Eritreans in America

Sex and age	
Male	50.7%
Female	49.3%
Median age	36.4
Citizenship	
Naturalized U.S. citizen	47.3%
Not a U.S. citizen	52.7%
Educational Attainment	
High school graduate or higher	72.2%
Bachelor's degree or higher	19.9%
Employment and Major Occupations	
In labor force	70.8%
Management, professional, and related occupations	23.8%
Service occupations	24.9%
Sales and office occupations	26.0%
Production, transportation, and material moving occupations	22.2%
Income	
Median household income	$33,284
Median family income	$38,100

Source: U.S. Census Bureau, Census 2000 Special Tabulations.

Appendix III: Notable Eritrean Americans

Mr. Kassahun Checole is the founder and proprietor of the Red Sea Press, Inc. and the Africa World Press, Inc. Since 1983, the two sister presses have published thousands of high-quality volumes on the history, culture, politics, arts, and literature of Africa and the Diaspora. In addition to its main publishing house in Trenton, New Jersey, the Red Sea Press, Inc. also has an office in the Eritrean capital, Asmara. The Web site of the press is www.africaworldpressbooks.com.

Ruth Iyob earned her PhD from the University of California, Santa Barbara. She is now associate professor of political science and research fellow in the Center for International Studies at the University of Washington, St. Louis. She has published widely on African politics, including the acclaimed volume *The Eritrean Struggle for Independence: Domination, Resistance, and Nationalism, 1941–1993* (Cambridge University Press, 1995). She was an observer in the United Nations-sponsored referendum on Eritrean independence in 1993. She has also held both a Mellon Fellowship and a Fulbright Fellowship.

Bereket Habte Selassie is William E. Leuchtenburg Professor of African Studies and professor of law at the University of North Carolina, Chapel Hill. Perhaps best known for his role in drafting the Eritrean Constitution, he also teaches courses in African civilizations and comparative constitutional law at UNC-Chapel Hill. He has published widely on the historical, cultural, political, and legal issues in Africa and is a highly respected advocate for civil and human rights.

Okbazghi (Obi) Sium earned a master of science degree in mechanics and hydraulics from the University of Iowa in 1975 and for 30 years has served as a water resources engineer, first with the Iowa Geological Survey and then the Minnesota Department of Natural Resources (DNR). In 2006, he ran for the Minnesota 4th Congressional District on the Republican Party ticket against incumbent Betty McCollum (D).

Saleh Younis came to the United States as a resettled refugee in 1982. From 2002 to 2005, he founded and operated a computer aided design drafting (CAD) school called Adulis College, in Sacramento, California, and in 2005 he became president of Pinnacle College, the nation's first audio engineering institution. Within the Eritrean American community, he is perhaps best known as a founding member of the Awate Foundation and the popular Web site www.Awate.com. He is a prolific and talented writer on matters of Eritrean culture, history, and politics, as well as issues facing the Eritrean American community. He has authored hundreds of essays over the years and in the mid-1990s produced a quarterly magazine called the *Eritrean Exponent*.

Glossary

Abune: Patriarch (of the Orthodox Church).

Amiche: An Eritrean person born and raised in Ethiopia.

Berbere: Spicy red pepper blend.

Boon: Coffee.

Djebena: Clay coffee pot.

Eid: Muslim holiday; final day of Ramadan.

Enda Hazen: Funeral wake.

Equb: Informal, mutual rotating credit.

Fasika: Orthodox Easter.

Fool: Fava beans.

Frittata: Fried egg dish with onions, tomatoes, and spicy green pepper.

Gorsha: A bite of food placed in a companion's mouth as a sign of affection.

Gwyla: Circular dancing.

Hembasha: Round, thick, semi-sweet bread.

Injera: Flat, spongy pancake bread.

Kebessa: Highlands.

Keboro: Drum.

Kraar: Stringed instrument similar to a lyre.

Ledet: Christmas.

Ma'alti Natsinet: Independence Day, May 24.

Ma'alti Sema'tat: Martyrs' Day, June 20.

Melsi: Second day of wedding festivities.

Mera'a: Wedding.

Meskel: Day of the True Cross (Orthodox Christian holiday).

Mesob: Large colorful basket used as a table.

Metahit: Lowlands.

Mies: Honey wine.

Ramadan: Muslim holy month.

Sewa: Mead.

Shahi: Tea brewed with spices.

Teff: Native grain to Eritrea and Ethiopia, used to make injera.

Tesmi: Spiced butter.

Tewahdo: Orthodox Church.

Timkat: Baptism of John the Baptist (Orthodox Christian holiday).

Tsebhee: Meat stew.

References

Amnesty International. 2005. "Religious Persecution in Eritrea." AFR 64/031/2005. December 5.

Amnesty International. 2008. "Egypt Continues to Deport Eritrean Asylum Seekers." June 13. [Online article or information; retrieved 7/5/09.] http://www.amnesty.org/en/news-and-updates/news/egypt-must-stop-flights-to-torture-in-eritrea-20080613.

Balsvik, Randi Rønning. 1985. *Haile Sellassie's Students: The Intellectual and Social Background to Revolution, 1952–1977.* East Lansing: African Studies Center, Michigan State University.

Bariagaber, Assefaw. 2006. *Conflict and the Refugee Experience: Flight, Exile, and Repatriation in the Horn of Africa.* Aldershot: Ashgate.

Bernal, Victoria. 2000. "Equality to Die For? Women Guerrilla Fighters and Eritrea's Cultural Revolution." *Political and Legal Anthropology Review (PoLAR)* 23: 61–76.

Cliffe, Lionel, and Basil Davidson, eds. 1988. *The Long Struggle of Eritrea for Independence and Constructive Peace.* Trenton, NJ: Red Sea Press.

Connell, Dan. 1997. *Against All Odds: A Chronicle of the Eritrean Revolution.* Lawrenceville, NJ: Red Sea Press.

Denison, Edward, Guang Yu Ren, and Naigzy Gebremedhin. 2003. *Asmara: Africa's Secret Modernist City.* London and New York: Merrell Publishing.

Favali, Lyda, and Roy Pateman. 2003. *Blood, Land and Sex: Legal and Political Pluralism in Eritrea.* Indianapolis: Indiana University Press.

Fessehatzion, Tekie. 2005. "Eritrea's Remittance-based Economy: Ruminations and Conjectures." *Eritrean Studies Review* 4 (2): 165–83.

Harmon-Gross, Elizabeth. 2009. "Seeking Resettlement and Navigating Transnational Politics: The Intersection of Policies, Individuals, and Human Rights in Shimelba Refugee Camp." M.A. thesis, University of Tennessee.

Hepner, Tricia Redeker. 2009. *Soldiers, Martyrs, Traitors and Exiles: Political Conflict in Eritrea and the Diaspora.* Philadelphia: University of Pennsylvania Press.

Hepner, Tricia Redeker, and Bettina Conrad. 2005. "Introduction: Eritrea Abroad." *Eritrean Studies Review* 4 (2): v–xvii.

Hepner, Tricia Redeker, and Lynn Fredriksson. 2007. "Regional Politics, Human Rights, and U.S. Policy in the Horn of Africa." *Africa Policy Journal* 3 (Spring): 22–48.

Iyob, Ruth. 1995. *The Eritrean Struggle for Independence: Domination, Resistance, Nationalism 1941–1993.* Cambridge: Cambridge University Press.

Killion, Tom. 1998. *Historical Dictionary of Eritrea.* African Historical Dictionaries No. 5. Lanham, Md., And London: Scarecrow Press.

Koehn, Peter. 1991. *Refugees from Revolution: US Policy and Third World Migration.* Boulder, CO: Westview Press.

Müller, Tanja R. 2005. *The Making of Elite Women: Revolution and Nation Building in Eritrea.* Boston, MA: Brill.

Murtaza, Niaz. 1998. *The Pillage of Sustainability in Eritrea, 1600s-1990s: Rural Communities and the Creeping Shadows of Hegemony.* Westport, CT: Greenwood Press.

Negash, Tekeste. 1987. *Italian Colonialism in Eritrea, 1882–1941: Policies, Praxis, and Impact.* Uppsala: Uppsala University Press.

Negash, Tekeste. 1997. *Eritrea and Ethiopia: The Federal Experience.* New Brunswick, NJ.: Transaction Publishers.

Pateman, Roy. 1993. *Eritrea: Even the Stones are Burning.* Trenton, NJ: Red Sea Press.

Pool, David. 2001. *From Guerrillas to Government: The Eritrean Peoples Liberation Front.* Oxford: James Currey.

Refugees International. 2008. "Eritrea-Ethiopia: Shimelba Refugee Camp's Intellectual Capital." [Online article or information; retrieved 7/5/09.] http://www.refintl.org/blog/eritrea-ethiopia-shimelba-refugee-camp%E2%80%99s-intellectual-capital.

Stewart, Emma. 2008. "Eritreans in Cyberspace: Mapping Diaspora Networks." Paper presented at the International Association for the Study of Forced Migration conference, Cairo, Egypt, January 5–12.

United Nations High Commissioner for Refugees. 2007. "Eritrean Refugees in Shimelba Camp, Tigray Region, Ethiopia." [Online article or information; retrieved 7/5/09.] http://www.unhcrrlo.org/BasicFacts/Docs/Eritrean%20Refugees%20in%20Ethiopia.pdf.

United Nations High Commissioner for Refugees. 2009. "Asylum Levels and Trends in Industrialized Countries 2008: Statistical Overview of Asylum Applications Lodged in Europe and Selected Non-European Countries." [Online article or information; retrieved 7/5/09.] http://www.unhcr.org/statistics/STATISTICS/49c796572.pdf. Accessed May 12, 2009.

United Nations High Commissioner for Refugees. 2010. "UNHCR Welcomes Ethiopian Decision to Relax Encampment of Eritrean Refugees." [Online article or information; accessed March 14, 2011.] http://www.unhcr.org/4c6128339.html.

U.S. Agency for International Development/U.S. Department of Commerce (Census Bureau). 2004. Global Population Profile 2002. http://www.census.gov/ipc/prod/wp02/wp-02.pdf. Accessed July 5, 2009.

U.S. Department of State, Bureau of Consular Affairs. 2008. "Eritrea: Country Specific Information." [Online article or information; retrieved 7/11/09.] http://travel.state.gov/travel/cis_pa_tw/cis/cis_1111.html.

Wilson, Amrit. 1991. *The Challenge Road: Women in Eritrean Revolution.* Trenton, NJ: Red Sea Press.

Woldemikael, Tekle M. 1998. "Eritrean and Ethiopian Refugees in the United States." *Eritrean Studies Review* 4 (2): 143–64.

Wrong, Michela. 2005. *I Didn't Do It For You: How the World Betrayed a Small African Nation.* New York: Harper Perennial.

Further Reading

Connell, Dan. 1997. *Against All Odds: A Chronicle of the Eritrean Revolution.* Lawrenceville, NJ: Red Sea Press.

An eyewitness account of the Eritrean struggle for independence, written by a veteran journalist and scholar of African politics who traveled with the EPLF and the ELF throughout the 1970s and 1980s.

Hepner, Tricia Redeker. 2009. *Soldiers, Martyrs, Traitors, and Exiles: Political Conflict in Eritrea and the Diaspora.* Philadelphia: University of Pennsylvania Press.

The first full-length ethnography of the Eritrean war for independence written by an American anthropologist. The book explores the construction of nationalism and political power from the perspective of both Eritrea and its U.S. diaspora.

Hill, Justin. 2002. *Ciao Asmara: A Classic Account of Contemporary Africa.* London: Abacus Books.

Written by a British teacher who lived and worked in Eritrea following the end of the independence war and prior to the Ethiopian-Eritrean border conflict, this book critically addresses Eritrean politics and history through sensitive firsthand narrative.

Iyob, Ruth. 1995. *The Eritrean Struggle for Independence: Domination, Resistance, Nationalism 1941–1993.* Cambridge: Cambridge University Press.

This book was the first comprehensive analysis to appear of modern Eritrean political history. It examines the origins and development of the nationalist movements and the groups contending for power within these movements, while addressing the regional and international context of the independence war.

Killion, Tom. 1998. *Historical Dictionary of Eritrea.* African Historical Dictionaries No. 5. Lanham, MD, And London: Scarecrow Press.

The only reference work of its kind, Tom Killion's *Historical Dictionary of Eritrea* provides a wealth of information on hundreds of topics, as well as a comprehensive and detailed chronology and original maps drawn by the author.

Mengisteab, Kidane, and Okbazghi Yohannes. 2005. *Anatomy of an African Tragedy: Political, Economic, and Foreign Policy Crisis in Post-Independence Eritrea.* Lawrenceville, NJ: Red Sea Press.

An analysis of postliberation Eritrea, this book provides a critical assessment of developments in Eritrea's political, economic, and foreign policy spheres. It addresses the structural and historical conditions and leadership patterns that have led to clear similarities between Eritrea and postcolonial African states.

Pateman, Roy. 1993. *Eritrea: Even the Stones are Burning.* Trenton, NJ: Red Sea Press.

This book provides a historical and political analysis of the Eritrean response to Ethiopian occupation and the impact of various foreign policies on the Horn of Africa region. In addition to the development of nationalism, the military strategies used during the independence war, and the guerrilla movements' objectives for a future state, the book also addresses the impact of famine and humanitarian disaster.

Pool, David. 2000. *From Guerrillas to Government: The Eritrean Peoples Liberation Front.* Oxford: James Currey.

The focus of this book is on the formation and development of the EPLF from the early 1970s to 1991, and its transformation from liberation front to ruling party and government of independent Eritrea. It provides an in-depth analysis of the historical, sociocultural, and political conditions that contributed to the nationalist movements.

Wilson, Amrit. 1991. *The Challenge Road: Women in Eritrean Revolution.* Trenton, NJ: Red Sea Press.

This book is a unique account of the experience of women fighters in the EPLF, as told largely through narratives collected among Eritrean women themselves during the long war for independence.

Woldemikael, Tekle M. 1998. "Eritrean and Ethiopian Refugees in the United States." *Eritrean Studies Review* 4 (2): 143–64.

A brief but comprehensive social scientific analyses of the demographic and ethnographic profile of Eritrean and Ethiopian refugees in the United States, this essay was among the first focused treatments of the diaspora and provides a benchmark in the study of Eritrean and Ethiopian Americans.

Wrong, Michela. 2005. *I Didn't Do It For You: How the World Betrayed a Small African Nation.* New York: Harper Perennial.

Written by a British journalist of Africa, this book addresses Eritrea as a case study in the colonial victimization and postcolonial trauma wrought on African countries subjected to European rule.

Ethiopian Immigrants

by Solomon Addis Getahun

Migration to the United States . . . may be seen as the complex and deeply ironic social consequences of the expansion of the nation to its post–World War II position of global hegemony. *As the United States has become more deeply involved in the world, the world has become more deeply involved in America.* Indeed, in diverse ways, it has come to America. (Rumbaut 1996, 24 [emphasis added])

Introduction

The presence of Ethiopians in the United States has primarily been the consequence of the commencement of a diplomatic relationship between Ethiopia and the United States. This relationship began in 1903. The United States was then an emergent power. A couple of years earlier, the United States engaged Spain over Cuba and the Philippines. Later on, it sent its fledgling navy, the so-called Great White Fleet, beyond what it traditionally considered its backyard, the Americas. Thus, the diplomatic ties with Ethiopia, it seems, was part of this global projection of power. Ethiopia was emerging from a relative isolation. Emperor Menelik II (r. 1889–1913) was reaching out to the West with greater intensity than his predecessors. His efforts bore fruit after he defeated Italy at Adwa in 1896. Since then, the Europeans were flocking to Addis Ababa, Ethiopia's capital, seeking economic opportunities and Menelik's good will; many congratulated him on his victory. In the eyes of the Ethiopians, the arrival of an American mission, the Skinner Mission (named after the head of the American delegation, Mr. Robert P. Skinner, America's Consul-General in Marseilles, France) in 1903, was part of the presence of Europeans in Ethiopia (Skinner 1906).

In addition to establishing commerce between the two countries, Skinner advised the emperor on the advantages of modern education and the possibility of sending Ethiopians for education to the United States. Menelik appreciated Skinner's proposal and promised to send Ethiopians to America. It was, however, his daughter Empress Zawditu (r. 1916–1930) who sent the first two Ethiopian students to attend schools in America. The sending of Ethiopian students that began in the

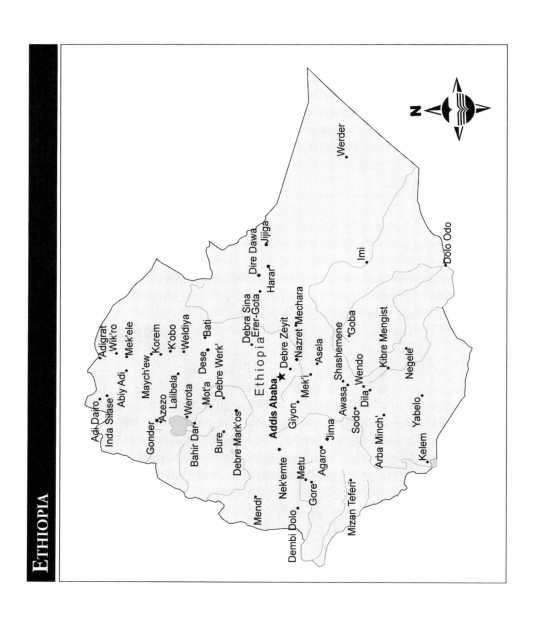

ETHIOPIA

1920s continued in the 1930s as well, though still a very limited number—five students—were sent. It was the post–1940s period that saw the presence of an ever-increasing number of Ethiopian students in the United States. By 1973, there were more than a thousand Ethiopian students in America, which made Ethiopia one of the African countries with the largest number of students in America, following Nigeria and Egypt. Between the 1920s and 1975, the United States educated some 7,000 Ethiopian students (Getahun 2007a).

In 1953, the United States and Ethiopia signed a mutual defense pact. As a consequence, between 1946 and 1972, the United States provided more than $180 million in military aid—a military assistance that made Ethiopia the largest recipient of U.S. military aid in Africa south of the Sahara. This aid accounted for 60 percent of the total U.S. military assistance for sub-Saharan Africa. Between 1950 and 1968, out of the 3,753 Africans trained under the International Military Education Training (IMET) program in the United States, 2,646 were Ethiopians. Of the 1,670 African military trainees who attended school in the United States between 1972 and 1976, more than half of them were Ethiopian officers. In sum, the number of Ethiopian military officers trained in the United States between 1950 and 1978 was almost 4,000. This figure remains even today the largest number for U.S.-trained military personnel in sub-Saharan Africa. By the time of the revolution, in 1974, the Ethiopian Armed Forces were totally dependent on the United States (Agyeman-Duah 1994; Marcus 1983).

As Haile Selassie's quest for more weapons and trained manpower continued, the number of Americans sojourning in Ethiopia also increased. By 1970, there were about 170 members of American Military Advisory & Assistance Group (MAAG); and the number of the U.S. military personnel at Qagnaw Station (America's military base in Asmara, Eritrea) increased from 1,300 in 1964 to 3,300 in 1970. In addition to the MAAG and Qagnaw military staff, there were 87 naval personnel working with the U.S. Naval Medical Research Unit in Ethiopia. There were also 2,800 American business people and educators attached to the Agency for International Development. Furthermore, in the same year about 1,500 nonofficial Americans resided in Ethiopia.

When the 1974 Ethiopian Revolution began taking a more radical posture that involved mass arrest and extrajudicial killings, almost all Ethiopians in America opted to stay in the United States. In the mean time, Ethiopian–American relations began to cool off. The military junta informed the State Department to close off the military base in Asmara and demanded that all Americans (now agents of U.S. imperialism) leave the country. These Americans, besides advocating for Ethiopian students who had now become asylum seekers in the United States, began providing shelter and assistance for some of these Ethiopians while others began sponsoring Ethiopians from abroad. These Ethiopians became the first immigrants and asylum seekers in America.

Following the revolution, the country was beset with draught, famine, and civil wars. The situation was further exacerbated by Somali's invasion of Ogaden, Ethiopia's southeastern territory, in 1977. The instability in Ethiopia gave rise to another wave of Ethiopian migration to the United States, the refugees. These refugees were diverse in origin and levels of education. Through various resettlement agencies, some 30,000 Ethiopians were resettled between the 1980s and early 1990s from the neighboring countries, mainly Sudan. Until recently, these refugees accounted for the largest group of Ethiopians in America (Getahun 2007a, 2007b).

In 1990, the U.S. government, through the Immigration Act of 1990, introduced the Diversity Visa Lottery program (DV), also known as Green Card Lottery. As a result of this program, an average of 4,000 or more Ethiopians are coming to the United States annually. Ethiopian DV winners comprise the third wave of Ethiopians in America. Various Ethiopian Community Association claim that today there are about a quarter of a million Ethiopians in America, though official U.S. figures for Ethiopians in America is much less than what Ethiopians assert. Be that as it may, Ethiopians account for the third-largest group (next to Nigeria and Egypt) of post–1960s African immigrants in the United States (Getahun 2007a).

Chronology

3.4 million years ago	*Dinqnesh* (Lucy), of the *Australopithecus afarensis* species, one of the oldest human ancestors, lives in Afar, in northeastern Ethiopia. (Fossils from her body are found in Ethiopia in 1975).
6000–3000 B.C.E.	The development of agricultural communities on highland Ethiopia. The domestication of teff *(Eragrostis tef)*, enset *(Ensete ventricosum)*, and coffee begins around this time.
950 B.C.E.	The Queen of Sheba, otherwise known as Makeda, rules Ethiopia. The legend has it that she has a son, Menelik I, by King Solomon. Ethiopian kings claim to be descendents of Menelik I.
10th–8th century B.C.E.	D'mt kingdom, a precursor of the Axumite Kingdom.
1000–500 B.C.E.	South Arabian laborers migrate to Ethiopia as employees of the royal court.
500 B.C.E.–100 C.E.	Rise of Axumite Kingdom.
fourth century C.E.	Ezana invades and destroys Meroe.

325–360	Emperor Ezana is converted to Christianity
fifth century	King Caleb conquers Arabia.
615	Ethiopia gives refugee for the relatives of the Prophet Mohammed—Islam is introduced into Ethiopia.
900–1000	The decline of Axum.
1137–1270	Ethiopia under the Zagwe Dynasty.
1270–1974	Ethiopia under the Solomonic Dynasty.
1434–1438	Emperor Zara Yaqob institutionalizes "Ethiopian" feudalism. He creates the Bahire-Negash title for the Bahir-Milash (Midr-Bahire) territory, present-day Eritrea.
1527–1544	Ahmad Gragn, otherwise known as Ahmad Ibn Ibrahim Al-Ghazi, defeats the Christian kings of Ethiopia and rules the country.
1541	A Portuguese military expedition led by Christopher da Gamma comes to Ethiopia to help the Christian king/queen of Ethiopian.
1540s	The beginning of the Oromo migration to the highlands of Ethiopia.
1557–1589	Ottoman Turks annex Ethiopia's coastal lands.
1599–1692	Zera Yacob (1599–1692), an Ethiopian philosopher, writes his 1667 treatise, *Hatata.* He is often compared with the French philosopher, René Descartes.
1620s–1630s	Catholicism becomes a state religion.
1630–1769	The restoration of Orthodox Christianity and the development of Gondar as a permanent capital of Ethiopia.
1769–1855	The Era of Princess, the *Zemena Mesafint,* the decline of central authority in Ethiopia.
	Oromos begins to play a prominent role in Ethiopian politics.
1855–1868	The rise of Tewodros II to the imperial throne and the reunification of Ethiopia.
1868	The British invade Ethiopia and defeat Tewodros at Magedla.
1869	An Italian shipping company purchases the port of Assab from Sulatan Ibrahim, a local chief.

1869	Yohannis IV succeeds Tewodrs II as emperor of Ethiopia.
1875	Yohannis defeats the Egyptians at Gundat (also called Guda-gude), in Eritrea (the Battle of Gudat).
1876	Yohannis foiled another Egyptian attempt to annex parts of Eritrea at Gura (the Battle of Gura).
1870s	Ras Alula Aba Nega, the famous general of Emperor Yohannis IV, establishes Asmara and makes it his capital.
1884	Yohannis signs the Adwa (Hewitt) Treaty with the British. The latter promises Yohannis to have access to the sea.
1885	The Italians, with the tacit approval of the British, annex Massawa and proceed toward the highlands of Eritrea.
1887	Yohannis defeats the Italians at Dogali, Eritrea (the Battle of Dogali).
1889	Menelik of Shoa signs the infamous Wuchale Treaty with Italy.
	Yohannis IV dies at Metema, fighting the Mahdists.
	Menelik becomes King of Kings of Ethiopia.
1896	Menelik defeats the Italians at Adwa (the Battle of Adwa).
	Menelik gives the Bahire-Negash territory (Eritrea) to the Italians.
1900	Italians officially claims the Bahire-Negash territory and renames it Eritrea.
1913	Menelik dies and Lij Iyasu assumes power.
1916	Lij Iyasu is deposed, and Empress Zewditu becomes ruler of Ethiopia.
	Tefere becomes regent.
1930	Tefere is crowned as Emperor Haile Selassie I and begins ruling Ethiopia.
1936–1941	Italians invade and occupy Ethiopia.
1941	Ethiopians defeat Italy with the help of the British.

1941–1952	England retains Ogaden and Eritrea as occupied enemy territory (OET).
1952	Eritrea is federated with Ethiopia.
1953	Ethiopia sends four battalions to Korea to fight beside the UN.
1960	Mengestu Niway attempts a military coup.
1962	Haile Selassie ends the Eritrean federation.
	Eritrean Liberation Front (ELF) launches the secessionist war.
1964	First Somali invasion of Ethiopia to annex Ogaden.
1974	Haile Selassie is overthrown—the end of the Solomonic Dynasty.
	A military junta, the Derg, takes power.
1974	The beginning of refugee flow from Ethiopia.
1977	Second Somali invasion of Ethiopia to annex Ogaden.
1977–1979	The Era of the Red Terror in Ethiopia.
	Tens of thousands of Ethiopians leave their country.
	The secessionist war intensifies in Eritrea.
	Qagnaw Station, the U.S. military base in Ethiopia, is closed.
1980	United States passes the Refugee Act.
1981	The beginning of Ethiopian refugee resettlement in the United States.
1991	The Ethiopian People's Revolutionary Democratic Front (EPRDF) and Eritrean People's Liberation Front (EPLF) liberate Ethiopia.
	EPRDF establishes an ethnic-based federation.
	Eritrea becomes a de facto state.
1993	UN observed referendum for Eritrean secession from Ethiopia is held.
1998–2000	Eritrea invades and occupies parts of Ethiopia.
	Operation Sunset ends Eritrean aggression and reclaims Ethiopia's territory.
2005	Election-related political turmoil in Ethiopia.

2007–2009	Ethiopia intervenes in Somalia.
2010	Disillusionment against the EPRDF continues in parts of Oromia and Ogaden.
	Ethiopian refugee flow continues though at a much smaller scale compared to the 1970s and 1980s.
	Network migration continues at an increasing rate.

Background

Geography of Ethiopia

Ethiopia is located in the Horn of Africa. The country covers 695,738 square miles, which is twice the size of Texas or France and four and half times the size of Great Britain. Ethiopia's neighbors are Eritrea in the north and northeast, Somalia in the south and southeast, Djibouti in the east, Kenya in the south, and Sudan in the west and southwest.

The Ethiopian Rift Valley, which is part of the Great Rift Valley that starts from Saudi Arabia and extends as far as South Africa, bisects the country from north to south. Ethiopia's Rift Valley is a home of diverse fauna and flora, as well as eight lakes. Of these lakes, Abaya (722 square miles) is the largest while Shala (204 square miles) is the deepest. It is in the Rift Valley that the Dalol Depression, one of the lowest altitudes in the world (-100 meters below sea level), is found.

Though the country is located 150 degrees north of the equator. It has mild climate due to its high altitude. In the highland plateau, the average temperature is around 65 degrees Fahrenheit. The country is full of mountains and plateaus. One of the tallest mountains in Africa, Ras Degen (Ras Dashen), which is part of the Semen Mountains, is more than 14,928 feet above sea level. The Ethiopian plateau is surrounded by lowlands whose temperature, during the summer season, can reach as high as 100 degrees Fahrenheit. Consequently, due to its elevation and location, the country has three climatic zones: *Dega* (colder), *Winadega* (temperate), and *Qolla* (hotter) (Mesfin 1972).

Ethiopia is often referred as the "water tower of Africa." And indeed, it is the source of more than seven international rivers, including the Blue Nile. The Blue Nile contributes 85 percent of the waters of the Nile, on which Egypt and Sudan depend for their survival. The source of the Blue Nile, locally known as Abbay, is Lake Tana, found in northwest Ethiopia. Except for the Baro River, none of Ethiopia's rivers are navigable.

Due to its diverse climate and topography, the country is endowed with one of the most diverse animal and bird species in the world. It is a home for 924 species of birds of which 42 are endemic to the country and 3 are rare. Ethiopia is also ranked first in the number of cattle in Africa while it is among the top ten countries in the world. Among the wild animals, seven are endemic. The country has three animal sanctuaries, nine national parks, and eight game reserves ("Wildlife" 2010).

History of Ethiopia

Ethiopia is one of the oldest countries on earth. Its history, some argue, could be traced to Lucy, *Australopithecus afarensis,* whose fossilized remains were discovered by American and Ethiopian archaeologists. Lucy, Ethiopians refer to her *Dinqnesh,* which means "the beautiful," is believed to have lived in the Afar region of northeastern Ethiopia some 3.4 million years ago. Others, though they appreciate the Lucy connection, prefer to mark Ethiopia's beginnings with the meeting of the Queen of Sheba and King Solomon. Yet still, there are some who claim that Ethiopia, like the rest of African states, is a by-product of European colonialism, and thus, they contend, Ethiopia's history, as such, begins in the 1800s. They argue that Ethiopia is the result of Emperor Menelik II's (r. 1889–1913) imperial endeavor that *conquered* the greater half of present-day Ethiopia; and therefore, Ethiopia is a hotchpotch that was sewn together by sheer force, and the 80 or so ethnic groups and nationalities found in Ethiopia were and still are constantly vying for dominance amongst themselves (Teshale 1996; Marcus 2002; Sergew 1972).

The diametrically opposing views regarding the history of Ethiopia reveal that Ethiopia, the nation-state, is unfinished business. It is a process in the making. This process, just looking at Ethiopia's very recent past, has included military coups d'état and the emergence of half dozen secessionist movement or national liberation movements, whichever way one wants to look at it.

The 1960s was an important decade for Ethiopia as it was for Africa as a whole, for different yet interrelated reasons. For Africa, the 1960s was a period of independence and thus of hope and optimism that was soon, however, followed by cynicism and apprehension. The continent was plagued by a series of military coups d'état and civil wars that dashed the hopes and aspirations of newly independent African countries. Ethiopia, though not colonized, had gone through many of the miseries that Africans suffered. Like many African countries, Ethiopia experienced a military takeover. The first military putsch was effected in December 1960. The coup makers were the Neway brothers, Germame and Mengistu Neway, and Worqneh Gebeyehu. The latter two were high-ranking military officers of the prestigious and the privileged section of the Imperial Ethiopian Armed Forces, the Imperial Bodyguard. The bodyguard's main task was guaranteeing the safety of Emperor Haile Selassie's monarchy—a monarchy that traces its origin to the Queen of Sheba and King Solomon.

Both officers and their accomplice, Germame, were products of Ethiopia's unequal association and partnership with the West, mainly the United States. Despite Haile Selassie's trust in them and their close association with the West, the coup makers, like their contemporaries in Africa, the new African educated elite, were dissatisfied with the way things were. They saw corruption and mismanagement of resources of their country by the rulers. The coup makers promised to rectify the injustice by redistributing land and doing away the *ancien* regime. They aspired to establish a republic. Haile Selassie easily squashed the military coup. Some of the plotters were sent to jail; some died battling their pursuers; and Mengistu was hanged (Greenfield 1965; Clapham 1968).

Though the coup failed, it showed the Ethiopian masses that the Solomonic Dynasty was no longer infallible. It could be challenged. Students of the Haile Selassie I University (HSIU) took the lead in confronting the old order. Something unique also happened following the 1960s coup d'état. After the coup, many people in Ethiopia as well as abroad believed that Haile Selassie would make certain reforms. Alas, their hopes were dashed as the emperor continued to crack down on his opponents and strengthen his hold on power. One such disappointed person was Brihanu Dinque, the Ethiopian Ambassador to the United States. In protest against Haile Selassie's rule, Birhanu resigned from his post and sought asylum in the United States—an event that got little attention at that time but was a watershed for events yet to come in Ethiopia. The ambassador was the first asylum seeker of Ethiopian origin in the United States.

Like many African countries, Ethiopia, too, experienced secessionist war or a war for national determination, depending on whichever way one wants to look at it. Two years after the attempted coup d'état, Haile Selassie ended the Ethiopian-Eritrean federation, albeit with the support of some Eritreans. Present-day Eritrea was part of Ethiopia since time immemorial. In fact, with present-day Tigray, Eritrea constituted the nucleus of Ethiopia, the Axumite Kingdom—a kingdom that roughly existed between 500 B.C.E. and 900 C.E. At its height, Axum conquered the Kingdom of Meroe and ruled parts of southern Arabia.

Axum was also one of the earliest Christian nations. Christianity was introduced into Ethiopia around 336 C.E. Axum was also one of the first to welcome Islam. The Prophet Mohammad, while he was being persecuted by his own Quraysh Tribe, sent his uncle to seek refugee in Ethiopia. The Axumites welcomed Mohammed's uncle and his entourage and gave him refuge. Yet, the emergence of a strong Islamic state across the Red Sea dealt a mortal blow to Axum's maritime trade and its dominance on the Red Sea. Due to this and internal disturbances, the Axumite Empire declined and finally collapsed around the 10th century. Though Axum was succeeded by the Zagewe Dynasty (1137–1270), which made its seat at Roha, Lalibella, located a few hundred miles south of Axum, the empire lost its hold on the Red Sea ports such as Adulis, at roughly present-day Mitswa (Massawa) (Sergew 1972; Kobishchanov 1979).

The Solomonic Dynasty, interchangeably known as Amhara or Shoa Dynasty (1270–1974), which succeeded Zagwe, was able to restore Ethiopia's glory of the Axumite times. Some of its emperors such as Amda Tsion (1314–1344) and Ze'ra Ya'kob (1434–1468) regained control of Ethiopia's Red Sea coast. Ze'ra Ya'kob, who is credited for institutionalizing "Ethiopian" feudalism, assigned a governor over what is now Eritrea. While the title of the governor was *Bahire-negash* (king or ruler of the sea), the territory was named *Bahir-milash* or *Midire-bahire* (land adjoining the sea, or land off the sea). Though the rise of the Ottoman Empire and later on, Egypt denied Ethiopia of its coastal towns and ports. Highland Eritrea, especially the three districts such as Serae', Hamsen and Aka'le Guza'i, remained parts of northern Ethiopia until 1896. In that year, though Emperor Menelik II successfully defeated the Italians at the Battle of Adwa, he gave up the Bahire-negash territory to the Italians. Menelik's action has remained a controversial issue in Ethiopian history. Noted historians (Marcus 1995; Paulos and Getachew 2005) have argued that the Battle of Adwa was fought after the Great Ethiopian Famine of 1889. This famine totally devastated the country, especially northern Ethiopia, and thus when Adwa was fought on March 1, 1896, Ethiopians had not yet recovered fully from the scars of the famine. So much so, on the day of the battle, not all Ethiopian forces engaged the Italians. Some were looking for supplies in places as far as Telemt, southwest of Adawa, in Gondar province. Thus, had the war continued longer, Menelik would have found himself in a quagmire, to say the least. It was also in this circumstance that Menelik heard about the arrival of 15,000 fresh Italian solders at Asmara under General Antonio Baldissera. This, coupled with the war-fatigued rag-tag Ethiopian army's desire to return home after eight months of grueling military campaign, convinced Menelik to return to Addis Ababa, his capital, than pursue the Italians and chase them out of Eritrea. Accordingly, Menelik decamped on March 20, 1896, and commenced his return journey. While the aforementioned variables were the reality on the ground, his return to Addis without reclaiming Eritrea (despite an enthusiastic support from Eritreans and the willingness of Ras Mengesha Yohannis and other notables of Tigray to continue fighting the Italians and dislodge them from Eritrea), had been viewed by some Ethiopians and Eritreans as sinister. Leaving Eritrea in Italian hands was advantageous for Menelik. It would divide Tigrigna-speaking Ethiopians into two, Tigray and Italian-colonized Eritrea, and thus weaken them from becoming a viable threat to Menelik. It should be noted that when Emperor Yohannis died at the Battle of Metema in 1889, the imperial throne should have been passed to his son, Mengesha. But, the Shoan king, Menelik, who was in a better military position than the embattled Mengesha Yohannes, proclaimed himself King of Kings of Ethiopia. Since then, Mengesha and the Tigray nobility were at loggerheads with Menelik. So much was their bitterness against Menelik, Mengesha and the Tigrian notables approached the then Italian governor of Eritrea, General Giuseppe Gandolfi, and signed the Mereb Convention in 1891. The convention was meant to create an alliance between Italy and Mengesha against Menelik. The alliance, however, did not materialize. When Mengesha and the Tigrian nobility realized the Italian insatiable appetite for colonies and their encroachment on Tigrian territory, they made peace with Menelik, the lesser evil, and bravely fought against the invading colonial army at Adwa (Marcus 1995; Paulos and Getachew 2005).

After the signing of the Addis Ababa Peace Treaty between Menelik and the Italians, the latter changed the name of the province from Bahire-milash to Eritrea in 1900 and ruled it until 1941. After the defeat of the Italians in 1941, Ethiopia claimed Eritrea on historic grounds. But the British were reluctant to give up Eritrea. In fact, they claimed that both Ethiopia (it had been occupied by Italy between 1936 and 1941) and Eritrea were occupied enemy territories and thus should be under British administration until the end of World War II—a war that just began in Europe and who's victors were not yet known!

Haile Selassie, with the help of the emergent superpower, the United States was able to compel the British to relinquish Eritrea. Thus, after a UN–observed referendum, the majority of Eritreans voted to be federated with Ethiopia in 1958. However, from the beginning, the federal arrangement was doomed. The Soviet Union, who saw the federal arrangement as one more American success in the Cold War scheme of global dominance, was against it. The Muslim Arab world, which then was spearheaded by Egypt, considered Eritrea's federation with Ethiopia as a continued domination of fellow Muslims by a Christian (the ELF to some degree the EPLF and the Arab world regarded Eritrea as Arab); and an obstacle to the centuries-old aspiration of Arabs that desires making the Red Sea an Arab lake. Egypt also felt that a united and strong Ethiopia was a grave threat to the flow of the waters of the Nile without which Egypt cannot exist (Ethiopia is the source for 85% of the Nile). The Unionist Party of Eritrea, which companied for absolute unity with Ethiopia, was unhappy by the UN decision. The Muslim League Party of Eritrea that battled for independence was also discontented by the federal formula. The Liberal Progressive Party, too, was not satisfied. Its objective was to establish an independent but Greater Eritrea that included the Tigrigna-speaking part of Ethiopia, the Tigray province. The emperor, who envisioned himself as Louis the XIV of Ethiopia, on his part, saw a federated Eritrea as an anomaly and an affront to his absolute imperial power. He was also afraid that Eritrea could set a "bad" example for the rest of Ethiopia—some, if not all, provinces might follow Eritrea's example or demand autonomy. Therefore, all concerned parties immediately began working against the federal arrangement (Shumet 2007; Daniel 2005).

It was Haile Selassie in particular and members of the Unionist Party in general that ultimately succeeded in undoing the federation. In 1962, Haile Selassie, with the help of members of the Unionist Party and with the tacit approval of the United States (it had established a military base in Asmara, the capital of Eritrea),

Exiled Ethiopian leader Haile Selassie speaks before the League of Nations in 1936, urging the group to renounce Italy's claim on Ethiopia. (Library of Congress)

abrogated the federation, dissolved the Eritrean parliament, and united Eritrea with Ethiopia. In the same year, some Eritreans took up arms and commenced the liberation struggle. While Egypt provided radio station and diplomatic support to the Eritrean Liberation Movement, Sudan served as a base of operation, a place to recoup, and a shelter in face of an Ethiopian attack. Nevertheless, due to Haile Selassie's political stature in Africa and the world, the Organization of African Unity's (OAU) opposition to secessionist war, and the lack of mass support from among Eritreans, the secessionist war remained unnoticed in Ethiopia and beyond, until the 1974 Ethiopian Revolution. However, the beginning of the secessionist struggle, like the 1960s coup, resulted in migration, though limited. Some leaders of the liberation struggle fled Ethiopia for the neighboring countries such as Sudan, Somalia, Yemen, and Egypt.

The monarchial system that began cracking in 1960 finally caved in 1974. Once again a group of army officers rebelled, this time supported by university students and the urban poor, and overthrew the Solomonic Dynasty in September 1974. The emperor was whisked away from his grand palace in a Volkswagen Beetle.

The Ethiopian military, like all military regimes in Africa and parts of the world, promised to handover power to civilians as soon as possible. Meanwhile, it established a provisional military administration and named itself, Derg, meaning "committee," and declared socialism—Ethiopian socialism—as its political ethos. The civilians, headed by Haile Selassie I University (now Addis Ababa University) and high school students, teachers, and others, demanded for the establishment of Provisional Peoples' Government (a slogan that resonates among members of the Ethiopian diaspora in the United States even today), redistribution of land, nationalization of property, democratic rights, and the right of nations and nationalities up to and including secession (Andargachew 1993; Gebru 2009; Balsvik 1986).

Soon, civilian political organization such as the EPRP, the All-Ethiopian Socialist Movement (AESM), and EDU appeared in the political arena. Individuals with ethno-national aspirations, who saw very little hope in the national political discourse or who were disillusioned with it, organized ethnic-based organizations. These included the Tigray Liberation Front (TLF), Tigray Peoples Liberation Front (TPLF), the Oromo Liberation Movement, the Ogaden Liberation Movement, and so forth. The whole country began seething. Somalia, which have had an irredentist aspiration over Ethiopia's Ogaden territory, sought an opportunity in this turmoil. It launched a military campaign against Ethiopia in 1977. The situation was further aggravated by Cold War politics. Ethiopia is adjacent to the strategic waterways of the Red Sea and the Indian Ocean. This made the country in particular and the Horn of Africa in general a prime real estate for contending superpowers. Adding to the unrest was the instability caused by the country's climate, which makes it prone to periodic droughts and famine. In fact, one of the immediate causes for the downfall of Haile Selassie's regime was the 1974 famine in Ethiopia's northeastern province, Wallo. Hundreds of thousands of peasants left their villages in search of food, some reaching Addis Ababa, the country's capital.

Therefore, the asylum seeking that started following the 1960 coup and picked in volume with the commencement of the Eritrean liberation struggle grew in the 1970s and 1980s.

Causes and Waves of Migration

Revolution in Ethiopia: The Beginning of Migration and the Refugee Exodus to the United States

By late 1970s, Ethiopian tourists, government functionaries, and students in the United States stood at about 5,000. The Ethiopian Community Development Council, which coordinated Ethiopian community associations' activities and oversees refugee resettlement in America, estimated that between 15,000 and 25,000 Ethiopians resided in the United States in the mid-1980s. Some scholars who have studied the flight of educated Ethiopians believe that there were some 30,000 Ethiopians in America prior to the 1974 Revolution (Getachew and Maigenet 1991; Akalou 1989).

Ethiopians in America and elsewhere were alarmed by the brutal measures of the military junta, Provisional Military Administrative Council (PMAC), otherwise known as the Derg. During the first four years of the revolution, the junta was believed to have executed more than 30,000 people. As a consequence, by the early 1980s the majority of the students, businessmen, and Ethiopian tourists in America declined to return to Ethiopia, letting their temporary nonimmigrant visas expire. The migration of Western-educated Ethiopians and government functionaries had commenced. By 1986, an estimated 22 ambassadors, 40 senior diplomats, and 14 cabinet ministers had defected to the West, mainly to the United States. These became the first permanent Ethiopian Americans.

Meanwhile, the struggle for power between the civilian political organization, such as the EPRP, the Ethiopian Democratic Union (EDU), and the AESM, on one hand, and the military junta, on the other, intensified. The Derg, in order to squash opposition against its rule, banned peaceful demonstration and freedom of expression. It began what is known as the Red Terror, a period of extrajudicial killings and mass detention. The Red Terror coupled with the intensification of the secessionist war in Eritrea and Tigray and the Somali irredentist war in eastern and southeastern Ethiopia further aggravated the already tense political situation in the country.

The Eritrean secessions movement that evolved into the EPLF and the ELF began fighting each other for supremacy in the province. At the same time, EPRP, EDU and the TPLF began fighting amongst themselves in northern and northwestern parts of the country.

One consequence of the civil war was the mass flight of Ethiopians, educated and the uneducated, seeking refugee in neighboring countries, especially Sudan. In the early 1980s, there were about 2 million Ethiopian refugees in the neighboring countries. At the same period, Ethiopians comprised the largest group of refugees and the internally displaced people of any country in Africa. In August 1985, at the height of the Derg's military offensive in Eritrea, between 400 and 700 refugees were flocking to Sudan every day. This was in just less than a decade after the Ethiopian Revolution (Koehn 1991; Getahun 2007a, 2007b)

The Coming of Refugees to America

After the Derg's seizure of political power in Ethiopia, diplomatic relations between Ethiopia and Western countries, especially the United States, cooled off. Because of this and for ideological reasons, the Derg restricted permits to Ethiopians who were leaving the country for Western Europe and America. Anyone who attempted to immigrate to the west was considered a lackey of imperialism and thus reactionary. As a result, during the reign of the Derg many Ethiopians took the arduous journey across the porous border illegally. Many well-off Ethiopians who had relatives in America and Europe, and those who had successfully resettled in the United States and other places, encouraged their families in Ethiopia to leave for Sudan. From there, it was relatively easy for Ethiopians residing in America to sponsor relatives. American and other refugee agencies, such as the International Catholic Migration Committee (ICMC), the International Committee for Migration (ICM), and the International Rescue Committee (IRC), came to Sudan with the express purpose of facilitating the resettlement of Ethiopians to America; the presence of these agencies in Sudan further intensified the attraction of Ethiopians towards Sudan. While the Ethiopian government considered Ethiopian refugees as counterrevolutionaries, the United States regarded these Ethiopians as people who voted against communism with their feet. Therefore, in early 1980s, the United States government decided to admit large numbers of Ethiopian refugees. Between October 1, 1980, and September 1981, the Immigration and Naturalization Services (INS, now U.S. Homeland Security) approved 3,500 Ethiopians for resettlement in the United States. Since then, though the number varies, the United States continued to accept Ethiopian refuges and immigrants. As Figure 14 shows, between 1980 and 2008, an average of 1,660 Ethiopian refugees were admitted into the United States annually (U.S. Department of Homeland Security, 2009).

The higher number of Ethiopian refugees that left their country between 1980 and 2008 reflected the degree of political turmoil in Ethiopia. While the number of early 1980s refugees mirrors the immediate effects of the Red Terror and the military campaigns of the Derg against Somalia and the Eritrean secessionists, the number of refugees in the early 1990s points to the chaotic political atmosphere and the relative uncertainty associated with the ouster of the Derg and EPRDF's ascent to the helm of power in 1991.

The total number of refugees and asylum seekers who were admitted into the United States between 1944 and 2002, according to the 2002 INS report, were 40,555. While there was no figure for the years 1946–1950, there were 61 individuals for the years 1951–1960; and two individuals for the years 1961–1970. However, the largest number of Ethiopian refugees and immigrants were admitted after the 1974 revolution. Between 1981 and 1990, some 18,542 Ethiopians were admitted; and between 1991 and 2000, 17,865 were accepted. (See Figure 14, "Ethiopian Refugees by Year of Entry into United States.")

The continuous decline of Ethiopian refugees admitted into the United States after 1993 reflects the relative peace and stability that prevails in Ethiopia and the ease with which Ethiopians can leave their country. Unlike the Derg, the EPRDF does not restrict Ethiopians from leaving their country. Passport, unlike earlier times, was not a privilege that few has access to. In the new Ethiopia, passport is considered a mere identification card. In today's Ethiopia, there is no visa restriction. Anyone who can afford to travel can have it too. The other reason is variations in U.S. refugee admittance policies. Aside from Cold War politics, the American government does not often accept refugees from "friendly" states. Therefore, while the United States viewed the Derg regime as Russia's clique, and thus an unfriendly state, it considers the EPRDF government as one of the most dependable allies in the Horn of Africa. Due to America's belief that peace and stability have prevailed in Ethiopia since EPRDF's takeover of power, it does not accept as many refugees and asylum seekers as before. Even if America accepts refugees from Ethiopia, the number is limited and the process arduous.

One fascinating consequence of such U.S. policy, which was also partly strengthened by events related to the September 11 terrorist attack on New York City, was that as the possibility of being admitted as a refugee into the United States became more difficult, some Ethiopians who were at loggerheads with the EPRDF sought other venues. Instead of waiting in refugee comps, they landed in America—seeking asylum. This alternative strategy, which costs a lot of money, including embarking on a more perilous journey across continents that involve human smugglers and traffickers in order to enter into the United States, circumvents the bureaucratic delays, various obstacles, and uncertainties that refugees encounter. (See Table 101.)

Demographic Profile: A Socioeconomic and Cultural Profile

The local origin of the pre-1980s Ethiopians in America indicates a preponderance of people from Shoa (central Ethiopia, the province from where the majority of the ruling elite came from), followed by Eritrea (northern Ethiopia), and Wallega (western Ethiopia) provinces. This was so due to the availability and accessibility of modern education in these provinces, especially in Shoa. Kinship ties, which largely determined recruitment and promotion in government offices and awarding of scholarships, also favored people from Shoa. Consequently, throughout Emperor Haile Selassie's rule, Shoa had the largest number of schools and universities. It also constituted more than two-thirds of Ethiopian officials, both noble and educated. The remaining officials were primarily from Eritrea and Wallega. The two provinces, in addition to the marital alliance with the Shoan ruling elite, were beneficiaries of missionary education. Protestant missionaries from Scandinavian countries and the United States had been operating in the said locals since the 19th century (Teshome 1990; Markakis 1974).

In terms of education, while Ethiopian refugees in America represent a sizable group of the illiterate, semi-literate Ethiopians, the immigrants and asylees are, by and large, highly educated professionals. The Ethiopian refugees admitted in the 1980s, in addition to the educated, included a large number of illiterate peasants who left their domicile due to famine, those who fled from government-sponsored resettlement programs, and those who escaped the infighting between the various liberation fronts in northern and northwestern Ethiopia. There were also some peasants who sought refuge in Sudan and elsewhere rather than being recruited into the partisan armies. Nevertheless, given the U.S. criteria for winning/applying for Diversity Lottery (the lottery has been in place since 1990), almost all Ethiopian immigrants have completed high school, to say the least. Consequently, Ethiopians, like their fellow African immigrants in America, are among the most educated recent arrivals into the United States. According to the 2000 U.S. Census, more than 95 percent of Africans aged 25 and over have completed high school and more. The figure for the high school completion rate for the foreign born from Asia, Europe, and South America is 83.8 percent, 81.3 percent, and 79.6 percent respectively. This makes Africans one of most educated immigrant groups in America. Yet, the figure for income by household does not correspond with educational attainment. The African household income for the said period was $36,371 while it was $41,773 for Europeans, $51,633 for Asians, and $40,480 for South Americans (U.S. Census Bureau 2001).

The age profile of Ethiopian refugees and immigrants in the United States indicates that the majority are between 20 and 45 years old. This segment is the most productive section of the population. Given the pyramidal population structure of Ethiopia, which is dominated by the 0–19 years age group at its base, the loss of the 20 and above age group is very extensive.

Males dominate the pre-1970s and the 1980s refugee and immigrant Ethiopians in America. In pre-revolution Ethiopia, social and cultural norms favor males over females. While boys were encouraged to be aggressive, to go to school, and to engage in the outdoor lifestyle, girls were taught to be meek and submissive, and to learn domestic chores including how to be a good mother and wife. As a result, the country's educational establishments, which were very few in number, were dominated by males in every level. The imbalance between males and females who were attending schools was even greater at the tertiary level. Fewer females were found in colleges and universities and even more so in graduate and postgraduate education. Because America's refugee and immigrant admittance policy favors the educated, there are fewer Ethiopian females than males living in the United States. Nevertheless, as the availability of education increased and government and nongovernment agencies embarked in rectifying the gender inequity in education and other areas, more girls began attending schools in Ethiopia. The ratio between Ethiopian American females and males is narrowing. Also, these days, migration of Ethiopians to the United States has become more network driven than before. Consequently, the gender disparity among Ethiopians in America is narrowing.

Adjustment and Adaptation

Ethiopians are found in almost every part of the United States, including Alaska. However, the Greater Washington area (District of Colombia, Virginia, and Maryland), California (Los Angeles and the Bay Area—San Francisco, Oakland, and

San Jose), Washington (Seattle), Chicago (Illinois), and Atlanta (Georgia) account for the largest concentrations of Ethiopians in the United States. Of these, Los Angeles and Washington, D.C., compete for supremacy for being the largest hub for Ethiopians outside of Ethiopia, except Israel. The two cities allege to have more than 100,000 Ethiopians and have taken steps to host their own Little Ethiopias. In Los Angeles, Little Ethiopia, situated between Fairfax and Pico Avenues, and in Washington, Adams Morgan, between 18th and Columbia Avenue, are business centers for Ethiopians. However, in Washington, D.C., the Ethiopian community's quest to officially claim Adams Morgan and its environs as Little Ethiopia met a stiff resistance from the African American community (Getahun 2007a).

Los Angeles and Washington, D.C., strive for leadership, on political as well as religious issues that affect Eritreans and Ethiopians. They host the largest number of radio stations, they have the largest number of Ethiopian Orthodox Churches in America, and both host Ethiopian Embassy officials and offices. Both cities are in the forefront in staging either pro- or antigovernment events.

The evolution and development of Little Ethiopias in American cities, in addition to displaying the growing influence and contribution of the Ethiopian refugee-

Wetbu Fikru (left) a native of Ethiopia, holds a poster of Ethiopian musician Dereje Degefaw with Hanna Addis, also from Ethiopia, as they decide where to post it at this music shop on Ninth Street in Washington, D.C., May 25, 2007. The neighborhood is home to a large Ethiopian community. (AP Photo/Jacquelyn Martin)

immigrant community in America, entails determinants of settlement patterns. American society is a race conscious society. Accordingly, a closer look at these Little Ethiopias and other areas where Ethiopians are found such as in Seattle (Washington), Chicago (Illinois), Dallas (Texas), and so forth, reveals that Ethiopians were resettled in neighborhoods primarily occupied or settled by African Americans. In so doing, refugee resettlement agencies paved the way, intentionally or innocently, for racial solidarity between Ethiopian immigrants and refugees and African American communities. This is especially true for second-generation Ethiopians. The second-generation Ethiopian Americans who grew up in a society that defines race in binary terms are more conscious of their blackness than their parents who did not experience the racial prejudices that their children encountered in schools and other arenas in America. Many first-generation Ethiopians, through their mutual community associations, churches, and social occasions, maintained a separate identity. Their children, however, often felt left out for they had very little in common with their parents. They are not sentimentally attached and thus nostalgic of their parents' country of origin—despite their parents' effort to make their offspring remain true to their Ethiopian identity.

Minneapolis, Minnesota, and Columbus, Ohio, expose the prevalence of ethnic chasm and polarization among Ethiopians in America. While Minnesota is often referred to as the "Oromia capital in America," Tigrigna-speaking Ethiopians, from Tigray, Gondar, and Wallo provinces, claimed Columbus as theirs. The Oromo, otherwise known as Galla (it has become a pejorative term as of late), are one of the major ethnic groups in Ethiopia. In both Minneapolis and Columbus, a sizable number of ethnic Somalis from Ethiopia's Ogaden region and Somalia proper are found. Like Washington, D.C., and Los Angeles, Minneapolis hosts mosques that both Oromos and Somalis use and political events that entertain either Somali or Oromo issues exclusively.

Ethiopian communities in America are faced with religious division. Since the fourth century c.e., Ethiopia had been follower of the Orthodox Christen faith. Until the 1974 socialist revolution in Ethiopia, Orthodox Christianity was a state religion. So much so, despite the existence of a sizable Muslim population and a few hundred thousand Jews, the country was depicted, both by its leaders and foreigners, as a Christian island encircled by hostile Muslim neighbors and heathens. This erroneous picture alienated the Muslims of Ethiopia, the majority of whom are ethnic Oromos and Somalis. Upon coming to America, one of the things that Ethiopian Muslims did was to exercise their religious freedom, something that barley existed in prerevolutionary Ethiopia. Yet, compared to their Orthodox Christian brethren, Muslim Ethiopians are fewer in number. Their lack in numbers, which prevented them from having their own religious establishment, mosques and *medrasas,* encouraged Ethiopian Muslims to join their co-religions of other countries. The sense of "brotherhood" among Muslims is also another factor that made it easier for

Ethiopians to join other Muslims in America, especially in the post–9/11 America. Muslims of Ethiopian origin (Oromos and Somalis) are increasingly being radicalized as a result of their association with other Muslims and Ethiopia's active role in the war on terror. Ethiopians are followers of the Sunni Islamic sect, which is the dominant form of Islam in the world (Getahun 2007a).

Until the secession of Eritrea in 1993, Ethiopian and Eritrean communities attended the same Orthodox Church. However, after the Eritrean independence, the immigrant-refugee church split between Eritrean and Ethiopian, though there were Ethiopians and Eritreans who attended the "other" church. The troubles of the Ethiopian Orthodox church in America did not end there. Due to the institutionalization of ethnic federalism in Ethiopia under the EPRDF government, followers of the Ethiopian Orthodox church are further divided based on ethnicity. Regional origin, and context of departure and arrival into the United States are other divisive variables. Thus, in a single American city, one often finds multiple churches bearing different (though at times similar) saint names dominated by a single ethnic group or refugees or immigrants and people from a certain province. Yet, in the eyes of an outsider, it sends the wrong idea—Ethiopians are very pious Christians who sacrificed a lot to build so many churches. But the reality, religious devotion aside, is that the proliferation of Ethiopian churches in the United States is partly a consequence of the continued division among Ethiopians.

Religious institutions offer spiritual guidance and thus could provide a soft cushion for Ethiopian immigrant and refugees landing in America; however, due in part to the weakening of religious institutions, tensions between old and young generations of Ethiopian Americans and confrontations between spouses have often been left unattended. Like many immigrant and refugee communities in America, squabbles in Ethiopian families often arise due to "role reversal." In patriarchal societies like Ethiopia, the young were groomed to be timid, modest, and respectful of elders, and not to speak unless spoken to. In America, however, children are encouraged to speak their mind. In America, often times, Ethiopian children serve as interpreters to parents who are illiterate in the English language. Such change empowers Ethiopian immigrant-refugee children. Ethiopian husbands, who were the sole bread winners in their country and thus the sole decision makers, often lose this privileged position in America. Professional accreditation requirements sometimes prevent husbands from securing better jobs vis-à-vis their semi-educated or illiterate spouses. In Ethiopia, due to cultural norms, females were not encouraged to be independent, and they were not provided with equal educational and job opportunities. In America, spouses could end up working similar jobs regardless of differences in their educational attainment. At other times, due to the relative availability of opportunities for women, wives could end up being the sole bread winner in America. Or, because women could work and earn a living in America, they may demand more respect and power within the relationship.

The growing power of Ethiopian American women threatens the status quo, which in turn sets off marital disputes. The lack of community or religious intervention to stave off such problems and the culturally uninformed intervention of county, city, and state authorities in America make matters worse. As a result, many Ethiopian families end up in divorce, which in turn has made the divorce rate among Ethiopians in America much higher than the host society.

Besides churches and mutual community organizations, Ethiopians in America have established a soccer federation, the Ethiopian Sports Federation in North America (ESFNA). The federation, which primarily facilitates soccer tournaments annually in one of the major American and Canadian cities, was established in 1982. Since then, it has become one of the most enduring Ethiopian immigrant associations in America while many others have failed. When established, it had less than five clubs but today it has more than 24 first- and second-division clubs (Getahun 2009).

The soccer tournament has become more than just an event where various clubs engage in a soccer match. By bringing noted Ethiopians from Ethiopia and other parts of the world, the tournament introduces these distinguished Ethiopians to second-generation Ethiopian Americans. The communal aspect of the tournament encourages the younger generation to emulate these prominent Ethiopians and strengthens the bond between the country of origin and the settlement.

An observation of the event reveals a community in the process of transition or Americanization. One notices Ethiopian traditional foods such as *injera* (a spongy, pita-like bread made of *teff*) with various types of *wot* (stew), *kitfo* (minced beef mixed with spiced butter), and so forth, competing against or supplementing American foods such as hotdogs, burgers, smoothies, and so forth. The tournament is indeed one place where one can observe Ethiopian identity affirmed as well as challenged by and reshaped into Ethiopian American identity.

ESFNA is one of the multiethnic and religious organizations with little or no political affiliation either with the government or the opposition in the diaspora. However, like the Ethiopian Orthodox Church in America, it has its share of uncertainties. One such predicament occurred with the independence of Eritrea in 1993. Until that time many Eritreans played in one of the Ethiopian soccer clubs in America. However, after independence, these Eritreans were observed playing for Eritrean soccer clubs—Eritreans, too, have established their club after independence. While many Ethiopians felt betrayed by the actions of the Eritrean soccer players who also played for Eritrea, they were willing to forgive. But, the Eritrean sports federation was not as forgiving as the Ethiopians. Ethiopians who played soccer in Eritrean teams were purged. Faced with such problems and trying to maintain its apolitical stance, the ESFNA left the decision to keep or purge Eritrean players in their club to individual clubs—a smart judgment that saved the federation from disintegration.

Redwan Hamza, spokesman for the Oromo Community of Minnesota, speaks in his office in Minneapolis about the influx of Ethiopians to Minnesota, July 14, 2006. Ethiopian refugees arriving in the state in 2005 increased 63 percent from the previous year. (AP Photo/Janet Hostetter)

In a similar fashion with Eritreans, Oromos, especially those who support the Oromo Liberation Movement (the organization fights for the independence of the Oromia state from Ethiopia) established Oromo Sports Federation in North America (OSFNA) in the 1990s. They, too, discouraged ethnic Oromos from playing for ESFNA. To dissuade some Oromo soccer players and fans from attending the ESFNA event, which was held in the week of July 4, the OSFNA often held their tournament in the same weekend. Despite such politically driven polarization, the majority of Ethiopians, Eritreans, and Oromos attend the soccer tournament regardless (Getahun 2009).

Integration and Impact on U.S. Society and Culture

The 1990s in general and 1991 in particular was a critical period in Ethiopian history. The military junta that ruled the country for almost two decades was overthrown. In its place, a coalition of ethno-nationalist rebel movements, the EPRDF, came to power. For many Ethiopians in the diaspora, EPRDF's ethnic policies and its willingness to accept the secession of Eritrea from Ethiopia was unforgivable. Many Ethiopians in America also regarded the policies of the EPRDF government as anti-Ethiopian and undemocratic. Hence, for many Ethiopian refugees and asylees in America and elsewhere the hope and desire of going back to Ethiopia for good died with the coming to power of EPRDF. This could be best witnessed from the dramatic increase in the number of Ethiopians who become naturalized American citizens since the 1990s. There were less than 5,000 Ethiopians who became citizens prior to the 1990s, though there were Ethiopians who had been in the United States for more than two decades (U.S. Department of Homeland Security 2009) (see Table 102).

The Ethiopians who came to America before 1990, like many refugees and asylum seekers from other countries, had regarded their stay in America temporary. They believed that one day, when things get better back home, they would return. Thus, they were sojourners. Very few desired to be naturalized Americans despite the bleak political situation in Ethiopia between 1974 and 1991. But once their hope for returning to Ethiopia was shattered with the coming of EPRDF to power in 1991, many opted to become Americans.

Aside from the continued antigovernment posture of Ethiopians in America, there are other variables that convinced Ethiopians to seek American citizenship. Like many immigrants and refugees that came to America before them, Ethiopians love America. As they enjoy the fruits of American democracy and the opportunities that America offers, they also want to contribute their share; and one of the best ways that they can return what America gave them is by becoming its citizen.

Upon coming to power, the EPRDF, unlike the Derg that prevented the return of members of the Ethiopian diaspora to Ethiopia, was willing to accept Ethiopian returnees as visitors or for good. Yet, those Ethiopians who sought asylum or refugee status in the United States can no longer claim political persecution if they visit their country. The EPRDF government also enticed members of the diaspora, regardless of their political opinion, with free urban land and investment opportunities in Ethiopia. To have security while in Ethiopia and to facilitate their travel, many Ethiopians became naturalized American citizens. The 1998–2000 Eritrean and Ethiopian boundary conflict that evolved into a full-fledged battle made some Ethiopian asylees and refugees in America stateless. It should be noted that until 1993, Eritreans asylum seekers and refugees came to the United States as Ethiopians or immigrated to the United States with an Ethiopian passport. Even after the independence of Eritrea, there were many Eritreans who remained Ethiopians. However, as the war progressed, both Ethiopia and Eritrea began deporting each others' citizens from their respective countries. The government of Ethiopia revoked Ethiopian citizenship of Eritreans who voted positively in Eritrea's referendum for independence. In light of these circumstances, Eritreans of Ethiopian origin have two choices, either to become American or have the new Eritrean passport. Some chose the former. The post–Cold War period, which is often dubbed the Age of Globalization, also encouraged Ethiopians to seek American citizenship. American passport guarantees a relative safety and facilitates travel better than an

Ethiopian passport. Also, 9/11 made it harder for asylum seekers, refugees, and immigrant aliens to find jobs. The best remedy was to become an American citizen. Since the introduction of the DV in early 1990s, many Ethiopians have benefited from it. Unlike the Ethiopian refugees and asylees of the pre-1990s, DV winners come to the United States willingly and thus are more eager to become naturalized Americans. Therefore, the number of Ethiopians who are becoming naturalized citizens of America is continually increasing. By 2008, their number eclipsed the total figure for Ethiopians who had been naturalized between 1940s and 1990.

The Second and Later Generations

By and large, the Ethiopian society is patriarchal. Though women may have say in domestic affairs, men are the sole bread winners and hence the final decision makers. Social and cultural norms favor males over females. While boys are encouraged to be aggressive, go to school, and engage in outdoor activities, girls are taught to be meek and submissive, and to learn domestic chores including how to be a good wife and mother. While such norms reveal the prevalence of gender inequality in Ethiopia, there is also inequality based on generation. Overall, children are expected to be quiet, obedient, submissive, and respectful of elders. Children are instructed not to speak unless spoken to. American culture, relatively speaking, encourages equal opportunity regardless of gender and age. It encourages children to be self-reliant, expressive, and assertive. In light of this, second-generation Ethiopians are compelled to live in two different worlds, the world at home and that at school (McAdoo, Young, and Getahun 2007).

Though the patriarchal order of things at home might vary depending on the Ethiopian parents' level of education and degrees of exposure to Western culture prior to arrival to United States, fear of the unknown in America and the negative image that the media projects regarding African Americans, further strengthens patriarchy at home. Refugee resettlement agencies often resettle refugees in inner cities where the majority of the residents are African American and another ethnic minorities. Settlement in rundown ethnic-minority dominated neighborhoods often exposes second-generation Ethiopians, especially boys, to the harsh realities of the inner-city life. Consequently, Ethiopian parents continue to employ firm parental control. In the meantime, they also adapt a less engaging posture toward African Americans and other ethnic minorities. Thus, for Ethiopian parents as well as other Africans (depending upon their class and race consciousness) attaining the American dream means lessening their assimilation into the black American society. Despite parents' desire to keep their children separate from African American culture, as indicated in previous sections, like other African immigrants, Ethiopian American immigrants are often swept up into the African American experience, often

---

Youth Profile

A Victim of the Military, She Speaks and Writes for Others

Maaza Mengiste, whose family was one of the victims of the military junta, otherwise known as the Derg, left Ethiopia when she was four years old. Maaza graduated with an MFA in creative writing from New York University. Her first novel, *Beneath the Lion's Gaze,* intimately relates the odyssey in an Ethiopian's exile following the downfall of Haile Selassie and the rise of the military junta. Her book follows the path of her contemporaries, Dinaw Mengestu (*The Beautiful Things That Heaven Bears*) and Nega Mezlekia (*Notes From the Hyena's Belly*), who are victims of the brutal rule of the Derg. All three writers left their country and live in exile in Europe and North America. Maaza received reviews that often complemented and compared her with young African writers the likes of Nigeria's Chris Abani, Chimamanda Ngozi Adichie, Helon Habila, Uwem Akpan, and Uzodinma Iweala, as well as Sierra Leone's Aminatta Forna. Maaza is often sought as a speaker by young Ethiopians attending schools throughout the United States. Maaza lives and works in Brooklyn, New York.

Source: "*Beneath the Lion's Gaze* Book Review." *NewsDire.* [Online article retrieved 6/10.] http://www.newsdire.com/news/60-beneah-the-lions-gaze-by-meaza-mengiste-book-review.html.

---

times by choice and other times by default or external ascriptions. This is especially true of second-generation Ethiopians. The second-generation Ethiopian Americans who grow up in a society that defines race in binary terms are more conscious of their blackness than their parents who do not understand the racial prejudices that their children encounter in schools and other areas in the American society. Most often first-generation Ethiopian immigrants, through their mutual community associations, churches, and social occasions, are able to maintain their separate identity. Their children, however, can feel left out for they have very little in common with their parents. The Ethiopian Orthodox Church employs Geez, an ancient liturgical language, which few of its laity understands. It does not at all appeal to the younger generation. Going to church, the young generation often remarks, "is boring." Community organizations have not yet given due attention to second-generation Ethiopian Americans. Almost all community associations in America are run by the old guard that still believes in authoritarian parenting and are very much involved in the politics at home rather than the well-being of the younger generation in America. Therefore, many second-generation Ethiopian Americans are not sentimentally attached to Ethiopia and thus lack their parents' nostalgia for their country of origin—despite their parents' efforts to make their offspring remain true to their Ethiopian identity (McAdoo, Young, and Getahun 2007).

The existence of divergent cultural norms between Ethiopian parents and their children also has a bearing on socialization and marriage. The issue is further complicated for the following reasons. Like the rest of African immigrants and refugees in America, Ethiopians are ethnically diverse, and at times are acutely divided in terms of regional or ethnic origin. Ethiopians identify themselves, especially after 1991, as Amhara, Oromo, Tigray, and so forth. Accordingly, Ethiopian parents want their children to marry or socialize with Ethiopians, and after the secession of Eritrea from Ethiopia and the heightened sense of ethno-nationalism among the old generation Ethiopians since then, parents prefer their children to socialize with their co-ethnics. The issue becomes very dicey when the children are of mixed parents. For instance, children of Eritrean and Ethiopian parents are expected to marry into the respective co-ethnics by both parents. If that is not possible, parents want their children to marry at least a person from their home province such as Shoa, Gondar, Eritrea, Wallega, Tigray, and so forth. In light of this, dating or marrying a *fereng* (an American or European) is unacceptable. However, the overall preponderance of single male Ethiopians vis-à-vis single female Ethiopians in America poses additional difficulty for the young generation. Thus, regardless of their parents' desires, the children of Ethiopian immigrants who grow up in the United States seek mates who can relate to their own experiences. However, this is further complicated based on their area of residence; they often encounter difficulties if they don't reside in one of the large metropolitan cities where a large proportion of Ethiopian immigrants reside. The second generation must choose whether they want to marry someone directly from their parents' home country, someone more assimilated into the American society with a background similar to theirs, or whether they want to marry outside of their national and racial group altogether.

In Ethiopia, education is the only means for upward mobility. In America, too, Ethiopian parents stress education as a means of upward mobility and emphasize the value of education to their children. They also advise their children to disregard racial discrimination and focus on their education in order to be successful, though success in education might not be as rewarding in America as it is in Ethiopia.

The primary reason for the migration of many Africans, including Ethiopians, to America is political repression. Thus, Ethiopian immigrant parents in America, like many immigrants before them, are actively involved in politics at home. They want their children to be equally engaged with politics in Ethiopia. What these parents overlook is that their children are Americans with little or no sentimental attachment to the country of origin. Besides, the fractious political environment among Ethiopians discourages the younger generation from getting involved. For instance, while their parents are divided into Eritrean, Oromo, Tigrian, and so forth, and organize themselves as such, the younger generation prefer to coalesce under

---

An Organizer for Grassroots Political and Civic Engagement

Menna Demessie left Ethiopia at an early age with her father Engineer Akililu Demessie. Her life story, like Maaza's, is intertwined with events related to the 1974 revolution in Ethiopia. Menna graduated with a BA degree in economics and law and society with honors from Oberlin College. In the college, she had served as a senior class president. Menna received her PhD in political science from the University of Michigan in 2010. Her dissertation was on legislative behavior, racial and ethnic politics, immigration, and the political participation of African immigrants in the United States. Menna was the 2006 Walter Rodney Prize Recipient at the University of Michigan. In 2005, she was part of the Ford School Public Policy team that traveled to Ethiopia to conduct social and economic analyses prior to the 2005 elections. She has also spoken at Capitol Hill about the need for grassroots political and civic engagement of Ethiopian Americans in the United States.

Menna is the national youth coordinator of the Society of Ethiopians Established in the Diaspora (SEED). The organization is a nonprofit entity established in 1993 in the United States. It strives to enhance and cultivate the lives of Ethiopians and Ethiopian Americans in order for them to become productive citizens of society.

Source: [Online article retrieved 6/10.] http://sitemaker.umich.edu/menna/home.

---

a pan-Ethiopian, pan-African, or African American identity. A good instance of this is the establishment of Ethiopian-Eritrean student association at Stanford University. The organization includes anyone from Ethiopia; however, the majority of the members are second-generation Ethiopian Americans. The formation of the East African gang in Seattle, Washington, whose membership includes Ethiopians, Somalis, and Eritreans, is a further testimony that the younger generation of Ethiopians, Eritreans, and Somalis are averse to division.

The previously mentioned circumstances highlight the predicament that second-generation Ethiopian Americans might face. Yet, there is little study conducted on second-generation Ethiopian Americans. In fact, there is no research that examines Ethiopian immigrants on ethnic lines—though some Ethiopians will view such an endeavor as divisive and counterproductive. Until such study is conducted and the community is informed of the results, the predicaments of the younger generation will continue for sometime.

Two young girls watch from the front seat of a car as several hundred Ethiopian demonstrators protest outside the World Bank in Washington, D.C., on May 13, 2002. The protestors were expressing their outrage at Ethiopia's Tigray People's Liberation Front (TPLF) regime and the World Bank activity in Ethiopia. (Paul J. Richards/AFP/Getty Images)

Issues in Relations between the United States and Ethiopia

The migration of Ethiopians to the United States, which began with a handful of students in 1920s, has dramatically changed in the past four or so decades. Initially, asylees and refugees were dominant among the Ethiopian immigrant community in America. In the past 10 years or so, however, the pattern increasingly shifted from asylees and refugees, who were reluctant sojourners in America, to network migrants. Consequently, either through family reunion or as DV lottery winners, an average of 5,000 Ethiopians are entering the United States annually since 1991. Today, Ethiopians in America account for the third-largest immigrant group from Africa. Also, unlike earlier times, more Ethiopians are becoming naturalized U.S. citizens (Getahun 2007a).

In addition to the immigrant community, the global war on terror and regional stability are issues that will bind Ethiopia and the United States together for years to come. As in the Cold War period, the region has caught global attention. At first glance, the reason for the current attention to the region seems different than that of the past, but fundamentally, the issue remains the same: it has been and continues to be difficult to bring democratic governance and meaningful and substantial change to the multitude in the region. One of the casualties in the area is Somalia—it imploded. The country is now a battleground between Islamic fundamentals, who transcends clan- and state-based loyalties, and those who adhere to clan loyalty and those who try to resurrect the territorial-state. The dissolution of the territorial-state in Somalia, in addition to providing fertile ground for the radicalization of Islam in that country, resulted in the development of piracy as a means of sustenance.

Sudan, though not imploded, is also on the verge of becoming another failed state. It is a country that has been oscillating between Arab and African identities and nationalisms. Such developments, which can be traced to its colonial past, might ultimately break the country into two: North and South Sudan. If this happens, there is no guarantee that Darfur and the Eastern Sudan will not follow the example of the South. Radical Islam has strong roots in Sudan. Hassan al-Turabi's party is opposed to a secular state. Al-Turabi espouses a Muslim state for Sudan. At one time, Sudan served as a refuge for Osama bin Laden.

The leader of the newly independent Eritrea, Isayas Afewerqi, squandered the goodwill of the world. Besides establishing a one-man rule in the mold of Mugabe, he instigated wars against his neighbors, Yemen, Ethiopia, and Djibouti. His undemocratic practices, coupled with unfulfilled expectations on the aftermath of the country's independence from Ethiopia, are making Eritrea vulnerable for ethnic as well as religious strife. Eritrea is a home for nine ethnic groups; the groups follow Islam, Christianity (Orthodox, Catholic, and Protestant), and animism. Of these, Muslims, who roughly account for half of the population, are complaining of unfair treatment under Isayas Afewerqi's Eritrea.

Kenya, like its neighbors, is also susceptible to crisis. Recent events in Kenya revealed that the country is not immune from either the threats of Islamic radicalism or ethnic tensions.

Ethiopia, though currently stable, is not an exception. The absence of democratic governance and lack of economic progress had already cost it a lofty price—Eritrea seceded. Unless the country's leaders honor their promises of establishing a democratic order in Ethiopia, the country is vulnerable to the path that the Somalis took. In Ethiopia, the threat of Islamic fundamentalism is real. Like the United States, Ethiopia has a legitimate concern. The majority of Ethiopian Muslims reside in Oromia and Ogaden (Ethiopia's Somali region). The regions adjoin the defunct Somali state where the *al-shabab,* which has close ties with *al-qaida,* operates. The *al-shabab* also claims Ethiopia's Ogaden as part of Somalia; and people of the two regions who felt oppressed under the EPRDF regime have established the Ogaden and Oromo Liberation Fronts.

Therefore, for its own survival and interest, Ethiopia is a party to the war on terror. As events in Somalia demonstrated, the implosion of Sudan or Eritrea is detrimental to its interest. Beside the burden for hosting millions of refugees, these countries could become a staging ground for radical Islam and for proxy wars. For the United States, finding a stable ally in one of the most unstable, yet strategically important parts of the globe, is vital to its strategic interest.

Yet, anchoring U.S. foreign policy options on the war on terror alone could be counter-productive. America's promises of upholding democracy and civil liberties in the post-Cold War era should not be sidelined or simply become a rhetoric designed for local consumption. African leaders, who are willing to join the war on terror," though they are noted for terrorizing their own people, are being touted as "new breed" and "visionary" leaders by the United States and given a red carpet welcome at Capitol Hill. The United States should condemn such leaders, to say the least. So far, as records of U.S. foreign policy toward Africa reveal, it is riddled with duplicity. America has a tendency to look the other way when African dictators trample upon human liberties as long as they serve its global politico-military strategic interest. Such leaders were and still are provided with substantial American military, economic as well as humanitarian aid.

Nevertheless, such an oversight, on America's part, is being challenged by transnational civic movements, organizations, and an increasing number of African immigrants (including Ethiopian Americans) who became naturalized U.S. citizens and thus use their vote to dissuade American foreign policy makers from following the well-trodden path.

Appendix I: Migration Statistics

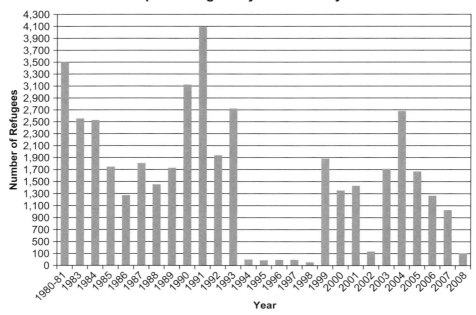

Figure 14 Ethiopian refugees by year of entry into United States

Source: U.S. Department of Homeland Security, *Yearbook of Immigration Statistics: 2008* (Washington, D.C.: U.S. Department of Homeland Security, Office of Immigration Statistics, 2009).

Table 101 Ethiopian asylum seekers in the United States by year of entry

Year	Asylum seekers
1996	823
1997	451
1998	551
1999	1,129
2000	1,439
2001	1,166
2002	1,047
2003	569
2004	750
2005	460
2006	430
2007	494
2008	588

Source: U.S. Department of Homeland Security. *Yearbook of Immigration Statistics: 2008* (Washington, D.C.: U.S. Department of Homeland Security, Office of Immigration Statistics, 2009).

Table 102 Ethiopian immigrants admitted into the United States between 1992 and 2002

Year	Immigrants
1992	4,602
1993	5,191
1994	3,887
1995	5,960
1996	6,086
1997	5,904
1998	4,205
1999	4,272

Source: U.S. Department of Homeland Security, *Yearbook of Immigration Statistics: 2002* (Washington, D.C.: U.S. Government Printing Office, 2003)

Table 103 Persons obtaining legal permanent resident status by region and country of birth (Ethiopia): Fiscal years 2000 to 2009

Region and country of birth	2000	2001	2002	2003	2004	2005	2006	2007	2008	2009
Total	841,002	1,058,902	1,059,356	703,542	957,883	1,122,257	1,266,129	1,052,415	1,107,126	1,130,818
Ethiopia	4,053	5,092	7,565	6,635	8,286	10,571	16,152	12,786	12,917	15,462

Source: U.S. Department of Homeland Security, Office of Immigration Statistics. 2010. Adapted from Table 3.

Appendix II: Demographics/Census Statistics

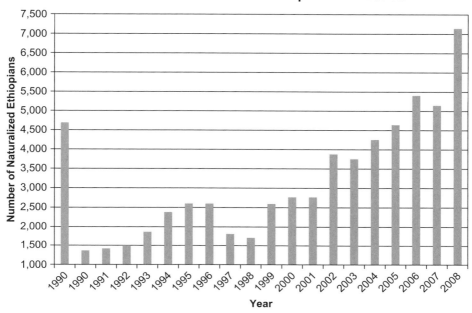

Figure 15 Number of naturalized Ethiopians in America
Source: U.S. Department of Homeland Security, *Yearbook of Immigration Statistics: 2008* (Washington, D.C.: U.S. Department of Homeland Security, Office of Immigration Statistics, 2009).

Table 104 Ethiopian persons obtaining legal permanent resident status during fiscal year 2009

Characteristic	Total	Male	Female
Leading states of residence			
Arizona	233	114	119
California	1,414	667	747
Colorado	718	345	373
Florida	193	98	95
Georgia	931	435	496
Illinois	393	210	183
Maryland	1,440	726	714
Massachusetts	371	184	187
Michigan	196	107	89
Minnesota	1,614	789	825
Nevada	508	234	274
New Jersey	107	51	56
New York	337	168	169
North Carolina	216	115	101
Ohio	473	246	227
Pennsylvania	274	132	142
Texas	1,025	490	535
Virginia	1,302	643	659
Washington	1,168	571	597
Other	2,549	1,290	1,259

Source: Adapted from U.S. Department of Homeland Security, *Profiles on Legal Permanent Residents: 2009*. Cobbook 73. 2010.

Appendix III: Notable Ethiopian Americans

Much of the information for notable Ethiopian Americans is gleaned from *Tadias,* an online magazine that caters to the younger generation Ethiopians. For further information, see http://www.tadias.com/12/27/2009/tadias-top-20-most-read-stories-of-the-year/. See also Cyber Ethiopi@ at http://cyberethiopia.com/home/content/view/87/1/.

Dr. Aklilu Habte served from 1958 to 1974 at the Haile Selassie University in many capacities including as a president of the university—the only university in the country in those days. Due to the military takeover of the country in 1974, Dr. Aklilu left Ethiopia for the United States. He joined the World Bank, where he served as the director of the education and training department and as special advisor in human resources development to the vice president of the African region from 1987 to 1990. Between 1990 and 1993, he worked for the UNICEF as chief of education division and special advisor to the executive director of UNICEF.

Dr. Gebisa Ejeta came to the United States in the 1970s for graduate studies and is a professor at Purdue University. In 2009, he won the World Food Prize for developing a sorghum hybrid. His research has increased the production and availability of one of the world's five main grains and improved the food supply of hundreds of millions of people in sub-Saharan Africa as well as the world.

Dr. Getachew Haile was an educator and researcher at Haile Selassie I University. After he had been tortured by the military junta that ruled the country between 1975 and 1991, he left for the United States in the early 1980s. He is currently a regents professor of medieval studies and cataloguer of oriental manuscripts at Hill Monastic Manuscript Library, College of St. Benedict, Saint John's University (Minneapolis).

Dr. Haile Gerima came to the United States in the 1960s. He studied film at UCLA. While there, he was a member of the Los Angeles School of Black Film Makers. He is currently a professor of film at Howard University. His cinema primarily focuses on Ethiopia's past and the African American experience. He is one of a handful of African filmmakers to earn international fame and accolade.

Dr. Ingida Asfaw came to Wayne State University and the Detroit Medical Center in 1967 for his general surgery residency. However, he decided to remain in the United States due to the political turmoil in Ethiopia. Since then, Dr. Ingida has become a prominent U.S. cardiac surgeon. In 2000, he and fellow Ethiopian medical professionals established the Ethiopian North American Health Professionals Association, which annually provides a team of experts to conduct open heart surgery in Ethiopia for free. Dr. Ingida is the recipient of the Volvo for Life Award. (It is interesting to note that there are more Ethiopian medical doctors in the Washington, D.C., area alone than in Ethiopia.)

Julie Mehretu came to the United States at early age with her father, Professor Assefa Mehretu in the 1970s. She studied art in the United States and Africa, and her work is featured at the Museum of Modern Art, New York—she is the only Ethiopian artist featured there. The subject of a *PBS* documentary that aired on October 28, 2009, she has had her art exhibited in many internationally recognized art venues such as the Whitney Biennial, the Istanbul Biennial, the Busan Biennale in Korea, and the Walker Art Center, and her work is currently on display at the San Francisco Museum of Modern Art and the Museum of Contemporary Art in San Diego.

Brig. General Legesse Tefera is often considered the hero of Ethiopia. He is a graduate of the prestigious Harar Military Academy, sometimes known as Haile Selassie Ist Military Academy. During the 1977 Somali invasion of Ethiopia, using his F5E fighter-interceptor plane, Legesse shot down two of Somali's most advanced MIG 23 over its airspace; and then he bombed a factory deep inside Somalia where he was shot down and remained in captivity for 11 years. For his valor, Ethiopia honored Legesse with the highest military award. Since the 1990s, he and his family have lived in America. Many high-ranking officers of the Ethiopian Armed Forces reside in America.

Liya Kebede, born and raised in Ethiopia, studied modeling in France and moved to the United States. In addition to being one of the highest paid top fashion models in the United States, Liya is a clothing designer and an actress. She is the first black face of *Estée Lauder.* In 2006, she set up the Liya Kebede Foundation, whose mission was to reduce maternal, newborn, and child mortality in Ethiopia and around the world. She has served as the WHO's ambassador for maternal, newborn, and child health

Chef Marcus Samuelsson was born in Ethiopia, and adopted and raised by Swedish parents. Samuelsson is one of the most noted chefs in New York City. U.S. President Obama invited him to prepare his first state dinner honoring the Indian prime minister, Manmohan Singh. First Lady Michelle Obama called Samuelsson "one of the finest chefs in the country." He has recently opened a new restaurant in Harlem, where he now lives.

Dr. Mehret Mandefro, who received a BA degree in anthropology and an MD from Harvard University, and an MS in public health from the London School of Hygiene and Tropical Medicine as a Fulbright scholar, is a primary care physician and HIV prevention researcher. President Obama named Mehret as one of the 2009/2010 White House Fellows for her research and accomplishments. She is also the founder of a nonprofit organization, TruthAIDS, which primarily deals with health literacy efforts among vulnerable populations.

His Holiness Abune Merkorios was elected the fourth patriarch of the Holy Synod of the Ethiopian Orthodox Church in 1988. He is widely regarded as a liturgical expert. In 1991, he went into exile while others allege that he abdicated. Nevertheless, he still claims to be the legitimate Patriarch of Ethiopia and many in the diaspora, especially in America and Europe, consider him as such.

Mimi Alemayhu has been nominated by President Obama to serve as executive vice president of the Overseas Private Investment Corporation. She has served the U.S. government at various capacities in and outside of the United States. She was also the founder and managing partner of Trade Links, LLC, a development consulting firm that worked with clients on emerging markets issues and promoting African exports under the African Growth and Opportunity Act.

Judge Nina Ashenafi is the daughter of the late Professor Ashenasi Kebede. He was the director of the Center of African-American Culture at Florida State University (Tallahassee). Nina came to the United States at an early age with her father Prof. Ashenafi Kebede, an ethno-musicologist and composer. Judge Ashenafi is the first African American woman to head the Tallahassee Bar Association and the first African American to lead the Tallahassee Women Lawyers.

Dr. Noah Samara was the founder, chairman, and the executive director of WorldSpace, an internationally known satellite company, at age 34. A graduate of Georgetown Law School, he played a prominent role in the establishment of the XM Satellite Radio.

Dr. Sossina Haile came to the United States with her father Prof. Getachew Haile at an early age and received her BS and PhD (1992) from the Massachusetts Institute of Technology. She is currently a professor at UCLA. Sossina has received numerous awards and has been called "the power behind cooler, greener energy" in *Newsweek* magazine (Murr 2007).

Dr. Teshome Wagaw is a professor of African and African American studies at the University of Michigan. Before he came to the United States in the early 1970s, he was the dean of students at the Haile Selassie I University (renamed Addis Ababa University). He has published numerous books and articles on the history of higher education in Ethiopia and the Ethiopian Jewish experience in Israel. In addition, Teshome is one of the founding members of the Ethiopian American Foundation—a nonprofit organization that provides help to students, universities, and colleges in Ethiopia.

Dr. Yared Tekabe studies cardiovascular disease detection and prevention at Columbia University, and he has worked on a non-invasive atherosclerosis detection and molecular imaging technique. Dr. Yared hopes that in a few years time his work can help heart disease prevention efforts and early detection of atherosclerosis in humans.

Glossary

Abba: Father.
Abun: Pope.
AESM: All-Ethiopia Socialist Movement.
COR: Sudanese Commission of Refugees.

Derg: Committee.

ECDC: Ethiopian Community Development Council.

EDU: Ethiopian Democratic Union.

ELF: Eritrean Liberation Front.

EOC: Ethiopian Orthodox Church.

EPLF: Eritrean People's Liberation Front.

EPRDF: Ethiopian People's Revolutionary Democratic Front.

EPRP: Ethiopian Peoples Revolutionary Party.

ERA: Eritrean Relief Association.

ESFNA: Ethiopian Sport Federation in North America.

ESUNA: Ethiopian Students Union in North America.

ICMC: International Catholic Migration Committee.

INS: Immigration and Naturalization Services.

IRC: International Rescue Committee.

IRCA: Immigration Reform and Control Act.

MAG: Military Advisory Group.

OAU: Organization of African Union.

OLF: Oromo Liberation Front.

PFDJ: People's Front for Democracy and Justice.

PMAC: Provisional Military Administrative Council.

PMGE: Provisional Military Government of Ethiopia.

RST: Relief Society of Tigray.

SPLA: Sudanese Peoples Liberation Army.

TLF: Tigray Liberation Front.

TPLF: Tigray Peoples Liberation Front.

UNHCR: United Nations Higher Commission for Refugees.

References

Agyeman-Duah, Baffour. 1994. *The United States and Ethiopia: Military Assistance and the Quest for Security, 1953–1993*. Lanham, MD: University Press of America.

Akalou, Wolde Micael. 1989. "Ethiopians and Afghans in the United States: A Comparative Perspective." *Journal of Northeast African Studies* 2(1): 55–74.

Andargachew, Tiruneh. 1993. *The Ethiopian Revolution, 1974–1987: A Transformation From an Aristocratic to a to Totalitarian Autocracy*. Cambridge: Cambridge University Press.

Balsvik, Randi Rønning. 1985. *Haile Selassie's Students: The Intellectual and Social Background to Revolution, 1952–1977.* East Lansing: African Studies Center, Michigan State University.

Clapham, Christopher. 1968. "The Ethiopian Coup d'état of December 1960." *The Journal of Modern African Studies* 6(4): 495–507.

Daniel, Kendie. 2005. *The Five Dimensions of the Eritrean Conflict, 1941–2004: Deciphering the Geo-Political Puzzle.* Prairie View, AR: Signature Book.

Gebru, Tareke. 2009. *The Ethiopian Revolution: War in the Horn of Africa.* New Haven, CT: Yale University Press.

Getachew, Metaferia, and Shifferraw Maigenet. 1991. *The Ethiopian Revolution of 1974 and the Exodus of Ethiopia's Trained Human Resources.* Lewiston, NY: E. Mellen Press.

Getahun, Solomon Addis. 2007a. *The History of Ethiopian Immigrants and Refugees in America, 1900–2000: Patterns of Migration, Survival, and Adjustment.* New York: LFB Scholarly Publishing.

Getahun, Solomon Addis. 2007b. "Determinants of Ethiopian Refugee Flow in the Horn of Africa, 1970–2000." In *The Human Cost of African Migrations,* edited by Toyin Falola and Niyi Afolabi, 359–80. New York: Routledge.

Getahun, Solomon Addis. 2009. "A History of Sport in Ethiopia." In *Proceedings of the 16th International Conference of Ethiopian Studies,* edited by Svein Ege, Harald Aspen, Birhanu Teferra, and Shiferaw Bekele, 409–18. Trondheim: Norwegian University of Science and Technology.

Greenfield, Richard. 1965. *Ethiopia: A New Political History.* New York: Frederick A. Praeger.

Kobishchanov, Yuri M. 1979. *Axum.* University Park: Pennsylvania State University Press.

Koehn, Peter H. 1991. *Refugee from Revolution: U.S. Policy and Third-World Migration.* Boulder, CO: Westview Press.

Marcus, Harold G. 1983. *The Politics of Empire: Ethiopia, Great Britain, and the United States, 1941–1974.* Berkeley: University of California Press.

Marcus, Harold G. 1995. *The Life and Times of Menelik II: Ethiopia 1844–1913.* Lawrenceville, NJ: Red Sea Press.

Marcus, Harold G. 2002. *A History of Ethiopia.* Berkeley: University of California Press.

Markakis, John. 1974. *Ethiopia: Anatomy of a Traditional Polity.* Oxford: Clarendon Press.

McAdoo, Harriet P., Young, and Solomon A. Getahun. 2007. "Emerging Patterns and Characteristics of Parenting, Marriage and Socialization of Native African Americans, Contemporary African, and Caribbean Immigrants." In *The Other African Americans: Contemporary African and Caribbean Families in the United States,* edited by Yoku Shaw-Taylor and Steven A. Tuch, 83–116. New York: Rowman Littlefield.

Mesfin, Wolde-Mariam. 1972. *An Introductory Geography of Ethiopia.* Addis Ababa: Addis Ababa University.

Murr, Andrew. 2007. "Sossina Haile: The Power Behind Cooler, Greener Energy." *Newsweek,* December 22. [Online article retrieved 6/10.] http://www.newsweek.com/2007/12/22/sossina-haile-the-power-behind-cooler-greener-energy.html.

Paulos, Milkias, and Metaferia Getachew. 2005. *The Battle of Adwa: Reflections on Ethiopia's Historic Victory against European Colonialism.* New York: Algora Publishers.

Rumbaut, Ruben G. 1996. "Origins and Destinies: Immigration, Race, and Ethnicity in Contemporary America." In *Origins and Destinies: Immigration, Race, and Ethnicity in America,* edited by Silvia Pedraza and Ruben G. Rumbaut, 21–42. Belmont: Wadsworth.

Sergew, Hable Selassie. 1972. *Ancient and Medieval Ethiopian History to 1270.* Addis Ababa: Union Printers.

Shumet, Sishagne.2007. *Unionists and Separatists: The Vagaries of Ethio-Eritrean Relation 1941–1991.* Hollywood: Tsehai Publishers and Distributors.

Skinner, Robert P. 1906. *Abyssinia of To-day: An Account of the First Mission Sent by the American Government to the Court of the King of Kings, 1903–1904.* New York: Longmans, Green.

Teshale, Tibebu. 1996. "Ethiopia: The 'Anomaly' and 'Paradox' of Africa." *Journal of Black Studies* 26(4): 414–30.

Teshome, G. Wagaw.1990. *The Development of Higher Education and Social Change: An Ethiopian Experience.* East Lansing: Michigan State University Press.

U.S. Census Bureau. 2001. *Profile of the Foreign-Born Population in the United States: 2000.* Current Population Reports, Series P23–206. Washington, D.C.: U.S. Government Printing Office.

U.S. Department of Homeland Security. 2009. *2008 Year Book of Immigration Statistics.* Washington, D.C.: Office of Immigration Statistics.

"Wildlife." *Selamta.* [Online article retrieved 06/10.] http://www.selamta.net/wildlife.htm.

Wolde-Mariam, Mesfin. 1972. *An Introductory Geography of Ethiopia.* Addis Ababa: Addis Ababa University.

Further Reading

Andargachew, Tiruneh. 1993. *The Ethiopian Revolution, 1974–1987: A Transformation From an Aristocratic to a to Totalitarian Autocracy.* Cambridge: Cambridge University Press.

The monograph is one the most comprehensive works on the Ethiopian revolution. Using primary sources written in Amharic and other languages, Andargachew provides a balanced view of the genesis of the revolution, the role of the various political parties and superpowers in the revolution, and the impact of the revolution on Ethiopian society.

Agyeman-Duah, Baffour. 1994. *The United States and Ethiopia: Military Assistance and the Quest for Security, 1953–1993.* Lanham, MD: University Press of America.

The book is among one of the two studies done by an African (from Ghana) on Ethiopia. The monograph reveals the deep involvement of the United States in Ethiopia during the height of the Cold War. The book examines in detail U.S. military assistance to Ethiopia.

Getahun, Solomon Addis. 2007. *The History of Ethiopian Immigrants and Refugees in America, 1900–2000: Patterns of Migration, Survival, and Adjustment.* New York: LFB Scholarly Publishing.

This is one of the very few monographs that comprehensively examines the causes and process of migration of Ethiopians to the United States. In addition, Getahun provides an insight into the development or lack of Ethiopian community organizations in the United States and the impact of Ethiopian Americans on the country of origin.

Greenfield, Richard. 1965. *Ethiopia: A New Political History.* New York: Frederick A. Praeger.

So far, Greenfield's work has remained the only published monograph that comprehensively discusses the 1960s military coups d'état against Haile Selassie's monarchial rule.

Tareke, Gebru. 2009. *The Ethiopian Revolution: War in the Horn of Africa.* New Haven, CT: Yale University Press.

This book is an impartial and a critical examination of socioeconomic, political, and military conditions in Ethiopia in relation to the success of the EPRDF and EPLF. The author displays the weakness and strengths of the various political parties in Ethiopia.

Marcus, Harold G. 1983. *The Politics of Empire: Ethiopia, Great Britain, and the United States, 1941–1974.* Berkeley: University of California Press.

Marcus examines Haile Selassie's Ethiopia on the immediate aftermath of the Italian defeat and clearly displays the intricacies and the shaping of the post–World War II period. The struggle between the emergent global powers, the United States and USSR, and the declining colonial powers, England and Italy, and their desire to dominate the Horn of Africa, especially Ethiopia, has been aptly presented by Marcus.

Marcus, Harold G. 1995. *The Life and Times of Menelik II: Ethiopia 1844–1913.* Lawrenceville, NJ: Red Sea Press.

This is one of the two books written on the political biography of Menelik. Marcus's work examines the circumstances that led to the Battle of Adwa and the socioeconomic and political developments of its aftermath. It also exhibits Menelik's Machiavellian skills in dealing with Emperor Yohannis, the Mahdists, the French, and the Italians.

Marcus, Harold G. 2002. *A History of Ethiopia.* Berkeley: University of California Press.

The book is an exceptionally comprehensive and up-to-date text for Ethiopian history. Anyone who wants to learn about Ethiopia from pre-history to present, Marcus's work is a must have.

Medhanie, Testfatsion. 1986. *Eritrea: Dynamics of a National Question.* Amsterdam: B. R. Grüner.

An exception among Eritrean intellectuals, Testfatsion Medhanie portrays the Eritrean struggle as a national a question that can be solved through class struggle instead of an ethno-nationalist revolt. His book remains one of the most influential works that has impacted the student movement in Ethiopia.

Sergew Hable, Selassie, 1972. *Ancient and Medieval Ethiopian History to 1270.* Addis Ababa: Union Printers.

It is an important monograph that provides a detailed account of Ethiopia from pre-Axumite times to the Zagwe Dynasty, roughly starting from 500 B.C.E. to 1270 C.E. The author tries to show Ethiopia's strong ties with Judaism and the Semitic origin of Ethiopian civilization.

Shumet, Sishagne. 2007. *Unionists and Separatists: The Vagaries of Ethio-Eritrean Relation 1941–1991.* Hollywood, CA: Tsehai Publishers and Distributors.

Shumet's work primarily deals with the events that led to the union between Ethiopia and Eritrea; he also explores how political actors from all sides (Ethiopians, Eritreans, the Arab, and Socialist world) worked to undo the federal arrangement. He presents an objective account of the genesis of the armed struggle in Eritrea.

Skinner, Robert P. 1906. *Abyssinia of To-day: An Account of the First Mission Sent by the American Government to the Court of the King of Kings, 1903–1904.* New York: Longmans, Green.

Skinner was the first American representative in Ethiopia. He provides invaluable first-hand information regarding early 20th-century Ethiopia, especially Menelik's personality and his royal court and Ethiopia's potential as a market for American goods.

Tadesse, Medhane. 1999. *The Eritrean-Ethiopian War: Retrospect and Prospects, 1991–1998.* Addis Ababa: Mega Printing.

Tadesse's work highlights the circumstances that led to the so-called border war between Ethiopia and Eritrea, 1998–2000. He faults the inability of the EPLF, now the PFDJ (People's Front for Democracy and Justice) to transform itself from a guerrilla movement to a viable state as one of the major causes of the war.

Teshale, Tibebu. 1996. "Ethiopia: The 'Anomaly' and 'Paradox' of Africa." *Journal of Black Studies* 26(4): 414–30.

The article is a synopsis of his book, *The Making of Modern Ethiopia, 1896–1974.* The author's unique contribution to Ethiopian historiography is in his attempt to include the centrist and ethno-nationalist paradigms in understanding modern Ethiopia.

Filipino Immigrants

by Maria Paz Gutierrez Esguerra

Introduction

There are 2,364,185 Filipino Americans in the United States according to the 2000 U.S. Census. Representing almost 18 percent of the Asian American population, Filipino Americans are the second-largest Asian American group in the United States. The history of Filipino settlement in the United States began as early as the 18th century, but it was not until the 20th century, after U.S. annexation of the Philippines, that Filipino immigrants came in greater numbers. The consequences of America's empire in the Philippines have shaped Filipino experiences of migration to and settlement in the United States. Today Filipinos in the United States make up the largest population of Filipinos living outside the Philippines.

Chronology

1763	Earliest known Filipino settlers in America establish fishing villages in the bayous of Louisiana.
1896	Emilio Aguinaldo leads a Filipino revolt against the Spanish rule that has colonized the Philippines since the 16th century.
1898	Spanish-American War ends.
	The United States signs the Paris Peace Treaty, and Spain cedes the Philippines for $20 million. The United States also annexes Cuba, Guam, Hawaii, and Puerto Rico.
1899	Philippine-American War begins.
1900	President William McKinley establishes Philippine civil government and appoints William Howard Taft as governor-general of the Philippines.
1903	*Pensionado* program is established in the Philippines to provide educational scholarships to Filipino students for education in the United States.

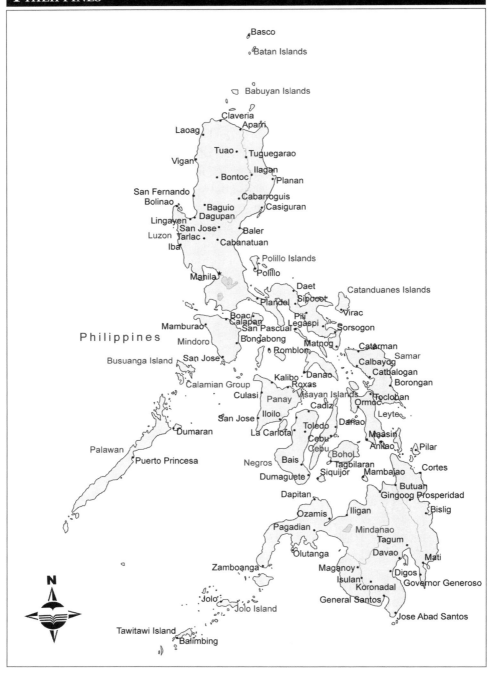

Basco

Batan Islands

Babuyan Islands

Claveria
Laoag
Aparri
Tuao
Tuguegarao
Vigan
Ilagan
Bontoc
Planan
San Fernando
Cabarroguis
Bolinao
Casiguran
Baguio
Dagupan
Lingayen
San Jose
Baler
Luzon
Tarlac
Cabanatuan
Iba

Polillo Islands
Polillo

Manila
Daet
Catanduanes Islands
Sipocet
Plandel
Pili
Virac
Boac
Legaspi
Mamburao
Calapan
San Pascual
Sorsogon
Bongabong
Mindoro
Matnog
Philippines
Romblon
Catarman
Busuanga Island
Samar
San Jose
Calbayog
Calamian Group
Kalibo
Catbalogan
Roxas
Danao
Borongan
Culasi
Panay
Visayan Islands
Cadiz
Tacloban
Iloilo
Ormoc
San Jose
Toledo
Danao
Leyte
La Carlota
Cebu
Maasin
Dumaran
Cebu
Anilao
Pilar
Palawan
Bohol
Negros
Bais
Tagbilaran
Cortes
Puerto Princesa
Dumaguete
Siquijor
Mambajao

Butuan
Dapitan
Gingoog Prosperidad
Ozamis
Iligan
Bislig
Pagadian
Mindanao
Tagum
Olutanga
Davao
Zamboanga
Maganoy
Mati
Isulan
Digos
Jolo
Koronadal
Governor Generoso
Jolo Island
General Santos
Tawitawi Island
Jose Abad Santos
Balimbing

N

1904	U.S. Navy begins recruitment of Filipinos.
1906	The Hawaiian Sugar Planters Association (HSPA) begins recruitment of Filipino laborers with recruitment centers in Vigan, Ilocos Sur, and Cebu. First Filipino laborers arrive in Hawaii.
1909	Payne-Aldriff tariff establishes free trade between the United States and the Philippines.
1911	Filipino Federation of Labor founded in Hawaii.
1928	Filipino workers driven out of Yakima Valley, Washington, by mob violence.
1929	A mob of 300 men storm a Filipino labor camp and drive out 200 Filipino workers in a race riot in Exeter, California.
1930	Race riot in Watsonville, California, is recorded as the most explosive anti-Filipino riot in the United States. Racial tensions over employment disputes and white-Filipino interracial relations fuel the tension in the town of Watsonville. The two-day race riot resulted in the death of Fermin Tobera, a 22-year-old Filipino laborer.
1933	The state of California adds "Malay" as a category to its anti-miscegenation laws, and California Civil Code Sections 60 and 69 prohibit marriages between whites and Filipinos. In addition to California, 12 other states have anti-miscegenation laws against Filipinos.
1934	Tydings-McDuffie Act, also known as the Philippine-Independence Act, is enacted into law. It allowed for a 10-year transition to full independence and restricts immigration from the Philippines to a quota of 50 persons per year. Independence is delayed until 1946 due to World War II.
1935	Welch Repatriation Act offers Filipinos in the United States free one-way passage to return to the Philippines. Approximately 2,190 Filipinos repatriate.
1941	December 7: Japan bombs Pearl Harbor, and the United States gets involved in World War II.

December 8: Japan attacks Clark Air Field and invades the Philippines.

1942	President Franklin D. Roosevelt signs the Selective Service Act, which permits Filipinos to serve in the U.S. Army without American citizenship. The 1st and 2nd Filipino Infantry

	Regiments of the U.S. Army forms with more than 7,000 Filipino and Filipino American soldiers serving.
1946	Philippine Independence proclaimed on July 4. War Brides Act and Fiancées Act permit entry of Filipino women into the United States despite quota restrictions. Luce-Celler Bill passes and allows Filipinos who arrived before the passing of the Tydings-McDuffie Act to apply for naturalized citizenship. Approximately 10,764 Filipinos become citizens.
1948	California repeals antimiscegenation law and becomes the first state to declare it unconstitutional.
1952	McCarran-Walter Immigration and Nationality Act ends anti-Asian immigration policies and lifts the ban on Asian exclusion. The 1952 Act also eliminates laws that prevent Asians from becoming naturalized citizens.
1965	Immigration and Nationality Act of 1965, also known as the Hart-Celler Act, passes in Congress. It abolishes the nationality quota system and establishes a preference system based on family reunification and occupational skills, which allows for larger numbers of Filipino professionals and families to migrate to the United States outside the yearly country limit of 20,000 people.
1972	President Ferdinand Marcos declares martial law in the Philippines resulting in political demonstrations and massive protests.
1986	People Power Revolution in the Philippines overthrows the Marcos regime and ends decades of martial law. Corazon Aquino becomes first female president of the Philippines.
1990	Immigration Act of 1990 increases total under flexible annual cap of 675,000 but ends unlimited immigration of immediate relatives of U.S. citizens. The act revises all grounds for exclusion, amending the McCarran–Walter Act of 1952. Filipino World War II veterans are naturalized under the Immigration Act of 1990.
1992	Last U.S. military base closes in the Philippines.
1994	Benjamin Cayetano becomes first Filipino American elected as governor in the United States.
2000	U.S. Census records show 2.4 million Filipinos in the United States.

2003	The Citizenship Retention and Reacquisition Act of 2003 allows natural-born Filipinos naturalized in the United States and their unmarried minor children to reclaim Filipino nationality and hold dual citizenship.
2006	U.S. Congress passes legislation that commemorates 100 years of Filipino migration to the United States.
2009	President Barack Obama signs the stimulus bill, known as the American Recovery and Reinvestment Act of 2009, which provides Filipino World War II veterans with lump-sum compensation for their service to the United States. H. Res. 780 passes in U.S. Congress recognizing the celebration of Filipino American History Month during the month of October.

Background

Geography of the Philippines

The Republic of the Philippines is an archipelago located in Southeast Asia that spans 1,152 miles north to south and 688 miles east to west. It is surrounded by the Philippine Sea in the east, the China Sea in the west, and the Celebes Sea in the south. Comprised of over 7,000 islands the country is divided into three major geographic island clusters: Luzon, Visayas, and Mindanao. Luzon, located in the north, is home to the capital city of Manila; 6,000 islands including some of the largest—Palawan, Leyte, Samar, Bohol, and Cebu—make up the Visayan region. In the south, Mindanao is the easternmost island of the country.

The geography includes coastal plains, valleys, dense rain forests, and mountain ranges. The Sierra Madre on the northeast coast island of Luzon is the longest and the largest landform in the country. Mt. Apo at 9,690 feet is a stratovolcano on Mindanao and the highest peak. The islands of the Philippines are chiefly of volcanic origin, and they are a part of a western Pacific arc comprised of active volcanoes. As such, the country is prone to earthquakes.

Climate in the country differs by region although generally the Republic of the Philippines has a tropical marine climate that averages 80 degrees Fahrenheit. There are three seasons in the year, which can include rainy monsoons, hot humid weather, and a dry season.

History of the Philippines

Present-day Philippines is the product of a long history of migration, settlement, and colonialism that began as early as the 14th century, when Arab traders from

Malay and Borneo arrived to the southern islands. This was followed by early migration from neighboring countries like India and China who brought with them their religions, languages, foods, and culture. Filipino natives adopted some of these customs and incorporated them to native ways of life; many of these influences are still evident in contemporary Philippines.

In pre-Spanish society Filipinos lived in small settlements called *barangays,* which consisted of families who lived together and supported one another. A chieftain, who was responsible for the protection of and the overall welfare of its members, ruled it. Agriculture was the main source of livelihood for the *barangay* as farmers grew rice, vegetables, and fruits for sustenance. Industries included lumbering, fishing, mining, and weaving, and the settlers sometimes traded these goods with neighboring countries like China, Siam (Thailand), Borneo, and Sumatra (Bautista 1998, 17). Religion also played an important role in *barangay* life. Natives practiced a religion that revered a supreme god known as Bathala, who created the heavens, Earth, and man. They honored the spirits of their ancestors with sacrifices and believed in the immortality of the human soul. Thus, prior to the arrival of Portuguese explorer Ferdinand Magellan in 1521, who claimed discovery of the Philippines, Filipino society, religions, and culture were already established and well developed.

Magellan stumbled upon the Philippines during a Spanish expedition to circumnavigate the globe but it was in a battle with a local leader, Lapu-Lapu, that he met an untimely death. Other Spanish expeditions followed including one led by Lopez de Villalobos, who named the archipelago after a young Philip II of Spain in 1542. Spanish settlement and colonization did not begin until the arrival of another expedition in Cebu Island in 1565. The expedition led by Miguel Lopez de Legazpi was comprised of approximately 400 men. They established themselves in a small town called San Miguel (Rodell 2002, 10). By 1751 Legazpi and his troops had moved up to Luzon Island in Manila, where the Spanish colony would flourish. Manila grew as an international port that served Spain's galleon trade between the Philippines and Mexico, which became the primary business for Spanish colonists in the Philippines.

Most of the Spanish trade remained in Manila while Spanish missionaries dispersed throughout the archipelago to secure Spain's goal of Christian conversion. Religious orders established themselves in small towns as they converted Filipino natives to Roman Catholicism. With the support of the Spanish crown, priests also oversaw all municipal affairs, which gave them both religious and political power and control over the towns and villages they lived in. The project of religious conversion was successful but destructive to established Filipino society. By the late 19th century, almost 80 percent of the population had converted to Christianity with the exception of Muslim peoples in the southern region of the country who resisted missionary efforts (Rodell 2002, 11).

Spanish colonization did not go without Filipino resistance. Throughout much of Spain's rule in the Philippines there were constant revolts and protests against

Spanish abuse. From 1565 to 1600 alone, there were 13 revolts (Bautista 1998, 34). Between the 16th to 19th centuries, the Spanish colonial government recorded approximately 124 revolts throughout the islands (Bautista 1998, 34). By the mid-19th century, native priests were beginning to openly defy Spanish clergy while educated Filipino elites like national hero Jose Rizal critiqued Spanish colonial practices in his writings. Although sentiments of revolution brewed within nationalists, patriots, and secret societies, it was not until the Philippine Revolution in 1896 that Filipinos organized and fought against Spanish troops in military battle. Filipino nationalist and revolutionary Andres Bonifacio led the *Katipuneros* in battle although the superiority of Spanish weapons, skills, and resources caused the ultimate defeat of Filipino revolutionaries.

In the meantime, international events involving the United States and Spain with regards to Cuba, another Spanish colony at the time, would change the trajectory of Philippine independence. U.S. intervention in the Philippines would be the result of the Spanish-American War, which began when the U.S. battleship *Maine* exploded in Cuba's Havana Harbor in 1898 (Rodell 2002, 15). Filipino resistance against Spanish colonialism would attract U.S. attention, and Filipinos and American troops would ally together in the Philippines to defeat Spain. In June 12, 1898, Filipino independence leader Emilio Aguinaldo declared Philippine independence making it Asia's first democratic government (Rodell 2002, 15). It was a short-lived victory as Spain ceded possession of the Philippines to the United States under the Treaty of Versailles.

What followed was an oft forgotten event in American history: the Philippine-American War of 1899, which resulted in the death of an estimated million Filipinos, the destruction of cities, and the territorial annexation of the Philippines (Espiritu 2003, 23). An expansion of the United States' policy of Manifest Destiny, American forces immediately took over different parts of Philippine society and established a government structure that mimicked its own. To support American military forces, the colonial government also established military bases in the islands. But the impact of American colonization was most evident in Philippine cultural life (Roddell 2002, 17) where Filipinos were taught to embrace American culture. It introduced an American education system where English was its primary language of instruction. Filipino education under the tutelage of American teachers taught them a new culture and a way of life in which the United States was considered the measure of modernity and civilization.

The relationship between the two countries was often tenuous, and American attitudes towards the annexation of the Philippines were ambiguous at best. U.S. colonialism was executed through "benevolent" means that were intended to win Filipino support, but Americans themselves were unsure about the role that the United States would play in empire. For Filipinos U.S. presence in the first half of the 20th century represented a barrier to full independence. Filipino aspirations

Filipino prisoners during the Philippine-American War, about 1899. The United States helped liberate the Philippines, a possession of Spain since 1521, in the Spanish-American War of 1898. When the United States annexed the islands and refused to recognize Filipino revolutionary leader Emilio Aguinaldo's authority as president, Aguinaldo and his rebel troops took up arms against their erstwhile "ally" and precipitated a bloody insurrection that ended with Aguinaldo's capture in 1902. (Library of Congress)

for independence never dissipated as the colonial government had hoped and instead remained despite continued American efforts to "Americanize" and "civilize" them. Transition to self-rule began in 1916 under President Woodrow Wilson with the passage of Jones Law, which provided the guidelines for Philippine independence, although it was not achieved until 1946, following the end of World War II. Even after the Philippines declared its independence, the influence of the American government, economy, military, and culture remained embedded in Philippine society.

Immediately following the declaration of independence, Filipinos established a democratic government that mimicked the American model. Reconstructing the war-torn country was challenging not only due to the need for resources but also the uprising of Communist-dominated *Hukbalahap* guerrillas. Despite the support of the American government and the Central Intelligence Agency, the Philippine government did not capture the guerillas' leader until 1964. Ferdinand E. Marcos became the president in the following year, and his popularity increased as programs helped to improve living conditions. Unfortunately, conditions deteriorated by the 1970s. On September 21, 1972, President Marcos declared martial law based on the growing threat of Communist movements in the country.

Poverty and governmental corruption increased in this period, and it began to look as if President Marcos was using the martial law to remain in office beyond the expiration of his presidency as well as to silence any political opposition, especially Senator Benigno "Ninoy" Aquino (Rodell 2002, 21). Aquino, who was a popular political leader, was a strong critic of the Marcos regime. Aquino's assassination on August 21, 1983 at the Manila International Airport made him a martyr in death, and his assassination became the catalyst for a new political movement. This movement was headed by an unlikely candidate—the widow of Senator Aquino, Corazon "Cory" Aquino.

Amidst controversy and government corruption but with the general support of the people, Cory Aquino emerged victorious after a contentious election and was inaugurated as the first female president of the Philippines in 1986. Her presidency faced tough challenges as it sought to rebuild the government, develop the economy, and improve living conditions for Filipinos who suffered under poverty and corruption. Much of the successes of President Aquino's presidency were due to massive public support, foreign aid, and the loyalty of the Armed Forces of the Philippines (Roddell 2002, 24). In 1992, President Aquino declined to run for re-election, and former Army Chief of Staff Fidel Ramos succeeded her in office.

President Fidel Ramos sought to revitalize the nation's economy through private investments and the deregulation of government. It was during his term that the geological disaster of Mount Pinatubo on the island of Luzon occurred, killing hundreds of people and destroying thousands of homes and businesses including the Clark Air Base. U.S. evacuation of military bases in 1992 followed after the Philippine Senate voted not to renew the contract. Jose Marcelo "Erap" Estrada won the presidency in 1998, but an illegal gambling scandal in 2000 led to his impeachment. Vice President Gloria Macapagal-Arroyo succeeded him, and in 2004 she was elected into a full term in office. Her administration, however, was marred with controversy as allegations that she rigged election votes spread. Numerous attempts to impeach President Macapagal-Arroyo failed, but these reflected popular discontent about the integrity of her administration. In the most recent election in 2010 Benigno "Noynoy" Aquino III was elected into office. He is the son of late President Corazon Aquino and late Senator Benigno Aquino, Jr.

Causes and Waves of Migration

Early Immigration

The earliest known Filipino settlers in the United States were subjects of the Spanish crown employed as sailors and crewmen of Spanish galleons that transported trade goods between Manila and the New World. Driven by a desire to escape harsh treatment from their colonial rulers, many of these men jumped ship to various ports in Mexico, California, Mississippi, and Louisiana. In the bayous of Louisiana, Filipino fishing and shrimping villages emerged, of which Saint Malo was the earliest (Espina 1988). Known as Louisiana's "Manilamen," these settlers constructed "communities of houses upon stilts . . . built in true Manila style, with immense hat-shaped eves and balconies" (Hearns 1883, 198). In these villages, the Manilamen lived in a homosocial world of men. Lafcadio Hearn, a journalist for *Harper's Weekly,* provided the first-known written account of this lacustrine settlement of "Malay fishermen—Tagalas from the Philippine Islands" in 1833. Unfortunately, in 1915 a strong hurricane destroyed Saint Malo and along with it further evidence of its history. Although other villages like Saint Malo continued to exist into the 19th century, many of these communities met eventual decline.

Despite an early history of Filipino settlement in the United States, it was not until after American colonization that migration to America increased. The early decades of the 20th century witnessed a sudden rise in Filipino migration to Hawaii and the continental United States, especially after the end of the Philippine-American War in 1902. The American colonial government encouraged much of this early migration beginning with a government-sponsored education program that sent hundreds of Filipino students to study in select American colleges and universities.

Termed *pensionados* for the scholarship funds they received, these students came as early as 1903 after Governor-General William Howard Taft's administration approved the Pensionado Act. The program's selectivity and the availability of funds limited the number of *pensionados* in the United States. During the program's tenure the *pensionado* program sponsored over 500 Filipino students. As government-sponsored students they were required by the colonial government to return to the Philippines immediately after the completion of their degrees. Upon their return many of these *pensionados* served in different administrative, cultural, economic, and government positions with the aim of developing the insular country. By 1910, a majority of these students had returned to the Philippines.

In addition to *pensionado* students, there were also non-sponsored students who came to United States with hopes of obtaining college degrees. Inspired by the successes of *pensionados* before them, these students migrated to the United States independently and without any funding from the colonial government. In America they attended universities throughout the country in metropolitan cities like Chicago, Los Angeles, New York, and Seattle. To fund their education many worked while attending school but lack of money, the demands of work life, and early encounters with discrimination limited their accomplishments. While some returned to the Philippines, many transitioned into full-time employment and later settled in the United States.

Recruitment of Filipino laborers into Hawaiian plantations helped to boost the numbers of Filipino immigrants beginning as early as 1906. American companies desperate for cheap laborers turned to the newly acquired colony as a source of immigrant labor. Impending labor strikes in Hawaii and stringent anti-Asian immigration policies halted the supply of Chinese, Korean, and Japanese labor, which posed a dilemma for an agricultural industry that relied heavily on it. The American annexation of the Philippines as a territory offered a solution to Hawaii's plantation owners. Filipinos were particularly attractive to the Hawaiian Sugar Planters Association (HSPA) because of their unique legal status as "American nationals." As nationals, Filipinos enjoyed special privileges that allowed them to travel freely between the Philippines and the United States.

By the mid-1910s and into the 1930s, Filipino migration continued to rise due to increasing recruitment of Filipino immigrant workers to Hawaii. The migration wave of non-sponsored students and workers in this period differed markedly from early *pensionados* in education, socioeconomic status, and Filipino ethnic affiliation. These migrants came from farming and working-class communities with large numbers from Ilokano-speaking provinces of northern Luzon. Economic and political circumstances in this region and the Philippines in general as a result of U.S. occupation had altered political and economic circumstances forcing workers to find alternative sources of employment. The combination of push-pull factors ensured that Hawaiian plantations had a steady and reliable labor source. Between 1909 and 1934, it is estimated that the HSPA recruited over "118, 556 *sakadas* into Hawaii—103,513 men, 8,952 women, and 6,091 children" (Posadas 1999, 15).

Labor recruitment in Hawaii opened up other opportunities for Filipino migrants who sought employment in Western states like California, Washington, Oregon, and Alaska. In the mainland United States many Filipinos continued to work in the agricultural industry, and when the harvest was out of season, these same men went as far north as Alaska to secure jobs as miners and as workers in Alaska's canneries. By the 1920s Filipinos were the largest group of Asian farm workers in the West Coast, while Filipinos in urban cities like Chicago, Los Angeles, San Francisco, and Seattle found work in hotels, restaurants, and domestic service.

The United States Navy also recruited Filipinos into service; they were the only Asian ethnic group to serve in the U.S. armed forces without U.S. citizenship. The establishment of three U.S. military bases in the Philippines immediately following U.S. occupation made available certain opportunities for Filipinos in the navy. As U.S. nationals, Filipinos were able to secure work in Navy yards in a variety of occupations such as stewards, seamen, petty officers, machinists, and firefighters (Espiritu 2003).

As a result of heavy labor recruitment and educational opportunities that were geared specifically towards young single Filipino men, it is not surprising that the Filipino immigrant population in the early decades of the 20th century was markedly skewed in age, gender, and occupation. This was evident in the disparity between the numbers of Filipino men and Filipina women who migrated in this early period. While a large number of Filipino men migrated for school and work, few Filipina women migrated independently or with their families. A few Filipina women who migrated between the 1920s and 1930s came as schoolteachers, pharmacists, and secretaries, but their numbers remained small (Cordova 1983). For example, in 1920s California, where the Filipino immigrant population was highest, 93.3 percent of Filipinos admitted into the state were men while only 6.7 percent were female (U.S. Department of Labor 1930, 32). A combination of family tradition, gender roles, and labor recruiting practices kept the Filipino female population low, and it was not until after World War II that their numbers would increase.

Immigrant Culture/Early Issues of Assimilation and Separatism

The unique relationship between the United States and the Philippines meant that Filipinos exercised special privileges that were unavailable to other immigrants in the early 20th century. As "American nationals," they were able to migrate between the United States and the Philippines without restriction during a period of extreme anti-Asian immigration exclusion. Despite their unique status, however, many Filipinos found that they were not welcome in the United States as equal citizens. As native-born Filipinos, access to citizenship through naturalization was barred to them just like other Asian immigrants.

As the number of Filipino immigrants in the mainland United States increased into the 1920s and the 1930s so did nativist resistance to Filipino migration. In the American West, where Filipino immigrant populations were highest, instances of social, economic, and legal harassment became commonplace (Melendy 1967, 144). Labor discrimination forced Filipinos into the agriculture and service industries where they worked as field hands, waiters, porters, and domestic servants while housing discrimination ensured that they lived in urban slums, rooming houses, and sheds (Burma 1951, 44; Melendy 1967, 146). Hostile propaganda against Filipino labor sometimes resulted in violent confrontations between whites and Filipino immigrants with some of the most infamous race riots against them occurring in the Western states of California and Washington state. Sociologists found that labor competition and Filipino-white interracial relations between men and women were some of the main causes for white disapproval (Melendy 1967, 144–45).

Filipino experiences with discrimination during this period stood in direct conflict with what they learned about American values of equality, democracy, and freedom from their American teachers in the Philippines. And although President Theodore Roosevelt claimed Filipinos as America's "little brown brothers," in reality the U.S. annexation of the Philippines produced mixed reactions about territorial expansion. Discussions about what to do with the Philippines as a U.S. possession preoccupied much of the political debates in the 1930s. Concerns about unemployment and increasing migration from the Philippines at the onset of the Great Depression shaped much of these debates, with exclusionists lobbying for Filipino exclusion as one solution to the growing so-called Filipino Problem. Thus although Filipino migrants enjoyed the benefits of their special status as American nationals, it did little to protect them from the harsh realities of the racial discrimination they experienced. Ironically, Filipinos found little government support and protection in being a ward of the United States.

By the mid-1930s economic and social discrimination manifested itself into law consequently making it difficult for Filipinos to own land, obtain marriage licenses, and naturalize. In 1934 the U.S. Congress passed the Philippines Independence Act, also known as the Tydings-McDuffie Act, which marked a dramatic shift in the relationship between the Philippines and the United States. While it promised a 10-year transition into full independence, it also immediately restricted Filipino migration to 50 people per year (Posadas 1999, 23). The Tydings-McDuffie Act was quickly followed by a piece of legislation introduced by Congressman Richard Welch. The Welch Repatriation Act of 1935, administered by the Immigration and Naturalization Services, would provide the financial means for Filipinos to voluntarily return to the Philippines (Ngai 2002). Approximately 2,190 Filipinos returned.

Later Waves of Immigration

Phases to 1965 Immigration Act

The period between 1945 and 1965 marked a period of important transformations for Filipinos both in the Philippines and the United States. Philippine independence, access to naturalized citizenship, formation of Filipino American families, and the expansion of Filipino American ethnic communities shaped the future of Filipinos in the United States.

The beginning of World War II was an important turning point as Filipinos saw a shift in U.S.–Philippine relations. Because the Philippines was an American ally in the war, American hostilities against Filipinos lessened as U.S. involvement in World War II increased. Filipino loyalty to the United States during the war against Japan won American praise. Philippine involvement in World War II led to major policy decisions that incorporated the Philippine Armed Forces into the United States Armed Forces in the Far East (USAFFE); this merger led to a massive recruitment of Filipinos into military service. In 1942 President Franklin Delano Roosevelt signed executive orders that allowed Filipino citizens to enlist for military service without citizenship. They would become the only immigrant group in the history of the U.S. military that would be allowed to do so. The Selective Service Act enabled Filipino noncitizens to serve in the segregated 1st and

2nd Filipino Infantry Regiments. In an attempt to display U.S. commitments to "democracy," rights to naturalization were also extended to Filipino service men that served during World War II. Approximately 10,737 Filipinos were naturalized (Posadas 1999, 26). Immediately following the end of the war, the United States granted Philippine independence on July 4, 1946, and Congress passed the Luce-Celler Bill, which enabled all remaining Filipinos who arrived before the passage of the Tydings-McDuffie Act to naturalize.

But this moment was also rife with tensions and contradictions for Philippine–U.S. relations. While the Luce-Celler Act offered opportunities for American citizenship, it simultaneously limited future Filipino immigration to 100 persons a year. Despite the quota, Filipinos found other opportunities for migration based on family and occupational preferences (Posadas 1999, 27). War brides and nurses accounted for a large amount of Filipino migration in the period following the passage of the Luce-Celler Bill. The Military War Brides Act of 1945 and the Fiancées Act of 1946 allowed for the migration of U.S. military servicemen's Filipina wives and fiancées in numbers that exceeded the established quota of the Luce-Celler Bill. Approximately 118,000 spouses and children arrived due to this legislation (Posadas 1999, 28). In addition the Exchange Visitor Program (EVP) administered by the State Department in 1948 offered Filipino nurses the unique opportunity to pursue postgraduate study in American hospitals. The Philippines immediately became an important EVP partner for the United States due to previous colonial ties (Choy 2003).

A visible result of the EVP, the War Bride Act, and the Fiancées Act was the increased migration of Filipina women who were absent in the early 20th century. New changes in immigration policies in the post–World War II period offered loopholes that would enable Filipinos to migrate to the United States outside the yearly quota. These new programs and laws also gave Filipino women a unique opportunity to migrate as independent migrants whether as students or professionals; or wives, or fiancées who were waiting to reunite with their families.

In 1952 the United States passed the McCarran-Walter Immigration and Nationality Act, which ended anti-Asian immigration policies and lifted the ban on race and sex as bars to exclusion. It also eliminated laws that prevented Asians from becoming naturalized citizens although it maintained race-based quotas previously in place. This act would once again transform international relations between the United States and the Philippines.

Immigration Act of 1965 and Succeeding Legislation

Amendments to U.S. immigration policies and changing conditions in the Philippines shaped contemporary Filipino migration in the post-1965 period. The Immigration and Nationality Act of 1965 abolished national quotas implemented in the early 1920s, which it replaced with hemispheric caps instead. The annual cap for the Eastern Hemisphere was 170,000, and the Western Hemisphere was 120,000 with a limit of 20,000 annually for every country (Daniels 2008). Dramatic changes in the social, political, and economic conditions in the Philippines also played an important role in Filipinos' decisions to migrate. Increasing political turmoil and unrest prompted by the regime of President Ferdinand Marcos resulted in economic instability and unemployment. This unstable government and the country's unpredictable future forced many Filipinos to migrate to the United States. The implementation of the new immigration law aided this process.

The 1965 Act established a set of preferences that facilitated family reunification and the recruitment of trained professionals. Two patterns of chain migration emerged from this: (1) family members in the Philippines came to reunite with Filipinos who had come to the United States prior to 1965 and (2) highly trained professionals came to seek out better work opportunities (Liu, Ong, and Rosenstein 1991, 488). Filipino immigrants unable to bring family members due to previous immigration restrictions took advantage of the new preferences and petitioned for relatives to join them in the United States. At the same time, shortages of medical professionals set in motion the recruitment of Filipino nurses, doctors, and other health-related professionals into American hospitals. The post-1960s migration differed markedly from previous waves of migration in this way. Unlike earlier Filipino immigrants who were primarily unskilled single male workers, post-1960s Filipino migrants came as highly trained skilled professionals indicating a dramatic shift in the demographics of new migrants' occupations and marital statuses.

The arrival of Filipina women in greater numbers also changed the demographic of this immigrant population. For the first time in Filipino immigration history, women comprised the larger group of migrants in the post-1965 era. Between 1966 and 1971, Filipino women in the United States far outnumbered men—66,517 to 47,599 (Takaki 1989, 432). A combination of families migrating as well as women dominating the health professional field contributed to this increase. Filipina nurses especially had become a principal part of the so-called brain drain generation with an estimated one-fifth of the 20,000 nurses graduating from Philippine schools migrating to the United States (Bautista 1998, 115). It was during this period that the Philippines became a major source of foreign-trained nurses in the United States.

The arrival of families and professionals revitalized what were once declining Filipino American communities throughout the United States. Over 230,000 Filipinos migrated to the United States in the decade immediately following the 1965 Act (Posadas 1999, 35). By the 1970s the Philippines had sent the highest number of new immigrants to the United States from Asia (Liu, Ong, and Rosenstein 1991).

Through IRCA to the Present

The Immigration Reform and Control Act (IRCA) was an attempt to address issues regarding illegal immigration during the 1980s. The new law sought to do three things: (1) restrict illegal immigration through more stringent enforcement, (2) enforce stricter penalties for employers who knowingly employ ineligible workers, and (3) provide amnesty for undocumented immigrants who have continuously resided in the United States since January 1, 1982 (U.S. Citizenship and Immigration Services n.d.). While Filipino immigrants were not the intended targets of the law, it did affect a small population of Filipinos who were living in the United States as undocumented immigrants. Many of them had entered the United States legally but "over stayed" past the expiration date of their tourist and temporary working visas (Posadas 1999, 130). By staying in the United States, these temporary migrants hoped that they would be able to accelerate the process of applying for permanent residency. Others chose different routes like entering into contracted marriages that enabled the undocumented immigrant to gain citizenship through a spouse. Between 1986 and 1999, approximately 27,696 Filipinos gained legal immigrant status under the IRCA (Posadas 1999, 40).

The enactment of the IRCA was followed by amendments to existing immigration legislation. The Immigration Act of 1990 increased the number of legal immigrants allowed to enter the United States. As a result, changes in the preference system doubled the number of Filipinos admitted into the United States. The Immigration Act of 1990 also included a section that directly affected Filipino veterans. Section 540 allowed for the naturalization of surviving Philippine-born World War II veterans who fought for the U.S. Armed Forces between September 1, 1939, and December 31, 1946 (Posadas 1999, 43). Veterans of the U.S. Armed Forces in the Far East (USAFFE), the Philippine Army, and the Philippine Scout Rangers were granted the rare opportunity to apply for U.S. citizenship.

In the 1990s the issue of illegal immigration resurfaced once again. The Illegal Immigration Reform and Immigrant Responsibility Act (IIRIRA), passed in 1996, drastically changed the grounds for exclusion and deportation of legal and illegal immigrants. It enforced harsh penalties against identified undocumented immigrants and barred them from future entry into the United States. Although the IIRIRA was intended as an illegal immigration bill, its policies affected legal immigration as well. Legal immigrants faced stricter conditions that made sponsorship of new immigrants more difficult to achieve. Other aspects of the law underscored the importance of "immigrant responsibilities" intended to deter legal immigrants from access to the benefits of social services (Posadas 1999, 142). Overall the IIRIRA was designed to implement immigration policies that would restrict migration, deter illegal immigration, and impose stringent penalties on those who violated these laws.

Demographic Profile

Size and Composition of Community

U.S. census data provides the best estimates of the Filipino population in the United States. In 2000 the U.S. Census Bureau identified Filipinos as the second-largest detailed Asian group representing approximately 19.8 percent of the total Asian population in the United States. There is an estimated 2,364,815 people who identified as Filipino alone or in combination with one or more races making up almost 1 percent of the U.S. population (U.S. Census 2000a). Despite a long history of disproportioned male migration, the sex ratio amongst Filipino Americans is now in favor of women. Males make up 46 percent while women represent 54 percent of the total adult Filipino American population (U.S. Census 2000a).

Filipino Americans live throughout the United States, but the West region has the highest concentration of the population with 68 percent. Approximately 14 percent of Filipino Americans live in the Southern region, while 10 percent are in the Northeast. The Midwest has the lowest percentage of the population with only 8 percent (U.S. Census 2000a). The top ten states with the highest population of Filipino Americans include: California (1,098,321), Hawaii (275,728), Illinois (100,338), New York (95,144), New Jersey (95,063), Washington (91,765), Texas (75,226), Florida (71,282), Virginia (59,374), and Nevada (51,318) (U.S. Census 2000a). Metropolitan regions and cities with the highest numbers of Filipino Americans are Los Angeles/Riverside/Orange County, California; San Francisco/Oakland/San Jose, California; Honolulu, Hawaii; New York/Northern New Jersey/Long Island, New York; San Diego, California; Chicago, Illinois/Gary, Indiana/Kenosha, Wisconsin; and Seattle/Tacoma/Bremerton, Washington. (U.S. Census 2000a).

Age and Family Structure

In 2000 Filipinos had a median age of 35.5 years, which is half a year older than the national median of 35 years. Following the trend of the overall population of the United States, 73 percent of Filipino Americans are over 18. Compared to other Asian ethnic groups the Filipino American population shows little signs of aging with only 8.7 percent of the population over 65 years old while children under 18 constitute 22.1 percent of the overall population (Reeves and Bennett 2004, 9).

The family unit occupies a central space in Filipino American lives. It is a nuclear one that includes the father, mother, and their children. In 2000 approximately 58.8 percent of Filipino Americans of marriageable age were married, 61.7 percent of which maintained Filipino American households (U.S. Census 2000b). In addition to this nuclear family structure, the Filipino kinship structure is also a "bilateral" one that incorporates relatives from the maternal and paternal lines. Thus it is not unusual for Filipino American families to include grandparents, uncles, aunts, and cousins—both blood and fictive kin—within their households. This kind of extensive family structure accommodates multigenerational families into a household; a rate that is higher in Filipino American communities when compared to other immigrant groups. When compared with other Asian ethnic groups, Filipino Americans were more than twice as likely to live in families with six or more members (Barnes, Adams, and Powell-Griner 2008).

Educational Attainment

Filipino Americans have a deep regard for education, which they view as a primary avenue for upward economic and social mobility. Historically the goal of obtaining a college degree has been a main driver for Filipino immigration to the United States beginning with American-sponsored *pensionados.* In contemporary times, Filipino immigrants continue to pursue the completion of college degrees or higher forms of education to achieve economic success and stability in the United States. It is believed that a good education presents opportunities for better jobs.

In 2000 approximately 87.3 percent of Filipino Americans 25 and older had at least a high school education. For 37 percent of Filipino Americans a high school diploma was the highest level of education attained. Over 43 percent had a bachelor's degree while 43.8 percent reported having achieved a bachelor's degree or higher. Of the total population of Filipino Americans 25 and older, only 13 percent have less than a high school degree compared to 20 percent of the general U.S. population (Reeves and Bennett 2004, 12).

The relatively high educational attainment of Filipino Americans can be attributed to selective migration, which has been a direct result of post-1960s Filipino immigration (Bankston 2006). As Filipino professionals arrived as a part of the brain drain of the 1960s, they came with high levels of education and training. Rates of educational attainment are especially high for foreign-born Filipino Americans when compared to their native-born counterparts. While 42.4 percent of foreign-born Filipino Americans hold a bachelor's degree or higher, only 22.3 percent of the native-born Filipino American population have achieved the same level of educational attainment (Posadas 1999, 103).

Economic Attainment

Occupation and Income Patterns

In general Filipino American families have achieved a relatively comfortable economic attainment. The median family income for Filipino Americans in 1999 was $63,057, which is approximately $21,000 higher than the median income for the general U.S. population (U.S. Census 2000c). A relatively high median annual income for Filipino Americans can be attributed to their educational attainment as discussed earlier as well as the concentration of Filipino Americans in professional occupations. Another factor contributing to the higher median family income is the higher numbers of family members who work within the household. Seventy-one percent of Filipino American men above the age of 16 years old reported participating in the labor force earned $35,560 on average. Among women in the detailed Asian groups of the 2000 Census, Filipino American women had the highest labor force participation rate at 65.2 percent (Reeves and Bennett 2004, 13). The percentage of Filipino American women in the labor force exceeded that of all Asian ethnic women. On average Filipino American women earned $31,450 annually.

In 1990 approximately 38 percent of Filipino Americans were employed in management and professional type occupations. Approximately 13.9 percent worked in the service industry, and 20.8 percent were in sales and office. Less than 20 percent of the total Filipino American population worked in the farming, construction, and production transportation industries (Reeves and Bennett 2004, 14). Although Filipino Americans are concentrated in professional occupations, they are

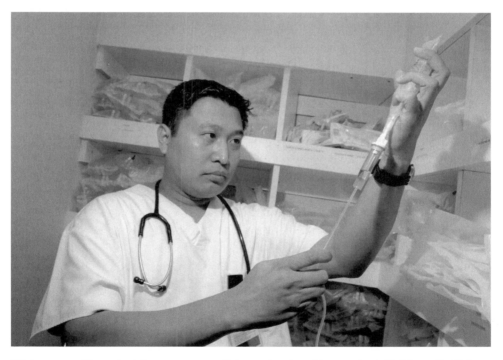

Filipino nurse Elmer Jacinto prepares medicine as he does his rounds at St. Vincent's Midtown Hospital in New York, September 21, 2006. Jacinto could have remained a doctor in the Philippines but chose to become a nurse in the United States, making a higher salary than physicians in his homeland. (AP Photo/Paul Hawthorne)

underrepresented in high-ranking leadership positions in both the public and private sectors. Filipinos are also less likely to become entrepreneurs and own businesses when compared to other Asian ethnic groups.

Despite relatively high economic success, however, approximately 7 percent of Filipinos in the United States live below the federal poverty line (U.S. Census 2000c). Filipino Americans have a lower per capita income of $19,259 when compared to whites, who have an average of $24,819 (Asian Pacific Islander Health Forum [APIAHF] 2005). Research shows that native-born Filipino Americans tend to have higher poverty rates than the foreign born. Filipino Americans who lived in ethnic enclaves in Los Angeles were more likely to live in poverty than Filipino Americans who lived in other regions of the country (Bankston 2006, 193).

Health Statistics and Issues

Health statistics for Filipino Americans offer limited findings because general studies on the Asian American population often do not differentiate between ethnic Asian groups (APIAHF 2005). Thus although Filipino Americans are the second-largest Asian ethnic group in the United States, few studies have examined specific health issues that impact their community members. Because the U.S. Census does not collect health information on the U.S. population, the National Center for Health Statistics (NCHS), which functions under the direction of the Center for Disease Control and Prevention (CDC), offers the best analysis of Filipino American health characteristics.

In 1994, according to the National Health Interview Survey (NHIS), 37 percent of Filipino Americans interviewed described their health as "excellent," 32 percent as "very good," 24 percent as "good," and 7 percent as "fair or poor" (APIAHF 2005). Reports on the general health conditions of Filipino American adults are good. The NCHS reports that 51 percent of the Filipino American adult population are in the healthy weight range and consumption of alcohol and rates of drug use are lower for Filipino American adults. But studies have also shown that amongst the Asian American population, the prevalence of obesity is higher with Filipino Americans. They are more than twice as likely to be obese (at 14%) when compared to other Asian ethnics (Barnes, Adams, and Powell-Griner 2008). There is also a high prevalence of diabetes amongst Filipino American adults. Heart disease is the leading cause of death while cancer is the second leading cause. Because there are relatively high rates of hypertension for both Filipino American men and women, they are at risk for stroke, which is another cause of mortality (APIAHF 2005).

Access to proper health care and preventive treatment are keys to addressing such health issues. Like most Americans, Filipino Americans rely on job-based insurance coverage. A study done by the UCLA Center for Health Policy on racial and ethnic disparities and access to health care found that although Filipinos have the same employment-based coverage as whites (74% and 75% respectively), they have lower rates of Medicaid coverage and generally have higher uninsured rates (Brown, Ojeda, Wyn, and Levan 2000, 44, 59). The study concluded that factors related to ethnic background and socioeconomic status such as language proficiency, immigration status, and income contributed to disparities in health status and disproportionate access to health care.

Adjustment and Adaptation

Family, Culture, and Life-Cycle Rituals

The most important life-cycle events for Filipinos include birth and baptism, marriage, and death. In celebrating life-cycle rituals religion plays a significant role, and many Filipino Americans honor rituals as prescribed by their respective religion. Because of the cultural, religious, and social significance of these events, it is generally celebrated in the presence of one's extended family and kin network. The universal importance of these events in Filipino American lives often transcends the boundaries of class, regional loyalties, and religions.

The arrival of a new baby is viewed with joy, as they are believed to complete the family unit and redefine familial roles. A childless couple assumes the responsibilities of parents and transitions from husband and wife to that of father and mother. Similarly, grandparents also take on new roles to support the newborn child. The naming of children is the first important event in the child's early life. Filipino American families often assign a given first name, a middle name, and a family surname that often reflect one's lineage, national heritage, and kinship ties (Posadas 1999, 48). In addition to their given names, many Filipinos also assign a nickname to their children that follows them into adulthood as a sign of affection and endearment. Filipino names are the product of the country's diverse history. While some names may be considered "indigenous," others are derived from Chinese and Spanish influences dating back to the period of colonization. This accounts for the majority of Spanish Filipino surnames. The arrival of Americans in the islands introduced Filipinos to the American versions of their Spanish first names, which some Filipinos have adopted. In the United States, Filipinos continue to name their children to reflect their Filipino heritage, which is often combined with more American first names. Because Filipinos inherit their parents' religion, baptism is another significant event in a child's young life. For Filipino Christians, baptism marks one's transition from being non-Christian to becoming a Christian. The ritual is performed in accordance with the mandates of the church and in the presence of the family and the child's sponsors. A celebration follows the church ceremony, as the child is welcomed into the faith community.

The coming of age for young Filipinos is sometimes celebrated with a debut. A debut is a debutante ball that is held in honor of the young Filipino man or woman who is turning 18 years old. The purpose of the debut is to present the young woman or man to society. The tradition has its roots in the Philippines but Filipinos in the United States have embraced it also. The debut is often held in a ballroom where the celebrant has her cotillion court comprised of nine girls and nine boys. There is a cotillion dance, which is followed by a cake cutting ceremony and a formal dinner in honor of the debutante. Debuts, however, can be costly and can cause an economic strain on the family's finances. Therefore, it is not something that everyone chooses to celebrate formally, and debuts have become optional celebrations for Filipino American families.

As young adults transition into adulthood, they look to marriage as the next important rite of passage. The bonds of marriage and family are central components of Filipino American values and are special occasions for celebrations within the Filipino American community. Filipino Americans place a high value on the importance of marriage and family and see one's marriage as an opportunity to establish new familial connections as well as expand the network kin. Thus marriage is foundational to the notion of family. Due to this Filipino Americans in general are less likely than the total population to be separated or divorced. Among Filipino Americans only approximately 12 percent of the total population are separated, widowed, or divorced (Reeves and Bennett 2004, 7).

In the United States, as it is in the Philippines, marriage is preceded by a courtship and an engagement. Practices of courtship can sometimes be challenging when an individual decides to marry someone of another religion, another Asian ethnic group, or race. Filipino preferences for an endogamous marriage create difficult challenges for the couple and their families. Cultural differences and conflicting values are central to these concerns. Despite this, intermarriage rates for Filipinos in the United States are steadily increasing although their numbers are still lower when compared to other Asian ethnic groups. Between 1982 and 1990, 56 percent of U.S.-born Filipino American women and 48.4 percent of men in California married a non-Filipino American (Posadas 1999, 150). Among Asians, Filipino Americans are more likely to marry someone who is Caucasian rather than someone of the same ethnicity (National Healthy Marriage Resource Center 2009).

Once the couple decides to marry and meets the approval of their families, weddings are performed in accordance with the law and the couple's religion. Due to the influences of Spain and the United States, wedding celebrations often follow a Christian Western tradition. A religious ceremony precedes a dinner reception that celebrates the couple's union. Filipino custom requires that the groom's family is responsible for the costs of the wedding. In the United States, Filipino Americans continue to follow this tradition although the second and later generations are increasingly sharing wedding costs.

While weddings are met with jubilation, the death of a relative or friend is an occasion of extreme sorrow. To honor the dead, Filipinos follow mandates of their religious affiliations. For Filipino Catholics, this includes the observance of a funeral mass in a Catholic church. In the United States, Filipino Americans have included Filipino traditions of family visits, food preparation, and collective prayers as significant components of honoring one's passing. Mourning is seen a collective and community process for the family and its community.

Families and Changing Gender Relations

Filipino Americans place a high value on family orientation, which is evident in the composition of their families and their extensive kinship networks. Due to colonial Spanish and American pasts, traditional notions of gender roles and familial responsibility influence the definitions of the family structure. Filipino tradition dictates a hierarchy in the family that requires familial responsibility to take precedence over personal preference or civic responsibility. Authority within the family is also often given to its adult members with respect to a hierarchy in gender and age.

In the United States, these family structures are being challenged by contemporary American society and culture. Generational tensions and cultural conflicts between parents and their children have become contributing factors to these changing family dynamics. Differences in experiences, moral values, and cultural norms between the two generations have also presented conflicting definitions of responsibility to the family unit. As a result, relations and hierarchies within the family structures are shifting as Filipino American youth and their parents negotiate new boundaries.

Gender relations between men and women are also changing. While authority has traditionally been ceded to the men of the family; in the United States, different demands of work and everyday living enable women to be equal partners in the family decision-making. In Filipino American households, an inversion of gender divisions in labor is beginning to take place. The predominance of Filipino American women in the workforce contributes to these changing dynamics and the negotiation of gender roles within family units.

Retaining a Sense of National Culture and Identity

Because of the diversity of America's overall population, Filipino Americans throughout the United States have found a number of ways to maintain a sense of cultural identity. Advanced technology in the post-1960s period has made this process easier especially for recent immigrants. Sending remittances, communicating by telephone and Internet, as well as taking return trips home keep Filipino Americans connected to their country of origin. In the United States, community

Children from the Filipiniana Dance Troupe wearing traditional Filipino dress prepare to perform a *putong,* or welcome dance, at the opening of the Filipino Community Center in Honolulu, Hawaii, on June 11, 2002. (AP Photo/B.J. Reyes)

building through formal means such as membership in social organizations, religious groups, and cultural celebrations have also played an important role in creating a sense of community. In regions and cities where large populations of Filipino Americans exist, hometown associations and community organizations provide formal spaces for community members to gather and celebrate. Informal networks based on ethnic affiliation and friendships also offer opportunities to maintain cultural ties to their home country. In addition the celebration of holidays, the performance of rituals, and the preparing and sharing of Filipino food also help to reinforce one's ethnic identity.

Continued Links to the Philippines

Filipino Americans exhibit a strong sense of loyalty to their country of origin, which is reflected in their continued involvement and support of the Philippines. For many foreign-born Filipino immigrants, this can mean financially supporting family members they left behind through the remittance of money. These remittances, which are intended to help families with living expenses, education, and medical care, reinforce the immigrants' relationship not only to their own families but also to the Philippines. Remittances boost the foreign direct investment (FDI) of the home country's economy, which the Philippines has increasingly relied on from overseas Filipinos. In addition to remittances in the form of money, Filipino Americans also send *balikbayan* boxes to family members that contain consumer goods such as clothes, toys, electronics, and even food. To cater to this need to send boxes to the Philippines, an industry of international shipping companies like Forex and LBC Mabuhay has emerged to serve the ethnic community. In addition to serving Filipino Americans these door-to-door delivery companies also serve Filipinos in Europe, the Middle East, Australia, and different parts of Asia.

When possible Filipino Americans prefer to return to the Philippines for periodic visits or vacations. The "homecoming" of the *balikbayan* renews pre-existing bonds not only with the Philippines but also their families. Filipino Americans as *balikbayans* return with *pasalubong*, or gifts for family members and friends—a display not only of one's generosity but also a reflection of one's successes in the United States. But the notion of the *pasalubong* is also an expected responsibility from the *balikbayan,* which families anticipate and rely on. The financial strain on the *balikbayan* due to this is evident, sometimes forcing some Filipino Americans to hold off on visiting and deciding to send boxes home instead. On the occasion that they decide to return, the homecoming of the Filipino can be symbolic. In returning the Filipino maintains links between themselves and their country of origin. In this way the relationship of the *balikbayan* to the country is strengthened while familial relationships are restored. Due to the financial costs of taking a return trip back, however, not everyone is able to afford a trip to the Philippines.

Thus for many Filipino Americans communicating by telephone and through the Internet is the most affordable way to maintain ties with family in the Philippines. Advanced technology has made this easier when return visits home are not possible. Filipino Americans rely on cheap phone plans to ensure that they can regularly communicate with family members although sending emails and text messages, video chatting, and connecting through social networking sites have also become commonplace.

Social Organizations Based on National/Ethnic Background

Filipino American community organizations have played a significant role in the experiences of immigrants in the United States. In the early period of Filipino American settlement, social organizations served a number of purposes. The wide variety of associations and clubs affirmed ethnic ties and allowed its members to express their cultural identity in society that was determined on marginalizing them. In the early 20th century, Filipino fraternal organizations like the Caballeros de Dimas-Alang, Legionarios del Trabajo, and Jose Rizal societies were very popular. Much like other Asian immigrant community organizations of that time, fraternal organizations emphasized mutual aid, cultural preservation, and community building for its members. Equally important were hometown associations where membership was based on common locality or affiliation in the Philippines. During a period in which many immigrants were without community and familial ties these social organizations provided a necessary space for communal participation and belonging.

In addition to "community," membership also afforded access to financial and emotional support in times of crises. Mutual aid became synonymous with community, and Filipino immigrants found necessary support within their own. These organizations also provided spaces for the communal celebration of life-cycle rituals like births and baptisms, weddings and anniversaries, as well as the commemoration of important Filipino holidays. While very popular in the 1920s and 1930s, these organizations met a slow decline in numbers in the period following World War II. A combination of restrictive immigration laws and a declining population halted their growth, and participation in organizations would not again increase until after the post-1960s period.

The post-1965 wave of Filipino immigration did much to revitalize these communities. In Hawaii and in the mainland United States new immigrants either created new organizations or revived inactive ones (Okamura 1984). But while Filipino American social organizations continued to play an important role in communities, their aims, goals, and purposes changed. Social organizations were no longer the central site for mutual aid or surrogate family support but were transformed in a way that met the new needs of its post-1965 community members.

New Filipino American social organizations focused on the promotion and preservation of Filipino culture, youth education, and community gathering. Hometown associations—organized by regional and provincial affiliations—became the primary vehicles for this form of community building. They hosted the celebrations of Filipino holidays and hometown festivals, beauty pageants, banquets, picnics, and cultural performances to raise funds for community projects (Bonus 2000). Many associations used these funds to erect monuments and build schools, libraries, and even hospitals in their hometowns. When the construction of buildings was not possible or affordable, Filipino American groups sponsored local students and supported their schooling into their college years instead.

Despite the popularity of social organizations, not all Filipino Americans joined, for a variety of reasons. Sometimes there was no need for association membership due to an extensive kin network. Others lived in cities and regions where the overall population was too scattered or too small. Many working-class immigrants found that they had limited time to commit to community membership while others expressed a general lack of interest in joining formal organizations. Instead, they connected to the community in more informal ways like getting together with Filipino American friends and engaging in different forms of ethnic affiliation such as attending cultural shows, watching Filipino movies, reading ethnic newspapers, and sending remittances home (Bonus 2000).

Religion

Filipinos inherit the religion of their parents and bring it with them as they migrate to the United States. The impact of Spanish colonial Christianity in the Philippines remains to this day and is still an influential force in Filipino religious practices. American presence in the Philippines in the early 20th century introduced Protestantism (Baptist and Presbyterian churches), which later gave rise to other evangelical groups such as Iglesia ni Kristo and Aglipayan. After World War II, Christian sects that included Mormons, Jehovah's Witnesses, and Seventh-Day Adventists successfully proselytized in the Philippines. Due to these influences, the Philippines is the only predominantly Christian country in Asia. Today approximately 85 percent of the population are Christian, 10 percent Muslim, and 5 percent "other" religions (including Taoist-Buddhist, Agnostic, and "indigenous" religions).

In the Philippines the church serves as an important space for community building and sociability that transcends social classes and provincial affiliations. In the United States church membership can bring Filipinos together in an ethnic community that helps to strengthen their ties to their homeland. Church activities and religious celebrations such as baptisms, weddings, and funerals are important opportunities for ethnic reinforcement and community building. Within these communities religion becomes more than just an affirmation of faith but also an affirmation of one's ethnic identity.

Language Issues

In general Filipino Americans exhibit a high proficiency of the English language, one of the highest amongst all Asian ethnic groups. In the 2000 Census, 47 percent of Filipino Americans aged 5 and older reported speaking English "very well" while almost 30 percent reported speaking only English at home (Reeves and Bennett 2004, 11). Filipino Americans' strong proficiency of the English language can be seen as a legacy of their American colonial past that contributes to their strong command of the English language. In 1987 the Philippine Constitution declared Filipino and English as the two official languages of the country. Because of this, language proficiency amongst the Filipino foreign-born population in the United States is relatively high. Still, 24 percent of the Filipino American population reported speaking English "less than very well" with 7 percent of the foreign-born population reporting limited or no knowledge of English (U.S. Census 2000b).

In the United States, Tagalog is becoming one of the most popular non-English languages spoken (Bankston 2006, 196). With over 1.2 million speakers it is the fifth-most spoken language in the United States. In the 2000 Census over 70 percent of the Filipino American population reported speaking a language other than English in their homes. Filipino Americans speak a variety of Filipino languages and dialects that include Tagalog, Ilokano, Kapampangan, and different variations of Visayan languages.

National/Regional-Language Press and other Media

The Filipino American media in the United States began with local ethnic newspapers and magazines published in the early 20th century. Sociologist Emory Bogardus observed that in Los Angeles alone there were up to eight Filipino American newspaper-magazines in publication during the 1930s (Bogardus 1934). Almost all of them were small operations and often short lived due to lack of financial resources, but sociologists saw it as a testimony to "considerable intellectual activity" within the community (Bogardus 1934, 584). Geared towards the immigrant Filipino, the press focused on political matters that concerned Filipinos in the United States such as Philippine independence and U.S. colonialism. It sought to expose discrimination and inform readers about the social conditions of Filipino students and workers. The newspaper-magazines also included op-ed pieces, photographs, and literature. Most of the printed pieces were in English due to their facility of the language but occasionally included articles in Tagalog and other Filipino languages.

In a period of limited technology and communication, these newspapers offered a community and a space where conversations about the state of Filipino America and the Philippines took center stage. Unlike mainstream papers that discussed little of what mattered to immigrants, these local ethnic newspapers catered to a specific population that longed to be in conversation with their homeland. Changes in the political state and Philippine-U.S. relations, however, altered the directions and purposes of the Filipino American press. In the period following World War II, with a smaller Filipino American population, the number of these community papers dwindled and did not rise again until the post-1965 era.

In the post-1960s period, Filipino American newspapers continue to serve the population by providing local as well as international news. There is no national paper that is distributed throughout the country. Instead, states with high numbers of Filipino Americans publish and distribute their papers. In California, for example, there are approximately 11 newspapers in print that are distributed throughout Southern California and the Bay Area. Despite the proliferation of ethnic newspapers, however, access to the media in the age of the Internet and advanced technology has also changed the ways in which Filipino Americans gain access to the news. Today, Filipino Americans use the Internet to not only access online newspapers in the United States but also ones from the Philippines. In addition, Internet radio has become another popular news source. Radio Manila, based out of Los Angeles, offers programming that informs listeners all over the country about local news, immigration, religion, politics, and public affairs. The use of e-mail and the Internet also allows Filipinos throughout the world to communicate with each other. Blogs, Listservs, and social networking sites are increasingly becoming the most popular way of communicating, especially with Filipino American youth.

But it is the Filipino cable networks that have brought the Philippines to every Filipino American home. ABS-CBN, the Philippine-based multimedia conglomerate, introduced The Filipino Channel (TCF) to cable subscribers in 1994. What started as a small and ambitious endeavor has transformed into a 24-hour cable network that airs Filipino movies, variety shows, news reports, TV sitcoms, and dramas. Other Filipino broadcast companies have since done the same. GMA Pinoy TV is a recent addition to American cable channel lineups. This premier international broadcasting channel offers 24 hours of Filipino programming that is not only broadcast in the United States but also anywhere in the world where potential Filipino subscribers might be. Together TFC and GMA Pinoy TV have revolutionized the Filipino American cable networks as Filipinos throughout the country have relied on these channels to keep them updated on everything that is happening in the Philippines.

Celebration of National Holidays

In the United States, Filipino Americans celebrate July 4 not only as an American Independence Day but also as Philippine-American Friendship Day. Philippine independence from Spain is celebrated on June 12 every year. In addition, on December 30 each year, Filipino American clubs and associations celebrate Jose Rizal Day, which commemorates the Philippine national hero Jose Rizal. Filipino Americans have been observing this holiday since the early 20th century; it is a tradition that young Filipino students began in college campuses (Guyotte and Posadas 1995). The celebration of Rizal Day is more than just the remembering of a national hero. In honoring this holiday, Filipino Americans are also celebrating Filipino history and culture in the United States. These holidays are often observed with picnics, banquets, or cultural shows that combine its political and cultural significance.

In addition to Filipino national holidays, Filipino Americans also celebrate provincial and religious holidays as is done in the Philippines. For example, hometown associations will observe their hometown's local patron saint with a feast and a program that honors the saint and their local history. Combining cultural and religious celebrations is not uncommon for Filipino American communities in the United States. The celebration of Filipino holidays serves not only to affirm one's ethnic identity but also to connect overseas Filipinos to the Philippines.

The recent passage of H.R. 780 in Congress, which recognizes October to be Filipino American History month, adds to this list of Filipino national holidays. The dedication of October to Filipino American History month will allow for a full-month commemorative celebration of Filipino American history and culture. Advocates of the resolution see this as a small victory in honoring and memorializing the long history of Filipino immigrants in the United States.

Foodways

The geography of the Philippines has shaped the staple diet of Filipinos. As in most countries in this region of Asia, rice serves as a staple with a typical meal consisting of rice and a meat or vegetable dish that supplements it. Filipinos customarily eat three meals a day that include breakfast, lunch, and dinner accompanied by a small snack at midday called a *merienda*.

The popularity and preparation of Filipino dishes vary by region as they are influenced by its geographic location and its local history. Methods of preparing Filipino food range from simple boiling and frying to more complicated forms of stewing and roasting meats. One of the most popular Filipino dishes is the Filipino *adobo*. The preparation of the Filipino *adobo* differs remarkably from the Latin American variety of a similar name. This uniquely Filipino dish features the salty and sour combination of a soy sauce and vinegar marinade infused with crushed garlic and pepper. Pork and chicken are two popular meats often used in the dish, but Filipino cooks alter its style and tastes by using different ingredients available in mainstream grocery stores in the United States. Equally popular is the *sinigang,* which is a stew known for its sour broth base of tamarind, guava, or tomatoes. *Sinigang* is an adaptable dish that can include any meat, fish, or vegetable that the cook has readily available. Due to their adaptability and ease of preparation, *adobo* and *sinigang* are popular dishes in Filipino American households and restaurants.

Filipino cuisine is also a fusion of Malayan, Chinese, and Spanish culinary influences that reflects a long and diverse history of cultural exchange and adaptation in the Philippines. The early migration of Malayan peoples from adjacent islands is among one of the earliest foreign influences on Philippine cuisine. Dishes of Malay origin—infused with spicy chili and prepared with coconuts and coconut milk—were incorporated into local Filipino dishes during these early encounters. The arrival of Chinese merchants into the Philippines also contributed to this early influence as new settlers introduced its Filipino trading partners to unique cooking and flavor styles, which natives adopted into the local cuisine. Filipinos slowly incorporated different variations of Chinese noodle and rice dishes, egg rolls, and steamed buns into Filipino cuisine, and these dishes continue to be some of the most popular dishes in the Philippines and in the United States today.

During the period of Spanish colonization, Spanish cuisine became another culinary influence but only within an elite group. Because it was the cuisine of the colonizer, Spanish food was reserved for the upper classes. Spanish cooking also required distinctive ingredients such as olives, capers, and Spanish meats, which were not readily available in the islands. Prepared with unique spices, succulent meats, and seafood, these elaborate Spanish dishes were often reserved for fiestas and the celebration of very important occasions.

Foreign culinary influences are also evident in Filipino desserts. While desserts are not a part of everyday meals due primarily to their tedious preparations they are still an important part of the Filipino culinary experience. Desserts like *bibingka, kutsinta, biko, palitaw,* and *sapin-sapin* are only a few examples of the regional varieties of rice cakes and puddings made with sticky rice mixed with fruits, grated coconut, and sweet beans. Other popular desserts include *halo-halo* (mix-mix), a sundae made with shaved ice, sweet beans, jackfruit, ice cream, and evaporated milk; *leche flan,* a caramel custard made of eggs, milk, and sugar with Spanish origins; and *sorbetes,* a uniquely Filipino type of ice cream.

Filipinos have incorporated many of these foreign influences into the preparation of local dishes, which have become an important part of contemporary Filipino cuisine. In the United States, Filipino Americans find new ways to further adapt Filipino dishes and rituals into their daily lives. Cooks often prepare traditional dishes using American ingredients as substitutes. Filipino American families also incorporate typical American fare into regular meals based on convenience and preferences.

As the population of Filipino Americans increases, so do the number of Filipino restaurants and markets, especially in the American West Coast. As a result, the availability of uniquely Filipino ingredients and prepared dishes has increased considerably in the recent past. In cities where Filipino oriented markets and restaurants are lacking, shopping online for Filipino groceries have become popular and have made these ingredients readily accessible.

Music, Arts, and Entertainment

The knowledge and performance of Filipino music, dance, and art is perhaps one of the most popular ways in which Filipinos maintain a sense of ethnic and cultural identity. A staple in every Filipino American celebration, the performances of Filipino dance and music has become a part of their cultural landscape in the United States. These public expressions of cultural identity allow members of the community to participate as performers or as members of the audience.

Traditional dance is popular especially with Filipino American youth. Whether performed in community centers or college campuses, dance offers young Filipino Americans an opportunity to participate in cultural preservation and celebration.

Dance also allows for Filipino American interpretations of costumes and movements that reflect their experiences in the United States. Much like other forms of Filipino art and culture, these dances are highly influenced by the diversity of Filipino history. Dances that are popularly performed include *tinikling* (bamboo dance), *singkil* (Muslim royalty dance), and *pandanggo sa ilaw* (dance of lights). Sometimes these dances are infused with more contemporary dance styles and music, which reflect the multiple identities of Filipinos in the United States.

The performance of Filipino music often accompanies the dance. The *rondalla,* a traditional form of Filipino folk music, is performed with stringed instruments and often consists of the guitar, the *banduria,* the *laud,* and the bass guitar. Another form of music that is popular in the United States is the *kulintang,* which originates from the southern region of the Philippines and is traditionally performed with gongs and drums, reflecting early Islamic influence. In addition to these more traditional forms of music, more contemporary genres include the original Pilipino music (OPM), Filipino rock, Pinoy hop-hop, and Philippine choral music.

Through the performance of Filipino dance and music, Filipino Americans express a sense of ethnic identity that encourages their preservation and renewal. This is especially true for Filipino American youth who see these forms of art as an opportunity to explore and affirm their cultural identities. Filipino dance and music

Tinikling dance performed by Filipino American students in Celebration of Filipino Culture at California State University, San Bernardino. (Courtesy of Kathleen Nadeau)

OPM: Old Pilipino Music

In the years following Philippine Independence and into the 1960s Filipino music showed evidence of heavy American influence. The emergence of OPM as a uniquely Filipino genre of music introduced Filipinos to artists such the Apo Hiking Society, Basil Valdez, Freddie Aguilar, Rico J. Puno, Rey Valera, and Florante. These artists sang Tagalog songs that reflected their own experiences of love, home, and culture. The songs touched many Filipinos in the Philippines and abroad. As migration from the Philippines to the United States increased in the post-1965 period, many Filipinos brought this music with them. In the United States, OPM took on a new significance for Filipino Americans who saw it as a link back to the home country. In a period in which Filipinos were migrating to the United States en masse, OPM was a piece of home that they could bring with them. Today early OPM has become a part of classic Filipino music, and performers of this genre continue to entertain Filipino audiences with live concerts both in the Philippines and in the United States.

also brings the community together and often links the younger and older generations together. In the United States, cultural performances of Filipino dance and music have been incorporated into public holiday celebrations as well as Philippine Cultural Nights, which are popular in high schools and colleges across the country. For Filipino Americans this is significant because it offers a necessary link to the home country. Dance and music become a component of one's group identity, a basis for sociopolitical and ethnic claims.

Integration and Impact on U.S. Society and Culture

Paths toward Citizenship

Naturalization

Historically the path towards American citizenship for Filipinos has been one that is rife with contradictions reflecting a complex relationship between the United States and the Philippines. It was not until the passage of the McCarran-Walter Immigration and Nationality Act in 1952 that Filipinos, like other Asian immigrants ineligible for citizenship, were able to apply for naturalization. This was something that many Filipinos who arrived in the early 20th century took advantage of. It is the same for post–1965 immigrants who have applied for U.S. citizenship in high numbers. According to estimates by the 2000 U.S. Census, over 73.9 percent of the Filipino American population are American citizens, of which 41.6 percent are foreign-born naturalized citizens (U.S. Census 2000b). Approximately 32.3 percent of the overall Filipino American population is native born, while only 26.1 percent are noncitizens. Among Asian ethnic groups, Filipino Americans have the lowest proportion of noncitizens (Reeves and Bennett 2004, 9).

The high rates of naturalization can be attributed to a number of different factors. Naturalization secures their legal residency in the United States and affords the foreign-born rights that are reserved only for American citizens, such as access to certain health care benefits and social services. Citizenship also allows Filipino Americans to petition for family members in accordance with the family reunification preferences of post-1965 immigration laws. Sometimes Filipino Americans' decision to naturalize is tied to their dissatisfaction with the overall political and economic conditions in the Philippines even though obtaining American citizenship and pledging allegiance to the United States do not stop them from participating in homeland politics.

Dual Citizenship

Dual citizenship was not permitted for Filipinos who obtained foreign citizenship prior to 2003. It was not until Philippine President Gloria Macapagal-Arroyo signed into law a bill that made permanent the national citizenship of Filipino citizens even after they acquired foreign citizenship. The Citizenship Retention and Reacquisition Act of 2003, popularly known as the Dual Citizenship Law, restored the rights of former Filipino citizens who lived or worked overseas. For Filipino Americans, this bill enables them to keep dual U.S. and Philippine citizenships without renouncing allegiance to the Philippines, as previously required. For Philippine citizens who may have lost their citizenship prior to 2003, the new law allows them to reacquire their citizenship by taking an oath to support and defend the Constitution of the Republic of the Philippines and to follow its laws.

Retention of Philippine citizenship does two things: (1) it restores the Filipino American's access to civil and political rights, and (2) it strengthens bonds of national belonging to the Philippines. Under the Dual Citizenship Law, Filipino citizens will be able to again own property in the Philippines, acquire a Philippine passport, practice their profession, and engage in business and commerce as a Filipino national. Individuals who are eligible to vote can now also exercise their right to suffrage by submitting an absentee ballot in accordance with the Overseas Absentee Voting Act of 2003. The Citizenship Retention and Reacquisition Act of 2003 has been seen as a step towards amending ties with overseas Filipinos who were alienated once they attainted foreign citizenship. This bill ensures that relationships between Filipinos and their country of origin are amended and restored.

Intergroup Relations

While Filipino Americans may be viewed as a homogeneous Asian immigrant group, the reality is quite the opposite. Post-1965 Filipino immigrants have come from all regions of the Philippines adding to the cultural, ethnic, linguistic, and religious diversity of the overall population. The proliferation of hometown associations and community organizations attest to the diversity of the Filipino American community in the United States and serves as one way to measure the state of relations amongst its members. Membership in Filipino American ethnic organizations illustrate immigrant loyalties to their hometowns and challenges American tendencies to "lump" all Filipinos together regardless of their hometown, regional affiliation, language or dialect spoken, and religion (Bonus 2000). Ethnic identities and shared experiences of migration, however, are not enough to determine intergroup relations because not everyone is a member of a community organization. Social organizations based on ethnic background have also been sites of tensions and divisions amongst its members due to competing ideas of identity and community.

These conflicts are often rooted in personal differences that include one's citizenship status, gender, educational attainment, class and occupation, political views, and even whether one is foreign or native born. Intergenerational conflicts mean that Filipino immigrants have unique perspectives shaped by their migration history and therefore experience the United States differently than those who are native born. Similarly, education and class differences can influence how Filipino Americans relate to one another; if simply on the basis of the work they do. In the post-1965 period, class differences between Filipino immigrants have become more dramatic between professionals and the working class (Espiritu 2003, 116).

Tensions and conflicts concerning class can even arise within Filipino American families (Posadas 1999, 150). While differences highlight the disparateness in the community, this is also evidence of a growing diversity in Filipino American identities. Thus, within post-1965 Filipino American communities in the United States, there exists competing ideas of "cohesion and fragmentation" that have determined intergroup relations (Posadas 1999, 149).

Forging a New American Political Identity

Legislative discrimination beginning with the Naturalization Act of 1790 made Asian immigrants ineligible for citizenship thus also ineligible to vote. Filipino access to naturalization was inconsistent prior to the 1960s and was subject to the changing political relationships between the United States and the Philippines. The inconsistencies on which Filipino immigrants could naturalize (and when) had a profound affect on their belief in the political system. Without being able to secure American citizenship, suffrage would have little meaning. But Filipino American political identity has not been defined simply by their ability or inability to vote but also by other (informal) forms of political participation. For many Filipinos political organizations, interest groups, and coalition politics provide alternative but necessary avenues to address important issues within their communities.

Political Associations and Organizations

Limited opportunities available to Filipino Americans required that they seek alternative forms of political participation. For many Filipinos in the early 20th century, participation in labor politics became the main vehicle for political membership. As anti-immigration campaigns increased and work conditions worsened, Filipino labor leaders like Pablo Manlapit and Philip Vera Cruz encouraged immigrant political involvement by fighting discriminatory labor policies targeting migrant laborers. Thus labor politics became an important arena in which political battles would be fought. Although Filipino American labor activists worked outside the main arena of American politics, they displayed high levels of participation in the political process. Historically, labor organizing has been the most successful in advancing Filipino Americans' economic and political interests.

Filipino community associations and fraternal groups also filled in the gaps as Filipino Americans turned to local communities as a space for political involvement. Without the ability to attain leadership positions in mainstream American political organizations, Filipino Americans secured them through more local means. Because leadership positions are closed off to most Filipino immigrants, hometown and local Filipino American organizations have become important public venues in which to achieve political influence. This has been especially true for post-1965 immigrants who find limited options in the political arena. Joining Filipino community associations and securing a leadership position as president, vice-president, secretary, or treasurer is a popular way to ensure one's position within the community. But because these leadership positions are limited, elections have been a source of tension within the groups themselves as members vie for a limited pool of political power (Okamura 1984). In reality, the extent of political power and influence afforded by these positions is restricted and often does not extend beyond the boundaries of the local group or community.

Civil and Electoral Politics

The proliferation of Filipino community organizations and active labor activism set the stage for contemporary Filipino American politics. Instead of using political organizations and electoral politics as a way to address issues, Filipino Americans used grassroots organizing strategies. This kind of homegrown grassroots politics grew out of and in conjunction with a pan-Asian political movement in the late 1960s, organized around issues of community needs (Espiritu 1993). Filipino American youth in college campuses joined with local Filipino American community activists as well as other Asian ethnic minority groups to address growing political, social, and economic issues (Espiritu 1993; Posadas 1999, 85). This pan-Asian ethnic coalition provided the foundation for a different kind of political empowerment. In this way, participation in electoral politics was a relatively new concept to Filipino Americans, who had found that voting did not guarantee effective results in their communities. Thus, despite higher rates of citizenship and naturalization amongst Filipino Americans, few exercise their right to vote.

A long history of political exclusion plays a significant role in this disinterest and distrust in American politics. Filipinos in the early 20th century despite their status as "American nationals" were prohibited from applying for naturalization in accordance with the 1790 Naturalization Act. Without access to citizenship, Filipino nationals found that they wielded little political power without the vote. Anti-immigrant campaigns and exclusion movements in the early 20th century further discouraged Filipino political participation marking them as outsiders to the process. This long history of political exclusion has shaped Filipino American attitudes about electoral politics as a means of affecting change in their communities. Today, low voting turnouts in local, state, and national elections are commonplace. As a result, Filipino American voters are not viewed as "politically aggressive" and therefore lack power as a voting bloc (Posadas 1999, 90).

But a history of exclusion is only one explanation to this quandary. Lower participation in American politics is also affected by other factors such as the population's age, noncitizen status, and the role of homeland politics in political identities. In 2000, 22.1 percent of Filipino Americans were under 18 years old, and 26.1 percent of the population over 18 years old were noncitizens (Reeves and Bennett 2004, 6, 9). Thus despite higher rates of naturalization compared to other Asian immigrant ethnic groups, a total of 48.2 percent of the overall Filipino American population was ineligible to vote.

Participation in homeland politics especially for the foreign born can detract from participation in American electoral politics. Whether by voting overseas through an absentee ballot or by following international news, Filipino Americans continue to follow contemporary political conditions in the Philippines. While not unique to Filipino Americans, participation in the home country politics is one way in which they have maintained closer ties to their country of origin. During the 1970s and 1980s, for example, Filipino Americans became involved in political activism against U.S. government support of the Marcos regime. Many Filipino Americans showed their support for their fellow countrymen by raising awareness of political conditions in the Philippines, holding rallies, and publicly protesting U.S. support of a corrupt Filipino government.

Public Policies and Political Representation

For Filipino Americans voting alone does not ensure political power. Instead Filipino Americans have pursued other means of political engagement by participating in local interest groups that are directed toward local community empowerment. There is a growing concern about issue-oriented causes in Filipino American communities such as affirmative action, voter registration, health care, education, citizenship, and immigration policies especially with the increase in anti-immigrant legislation in the 1990s (Bonus 2000, 52). Advocacy organizations and civil rights groups have been instrumental in promoting economic and political concerns. As a result, not only are Filipino Americans beginning to become more involved they are also becoming more visible within their local and regional communities. Advocating for what might seem like simply local issues has had the effect of forcing public officials to recognize the needs of their Filipino American constituents.

Some believe, however, that voting a Filipino American into office could lead to increased political power. The desire for a Filipino American representative is based on the hope that elected officials can more successfully advocate for community needs, which can result in increased social services and funding for community programs (Espiritu 1993). Although voting "one of their own" into a public office would be ideal, doing so presents a number of challenges. The candidate must not only secure Filipino American votes but also those of the general population by advocating for programs that cut across racial, gender, and class lines. Therefore, although some political candidates have been successful in securing a primary bid, they find it difficult to secure a victory in the general election that would put them in office. Not surprisingly, the number of Filipino American representatives in public office remains small and reflects a disproportion to the population. The election of Benjamin Cayetano in 1994 as Governor of Hawaii made him the first Filipino American governor in the country. A handful of Filipino Americans have been elected into government positions in states like California and Hawaii, where populations of Filipinos are higher, but instances like these are still uncommon (Bonus 2000, 59).

Return Immigration

As conditions in the Philippines continue to deteriorate into the 21st century, the chances of Filipino Americans' permanent return to the Philippines are becoming more and more unlikely. Unlike previous waves of migration who came under more temporary terms, the majority of post-1965 Filipino immigrants have settled permanently in the United States. Although they become permanent residents and citizens of the United States, many Filipino Americans continue to visit their homeland as *balikbayans*. This is typical for Filipino Americans with close connections to their families in the Philippines. For many, "going home" is necessary to maintain familial and ethnic ties after long absences. For others who do not have a similar connection visiting the Philippines can still be a unique experience, which serves to reconnect them or introduce them to their roots. Overall rates of permanent return migration are low for Filipino Americans when compared to other immigrant groups in the United States.

The Second and Later Generations

Ethnic Identity

Filipino American youth ethnic identity is derived primarily from the family unit, which serves as a primary introduction to their Filipino heritage. The intimacy of the family determines how much Filipino American youth will identify with their ethnic heritage. The family also plays a key role in one's introduction to the larger ethnic community because the presence of a strong ethnic community can affect how young Filipino Americans locate themselves within this space. While belonging in an ethnic community may be important for some, others are less inclined to do so especially when they live in cities where the general Filipino American population is relatively low. To supplement this void, Filipino American youth have turned to alternative forms of ethnic and community building. They supplement their ties to the ethnic community by forming relations with groups that fall outside the boundaries of their ethnic identity. This could mean developing relationships with non-Filipino friends or joining social and cultural organizations that are based on other interests. In expanding their social networks to include friendships and relationships that cross racial and class lines, Filipino American youth develop different aspects of their ethnic identity through various relationships with family, friends, and surrounding communities.

Educational Attainment

Although Filipino Americans as a whole show high levels of educational attainment, the achievement level for Filipino American youth is somewhat lower when compared to other Asian ethnic groups. Second-generation Filipino Americans experience higher rates of high school dropout rates and lower rates of college admission (Posadas 1999, 105). The 2000 Census showed that there is a gap in educational achievement between the foreign and native born. Foreign-born Filipino Americans in general maintain a higher level of educational attainment than the native born. According to the census, approximately 41.1 percent of foreign-born Filipino American men and 46.9 percent of foreign-born Filipino American women received college degrees compared to 30.7 percent of second-generation

Youth Profile

The Filipino Founder of the Black Eyed Peas

Allan Pineda Lindo, popularly known as apl.de.ap, is a founding member of the international hip-hop group Black Eyed Peas. Born in Angeles City, Pampanga, Philippines, Lindo is the son of a Filipina mother and an African American father. He came to the United States when he was 14 years old with the help of the Pearl S. Buck Foundation, an organization that advocates for Amerasian children. An adoption allowed Lindo to migrate to the United States, where he lived with his adoptive father Joe Ben Hudgens in Los Angeles, California. While the adoption separated him from his immediate family in the Philippines, Lindo continues to maintain close ties with them.

In his work, Lindo incorporates his Filipino heritage into the music he produces as a way of introducing Filipino history and culture into the American mainstream. In 2003, he released "The Apl Song" in the Black Eyed Peas album *Elephunk*; and the 2005 Black Eyed Peas album *Monkey Business* included an all-Tagalog song "Bebot." Lindo also added a dance song called "Mare" to their latest release. With a focus on Filipino and Filipino American cultures, these songs are tributes to the myriad experiences of Filipinos in the United States. In addition to working with the Black Eyed Peas, Lindo has launched his own music label, Jeepney Music, based out of Silver Lake, California. Under this label, Lindo has released songs such as "Mama Filipina," "U Can Dream," "Islands," and "Take Me to the Philippines," in which his Filipino heritage is featured prominently. More importantly, these songs touch on themes of belonging, identity, and homecoming. Lindo is also the founder of the Apl Foundation, a nonprofit organization that is committed to helping children and their communities in the Philippines. The foundation's mission is to provide educational, financial, and material support to on-site charities that do work within local communities.

Filipino American men and on 32.3 percent of Filipino American women (Bankston 2006; U.S. Census 2000b). Post-1965 immigration accounts for the disparity in the educational attainments between the two generations and shows a trend that is unique to the Filipino American population when compared to other Asian American groups.

Cultural Identification

For many Filipino American youth, culture is an important marker of one's identity that offers a way to locate one's place within the Filipino American community and restores ethnic ties to the Philippines. Participation in cultural shows, which are highly popular in American high schools and colleges, is one way to reaffirm cultural ties with the Filipino American community. It allows Filipino American youth to participate in cultural production by reinventing and re-imagining their place within a larger diaspora made up of Filipinos all over the world. Sometimes traditional Filipino dance and music are performed simultaneously with more popular contemporary American hip-hop or pop music. Reinterpretations of Filipino culture allow them to actively engage in a way that reflects their experiences as Filipino Americans. The combination of different cultures embraces both their Filipino and American identities.

Filipino cultural identity can also be measured by one's knowledge of Philippine history and a Filipino language or dialect. The ability to express this knowledge, however, can simultaneously act as a marker of belonging or exclusion from the ethnic community. Knowledge of a Filipino language, for example, can immediately mark one as a community member while one's inability to speak a language can act as a barrier to belonging. The question surrounding "authenticity" is often at the center of these concerns. Does one's ability to speak a Filipino language really mean that they are more Filipino than someone who cannot? Sometimes generational conflicts between first- and second-generation Filipino American youth can arise out of these cultural differences. To address these issues some Filipino American community centers hold classes on Philippine and Filipino American history for the younger generation. Some of these community centers also have language programs where Filipino is taught to students who are interested. The hope is that these classes can help reconnect Filipino American youth to their culture, their history, and their communities.

Issues in Relations between the United States and the Philippines

Forecasts for the 21st Century

Deep economic, military, political, and cultural ties with the United States ensure that ties between both countries will continue well into the 21st century. As economic and political conditions in the Philippines continue to deteriorate, the United States will remain an attractive option for the next generation of Filipino immigrants. Assuming that similar factors in Filipino immigration persist, Filipino migration will predictably continue to rise in the following decades. With the persistent immigration of Filipinos into the United States, demographers project that Filipino Americans will likely become the largest Asian American ethnic group in the United States. Growing anti-immigrant sentiment and the desire for stricter immigration policies, however, means that newly arrived Filipino immigrants and

Filipino Americans can expect to experience some resistance and backlash against contemporary Filipino migration.

Appendix I: Migration Statistics

Table 105 Filipinos in the United States, 1910–2000

Year	Population in United States
1910	160
1920	5,603
1930	45,208
1940	45,563
1950	61,636[a]
1960	176,310
1970	343,060
1980	774,652
1990	1,406,770
2000	2,364,815

Source: Gibson, C., and K. Jung. 2002. *Historical Census Statistics on Population Totals By Race, 1790 to 1990, and By Hispanic Origin, 1970-1990, For The United States, Regions, Divisions, and States.* Washington, D.C.: U.S. Census Bureau.

[a]This number is an estimate. In 1950 the census data on Filipinos was not published in the general census volumes although the census did include a subject report on the geographic regions with the highest Filipino population in the United States.

Table 106 Persons obtaining legal permanent resident status by region and country of birth: Fiscal years 2000 to 2009

Region and country of birth	2000	2001	2002	2003	2004	2005	2006	2007	2008	2009
Total	841,002	1,058,902	1,059,356	703,542	957,883	1,122,257	1,266,129	1,052,415	1,107,126	1,130,818
Philippines	42,343	52,919	51,040	45,250	57,846	60,746	74,606	72,596	54,030	60,029

Source: U.S. Department of Homeland Security. Office of Immigration Statistics. 2010. Adapted from Table 3.

Table 107 Persons obtaining legal permanent resident status during fiscal year 2009. Leading states of residence region/country: Philippines

Characteristic	Total	Male	Female
Total	60,029	22,307	37,722
Arizona	877	282	595
California	24,937	9,981	14,956
Connecticut	370	138	232
Florida	2,193	735	1,458
Georgia	568	173	395
Hawaii	4,013	1,661	2,352
Illinois	2,553	994	1,559
Maryland	1,157	442	715
Massachusetts	362	125	237
Michigan	586	177	409
Minnesota	383	109	274
Nevada	2,080	743	1,337
New Jersey	2,509	1,009	1,500
New York	2,572	971	1,601
North Carolina	506	139	367
Ohio	614	197	417
Pennsylvania	544	147	397
Texas	2,797	971	1,826
Virginia	1,503	532	971
Washington	2,169	771	1,398
Other	10,749	3,671	7,078

Source: Adapted from U.S. Department of Homeland Security. Profiles on Legal Permanent Residents: 2009. State of Residence, Stbk 15. 2010.

Appendix II: Demographics/Census Statistics

The U.S. census provides the most accurate and detailed information on Filipinos in the United States. It defines the category of "Filipino" to include individuals "who indicate their race as 'Filipino' or who report entries such as Philipino, Philipine, or Filipino American" (U.S. Census 2000a, B-39). The census began to enumerate Filipinos beginning in 1910. It was in this decennial census that Asian and Pacific Islander categories such as Filipino, Hindu, and Korean were added to Chinese and Japanese.

The census data collected on race in 1990 differs from the 2000 Census. The "Filipino" population had been identified under the race category of "Asian or

Pacific Islander" until 2000, when the U.S. Census Bureau separated it into "Asian" and "Native Hawaiian or Other Pacific Islander" (Reeves and Bennett 2004, 2). Due to these changes, census data on race in the 2000 Census cannot directly compare with that from 1999. It was also in this decennial survey that respondents were able to report more than one race for the first time. Filipinos who identified with more than one race category were referred to as the "race in combination population." As a result, the population number between 1990 and 2000 increased dramatically within the decade to reflect single-race Filipinos and the "race in combination" population, which includes Filipinos who identify with another Asian ethnic population or another race.

Table 108 Primary census data in 2000

Subject	Number
Total population	2,364,815
Male	1,085,441
Female	1,279,374
Race	
One Asian category only: Filipino	1,850,314
One or more Asian categories only: Filipino	57,811
One or more Asian categories only: Filipino and another race	514, 501
Age	
Median age (years)	31
Under 5 years	191,793
18 years and over	1,681,674
65 years and over	180,176
Household	
Household population	2,325,284
Average household size	3
Average family size	4
Median household income	$58,323
Median family income	$63,057

Source: U.S. Census Bureau, Summary File 2 (SF2) and Summary File 4 (SF4).

Table 109 Occupation distribution of Filipino Americans in 2000 (employed civilian population 16 years and over)

Occupation	Male	Female	Total
Management, professional, and related occupations	167,125	248,405	415,530
Service	85,215	113,260	198,476
Sales and office	118,054	206,192	324,246
Farming, fishing, and forestry	3,303	2,269	5,572
Construction, extraction, and maintenance	48,235	2,912	51,147
Production, transportation, and material moving	82,053	46,194	128,247
Employed civilian population 16 yrs and over			1,1,23217

Source: U.S. Census Bureau, Summary File 4 (SF4).

Appendix III: Notable Filipino Americans

Carlos Bulosan (1913–1956) is a renowned writer and poet who documented Filipino American experiences through his writings. Born in a small town in the Pangasinan province of Luzon, Bulosan migrated to the United States in 1930. Best known for his semiautobiographical work *America Is in the Heart,* Bulosan sought to expose the struggles and hardships experienced by Filipino immigrants in the early 20th century. His other works include *The Laughter of My Father* as well as his posthumously published *The Cry and the Dedication.*

Benjamin Cayetano (1939–), governor of Hawaii, was the first governor in the country to be of Filipino ancestry. He is a graduate of the University of California, Los Angeles, where he received a bachelor's degree in political science, and the Loyola Law School in Los Angeles, where he earned his juris doctorate. Prior to his election as governor, he served 12 years in the Hawaii state legislature.

John Robert "J.R." Celski (1990–) is a two-time medalist short track speed skater. He is the Polish Filipino American son of Robert and Sue Celski. He achieved international acclaim as a short track speed skater at the 2010 Winter Olympics in Vancouver, where he won a pair of bronze medals in the 1,500 meter and the 5,000 meter relay. Prior to his Olympic victories Celski held world championship titles in various short track speed skating events.

Cristeta Comerford (1962–) has been the executive chef at the White House since 2005. She is the first woman to occupy this position and also the first to be of Filipino descent. After an extensive career as a chef in restaurants in

Chicago and Washington, D.C., Comerford joined the White House staff during the Clinton administration in 1995.

Victoria Manalo Draves (1924–2010) made history by winning two gold medals in the 1948 Olympics in London held after World War II. She became the first woman to win two gold medals in diving. To honor her achievements, in 1969, she was elected into the International Swimming Hall of Fame in Fort Lauderdale, Florida. Draves died at the age of 85 in April 2010.

Roman Ildonzo Gabriel, Jr. (1949–) was the first Filipino American to start as a National Football League (NFL) quarterback. An alumna of North Carolina State University, Gabriel was an Academic All-American who was inducted into the College Football Hall of Fame in 1989. He began his professional career with the Los Angeles Rams in 1962. During his career with the Rams, he led the team to two division championships and was voted the NFL's Most Valuable Player in 1969. After his retirement, Gabriel pursued a short acting career in Hollywood, and then he went on to become a sports analyst for CBS.

Jessica Hagedorn (1949–) is a celebrated Filipino American poet, writer, and playwright. Her first novel, *Dogeaters,* won the American Book Award from the Before Columbus Foundation and was nominated for the 1990 National Book Award. Prior to the success of *Dogeaters,* Hagedorn began her career as a poet in San Francisco, where she published her first books of poetry. In 1993, she edited *Charlie Chan Is Dead: An Anthology of Contemporary Asian American Fiction.* Her second novel, *The Gangster of Love,* was published in 1996.

Allan Pineda Lindo (1974–), popularly known as apl.de.ap, is a member of the international hip-hop group the Black Eyed Peas. Lindo continues to celebrate his Filipino heritage through his music. Black Eyed Peas' albums *Elephunk* in 2003 and *Monkey Business* in 2005 both released two all-Tagalog songs entitled the "Apl Song" and "Bebot."

Michelle Malkin (1970–) is a columnist, political commentator, and blogger. Born in Philadelphia, Michelle Malkin is the daughter of Filipino citizens who came to the United States in 1970. Her career as a journalist began when she was a student at Oberlin College, and after graduation, she pursued a career in newspaper journalism with the *Los Angeles Daily News*. She is best known for her non-apologetic conservative political views. Malkin maintains a blog and a weekly syndicated column online and in newspapers across the country.

Philip Vera Cruz (1904–1994), a long-time farm worker and labor leader, is best known for his activism and crusade to improve the lives of migrant workers. He helped to found the United Farm Workers Union, where he served as its second vice-president. However, he resigned in 1977 to protest the leadership of Cesar Chavez. He spent much of his life and career working to unite Filipino and Mexican labor unions and achieved much success through a series of labor strikes he helped to organize. In 1988, President Corazon Aquino bestowed upon him an award for his service to Filipinos in the United States. Vera Cruz died at the age of 89 in 1994.

Glossary

Adobo: A popular dish of meat marinated in a sauce of vinegar, soy sauce, garlic, and pepper.

Balikbayan: An overseas Filipino returning to the Philippines; also refers to a "homecoming."

Hiya: Shame or embarrassment.

Kababayan: Fellow Filipino or someone who hails from a similar home city or town.

Katipunero: Members of Andres Bonifacio's revolutionary group Kataastaasang Kagalanggalangang Katipuanan ng mga Anak ng Bayan (KKK) established against Spanish rule in 1892.

Lechon: A whole roasted pig.

Leche flan: A rich egg custard with a soft caramelized topping of Spanish origin.

Lumpia: A type of egg roll filled with meats and vegetables; can be served fried or fresh.

Merienda: Mid-afternoon snack often eaten between lunch and dinner.

Pakikisama: Cooperation; to get along with others.

Pancit: Noodle dish with Chinese origin cooked with a variety of meats and vegetables.

Pasalubong: Gifts to family and friends.

Pensionado: U.S. government–sponsored students who came to the United States in the early 20th century to study in American colleges and universities.

Pinoy: Slang term referring to Filipino men.

Pinay: Slang term referring to Filipina women.

Rondalla: A form of traditional Filipino music played by a string ensemble.

Sakada: Filipino agricultural workers recruited to Hawaii by plantation owners in the early 20th century.

Sawsawan: Any kind of condiment or dip used to enhance the flavor of Filipino dishes.

Singkil: Traditional dance from the southern region of Mindanao that depicts the dance of Muslim royalty.

Tinikling: National dance of the Philippines; an indigenous dance involving two people tapping a set of bamboo poles on the ground while dancers step over and dance in between the poles.

Utang na loob: Debt of gratitude.

References

Asian Pacific Islander Health Forum. "Filipinos in the United States." [Online article retrieved 12/24/10.] http://www.apiahf.org/images/stories/Documents/publications_database/Filipinos_in_the_United_States.pdf.

Bankston III, C. L. 2006. "Filipino Americans." In *Asian Americans: Contemporary Trends and Issues Second Edition,* edited by P. G. Min. Thousand Oaks, CA: Sage Publications: 178–206.

Barnes, P. M., P. F. Adams, and E. Powell-Griner. 2008. "Health Characteristics of the Asian Adult Population: United States, 2004–2006." [Online article; retrieved 3/23/10.] www.cdc.gov/nchs/data/ad/ad394.pdf.

Bautista, V. B. 1998. *The Filipino Americans: From 1763 to the Present Their History, Culture and Traditions.* Farmington Hills, MI: Bookhaus Pub.

Bogardus, E. 1934. "The Filipino Press in the United States." *Sociology and Social Research* 18 (6): 581–85.

Bonus, R. 2000. *Locating Filipino Americans: Ethnicity and the Cultural Politics of Space.* Philadelphia: Temple University Press.

Brown, E. R., V. D. Ojeda, R. Wyn, and R. Levan. 2000. *Racial and ethnic disparities in access to health insurance and health care.* [Online article; retrieved 8/11/10.] http://www.healthpolicy.ucla.edu/pubs/files/RacialandEthnicDisparitiesReport.pdf

Burma, J. H. 1951. "The Background of the Current Situation of Filipino-Americans." *Social Forces* 30 (1): 42–48.

Choy, C. 2003. *Empire of Care: Nursing and Migration in Filipino American History.* Durham: Duke University Press.

Cordova, F. 1983. *Filipinos, forgotten Asian Americans: A Pictorial Essay, 1763-circa 1963.* Dubuque: Kendall/Hunt Pub.

Daniels, R. 2008. "The Immigration Act of 1965: Intended and Unintended Consequences of the 20th Century." [Online article; retrieved 12/24/09.] http://www.america.gov/st/educ-english/2008/April/20080423214226eaifas0.9637982.html

Espina, M. 1988. *Filipinos in Louisiana.* New Orleans: A. F. Laborde.

Espiritu, Y. L. 1993. *Asian American Panethnicity: Bridging Institutions and Identities.* Philadelphia: Temple University Press.

Espiritu, Y.L. 2003. *Homeward Bound: Filipino American Lives Across Cultures, Communities, and Countries.* Berkeley: University of California Press.

Gibson, C., and K. Jung. 2002. *Historical Census Statistics on Population Totals By Race, 1790 to 1990, and By Hispanic Origin, 1970–1990, For The United States, Regions, Divisions, and States.* Washington, D.C.: U.S. Census Bureau.

Guyotte, R., and B. Posadas. 1995. "Celebrating Rizal Day: The Emergence of a Filipino Tradition in Twentieth Century Chicago." In *Feasts and Celebrations in North American Ethnic Communities,* edited by R. Gutierrez and G. Fabre, 111-27. Albuquerque: University of New Mexico Press.

Hearns, L. 1883. "Saint Malo: A Lacustrine Village in Louisiana." *Harper's Weekly*, March 31, 196–99.

Liu, J. M, P.M. Ong, and C. Rosenstein. 1991. "Dual Chain Migration: Post-1965 Filipino Immigration to the United States." *International Migration Review* 25 (3): 143–69.

Melendy, B. 1967. "California's Discrimination Against Filipinos, 1927–1935." In *The Filipino Exclusion Movement, 1927–1935*, edited J.M. Saniel, 141–51. Quezon City: University of the Philippines Press.

National Healthy Marriage Resource Center. 2009. "Marriage and Intermarriage Among Asian Americans: A Fact Sheet." [Online information; retrieved 8/11/10.] http://www.acf.hhs.gov/healthymarriage/pdf/marriageamongasianamericans.pdf.

Ngai, M. 2002. "From Colonial Subject to Undesirable Alien: Filipino, Migration, Exclusion, and Repatriation, 1920–1940." In *Re/collecting Early Asian America: Essays in Cultural History*, edited by J. Lee, I. Lim, and Y. Matsukawa, 111–26. Philadelphia: Temple University Press.

Okamura, J. 1984. "Filipino Voluntary Associations and the Filipino Community in Hawaii." *Ethnic Groups* 5(4): 279–305.

Posadas, B. 1999. *The Filipino Americans*. Westport, CT: Greenwood Press.

Reeves, T.J., and C. Bennett. 2004. *We the People: Asians in the United States*. U.S. Census Bureau.

Rodell, P. 2002. *Culture and Customs of the Philippines*. Westport, CT: Greenwood Press.

Takaki, R. 1989. *Strangers from a Different Shore: A History of Asian Americans*. Boston: Little Brown.

U.S. Census. 2000a. "Census 2000 Summary File 1 (SF 1)—2000 Census of Population and Housing." [Online information retrieved 2/7/10.] http://www.census.gov/prod/cen2000/doc/sf1.pdf.

U.S. Census. 2000b. "Census 2000 Summary File 4 (SF 4)—Sample Data." [Online information retrieved 3/23/10.] www.census.gov/prod/cen2000/doc/sf4.pdf.

U.S. Census. 2000c. "Census 2000 Demographic Profile Highlights: Selected Population Group: Filipino Alone or In Any Combination." [Online information retrieved 11/27/09.] http://factfinder.census.gov/servlet/SAFFIteratedFacts?_event=&geo_id=01000US&_geoContext=01000US&_street=&_county=&_cityTown=&_state=&_zip=

&_lang=en&_sse=on&ActiveGeoDiv=&_useEV=&pctxt=fph&pgsl=010&_submenu
Id=factsheet_2&ds_name=DEC_2000_SAFF&_ci_nbr=019&qr_name=DEC_2000_
SAFF_R1010&reg=DEC_2000_SAFF_R1010%3A019&_keyword=&_industry=.

U.S. Citizenship and Immigration Services. "Immigration Reform and Control Act of 1986
(IRCA)." [Online information retrieved 11/28/09.] http://www.uscis.gov/portal/site/
uscis/menuitem.5af9bb95919f35e66f614176543f6d1a/?vgnextchannel=b328194d3e88
d010VgnVCM10000048f3d6a1RCRD&vgnextoid=04a295c4f635f010VgnVCM100000
0ecd190aRCRD.

Further Reading

Bonus, R. 2000. *Locating Filipino Americans: Ethnicity and the Cultural Politics of Space.*
Philadelphia: Temple University Press.

In this ethnographic study of Filipino American communities in Los Angeles and San
Diego, Rick Bonus focuses on commercial establishments and the media as public sites
of ethnic immigrant identity formation. Through interviews, he examines the spatial
and social meanings of places like "Oriental stores," community centers, and newspapers that cater specifically to the Filipino and Filipino American population in Southern California. Place making, he argues, is an important part of Filipino American
experiences.

Bulosan, C. 1974. *America Is in the Heart: A Personal History.* Seattle: University of
Washington Press.

Famed novelist and poet Carlos Bulosan is best known for this semiautobiographical
book. *America is in the Heart* offers an unparalleled Filipino immigrant perspective on
early 20th-century America.

Choy, C. 2003. *Empire of Care: Nursing and Migration in Filipino American History.* Durham, NC: Duke University Press.

Notions of empire, labor, gender, and migration all come together in this transnational
analysis of Filipina nurse migration. *Empire of Care* is a unique look at the labor migration of Filipina nurses to the United States that offers a compelling historical account of
the processes behind the recruitment of Filipina women into American hospitals.

Cordova, F. 1983. *Filipinos, Forgotten Asian Americans: A Pictorial Essay, 1763-circa
1963.* Dubuque: Kendall/Hunt Pub.

A pictorial essay dedicated to documenting the settlement of the Filipino "old timers"
generation, this book is a great introduction to Filipino American culture and history.

Fujita-Rony, D. 2003. *American Workers, Colonial Power: Philippine Seattle and the
Transpacific West, 1919–1941.* Berkeley: University of California Press.

American Workers, Colonial Power is a transnational look at the dual legacies of U.S.
colonialism in the Philippines and the United States. This project examines how U.S.
colonialism transformed the Filipino American community in Seattle and how in turn,
this immigrant population influenced the colonial metropolis of Seattle.

Gonzalez, J.L. 2009. *Filipino American Faith in Action: Immigration, Religion and Civic Engagement.* New York: New York University Press.

The discussion of religion as a part of Filipino American experiences is an understudied one. In this work, Gonzalez examines the Filipino American spiritual experience as a lens in which to consider the social, political, and cultural integration of Filipino immigrants into American society. Its focus on Filipino American religious experiences offers a unique insight to their experiences of migration, adaptation, and settlement in the United States.

Kramer, P.A. 2006. *The Blood of Government: Race, Empire, the United States, and the Philippines.* Chapel Hill: University of North Carolina Press.

In this comprehensive study on race and government in the Philippines during the American colonial period, Paul Kramer presents a unique look at the complexities behind U.S.–Philippine relations.

Melendy, H.B. 1977. *Asians in America: Filipinos, Koreans, and East Asians.* Boston: Twayne Publishers.

This book, which deals primarily with early 20th-century history, examines the experiences of Filipino, Korean, and East Asian immigrants to the United States. It is filled with informative chapters on Filipino immigration history, adaptation, and discrimination against Filipinos. These chapters deal specifically with the pre-1965 Filipino immigration.

The Philippine History Site. [Online information; retrieved 3/23/10.] http://opmanong.ssc.hawaii.edu/filipino/index.html.

This site is dedicated to documenting Filipino and Filipino American history. Its content focuses specifically on the Philippine Revolution, the Philippine-American War, and Filipino migration to the United States.

Posadas, B. 1999. *The Filipino Americans (The New Americans).* Westport, CT: Greenwood Press.

This book offers a detailed introduction into the history of Filipinos in the United States and serves as an important reference on Filipino American history.

Shaw, A.V., and L.H. Francia. 2002. *Vestiges of War: The Philippine—American War and the Aftermath of an Imperial Dream, 1899–1999.* New York: New York University Press.

This collection of essays, visual art, poetry, and literature explores U.S. intervention in the Philippines. *Vestiges of War* departs from traditional texts on the topic but brings a uniquely different perspective on U.S. colonization that addresses the complexities of this oft forgotten event.

Smithsonian Filipino American Heritage Website. [Online information; retrieved 2/7/10.] http://filam.si.edu/.

This site commemorates the centennial of Filipino migration to the United States. It includes a curriculum project that is designed to teach teachers and students about Filipino American history and culture.

Ghanaian Immigrants

by Baffour K. Takyi

Introduction

Even though the majority of Ghanaians move within the West African region, over the past two decades the number of Ghanaians who have moved beyond this region and have settled in countries such as the United States has also increased dramatically. Prior to the 1980s, the few Ghanaians in America were mostly foreign students or diplomats and government officials who were here for a specified time period. This pattern has changed in recent years as the Ghanaian community has increased significantly to encompass other social groupings besides those previously mentioned, and many of the newly immigrated Ghanaian Americans are less likely to consider themselves as "sojourners" and more likely to consider the United States as home. Recent Department of Homeland Security statistics show that the number of Ghanaians who have become permanent residents in America have nearly doubled between 2000 and 2009 (U.S. Department of Homeland Security 2010). This chapter provides some insights about these newly immigrated Ghanaians, thereby contributing to the emerging discourse on America's recent immigrant communities.

In highlighting the Ghanaian immigrant experience in America, I take into cognizance the fact that the African immigrant community is not monolithic. They differ for example, on the way they arrived in America, their reasons for coming, their settlement patterns, and their mode of acceptance and incorporation into American society (see, e.g., Takyi 2000; Takyi and Boate 2006). My other reason for focusing on the Ghanaian diaspora is that the recent influx of immigrants from Africa to America is dominated by a select number of countries—primarily from Anglophone Africa. Ghana is one of these countries that have emerged as a major sender of African immigrants to the United States. As of 2000, Ghanaians were the sixth-largest group of recent immigrants from the continent of Africa in America. By 2007, it ranked fifth in terms of admissions. If the emphasis shifts to the black population only, then Ghana is ranked third in terms of the composition of African-born immigrants in the United States (Kent 2007, 8).

As the Ghanaian community in the United States grows, scholars need to examine their pre- and post-immigration experiences. The aim of this chapter is to fill this knowledge gap and contribute to the literature on the major immigrant groups

GHANA

from Africa to America. To provide a backdrop for looking at the Ghanaian experience in America, I provide the reader with some geographical and historical information about the country Ghana. Next, I explore the reasons why Ghanaians have come to America, the size of the community, as well as their adjustment process into American society.

Chronology

1820	Gold Coast—the colony comes under British Protectorate.
1900	Most areas of what is now Ghana become a British Protectorate.
1940s	Ghanaians who wish to pursue higher education go to England to further their education.
	Some Ghanaians, including Nkrumah, the future president of Ghana, come to school in the United States.
	Agitation for independence begins in earnest.
1957	End of British colonial rule in Ghana. Nkrumah assumes power.
	Ghanaian immigration to the United States is a trickle despite USAID scholarships to Ghanaians to study in America.
1966	The military overthrows Dr. Nkrumah's government.
1970s	Ghana's economy begins its slide and decline.
	Promulgation of the Alliance Compliance Order in Ghana.
	Exodus of large numbers of non-Ghanaians in the country.
	Formation of the Economic Community of West African States (ECOWAS).
1980s	Economic decline and the political instability lead to the beginning of mass population movements of the people.
	Nigeria and Côte d'Ivoire become favorite destinations for Ghanaian migrants.
	Movement to these countries facilitated by the passage of the ECOWAS treaty; one of the treaty's principles is the freedom of movement for citizens of member countries.
1983	Nigeria deports its nonresident immigrants. Ghanaians are among the most affected West Africans who were deported. Prior to the 1980s, student migration to United States

dominated. But Nigeria's deportation of nonresidents begins the onset of massive waves of Ghanaian emigration to other parts of the world, including the United States—especially for those who could afford it.

1986   The Immigration and Reform Control Act of 1986 (IRCA) regularizes the status of undocumented immigrants in the United States.

Several Ghanaians whose immigration status have changed since coming to the United States benefit from the amnesty and adjusts their status. These beneficiaries of IRCA begin to reunite with their families.

1990   Diversity lottery promulgated. Ghana becomes a major recipient of visas under the program.

The number of Ghanaians in America increase significantly—due mainly to the diversity lottery.

1992   Ghana returns to Multi-Party Democracy (Fourth Republic). Passage of Dual Citizenship Act.

2000   The 2000 Census identifies over 60,000 Ghanaians in America.

2000s   Dual Citizenship Regulation Act passed in Ghana.

Passage of Representation of the Peoples Amendment (ROOPA) bill in Ghana's parliament.

Background

Geography of Ghana

The Republic of Ghana is located along the west coast of Africa. Geographically speaking, it covers an area of approximately 92,098 square miles and shares borders with Côte d'Ivoire in the west, Burkina Faso in the north, Togo in the east, and the Gulf of Guinea (Atlantic Ocean) in the south. For administrative purposes, the country is divided into 10 regions, and Accra is the main city and its capital. Besides Accra, the major cities in Ghana include the following: Kumasi, Tema, Tamale, Sekondi-Takoradi, Koforidua, and Sunyani. As in many Third World nations, Ghana is a raw material producer. Cocoa, timber products, gold, diamonds, bauxite, and manganese are among its main exports. Indeed, it is the world's second-biggest cocoa producer and Africa's second-biggest gold exporter. Recently, tourism has become one of its major foreign exchange earners as well, and the country is set to become the continent's newest oil producer very soon.

Ghana has an estimated population of 24 million people as of 2009, of which nearly 40 percent live in urban areas, making the country one of the most urbanized in Africa. Like most African nations, its population has been growing rapidly during the past four decades. At current rate of growth, it is projected that the number of Ghanaians will increase at a rapid pace, as with those who live in urban areas (the result of natural increase and rural-urban migration). In the 1960s Ghana's population was 6.6 million people. The rapid population growth since the 1960s, which has averaged between 3 to 4 percent, is attributed to high birthrates and low contraceptive use patterns. More recently, fertility levels (measured by the total fertility rate [TFR], the average number of births to a woman if she were to live through her reproductive years [ages 15–49]) have begun to decline: from a reported high of 6.47 in 1980 to 4.55 by the late 1990s. Indeed according to preliminary data from the latest Ghana Demographic and Health Survey, which was conducted between June and July of 2008, TFR has declined further to about 4 births per woman.

History of Ghana

Formerly called the Gold Coast, Ghana is a young republic and in 1957, it became the first black African nation to attain its political independence, after over 100 years of British colonial rule. It has to be pointed out that Ghana itself is a colonial creation, pieced together from numerous indigenous societies and ethnic groups that were living in various parts of modern-day Ghana prior to European colonial rule. While little written documentation exists of the region's past before the advent of the Portuguese, the first Europeans to arrive on the shores of modern Ghana in the 15th century (due primarily of its riches in gold and other raw materials, later to include slaves) met some powerful inland kingdoms that had developed especially among the various Akan-speaking groups and neighboring groups. These developments invariably led to clashes between these indigenous powers and the various European powers (such as the Dutch, the Danes, and the British) between the 15th and 20th centuries. By the mid-19th century, the British had consolidated their position and had become the main power that ruled the region that later, after its independence, became known as Ghana.

At the time of its independence in 1957, Ghana was one of the richest nations on the African continent: the world's leading cocoa exporter and a major producer of a significant amount of the world's gold and diamonds. Unfortunately, as the case is in many African countries, the postcolonial challenges that came with Ghanaian political independence were quite daunting and have led to failed promises and hopes for the people. Indeed, the political history of Ghana typifies the political turmoil and instability that has characterized several African countries since the 1960s. At different times since its political independence from Britain, it has been ruled by military governments: four military coups and the collapse of three republics.

Indeed, its first coup occurred in 1966 when its first president and pan-Africanist hero, Dr. Kwame Nkrumah, was deposed. The end of his rule was followed by years of mostly military rule. In 1981 Flight Lieutenant Jerry Rawlings staged his second coup that deposed the then-civilian administration of Dr. Limann.

Since 1992, when the military government at the time (led by Flight Lieutenant Jerry Rawlings) agreed to a multi-party system of rule, it has successfully conducted five general elections that have been deemed fair and transparent by international and local observers. More importantly, the country has evolved an orderly political succession and a vibrant democratic culture; has been able to transfer power between two different parties during this period; and has been devoid in large part of the widespread fraud that was common in many African countries. Party elections have now become so routine and common in Ghana that it has become a beacon of hope for democratic activists in sub-Saharan Africa.

One interesting aspect about Ghana's postcolonial social and economic history that provides a context for scholars studying its migratory history is that the economic stagnation and political instability that characterized much of its early postcolonial period, and perhaps till today, have played a large role in decisions about whether its citizenry stay home or travel outside for the proverbial "greener

Dr. Kwame Nkrumah, standing on stool, being sworn in by Arku Korsah as the first president of the Republic of Ghana, in Accra, 1960. (Library of Congress)

pastures." While it is true that Ghana was among the first African nations to experience political upheavals and later economic decay and stagnation, it was also one of those countries in the 1980s and 1990s that implemented an Economic Recovery Program (ERP) comprising of Structural Adjustment Programs (SAP) (with the support of the World Bank, the International Monetary Bank [IMF], the African Development Bank, and the United Nations Development Program) to reverse its economic misfortunes. These programs led to improvements in its macro indicators, but they led to massive layoffs of public sector employees as well. This is significant given that the public sector continues to be the major employer of Ghanaians—especially of the educated class—till today. Moreover, while the country was reporting some success at the macro levels, these changes did not translate into improved living conditions for the average Ghanaian. For the reasons cited above—retrenchments, limited job opportunities for its teeming youth and college graduates, political instability, and the absence of significant improvements in their well-being—many Ghanaians had no choice than to leave the country in search of greener pastures elsewhere.

Causes and Waves of Migration

Immigration scholars have observed that the face of the United States is changing rapidly (see, e.g., Pedraza 2000). These changes in large part reflect the growing number of immigrants who have moved to the country during the past 40 years or so. Equally important is that the majority of these recent immigrants come primarily from non-European or Third World countries (Bouvier and Gardner 1986).

As is happening among the general population, America's black population and identity is also changing somewhat as a result of these recent waves of Third World immigration (see, e.g., Bryce-LaPorte 1977, 1993). This is especially the case with respect to immigration from Africa and other world regions—especially the Caribbean and Latin America—with a significant proportion of people of African ancestry. Based on recent developments and trends, some studies have indicated that about 7 percent of America's total black population now consists of foreign-born blacks—up from 5 percent in 1990 (Logan, 2007; Dean and Logan 2003; Waters 1999). Admittedly, although the majority of these new foreign-born blacks are Afro-Caribbean, significant numbers have come from the continent of Africa itself. Among these recent African immigrants are Ghanaians.

Historically speaking and until quite recently, Ghana was considered an immigrant receiving nation (Zachariah and Conde 1981). As a result of this history, it should come as no surprise that over 800,000 foreign-born nationals (representing 12% of its total population) were counted in its first postcolonial census, which was conducted in 1960. Some of these immigrants, however, left Ghana when it promulgated an Aliens Compliance Oder in the early 1970s during the administration of Dr. Busia's Progress Party. As Ghana's economic fortunes began to wane in the 1970s, some of its foreign-born population who had stayed after the promulgation of the Aliens Compliance Order also left the country. As a result of recent political and civil upheavals and wars in the West African region (especially during the 1980s and 1990s), several refugee groups from the region have found their way back to Ghana. This is especially true with Liberians. As a result, Ghana now hosts one of the largest refugee populations in the West African region (International Organization of Migration [IOM] 2009).

Thus, for most of its history, until quite recently, Ghana received (rather than sent) people to other parts of the world. Due in part to the fact that it was a former British colony and its institutions were similar to what existed in Great Britain, the latter was the traditional destination of choice for most Ghanaians who traveled outside the country. The Ghanaians who left for a variety of reasons, but mainly for higher education. Because of limited and underdeveloped communication between Africa and America, during the colonial and early postcolonial period, those Ghanaians who had the chance to pursue higher education invariably went to England than the United States. A few people, including Kwame Nkrumah, found their way to America to attend universities, but in this first wave of immigration, the number of Ghanaians coming to America was quite small. Anarfi and Kwankye (2003) point to four different phases of emigration: minimal emigration, initial emigration, large-scale emigration, and massive emigrations. After independence, a few Ghanaians were sponsored by the government or were offered scholarships through the USAID and the Ford Foundation to attend American universities. These earlier immigrants tended to go back to Africa after their studies—due in large part to the fact that they had little problem securing well-paying jobs in the many state agencies or in the public sector at large. After all, not many Ghanaians had the higher level education that was needed at that time for the many positions that had become available with the departure of some European colonial workers.

Though the historically established patterns has not changed that much as the United Kingdom continues to attract significant numbers of Ghanaians, in more recent years, the United States, Canada, Australia, the Middle East and other non-European countries have increasingly become major destinations for Ghanaian immigrants. Now, partly as a result of several push factors (economic hardships and the demand for higher education) and pull factors (policy changes such as the diversity lottery), America is home to some 65,000 or more Americans of Ghanaian origin, the majority of whom are recent immigrants, having emigrated since the 1980s (Takyi 2002). Indeed Taylor (2009) points out that the United States and Canada have overtaken Europe as the preferred destination of Ghanaian immigrants in recent years. Orozco (2005) cites data on remittances to support the observation that there may be over 300,000 Ghanaians currently in America. These shifting patterns also correspond in no small way to the changing economic and political fortunes of Ghana during the 1970s, 1980s, and 1990s, decades that coincide with new waves of emigration to America and the other parts of the world.

Overall, Ghanaians in America are part of a growing number of African immigrants who now call Europe and North America home, estimated to number over 3 million today, (IOM 2003, Dean and Logan 2003). In America, it is estimated that about 1 million or more Africans have relocated to this country in recent years (see, e.g., Zeleza 2009, 2005; Konadu-Agyemang, Takyi and Arthur 2006; Dixon 2006; Roberts 2005; Eissa 2005; Dodoo and Takyi 2002; Takyi 2002; Gordon 1998; Dodoo 1997; Takougang 1995), with the bulk of these Africans coming in the 1980s and 1990s. In his analysis of recent data from the American Community Survey, Terrazas (2009) reported that the number of African immigrants in the United States grew nearly fortyfold between 1960 and 2007, from 35,355 to 1.4 million. Most of this growth, he concluded, has taken place since 1990. A recent *New York Times* article about the growing presence of African immigrants in New York suggested that more Africans have moved to this country voluntarily since the 1990s than at any other period since the abolition of the slave trade in 1807 (see Roberts 2005).

Joseph Mataley, a Ghanaian immigrant, poses with his four daughters, from left, Susana, Josephine, Beatrice, and Rosina, at their home in Denver, Colorado, on July 27, 2006. (AP Photo/Ed Andrieski)

The New York City region is not the only place where these Africans can be found. Indeed, they have settled throughout the continental United States; however, the eastern seaboard region—especially New York/New Jersey, Massachusetts, and the Washington, D.C./Maryland/Virginia metropolitan areas seem to be the main destination for a significant number of Africans (Takyi 2002). Also some studies have reported that in all the top metropolitan regions that they have settled, their growth rate has exceeded the 100 percent threshold: in Washington, D.C., Maryland, and Virginia, 148.9 percent; New York City, 134.2 percent; Atlanta, 284.6 percent; Minneapolis–St. Paul, 628.4 percent; Houston, 129.1 percent; Chicago, 122.5 percent; Boston, 102.1 percent; Dallas, 159.5 percent; and Philadelphia–New Jersey, 220.6 percent (see, e.g., Dean and Logan 2003).

At the early stages of these population movements out of Ghana (later to become an "exodus" as a result of the sheer number of Ghanaians who were involved), the West African region, particularly the Côte d'Ivoire and the then-booming oil-rich nation of Nigeria, were the main destinations for these migrants. It is believed that between 1974 and 1981 about a million or more Ghanaian workers left Ghana; their primary destinations were Nigeria and Côte d'Ivoire. Skilled Ghanaians such as teachers, doctors, and administrators moved to Nigeria, Uganda, Botswana, and Zambia. As of the mid-1980s, Ghanaians have increasingly migrated to a range of destinations in Europe and North America (Bump 2006). This is especially the case with some of the Ghanaian technocrats who fled Ghana for a variety of reasons (economic and political) during Flight Lieutenant Jerry Rawlings's provisional National Defense Council (PNDC) administration. Following the deportation of non-Nigerian nationals from Nigeria in 1983, some of those "deportees" who were able to do so left the African shores for Europe and North America. The United Nations reported that approximately 1.2 million Ghanaians returned to their homeland, either on land through Togo and Benin, or by sea during this expulsion (see, e.g., Brydon 1985). Some members of the latter, plus those few Ghanaians who came to America before the 1980s, were to serve as the seed for the growing community of Ghanaians now resident in America.

Even though some consider the 1970s as a period of mass emigration from Ghana (the second wave), as a result of poor record keeping and the fact that some of these moves were undocumented, we know very little about the extent of the outflow during this era. Although the number of Ghanaians who left during this period, and continue to leave Ghana now, are still unknown, it appears that the Ghanaian diaspora is quite large and, as a community, very vibrant. The evidence for this assertion comes from the presence of many Ghanaian associations and organizations—town unions, ethnic associations, churches, and old student associations (e.g., town and ethnic associations, old boys/girls unions, etc.). For instance, the Ghanaian-Canadian Business Directory published in Toronto, Canada, is even bigger than some city telephone directories in the United States. More importantly, in the case of the

United States, anecdotal evidence and other informal sources suggest that most of the winners of its diversity lottery actually did move out of Africa.

In her study of Ghanaian immigrants based on data from the 1980s, Peil (1995) noted that about 10 percent of Ghana's population of about 12 million in 1984 lived outside of Ghana. Data from several rudimentary sources—including those from Europe, Canada, and other parts of the world—suggest that the Ghanaian diaspora is quite large. Considering the fact that large-scale emigration has continued unabated since the beginning of the new century, it is true to suggest that at the moment, significant numbers of Ghanaians live outside the shores of West Africa. More important, and based largely on the locations where Ghanaians have settled in recent years, it is equally true that the destination for these immigrants have also become more diverse and not limited to traditional gateways and destinations in Europe, such as the United Kingdom. Indeed the existence of significant numbers of Ghanaian communities have been found in many places, including Canada, Japan, South Korea, and also China and many countries in the European Union (EU) (see, e.g., Bump 2006; Nieswand 2005; Ter Haar 1998.) Taylor (2009) points out that the United States and Canada have overtaken Europe as the preferred destination of Ghanaian immigrants in recent years. However, Orozco (2005) also suggests that there may be over 300,000 Ghanaians currently residing in America.

A second aspect of the recent emigration trends that is different from earlier waves is that the majority of those who left Ghana prior to the 1970s invariably returned to the home country on a permanent basis. This is particularly true with respect to the educational migrants (i.e., students). This is not necessarily the case with recent waves of immigration as several of these people have become permanent fixtures in their adopted countries of residence. In large part it is those who fall within the purview of the recent wave that have become the foundation of the growing Ghanaian diaspora community. While the reported numbers in America may underestimate the true size of the Ghanaian diaspora, anecdotal evidence suggest that the community is growing quite rapidly, due in large part to their increased representation in the diversity lottery program, and the fact that the established immigrants have been bringing their family members to join them, given that American immigration policies still give preference to family reunification (see, e.g., Kent, 2007; Lobo, 2006). Based on these expectations, it is no surprise that more recent data from the American Community Survey suggests that there may be more Ghanaians in the country than has been earlier reported, with the largest concentrations found in the New York/New Jersey and Washington, D.C./Virginia regions.

A third important difference between the earlier and recent waves of Ghanaian immigrants in North American cities such as Toronto and New York is that those who arrived in the 1980s were more diverse in terms of their social class and gender. In contrast, those Ghanaians who came to America before the 1980s were predominantly male students (Donkor 2005). Moreover, as Donkor notes, their reason for coming to America itself varies from period to period. For example, given that their earlier waves were composed of mainly students, they came here primarily to study. For the recent arrivals or cohorts (i.e., post 1980s), the group consists of students and non-students alike. The latter include economic and political refugees looking for job opportunities and a safe haven from the political instabilities of the 1980s and 1990s.

Explaining the Recent Waves of Ghanaian Emigration

Why are more Ghanaians leaving that country to come to the United States? Answers to this simple question are not easy to come by and are multifaceted. Indeed as has been indicated earlier in this chapter, the appeal of America to many Ghanaians can be considered as a recent development or phenomenon (Arthur 2000, 2008, 2009; Takyi 2000, 2009; Manuh 1998; Ter Haar 1998; Owusu 1998; Peil 1995; Killingray 1994). This statement is particularly true when one considers Ghana's social and political history. During its long colonial and early postcolonial history, Ghana's relatively vibrant and booming economy (prior to the 1970s) made it an attractive destination for other Africans and non-African's alike to settle in that country (Zachariah and Conde 1981).

Ghanaian Mary Gyimah is sworn in as a U.S. citizen during a naturalization ceremony on the National Mall in Washington, D.C. (Chris Maddaloni/Roll Call/Getty Images)

So far, researchers who have examined Ghana's immigration patterns draw in large part on some of the general reasons that have been identified in the literature to explain international migration (see, e.g., Arango, 2000; Massey 1999). Thus, as the case is with other immigrants in general, one cannot point to a single factor to explain recent migratory flows and patterns: both internal and external factors play key roles in the reasons behind migration flows (see, e.g., Takyi 2009; Peil 1995).

Among the internal processes that have served as a catalyst for leaving Ghana, one can but only conclude that economic considerations—that is, the betterment of one's economic situation—seem to be paramount when it comes to the decision to emigrate or not. For example, since the mid-1970s, and especially following the 1973 oil crisis, Ghana's once buoyant economy began to strain and deteriorate. As a result, throughout the 1970s and 1980s, the country went through a series of economic hardships, including high inflation, shortages of goods, and a rise of the unemployed and underemployed. These developments were compounded by severe droughts and bush-fires that swept the countryside in the early 1980s, destroying food and cash crops in many parts of the country, thereby straining the already critical food situation further. The changing economic fortunes of the nation also affect the educated class. Indeed, the rising educational levels and aspirations, as well as graduate unemployment and underemployment during this period when the economy stagnated (or contracted in some cases), created some of the pressures for the mass emigration that occurred during the 1970s and early 1980s—whether to neighboring countries or to countries outside Africa.

Equally important in the discussion of education is the type of education Ghanaians and, for that matter, most Africans inherited from their colonial "masters." Colonial and postcolonial education tend to prepare Africans for jobs that do not exist in their own countries, helping to fuel what others call the "brain drain." A case in point is the fact that most Ghanaian University graduates are more likely to write and speak English better than their own native languages. Not surprisingly, graduates tend to know more about the Western societies than their own country.

Some scholars also blame the IMF-sponsored SAPs, which were aimed at reversing Ghana's economic decline and stagnation in the 1980s for contributing to the recent outflow of Ghanaians to other parts of the developed and developing world. According to those who subscribe to this view, the SAP initiatives had an unintended effect on employment patterns in the country; not only did the Ghana government downsize and de-emphasize its role in the country's economy as a result of SAP, the downsizing trimmed the state bureaucracy, the main employer of university graduates in Ghana. Awuah (1997) has estimated that over 300,000 civil and public workers and those from the state-owned enterprises (SOEs) were retrenched during the 1980s. These retrenchments increased the pool of unemployed people in the country and contributed in no small way to the exodus to the neighboring countries such as Nigeria and Côte d'Ivoire, and other parts of Africa, especially during the 1980s.

Some evidence exists to support the economic motive for leaving Ghana. In his study of Ghanaians in Cincinnati, Ohio, Yeboah (2008) reported that a frequently cited reason among those he studied for coming to America was economic considerations. He noted that those surveyed suggested that their move was part of their overall strategy of improving their living standards and also bettering themselves and their families. To these Ghanaians, the availability of jobs in America and the opportunities available in this country for higher education, especially postgraduate education, appealed to them as they made their decisions to leave Ghana for America. Similar observations have been reported by Arthur (2009) in his study of some Ghanaians in the Minneapolis, Minnesota, area. On the question of "educational immigrants," their situation has been facilitated by the fact that in the case of Ghana and those from the Anglophone world, the use of English in American universities means it is somewhat easier for them to study in the many universities dotted all over America. After their studies, some of these students—having landed jobs—did not go back to Ghana and choose instead to settle permanently in this country.

In addition to economic factors, political instabilities and considerations have played a role in migratory decisions of some people, especially as pertains to immigrants who arrived post 1970s. During the late 1970s and the early 1980s, the military regime at the time, the Armed Forces Ruling Council (AFRC) and later the Provisional National Defense Council (PNDC), carried out many arrests of people considered to be "economic and political saboteurs." Among these perceived saboteurs were politicians, traders, and some intellectuals. The fear of arrest or persecution led to some Ghanaians fleeing the country during this period to settle in America. Not only that, throughout the 1980s and 1990s, those who were opposed to military rule became "enemies" of what was called the "revolution." Some were persecuted and others became threatened enough to emigrate.

Other researchers such as Massey (1995) and Amin (1974) have also argued that the current migratory patterns around the world draw from the outcome of colonial and neocolonial penetrations into the Third World regions. The thesis here is that the imposition of capitalism has led to unequal exchange, uneven development, and the neglect in world affairs of Third World regions such as Africa. As Amin (1974) argues, the uneven development was not only between Africa and the West, but also between the rural and urban areas. The colonial and postcolonial developmental policies' emphasis on urban areas means rural folks often have to move to urban centers if they want to improve their quality of life. Because these policies are not decided by the people, it is accurate to suggest that internal and international migration of Africans may not necessarily be voluntary; the migration may simply be a response to the established unequal relationship that exist between the rich

North (Western and industrial nations) and the poor South (Africa). These patterns have also been helped in no small ways by changes in technology and communication that have made it easier and cheaper for Africans to communicate or travel to America. The cultural expectations of Ghanaians also contribute to the outflow. This is because some are forced to leave the country in pursuit of a better life to safeguard against ridicule for being considered failures. This is true considering that until quite recently, educated people in Ghana were "expected" to be employed in the formal sector and be gainfully employed. This unrealistic expectation has forced a lot of people to leave Ghana for Europe and America to do jobs, in some cases, that are unrelated to their educational or vocational training. For some also, the whole idea of foreign travel (*aburokyire*) is captivating enough to force them to leave Ghana regardless of the obstacles that they go through in order to arrive at their destinations. Given the Ghanaian obsession with anything that is foreign, those who go to Europe and America tend to be treated with special respect and given recognition. In some cases, this has in recent years even affected the type of people that communities are willing to select to become traditional leaders (chiefs) in many parts of West Africa. All these factors have created a psychology of migration in most African societies whereby people are willing to abandon their home countries to undergo the challenges of moving to foreign countries, especially Europe and America.

With respect to the external factors that have served as inducement for Ghanaians to come to the United States, changes in U.S. immigration policies and laws have had one of the major effects of drawing Ghanaians to America. For example, the passage of the 1965 Immigration and Nationality Act repealed the national origins quota system that was put in place in the 1920s to limit non-European immigrations. The abolition of these laws paved the way for overall immigration from what is called the Third World regions. A second law that is important for African immigrants in general is the Immigration and Reform Control Act of 1986 (IRCA), which regularized the status of those who were here "illegally" and came before 1982 and the 1990 Immigration and Nationality Act. A more recent legislation, which is particularly relevant to African immigrants in America, is the 1990 Immigration Reform and Nationalization Act. In addition to increasing the numbers of immigrants who could come in as "family sponsored," this law has single handedly led to an increase in immigration from Africa. This is due to the fact that one of the provisions of the act created what has become known as the "Diversity Lottery," which has benefited many Africans. Under the diversity immigrant visa program, which is based on a lottery system, 50,000 visas are made available annually to a select number of countries that are deemed as sending few immigrants to the United States. The winners are drawn randomly from entries from individuals from those selected countries. Indeed, since the early 1990s when this act became effective, more than 20,000 Africans have been granted permission to immigrate to the United States each year. While it is not clear whether all those who qualified and won the lottery under the system actually immigrated to the United States, it appears that most of the winners did leave Africa. If current patterns continue, the expectations are that the "neo-diaspora" of African immigrants will change significantly in size and dynamism.

At the same time that U.S. immigration laws were becoming more open and liberal, the rules and regulations under which colonial subjects had used to emigrate in large numbers to European capitals were changed as part of overall immigration restrictions in the EU regions. With restrictions on immigration from their former colonies and the traditional destination for most Africans curtailed, other choices had to be found; and the United States became one of these new destination points. Thus, with the United States liberalizing its immigration policies, it emerged as a major country for higher learning and as a major recipient of refugees and political asylees; and Africans have turned increasingly to the United States as they flee their own countries for a variety of reasons. Improvements in communication between Africa and the rest of the world and also established networks of family and friends have all helped to facilitate African immigrations to America in recent years.

Demographic Profile

A Snapshot of the Ghanaian Diaspora in America

The recent attention to Ghanaian immigrants, and for that matter, African immigrants as a whole in America has something to do with their increasing numbers and its implication for black relations and interracial discourse in this country. Yet, as is true with America's foreign-born population as a whole, accurate figures on the size of the Ghanaian diaspora in America are hard to determine. However, by all accounts this number ranges from the reported 65,000 who were enumerated in the 2000 Census to over 300,000 or more as reported by Orozco (2005), who used data on money transfers to Ghana. Relatively small by comparison to black immigrants from the Caribbean region, the number of Ghanaians who consider America as home now has increased sharply since the 1990s and continues to grow at the end of the first decade of this century.

By all accounts, the recent increases have occurred mainly within the past decade. Its newness is quite striking. Indeed of the more than 60,000 Ghanaians who were enumerated in the 2000 Census, more than half (60.5%) came to America in the 1990s, nearly a quarter (24.3%) came during the 1980s, and less than a fifth (15.2%) came before the 1980s. In his analyses of 1990 and 2000 U.S. Census data, Takyi (2009, 2000) found that prior to the 1980s there were less than 10,000 Ghanaians in America, with this figure increasing to 20,863 (a 40% increase) in

1990, and rising sharply to 68,122 by 2000. No doubt the growth that is evident since the 1990s is attributed in large part to the diversity visa, something that Lobo (2006) and others (see, e.g., Konadu-Agyemang, Takyi, and Arthur 2006) have alluded to in their studies on African immigrants. Based on the available data, it is accurate then to suggest that the number of Ghanaians admitted to the United States has increased every 10 years since the 1980s. Indeed, the rate of growth has more than doubled between 1990 and 2000 (Tables 115 and 116). For example, in 1990, about 15,950 Ghanaians were enumerated in the census. By 2000, this figured had risen to 39,685.

How They Came

Though a community of Ghanaian immigrants has grown in recent years, how they have arrived on the shores of America is interlaced with a host of problems, including, for example, visa restrictions and regulations that limits who can come in and who cannot. As a result, these immigrants have relied on a variety of ways to arrive in America: some legal, others not. Some Ghanaians who came into the country legally (e.g., students) have found themselves for a variety of reasons in an undocumented status.

Based in large part to the liberalization of visa requirements, many recent educational "immigrants" often come directly from Ghana; however, some studies have also reported that those who emigrated before the 1990s may have used a stepwise approach in coming to America (Konadu-Agyemang, Takyi, and Arthur 2006). According to this thesis, those who used this approach lived in another country (e.g., Nigeria, Zimbabwe, or South Africa) prior to either enrolling in American schools or settling permanently in America. While in these countries, these Ghanaians worked (as teachers or in the health sectors), saved money, and used their savings to obtain the necessary papers to emigrate. In some cases, though, not all these immigrants moved to other countries before coming to the United States. Rather, they moved from Ghana's rural areas to the urban centers and worked hard to save enough to facilitate their departure.

Some evidence exists to support the stepwise-migratory patterns. In their analysis of data on a sample of Ghanaians living in several northeastern cities, Konadu-Agyemang and Takyi (2001) and Konadu-Agyemang, Takyi, and Arthur (2006) concluded that several of the people they interviewed reported living in another country before coming to America. These immigrants, they pointed out, were more likely to have lived in the West African sub-region (especially Nigeria) first, made some money, and then continued their move out of the continent. More recent, Yeboah (2008) has also reported that among the Ghanaians he studied in Cincinnati, Ohio, a sizable proportion indicated to him that they arrived in the United States by a stepwise process. Finally, a good number of Ghanaians, he reported, arrived as visitors or students and ultimately overstayed their visa status and become part of the undocumented Ghanaian community. Fortunately for some of these undocumented immigrants, especially those who came here before the mid-1980s, the IRCA legalization program was used to regularize their stay.

Another observation about the Ghanaian community, which contradicts with the popular view about African immigrants, is that very few came here as refugees. Citing data from a number of sources (e.g., the International Institute for Education [IIE]), Kent (2007) reported that Ghana is among the sub-Saharan African countries that send substantial number of foreign students, not refugees, to the United States. Between 2001 and 2005, for instance, she notes that about 3,053 Ghanaian students enrolled in American universities (see Kent 2007), which means several came here legally. After analyzing U.S. Immigration data, Eissa (2005) concluded that of all the refugees who were admitted to the United States between 1990 and 2000, only 10 percent were from Africa. He also points out that of the African immigrants in America who adjusted their status in 2003, only 16 percent were refugee and asylum adjustments. Indeed, the majority of recent Africans as a whole have come here by way of the diversity lottery visa, a pattern that applies to Ghanaians as well. In the case of Ghana, it is one of the major recipients of visas under the program. Arguably those Ghanaians who came prior to the tumultuous 1980s may have come as refugees, but the available data show that they do not matter with respect to refugee immigration from Africa (Kent 2007).

Where They Are Now: Settlement Patterns

Researchers have observed that America's immigrants tend to concentrate in a few immigrant receiving states. To a large extent, this general observation is rather true about the Ghanaian diaspora community in America. Although increasing numbers of Ghanaians have begun to move from the main gateway cities of New York and the Washington, D.C./Virginia areas to other midsize cities such as Columbus and Cincinnati, Ohio (Yeboah 2008) and Minneapolis (Arthur 2009), the majority of Ghanaians in America have settled in only a handful of states. In their analysis of 1990 and 2000 U.S. Census data, Takyi (2000) and Takyi and Boate (2006) found that almost half (48%) of all Ghanaians live in the Northeastern region, with the highest concentrations reported in major metropolitan regions in the New York/New Jersey area, Maryland/Virginia region, and Massachusetts as well (Table 114). Not only that, Takyi (2009) concluded that a significant number (35%) reside in the central cities. But the picture becomes more interesting the deeper one looks at residential patterns by state and metropolitan region. In the Washington, D.C., area for instance, Kent (2007) reports that Africans are more likely to reside in the inner suburbs and central city than in the outlying regions.

Who Is Here: Characteristics of Ghanaians in America

Consistent with studies dealing with contemporary international migrations, women feature prominently among the Ghanaians in America. As a result of selectivity, earlier waves of immigrants tended to be men. Thus of the more than 60,000 Ghanaians enumerated in the 2000 Census, slightly more than half were male (56%), but about 44 percent were female. This suggests that women have increasingly become major players in the emerging diaspora as well. Since migration tends to favor the young and the more agile, it is also not surprising that the majority of Ghanaians are young and in their working ages (18–64). Arthur (2008) reports that the Ghanaian community is made up of young people; especially those aged 25 to 35 years.

One of the most pernicious images of Africa—at least as portrayed in the American media—is that it is a continent full of poor and uneducated people who are always fighting among themselves. As a result of their poverty levels and their high degree of intolerance, these Africans are always on the move—out of the continent when the opportunity arises. Suffice it to say that this portrayal does not accurately capture the realities of the Ghanaian community, which comprises of people from all walks of life, including a significant number of professionals (skilled immigrants). Going by educational credentials, 2000 Census data shows that 87.4 percent of the 53,245 Ghanaians aged 25 and over had a high school or higher level of education. Focusing specifically on higher education, the same data indicate that nearly a third (31.6%) of all Ghanaians have a bachelor's degree or higher (see Table 117). This reported figure is slightly below the reported 38 percent for all Africans in America, but higher than those for all foreign-born residents (26%) and native-born Americans (16%) (Kent 2007).

Indeed, it is the size of the so-called educated class, particularly that of skilled workers (e.g., engineers, accountants, computer scientists) and professionals (e.g., attorneys, physicians, nurses, teachers, professors) that has provoked a lively debate among many scholars and funding agencies as to the implications of such losses for Africa's socioeconomic development (see, e.g., Kaba 2007; Ozden and Schiff 2006; Dodoo, Takyi, and Mann 2006; Saravia and Miranda 2004; Adepoju 2000; Carrington and Detragiache 1999; Logan 1990). This pattern of brain-drain is equally true of the Ghanaians who have left Africa to work in America as significant numbers work in professional settings (Table 118). According to a recent article in the *New England Journal of Medicine,* there are 532 Ghanaian doctors practicing in the United States. Although they represent a tiny fraction of the 800,000 U.S. physicians, their number is equivalent to 20 percent of Ghana's medical capacity, for there are only 2,600 physicians in Ghana (Mullan 2007).

Adjustment and Adaptation

Culture: Foodways, Music, Art, and Celebrations

As Africans living in America, Ghanaians are confronted daily with the negative images that are often portrayed in the U.S. media about Africa. It has been suggested that black immigrants in general are confronted with a host of issues when it comes to acculturation; one major issue concerns conforming to the larger American society or to black American society (see, e.g., the works of Bryce-Laporte). Notwithstanding the images about Africa and the pressures to conform to mainstream American or African American culture, researchers have observed that the typical Ghanaian immigrant is yet to do away with his/her "African or Ghanaian identity or culture" in America.

Studies have reported, for instance, that Ghanaians in the diaspora, including those in America, have organized themselves into ethnic or national community groups to help fill in the void of their absent extended family members (see, e.g., Konadu-Agyemang, Takyi, and Arthur 2006; Donkor 2005). Members from such organizations have been instrumental in the provision of social support to their members in a variety of ways; including counseling the youth, resolving domestic conflict among families, and providing moral and financial support in times of crisis or death. In addition, members help each other celebrate joyous events such as weddings, births, and graduations. During celebrations, most Ghanaians showcase their traditions and culture to the wider audience of Americans. These events also provide a unique opportunity for their children (the second generation) to learn the traditions and values of their parents. This is especially true for the second-generation Ghanaians whose ties to Ghana may be tenuous or weak.

Whether at birthday celebrations, wedding and cultural celebrations, or funeral services, popular Ghanaian dishes and foods are served liberally by the host. Traditional African practices and invocations are also used liberally to showcase the significance of the occasion. Guests listen and dance to Ghanaian music—from the traditional and popular highlife to its new forms, including hiplife (a variant or amalgam of highlife and hip-hop music popular in the United States). More likely than not, participants of these events tend to wear African/Ghanaian clothes—be it *kente* (for birthdays, church service, and other celebrations) or the black and red clothes favored for funeral and burial services. African and Ghanaian clothes and paraphernalia such as music and movies (DVDs) are readily available in the United States (through the mail/Internet) or can be bought from the many Ghanaian/African and ethnic stores that are found in cities such as New York and the metropolitan Washington, D.C., region, where many Ghanaians have settled. Many shops sell clothes, basic African cooking ingredients, familiar foodstuffs, meat, fish, and groceries from Ghana as well as the latest hits from Nollywood and

Ghallywood, the Nigerian and Ghanaian equivalents to India's Bollywood and America's Hollywood.

Another context where Ghanaian culture is likely to be displayed is in the churches. Indeed, the many Ghanaian Churches (especially mainstream Christian groups and Evangelical/Pentecostal ones) that have sprung up in the diaspora provide yet another environment (beside the home) for Ghanaians to speak their local dialects and wear their African clothes. Church services in some of these Ghanaian churches in the diaspora are conducted in English, but the use of the local Ghanaian dialects such as Twi (Akan) is also quite common.

Family and Intimate Life and Adjustment-Related Issues

Numerous studies have pointed to the centrality of family to the lives of many Africans (see, e.g., Oheneba-Sakyi and Takyi 2006; Takyi and Dodoo 2005). The attachment to married and family life can equally be discerned among the Ghanaian diaspora as well. In a context where marriage is considered the preferred mode of reproduction, and where marriage is highly regarded, it should come as no surprise then that a good number of Ghanaians in America are married or live in married couple households. An analysis of family and household structure finds that about 57 percent of these immigrants were married and the rest were unmarried (including the widowed, the divorced, and the separated). Nearly 60 percent of Ghanaian households have young children. Only 2 percent of the households have no children. The average family size of the community is estimated at about four children, with levels of education attainment being a key factor in determining the size of the family. In a family where either of the parents, especially the wife, has postgraduate level of education, the average number of children is two. More important, the children of these Ghanaians tend to live in two-parent households. About 20 percent of the households have grandparents. These are at times first-generation immigrants or elderly parents of recent immigrants who in some cases have been invited by their married children in the diaspora to assist in taking care of their children (Arthur 2008, 47). The role of the elderly or grandparents in the Ghanaian immigrant households is economically beneficial as the husband and the wife can have free time to concentrate on their economic activities. For most households the presence of the grandparents also is an opportunity for the children to learn their native language and culture.

Family life is central to many Ghanaians; however, by no means do we suggest that all their unions are stable. Scattered reports abound in the popular press and on the Internet that suggest that the Ghanaian family life in the diaspora may be under stress. There are indications of high levels of divorce and separation. Unfortunately, accurate data on marital and divorce patterns appears to be nonexistent. Going by the household composition, though, one can say that the percentage of households headed by females is not that large.

Integration and Impact on U.S. Society and Culture: Intergroup Relations

There is some interest in the nature and context of the relationships that exists between the new African immigrants and the "old" (native-born) African Americans or other people of Africa in the diasporas. Unfortunately, given the recent arrival of the Ghanaian diaspora in America, very few studies have looked at interethnic relations between these immigrants and their native-born counterparts, especially their African American brethren. Some studies, however, have pointed out that there may be some degree of misunderstanding and communication gaps between African immigrants and African Americans (see, e.g., Apraku 1991; Waters 1995; Takougang 1995). In part, these misunderstandings often deal with the issue of acceptance by their native-born black Americans as foreign-born African Americans are at times thought of as having sold their ancestors into slavery. Also, one cannot ignore the tension among the two groups over access to valued resources in our society. A typical example is the idea that these new immigrants and their children are unfairly benefitting from the legacies of the civil right movement, such as affirmative action programs.

But as Yeboah (2008) notes in his work of Ghanaians in Cincinnati, recent immigrants of African origin are compelled by the realities of their new environment to negotiate their African heritage with their American experience. Among these daily realities are issues of race and identity. Just as native-born black Americans are burdened with stereotypes and discrimination that are associated with "blackness" in America, so too are foreign-born black Americans. However, in the case of foreign-born blacks, they also suffer from the negative images that are often associated with contemporary African societies. Moreover, African-born immigrants also are confronted with the problems and negative views some hold about immigrants in general. Yeboah claims that Ghanaians may be creating new or hybrid cultures that in large part are a reflection of how well they have adapted into American society.

On the whole, Ghanaians feel welcomed in their communities, making, in some cases, their integration less traumatic. This is due in part to the fact many African Americans are also adopting African traditions. Indeed, for those Ghanaians who live in the big cities of New York and Washington, D.C., which have significant black populations, it is often difficult to tell who was born in Africa and who was not. People have interacted positively like brothers and sisters—on many levels. For example, one can see many African Americans eating in African restaurants around Harlem. But it is also true that some have questioned the overrepresentation of second-generation African immigrants in the Ivy League schools (Massey et al. 2007).

On the political front, Ghanaians in the diaspora have become major players in the political process and discourse back home. Some have gone home to stand for elections, while others have donated their money and resources for the major political parties in the country: the National Democratic Congress (NDC) and the New Patriotic Party (NPP). These American branches of political parties have hosted most of the leadership who regularly come over to brief their "overseas" branches of developments back home and also to raise funds for campaigns. Using existing political structures back in Ghana, those in the diaspora are increasingly becoming involved in the on-going democratization that is currently underway after decades of military rule in Ghana. To the extent that this trend will continue, especially among the second generation is a subject of debate.

The Ties that Bind: Linkages and Other Issues Relating to Ghana

Diasporan Ghanaians have not completely detached themselves from their towns and villages in Ghana. Even though nearly a third (31%) are naturalized citizens, when some are asked about where they consider "home," often times they point to 'here" and "there" (Africa, specifically Ghana) as their homes. As a result of living in America (based on how long they have been here), some Ghanaians have adopted some values, manners, and personality attitudes associated with America—including hard work and individualism. However, that has not meant that they have completely been detached from Ghana. Modern technology has made it easier today for immigrants to communicate with families and friends on the continent. Their affinity to Ghana is strong, and they are passionate and proud of their heritage as evidenced by their dressing habits, food preferences, and interest in "anything" to deal with Ghana. Indeed, the notion of separation which has been observed among some immigrant groups in America appears to be less applicable to this community of Ghanaians. Even some Ghanaians who die here have had their bodies shipped home for burial—the ultimate pride of most Ghanaian families.

Ghanaian Americans have not completely ignored what goes on in Ghana itself as they are active participants in some of the sociopolitical developments back home. Indeed, some scholars have noted the extensive contacts that exist between Ghanaians in the diaspora and those back home in Ghana as these Ghanaians have continued to maintain strong cultural and sociopolitical ties in the United States as a means of cultural preservation and mutual support. This is particularly true about the first-generation Ghanaians in the diaspora whose ties to the "homeland" are more recent. Owusu (2003) and many others have reported that those in the diaspora have maintained strong ties to Ghana. This is evidenced, for example, by the number of homes they have built and maintained in Ghana. Indeed, it is believed that the on-going housing boom (especially the high-end houses in expensive neighborhoods such as East Legon in Accra) has something to do with the activities of Ghanaians in the diaspora. More importantly, a real estate market has arisen that caters for the housing needs of those in the diaspora as well.

The need to maintain ties with Ghana and also develop a network of social support system in America (for cultural values and identity reasons) has led to the establishment of various voluntary associations (ethnic, religious, professional, political, and others) in many parts of North America where Ghanaians are found (Owusu, 2003; Agyemang and Atta-Poku 1996). In spite living abroad, Ghanaian Americans have never lost their sense of community, a phenomena that can be attributed to the cherished extended family systems and perhaps a slogan of "one people with a common destiny." It is quite common to find these associations raising funds to help develop their communities of origin in Ghana. A typical example of this is my own hometown association: the Duayaw-Nkwanta Association of the United States and Canada (there is an international branch that also comprises other unions in Europe and around the world), which has been helping to initiate and fund development projects in that town in the Brong-Ahafo Region of Ghana. Under the auspices of The National Council of Ghanaian Associations (NCOGA), several ethnic and national activities have been organized in major cities such as New York and Chicago on national events. Events such as Ghana's Independence Day (March 6), Ghana's Fiftieth Independence Anniversary (Ghana at 50), and other cultural relevant programming showcase the rich and vibrant culture of the country, making it an attractive place for non-Ghanaian tourists.

Ethnic churches that cater primarily to immigrants have also sprung up and have become fixtures of the religious landscape in cities where Ghanaians have settled (e.g., Ghanaian Presbyterian Church of New York; the Black Catholic Apostolate of Albany, New York; and various Pentecostal and Evangelical denominations). Most churches, particularly those in the big cities, have separate services for different Ghanaian language groups, while others use English language for church service. Cadge and Ecklund (2007) observed that the Ghanaian Pentecostal churches in Chicago conduct services in English language so as to bridge the language gap and attract more people. These ties that these churches have established among themselves through their community and cultural organizations is perhaps one way for them to cope with the realities of their new environment and establish social networks that in the long run help in their adjustment to American society. It may also be that these people see themselves as sojourners who will one day go back to Ghana and as such want to maintain some ties in both worlds.

Additionally, there has emerged an entrepreneurial class, one devoted to the provision of the traditional needs and foodstuffs of these immigrants. Consequent upon this, some Ghanaian immigrant entrepreneurs have recognized the business opportunities that the increase in the size of the community provides (see, e.g., Yeboah 2008; Amankwaa 2004). Thus, one can see several mom-and-pop shops or businesses that have been established in faraway places such as Columbus and Cincinnati, Ohio. Even though the profit motive is behind the establishment of these businesses, at the same time they provide a direct link between those in the diaspora

Home Away from Home: Ghanaian Voluntary and Ethnic Associations

Over the past 15–20 years, many Ghanaians have settled in America. Among the Ghanaian community in America, one of the popular things to do is to belong to ethnic/hometown associations or other forms of voluntary associations (church, professional, etc.). As in other parts of the world where Ghanaians can be found, these hometown associations often draw their membership from migrants from the same place of origin or ethnic background. Even though ethnic affiliation is often a criterion for belonging to some of these associations, they do not necessarily rule out interaction with people of other backgrounds. This is to be expected as intermarriages and friendship ties (such as attending the same boarding schools, etc.) has led to the forging of identities and ties that cut across ethnic lines. Thus, despite the goals of the some of these ethnic associations, membership of the group can be viewed as opened or closed. An important feature of these ethnic associations is that most communicate in the local language spoken in the immigrants' place of birth or origin.

Why the need for these voluntary associations in the first place? First, as Ghanaians who have left their ancestral home, these voluntary associations provide members the opportunity to recreate their lost traditional families back home here in America. Second, like with the Ghanaian family, these organizations provide some form of socialization to members, including inculcating the values and culture of their specific cultural group to their children. Third, ethnic organizations such as the Duayaw-Nkwanta Citizens Union tend to come to the aid of their members when the need arises—both in joyful and sad moments. Members often share festive occasions such as births and marriages together and offer support in emergency situations (e.g., deaths, illness, or accidents) by offering community care and visits in some cases. Fourth, some of the ethnic associations have a developmental agenda as well. They help to mobilize their members to support or initiate development projects back home in Ghana. Fifth, at times, members devote attention to economic or political issues facing their areas and serve as a needed pressure group for monitoring socioeconomic developments back home in Ghana.

Of the many benevolent roles these associations play, the provision of help for newly arrived immigrants and their families of members in times of distress may be considered one of the most important roles for their existence. For the most part, the various associations that have been formed by the diasporan Ghanaians are run by volunteers and are headed and staffed by officials elected by the membership as a whole. Through group activities, the associations are able to showcase their rich cultural heritage to the second generation and also the larger audience of Americans. More important, they also provide a useful link for Americans wanting to travel to Ghana or learn more about Ghanaian culture and history.

and back home. They are places where Ghanaian foods and produce are transacted between those in Ghana and in the diaspora. More importantly, some of these businesses provide immigrants the opportunities to remit to their folks back home, or start a home—something most of these Ghanaians aspire to back home.

One of the areas where the diaspora Ghanaian has contributed in no small way has to do with remittances. Several studies indicate that remittances of Ghanaians in the diaspora account for a significant part of the nongovernmental foreign direct investment. A recent report by the International Organization for Migration (IOM) estimates that the Ghanaian diaspora, which is estimated to include between 1.5 million and 3 million people, is contributing financially to the well-being of the Ghanaian economy. The report quotes data from the Ghana Central Bank to indicate that Ghanaians abroad contributed about $2 billion in remittances in 2009, a huge increase compared to the $476 million they remitted in 1999.

According to Akurang-Parry (2002), Ghanaian expatriates' remittances to families and loved ones is one of the significant net gains from the brain drain. Diaspora remittances have helped Ghana in several ways as the projects they finance provide jobs for the otherwise jobless masons, electricians, carpenters, and many others in the country. These remittances intended for building projects, community development efforts, and educational and health facilities are the ultimate infrastructure in most rural areas abandoned by the central government, which tends to focus more on the urban areas. More importantly, and in several cases, these remittances to family members back home serve as the main source of income for many rural dwellers.

Equally important besides remittances are the symbiotic, collaborative connections that have emerged between home-based Ghanaian professionals and their non-resident counterparts. Apart from books and articles, collaborative work between home-based professionals and expatriates has also been established in some cases. Indeed, several Ghanaian professionals, medical doctors, and university professors have been instrumental in helping to set up various exchange programs between Ghana and American institutions (e.g., the Regional Institute of Population at the University of Ghana and the Pennsylvania State University at State College). Others such as the EO group, for example, have been instrumental in linking up American businesses and their Ghanaian counterparts or the government itself (as is the case with Kosmos of Texas, the company that is involved in Ghana's nascent oil industry). Thus, there have been some gains for Ghana as a result of the brain-drain.

The Second and Later Generations

International migration has emerged as one of the major social forces in the early part of the 21st century and has led to transformations in many societies around the world. In the case of the United States, immigration from Africa is also helping to redefine black identities and social relations. Even though very little is known about the second generation of Ghanaians—partly due to the recent nature of their parents immigration and the relative small size of the community; which makes it difficult to get adequate and reliable sample size to study such a group—the limited studies that exist suggest that in terms of education, they may be doing relatively well. For example, like the educational experience of President Barack Obama (son of a Harvard-educated Kenyan father and a white American mother), a typical second-generation African in America is in many ways part of a new phenomenon that some scholars have observed with respect to higher education among black Americans—it has been noted that about 13 person of black students in elite colleges are first- or second-generation African immigrant such as Ghanaians. How these second-generation Ghanaian Americans will identify or relate to the mother country (Ghana) over time will need to be studied in the coming years. Will they see themselves as Americans first and Ghanaians second? Will they continue the tradition of remitting to relations back in Ghana or building homes in Ghana (something many first-generation Ghanaian immigrants cherish)?

Toward the Future

Political boundaries that differentiate one African country from another have made it somewhat difficult to travel from one part of the continent to another. Despite the difficulties, the majority of African population movements are within the African region itself. Increasingly, this pattern is changing as there has been a significant increase in the number of Africans, including Ghanaians, who have moved beyond the borders of Africa to seek their fortunes in America. The new trend is attributed to a host of interrelated factors, including changing U.S. immigration policies that have eliminated restrictive laws, and growing economic and political problems in Africa that serve as a push factor for emigration.

Overall, Ghana's share of the total African immigrant population in the United States has increased over the past couple of decades. Still, the community is a recent development, given that very few have deep roots in America, if we define "roots" to imply years of residence in America. Going beyond the debate about the brain-drain that has dominated the discourse on African immigrations in recent years, one can observe the diversity that is evident among the Ghanaian community as it encompasses all age and socioeconomic groupings. Finally, and as is also true with many new immigrant groups, these Ghanaians so far still see themselves as Ghanaians. They have, for the most part, not forgotten about their roots and have maintained and continued to maintain a strong attachment to their home country and have been engaged in some of the sociopolitical developments currently underway in Ghana. They continue to participate in the activities of the home country through several means, including remitting, joining political groupings, and

A 19-Year-Old Scholar-Athlete

University of Akron's Kofi Sarkodie points to the sky after scoring during an NCAA college soccer match against Michigan, December 10, 2010. (AP Photo/Mark J. Terrill)

Kofi Sarkodie is a junior at the University of Akron, Ohio, and is a soccer player for the highly ranked University of Akron Team called the Zips. Kofi played in the 2009 NCAA finals for the No. 1–ranked Zips soccer team that went to the finals last year. He also featured for the Zips soccer team that won the Mid-Atlantic Conference Champions in its 2009 season during his sophomore year.

Kofi Sarkodie was born to Ghanaian immigrant parents and grew up outside of Dayton, Ohio. Even though his parents, Amaning and Olivia Sarkodie, are originally from Kumasi, Kofi (like his senior brother Ofori, also a soccer player) was born in the United States.

According to Kevin Crater, a sportswriter for the *Akron Buchetlite* (the student newspaper), Kofi is a versatile player as he can play in the back and the midfield and also as a forward player. Kofi has represented the United States in various capacities; including being a member of its Youth National team. He spent the summer of 2008 competing in South America with the U-18 national team that played in the U-17 World Cup.

Beyond his soccer skills, Kofi is a scholar-athlete as well. He is a member of the University of Akron's Honors College. The prestigious Honors College caters primarily to highly motivated and achieving students who have demonstrated their abilities to excel. Only students with high GPAs are admitted into the honors program. He is quite sociable and gets along well with colleagues and faculty alike. Kofi Sarkodie aims to turn pro after college and anticipates a professional soccer career after graduating from Akron.

also participating in voluntary organizations. To the extent that this high degree of engagement will continue is something one cannot easily predict—even though it may be relevant for future discourse on engagements with the mother country—especially with respect to the issue of remittances, which has become a major source of revenue to Ghana. However, as the first generation, with its strong attachment to Ghana, gets older and passes on, their children may be less likely to see themselves as Ghanaians to the extent that their parents viewed themselves but rather they may be more likely to see themselves as simply African Americans. If this occurs, perhaps these second- and third-generation Ghanaian Americans may be less likely to be so involved in some of the activities that their first-generation parents have been engaged in while here (e.g., homeownership in Ghana and remitting to family members back home). This could in turn change the nature of the relationship between those in the diaspora and in Ghana itself.

As the community becomes bigger and more established, there are several unknown areas of study to be explored. For example, it is not clear how the second generation will feel about their ties to Ghana. Many first-generation Ghanaians in the United States also encounter racial discrimination; however, their attitudes toward race at times may be somewhat different from those of black Americans—given their different historical experiences. Studies are needed to understand how these attitudes affect their adaptation and acculturation into American society. Looking ahead, there is the need for valuable studies that provide in-depth analyses of a host of issues facing the Ghanaian community as they integrate into American society.

Appendix I: Migration Statistics

Table 110 Persons obtaining legal permanent resident status by region and country of birth: Fiscal years 2000 to 2009

Region and country of birth	2000	2001	2002	2003	2004	2005	2006	2007	2008	2009
Total	841,002	1,058,902	1,059,356	703,542	957,883	1,122,257	1,266,129	1,052,415	1,107,126	1,130,818
Ghana	4,339	4,023	4,248	4,410	5,337	6,491	9,367	7,610	8,195	8,401

Source: U.S. Department of Homeland Security. Office of Immigration Statistics. 2010. Adapted from Table 3.

Table 111 Trends in international migrant stock, Ghana

	1990	1995	2000	2005	2010
Estimated number of international migrants at mid-year	716,527	1,038,349	1,504,715	1,669,267	1,851,814
Estimated number of refugees at mid-year	4,102	98,433	12,991	47,795	39,948
Population at mid-year (thousands)	14,968	17,246	19,529	21,915	24,333
Estimated number of female migrants at mid-year	317,902	447,152	628,951	697,731	774,034
Estimated number of male migrants at mid-year	398,625	591,197	875,764	971,536	1,077,780
International migrants as a percentage of the population	4.8	6.0	7.7	7.6	7.6
Female migrants as percentage of all international migrants	44.4	43.1	41.8	41.8	41.8
Refugees as a percentage of international migrants	0.6	9.5	0.9	2.9	2.2
	1990–1995	1995–2000	2000–2005	2005–2010	
Annual rate of change of the migrant stock (%)	7.4	7.4	2.1	2.1	

Source: United Nations, Department of Economic and Social Affairs, Population Division (2009). The 2008 Revision, United Nations database, POP/DB/MIG/Stock/Rev.2008.

Table 112 The distribution of refugees in Ghana by country of origin, 2001–2008

Country of origin	2001	2002	2003	2004	2005	2006	2007	2008
Liberia	8,865	28,298	42,466	40,853	38,684	35,653	26,967	15,797
Sierra Leone	1,998	4,316	943	632	125	103	101	132
Sudan	16	23	3	12	579	600	595	392
Togo	842	819	534	542	14,136	8,517	7,243	1,796
Other	70	48	1	14	13	65	52	89
Total	11,791	33,504	43,947	42,053	53,537	44,938	34,958	18,206

Source: IOM (2009, Table 15).

Table 113 Ghanaians living in Europe and North America, 1999–2006

	Emigrants	Year
UK	96,650	2006
USA	67,190	2000
Italy	34,499	2005
Germany	20,636	2004
Canada	17,070	2001
Netherlands	12,196	2007
Spain	12,068	2006
France	4,096	1999

Source: IOM (2009, Table 20)

Table 114 Persons obtaining legal permanent resident status during fiscal year 2009. Leading states of residence region/country: Ghana

Characteristic	Total	Male	Female
Total	8,401	4,371	4,030
Arizona	57	31	26
California	257	129	128
Colorado	151	82	69
Connecticut	203	110	93
Florida	156	89	67
Georgia	465	257	208
Illinois	301	149	152
Maryland	692	338	354
Massachusetts	498	240	258
Michigan	73	35	38
Minnesota	154	77	77
New Jersey	745	384	361
New York	1,926	983	943
North Carolina	216	119	97
Ohio	538	308	230
Pennsylvania	251	125	126
Texas	323	176	147
Virginia	605	294	311
Washington	86	44	42
Other	704	401	303

Source: Adapted from U.S. Department of Homeland Security. Profiles on Legal Permanent Residents: 2009. Cobbook 82. 2010.

Appendix II: Demographics/Census Statistics

Table 115 Ghanaians living in America

	1980	1990	2000	Total
Total number of Africans	155,444	226,929	498,927	881,300
Total number of Ghanaians	9,935	15,950	39,685	65,570
As a percent of all Africans	6.4	7.0	8.0	7.4

Source: Author's Analysis of U.S. 2000 Census Data.

Table 116 When they came: Ghanaians in America 2000

	Number	Percent
All Ghanaians	65,570	100.0
Entered between 1990 and 2000	39,685	60.5
Entered between 1980 and 1989	15,960	24.3
Entered before 1980	9,935	15.2

Source: Author's analysis of U.S. 2000 Census Data.

Table 117 Educational attainment of Ghanaians in America, 2000

	Number	Percent
Educational attainment (population 25 years and over)	53,245	100.0
Less than 9th grade	2,010	3.8
9th to 12th grade, no diploma	4,680	8.8
High school graduate (includes equivalency)	13,665	25.7
Some college, no degree	10,505	19.7
Associate degree	5,570	10.5
Bachelor's degree	9,000	16.9
Graduate or professional degree	7,815	14.7
Percent high school graduate or higher		87.4
Percent bachelor's degree or higher		31.6

Source: U.S. Census Bureau, Census 2000 Special Tabulations (STP-159).

Table 118 Occupational distribution of Ghanaian immigrants in America, 1972–2000

	Period		
	1972-1977	**1978-1989**	**1990-2000**
Annual average flow	237	528	1,271
Occupation (percent)			
Professional, managerial, and technical	40.8	28.3	31.7
Sales and adminstrative support	21.3	18.5	16.5
Precisiion, production, craft, and repair	6.7	9.1	18.8
Operators, fabricators, and laborers	18.1	18.1	7.8
Farming, forestry, and fishing	0.4	1.0	2.3
Service occupations	12.7	25	22.9
Total	100.0	100.0	100.0

Source: Lobo (2006, Table 11.2)

Table 119 Marital status and household structure of Ghanaians in America, 2000

	Number	**Percent**
Panel I		
Marital status		
Population 15 years and over	61,400	100.0
Never married	17,065	27.8
Now married, excluding separated	34,975	57.0
Separated	3,515	5.7
Widowed	1,030	1.7
Female	820	1.3
Divorced	4,820	7.9
Female	2,070	3.4
Panel II		
Households by type		
Total households	30,010	100.0
Family households (families)	20,820	69.4
With own children under 18 years	13,495	45.0
Married-couple family	14,180	47.3
With own children under 18 years	9,685	32.3
Female householder, no husband present	3,515	11.7
With own children under 18 years	24,50	8.2
Nonfamily households	9,190	30.6
Householder living alone.	6,900	23.0

Source: U.S. Census Bureau, Census 2000 Special Tabulations (STP-159).

Table 120 Household income of Ghanaians in America, 2000

	Number	Percent
Income in 1999		
Households	30,010	100
Less than $10,000	2,495	8.3
$10,000 to $14,999	1,410	4.7
$15,000 to $24,999	3,875	12.9
$25,000 to $34,999	4,335	14.4
$35,000 to $49,999	5,380	17.9
$50,000 to $74,999	6,370	21.2
$75,000 to $99,999	2,930	9.8
$100,000 to $149,999	2,230	7.4
$150,000 to $199,999	550	1.8
$200,000 or more	430	1.4
Median household income (dollars)	42,016	

Source: U.S. Census Bureau, Census 2000 Special Tabulations (STP-159).

Table 121 U.S. citizenship and period of entry, Ghanaians in America 2000

	Number	Percent
Total population	65,570	100.0
U.S. citizenship and period of U.S. entry		
Naturalized U.S. citizen	20,655	31.5
Entered 1990 to 2000	4,210	6.4
Entered 1980 to 1989	8,945	13.6
Entered before 1980	7505	11.4
Not a U.S. citizen	44,915	68.5
Entered 1990 to 2000	35,475	54.1
Entered 1980 to 1989	7,015	10.7
Entered before 1980	2,430	3.7

Source: U.S. Census Bureau, Census 2000 Special Tabulations (STP-159).

Table 122 Classes of admission, African immigrants to the United States by country of birth and period of arrival

	Annual average immigrant flow			Annual average changes between	
	1972–1977	1978–1989	1990–2000	1972–1977	1978–1989
					Growth
Africa	7,420	15,466	35,080	8,046	100.0
Family	4,356	11,340	16,953	6,984	86.8
Employment	2,751	2,029	3,693	−722	−9.0
Refugee	204	17,78	4,896	1,574	19.6
Diversity	0	10	9,178	10	0.1
Ghana	370	989	3,135	619	100.0
Family	287	861	1,661	574	92.7
Employment	80	100	176	20	3.2
Refugee	0	8	44	8	1.3
Diversity	0	0	1,215	0	0.0

Source: Lobo (2006, Table 11.1).

Appendix III: Notable Ghanaian Americans

Freddy Adu was top overall pick in the 2004 Major League Soccer draft for D.C. United. Adu represented the United States at the World under 17 and under 20 soccer cups. Indeed, he was the youngest person to play for the U.S. national soccer team when the United States played against Canada in January 2006. His soccer abilities made him one of the world's most sought after players by the time he was 13.

Reverend Bismarck Akomeah is the pastor of Jesus Power Assembly of God Church in Columbus, Ohio. He was ordained a reverend minister by the Ohio District Council of Assemblies of God in September of 2005. In that same year, the Jesus Power Assembly of God was recognized as one of the 14 Transformational churches by the General Council of Assembly of God, USA. Under his stewardship, his church has grown tremendously. He has also opened affiliate branches of his church in Atlanta, Georgia, and Cincinnati, Ohio. Not only that, he has also opened Swahili and French churches in Columbus, Ohio, and membership in his churches includes people from Nigeria, Togo, Benin, Sierra Leone, Kenya, Tanzania, Haiti, St. Lucia, the United States, and Ghana.

Professor Kwame Anthony Appiah was born in London to a Ghanaian father and a British mother. He moved to Ghana as a young child. He is currently a professor of philosophy at Princeton University in New Jersey and a member of the American Academy of Arts and Sciences. Prior to his current post, he taught at Duke University and also at Harvard. Professor Appiah has published widely in African and African American literary and cultural studies. His published works include the following: *In My Father's House, Color Conscious: The Political Morality of Race,* and *Bu Me Bé: Proverbs of the Akan* (co-edited with his mother). He has served on several boards, including the American Academy in Berlin, and was a trustee of Ashesi University College in Accra, Ghana, until 2009.

Professor George Ayitteh is currently a distinguished Economist in Residence at the American University. And also the president of the Free Africa Foundation, a think tank devoted to reforms in Africa. He earned a B.Sc. degree from the University of Ghana, Legon; and an M.A. from the University of Western Ontario. He also holds a Ph.D. from the University of Manitoba in Canada. Among his publications are the following: *Africa Betrayed, The Blueprint For Ghana's Economic Recovery, Africa In Chaos,* and *Africa Unchained: The Blueprint for Development.*

Kofi Boateng is the director of the Africa-America Institute in New York City. His undergraduate degrees are from Yale University. He also has an M.S. degree from Northeastern University Graduate School of Professional Accounting. He is a certified public accountant, a chartered life underwriter, and a chartered financial consultant. He is a member of the American Institute of Certified Public Accountants. He is an active member in the Ghanaian diaspora community.

Dr. Kwame Bawuah Edusei is a medical practitioner, and he was Ghana's Ambassador to the United States (2004–2008). He holds an M.D. from the Kwame Nkrumah University of Science and Technology in Kumasi, Ghana. After completing his M.D., he proceeded to the United States, where he did his medical residency in family medicine at the Howard University Hospital in Washington, D.C. Prior to his appointment as ambassador to the United States, he served as a medical practitioner, businessman, and humanitarian both in Ghana and in the United States.

Dr. Ave Kludze is one of NASA's top strategists and engineers. He had his early education at Adisadel College in Cape Coast, from where he proceeded to the Rutgers University of New Jersey to further his studies. After receiving his bachelor of science degree in electrical and computer engineering, he proceeded to the John Hopkins University, where he obtained his master's of science degree in engineering. For nearly 15 years he has helped develop and launch spacecraft for NASA. He has also worked at NASA's Langley Research Center in Virginia and the NASA/Goddard Space Flight Center in Maryland.

George Y. Owusu co-founded the EO Group, which deals with oil-related services. The EO group is a shareholder in Ghana's nascent oil industry. Mr. Owusu served as the representative for Kosmos Energy in Ghana.

Ms. Rose Quarshie is the current executive secretary general of the National Council of Ghanaian Associations (NCOGA). NCOGA is an umbrella organization that represents various associations of Ghanaians living outside Ghana. It serves as a clearing house for many Ghanaian ethnic and non-ethnic organizations (e.g., hometown associations) in America.

Dr. David Sam is president of Elgin County Community College (Chicago). He attended Mfantsipim Secondary School in Cape Coast before enrolling for his undergraduate degree from the Illinois State University. He also holds a Ph.D. in international economics and political relations from the Fletcher School of Law and Diplomacy at Tufts University, an M.B.A. from the Kellogg School of Management at Northwestern University, and a J.D. degree from the University of Akron Law School. Before his current position, he was the president of North Harris College in Houston (Texas) and dean of the Community and Technical College (now Summit College) at the University of Akron, Ohio. He also served as the vice-president for faculty and instruction at Harrisburg Area Community College in Pennsylvania.

Glossary

Armed Forces Ruling Council (AFRC): The military junta that overthrew the political administration in Ghana in 1979. The junta was led by Flight Lieutenant Jerry Rawlings. It ruled for a short period and handed over power to the civilian administration after conducting what it termed a house-cleaning exercise.

Aliens Compliance Order: An act promulgated in November 1969 that required foreign nationals in Ghana to either obtain residential and working permits or face deportation. The period subsequent to the passage of the law saw many foreign nationals leaving the country.

Akans: People who speak the Akan (Twi) language. The Akans are the largest ethnic group in Ghana. Thus, a significant number of Ghanaians speak or understand the Akan language.

Economic and political saboteurs: A term used to describe people whose actions were thought to have brought about economic stagnation and political instability in

Ghana during the military regimes in that country. These people experienced a lot of persecutions and had to run away from the country.

Ethnic associations: Nonprofit social- or ethnic-based organizations formed by the Ghanaian immigrant community (e.g., Duayaw-Nkwanta Citizen Unions of the United States and Canada). These ethnic groupings maintain their respective ethnic cultural identity.

Ghanaian diaspora: The Ghanaian community residing outside Ghana. The majority of the Ghanaian diaspora can be found in Europe and recently North America, especially Canada and the United States. Recently there has been considerable number of Ghanaians living in Asia and the pacific regions. The Ghanaian diaspora still maintain strong ties to their home country.

Inland kingdoms: The traditional ethnic states of the precolonial era. Notable among these kingdoms were the Ashanti, the Bono, the Gonja, and the Akims. These kingdoms still exist and function alongside the modern constitutional system.

Provisional National Defense Council (PNDC): A revolutionary group led by Flight Lieutenant Jerry Rawlings, who overthrew the civilian administration in 1981. It ruled Ghana until 1992, when Ghana returned to civilian administration.

State-owned enterprises (SOEs): These are businesses owned and run by the Ghanaian government. Most of these enterprises were established after political independence. In the early years of the 1980s, most of these government-owned businesses were considered inefficient due to large size of employees, corruption, and political interference.

References

Adepoju, A. 2000. "Issues and Recent Trends in International Migration in sub-Saharan Africa." *International Social Science Journal* 52: 383–94.

Agyemang, Atta-Poku. 1996. "Asanteman Immigrant Ethnic Association: An Effective Tool for Immigrant Survival and Adjustment Problem Solution in New York City." *Journal of Black Studies* 27: 56–76.

Akurang-Parry, Kwabena O. 2002. "Passionate Voices of Those Left Behind: Conversations with Ghanaian Professionals on the Brain Drain and Its Net Gains." *African Issues* 30 (1): 57–61.

Amankwaa, Benjamin. 2004. "Small Businesses of Immigrants: The Ghanaian Experience in Columbus, Ohio." Master's thesis, Miami University, Oxford, Ohio.

Amin, Samir. 1974. *Modern Migrations in West Africa.* London: Oxford University Press.

Anarfi, J., and S. Kwankye, with O-M. Ababio, and R. Tiemoko. 2003. "Migration from and to Ghana: A Background Paper." Development Research Centre on Migration, Globalisation and Poverty, Working Paper #4: Sussex.

Apraku, Kofi. 1991. *African Émigrés in the United States.* New York: Praeger.

Arango, Joaquin. 2000. "Explaining Migration: A Critical View." *International Social Science Journal* 52: 284–96.

Arthur, John A. 2000. *Invisible Sojourners: African Immigrant Diasporas in the United States.* Westport, CT: Greenwood/Praeger.

Arthur, John A. 2008. *The African Diaspora in the United States and Europe: The Ghanaian Experience.* London: Ashgate.

Arthur, John A. 2009. "Immigrants and the American Justice System: Perspectives of African and Caribbean Blacks." In *The New African Diaspora*, edited by Isidore Okpewho and Nkiru Nzegwu, 215–35. Bloomington: Indiana University Press.

Awuah, E. 1997. "Mobilizing For Change: A Case Study of Market Trader Activism in Ghana." *Canadian Journal of African Studies* 31: 401–23.

Bouvier, Leon, and R. Gardner. 1986. "Immigration to the U. S: The Unfinished Story." Washington, D.C.: Population Reference Bureau. *Population Bulletin* 41(4).

Bryce-LaPorte, Roy. 1977. " Visibility of the New Immigrants." *Society* 14: 18–33.

Bryce-LaPorte, Roy. 1993. "Voluntary Immigration and Continuing Encounters between Blacks: The Post-Quincentenary Challenge." *The ANNALS of the American Academy of Political and Social Science* 530: 28–40.

Brydon, Lynne. 1985. "Ghanaian Responses to the Nigerian Expulsions of 1983." *African Affairs* 84: 561–85.

Bump, Micah. 2006. "Ghana: Searching for Opportunities at Home and Abroad." Washington, D.C.: Institute for the Study of International Migration, Georgetown University. [Online information retrieved 09/09.] http://www.migrationinformation.org/USfocus/display.cfm?ID=381.

Cadge, Wendy and Ecklund, Elaine. 2007. "Immigration and Religion." *Annual Review of Sociology* 33: 359–79.

Carrington, W. J., and Enrica Detragiache. 1999. "How Extensive Is the Brain Drain?" *Finance and Development* 36: 46–49.

Dean, Glenn, and John Logan. 2003. *Black Diversity in Metropolitan America.* Lewis Mumford Center for Comparative Urban and Regional Research. Albany, NY: University at Albany.

Dixon, D. 2006. "Characteristics of the African Born in the United States." Migration Information Source. [Online information retrieved 06/11.] http://www.migrationinformation.org.

Dodoo, F. Nii-Amoo, and Baffour K. Takyi. 2002. "Race and Earnings: Magnitude of Difference among American Africans." *Ethnic and Racial Studies* 25: 913–41.

Dodoo, F. Nii-Amoo, Baffour K. Takyi, and Jesse R. Mann. 2006. "On the Brain Drain of Africans to America: Some Methodological Observations." *Perspectives on Global Development and Technology* 5: 155–62.

Donkor, Martha. 2005. "Marching to the Tune: Colonization, Globalization, Immigration, and the Ghanaian Diaspora." *Africa Today* 52(1): 27–44.

Eissa, Salih O. 2005. *Diversity Transformation: African Americans and African Immigration to the United States.* Washington, D.C.: Immigration Policy Center Publication.

Ghanaweb. 2005. "Ghana second in brain drain." *General News of Sunday.* October 30. [Online information retrieved 06/11.] www.ghanaweb.com.

Gordon, April. 1998. "The New Diaspora: African Immigration to the United States." *Journal of Third World Studies* 15: 79–103.

International Organization for Migration. 2009. *Migration in Ghana: A Country Profile.* International Organization for Migration: Geneva, Switzerland.

Kaba, Amadu J. 2007. "The Two West Africas: The Two Historical Phases of the West African Brain Drain." *Journal of Pan African Studies* 1(8): 77–92.

Kent, Mary Mederios. 2007. "Immigration and America's Black Population." *Population Bulletin* 62(4): 1–18.

Killingray, David, ed. 1994. *Africans in Britain.* London: Frank Cass.

Konadu-Agyemang, K., Baffour K. Takyi, and John Arthur, eds. 2006. *The New African Diaspora in North America: Trends, Community Building and Adaptation.* Lanham, MD: Lexington Books.

Lobo, Peter A. 2006. "Unintended Consequences: Liberalized U.S. Immigration Law and the Brain Drain." In *The New African Diaspora in North America*, edited by Kwadwo Konadu-Agyemang, Baffour K. Takyi, and John Arthur, 189–208. New York: Lexington Books.

Logan, I. 1990. "The Brain Drain of Professionals to the United States." *International Migration Review* 30: 289–312.

Logan, John. 2007. "Who Are the Other African Americans? Contemporary African and Caribbean Immigrants in the United States" In *The Other African Americans: Contemporary African and Caribbean Immigrants in the United States,* edited by Yoku Shaw-Taylor and Steven Tuch, 49–53. Boulder, CO: Rowman and Littlefield.

Manuh, Takyiwaa. 1998. "Diaspora, Unities, and the Marketplace: Tracing Changes in Ghanaian Fashion." *Journal of African Studies* 16: 13–19.

Massey, Douglas S. 1995. "The New Immigration and Ethnicity in the United States." *Population and Development Review* 21(3): 631–52.

Massey, Douglas S. 1999. "Why Does Immigration Occur? A Theoretical Synthesis." In *The Handbook of International Migration: The American Experience*, edited by Charles Hirschman, Philip Kasinitz, and Josh DeWind, 34–52. New York: Russell Sage Foundation.

Massey, Douglas S., Margarita Mooney, Kimberly C. Torres, and Camille Z. Charles. 2007. "Black Immigrants and Black Natives Attending Selective Colleges and Universities in the United States." *American Journal of Education* 113: 243–71.

Model, S., and D. Ladipo. 1997. "An Occupational Tale of Two Cities: Minorities in London and New York." *Demography* 34: 539–50.

Mullan, Fitzhugh. 2007. "Doctors and Soccer Players—African Professionals on the Move." *New England Journal of Medicine* 356(5): 440–43.

Nieswand, Boris. 2005. "Development and Diasporas: Ghana and Its Migrants." *Sociologus* 59: 17–32.

Oheneba-Sakyi, Yaw, and Baffour K. Takyi, eds. 2006. *African Families at the Turn of the 21st Century.* Westport, CT: Praeger/Greenwood.

Orozco, Manuel. 2005. *Diasporas, Development and Transnational Integration: Ghanaians in the U.S., U.K., and Germany.* Washington, D.C.: Institute for the Study of International Migration and Inter-American Dialogue.

Owusu, Thomas. 1998. "To Buy or Not to Buy Determinants of Home Ownership among Ghanaian Immigrants in Toronto." *Canadian Geographer* 42(1): 40–52.

Owusu, Thomas. 2003. "Transnationalism among African Immigrants in North America: The Case of Ghanaians in Canada." *Journal of International Migration and Integration* 4: 395–413.

Ozden, Caglar, and Maurice Schiff, eds. 2006. *International Migration, Remittances and the Brain Drain.* Washington, D.C.: The International Bank for Reconstruction and Development/World Bank.

Pedraza, Silvia. 2000. "Beyond Black and White." *Social Science History* 24: 697–726.

Peil, Margaret. 1995. "Ghanaians Abroad." *African Affairs* 94: 345–67.

Roberts, Sam. 2005. "More Africans Enter U.S. than in Days of Slavery." *New York Times.* February 21: A1.

Rumbaut, R. 1994. "Origins and Destinies: Immigration to the U.S. since World War II." *Sociological Forum* 9(4): 583–22.

Saravia, Nancy G., and Juan Francisco Miranda. 2004 "Plumbing the Brain Drain." *Bulletin of the World Health Organization* 82: 608–15.

Takougang, J. 1995. "Recent African Immigrants to the U.S.: A Historical Perspective." *Western Journal of Black Studies* 19(1): 50–57.

Takyi, Baffour K. 2000. "The African Diaspora: A Socio-Demographic Portrait of the Ghanaian Migrant Community in America." *Ghana Studies Journal* 2: 35–56.

Takyi, Baffour K. 2002. "The Making of the Second Diaspora: Emigration from Africa to the United States and Its Policy Implications." *Western Journal of Black Studies* 26: 32–43.

Takyi, Baffour K. 2009. *Africans Abroad: Comparative Perspectives on America's Postcolonial West Africans.* In *The New African Diaspora,* edited by Isidore Okpewho and Nkiru Nzegwu, 236–54. Bloomington: Indiana University Press.

Takyi, Baffour K., and Kwame Safo Boate. 2006. "Location and Settlement Patterns of African Immigrants in the United States: Demographic and Spatial Context." In *The New African Diaspora in North America,* edited by Kwadwo Konadu-Agyemang, Baffour K. Takyi and John Arthur, 50–67. Lanham, MD: Lexington.

Takyi, Baffour K., and Francis N. A. Dodoo. 2005. "Gender, Lineage, and Fertility-Related Outcomes in Ghana." *Journal of Marriage and Family* 67: 251–57.

Taylor, Linnet. 2009. *Return Migrants in Ghana.* Southampton, UK: Institute for Public Policy Research.

Ter Haar, G. 1998. *Halfway to Paradise: African Christians in Europe.* Cardiff, Wales: Cardiff Academic Press.

Terrazas, Aaron. 2009. *African Immigrants in the United States.* Washington, D.C.: Migration Policy Institute.

U.S. Census Bureau. 2000. Census 2000 Special Tabulations (STP-159) Table FBP-1 to 3. Profile of Selected Demographic and Social Characteristics: 2000—Ghana.

U.S. Census Bureau. 2007. American Community Survey 2007, Public Use Microdata, Washington, D.C.

U.S. Department of Homeland Security. 2010. Office of Immigration Statistics (Table 3).

Waters, Mary. 1994. "Ethnic and Racial Identities of 2nd-Generation Black Immigrants in New York City." *International Migration Review* 28(4): 795–820.

Waters, Mary. 1999. *Black Identities: West Indian Immigrant Dreams and American Realities.* Cambridge, MA: Harvard University Press.

Woldemikael, Tekle. 1996. Ethiopians and Eritreans. In *Refugees in America in the 1990s*, edited by David W. Haines, 147–69. Westport, CT: Greenwood Press.

Yeboah, Ian E. A. 2008. *Black African Neo-Diaspora: Ghanaian Immigrant Experiences in the Greater Cincinnati, Ohio Area.* Lanham, MD: Lexington Books.

Zachariah, K., and J. Conde. 1981. *Migration in West Africa: Demographic Aspects.* New York: Oxford University Press for the World Bank.

Zeleza, Paul T. 2005. "Rewriting the African Diaspora: Beyond the Black Atlantic." *Affairs* 104: 35–68.

Zeleza, Paul T. 2009. "Diaspora Dialogues: Engagement between Africa and its Diaspora." In *The New African Diaspora,* edited by Isidore Okpewho and Nkiru Nzegwu, 31–58. Bloomington: Indiana University Press.

Further Reading

Kent, Mary Mederios. 2007. "Immigration and America's Black Population." *Population Bulletin* 62: 1–17.

In this bulletin, the author who is senior demographic and editor of the *Population Bulletin* series analyzes current data to provide a portrait of immigrants from predominantly black countries in the United States. The author argues that recent immigrants from Africa and the Caribbean are a growing component of the U.S. population and are helping to transform racial and ethnic identities in the United States. Even though these immigrants are far outnumbered by nonblack Hispanic and Asian immigrants, Mary Kent argues that the number of black immigrants is growing at a remarkable rate. She notes that more than one-fourth of the black population in New York, Boston, and Miami is foreign born. Overall, this issue of the *Population Bulletin* looks at black immigrants to the United States—what countries they are coming from, which states and metro areas they are living in, and what factors have affected their entry into the United States.

Konadu-Agyemang, K., Baffour K. Takyi, and John Arthur, eds. 2006. *The New African Diaspora in North America: Trends, Community Building and Adaptation.* Lanham, MD: Lexington Books.

The authors of this edited volume have written extensively about recent African immigrants in America. Most of the contributors to this volume are social scientists from Africa who now work either in the United States or Canada. After an overview and a discussion of the theoretical debates about the causes of international migration as relates to Africans, the various chapters shed some light on the factors behind the increasing wave in African immigration to the United States and Canada; the socioeconomic characteristics of African immigrants; and their spatial distribution, obstacles, and adjustments patterns.

Okpewho, Isidore, and Nkiru Nzegwu, eds. 2009. *The New African Diaspora.* Bloomington: Indiana University Press.

This edited volume looks at the contemporary African immigrant in America. The book is the result of a symposium held at the Department of African Studies at Binghamton University in 2006 that dealt with the voluntary relocations or migrations of postcolonial Africans. The contributors, most of whom are African immigrants themselves, bring their own knowledge and firsthand experiences to discuss the new African diaspora.

Ter Haar, G. 1998. *Halfway to Paradise: African Christians in Europe.* Cardiff, Wales: Cardiff Academic Press.

For a variety of reasons, many Africans have left the continent to pursue their dreams outside Africa. The increased emigration has come at a time of an expanding Christianity in Africa. This book by Professor Gerrie Ter Haar, who has written extensively about religion in Ghana and Africa as a whole, looks at the growth of African Christian communities on the European continent (as a result of international migration). Her focus is on the large and growing Ghanaian immigrant community in the Netherlands, where several African-led churches, mostly founded by Ghanaians, have sprung up, particularly in the main cities. After providing a brief history of African migration to Europe, the book examines some of the African-led churches in the Netherlands, using data gathered in Ghana in 1994, and in the Netherlands since mid-1992. The book also examines the relationship that exist between the Dutch and African churches, pointing out that there is a general reluctance in both churches and other theological circles to enter into meaningful contact with African Christians and vice versa.

Yeboah, Ian E. A. 2008. *Black African Neo-Diaspora: Ghanaian Immigrant Experiences in the Greater Cincinnati, Ohio Area.* Lanham, MD: Lexington Books.

This book is an intensive study of the experiences of one specific African immigrant group, Ghanaians living in Cincinnati, Ohio. Yeboah looks at how Ghanaians in Cincinnati are renegotiating the nexus of Ghanaian and American cultures. He presents issues of migration trajectory, associational life, gender renegotiation, business experiences, and second-generation socialization.

Guatemalan Immigrants

by Timothy Steigenga and Sandra Lazo de la Vega

Introduction

Poverty is a fact of life for the majority of Guatemalans. The U.N. reports that 43 percent of children in Guatemala under the age of five suffer from chronic malnutrition. According to the 2009 Human Development Report, per capita GDP in Guatemala is $4,562, or approximately one-tenth of the $45,592 per capita GDP in the United States (United Nations Human Development Programme 2009). This figure is also less than one-third of the average annual per capita income reported for Guatemalans living in the United States (American Community Survey [ACS] 2008). Furthermore, Guatemala has a large and historically marginalized indigenous population. In Guatemala opportunities for upward social mobility for indigenous people are few. Given this scenario, it is not surprising that Guatemala ranks third in the list of countries sending undocumented migrants to the United States. Nearly 1 in 10 Guatemalans lives in the United States today.

Despite the relatively high numbers, elusiveness is one of the primary defining characteristics of the Guatemalan community in the United States. Because many Guatemalan migrants work in informal or migratory labor settings, live in neighborhoods that generally are intermixed with other Central American and Mexican immigrants, and are reported under different ethnic and geographic categories in various surveys, generating specific numbers on Guatemalan migration to the United States is far from a precise science. Despite these limitations, this chapter provides a general overview of the best available data on the history, profile, challenges, and accomplishments of Guatemalans living in the United States.

Chronology

1821	Independence from Spain: Central American countries (including Guatemala) declare independence from Spain and form the United Provinces of Central America.
1838	The United Provinces of Central America break up into different countries due to a civil war.

GUATEMALA

·Paxban

·Tikal

Flores ·

·Poptun

San Luis ·

·Rubelsanto

·Kaibil Balam   Modesto Mendez·   ·Livingston·
·Barillas   Francisco Vela·   ·Puerto Barrios
                                              Cahabon Santo Tomas de Castilla·
Guatemala   El Estor·
·Chajul   Coban·
Huehuetenango·   ·Morales
                    ·Sacapulas   ·Tactic
Ixchiguan   ·Los Amates
              Rabinal · ·Salama   Gualan·
San Marcos ·   ·Santa Cruz del Quiche   Zacapa·
              ·Totonicapan   ·El Progreso ·Chiquimula
Quezltenango· Solola ·
Coatepeque·   Chimaltenango·   Jalapa
Ocos· Retalhuleu· Mazatenango   Antigua ·Guatemala City
Champerico·   ·Concepcion las Minas
                                          ·Los Delores
Tulate·   Siquinala· ·Escuintla Cuilapa· ·Jutiapa
El Semillero Barra Nahualate   ·Chiquimulilla
                          ·San Jose
                    Las Lisas·

N

1870	Coffee becomes Guatemala's biggest export. During the Liberal Era that followed independence, exports of raw goods were a motor for development. In Guatemala export-production agriculture was focused on coffee, which continues to be the case until today.
1944	Jorge Ubico, dictator since 1931, is ousted by a coup d'état ushering in Guatemala's "ten years of spring."
1954	Jacobo Arbenz is ousted by a coup d'état backed by the CIA and the United Fruit Company.
1960	Civil war begins in Guatemala: Large portions of the population, especially the Maya, were displaced by the military. Over 40,000 Guatemalans fled their country during a war in which an estimated 200,000 were killed.
1976	Thousands die in a major earthquake that does great damage to the country's infrastructure. Migration out of Guatemala spikes following this earthquake.
1982–1983	Evangelical military general Efrain Rios Montt becomes president following a military coup, ushering in one of the bloodiest periods of the war.
1991	The American Baptist Churches (ABC) Settlement Agreement is reached, following a lawsuit filed against the Immigration and Naturalization Service (INS) claiming discrimination against Guatemalan and Salvadoran refugees and asylum seekers. Guatemalans who had been present in the United States prior to 1990 become eligible to have their asylum claims revisited.
1996	Peace accords are signed, officially ending the civil war.
1997	The Nicaraguan Adjustment and Central American Relief Act (NACARA) passed in the United States, allowing Guatemalans protected under the ABC Settlement to apply for legal permanent resident status in the United States.
1998	Hurricane Mitch hits Guatemala. The Recovery of Historical Memory (REMHI) report is released with statements from thousands of victims of repression during the civil war placing the blame for the vast majority of the violations on the government and the army. Bishop Juan José Gerardi is murdered two days after announcing the results of the report.

2001	The coffee crisis hits Guatemala: the prices for coffee, Guatemala's main export, drop to their lowest level in decades (below the cost of production).
2005	Hurricane Stan hits Guatemala.
2006	The Central American Free Trade Agreement (CAFTA) enters into effect in Guatemala.
2008	Nearly 300 Guatemalan immigrants are arrested in the largest immigration raid in U.S. history in a kosher meatpacking plant in Postville, Iowa. Families are abruptly separated, and those arrested are processed and deported within days of the raid. Controversy about the way in which the authorities handled the situation is cited as one of the reasons the Obama administration subsequently moved away from workplace immigration enforcement strategies.
2010	In December the number of Guatemalans deported from the United States reaches a new record of more than 28,051 during 2010.

Background

Geography of Guatemala

Guatemala's national territory spans a little over 40,000 square miles in Central America. It shares an extensive border with Mexico to the northwest, and smaller borders with Belize to the northeast and with Honduras and El Salvador to the south. Guatemala has a relatively small Caribbean coast and a much larger Pacific coast region. Approximately one-third of Guatemala is mountainous. The Cuchumatan mountain range in the western region of the country is the most rugged portion of the Guatemalan territory and is home to a majority of Guatemala's indigenous people (Handy 1984, 16). The ruggedness of the Cuchumatan mountains allows for a type of geographic isolation between villages or *municipios* within the Western Highlands. Due in part to this isolation, there are 22 different Mayan languages spoken today (Montejo 1999, 3).

The Pacific coast is also an important geographical feature of Guatemala's history of migration. Historically, peasants from the highlands migrated to the coast to work on seasonal crops of coffee, sugarcane, and corn (Handy 1984, 17). During the colonial period, indigenous people were forced to migrate with the crops, but after the colonial period, the system of seasonal migration to the coast became a standard survival strategy for highland farmers facing a shortage of land and poor crops (Piedrasanta 2007, 95–96).

Unlike the other regions of Guatemala, the lowlands of El Petén are not primarily agricultural. Rather, these lowlands are a tropical rainforest. Historically, this region has produced certain types of wood and rubber, and there has also been some limited production of oil (Handy 1984, 17). This area of the country is also the least densely populated area. In the past, the Petén region has been a destination for internal migrants in Guatemala. People came to the region following the different boom cycles (rubber, wood, etc.) and to work in construction.

Guatemala's geography has played an important role in its development and migratory history because the country is exposed and particularly vulnerable to multiple forms of natural disasters. Within Guatemala's mountains there are over 30 volcanoes, 4 of which are currently active. Guatemala's territory, which is divided between three plate tectonics, makes it prone to frequent tremors and earthquakes (Instituto Nacional de Sismología 2010). A spike in migration followed the particularly devastating earthquake that struck close to the capital city in 1976, killing thousands and destroying much of the country's infrastructure. Guatemala's location in the Caribbean also makes it vulnerable to hurricanes, frequent flooding, and landslides. Hurricane Mitch in 1998 and Hurricane Stan in 2005 caused massive flooding, landslides, thousands of deaths, and millions of dollars worth of damages (Reynoso, Castellanos, and Orantes 2005).

History of Guatemala

Prior to the arrival of the Spanish, the present-day Guatemalan territory was dominated by the Maya empire. The Maya were accomplished mathematicians, astronomers, and architects. The Maya empire, however, was already in decline when the Spanish arrived. The Spanish encountered internal conflict between different ethnic and linguistic groups in Guatemala. They took advantage of these divisions and made strategic alliances with different groups to carry out the conquest. Robert Trudeau (2000, 497) explains that the Spanish attacked the Maya three ways: with war, with disease, and with cultural disruption. The Spanish were able to conquer Guatemala and remained in power for over three hundred years.

In 1821, the Central American States declared their independence from the Spanish crown and formed the Federation of Central American States. This union was short-lived, as the modern Central American states broke away from the federation soon after its formation. The postcolonial period was a struggle of power between the conservatives and the liberals. Political power shifted from one side to the other, but the indigenous remained marginalized, subject to abuse and debt peonage long after the colonial period.

Guatemala was dominated by a series of military rulers for years. In 1931, General Jorge Ubico was elected president. Ubico came from a wealthy family, and his rise through the ranks of the military was accompanied by praise from representatives of the United States in Guatemala. As president, Ubico signed an agreement with the United States that allowed coffee and bananas to enter the United States duty-free. The main benefactor of this agreement was the United Fruit Company (Handy 1984, 94). By this time, the United Fruit Company had an overpowering presence in Guatemala, controlling the majority of agricultural land and the railroad systems, among other key assets.

Over time Ubico began to lose public support both within the country and from the United States. Facing violent protests of students, professionals, and young military officers in 1944, Ubico resigned and fled Guatemala (Handy 1984, 103). The decade that followed Ubico's overthrow is often referred to as the "ten years of spring" because Guatemala witnessed greater political freedoms and progress in the areas of labor rights and land reform.

In 1945, civilian Juan José Arévalo was elected to the presidency of Guatemala. Arévalo and his successor, Jacobo Arbenz, put several progressive measures into effect. These actions provoked strong criticism from the traditional elites. Arbenz's plan for agrarian reform also encountered strong opposition from the United Fruit Company, backed by the United States, which understood the land reform as a threat to private ownership within the context of the Cold War. In 1954 after a decade of reform, a coup d'état (in which the CIA was a major actor) overthrew the Arbenz government (Schleisinger and Kinzer 1982). The events surrounding the 1954 coup created an environment that contributed to the Guatemalan civil war and initiated a series of military governments that would last into the 1980s.

The civil war began in the early 1960s and officially ended with the signing of the 1996 peace accords. The primary conflict of the civil war was between a group of leftist guerrilla movements who eventually joined to form the Guatemalan National Revolutionary Unit (URNG) and the right-wing militarized state. A series of military leaders dominated Guatemalan politics, crushing any form of opposition from the political left. Paramilitary squads were used throughout this period to terrorize political opponents. Efraín Rios Montt was president during one of the deadliest periods of the war (1982–1983). A born-again evangelical Christian and retired officer from the Guatemalan army, Rios Montt launched a counterinsurgency campaign to suppress support for the URNG in the rural areas of Guatemala. As part of this campaign, entire villages were destroyed and tens of thousands of people, especially the rural Maya, were killed or disappeared (Montejo 1999). As Maya anthropologist Victor Montejo recalls: "the army's intent was to kill all suspected guerillas, and all Mayas were suspect" (52). The army created "model villages" that were modeled after strategic hamlets used by the United States in the Vietnam War. Tens of thousands of displaced Maya were forced to leave Guatemala as refugees. The persecution and displacement of the Maya during the civil war played a major role in the chain of migration to the United States.

Though civilian control of the executive returned with the election of Christian Democrat Vinicio Cerezo in 1986, the military remains a very strong presence in Guatemala. The 1996 peace accords officially ended the internal conflict and the URNG laid down its arms and became a political party. However, concerns about the impunity of former military leaders, growing violence, and the overall stability of the democratic process in Guatemala remain. In 1998, shortly after announcing the findings of a major inquiry that found the military to be responsible for most of the human rights violations that occurred during the war, Bishop Juan José Gerardi was bludgeoned to death in the garage of his home. Three military officers and a priest were eventually convicted for the crime in 2001.

Today, Guatemala continues to struggle to remain stable. As of March 2010, Alfonso Portillo, who was president from 2000 to 2004, was awaiting trial on charges of embezzlement and money laundering (Malkin 2010). Álvaro Colom (who became president on January of 2008) faced a short-lived political crisis in May of 2009, when, after the assassination of Rodrigo Rosenberg, a prominent Guatemalan lawyer, a video surfaced in which Rosenberg stated that he believed that he was going to be assassinated by orders of Colom and his associates.

Causes and Waves of Migration

Early Immigration

Until the late 1970s, migration from Guatemala was minimal and characterized primarily by upper- and middle-class Ladinos (Hong 2000, 767). However, following the 1976 earthquake and the subsequent forced displacement of hundreds of thousands of indigenous peoples in the civil war, immigration expanded rapidly, and Guatemala became the second-largest immigrant sending country in Central America (ACS 2008). The International Organization for Migration (IOM) reports that following the earthquake, migration to the United States increased steadily in the following decades so that by 1990 the number of Guatemalans in the United States was five times greater than in 1980 (IOM 2003, 2). One major cause of the increase in migration was the internal conflict in Guatemala. The indigenous population was routinely targeted and persecuted as the military destroyed or relocated entire indigenous villages in the 1980s. Looking for safety, Guatemalan refugees fled to Mexico, the United States, and Canada throughout the conflict.

Immigrant Culture/Early Issues of Assimilation and Separatism

The initial flow of post-1980 Guatemalan migrants was made up of primarily Mayan war refugees. For the most part, these migrants gravitated to cities and agricultural areas that already had established Latino communities. Los Angeles,

Houston, Chicago, New York, Washington, D.C., and some rural communities such as Indiantown and Immokalee in South Florida were early areas of settlement for Guatemalan immigrants. These early Mayan immigrants faced a host of daunting obstacles to the process of assimilation and acceptance. Because Spanish was not the first language of many of these individuals (and many did not speak or understand Spanish at all), early interactions with political and legal authorities, aid organizations, and even other Hispanic groups were strained and characterized by sometimes tragic misunderstandings. Allan Burns (2000, 166) recounts the story of a young Mayan mother in Indiantown, Florida, who was picked up by police and questioned while traveling to a clinic for treatment for postpartum depression. Unable to understand her, authorities placed her under psychiatric care claiming that she was "speaking in tongues" and held her for two weeks until she was located by someone from Indiantown. Such experiences were not uncommon for early Mayan migrants.

Language issues were further complicated by fear and mistrust of political and legal authorities among early Mayan immigrants. After experiencing severe political violence at the hands of both Guatemalan and Mexican security forces (according to Eisenman et al. 2003, a full 7% of the Guatemalan migrants they studied in Los Angeles were victims of torture), many immigrants sought to avoid any interactions that would bring them in contact with law enforcement or any political authorities. Crimes against Guatemalans frequently went unreported, and when Mayan immigrants did come into contact with immigration or other law enforcement representatives, fear and communication issues frequently led to incarceration or even deportation.

Language and cultural issues also impacted Mayan relations with other Hispanic groups. Mayan immigrants are frequently stereotyped as backward or unsophisticated by other Latinos. In some cases, other Latinos in positions as labor contractors, public notaries, or other intermediary roles actively exploited the new Mayan immigrants. Without their own established networks of support and immersed in communities with large Latino populations, Guatemalan migrants were both extremely vulnerable and largely invisible during the early stages of Guatemalan migration.

Later Waves of Immigration

There were three important pieces of legislation that impacted Guatemalan immigration in the 1980s and early 1990s: the Immigration Reform and Control Act (IRCA), the American Baptist Churches settlement (ABC), and the Nicaraguan Adjustment and Central American Relief Act (NACARA). In 1986, the IRCA made it illegal to knowingly recruit or hire immigrants who were not authorized to work in the United States, but it also allowed undocumented immigrants who were in the country before January 1, 1982 (as well as some agricultural workers who came to the United States after that date) to apply to adjust their status. The IRCA benefited over 59,000 Guatemalans (Smith 2006).

The second important piece of legislation is the ABC settlement. Post-1976 immigration was initially driven by the internal conflict. Unfortunately the cases of many Guatemalans seeking asylum in the United States were routinely dismissed without proper consideration by the INS. This situation ultimately led the American Baptist Churches (ABC) to file suit against the INS, charging that asylum status was being denied to Guatemalans (and other Central Americans) because the United States did not openly oppose the strongly anticommunist governments in the region at the time (Gzesh 2006). In 1991 the ABC case was settled, and the INS agreed to revisit the cases of thousands of Guatemalans whose asylum claims had been denied. In 1997 the NACARA was signed into law, further addressing the cases of Guatemalans and other Central American refugees. According to section 203 of NACARA, Guatemalans who had registered for benefits from the ABC settlement prior to 1991 or had entered the United States before 1990 were allowed certain immigration benefits, including the right to apply for permanent resident status (U.S. Citizenship and Immigration Services [USCIS] 2009).

Though migration from Guatemala was relatively high during the years of the civil war, it actually grew much more in the years after the peace accords (Smith 2006). In 2000 and 2001 the price of Guatemala's main export, coffee, dropped dramatically to its lowest point in decades. The price of coffee fell below the cost of production, which caused a grave economic crisis in the already shaken country (Varangis et al. 2003, 3). The postwar Guatemalan migrants have been called "economic refugees." Though the civil war may have ended, the long period of fighting left the country's economy and infrastructure badly damaged and incapable of providing opportunity for its citizens, which, combined with the coffee crisis, created ripe conditions for emigration. The International Organization for Migration (IOM) reports that in 2009, 91 percent of Guatemalan emigrants left because they were either looking for work or for better pay, while less than one percent were traveling to escape violence (IOM 2009, 65).

Demographic Profile

Size and Composition of Community

According to the U.S. Census Bureau's 2008 American Community Survey (ACS), there were 985,601 Guatemalans living in the United States in 2008 (ACS 2008). This figure likely undercounts the actual number of Guatemalans living in the United States for several reasons. First, many Guatemalans currently living in the United States are unlikely to respond, or even to be reached by formal surveys.

Many do not have regular status and consciously avoid polls or other forms of contact with the government. Also, the wording on surveys is unlikely to capture all people of Guatemalan origin given that many of them are Mayan, and they may not identify themselves as "Hispanic/Latino" or "Guatemalan." Many Mayan immigrants identify themselves by their specific Mayan ethnic identity (Kanjobal, Quiche, Jacaltec, etc.) or as "indigenous" (Palma, Girón, and Steigenga 2009).

The IOM reports different figures than the ACS. According to the IOM, there were 1,324,474 Guatemalans living in the United States in 2009. Unfortunately, because the IOM bases its count on surveys conducted with the family members of immigrants in Guatemala, these figures are also not completely reliable, but they are probably closer to the actual number than surveys carried out in the United States.

Age and Family Structure

Though migration from Guatemala has been dominated by men, the gender gap has been narrowing recently. The 2008 ACS reported that approximately 57 percent of the Guatemalan population in the United States was male and 43 percent was female. The IOM (2009, 27) reports similar numbers regarding the gender of Guatemalan migrants to the United States but also found that of Guatemalans who express the intention to migrate, 53 percent were women and 47 percent were men (IOM 2009, 53). Though these figures only represent intent to migrate, they point to a potential change in future trends. Finding work remains the most important reason for migrating, but more women may be traveling to reunite with their husbands, as family reunification is becoming one of the important motors driving Guatemalan migration (Palma, Girón, and Steigenga 2009).

Another defining characteristic of Guatemalan migration to the United States is that almost all the migrants are young. The ACS reports that the median age of the Guatemalan community in the United States is 28.1 years (ACS 2008), considerably younger than the 36.9 years of the general U.S. population. The IOM reports that 80.5 percent of Guatemalans who migrate are between 15 and 34 years of age (IOM 2009).

According to the ACS data (2008), about half (44.5%) of Guatemalans over the age of 15 living in the United States are married. It is possible that this figure undercounts the large number of transnational marriages. The IOM reports that 44.8 percent of Guatemalan migrants are married and that 20.8 percent have partners but are not yet married (IOM 2009, 65). Furthermore, the IOM reports that 47.6 percent of migrant households faced a rupture in family structure due to migration (58). For migrant families, being separated creates a great deal of stress and anxiety for both the migrants and their family members in the communities of origin. Family disintegration is one of the biggest concerns for migrants and the organizations that work with them both in Guatemala and the United States (Palma, Girón, and Steigenga 2009).

Educational Attainment

According to the 2008 ACS, approximately 54.1 percent of Guatemalans living in the United States have not obtained at least a high school diploma. The IOM (2009) reports that 48.8 percent of Guatemalans who migrated had at least some elementary education (31% had completed elementary school and 17.8% had not), while only 12.3 percent had finished high school and 3 percent had never gone to school at all. Most first-generation Guatemalans who migrate to the United States are focused on working (mostly in manual labor), thus, very little time is left for education. Furthermore, English is a third language for many Guatemalan migrants who speak one of the 22 Maya languages as well as Spanish. Education, however, remains an important part of migration because immigrants often see improved educational opportunities for their children as an important factor influencing their decision to migrate. Nevertheless, Cecilia Menjívar argues that many Guatemalan children, even those born in the United States, find their educational opportunities truncated because of their "liminal legality." In other words, though the legal status of their parents may not be an obstacle for children to complete high school, college may be out of reach because extensive documentation is required in order to obtain financial aid and other educational opportunities (Menjívar 2006, 1022–24).

Economic Attainment

Most Guatemalans who migrate to the United States report that looking for work is the main reason they decided to migrate. Young people migrate in order to work and send money back to their home country to support those they left behind. In 2009, the IOM reported that $4.2 billion in remittances from the United States entered Guatemala, making up over 10 percent of the GDP (9). Unfortunately, Guatemalans tend to find work at the bottom of the U.S. labor market. According to the 2008 ACS, the median per capita income for Guatemalans in the United States was only $14,657. The same survey reported that 21.7 percent of Guatemalans live in poverty in the United States, compared with 13.2 percent of the general U.S. population.

The IOM provides some figures on employment categories for Guatemalans, but these figures include all Guatemalans living outside the country. Based on the fact that 97 percent of the working-age population recorded in the survey lives in the United States, we roughly estimate the general employment categories breakdown for working-age Guatemalans in the United States to be: 35–40 percent as unskilled workers; 30–35 percent in manufacturing, machine operation, or artisanship;

15–20 percent in services and sales; 3 percent in agriculture; 3–5 percent as technicians, clerks, or other mid-level professionals; and a small percentage as professionals and executives (IOM 2009, 63).

These general trends are confirmed by the 2008 ACS data, though the absolute numbers and occupation categories vary slightly. The 2008 ACS reported 31.4 percent of Guatemalan respondents working in the service industry; 20.9 percent in production, transportation and material moving occupations; 21.6 percent in construction and maintenance; 14.7 percent in sales and as office employees; 9.5 percent as executives and professionals; and 1.9 percent in agriculture and fisheries. The higher figures for professionals and lower figures in agriculture are attributable to the respective sample biases in the IOM and 2008 ACS data. Since the IOM data is based on family member interviews in Guatemala, it likely undercounts the numbers of long-term Guatemalan residents working in professional positions. As we noted above, the ACS figures are likely biased in the opposite direction, severely undercounting the undocumented population, and therefore undercounting many Guatemalans who work in agriculture, processing, and other unskilled labor.

The primary defining characteristics of the Guatemalan niche in U.S. labor markets are the difficulty of working conditions, the vulnerability of the workers, the lack of job security, and low wages. The specific industries that heavily utilize the Guatemalan labor pool vary by geographic area but share the general trends of job insecurity and low wages. In the traditional destinations of Los Angeles and New York, the garment and textile industries have long histories of employing Central American immigrants. More recently, Guatemalan workers have taken jobs in the meatpacking and poultry processing industries in Nebraska, Iowa, Georgia, Arkansas, Delaware, Kentucky, Tennessee, and the Carolinas. As with textiles, these jobs offer dangerous working conditions, little access to affordable insurance, and low wages; and are known to actively discourage labor union organizing (Fink 2003).

To summarize, Guatemalans (along with other Central Americans) are primarily inserted at the bottom of what has become an increasingly polarized U.S. labor market. By polarization, we refer to the dual process of increased demand for flexible and low-wage labor along with the simultaneously growing population of aging high-income individuals who generate increasing demand for services and products. Thus, Guatemalans are frequently employed in the informal service sectors of the economy, working temporary jobs as day-laborers, maids, nannies, or other service jobs.

Health Statistics, Issues

Because looking for work is one of the primary motivations for Guatemalans to migrate to the United States, the Guatemalan population tends to be younger and relatively healthy. The 2008 ACS reports that the rate of physical disability within the

Guatemalan population is 4.7 percent, which is much lower than the 12.1 percent for the general U.S. population. At the same time, research suggests that the Guatemalan community is at a higher risk for some health complications. In the United States, many Guatemalan migrants have to cope with issues of family separation, and they often find themselves without a well-established support network to help them cope. Depression among the Guatemalan community may be aggravated by loneliness, lack of success in finding a job, shortages of money to send to relatives back home, and the general hardships of daily life as a migrant worker. Combined with fears of deportation, these stress factors contribute to potential psychological and substance abuse problems in the Guatemalan migrant population.

The general demographic characteristics of the Guatemalan population in the United States (high levels of poverty, low levels of education, etc.) also decrease access to health services (Carrasquillo, Carrasquillo, and Shea 2000). Even when services are available, they may not reach large portions of the Guatemalan community. For example, some studies suggest that though the prevalence of HIV/AIDS may be high within the Guatemalan community, HIV/AIDS education may not be effective unless it is presented in a way that better reflects the cultural framework of the community (Schoorman, Acosta, and Sena 2008).

Adjustment and Adaptation

Family, Culture, and Life-Cycle Rituals

The family is of central importance in Guatemala, and it also plays an important role in migration to the United States. For many migrants who are away from their loved ones, thinking of their families back home serves as both coping mechanism to withstand the hardships of the migrant life and a constant reminder of what has been left behind in their home communities (Palma, Girón, and Steigenga 2009). Not surprisingly, Guatemalan migrants who have the ability to do so seek either to reunite their families in the United States or have plans to return to their communities of origin after working for five or six years in the United States. Today, more Guatemalan women and children are migrating to re-establish families that have been broken apart in the process of migration.

Allan Burns notes that "life crisis events, such as births, baptisms, marriages and funerals are times when activities that are familiar parts of life in Guatemala can be adapted to life in the United States" (1993, 45). Baptism is one of the most important life-cycle rituals among Guatemalan migrants, not only because of its religious significance, but also because it strengthens bonds in a new community. Trying to recreate a sense of community, parents and couples who want to get married may ask their new friends in the United States to become the godparents of children during baptism or of the couple at a wedding. Burns argues that this bond of *compadrazgo* (godparenthood) is an effective tool to create networks of support for Guatemalan migrants in new places (46).

Another ritual common among Mayan migrants is the repatriation of the dead. Among the Jacaltec Maya population, for example, a collection is generally taken to fund the process of sending the bodies of migrants who die in the United States back to their communities of origin in Guatemala for burial. This process cements bonds and networks not only within the migrant community but also between the migrants and their community of origin (Steigenga, Palma, and Girón 2008).

Families and Changing Gender Relations

The centrality of the family unit in Guatemalan culture endures through the process of migration. Strong nuclear families are the ideal for Guatemalan migrants, but long periods away from family members can generate unrealistic expectations and other problems that may lead to conflict. Familial disintegration is a major area of concern reported by organizations who work in migrant sending communities.

Unfortunately, it is often women who experience the most negative impact of migration both in sending and receiving communities. In receiving communities, Guatemalan men may seek to reassert their dominant role in unacceptable ways. Guatemalan women who migrate to reunite their families are often dependent on

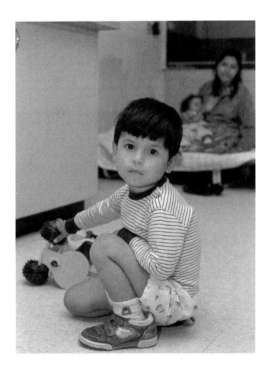

Marco Grijalba plays on the floor of a Red Cross shelter in Brownsville, Texas, as his mother and infant sister sit on a cot in the background, February 24, 1989. (AP Photo/Pat Sullivan)

their husbands (who may have more knowledge of life in the United States) and in some cases become victims of physical and emotional abuse (Palma, Girón, and Steigenga 2009). In communities of origin, women are affected by transnational gossip about their behavior that finds its way back to their husbands in the United States, in some cases causing them to isolate themselves in fear of risking their marriages. This isolation can cause many physical as well as psychological problems (Skolnik, Lazo de la Vega and Steigenga 2012).

Children of Guatemalan immigrants face the challenge of maintaining a balance between the traditional family roles and structure of their home community while simultaneously adapting to the new behavioral norms of the United States. Tensions frequently arise between parents struggling to raise "good children" and adolescents struggling to adapt and grow up in between worlds.

Retaining a Sense of National Culture and Identity

Guatemalans in the United States maintain their connections with their hometowns and cultural identity in a number of ways. Many Guatemalan migrants participate in hometown associations; organizations dedicated to maintaining contacts or projects in communities of origin. While the absolute number of hometown associations is uncertain, Manuel Orozco and Eugenia Garcia-Zanello (2009) note that the Guatemalan Ministry of Foreign Affairs counted 164 such Guatemalan organizations operating around the United States in 2006. Many of these organizations were initially organized as communities of migrants who came together to celebrate fiestas in honor of their town's patron saint. Organizing for the celebration of the fiestas frequently evolves into organizing for other goals in both communities of origin and destination (Palma, Girón, and Steigenga 2009).

As is the case in Guatemala, a large portion of community life for Guatemalan immigrants revolves around organized religion. While the majority of Guatemalan immigrants are Catholic, between 30 percent and 40 percent belong to various evangelical churches, with a majority of those in Pentecostal churches. Mayan Catholics from Guatemala maintain many of their traditional Mayan beliefs and customs within their practice of Catholicism, including the veneration of local saints, participation in dances and other elements of local fiestas (such as the dance of the deer), and other elements of *costumbre*.

Some Guatemalan Mayan groups in the United States have made attempts to maintain indigenous languages in the second generation and to teach younger Guatemalan Americans about their indigenous culture. For example, Ajaw Kab'Awil is a nonprofit organization based in Indiantown, Florida, that helps young people maintain their Mayan cultural identity through dress, dance, music, and language. Ajaw Kab'Awil provides a space where Maya children growing up in the United States can learn and maintain a sense of Mayan identity within the larger context of migration.

National/Regional-Language Press and Other Media

Spanish-language media in the United States is abundant, especially in states with large immigrant populations. Most commonly, Spanish-language media is targeted to the general Hispanic community, and not to people from one particular country. Some attempts, however, have been made by the Guatemalan community in the United States to publish newsletters that speak specifically to them as Guatemalans or as Maya, not just as Hispanic. The Movimiento de Immigrantes Guatemaltecos en los Estados Unidos (MIGUA) is an organization based in Chicago that publishes a monthly newsletter, *Nahual Migrante,* featuring news and articles for and about the Guatemalan immigrant community in the United States. The *Nahual Migrante* also features news from Guatemala, especially news relevant to the migrant community in the United States. The *Nahual Migrante* is available online through MIGUA's blog, which also publishes stories and articles pertaining to the Guatemalan migrant community in the United States. Other important media outlets for the Guatemalan community in the United States include the radio show *Hora Chapina,* which airs on Saturday mornings in several cities in California via KATD 900 AM out of San Francisco; the radio show *Noche De Fiesta Chapina,* which airs on Saturday evenings via La Grande 1010 SF and 990 in Sacramento; and the magazine *Enlace Guatemala,* a monthly publication based in Chicago. Also, *La Prensa Libre,* the most prominent newspaper in Guatemala, continues to be popular with Guatemalans in the United States. *La Prensa Libre* is available online, where people who want to follow the news in Guatemala can access it free of charge.

Celebration of National Holidays

The majority of holidays celebrated in the Guatemalan immigrant community relate to religious and regional celebrations. For Guatemalans of Mayan decent, celebrations of regional patron saints are critical annual events. For example, the Jacaltec community in Jupiter, Florida, celebrates the Virgin of Candelaria festival in February with a mass, a parade of the image of the Virgin of Candelaria, marimba, traditional dance, food, and a soccer game. Preparation for the celebration of the fiesta takes months and includes committees of volunteers to organize all aspects of the fiesta, including the food, flowers, dances, and so forth. The celebration in Jupiter takes place simultaneously with the celebration in Jacaltenango. Other Maya communities throughout the United States celebrate their regional holidays as well. Some Mayan immigrants in Houston, for example, travel to their home town to celebrate the Fiesta de Santiago, honoring their local patron saint (Hagan 1994).

Many of the holidays recognized by the Guatemalan embassy are religious holidays, such as Christmas, *semana santa* (Holy Week), and All Saints' Day. The most important nonreligious holiday is Guatemalan Independence Day on September 15. The same date marks the beginning of Hispanic Heritage Month in the United States, and Guatemalans participate in many pan-Hispanic celebrations on that day as well.

Foodways

Guatemalan cuisine is varied and readily available in the United States, especially in areas with high concentrations of migrants. Beans and corn tortillas are the staples of Guatemalan cuisine and remain popular with Guatemalan migrants. Traditional Guatemalan tortillas are relatively thick, formed by hand, and cooked on a *comal.* They accompany almost every meal. While in Guatemala fresh tortillas are either made at home or readily available at a local bodega, in the United States it is common for immigrants to buy premade tortillas, which are generally thinner than the handmade traditional tortillas.

For special occasions and celebrations *carne asada* and *pepián* may also be available. *Tamales* are also popular for important celebrations, especially Christmas. *Tamales* vary regionally across Guatemala but are typically made with corn dough or *masa* and stuffed with chicken, pork, turkey, or beef. The filling is wrapped in the dough, which is then wrapped in a corn husk and cooked in large pots.

Pollo Campero, Guatemalan Fried Chicken

The large influx of Guatemalan migrants to the United States has not gone unnoticed by the fast food industry. Pollo Campero, the most popular fried chicken chain in Guatemala, has recently expanded to the United States, opening 53 restaurants in 14 states and the District of Columbia (with a 54th restaurant scheduled to open in Walt Disney World in Orlando in late 2010). Not surprisingly, the state with the most Pollo Campero restaurants is California (14), where the majority of the Guatemalan population in the United States still resides. It took Pollo Campero only seven weeks to reach sales of $1 million in its first U.S. restaurant in Los Angeles in 2002 (Frumkin 2002). Undoubtedly these sales were propelled by the large Guatemalan population in the area. Pollo Campero is planning to continue its growth in the United States; some estimate a tenfold projected growth in the coming years (Arndt 2010). Pollo Campero's growth in the U.S. market has the potential to rival long-standing fast food chains such as KFC. Pollo Campero is relatively more expensive than its competitors, but in 2010 it launched its new value menu with the tag line "More Campero for Less Dinero." The tag line speaks to the desire of Pollo Campero to expand its market within the United States beyond its Guatemalan immigrant consumer base.

Music, Arts, and Entertainment

No traditional Guatemalan celebration would be complete without a marimba. Marimbas are large instruments that somewhat resemble xylophones, generally played by groups of three or four people rather than individuals. Marimbas are played at parties, special events, and cultural religious festivals by organizations of Guatemalan migrants all over the United States. Marimba classes and workshops have been used by migrant associations to reconnect young people with their home country (Burns 1993, 63).

While the marimba is very popular, Guatemala's most famous musician is the pop-rock singer Ricardo Arjona. Born near Antigua, Guatemala, Ricardo Arjona has become one of the most popular Spanish-language musicians in the United States and Latin America. Since starting his career in the early 1990s, Arjona has released 14 albums and won two Grammys. In 2005 he collaborated with Intocable (a Texano band) to make the song "Mojado" about the plight of undocumented immigrants who cross the U.S. border. The song became widely popular throughout the Americas.

Another important form of artistic expression in Guatemala is textile design and weaving. In 2008 the Phoebe A. Hearst Museum of Anthropology at the University of California Berkley hosted a year of Guatemalan educational programs. The year-long event started with an exhibit entitled "*Traje de la Vida*: Maya Textiles of Guatemala," showcasing some of the pieces from the museum's permanent collection on Guatemalan textiles along with photographs and videos on the subject.

Migration from Guatemala to the United States was the topic of the critically acclaimed film *El Norte*. Released in 1983, *El Norte* chronicles the journey of two young people (Rosa and Enrique) who escape their village in Guatemala during the civil war and make their way out of Guatemala, through Mexico, and into the United States, where they struggle to achieve the so-called American dream as undocumented migrants. The film contains dialogue in English, Spanish, and Quiche and delivers a realistic representation of the migrant journey. *El Norte* was released in DVD for the first time in 2009.

Integration and Impact on U.S. Society and Culture

Paths toward Citizenship

The paths that Guatemalans may take towards attaining citizenship depend on the context and timing of their migration to the United States. Only a small portion of Guatemalans who live in the United States today arrived as refugees fleeing the 36-year civil war. This group is eligible to file legitimate political asylum claims, which makes it the group of Guatemalans with the highest likelihood of legalizing their immigration status. However, the majority of Guatemalans in the United

States came after the civil war as economic refugees and therefore, very few have a clear path toward citizenship.

For Guatemalans who have become naturalized citizens of the United States, dual citizenship is not allowed by the Guatemalan constitution. The Oath of Allegiance that all naturalized American citizens must take requires that they renounce their allegiance to any other country (U.S. Citizenship and Immigration Service 2010). Decree 86–96 (which amends the citizenship section of the Guatemalan Constitution) explicitly states that Guatemalan persons who have become naturalized citizens of countries that require them to make such an oath automatically lose their Guatemalan citizenship (El Congreso de la Republica de Guatemala 1996). Article 144 of the Guatemalan Constitution grants Guatemalan citizenship to the children of Guatemalans born abroad (El Congreso de la Republica de Guatemala 1985). The Guatemalan state, however, requires that these U.S.-born children choose either Guatemalan or American citizenship upon reaching their 18th birthday (Menjívar 2002, 537).

Intergroup Relations

Guatemalans frequently arrive and settle in locations that are home to many other Central American as well as Mexican migrants. While there are some tensions between national groups and Mexicans often compete with Guatemalans in certain labor markets (such as the orange-picking industry in South Florida), there are also many shared events, spaces, and positive intergroup relations. In many communities around the United States, soccer fields bring these groups together either through formal leagues or in pick-up games. Intermarriage between Mexicans, Guatemalans, and other Central Americans is relatively common.

Group divisions within the Guatemalan community fall primarily along ethnic, class, and political lines. While the majority of business owners, managers, and other elites in the United States are Ladinos, the majority of Guatemalan immigrants come from Guatemala's 22 different Mayan groups. Mayan leaders frequently complain that they are poorly represented by the national organizations that claim to speak for Guatemalan migrants as well as the formal representatives of the Guatemalan state present in the United States. Divisions stemming from Guatemala's civil war also continue to impact group relations as victims of military violence, former guerrillas, and former military and civilian patrol members live in close proximity in many U.S. communities. Particularly in the Mayan communities, immigrants have to negotiate a continuing "minefield" of complex and painful relationships related to roles and events during the war.

Forging a New American Political Identity

Due to the diversity within the population, Guatemalans in the United States do not share a single common political identity or program. While the civil war continued in Guatemala, most Guatemalan immigrant organizations focused their work on assisting new refugees, condemning human right abuses in Guatemala, and opposing U.S. support to the Guatemalan military. Following the signing of the peace agreements in 1996, the Coalition of Guatemalan Immigrants in the United States (CONGUATE) brought various groups together around the issues of immigrant rights and immigration reform. Along with other Guatemalan organizations, CONGUATE lobbied for temporary protective status (TPS) for Guatemalans in the United States following Hurricane Stan. The Movement of Guatemalan Immigrants in the United States (MIGUA) also focuses its agenda on immigration reform and stopping the immigration raids and detentions that have recently led to as many as 25,000 deportations to Guatemala per year.

Return Immigration

The first major wave of return migration to Guatemala took place in the early 1990s through a refugee repatriation supervised by the United Nations High Commission on Human Rights. According to Victor Montejo (1999, 222–37) the process was fraught with complications and hurdles to resettlement for the refugees, many of whom had spent 10 years or more in Mexico or the United States.

Beginning in the mid-1990s the U.S. policy focus on border enforcement combined with increasing numbers of economic refugees from Guatemala created a context in which return migration was delayed for many Guatemalan migrants. While many undocumented Guatemalan migrants come to the United States with the intention of returning once they have made enough money to build a house or start a small business back in their home community, that dream has become increasingly elusive. The costs and risks associated with crossing the border have increased dramatically in the past 15 years, causing migrants to incur larger debts and stay longer to pay them off. For some migrants, return to their home communities becomes increasingly difficult after spending more than seven or eight years in the United States. There are many cases of Guatemalan migrants who have returned to their home communities only to return to the United States again within a period of months or years. These individuals report that they returned home to find little economic opportunity and a social and cultural environment to which they are no longer fully accustomed.

With the recent downturn in the U.S. economy, Guatemalan laborers have been particularly hard-hit. Because they occupy the most precarious positions in the labor market (frequently seeking work as day-laborers or part-time workers), Guatemalans were among the first to be let go as service industry companies began to cut back. The average monthly remittance amount that a household received in 2009 was $272, which is $73 less than in 2008 (IOM 2009, 68). Due to the difficult economic situation, increasing numbers of Guatemalans have decided to return home.

Deportation, however, is the main reason for return migration. According to a recent report by the U.S. Citizen and Immigration Services, Guatemala was the third-leading country in the number of people removed in 2008, when more than 28,000 Guatemalans were deported. New legislation (such as 287(g) that allows local law enforcement to act on behalf of Immigration Customs and Enforcement) has certainly contributed to an increase in the number of arrests and deportations among the Guatemalan population. A large portion of the Guatemalan migrant community lives in constant fear of deportation. Workplace immigration raids, such as the Postville, Iowa, incident, aggravate these fears.

The Second and Later Generations

Cultural and Ethnic Identity

The migrant experience adds another layer to the already complex issue of ethnic and cultural identity in the Guatemalan diaspora. There are many ethnic Mayan groups in Guatemala, each with their own dialect, dress, and customs. There is also a relatively small population of Garifuna people in Guatemala. Garifuna people are of mixed African, Carib, and Arawak descent and live primarily on the Caribbean coastal region of Guatemala and other Central American countries. The socially

Residents of the largely Guatemalan Westlake neighborhood in Los Angeles eat at a Guatemalan restaurant, September 9, 2010. (AP Photo/Damian Dovarganes)

Children Adopted from Guatemala

Up until 2008, tens of thousands of Guatemalan children were adopted by American families every year. The relative ease of the adoption process in Guatemala made it one of the top countries for adoptions in the United States, behind much larger countries such as China. The Department of State reported that the number of Guatemalan adoptions was rising every year until the law changed in 2008.

Adoptions became a lucrative business in Guatemala, with couples paying an average of $30,000 to private adoption agencies (Roig-Franzia 2007). Allegations of agencies and lawyers becoming "baby brokers" (buying babies from pregnant women in the countryside and then selling them to American couples) became rampant (Lacey 2006). In September 2008 the Guatemalan National Council on Adoption announced that it would not take any more cases in order to review the pending adoption cases and investigate allegations of illegal activities and infant trafficking. After a long period of investigation, international adoptions from Guatemala resumed in June 2010. The laws governing the process, however, have changed so that potential parents will be matched with a specific pool of available children (Llorca 2010).

Adoption visas granted to Guatemalans: 2003–2009

Fiscal year	Adoption visas
2003	2,328
2004	3,264
2005	3,783
2006	4,135
2007	4,727
2008	4,122
2009	756

Source: U.S. Department of State. 2010. "Adoptions from Guatemala to the United States."

dominant group in Guatemalan society is the Ladino group. Though the indigenous population is large, the Ladino population is disproportionally represented within the business and government elites. While large Mayan communities exist in Florida, Texas (Houston), North Carolina, and other states, the Garifuna Coalition USA (2010) estimates that the largest settlement of Garifunas in the United States is in the South Bronx, where approximately 200,000 Garifuna people live. Ladino Guatemalan migrants live spread throughout most of the major migrant-receiving communities from Los Angeles to the East Coast.

Depending on their own background and personal preference, second-generation Guatemalan youth may identify as members of their individual Mayan group (Mam, Kanjobal, etc.), as indigenous, as Guatemalan, as members of a pan-ethnic Hispanic/Latino group, as African American (in the case of Garifuna), or as American. Most large-scale studies of the second generation of immigrants in the United States tend to study "Hispanics/Latinos" as one group instead of disaggregating them by the country of birth of their parents. Ethnographic data from small groups, however, can shed some light on the issue.

Cecilia Menjívar (2002) carried out 26 in-depth interviews with Guatemalan children who were born in the United States or who migrated at a very young age. From her interviews, she concluded that while parents may encourage transnational activities and the maintenance of their ethnic identities, most of the second generation has little interest in these pursuits (indigenous Guatemalan migrants have marginally more success), choosing instead to focus on their lives in the United States. For example, most of the children in Menjívar's study did not speak Spanish

Marvin Velasquez (left), Andy Thomas (center), and Pedro Velasquez wear traditional Maya outfits as they wait for festivities to begin at the San Miguel Fiesta in West Palm Beach, Florida, September 30, 2006. (AP Photo/Lynne Sladky)

Youth Profile

Helping to Meet Community Needs

(Courtesy of Sandra Lazo de la Vega)

Jocelyn Skolnik was born and raised in Guatemala City. After high school, Jocelyn came to the United States to attend the Harriet L. Wilkes Honors College of Florida Atlantic University. During her college career, Jocelyn became involved with the Guatemalan immigrant community in South Florida, interning with a nonprofit organization (Corn-Maya Inc.) to coordinate and deliver services that met the community's needs. Jocelyn was recognized with numerous awards for her academic excellence and community involvement during her years at the Wilkes Honors College. Upon graduating in 2007, she was hired as coordinator of the El Sol Community Neighborhood Resource Center, a multifaceted 501(c)3 nonprofit whose mission is to assist Jupiter's immigrant population to become an active and integrated part of the larger Jupiter community and to build bridges among the different ethnic, cultural, and religious groups in Jupiter, Florida. In 2008, Jocelyn was recognized in the *Palm Beach Post* as a nonprofit "business person to watch." She was promoted to director of the center in 2009, where she now supervises three employees; directs a grant-writing team; manages the center's educational, legal, health, and labor programs; and oversees a budget of $200,000. Under Jocelyn's management, El Sol has become a model for other communities struggling to deal with issues of immigrant integration. Recognizing her achievements, Florida Atlantic University's Alumni Association named her the Harriet L. Wilkes Honors College distinguished alumna of 2010.

fluently and had limited desire or opportunity to visit Guatemala, and most only kept in touch with events in Guatemala through their parents, if at all.

The fact that the second generation of Guatemalans did not choose the ethnic identity of their parents does not mean that they fully embraced an American identity. Menjívar found that while the Spanish proficiency of her interviewees was limited, their English proficiency was not fully developed either. These Guatemalan children had developed the language skills necessary for communication with their immediate peers but "did not gain the language skills necessary to successfully participate in the wider society" (Menjívar 2002, 545). In other words, the second-generation Guatemalan youth that Menjívar studied suffer from what Portes and Rumbaut call dissonant acculturation or a "rupture of family ties and abandonment of ethnic community" (2001, 242).

Educational Attainment

The ability to give one's children greater opportunities is a major driving motor of Guatemalan migration to the United States. As is true of most immigrant groups, Guatemalan parents consider education a high priority for their children. Unfortunately, data on the education attainment of the second generation of Guatemalans in the United States is scarce, and what we do know does not measure up to the high expectations of Guatemalan parents.

There are several situational factors that affect the educational attainment of the second generation of Guatemalans in the United States. A large portion of the second generation is growing up in poor neighborhoods, with inadequate schools (Portes and Rumbaut 2001; Menjívar 2002). Even when students are resilient and manage to thrive academically, their educational options may be limited by their legal status. As Cecilia Menjívar (2006) explains, even if Guatemalan children are high achievers in high school, universities require legal residency in a state in order to qualify for in-state tuition rates, student loans, and other types of financial aid (1023). Furthermore, even if the student was born in the United States, extensive documents from parents are also needed in order to apply for financial aid, which parents either may not have or may be reluctant to produce for fear of deportation (1029).

Issues in Relations between the United States and Guatemala

Forecasts for the 21st century

Like other Central American countries, Guatemala's political history has been closely tied to trends in U.S. foreign policy. The Monroe Doctrine, the Alliance for Progress, CAFTA, and U.S. Immigration Laws have all impacted Guatemala's politics, development, economy, and ultimately the emigration of its citizens to the United States. In 1999, shortly after the release of the Guatemalan Truth and

Reconciliation Committee report, president Bill Clinton apologized for U.S. support of military violence in Guatemala during the civil war and pledged to support Guatemala in its peace and reconciliation process (Broder 1999). According to the U.S. State Department, supporting the implementation of the Peace Accords continues to be one of the U.S. policy objectives towards Guatemala, along with issues of economic development, trade, and security cooperation to combat international crime, drug trafficking, and money laundering. On the issues of international crime and drugs, Guatemala is participating along with other Central American countries and Mexico in the controversial Merida Initiative, a comprehensive public security package designed to improve citizen security in the region through fighting organized crime, gangs, and the drug trade. The Guatemalan portion of the package has drawn criticism for emphasizing aid and equipment to police units rather than institutional police reform.

In 2006 the CAFTA entered into effect in Guatemala. It lifted trade barriers between Costa Rica, El Salvador, Guatemala, Honduras, Nicaragua, the Dominican Republic, and the United States. One of the key effects of CAFTA is that it opens Central American markets to subsidized U.S. agricultural goods. In an economy driven by rural agriculture, this has meant dislocation for many Guatemalan farmers who cannot compete and look to migration as a survival strategy. The problem is compounded as those who migrate successfully inject remittances into the local economy in their home communities, driving up the price of land potentially encouraging further migration.

Migration is the most important issue pertaining to United States–Guatemala relations. With nearly one-tenth of Guatemala's population living in the United States, arriving at some type of favorable immigration reform should be one of the most pressing issues for the Guatemalan government. The Guatemalan National Council for Attention to Migrants (CONAMIGUA) was formed in 2007 to tend to the needs of Guatemalan migrants. According to its 2009 annual report, CONAMIGUA has and will continue to work to articulate a regional immigration reform proposal, asking for the regularization of the immigration status of Guatemalans and other Latin Americans currently living in the United States without the proper documents (Consejo Nacional de Atención al Migrante de Guatemala [CONAMIGUA] 2009). One of CONAMIGUA's main tasks is to lobby countries that receive Guatemalan migrants to adopt an immigration reform policy that includes legalization and a family reunification program (CONAMIGUA 2009). In the case of the United States, advocates for immigration reform have also focused on the impact of immigration raids on the Guatemalan community, the need for TPS for Guatemalan immigrants impacted by natural disasters, and the problems associated with immigration enforcement strategies that rely on local police and sheriffs to carry out federal immigration law.

Appendix I: Migration Statistics

Migration statistics about Guatemalans are notoriously unreliable. The IOM collects data on Guatemalan emigrants but does not disaggregate them per country of destination. The U.S. Department of Homeland Security collects some migration statistics about Guatemalans in the United States, but most experts agree that the numbers reported undercount the Guatemalan population. The following tables summarize the statistics reported by the U.S. Department of Homeland Security (specifically the U.S. Citizenship and Immigration Service) on the Guatemalan population in the United States.

Table 123 Legal permanent residents 2008

	Legal permanent residents		Legal permanent residents eligible to naturalize	
	Number	**Percent**	**Number**	**Percent**
Total in the U.S.	12,600,000	100	8,160,000	100
Guatemala	180,000	1.4	110,000	1.3

Source: Rytina 2009.

Table 124 Legal permanent residents: Fiscal years 2000 to 2009

Region and country of birth	2000	2001	2002	2003	2004	2005	2006	2007	2008	2009
Total	841,002	1,058,902	1,059,356	703,542	957,883	1,122,257	1,266,129	1,052,415	1,107,126	1,130,818
Guatemala	9,942	13,496	16,178	14,386	18,920	16,818	24,133	17,908	16,182	12,187

Source: U.S. Department of Homeland Security. Office of *Immigration Statistics. 2009.*

Table 125 Estimated unauthorized immigrant population: January 2009 and 2000

	Estimated population in January		Percent of total		Percent change	Average annual change
	2009	2000	2009	2000	2000–2009	2000–2009
All countries	10,750,000	8,460,000	100	100	27	250,000
Guatemala	480,000	290,000	4	3	65	20,000

Source: Hoefer, Rytina, and Baker 2010.

Table 126 Apprehensions: Fiscal years 2006–2008

	2008	2007	2006
Total apprehensions	791,568	960,756	1,206,457
Guatemala	22,670	23,907	25,135

Source: U.S. Department of Homeland Security Office of Immigration Statistics, Immigration Enforcement Actions: 2008. July 2009.

Appendix II: Demographics/Census Statistics

Question number five of the 2008 ACS asks respondents about "Hispanic, Latino or Spanish origin." The available answers include broad Hispanic origin groups (e.g., Mexican, Puerto Rican, and Cuban) as well as the option to write in individual answers, such as "Guatemalan." The following table contains data on those who wrote in "Guatemalan" in question number five in the 2008 ACS.

Table 127 Basic census demographics of the Guatemalan population in the United States

Subject	Guatemalan	Margin of error (+/-)
Total number of races reported		
Total population	991,871	32,016
One race	96.3%	0.6
Two races	3.4%	0.6
Three races	0.2%	0.1
Four or more races	0.0%	0.1
Sex and age		
Total population	991,871	32,016
Male	57.1%	1
Female	42.9%	1
Under 5 years	11.7%	0.7
5 to 17 years	18.0%	0.8
18 to 24 years	12.6%	0.7
25 to 34 years	23.2%	0.9
35 to 44 years	17.4%	0.7
45 to 54 years	9.7%	0.6
55 to 64 years	4.8%	0.5
65 to 74 years	1.7%	0.2
75 years and over	1.1%	0.2
Median age (years)	28.1	0.4
18 years and over	70.4%	1
21 years and over	65.7%	1
62 years and over	3.8%	0.3
65 years and over	2.7%	0.3
Under 18 years	293,722	14,953
Male	51.3%	1.7
Female	48.7%	1.7
18 years and over	698,149	23,316
Male	59.5%	1
Female	40.5%	1
18 to 34 years	354,590	16,376
Male	64.2%	1.4
Female	35.8%	1.4
35 to 64 years	316,315	12,569
Male	56.4%	1.6
Female	43.6%	1.6

(Continued)

Table 127 Basic census demographics of the Guatemalan population in the United States (*Continued*)

Subject	Guatemalan	Margin of error (+/-)
65 years and over	27,244	2,697
Male	34.4%	4.9
Female	65.6%	4.9
Households by type		
Households	247,786	7,991
Family households	78.2%	1.5
With own children under 18 years	50.4%	2
Married-couple family	46.5%	1.8
With own children under 18 years	32.5%	1.7
Female householder, no husband present, family	16.0%	1.3
With own children under 18 years	10.4%	1.1
Nonfamily households	21.8%	1.5
Male householder	15.2%	1.5
Living alone	6.7%	0.9
Not living alone	8.5%	1
Female householder	6.6%	0.8
Living alone	4.7%	0.8
Not living alone	1.9%	0.4
Average household size	4.01	0.09
Average family size	4.12	0.08
Marital status		
Population 15 years and over	735,923	24,211
Now married, except separated	44.5%	1.3
Widowed	2.2%	0.3
Divorced	5.0%	0.6
Separated	3.5%	0.4
Never married	44.8%	1.3
Male 15 years and over	435,752	17,048
Now married, except separated	43.5%	1.5
Widowed	0.9%	0.3
Divorced	3.6%	0.6
Separated	2.7%	0.5
Never married	49.4%	1.4
Female 15 years and over	300,171	11,528
Now married, except separated	45.9%	1.8

(*Continued*)

Table 127 Basic census demographics of the Guatemalan population in the
United States (Continued)

Subject	Guatemalan	Margin of error (+/-)
Widowed	4.1%	0.7
Divorced	7.1%	1
Separated	4.8%	0.7
Never married	38.2%	1.9
School enrollment		
Population 3 years and over enrolled in school	237,594	11,835
Nursery school, preschool	8.1%	1
Kindergarten	7.6%	1.1
Elementary school (grades 1–8)	46.2%	2
High school (grades 9–12)	21.8%	1.6
College or graduate school	16.3%	1.8
Educational attainment		
Population 25 years and over	573,206	19,535
Less than high school diploma	54.1%	1.7
High school graduate (includes equivalency)	21.6%	1.2
Some college or associate's degree	15.4%	1
Bachelor's degree	6.7%	0.6
Graduate or professional degree	2.1%	0.3
High school graduate or higher	45.9%	1.7
Male, high school graduate or higher	45.0%	2.2
Female, high school graduate or higher	47.2%	1.9
Bachelor's degree or higher	8.9%	0.7
Male, bachelor's degree or higher	8.6%	0.9
Female, bachelor's degree or higher	9.3%	1.1
Fertility		
Women 15 to 50 years	241,239	9,950
Women 15 to 50 years who had a birth in the past 12 months	20,118	2,415
Unmarried women 15 to 50 years who had a birth in the past 12 months	8,586	1,488
As a percent of all women with a birth in the past 12 months	42.7%	6.5
Veteran status		
Civilian population 18 years and over	695,982	23,228

(Continued)

830

Table 127 Basic census demographics of the Guatemalan population in the United States (*Continued*)

Subject	Guatemalan	Margin of error (+/-)
Civilian veteran	1.0%	0.2
Disability status		
Total civilian noninstitutionalized population	983,526	31,961
With a disability	4.7%	0.4
Residence 1 year ago		
Population 1 year and over	971,458	31,609
Same house	82.3%	1.3
Different house in the United States	15.5%	1.3
Same county	11.1%	1.2
Different county	4.3%	0.6
Same state	2.6%	0.5
Different state	1.7%	0.4
Abroad	2.2%	0.4
Place of birth, citizenship status and year of entry		
Native	310,981	16,542
Male	51.7%	1.8
Female	48.3%	1.8
Foreign born	680,890	22,314
Male	59.5%	1.1
Female	40.5%	1.1
Foreign born; naturalized U.S. citizen	159,491	8,090
Male	47.5%	2.1
Female	52.5%	2.1
Foreign born; not a U.S. citizen	521,399	19,982
Male	63.2%	1.2
Female	36.8%	1.2
Population born outside the United States	680,890	22,314
Entered 2000 or later	41.3%	1.6
Entered 1990 to 1999	27.9%	1.2
Entered before 1990	30.8%	1.3
Language spoken at home and ability to speak English		
Population 5 years and over	876,217	27,781
English only	8.9%	0.7

(*Continued*)

Table 127 Basic census demographics of the Guatemalan population in the United States (Continued)

Subject	Guatemalan	Margin of error (+/-)
Language other than English	91.1%	0.7
Speak English less than "very well"	60.9%	1.3
Employment status		
Population 16 years and over	723,849	23,598
In labor force	77.6%	1.1
Civilian labor force	77.3%	1.1
Employed	71.8%	1.2
Unemployed	5.5%	0.5
Percent of civilian labor force	7.1%	0.7
Armed Forces	0.3%	0.1
Not in labor force	22.4%	1.1
Females 16 years and over	295,510	11,230
In labor force	61.7%	1.8
Civilian labor force	61.5%	1.8
Employed	55.5%	1.8
Unemployed	6.0%	0.7
Percent of civilian labor force	9.8%	1.2
Occupation		
Civilian employed population 16 years and over	519,911	19,018
Management, professional, and related occupations	9.5%	0.8
Service occupations	31.4%	1.5
Sales and office occupations	14.7%	1
Farming, fishing, and forestry occupations	1.9%	0.4
Construction, extraction, maintenance, and repair occupations	21.6%	1.4
Production, transportation, and material moving occupations	20.9%	1.3
Male civilian employed population 16 years and over	355,867	15,052
Management, professional, and related occupations	7.2%	0.9
Service occupations	25.9%	1.8
Sales and office occupations	9.8%	1.1
Farming, fishing, and forestry occupations	2.3%	0.6

(Continued)

Table 127 Basic census demographics of the Guatemalan population in the United States (*Continued*)

Subject	Guatemalan	Margin of error (+/-)
Construction, extraction, maintenance, and repair occupations	31.1%	1.9
Production, transportation, and material moving occupations	23.6%	1.6
Female civilian employed population 16 years and over	164,044	8,664
Management, professional, and related occupations	14.5%	1.5
Service occupations	43.4%	2.5
Sales and office occupations	25.2%	1.9
Farming, fishing, and forestry occupations	0.9%	0.4
Construction, extraction, maintenance, and repair occupations	1.1%	0.4
Production, transportation, and material moving occupations	14.9%	1.7
Industry		
Civilian employed population 16 years and over	519,911	19,018
Agriculture, forestry, fishing and hunting, and mining	2.6%	0.6
Construction	18.9%	1.3
Manufacturing	13.5%	1.2
Wholesale trade	2.9%	0.5
Retail trade	9.1%	0.8
Transportation and warehousing, and utilities	4.1%	0.6
Information	0.8%	0.2
Finance and insurance, and real estate and rental and leasing	3.3%	0.4
Professional, scientific, and management, and administrative and waste management services	13.8%	1.3
Educational services, and health care and social assistance	8.9%	0.8
Arts, entertainment, and recreation, and accommodation and food services	12.9%	1.1
Other services (except public administration)	8.4%	0.6
Public administration	0.8%	0.2

(*Continued*)

Table 127 Basic census demographics of the Guatemalan population in the United States (*Continued*)

Subject	Guatemalan	Margin of error (+/-)
Class of worker		
Civilian employed population 16 years and over	519,911	19,018
Private wage and salary workers	87.8%	0.9
Government workers	3.9%	0.5
Self-employed workers in own not incorporated business	8.1%	0.8
Unpaid family workers	0.2%	0.1
Income in the past 12 months (in 2008 inflation-adjusted dollars)		
Households	247,786	7,991
Median household income (dollars)	41,225	1,241
With earnings	95.9%	0.7
Mean earnings (dollars)	51,535	1,556
With Social Security income	7.1%	0.7
Mean Social Security income (dollars)	10,555	899
With Supplemental Security Income	1.6%	0.4
Mean Supplemental Security Income (dollars)	7,464	1,007
With cash public assistance income	2.1%	0.5
Mean cash public assistance income (dollars)	4,905	1,014
With retirement income	2.8%	0.6
Mean retirement income (dollars)	13,562	4,333
With Food Stamp benefits	9.0%	1.1
Families	193,840	7,298
Median family income (dollars)	39,699	1,424
Married-couple family	59.5%	2
Median income (dollars)	46,229	1,717
Male householder, no spouse present, family	20.1%	2
Median income (dollars)	35,806	1,837
Female householder, no husband present, family	20.4%	1.6
Median income (dollars)	25,996	2,593
Individuals	991,871	32,016
Per capita income (dollars)	14,657	409

(*Continued*)

Table 127 Basic census demographics of the Guatemalan population in the United States (*Continued*)

Subject	Guatemalan	Margin of error (+/-)
With earnings for full-time, year-round workers:		
Male	269,803	11,741
Female	103,646	6,684
Mean earnings (dollars) for full-time, year-round workers:		
Male	30,836	865
Female	28,393	1,498
Median earnings (dollars) full-time, year-round workers:		
Male	25,238	586
Female	22,139	773
Poverty rates for families and people for whom poverty status is determined		
All families	19.3%	1.5
With related children under 18 years	24.5%	2
With related children under 5 years only	26.6%	4.2
Married-couple family	14.6%	1.7
With related children under 18 years	17.8%	2.3
With related children under 5 years only	17.2%	4.3
Female householder, no husband present, family	37.0%	4.5
With related children under 18 years	45.1%	5.4
With related children under 5 years only	52.3%	10.9
All people	21.7%	1.3
Under 18 years	28.1%	2.4
Related children under 18 years	27.8%	2.4
Related children under 5 years	30.4%	2.7
Related children 5 to 17 years	26.1%	2.9
18 years and over	19.0%	1.2
18 to 64 years	19.0%	1.3
65 years and over	19.6%	4.7
People in families	19.2%	1.5
Unrelated individuals 15 years and over	32.4%	2.4

Source: American Community Survey (2008).

Table 128 shows the leading states in the United States where those Guatemalans obtaining legal permanent residence in 2009 lived. Chief among them are California, Florida, New York, and Texas.

Table 128 Guatemalans obtaining legal permanent resident status during fiscal year 2009 by state

Characteristic	Total	Male	Female
Total	12,187	5,826	6,361
Arizona	189	109	80
California	4,282	1,981	2,301
Colorado	100	47	53
Connecticut	187	90	97
Florida	884	423	461
Georgia	368	189	179
Illinois	472	211	261
Maryland	308	153	155
Massachusetts	388	199	189
Minnesota	90	43	47
Nevada	227	115	112
New Jersey	499	238	261
New York	715	342	373
North Carolina	175	77	98
Ohio	91	41	50
Pennsylvania	110	45	65
Texas	641	298	343
Virginia	389	196	193
Washington	198	109	89
Other	1,874	920	954

Source: Adapted from U.S. Department of Homeland Security. Profiles on Legal Permanent Residents: 2009.

Appendix III: Notable Guatemalan Americans

David Campos, born in Izabal, Guatemala, came to the United States with his family when he was 14. Campos learned English and graduated at the top of his high school class in South Central California. He attended Stanford University, where he majored in political science and then went on to graduate from the Harvard Law School in 1996. Campos worked in the private sector for a few years before becoming a deputy city attorney in San Francisco. He continued in public service, where he has served as general counsel to the San Francisco Unified School District and as a member of the San Francisco Police Commission. Campos currently represents District 9 as a member of the San Francisco Board of Supervisors and is an elected member of the San Francisco Democratic County Central Committee (City and County of San Francisco Board of Supervisors 2010).

Francisco Goldman was born in Boston to a Guatemalan mother and an American father. Goldman is the author of several novels, including *The Long Night of White Chickens* (1992). He also wrote *The Art of Political Murder: Who Killed the Bishop?* (2007), a nonfiction work about the 1998 murder of the Guatemalan bishop Juan Gerardi. Goldman's work has been translated into 10 languages and he has received a multitude of awards, including the WOLA-Duke Award for the best book about human rights in Latin America for *The Art of Political Murder* (Fundación Nuevo Periodismo Iberoamericano 2010; Trinity News 2008)

Victor Montejo is a Jacaltec Maya who fled Guatemala in 1982 after his brother's assassination. In 1993, Montejo received his Ph.D. in anthropology from the University of Connecticut. Montejo's most important work is *Voices from Exile: Violence and Survival in Modern Maya History* (1999), which won the Race, Ethnicity and Politics Award from the American Political Science Association in 2000 (McConahay 2003; Native American Indigenous 2010).

Luis Vasques-Ajmac moved to the United States from Guatemala at the age of six. Vasques-Ajmac is the founder of MAYA, a marketing agency that targets multicultural audiences. Vasques-Ajmac named his company MAYA to pay homage to his heritage. He has received multiple awards for his accomplishments in business, including the 1999 Small Business of the Year Award, the 2003 Hispanic Businessman of the Year Award, and the 1999 Vision Award (Reynolds School of Journalism 2010; Browne 2005).

Luis von Ahn was born in Guatemala City. He is a professor of computer science at Carnegie Mellon University. He is best known for development of Captcha, a computer program that produces skewed images of letters that have to be transcribed by the user trying to access a variety of online services in order to thwart spambots. Captcha, ReCaptcha, and GWAP (Games With A Purpose), all created by Von Ahn, are used to garner the power of human intelligence to facilitate tasks that are too complex for computers to solve at this point, such as accurately scanning older texts to make them digitally available. Von Ahn is a recipient of the Macarthur Foundation Fellowship (2006–2011), *Businessweek* magazine called him a "pioneer of human computation," and *Discover* magazine listed him as one of the "50 Best Brains in Science" in 2008 (Von Ahn 2010).

Glossary

Comadre/compadre: Co-mother, co-father. When an individual becomes the godparent of a child, the individual and the child's parents become *compadres* or *comadres*.

Comal: A round cooking surface where tortillas are usually cooked.

Costumbre: "Custom" or traditional cultural practices. For many indigenous Maya, *costumbre* reflects a mix of precolonial and Spanish religious and cultural traditions or practices.

Ladino: In Guatemala Ladino is recognized as a formal (yet heterogeneous) ethnic group of mixed Hispanic and indigenous race who speak Spanish as their first language. In common usage, the term refers to nonindigenous Guatemalans as well as indigenous Guatemalans who have adopted nonindigenous forms of cultural expression (e.g., language, dress, etc.).

Municipio: A municipality or village.

Padrino/madrina: Godfather/godmother.

References

American Community Survey. 2008. "S0201. Selected Population Profile in the United States. Population Group: Guatemalan." [Online information, retrieved 03/15/10.] www.factfinder.census.gov.

Arndt, Michael. 2010. "At Pollo Campero, Growth is on the Menu." *BusinessWeek Magazine*. March 11.

Broder, John. 1999. "Clinton Offers His Apologies to Guatemala." *New York Times* March 11. [Online information retrieved 03/29/10.] www.nytimes.com.

Browne, Andrea. 2005. "Small Business 101." *The Washington Post,* November 11. [Online information, retrieved 03/29/10.] www.washingtonpost.com.

Burns, Allan. 1993. *Maya in Exile: Guatemalans in Florida.* Philadelphia: Temple University Press.

Carrasquillo, Olveen, Angeles I. Carrasquillo, and Steven Shea. 2000. "Health Insurance Coverage of Immigrants Living in the United States: Differences by Citizenship Status and Country of Origin." *American Journal of Public Health* 90(6): 917–23.

City and County of San Francisco Board of Supervisors. 2010. "Supervisor Campos-About." [Online information, retrieved 05/10/10.] http://www.sfbos.org/index.aspx?page=2127.

Consejo Nacional de Atención al Migrante de Guatemala. 2009. *Informe Ejecutivo de las Acciones de CONAMIGUA 2009.* Guatemala.

Eisenman, David P., Lilian Gelberg, Honghu Liu, and Martin F. Shapiro. 2003. "Mental Health and Health-Related Quality of Life Among Adult Latino Primary Care Patients Living in the United States With Previous Exposure to Political Violence." *JAMA* 290(5): 627–34.

El Congreso de la República de Guatemala. 1996. "Decreto Número 86–96: Reformas a la Ley de Nacionalidad, Decreto Número 1613 del Congreso de la República de Guatemala." [Online information, retrieved 03/29/10.] http://www.congreso.gob.gt/archivos/decretos/1996/gtdcx86–1996.pdf.

El Congreso de la República de Guatemala. 1985. "Constitución Política de la República de Guatemala, Título III, Capítulo II: Nacionalidad y Ciudadanía." [Online information, retrieved 03/29/10.] http://www.congreso.gob.gt/gt/constitucion2/Constitucion.pdf.

Fink, Leon. 2003. *The Maya of Morganton: Work and Community in the Nuevo New South.* Chapel Hill: University of North Carolina Press.

Frumkin, Paul. 2002. "Pollo Campero Takes Wing in the United States." *Nation's Restaurant News,* September 23.

Fundación Nuevo Periodismo Iberoamericano. 2010. *Francisco Goldman.* Nuestros Maestros. [Online information, retrieved 03/29/10.] http://www.fnpi.org/maestros/directores-de-talleres/francisco-goldman/.

Garifuna Coalition USA. 2010. [Online information, retrieved 03/29/10.] www.garifunacoalition.org.

Gzesh, Susan. 2006. *Central Americans and Asylum Policy in the Reagan Era.* Migration Information Resource. April. [Online information, retrieved 03/20/10.] http://www.migrationinformation.org.

Hagan, Jaqueline Maria. 1994. *Deciding to be Legal.* Philadelphia: Temple University Press.

Handy, Jim. 1984. *Gift of the Devil: A History of Guatemala.* Boston: South End Press.

Hoefer, Michael, Nancy Rytina, and Bryan C. Baker. 2010. "Estimates of the Unauthorized Immigrant Population Residing in the United States: January 2009." U.S. Department of Homeland Security, Office of Immigration Statistics. *Population Estimates,* January.

Hong, Maria. 2000. "Guatemalan Americans." In *The Gale Encyclopedia of Multicultural America,* 2nd Edition, edited by Jeffrey Lehman. Detroit: Gale. [Online information, retrieved 04/01/10.] http://www.everyculture.com/multi/Du-Ha/Guatemalan-Americans.html.

Instituto Nacional de Sismología, Vulcanología, Meteorología e Hidrología de Guatemala. 2010. "Sismología: Marco Tectonico para Guatemala." [Online information, retrieved 03/15/10.] www.insivumeh.gob.gt/geofisica/indice%20sismo.htm.

International Organization for Migration (Organización Internacional para las Migraciones). 2003. *Cuadernos de Trabajo Sobre Migración 17: Encuesta Nacional Sobre Remesas Familiares.* Guatemala: IOM.

International Organization for Migration (Organización Internacional para las Migraciones). 2009. *Cuadernos de Trabajo Sobre Migración 27: Encuesta Nacional Sobre Remesas 2009 Niñez y Adolescencia.* Guatemala: IOM.

Lacey, Mark. 2006. "Guatemalan System is Scrutinized as Americans Rush in to Adopt." *New York Times.* November 5.

Burns, Alan. 2000. "Indiantown, Florida: The Maya Diaspora and Applied Anthropology." In *The Maya Diaspora: Guatemalan Roots, New American Lives,* edited by James Loucky and Marylin Moors, 152–71. Philadelphia: Temple University Press.

Llorca, Juan Carlos. 2010. "Guatemala to Resume International Adoptions in June." *Associated Press.* March 17.

Malkin, Elisabeth. 2010. "Guatemala: Ex-President Arrested on U.S. Warrant." *New York Times.* January 26.

McConahay, Mary Jo. 2003. "American Maya Goes to Guatemalan Congress." *Pacific News Service: News Feature,* December 29. [Online information, retrieved 03/29/10.] http://news.newamericamedia.org.

Menjívar, Cecilia. 2002. "Living in Two Worlds? Guatemalan-origin Children in the United States and Emerging Transnationalism." *Journal of Ethnic and Migration Studies* 28(3): 531–52.

Menjívar, Cecilia. 2006. "Liminal Legality: Salvadoran and Guatemalan Immigrants' Lives in the United States." *American Journal of Sociology* 111(4): 999–1037.

Montejo, Victor. 1999. *Voices from Exile: Violence and Survival in Modern Maya History.* Norman: University of Oklahoma Press.

Native American Indigenous Studies Association. 2010. "Victor Montejo: Biography." [Online information, retrieved 03/29/10.] http://naisa.org/election/council/montejo.

Orozco, Manuel, and Eugenia Garcia-Zanello. 2009. "Hometown Associations: Transnationalism, Philanthropy, and Development." *Brown Journal of World Affairs* 15(2): 1–17.

Palma, Irene, Carol Girón, and Timothy Steigenga. 2009. "From Jacaltennago to Jupiter: Negotiating the Concept of "Family" through Transnational Space and Time." In *A Place to Be: Brazilian, Guatemalan, and Mexican Immigrants in Florida's New Destinations,* edited by Phillip J. Williams, Timothy J. Steigenga, and Manuel A. Vázquez, 57–79. New Brunswick, NJ, and London: Rutgers University Press.

Piedrasanta Herrera, Ruth. 2007. "Apuntes sobre transmigración y remesas entre los chuj de Huehuetenango." In *Comunidades en Movimiento: La migración internacional en el norte de Huehuetenango,* edited by Manuela Camus, 95–112. Antigua, Guatemala: INCEDES, PCS, PROGOBIH.

Reynolds School of Journalism News. 2010. "To Land a Job: Be Smart, Write Well and Keep a Positive Attitude." March 3. [Online information, retrieved 03/29/10.] http://journalism.unr.edu/latestnews.

Reynoso, Conié, Amafredo Castellanos, and Coralia Orantes. 2005. "Tormenta Stan peor que Mitch." *Prensa Libre,* Guatemala, October 9.

Roig-Franzia, Manuel. 2007. "Guatemala Moves to Tighten Adoption Rules." *Washington Post.* December 12.

Rytina, Nancy. 2009. "Estimates of the Legal Permanent Resident Population: 2008." U.S. Department of Homeland Security, Office of Immigration Statistics. *Population Estimates,* October.

Schlesinger, Stephen, and Stephen Kinzer. 1982. *Bitter Fruit: The Story of the American Coup in Guatemala.* New York: Doubleday.

Schoorman, Dilys, Maria Cristina Acosta, and Sister Rachel Sena. 2008. "Implementing Freirian Perspectives in HIV-AIDS Education Among Preliterate Guatemalan Maya Immigrants." *Journal of Thought* (Spring/Summer 2008): 41–54.

Skolnik, Jocelyn, Sandra Lazo de la Vega, and Timothy J. Steigenga. 2012. "El Chisme across Borders: The Impact of Gossip in a Transnational Guatemalan Community." *Migraciones Internacionales* 22.

Smith, James. 2006. *Guatemala: Economic Migrants Replace Political Refugees.* Migration Information Resource. April. [Online information, retrieved 03/20/10.] http://www.migrationinformation.org.

Steigenga, Timothy J., S. Irene Palma, and Carl L. Girón. 2008. "El transnacionalismo, la movilización colectiva de la comunidad maya en Jupiter, Florida. Ambigüedades en la identidad transnacional y la religión vivida" *Migraciones Internacionales* 4(4): 36–71.

Trinity News. 2008. "More Accolades for Francisco Goldman's *The Art of Political Murder.*" *Trinity News Press Release.* [Online information, retrieved 03/29/10.] http://www.trincoll.edu/AboutTrinity/News_Events/trinity_news/080808_Goldman.htm.

Trudeau, Robert H. 2000. "Guatemala: Democratic Rebirth?" In *Latin American Politics and Development,* 5th ed., edited by Howard J. Wiarda and Harvey F. Kline, 493–511. Boulder, CO: Westview Press.

United Nations Development Programme. 2009. *Human Development Report 2009, Overcoming*

Barriers: Human Mobility and Development. [Online information; retrieved 03/01/10.]

http://hdr.undp.org/en/media/HDR_2009_EN_Complete.pdf.

U.S. Citizenship and Immigration Services. 2009. *Immigration through the Nicaraguan Adjustment and Central American Relief Act (NACARA) Section 203.* [Online information; retrieved 03/11/10.] http://www.uscis.gov/portal/site/uscis/menuitem.5af9bb95919f35e66f614176543f6d1a/?vgnextoid=2ee215d27cf73210VgnVCM10 0000082ca60aRCRD&vgnextchannel=f39d3e4d77d73210VgnVCM100000082ca6 0aRCRD.

U.S. Citizenship and Immigration Services. 2010. "The Oath of Allegiance." In *A Guide to Naturalization*. [Online information, retrieved 03/29/10.] http://www.uscis.gov/files/article/M-476.pdf.

U.S. Department of Homeland Security Office of Immigration Statistics. 2009. "Immigration Enforcement Actions: 2008." July 2009.

U.S. Department of Homeland Security. 2010. "Profiles on Legal Permanent Residents: 2009." Downloadable MSExcel file "Cobbook86." [Online information; retrieved 03/16/10.] http://www.dhs.gov/files/statistics/data/DSLPR09c.shtm.

U.S. Department of State. 2010. "Adoptions from Guatemala to the United States." [Online information, retrieved 04/05/10.] http://adoption.state.gov/country/guatemala.html.

Varangis, Panos, Paul Siegel, Daniel Giovanucci, and Brian Lewin. 2003. *Dealing with the Coffee Crisis in Central America: Impacts and Strategies*. World Bank Policy Research Working Paper 2993.

Von Ahn, Luis. 2010. "Luis von Ahn's Home Page." *Carnegie Mellon University* [Online information, retrieved 03/29/10.] http://www.cs.cmu.edu/~biglou/.

Further Reading

Burns, Allan. 1993. *Maya in Exile: Guatemalans in Florida*. Philadelphia: Temple University Press.

Maya in Exile tells the story of Maya refugees in Florida. Beginning in the early 1980s, Florida began receiving hundreds of thousands of Maya refugees fleeing the civil war in their homeland. *Maya in Exile* is an excellent ethnography of their lives and struggles to live in the United States.

Handy, Jim. 1985. *Gift of the Devil: A History of Guatemala*. Boston: South End Press.

Gift of the Devil provides an excellent historical overview of Guatemala, from the pre-Columbian legacy until the 1980s, when Guatemala was in the midst of its civil war. *Gift of the Devil* portrays an indigenous society in perpetual defense mode from outside forces that seek to destroy or possess the resources available in Guatemala.

Marquardt, Marie, Timothy J. Steigenga, Philip J. Williams, Manuel Vásquez. 2011. *Living "Illegal": The Human Face of Unauthorized Immigration*. New York: New Press.

Living Illegal tells the stories of unauthorized Guatemalan and Mexican immigrants living in South Florida and Atlanta. The book details the process and forces propelling migration, tensions and mobilizations of migrants in new destination communities, and struggles to survive, integrate, and thrive in the face of an increasingly restrictionist national climate.

Montejo, Victor. 1999. *Voices from Exile: Violence and Survival in Modern Maya History*. Norman: University of Oklahoma Press.

Voices from Exile is also an excellent ethnography of Maya exiles living in the United States. Victor Montejo, a Maya exile himself, tells the story of a part of the modern Maya living in the United States today.

Migration Information Source. [Online article; retrieved 03/11/11.] http://www.migration information.org.

Migration Information Resource is an online resource provided by the Migration Policy Institute. It has valuable resources and information about different migrant groups, including Guatemalans who migrate to the United States. New articles with up-to-date information are routinely uploaded.

Organización Internacional para las Migraciones (International Organization for Migration). Guatemala Country Web site. [Online article; retrieved 03/11/11.] http://www. oim.org.gt/.

This Web site contains general information regarding migration issues in Guatemala. The OIM produces extensive yearly reports focused on one topic (women, children, climate change, etc.) within the larger context of migration out of Guatemala. The yearly reports include statistical data about the population of Guatemalans living abroad as well as their families in Guatemala.

Pew Hispanic Center. *Hispanics of Guatemalan Origin in the U.S.* [Online article; retrieved 03/11/11.] http://pewhispanic.org.

The Pew Hispanic Center's website has valuable information about Hispanics in the United States, as well as information about individual population groups (including Guatemalans). The Pew Hispanic Center's Web site also has general information about relevant topics involving the general Hispanic immigrant population in the United States, including religious behavior, voting trends, and so forth.

Schleisinger, Stephen, and Stephen Kinzer. 1982. *Bitter Fruit: The Story of the American Coup in Guatemala*. New York: Doubleday.

Bitter Fruit is a classic of Guatemalan history about the 1954 overthrow of Jacobo Arbenz. *Bitter Fruit* tells the history of the United Fruit Company and of Guatemalan politics long before the 1954 events. The overthrow of Arbenz and the political turmoil that followed are not just the source of many of Guatemala's present-day troubles, but they are also a main factor pushing immigration to the United States.

Williams, Phillip, Timothy Steigenga, and Manuel A. Vásquez, eds. 2009. *A Place to Be: Brazilian, Guatemalan, and Mexican Immigrants in Florida's New Destinations*. New Brunswick, NJ, and London: Rutgers University Press.

This edited volume contains vital information on religion and transnational communities. The chapters about Guatemala deal with important issues, such as the meaning and importance of family in the process of migration.

Guyanese (Indo-Guyanese) Immigrants

by Stephen J. Sills and Natassaja Chowthi

Introduction

Guyana is the only English-speaking country in South America. It is multiethnic and culturally Caribbean and has been nicknamed the "land of six peoples" due to its ethnic diversity. Guyana has been populated by Amerindians, white Europeans, Africans, Portuguese, Chinese, and East Indians. Most of these groups arrived in Guyana in the 17th century during its colonial period as a result of the British importation of labor. The largest of the ethnic groups in Guyana is from India. East Indian Guyanese are often referred to as Indo-Guyanese. This group has re-migrated from Guyana to the United States beginning in the 1960s in response to political changes, economic downturn, and interethnic conflict in Guyana. According to 2006 data from the American Community Survey of the U.S. Census Bureau, there are about 196,174 individuals of Guyanese ancestry in the United States. While they have encountered some barriers to upward mobility, over time Indo-Guyanese immigrants have achieved a high level of structural assimilation: they are well-educated, often own their own homes, and have multiple-income households with just above the median household income. Guyanese immigrants have established a transnational community in New York City known as Little Guyana. Their complex historical, ethnic, and national backgrounds are reconstructed within the United States and shaped by current conceptions of race, ethnicity, and immigration. The second generation, born in the United States, is characterized by its cosmopolitan, transnational, or hybrid identity. Although Indo-Guyanese are a new, and relatively invisible population, they are also a growing one. It was predicted that more Guyanese would reside outside of their country of origin than within by 2010.

Chronology

1498	Guyana is "discovered" by Spanish.
1580	Dutch trade outposts are established on Guyana.
1620	Dutch establish forts. West India Company imports slaves from Africa to work on the sugar plantations.

GUYANA

Mabaruma

Port Kaituma

Matthawa Ridge

Charity

Spring Garden

Parika

Georgetown

Arimu Mine

Bartica

Rosignol

Rose Hall

Peters Mine

Rockstorie

Linden

Mara
Corrivertorr

Issano

Kalkuni

Potaro Landing

Iluni

Takama

Mahdia

Kwakwaui

Orinduik

Guyana

Kumpukari

Surama

Good Hope

Lethem

Dadanawa

Iserton

N

1763	Berbice Slave Uprising.
1814	Anglo-Dutch Treaty: the British gain control of Guyana.
1831	Colonies of Demerara-Essequibo and Berbice are united as British Guiana
1838	Slavery is abolished in Guyana. First East Indian indentured servants arrive in Guyana.
1917	Last shipments of East Indians to Guyana.
1964	Forbes Burnham and People's National Congress (PNC) replaces Cheddi Jagan's Progressive Party.
1965	U.S. immigration amendment stimulates mass migration from Guyana.
1966	Guyana's independence, continued political corruption from the PNC.
1970s–1980s	Guyanese emigrate via backtrack rings. In the late 1980s, 10,000 to 30,000 Guyanese emigrate legally and illegally.
1990	Guyana's debt reaches U.S. $2 billion, one of the highest debts in the world per capita.
1992	First fair election in Guyana since the 1960s; the Jagans return to office.
1999	Bharrat Jagdeo (People's Progressive Party [PPP]) assumes presidency in Guyana.
2000	Over 160,000 documented Guyanese immigrants in the United States; nearly 70 percent of these immigrants in New York City alone.
2010	It is predicted that more Guyanese will reside outside of Guyana than inside it.

Background

Geography of Guyana

Guyana lies between Venezuela and Suriname. Brazil borders Guyana to the west and south. It is an area of approximately 133,576 square miles, about the size of Idaho. An Amerindian word that literally means the "land of many waters," Guyana has four main rivers, three of which share the name of Guyana's three counties: Berbice, Demerara, and Essequibo. Demerara is sandwiched between Berbice and Essequibo counties and is the most densely populated county. Essequibo is located in western Guyana, its boundaries roughly delineated by the Essequibo River. It is the largest county with the smallest population. Guyana's largest river, the Essequibo River, runs south from Brazil up north towards the Atlantic Ocean. This equatorial country has a tropical climate that is characterized by high temperatures, rainfall, and humidity.

Guyana is comprised of three primary geographical regions: the coastal plain, the sand belt, and the interior highlands. The coastal plain is an area of fertile land that supports most of Guyana's agriculture industry; over 80 percent of the rest of Guyana's land is largely uninhabitable tropical rain forest. The coastal plain area lies below sea level. Tidal flooding makes agriculture here a challenge, and the seawall and drainage systems must be constantly maintained. Most of Guyana's population is concentrated on this sliver of land and around Georgetown, the capital of Guyana. Markets, government offices, universities, and industries are centered here.

Guyana's tourism industry lags behind those of the more profitable Caribbean destinations such as Jamaica and Barbados. Between 1970 and 1990, Guyana's tourism sector grew not even 2 percent annually. Its muddy beaches and dense forests appeal less to regular tourists but more to ecotourists who travel to pristine areas to observe natural wildlife. The Kaieteur Falls, one of the world's largest waterfalls, is five times as large as Niagara Falls. Kaieteur Falls drops from the Potaro River at 741 feet. This majestic waterfall is located in the highlands region, a mostly unpopulated area consisting of dense forest, mountains, and plateaus. Amerindians mainly inhabited this area. The prominent Pakaraima Mountains, the rocky Kaieteur Plateau, and the low-lying Acarai Mountains dominate southern and western Guyana.

The sand belt is an area of plateaus, hills, and white sands that lies between the coastal plain and the highland region. Guyanese mine bauxite deposits along this sand belt. Guyana has one of the largest bauxite reserves in the world, and bauxite was one of Guyana's most important exports. However, bauxite production and exportation has stagnated in recent years. International competition from countries like China that produce bauxite at a lower price have caused layoffs at bauxite companies in Guyana. Other major exports in Guyana are gold, shrimp, rice, and sugar. The sugar industry was especially profitable in early Guyana. European colonialists imported slave labor to Guyana because of the abundance and profitability of sugar cane. In the 1980s, however, sugar production declined, harvests shrunk, and international competition grew. According to Guyasuco, Guyana's largest sugar corporation, production grew in the 1990s, hit its peak in 1999, and dropped significantly in 2000.

History of Guyana

Guyana's ethnic diversity stretches back to Dutch colonization and the importation of human labor beginning in the 17th century. Europeans sought to settle the

Caribbean islands because they were beautiful, pristine lands full of natural resources, and especially suited for the production of sugar cane. Cultivation required
a vast amount of human labor. When the Dutch first arrived, they enslaved the local
Amerindian population and forced them to work in sugar cane fields. The Amerindian population suffered mass epidemics and genocidal conditions as a result of
Dutch enslavement and exploitation. Lacking a sufficient labor force, the Dutch
imported African slaves in order to increase sugar production and maintain a strong
workforce. As a result of often brutal treatment, African slaves rebelled in 1763 in
what has become known as the Berbice Slave Uprising. Under the leadership of
a house slave named Cuffy (also spelled "Kofi" or "Coffy") more than 500 slaves
revolted. Cuffy is celebrated today as a national hero.

By the 1800s, Dutch economic and colonial power began to wane. In 1814, under
the terms of the Anglo-Dutch Treaty, the British gained control of Guyana. They
made it an official colony in 1831 and from then until independence in 1966, it
was known as British Guiana. Guyana, at the time of British colonization, shared
in a growing worldwide consciousness for emancipation. Slavery was abolished
in 1838, 27 years before emancipation in the United States. However, colonial
elites needed to ensure the continued prosperity of the agricultural sector, so they
brought workers from India. India, as another British colony, had been made politically and economically weak. Indians were cheap sources of labor that the British
could export to Guyana through a new indenture system. East Indian importation
ensued from 1838 to 1917. During this time period, the British recruited about half
a million East Indians to work under five-year labor contracts, though only about
200,000 made it to Guyana due to arduous travel conditions. Eighty-five percent
of these Indians were recruited from India's northern provinces of Bihar and
Uttar-Pradesh. The British also recruited laborers from Portugal between 1835 and
1882 and from China between 1853 and 1884. This influx of laborers added to the
diversity in the country.

Harsh living conditions, difficult work, and maltreatment characterized plantation life for indentured servants. Estate owners physically and verbally abused
workers, who were undefended and neglected by the justice system. Many immigrant workers died of diseases during travel and during residence in cramped
double-storied barracks. On the plantation, estate owners used divide-and-conquer
tactics to split the Indian and African groups against one another. Ethnic groups
vied for scarce economic resources. Perhaps due to their European background,
only the Portuguese fared well of all the ethnic groups in Guyana, securing economic wealth by controlling retail trade.

Colonial elites used ethnic differences to their advantage and maintained an inequi-
table distribution of resources causing tensions that remain until today. For example,
once indentured servants from India had fulfilled their labor contracts, they were promised return passage. However, estate owners needed these workers on their plantations.

To keep them, estate owners drew up subcontracts that offered land grants in lieu of return passage. Rather than returning to their homeland, many Indians accepted these land grants and settled in Guyana. Yet, these land grants sparked resentment among African laborers. After emancipation, estate owners wanted to limit the economic power of African residents. Policies were enacted that restricted Africans from purchasing land. Therefore, after emancipation, many Africans deserted the plantations and established autonomous villages. However, colonial elites did not provide the maintenance, infrastructure, and vital services for these villages, and as a result, many African villagers fell further into poverty. East Indians were relative newcomers to Guyana, and their ownership of land offended the Afro-Guyanese. Africans had lived in Guyana for over two centuries and felt as though Guyana should be more readily claimed as their land. Over a century later, disparities in property ownership were still apparent. In the 1960s, upon independence from England, 85 percent of land owners were Indo-Guyanese, while Afro-Guyanese only represented 13 percent of land owners.

Interethnic conflict crystallized in the form of ethnicity-based politics. In the 1950s and 1960s, Guyana was preparing for independence from the British. The colonial political authority in Guyana restricted democratic participation, yet workers demanded improved work conditions and better pay. They formed unions, held strikes, and struggled against colonial rule. Emerging from these unions were political parties that vied for control. Cheddi Jagan, an influential Indo-Guyanese political leader, created the Political Affairs Committee (alternately referred to as the Political Action Committee or PAC in some texts) that called for Guyanese self-governance. The committee attracted Guyanese laborers and union organizers, and appealed to both Indo- and Afro-Guyanese. Forbes Burnham was an influential politician of Afro-Guyanese descent. Burnham joined with Jagan to transform the committee into the People's Progressive Party (PPP) in 1950. Jagan built the party based on socialist principles, which the United States and Britain disfavored. They viewed Jagan and the PPP as being pro-communist during this Cold War period.

In 1953, Jagan, as the PPP candidate, was elected to chief minister under a pro-labor platform. International actors sought to dissolve the party internally in favor of a more conservative base. The British suspended the Guyanese constitution, declared a state of emergency, and installed an interim government. The PPP began to break up internally. Forbes Burnham's politics clashed with Jagan's, and, in 1957, Burnham split with the PPP forming the People's National Congress (PNC). British officials encouraged and advised Burnham in forming the PNC. They noted that working-class Afro-Guyanese were more likely to support the PNC, and that Burnham needed to attract middle- and upper-class Afro-Guyanese in order for his party to succeed in the 1964 election. Burnham thus began an appeal to co-ethnic solidarity in order to consolidate Afro-Guyanese votes (Abraham 2007; Federal Research Division 1992). Similarly, the PPP began to appeal to the Indian population. The political focus thus shifted from labor-based politics to ethnicity-based politics.

Cheddi Jagan attends his victory parade in Georgetown, following his win in British Guyana's general elections on August 23, 1961. (AP Photo)

The 1960s saw the most violent racial conflicts; the intensity of the conflicts came to their height around the 1964 elections. Historians note that almost all ethnicity-related violence in Guyana is rooted in this election period. During these times the Afro-Guyanese minority fought with the Indian majority in Guyana. The PNC supporters looted Indian businesses, rioted in the streets, and led strikes against PPP-supported unions. Interethnic violence forced the population into segregated communities. Europeans emigrated from Guyana, resulting in a substantial white flight. The PNC formed a coalition with another independent, minority party, and in 1964, Burnham won the election. The Indo-Guyanese criticized the election as being fraudulent.

In 1966, shortly after this contentious election, Guyana gained its independence from Britain. The country saw momentary stability, peace, and economic growth. However, Burnham's moderate politics turned sharply leftist as he converted the state into an instrument of the PNC. Burnham ensured that the PPP would not win another election. The government gerrymandered voting districts to guarantee that the PNC's political domination would be unsurpassed. For the next 20 years, Guyana remained under the authoritarian leadership of the PNC. During this period, many Indians were beaten and killed. The resulting ethnic division led some members of the Afro-Guyanese community to feel that "the PNC had betrayed the wishes of the African people to live in a multiracial society" (Abraham 2007, 117).

In 1985, Vice President Desmond Hoyte assumed office after Burnham's death. To rectify the corruption and equalize relations between the PPP and PNC, Hoyte conducted what was seen as the first fair elections since the 1960s. The Guyanese people voted Hoyte and the PNC out and elected PPP's Cheddi Jagan. Indo-Guyanese saw Jagan's return to office after 30 years as a victory. Yet, the 1992 and 1997 elections continued to spark election violence in Guyana. Today, Guyana is a semi-presidential republic. Since 1999, the country has been presided over by President Bharrat Jagdeo (PPP) and Prime Minister Samuel Hinds (PPP). Although Guyana moves towards democracy, it has continued to struggle economically.

During the reign of the PNC, the party had mismanaged the economic sector and Guyana became heavily indebted. From the late 1970s until the 1990s, living standards and the economy further declined. The Guyanese dollar (GYD) depreciated steadily. In 1985, one U.S. dollar was worth $4.25 GYD. As the currency slid, a U.S. dollar was up to about $40 GYD in 1990; and, by 2000, over $180 GYD. Guyana steadily became one of the poorest countries in the Western Hemisphere. By the 1980s, Guyana had already received millions of dollars in aid from the United States. For example, in 1988 the United States provided about U.S. $7 million to Hoyte's administration as part of an Economic Recovery Program. In 1990, Guyana's debt was about U.S. $2 billion, over seven times its GDP. The government resorted to further loans from neighboring countries as well as the International Monetary Fund and World Bank.

As a condition of borrowing more funds, the World Bank required them to implement structural adjustment programs. Structural adjustment programs are programs that reorganize the internal economic structure of struggling countries, especially developing and debtor countries. These set of policies were set forth in Washington and implemented by the International Monetary Fund and the World Bank, two of the largest international economic institutions in the world. By reforming the economy, fledgling nations could repay their debts to loaner countries, like the United States. Yet, these programs only further depreciated public services and the quality of life in Guyana. Structural adjustment programs required reduced spending on public programs, tax reform, and privatization of state enterprises. Essential services such as health and education were no longer properly funded. The declining quality of life further incited Guyanese to migrate to the United States.

Causes and Waves of Migration

Guyana suffered a tumultuous political and economic history, the after-effects of British imperialism and colonialism. Guyana's history resembles that of other postcolonial nations wherein dislocated peoples must reorganize a socially disoriented and economically exploited country. In response to the political corruption, terrorization of Indians, and depreciating economy, many Indo-Guyanese chose to emigrate to seek a better life. Indo-Guyanese sought residence in the United Kingdom, the United States, and Canada. Many have moved to other Caribbean islands. Beginning in the 1960s, Indo-Guyanese joined the wave of new migrants to the United States.

The Indo-Caribbean wave of migration in the United States is a relatively new migrant wave compared to other migrant groups. The term "Indo-Caribbean" refers to immigrants of Indian descent from Guyana, Trinidad, and Tobago, or other Caribbean islands. Indo-Guyanese moved in response to the ethnic conflict and instability in Guyana. Many Guyanese no longer trusted the government, and instead they "voted with their feet." They left a country in which they felt unsafe, unprotected, and underrepresented. Demographers estimate that as a result of this migration, more individuals of Guyanese ancestry reside outside of the country than within Guyana.

Post-1965 Migration

Changes in United States immigration policy stimulated movement from Guyana to America. In 1965, the United States lifted immigration restrictions and expanded immigration allowances to the global "south," a region which included Latin America and the Caribbean. The amendments to immigration legislation abolished the national origins quota system. Race and ancestry were no longer as important a basis for immigration. The new legislation allocated immigrant visas on a first-come, first-served basis. Preference was given to relatives of U.S. citizens and persons with special occupational skills, abilities, or training.

As a result of the liberalized policy, Indo-Guyanese intellectuals, medical professionals, and members of the Guyanese upper-middle class looked to the United States as a destination (rather than other countries in the British Commonwealth). Professionals migrated to seek better opportunities, and prospective students moved abroad to attend universities in the United States. The migration of Guyanese professionals and intellectuals resulted in a so-called brain drain in Guyana. After establishing residency, typically in the gateway city of New York, Guyanese immigrants then sent for their family members. Between the 1970s and late 1980s, over 10,000 Guyanese migrated per year. In 1976, 43 percent of Guyanese emigrants moved to the United States, 31 percent went to Canada, 10 percent migrated to Great Britain, and 9 percent moved to other Caribbean nations. In the late 1980s, 10,000 to 30,000 Guyanese emigrated per year both legally and illegally.

Indo-Guyanese who became naturalized citizens of the United States were eligible to obtain family visas. They sponsored families and relatives to come to the United States. These existing networks abroad lowered the costs and risks of migration, making migration easier for future Indo-Guyanese immigrants. Entrepreneurs and professionals in the receiving areas established institutions, businesses, and organizations to satisfy the needs of the new Indo-Guyanese population. Networks and institutionalization encouraged and facilitated future migration. These changes indicated a pattern of cumulative causation in which migration altered the receiving context and made additional movement more likely. Cumulative causation stimulated a momentum that made immigration more resistant to government regulation. In this way, Indo-Guyanese constantly flowed into the United States.

Backtracking

Once social networks had been established between professionals from Guyana living in the United States and those back in the home country, other social classes were able to migrate. A prospective immigrant to the United States could cash in on their assets and use the money to apply for a visa and purchase a home in the United States. They could also use the money to enter other immigration channels. For Indo-Guyanese, there are three typical paths to migration: through family sponsorship under U.S. immigration legislation; by obtaining a visa under immigration allowance; or through the "backtrack" method. Backtracking is an illegal enterprise that allows immigrants to enter through the "back door." A backtracker first pays a fee to smugglers before leaving Guyana. Smugglers provide a valid passport of an actual U.S. resident whose photo is replaced with that of the backtracker. The backtracker enters an intermediate, or "pipeline," country such as Brazil or Venezuela before arrival in the intended country. Backtrackers and other illegal immigrants also seek political asylum while in the United States. Political asylum may be granted to immigrants who flee their home country to escape political, religious, or other form of persecution.

Receiving Locations

Most Guyanese reside on the East Coast, as far north as New York and as far south as Florida. Other than New York, which has the highest Guyanese population, New Jersey, Maryland, Georgia, and Florida have significant Guyanese populations. Indo-Guyanese have settled mainly in "gateway cities," or large metropolises that tend to attract immigrants from around the world. The largest Indo-Guyanese community in the United States is in New York City, in an area called Richmond Hill. Richmond Hill is located in Queens, which is New York's most immigrant-populated borough. Locals in Queens refer to Richmond Hill as "Little Guyana." Other ethnic groups previously populated the area, mainly Italian, Irish, and German immigrants. Richmond Hill drew Indo-Guyanese because of affordable home ownership. Due to family networks and expanding Indo-Caribbean businesses, Richmond Hill has grown into the large Indo-Caribbean community that it is today.

Little Guyana in the Richmond Hill section of Queens, New York. (Courtesy of Natassaja Chowthi)

IRCA to the Present

Migration to the United States continues, both legal and illegally. Both the United States and the Guyanese governments maintain migration statistics; however, it is hard to obtain accurate statistics for Indo-Guyanese because of backtrackers who evade the migration process. The Immigration Act of 1990 increased the overall immigration cap to an allowance of 675,000 new persons annually. Out of these 675,000 new immigrants, 480,000 could be family-sponsored. Post-1990 legislation has focused on illegal immigrants, criminals, and immigrants who overstayed their visas. The United States began to deport non-citizens sentenced to a year or more in prison. In 2001, the United States government refused to grant visas to Guyanese officials until the Guyanese government agreed to receive over 100 Guyanese deportees. Between 1997 and 2004, the United States deported a total of 1,400 Guyanese to Guyana.

Demographic Profile

Demographics

According to the latest Guyanese census, the population of the country is just over three-quarters of a million. This is nearly the population of South Dakota. Guyana

Ethnic composition in Guyana, 2002

Ethnicity	Population	Percentage
East Indian	326,277	43.45
African/Black	227,062	30.2
Mixed	125,727	16.73
Amerindian	68,675	9.16
Portuguese	1,497	0.2
Chinese	1,396	0.19
White	477	0.06
Other	112	0.01
Total population	751,223	100

Source: Guyana Census 2002.

is comprised of multiple and diverse ethnic groups including East Indians, Africans, Chinese, Europeans, Portuguese, and Amerindians. Guyana's ethnic diversity makes up its rich cultural heritage yet has also been center focus for violence and political conflict. The two largest ethnic groups in Guyana are Indo-Guyanese and Guyanese of African descent, or Afro-Guyanese. In 2002, Indo-Guyanese made up about 43.5 percent of the population and Afro-Guyanese made up about 30 percent. About 9 percent of the population was Amerindian, and Europeans and Chinese comprised less than 1 percent of the population. About 17 percent of the remaining population were individuals of mixed heritage.

Size and Composition of Community in United States

According to the 2000 Census, over 160,000 persons reported "Guyanese" as their national background. Yet others view this figure as low and place the total population of Guyanese descent at more than 300,000. It is difficult to ascertain the number of Indo-Guyanese versus Afro-Guyanese in the United States because these statistics lump them together into a single category. In 2000, over 130,000 Guyanese (as much as 80% of the population) resided in New York City alone. According to New York City's Department of City Planning, Guyanese are the fourth-largest immigrant group in New York City. Thus, we will focus on data that comes from this area in order to provide a more accurate picture of this population.

What makes statistics on this population even less reliable is the fact that census forms do not provide race categories applicable to Indo-Guyanese. Based on the race categories on the 2000 Census, Indo-Guyanese can choose from "Asian" or "some other race," neither of which accurately describe Indo-Guyanese ethnic identity. The census also provides the option to select multiple categories or write

Demographic changes of Richmond Hill from 1990 to 2000

Race/Hispanic origin	Number	Percent change 1990 to 2000
White non-Hispanic	−26,206	−39.5
Black/African American	2,175	28.7
Asian and Pacific Islander	13,230	134.4
American Indian and Alaskan Native	652	192.3
Some other race	4,917	894.0
Hispanic	23,150	84.2
Total population in 2000	141,608	

Source: United States Census 2000.

in a race or ethnicity. However, the 2000 Census tabulated individuals who selected two or more races as "multiracial." In the Richmond Hill area, persons of "some other race" (thought to be primarily Guyanese immigrants) grew 894 percent between 1990 and 2000.

Age and Family Structure

Guyanese are a relatively new immigrant population in the United States. This population generally consists of families with children; educated, working adults; and home owners. Family households made up almost three-quarters of the population. Almost half of these families consisted of children under the age of 18. For example, in the Richmond Hill area the average household size was three to four persons. Nearly two-thirds of the population was under the age of 40, and nearly half of the population was under the age of 34. In 2005, the median age for Guyanese in New York City was 36, on par with the city's overall median age. The population structure also exhibited a "youth bulge" in which there were higher numbers of persons in the younger, middle-age groups (see Figure 16). Over 40 percent of the population was between 20 and 45 years old. This may indicate the age range at which most Indo-Guyanese immigrate.

Economic Attainment

American society expects immigrants to contribute to the economy. Like many new immigrants, Indo-Guyanese work hard in the United States. They face the challenge of incorporation into the American workforce. In Guyana, many were teachers, professionals, and entrepreneurs. They may hold certifications and degrees from institutions and universities in Guyana. In the United States, however, these credentials are not accepted as equivalent to credentials granted here. These professionals must begin a new earning new degrees and certifications in the United States in order to qualify for the same jobs they had in Guyana. Because some new immigrants cannot immediately afford the cost of tuition at an American university or cannot invest the time for classes, many must accept lower-wage work.

In 2000, the average Guyanese household in New York City had a median income of nearly $42,000, slightly higher than New York City's overall median household income of $38,293. However, per capita income, or the average income per individual, was only about $20,000 (below the per capita income of $22,402 for New York). This indicates that Guyanese households are usually multiple-income households. Indeed, data show that more Guyanese women participated in the labor force than other ethnic groups except for Filipinas, Jamaicans, and Trinidadians.

In New York City, immigrants are disproportionately represented in the manufacturing, construction, and service industries. A large percent also work in the educational, health, and social service sectors. Yet, about a quarter of the Guyanese in New York are employed in management and professional occupations. About 8 percent of Guyanese immigrants were unemployed, and a smaller proportion of Guyanese than native-born New Yorkers were in poverty in 2005. Guyanese were third, just behind Italians and Greeks, in home ownership. Guyanese had higher rates of home ownership because multiple-income households pool earnings to support mortgage payments and other living expenditures.

Many of the Guyanese households in the United States contributed a portion of their income to overseas relatives. On average, families remit about U.S. $200 per month to assist with living expenses and utilities for relatives in Guyana. Poorer families in Guyana rely on these remittances from overseas family members, who also send Christmas and holiday gifts. Seventy percent of these remittances are sent via money transfer services such as Western Union and MoneyGram. Guyana's economy also depends on these remittances. The Inter-American Development Bank estimates that in 2007 nearly 43 percent of the country's GDP came in the form of remittances. The percent of remittances to Guyana have increased with the rising out-flow of Guyanese to the United States and other countries. However, due to the effect of the economic crisis on working Guyanese families in the United States, remittances to Guyana have declined since 2008.

Educational Attainment

In 1990, Guyana had one of the highest literacy rates in the Western Hemisphere at over 98 percent. Guyana's education system was derived from the British colonial system, in which education is highly regarded as an avenue for upward social mobility. Being a schoolteacher in Guyana is an esteemed profession. Because of the high emphasis placed on education, most Guyanese emigrated with a degree from a secondary school. More Guyanese than any other ethnic group in New York City held a high school diploma.

Adjustment and Adaptation

For many immigrants, the initial experience after migrating to the United States is one of culture shock. When Indo-Guyanese began to migrate to the United States, it was a haven during the Burnham era in Guyana. They fled their country but continued to maintain links to Guyana. Little Guyana, the Indo-Caribbean transnational community in New York City, has a constant flow of information, people, and goods coming from Guyana, as well as information, remittances, and other resources streaming back to Guyana. Yet, New York City is also a new context with a high population density; a mix of ethnicities; and a colder, wintry climate as opposed to the warm, tropical climate of Guyana. When it comes to cultural adjustment, Indo-Guyanese do have several advantages over most immigrants. First, they are native English speakers and do not have the barrier of a foreign language. In addition, American culture is already an established influence in Guyana. Media and overseas relatives have, at least superficially, provided Indo-Guyanese with an idea of what American culture is like.

Family, Culture, and Life-Cycle Rituals

Indo-Guyanese religious practices are unique to Indo-Caribbeans and were shaped by social processes in Guyana. While the main religious affiliations among Indo-Guyanese are Hinduism, Christianity, and Islam, the majority of Indo-Guyanese are Hindu. The Hinduism practiced by Indo-Guyanese is a modification of orthodox Hinduism. During the period of indentured servitude, East Indians lived in plantation households where estate owners restricted contact with extended kin and members of the same caste. They were exposed to other East Indians of various castes, dialects, and social backgrounds. As a result of the social mixing, the caste system collapsed and practices related to caste diminished. In addition, the British imported very few East Indian women to Guyana, limiting men's choices for partners from their same caste and thus disrupting the inheritance of caste. East Indian transnational ties to India also faded during the postindependence Guyana as communications and travel were too expensive to maintain. As a result, the Indo-Guyanese practice a variation of Hinduism that lacks the strict caste structure and has evolved away from the practices on the Indian subcontinent.

Little Guyana supports and preserves the continuance of religious practice. In Richmond Hill there are several Guyanese Hindu temples where worship, prayer, and ceremony take place. These temples often serve as spaces for social events like weddings, religious holidays, and birthdays. The *pandit,* or Hindu priest, is highly regarded in the community. *Pandits* provide the spiritual guidance for Indo-Guyanese. They are involved in weddings and other life rituals, provide counsel to families, and organize cultural activities.

One of the key religious holidays for Indo-Caribbeans is Holi. This is a Hindu occasion that ushers in the new spring season in March. Holi is more popularly called Phagwah (pronounced "Pahg-wah"), a "festival of colors." In Little Guyana, Indo-Caribbeans celebrate the event through a series of cultural festivals at local Hindu temples or *mandirs*. The festivals include food, dancing, and musical performances. Thousands of Indo-Caribbeans congregate at the Phagwah parade on Liberty Avenue, where the main shopping and business activities occur. The parade attracts Indo-Caribbeans and family members from around the United States and even Guyana. Religious songs are performed from parade floats sponsored by local *mandirs*. After the parade, a crowd meets at a local park where the celebrators playfully throw colored powders onto one another in festivity. Baby powder or liquid dye sprayed from bottles is often used. The tradition of playing with these colored powders represents joy, unity, and the colorfulness of spring.

Tassa drumming is common at cultural and religious events. *Tassa* drums are specific to Indo-Caribbean culture. Drums are played in groups and range from

Indo-Caribbean cultural gathering at a *mandir*, or Hindu temple, in New York. (Courtesy of Natassaja Chowthi)

high- to low-pitched sounds. The drumming is improvised and rhythmic, and often accompanied by dancing. Indo-Caribbeans also play *tassa* drums at Hindu weddings. Indo-Guyanese marriages are seen as rites of passage and a step into adulthood. Traditionally, parents select the partner and arrange the marriage. Elaborate Hindu weddings signify social prestige. It is traditional at Indo-Caribbean Hindu weddings for the bride to wear a sari, a wrap made from a long piece of colorful material. Weddings typically take place at a temple and proceed according to religious tradition. Funerals are another type of life event that is attended by family and extended networks of kin, friends, and associates. Kin serve as a support system to the family of the deceased. Grief is publicly articulated at funerals and wakes.

Family

Indo-Guyanese families are typically patriarchic, or male-headed, and women and children are subordinate to the male. Marriage rates for Indo-Guyanese tend to be higher than that of Afro-Guyanese because Indo-Guyanese hold more conservative beliefs about relations between men and women. Many Indo-Guyanese practice Hinduism, which informs their beliefs regarding marriage. These beliefs also cast cohabitation, premarital sex, and adultery in a negative light. Family is important to Indo-Guyanese. Relatives who are newly arrived in the United States rely heavily on family who sponsor their migration. Family members work multiple jobs and pool earnings to contribute to the household. Relatives and grandparents may help with childrearing by looking after children while parents are at work.

American society imposes different laws and social norms that affect family life for Indo-Guyanese. For example, Indo-Guyanese, and other West Indians, believe in the physical discipline of children. When children misbehave, parents use corporal punishment as a tool for discipline. Laws in the United States that limit physical discipline may see these actions as child abuse. American Indo-Guyanese parents are thus restricted in the way they discipline children. They are also limited in their involvement in children's lives because of their busy work schedules. Parents may leave children temporarily unsupervised; therefore children have more freedom than they would in Guyana. In Guyana, support networks of kin, teachers, neighbors, and friends helped to raise children. There are villages in Guyana that shared beliefs and cultural context. In America, such villages do not exist in the way that they did in Guyana.

Changing Gender Relations

Differences between American and Indo-Guyanese culture also influence the treatment of Indo-Guyanese women. In Guyana, physical abuse towards women was a common problem that may be traced back to its colonial history. During the East Indian indenture period, Europeans imported more East Indian men to Guyana than women. There was an overabundance of men that provided women a wide choice among partners. To bind women to the family and restrict social mobility, men asserted power upon women via physical violence. Women were victims of wife-beating, sexual abuse, infidelity, and men's alcoholism. Alcoholism among Indians in Guyana has been problematic since the 1850s. During the indenture period, alcohol abuse was a response to the cultural disorientation of Indians and harsh living conditions on the plantation. There were reports of frequent intoxication and public drunkenness among Indian immigrant men during this time period. Today, drinking rum continues as part of Indo-Guyanese culture. Rum is often present at social events and is a custom especially among men.

In Guyana, men dictate a woman's life and restrict her decisions regarding employment and education. Women endure sometimes physically and emotionally abusive marriages because of religious beliefs, financial reliance on the husband, or the social stigma of divorce. While the Guyanese legal system prohibits domestic violence, the police poorly enforce the law. Indo-Guyanese women in the United States also experience many of the same abuses but are provided more protection and support options than in Guyana. In response to violence against women, several women's support groups formed to serve female victims in the Queens area. Sakhi, meaning "women friend," is an outreach organization against domestic violence that serves South Asian women in New York City. According to Sakhi's Web site, the largest percent of all survivors of domestic violence come to Sakhi from Queens, where Little Guyana is located. Organization members and outreach activists operate in the community to support women victims.

Although the family structure continues to be patriarchal, gender relations in Little Guyana are more equitable than those in Guyana. In Guyana, women achieve lower levels of educational attainment and face marginalization in the workforce. Indo-Guyanese women hold power only in the household realm and in managing relations with kin. Men, on the other hand, have free access to the public realms of the workforce and education. Yet, in New York City, more Guyanese women participate in the labor force than men. Women in New York City must work in order to provide enough earnings for the family. As a result, they gain more decision-making power in the United States than they had in Guyana. Indo-Guyanese women in Little Guyana manage businesses and own local shops and salons. More than homemakers, immigrant Indo-Guyanese women are actively involved in community organizations and a variety of occupations.

Retaining a Sense of National Culture and Identity

Like many other immigrant populations, Indo-Guyanese immigrants struggle to maintain their cultural identity in the United States. In Little Guyana, travel agencies advertise "rediscovery tours of India." Interested travelers book trips to India where they can learn about their ethnic and cultural heritage. Local newspapers also print advertisements for "Indian investments," in which moneyed investors can purchase acres of Indian land, reestablishing a tie to India. In the local context, Indo-Guyanese celebrate their heritage through cultural and national celebrations and maintain strong ties to Guyana via communications technologies and media.

In addition to being a religious holiday, Phagwah for Indo-Guyanese is a cultural and national celebration. Phagwah reflects Indo-Caribbean preservation of transnational ties between Guyana, America, and India. At these events thousands of relatives and friends from Guyana, Toronto, and around the United States come to rejoin family. During the Phagwah parade, Indo-Guyanese wave Guyanese and American flags. In 2007, New York City Mayor Michael Bloomberg declared May 26 Guyana Independence Day for the city. The event was celebrated with annual concerts and presentations in New York City. Guyanese of all ethnic backgrounds joined to celebrate Guyana's independence and culture. May 5 is annually observed as Indian Arrival Day, or the day in which indentured East Indians immigrated to Guyana in the 19th century. Indo-Guyanese celebrate this day as a reminder of their Indian ancestry. Another cultural event, the annual Duck Curry Competition, features West Indian foods, "chutney soca" dance performances, and other cultural events. Well-known Guyanese musicians often perform at these events. Another event, the Last Lap Lime is held annually in Toronto and attracts thousands of Guyanese from Canada and New York City. Events like these bring together Guyanese of all ethnic backgrounds and distant locations.

Communication technologies also allow Indo-Guyanese to maintain virtual transnational ties. YouTube posts, Facebook groups, and personal blogs are popular not only among Americans. Indo-Guyanese constantly update and access these communication sites. YouTube broadcasts local, amateur videos of Indo-Guyanese weddings, parties, or vacation footage. Indo-Guyanese youth can be seen wearing the latest American fashions or dancing to hip-hop music. Reunification sites are numerous. These sites help relatives and old high school friends reunite online. There are also online directories of Guyanese abroad who voluntarily list their contact information online in hopes of reconnecting with lost or distant loved ones. Sites like Guyanaoutpost.com provide links to directories of Guyanese on the Internet. Online newspapers and journals inform distant Indo-Guyanese on current events in Guyana's social and political scene. Stabroek News, Guyana Chronicle, and Kaieteur News are prominent online news sources in the Guyanese community. "Guyana community" Web sites feature travel information, recipes, Guyanese news, American news, and Guyanese literature and poetry. Many Indo-Guyanese cyber surfers have joined the intense online dialogue and comment on Guyanese issues.

There are also several social and cultural organizations for Indo-Guyanese like the Indo-Caribbean Federation and the Association for Guyanese Americans. Such organizations work to bring awareness to the local Indo-Caribbean and broader

Queens, New York, community. They promote education and Indo-Caribbean culture by hosting cultural events like Phagwah, Indian Arrival Day, and talent competitions. Local newspapers and journals such as the *Caribbean New Yorker* and *Guyana Journal* feature articles relevant to Indo-Caribbeans. These journals and newspapers connect Indo-Caribbeans in America to their West Indian and Indian roots. They include breaking stories and essays on Indian, West Indian, and American politics, government, and economy. Bollywood celebrity gossip and updates on international cricket matches contribute to the Indo-Caribbean community's entertainment.

Foodways, Music, and Entertainment

Liberty Avenue is the main shopping center in Little Guyana. Anything Guyanese can be bought or sold here. The area is especially busy in the summertime, when children are out of school, tourists are seeking a cultural spot to visit, and the weather is perfect for shopping. Numerous Guyanese restaurants, Indian clothing shops, open fresh-food markets, and stores that sell Guyanese gold line Liberty Avenue. Salons, real estate, mortgage, and insurance businesses are major services located in the area. Residential areas are located on either side of Liberty Avenue. These are mostly quiet, family-oriented neighborhoods. The A train runs directly over Liberty Avenue. It and the bus lines that run through this section of Queens provide the transportation for Little Guyana's residents.

Chutney soca and dancehall music resonates from the stereos of vehicles passing on Liberty Avenue. Chutney music is popular in Guyana, Trinidad, and in Indo-Caribbean communities abroad. This rhythmic dance music blends West Indian calypso with Indian folk songs (Warikoo 2005). Chutney soca music and Indian folk songs often accompany Indo-Caribbean events. Indian folk songs and songs from Bollywood films are popular among Indo-Caribbeans, a market for India's products. Older generations of Indo-Guyanese grew up watching Bollywood movies that consequently became part of Indo-Guyanese culture and entertainment. Local television stations in Little Guyana broadcast programming segments that feature Bollywood music videos and traditional Indian folk songs. Local shops also sell Bollywood movies and entertainment for the Indian and Indo-Caribbean communities. The Bollywood tradition that older generations were accustomed to has changed by becoming more westernized. Contemporary Bollywood movies incorporate hip-hop styled dances and more scandalous clothing for women, as opposed to traditional styles of dress.

Cricket is a prominent pastime in Little Guyana. This sport originated in Europe and became a part of Indian culture when India was under British rule. When East Indians arrived in Guyana, cricket traveled with them. It continues as a major leisure activity in Guyana and Little Guyana. Families and other spectators meet at park fields in Richmond Hill to watch local cricket matches. These fields in Richmond Hill are the typical sporting venue for cricket matches. Members of the community play and organize cricket clubs. Some clubs consist of local businessmen preparing for annual competitions. Cricket is a pastime that connects the players, supporting families, and the community.

One of the most distinct aspects of Indo-Caribbean culture is the uniqueness of the food. These foods combine Indian, West Indian, and Chinese ingredients and dishes. In Little Guyana, *roti* shops and Guyanese-Chinese restaurants receive high traffic daily. *Roti* is a round flatbread (similar to a tortilla) used for eating curry and other dishes. Curry and rice are common Indo-Guyanese dishes. Guyanese-Chinese food is Chinese food cooked Guyanese-style. It usually consists of fried rice, chow mein, and a mix of Indo-Guyanese foods, like Tandoori chicken. Tandoori chicken is an Indian dish in which chicken is marinated in a sauce that consists of spices, yogurt, peppers, and other various ingredients. Indo-Guyanese food also includes Caribbean foods like fried plantains and "cook-up." Cook-up is a stew made of rice, coconut milk, black-eyed peas, and meats. Pepperpot is another distinctly Guyanese dish. It is a stew derived from Amerindian culture that includes various meats, peppers, and *cassareep,* a molasses-like preservative from the cassava fruit. Guyanese food in general reflects the ethnic diversity and cultural richness of Guyanese people.

Integration and Impact of U.S. Society and Culture

Paths toward Citizenship

American society imposes certain expectations on immigrants, one of which is eventual naturalization. Naturalization entails continuous residence in the United States for five years and completion of a naturalization interview and application. Immigrants seeking naturalization must display certain qualities expected of American citizens. They must have entered the United States lawfully, show allegiance to the United States and understand the U.S. Constitution and history. They must also speak, understand, and write simple English (though some exemptions are made for those over 50 years old). One advantage that Indo-Guyanese have over many immigrants in that they are English speaking. In Guyana English is the official language. According to the Department of Homeland Security, in 2009, over 6,600 Guyanese immigrants obtained legal permanent resident status and nearly 75,000 Guyanese immigrants have obtained this status since 2000.

Intergroup Relations

Although Indo-Caribbeans in New York City mostly live in Little Guyana, they work and do business in the larger American public, where they encounter intergroup boundaries, stereotypes, and interethnic relations. The relations between ethnic groups in the United States differ from those in Guyana because there are different groups in America, especially in New York City. Here different groups delineate social territories, or "turfs" that are often crossed. "Turf" refers to the physical or social territory claimed by a group. It can be allocated according to certain rules and governed by social boundaries.

The United States provides new turf for Indo-Guyanese. In Guyana, the main ethnic conflict centered between Indo-Guyanese and Afro-Guyanese. In the United States, where there are other West Indians, Latinos, Asians, and many other race groups, the polarized Indo-Guyanese versus Afro-Guyanese conflict tends to recede. The new social context and wider social space lessens the conflict between the two groups. In addition, social interactions that occur during cultural or national celebrations create a shared sense of unity among Guyanese people. Indo- and Afro-Guyanese relationships and intermarriages are not unheard of; yet, group boundaries still remain. In New York City, these two groups continue to self-segregate.

Overt interethnic conflict, although not widespread, happens in Little Guyana. According to local news sources in Queens, residents accused the police of racially profiling Guyanese people in Richmond Hill. Guyanese have been disproportionately targeted for minor traffic offenses and arrests. After September 11, 2001, Sikh men (who wear a turban) and other Indo-Guyanese were the targets of hostilities and racial violence due to their appearance, which was mistaken as a resemblance to Middle Easterners. In 2007, a plot that involved three Guyanese and Trinidadian men at the JFK International Airport in Queens stirred commotion and conversation in the media. American media associated Guyanese immigrants with Islamic terrorists. The event startled Americans and Indo-Guyanese alike, who view Little Guyana and other Guyanese neighborhoods as peaceful and multicultural communities. Although final investigations did not link the JFK plot to Little Guyana or the Guyanese community, the event unfortunately contributed to negative images of Guyana nationals.

Indo-Guyanese immigrants also face the task of providing constant definitions of their ethnic identity for their American counterparts. Indo-Guyanese physically resemble other South Asians. However, their accent is West Indian. The geographical mismatch between Indo-Guyanese's Indian appearance and West Indian language confuses many Americans. Indo-Guyanese must explain their Indian ancestry and Guyanese nationality. Job applications and college forms only provide a few racial categories, usually white, African American, Asian or Pacific Islander, American

Indian, and Hispanic or Latino. Indo-Guyanese may select multiple categories that do not accurately fit their ethnic background. No category is specific to Guyana, which is culturally Caribbean, located in South America, but not Spanish-speaking.

The creation of an Indo-Caribbean enclave has allowed Indo-Guyanese to create a sense of identity. It also provides a sense of comfort and familiarity. Like their American counterparts who settled into communities across the United States, Indo-Guyanese became comfortable in their community and around other people who share their culture, experiences, identity, language, and traditions. Some Indo-Guyanese initially moved to Tampa, Florida, or other American cities, then later chose to move to New York because of the large Indo-Caribbean population there. Being among familiar faces makes the adjustment to American society less daunting than attempting to incorporate into a community of strangers.

Indo-Guyanese often talk to one another in "old talk." Old talk refers to the habitual, regional dialect in Guyana. This language is English, but it incorporates culture-specific words and phrases. This way of talking has its own rhythm and flow, and resembles other West Indian accents. Indo-Guyanese can make references to Guyana and tell stories to which Americans cannot relate. In addition, Indo-Guyanese participate in code switching. Code switching is the ability to converse in American Standard English when speaking to non-Guyanese Americans, then instinctively slipping into the Caribbean dialect or old talk when among family or close friends.

Political Associations and Organizations

Political organizations in Little Guyana support community empowerment and provide a representative voice for Indo-Caribbeans in Queens. Local politicians include attorneys, business professionals, and community leaders. They encourage Indo-Caribbean self-awareness, education, and participation during election seasons. Political clubs meet on a regular basis and provide an outlet for community dialogue. Unfortunately, however, the Indo-Guyanese population is not very active in participating in formal political affairs of Richmond Hill. The reason for this owes to their lack of trust in Indo-Caribbean politicians. Political mistrust stems back to the political context in Guyana, where political actors utilized race as a tool for party antagonism and national division. Indo-Guyanese who migrated during the 1960s remembered the victimization of Indians in Guyana by PNC supporters. Those who fled during the Burnham era emigrated to escape political corruption. Although the American political system rests on principles of a representative democracy and provides a new political context for emerging leaders in Richmond Hill, Indo-Guyanese continue to doubt Indo-Caribbean politicians. For those eligible to vote, the structure of daily life also limits their opportunity to vote. After having to work long or multiple shifts during the day, by the time many Indo-Guyanese commute home the polling stations are closed.

In Richmond Hill, some organizations eventually collapse under the problems of regulation and management. Local politicians and other interest groups often seek out these organizations and monopolize meetings to gain public visibility or seek donations. In addition, residents in the local community may view these meetings as spaces in which they can voice their community complaints, rather than contribute to the community dialogue. These issues frustrate community leaders and politicians who seek to give political voice to Little Guyana. Yet, local leaders continue to work and encourage local Indo-Caribbean involvement in the political process even going door-to-door to register voters in Richmond Hill.

As a result of limited political participation, Indo-Guyanese are not very well represented. American politicians lack the cultural expertise to reach out to the community, often overlooking the needs of Indo-Caribbeans. As a result, Richmond Hill lacks essential resources such as immigration support services, youth development facilities, and senior centers. After-school centers could provide a place for children who are unsupervised while parents are away at work. In the same way, when household members are out at work or in school, retired Guyanese immigrants remain home alone without medical assistance or social activities to engage them. Senior citizens are culturally integral to Indo-Guyanese families and the community because they help with child-rearing and pass along traditional values and cultural heritage. The inadequate senior centers in Richmond Hill are often underfunded and vandalized. Local Indo-Caribbean politicians try to bring these needs "to the table" during their campaigns, but without significant response from their constituents.

Religion often plays a role in the political affairs of Richmond Hill. Religion has historically been an integral force in guiding the politics in Guyana. In the 1950s, the Catholic Church in Guyana publicly disapproved of the PPP's socialist political stance. Other Christian denominations also censured the Guyanese government during the Burnham era. In the 1980s, religious councils and the government clashed on issues related to the failings of the PNC. In Richmond Hill, religion and politics continue their antagonistic relationship. Clergy perform the central role of leading the spiritual and social lives of Indo-Guyanese. When these leaders do not support particular Indo-Caribbean politicians, their stance influences those of the congregation. Religious and political leaders sometimes have conflicted on their interests for the community. Indo-Caribbean politicians often struggle in garnering support without the endorsement of religious leaders. At cultural events like Phagwah, parade organizers do not allow politicians to sponsor a float in the parade. The event is seen as a religious and cultural event and not a political one. Yet, the event does provide a space for local politicians to interact with residents.

While Indo-Guyanese are not active in formal governance, it does not mean that they lack political power altogether. The Indo-Caribbean cultural and political organizations in Richmond Hill openly acknowledge Indo-Caribbean political identity as the focus of their work. Their publications place emphasis on their identity as an Indian diaspora with transnational political connections to India, Guyana, and the United States. Through initiating and building upon community dialogue, they have begun to mobilize Indo-Caribbean political power. Several organizations have been successful in mobilizing the community to engage in a reflection of Guyana's political past in order to improve Indo-Guyanese Americans' political future.

Return Migration

In the 1990s the Guyanese government sought to re-attract overseas Guyanese through a "Remigration Scheme." The plan mostly attracted Guyanese professionals and business persons. Indo-Guyanese professionals also periodically returned to Guyana to maintain their overseas businesses. Some Indo-Guyanese return to attend cricket finals, while others return to visit with family. These visits are temporary and usually not a sign of permanent return migration. Guyana continues to lose population to emigration. In 1960, Guyana's population was about 630,000. By 1995, demographers estimated that it should have doubled to nearly 1.5 million. However, Guyana's population has been hovering at only around 750,000 since 2000.

Some Indo-Guyanese desire to return to Guyana. They experience a different America than the "melting pot" or "promised land" to which they looked forward. When they migrated to the United States, like many other Indo-Guyanese, they cashed in on their assets and used the money to purchase a home in the United States. In order to return to Guyana, they would have to resell their homes in Richmond Hill and use the money to re-purchase a home in Guyana. However, home values have inflated since they left Guyana leaving them unable to afford to repurchase a home in Guyana. They have become economically "stuck" in America.

Still, Little Guyana has become a home-away-from-home for many Indo-Guyanese. Since migrating, they have established businesses, started families, and created social connections in America. Older immigrant generations feel satisfied and rooted in Little Guyana. Little Guyana holds the potential as serving as a launching point for the second generation of Indo-Guyanese, who may eventually branch out into communities and cities across America if they follow a similar trajectory as other immigrant populations. The community provides resources and opportunities that allow future generations more opportunities than were available in Guyana. They can obtain jobs outside of Richmond Hill, enroll in American universities, and relocate to new cities in the United States. The older generation sees Little Guyana as a launching pad for younger generations' success.

The Second and Later Generations

The term "first generation" refers to the foreign-born group of Indo-Guyanese who migrated to the United States. Their children, born in the United States, are the second generation, and they have experiences, a culture, and an identity that is very different from that of their parents. In a recent study of the Indo-Guyanese community in Queens, a first-generation Indo-Guyanese interviewee expressed concern for the second generation:

> I'm kind of worried about my children. I grew up in a house that had no refrigerator. I mean ice for us was a big thing. You had to go to the store and buy ice. . . . And here my kids come home they open the refrigerator and there's cold stuff there, and it's like, and I'm not saying that they should be at a disadvantage, but I'm worried for them in the sense that—I never had a television in my house, we used to go to a neighbor's house and watch television. We went to the movies, yeah, but we don't come home and turn on the TV, you know, and were exposed to all these different things. And I think that help mold and shape who I am today. I don't know how its gonna turn out for my children and our future generation if we're living in conspicuous consumption or in an age of excess, I don't know. (Chowthi 2009)

The second generation did not experience life in Guyana. Although their parents told them stories about Guyana's circumstances and educated them about their ethnic history, the second generation grew up in American society. Here, life is easier than life in Guyana. The second generation also grew up in a technological era of cell phones, laptop computers, Internet, and Facebook. The first generation values hard work and wants their children to realize the opportunity that America presents. Thus, there exists a degree of tension between the generations.

The second generation also grew up in a racially diverse American society. At the schools they attend in New York City, they interact with many racial groups. Richmond Hill is not solely an Indo-Caribbean neighborhood; it is also comprised of Latinos, Asian Indians, African Americans, and whites. Indo-Guyanese youth can choose from various styles of dress, musical genres, and ways of communication from the diverse cultural tool kits available to them. They find a common way of interacting and find shared interests. Different styles of music other than chutney soca have become popular among Indo-Caribbean youth. As a result of diverse interactions and American cultural influence, second-generation youth in

New York City are more cosmopolitan than their non-Indo-Guyanese American counterparts.

Ethnic Identity

Second-generation Indo-Guyanese have a wide range of ethnic identities to select from. Identifying with just one racial or ethnic group is a challenge for these cosmopolitan youth. Like the first generation, second-generation Indo-Guyanese must create an identity for themselves within the context of the United States. They do not neatly fit into racial or ethnic categories like those presented on census forms; they form their own unique ethnic identity different than that of South Asians and other Guyanese. Indo-Guyanese who grow up in the United States have a fluid identity that is not easily defined. They incorporate diverse experiences and interactions with other ethnic groups into their sense of self, seeing themselves as Indo-Guyanese and Americans. They often identify with other Indian Americans and with Afro-Caribbeans. Indo-Guyanese youth do, however, draw boundaries around what they are not. In high school, youth refer to stereotypes, use racial epithets, and make group distinctions. The word "coolie" is used in Indo-Caribbean communities. The word was used historically to refer to Indian indentured servants; however, when used by non-Indians, the term is pejorative and offensive to Guyanese of Indian decent. However, Indo-Guyanese also use the word among themselves to describe certain cultural behaviors. One can behave very much "like a coolie," engaging in cultural-specific behaviors. Indo-Guyanese youth distinguish themselves from other groups; they are not entirely Indian, but of Indian ancestry. Similarly, they are not entirely West Indian or Guyanese because those labels hold the connotations of being of African ancestry. The second generation redefines itself in American society.

Cultural Identification

Indo-Guyanese are a small and new population in the United States, and the second generation is still relatively young. Research on the Indo-Caribbean second generation explores how youth feel pulled in the direction of the mainstream culture of the United States while simultaneously being drawn back by cultures of their own people. The Indo-Guyanese second generation experiences diverse interactions in New York City that fosters fluid, hybrid, or cosmopolitan identities. They feel pulled between two cultures and redefine what it means to be American and Guyanese.

Indo-Caribbean youth stay abreast of American trends, fashion, and popular culture. New immigrants learn about American culture through movies, music videos, and advertisements as sources of reference for the latest American trends. Indo-Guyanese youth incorporate the most recent fashion trend into their dress.

Shundell Prasad, Filmmaker

Shundell Prasad graduated from the highly acclaimed Tisch School of the Arts in New York, where she studied film and television production. She directed and produced *Once More Removed: A Journey Back to India,* her documentary film debut that tracked Prasad's ethnic ancestry back to India. Prasad began her travels in the Indo-Caribbean community in Queens, New York, after which she journeyed to Guyana, her country of birth. Prasad located her family's archived ship records and traced her heritage back to the Bihar province in India. The film reflects on the Indian diaspora, transnationalism, Indian indentureship, and the rich multicontinental cultural history of Indo-Guyanese people. Prasad pursued her ethnic lineage because of questions that she herself had about her ethnic identity, questions that she learned over 20 million other persons of the Indian diaspora shared.

Prasad's film career includes work with HBO's documentary division and as an associate producer for CNN. Prasad also worked for the *Wall Street Journal*, A&E/The History Channel, and on CBS's Emmy award–winning series *The Amazing Race.* Prasad has traveled to over 10 countries internationally, including Guyana, India, and countries in the Caribbean. She also speaks Hindi. Prasad is interested in issues of social significance such as Asian women's rights, poverty, and slavery. Among all of her accomplishments, Prasad was invited by the Indian government to speak on the Indian diaspora at an international conference in 2006. She met with Guyana's president Bharrat Jagdeo in working on her documentary film. In her mid-twenties, Prasad currently lives in New York and continues to travel and work in film. (http://www.oncemoreremoved.com/.)

Most recently, hip-hop clothing styles and basketball shoes are popular clothing styles among male youth. On Liberty Avenue, shoppers purchase American brands alongside Guyanese items. For Indo-Guyanese, American name brands are visible markers of identity. The fixation over these brand names was a common trend in Guyana influenced by the circulation between the countries. When a family member returned to Guyana to visit, they would "show off" their worldly, cosmopolitan lifestyle and status through their clothing. In this way, consumerism has become culturally ingrained among Indo-Guyanese and marks one's entrance as an American. Those who do not own material objects that mark their success and status are seen as "lesser and incomplete" persons.

The second generation in Little Guyana is more autonomous than youth in Guyana. Since both parents work and are unable to consistently monitor their child's school progress and social activities, they often leave children unsupervised. The child lacks the "village," or the tight network of neighbors, relatives, and community members that help with child-rearing in Guyana. While rum-drinking has always been a way of celebrating, especially during weddings, festivals, and family occasions in the Indo-Guyanese community, a new trend, especially among the younger second generation, is that of the party culture and nightclub industry. In Richmond Hill, Caribbean clubs, such as Club Tobago, are quite popular. At these clubs, DJs spin the latest dancehall and soca tracks. Newspapers and flyers use catchy slogans to advertise parties and special occasions. Celebration with alcohol combined with the nightclub industry keeps the "party lifestyle" a focus for many.

There is gender variation in the way Indo-Caribbeans feel about their traditional culture. For example, Indo-Caribbean boys and girls include various styles of dress into their personal appearance. According to a 2005 study of gender and ethnic identity, Indo-Caribbean girls tended to identify more with Indian culture, while boys distanced themselves from it (Warikoo). Indo-Caribbean girls were more interested in Indian clothing, movies, music, and traditions. Boys on the other hand viewed Bollywood movies and Indian clothing as being traditionally feminine things. Boys associated Indian-ness with powerlessness. Boys preferred to identify with American cultural aspects, like hip-hop clothing and music. They viewed these physical appearances as being more masculine and cool.

A group of boys, one sporting a Guyanese flag, at a Phagwah festival in New York. (Courtesy of Natassaja Chowthi)

However, at events like Phagwah, cultural, national, and transnational elements are woven together. In spite of the older generation's concerns that younger generations forget or take their culture for granted, younger generations actively engage in Indo-Guyanese culture. Youth groups participate in Caribbean cultural groups and school activities at their high schools. Teenagers perform *tassa* drumming. They also participate in pageants and perform traditional dances at cultural festivals. They know the words to Indian folk songs and can sing along. Large numbers of youth attend the Phagwah parade, after which they congregate at a local park to continue the celebration. They represent "the colors" by sporting Guyanese flags.

Issues in Relations between the United States and Guyana

In the past, the United States influenced Guyana's political, governmental, and economic problems. When Cheddi Jagan took office in 1953, the United States feared him to be a communist supporter and radical socialist. Jagan was born in Guyana but spent many years in the United States, where he attended Howard University and Northwestern University. When Jagan returned to Guyana, he used his political awareness and experience in America to form a party centered on labor union rights. He identified with several political ideologies, calling himself a "Marxist and a left-wing socialist" (Rabe 2005). In the 1950s, the United States was especially keen to monitoring potential communist threats around the world. Jagan and other PPP members had visited Germany and had contacts in communist countries. In addition, PPP members had been invited to Cuba during the Cuban revolution. While the PPP never posed an overt communist threat, the United States dispatched international officials into Guyana to report on PPP party dealings. President John F. Kennedy kept a watchful eye on the goings-on between Guyana and the Soviet Union. The fear was that Soviet Russia would ally with Guyana and build a military base. Guyana was within closer proximity to the United States than Russia and thus could pose a security threat to the United States and allies in Central or South America. When the PPP entered office, the United States sought to oust the party in favor of a more conservative base.

In the 1950s the British dispatched commissions to investigate the governmental affairs in Guyana. These commissions declared that PPP members were extremists, and Forbes Burnham was a less-threatening moderate, democratic socialist. These international commissions invited Burnham to leave the PPP or assume control of the party. London did not want to grant independence to a potentially dangerous and communist Guyana. In 1955, Burnham split with the PPP to form the PNC. International actors supported Burnham's move to take control and develop an anticommunist Guyana. In cooperation with the British, Eisenhower's administration provided nearly a million dollars to assist with infrastructure and industry development in Guyana.

While the Eisenhower administration merely supported the decisions made in London regarding Guyana's independence, the subsequent Kennedy administration was more aggressive in its intervention in Guyana. The administration was wary of Guyana's proximity to and sympathetic relations with Cuba. They warned against another "Castro" in the Western Hemisphere and organized CIA operations in Guyana. In 1961, Jagan met in Washington with President Kennedy and state department officials. Jagan assured the president of his democratic beliefs and asked for financial assistance for Guyana's future. Shortly after the meeting in Washington, arsonists and rioters burned down the capital city of Georgetown, Guyana. Afro-Guyanese terrorized Indians in the city streets, burned and looted Indian businesses. The city was in chaos, and PPP and PNC opposition aggravated ethnic tensions. Burnham organized mobs to "bring government down to the streets" (Rabe 2005). According to declassified CIA documents, the CIA aided in the Georgetown burning. The crisis prevented Jagan's efforts to ameliorate the United States' perceptions of the PPP. It also delayed Guyana's independence, providing international actors the time to help install the PNC government, a safer choice than the PPP.

State Department officials also influenced the result of the 1964 elections. Under the direction of the CIA, Burnham formed a coalition with a minority party, the United Front Party (UF) in order to win the majority of the vote. The CIA helped finance and advise the PNC-UF campaign. In addition, the Johnson administration offered over $10 million in economic aid after Burnham's election. In the 1964 election, Burnham and the PNC won the majority of parliamentary seats. After the election President Johnson granted aid to Burnham for infrastructural development. The racial violence continued in Guyana but was of little concern to the United States, who was mainly concerned with limiting communist threats in the region. In the years that followed, the United States cooled its position towards Guyana, and tension between the two countries subsided. However, the social and economic situation in Guyana worsened. Elections continued to be rigged to ensure that Burnham would stay in power, and Afro-Guyanese victimization of Indians led to mass emigration.

Guyana gained the most visibility by Americans not for its domestic ethnic tensions, nor its communist threat exaggerated by international actors, nor for its economic problems but for the sensational Jonestown Massacre of 1978. International media attention spotlighted Guyana when Reverend Jim Jones from San Francisco led over 900 American cult followers to their deaths in a mass suicide. The suicide plot was incited by Jones's attempt to escape investigation for the murder of California congressman Leo Ryan. Ryan had traveled to Guyana to investigate Jones and the small commune that he had established in Guyana. In the early 1970s, Jones moved his followers from San Francisco to a remote location in Guyana he named

Jonestown. Jones founded the small settlement in Guyana's western countryside, out of eyesight of the majority of the Guyanese population. However, the PNC was aware of the Jonestown settlement. During Ryan's investigation in Guyana, Jones and a cohort of supporters gunned down Ryan and his group. The event raised U.S. scrutiny of the PNC government.

The United States continues to monitor elections and politics in Guyana to ensure organized and democratic governance. International actors have increasingly focused on human rights issues. In a 2008 human rights report by the U.S. State Department, police brutality and unlawful killing, continued government corruption, and abuses toward women and children were found to be pervasive rights violations in Guyana. Guyana's inconsistent enforcement of laws has exacerbated the problems. Investigatory teams have been sent to observe the electoral process in Guyana. In a recent report from the Carter Center's Global Development Initiative, the electoral process in Guyana was found to be significantly improved since the Burnham regime and previous administrations. However, the improvements in the election process had not alleviated Guyana's economic dilemma, ethnic division, or government disorganization.

Forecasts for the 21st Century

Even though Guyana's government continues in its efforts towards rebuilding its economy and improving social relations, emigration will persist. By 2010 more Guyanese resided outside of Guyana than within the country. Migration to the United States from Guyana will continue to account for a large part of this diaspora. Political, economic, and social push factors will continue to fuel Indo-Guyanese mass movement to the United States. Migration will also be encouraged by the cumulative momentum of overseas networks and institutionalization in the United States. Naturalizations in the United States are expected to continue increasing. Likewise, the sociohistorical context of Guyana will continue to influence Indo-Guyanese migrants in the United States: their political views, racial identity, gender relations, and multifaceted culture. It will influence the way in which the identity of the second generation is constructed. Moreover, places like Little Guyana in Richmond Hill, New York, will continue to serve as transnational communities facilitating immigrant incorporation into the United States.

Appendix I: Migration Statistics

Table 129 Guyanese naturalizations, 1999–2008

Year	Number of naturalizations
1999	10,347
2000	10,794
2001	7,038
2002	7,220
2003	4,929
2004	4,877
2005	5,543
2006	7,434
2007	5,631
2008	8,290

Source: U.S. Department of Homeland Security.

Table 130 Persons obtaining legal permanent resident status by region and country of birth: Fiscal years 2000 to 2009

Region and country of birth	2000	2001	2002	2003	2004	2005	2006	2007	2008	2009
Total	841,002	1,058,902	1,059,356	703,542	957,883	1,122,257	1,266,129	1,052,415	1,107,126	1,130,818
Guyana	5,719	8,279	9,938	6,809	6,351	9,317	9,552	5,726	6,823	6,670

Source: U.S. Department of Homeland Security. Office of Immigration Statistics. 2010. Adapted from Table 3.

Table 131 States with highest Guyanese populations, 2000

State	Population	Percentage
New York	109,104	67.16
New Jersey	14,296	8.80
Florida	11,842	7.29
Maryland	5,315	3.27
Georgia	3,779	2.33
All others	18,120	11.15
United States total	162,456	100

Source: United States 2000 Census.

Table 132 Persons obtaining legal permanent resident status during fiscal year 2009 leading states of residence region/country: Guyana

Characteristic	Total	Male	Female
Total	6,670	2,932	3,738
Arizona	9	D	D
California	71	34	37
Colorado	12	5	7
Connecticut	104	39	65
Florida	614	272	342
Georgia	144	58	86
Illinois	16	5	11
Maryland	242	102	140
Massachusetts	58	25	33
Michigan	15	D	D
Minnesota	110	50	60
Nevada	6	D	D
New Jersey	547	231	316
New York	4,363	1,948	2,415
North Carolina	35	17	18
Ohio	37	14	23
Pennsylvania	75	34	41
Texas	58	23	35
Virginia	38	13	25
Other	116	49	67

Source: Adapted from U.S. Department of Homeland Security. Profiles on Legal Permanent Residents: 2009. Cobbook 88. 2010.
Note: D = Data withheld to limit disclosure.

Appendix II: Demographics/Census Statistics

It is difficult to ascertain the exact number of Indo-Guyanese in the United States. Backtrackers and other illegal immigrants are not counted in migration statistics. The statistics available may omit significant numbers of Indo-Guyanese. These statistics generally refer to the entire "Guyanese" population and include Guyanese of all ethnic backgrounds. According to the 2000 Census, over 160,000 persons reported "Guyanese" as their national background. Guyanese are the fourth-largest immigrant group in New York City. In 2000, over 130,000 Guyanese resided in the New York City area alone.

The relationship between the United States and Guyana is one of constant migration. In the late 1980s, 10,000 to 30,000 Guyanese emigrated legally and illegally. In 2008, over 8,000 Guyanese immigrants were naturalized. Over 60,000 Guyanese immigrants became naturalized citizens since 2000.

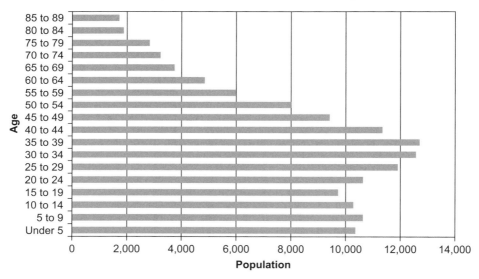

Figure 16 2000 population in Queens Community District 9.

Table 133 Demographic features of Guyanese in 2000

Official population size in United States	162,456
Median age	36
Median household size	3–4 persons
Median household income	$41,960
Home ownership	48.5% owner occupied
Poverty	13.4%
Education	65.4% high school graduate
Naturalizations in the United States	72,103 since 1999

Source: United States 2000 Census and 2005 American Community Survey.

Appendix III: Notable Indo-Guyanese Americans

Because Indo-Guyanese are a small and relatively new population in the United States, there are very few prominent Indo-Guyanese Americans. However, as the second generation ages and the population continue to grow, more notable Indo-Guyanese will emerge in United States. This list includes prominent Indo-Guyanese from the United States, Canada, and the United Kingdom.

Dave Baksh, Canadian, is former lead guitarist for Canadian rock band Sum 41. Sum 41 is also a rock band popular in the United States.

Albert Baldeo is a rising Indo-Guyanese politician in Richmond Hill. Baldeo was born in Guyana and migrated to New York City, where he pursued a career in law. His practice focuses on immigration rights and reform, real estate, and other areas that affect the Indo-Caribbean community. Baldeo nearly won a democratic seat in the New York State Senate race in 2006.

Shakira Caine is a former model, actress, and current wife of actor Michael Caine. Caine placed third in the 1967 Miss World pageant in London.

David Dabydeen is a poet, novelist, and critic. Dabydeen is a professor at the University of Warwick, where he is also director of the Centre for Caribbean Studies. Dabydeen's work has received numerous prizes and awards, including the Commonwealth Poetry Prize for his first book, *Slave Song,* a collection of poems, and the Anthony Sabga Prize for Literature in 2008. His work explores the history of Guyanese people and life experiences in Guyana. Dabydeen currently serves as the Guyanese Ambassador to UNESCO.

Shundell Prasad is a filmmaker in New York City. Her documentary film work traces her ancestry back to India.

Glossary

Amerindians: The native inhabitants of Guyana who lived in indigenous lands. There are Amerindian reservations in central Guyana to preserve Amerindian culture and lands.

Backtrack: An illegal enterprise that allows Guyanese immigrants to enter through the "back door." A backtracker first pays a fee to smugglers before leaving Guyana. They are provided valid passports of actual U.S. residents whose photo is replaced with that of the backtracker. The backtracker enters an intermediate, or "pipeline," country such as Brazil or Venezuela before arrival in the United States.

Chutney soca: a popular musical genre in Guyana, Trinidad and among other Indo-Caribbean people. This rhythmic dance music blends West Indian calypso with Indian folk songs.

Coolie: A term historically used to describe Indian indentured servants. Use of the term is usually pejorative and refers to individuals of Indian descent. The word "coolie" is both used as a racial epithet and to describe Indo-Guyanese cultural behaviors. To "act like a coolie" means to behave in a certain manner, or to act very Guyanese.

Indo-Guyanese: Refers to the ethnic identity of Guyanese persons of East Indian descent.

Pepperpot: A common Guyanese dish that derived from the Amerindian culture. Pepperpot is cooked by stewing various meats with peppers and *cassareep,* a seasoned molasses-like preservative from the cassava fruit.

Phagwah: A religious holiday from the Hindu religion. Also called "Holi," it is celebrated in March. Phagwah ushers in the new spring season and is celebrated by a "festival of colors." In Little Guyana, Queens, New York, the event is observed by a series of cultural festivals that are filled with food, dance, and musical performances. The Phagwah parade on Liberty Avenue attracts Indo-Caribbeans, family members from Toronto and Guyana, and local New Yorkers.

Tassa **drums:** Drums specific to Indo-Caribbean culture. Drums are played in groups and range from high- to low-pitched sounds. The drumming is improvised and rhythmic, and often accompanied by dancing.

References

Abraham, Sara. 2001. "The Shifting Sources of Racial Definition in Trinidad and Tobago, and Guyana: A Research Agenda." *Ethnic and Racial Studies* 24: 979.

Abraham, Sara. 2007. *Labour and the Multiracial Project in the Caribbean: Its History and Its Promise.* Lanham, MD: Lexington Books.

Berger, Joseph. 2004. "Indian Twice Removed." *New York Times*. December 14. [Online article; retrieved 9/24/08.] http://www.nytimes.com/2004/12/17/nyregion/17guyanese.html.

Canterbury, Dennis C. 1997. "The Impact of Neoliberalism on Labour in Guyana: A Case from the Caribbean." *Labour, Capital & Society* 30: 261–89.

Carter Center, "International Peacemaking and Human Rights Programs, Guyana." [Online article; retrieved 7/20/09.] http://www.cartercenter.org/countries/guyana.html.

Chowthi, Natassaja. 2009. *Changing Places and Questions of Identity: The Fluid Lives of First Generation Indo-Guyanese.* Master's thesis. [Online information; retrieved 5/27/11.] http://libres.uncg.edu/ir/listing.aspx?id=2436.

Clement, R., S. S. Singh, and S. Gaudet. 2006. "Identity and Adaptation among Minority Indo-Guyanese: Influence of Generational Status, Gender, Reference Group and Situation." *Group Processes & Intergroup Relations* 9: 289–304.

Dobnik, Verena. 2007. "Trying Times for NYC Guyanese Community." *Washington Post.* June 7. [Online article; retrieved 7/20/09.] http://www.washingtonpost.com/wp-dyn/content/article/2007/06/07/AR2007060700220.html.

Fasanella, Richard. 2000. "Converting Queens, Needed Shelter or Potential Danger?" *Queens Tribune.* [Online article; retrieved 7/20/09.] http://www.queenstribune.com/archives/featurearchive/feature2000/0217/index.html.

Federal Research Division of the Library of Congress. 1992. *A Country Study: Guyana.* Washington, D.C.: Federal Research Division of the Library of Congress.

Gowricharn, Ruben S. 2006. *Caribbean Transnationalism: Migration, Pluralization, and Social Cohesion.* Lanham, MD: Lexington Books.

Griffith, Ivelaw L. 1997. "Political Change, Democracy, and Human Rights in Guyana." *Third World Quarterly* 18: 267–85.

Guyana Bureau of Statistics. "Population Composition." *2002 Census.* Georgetown, Guyana. [Online article; retrieved 7/20/09.] http://www.statisticsguyana.gov.gy/census.html.

Guyana Chronicle. 2007. [Online article; retrieved 9/24/08.] http://www.guyanachronicle.com/.

Guyana Journal. 2009. Site maintained by Gary Girdhari. [Online article; retrieved 9/24/08.] http://www.guyanajournal.com/.

Guyana Outpost. 2009. Site maintained by Wayne Moses. [Online article; retrieved 9/24/08.] http://guyanaoutpost.com/guyana.shtml.

Halstead, Narmala. 2005. "Branding 'Perfection': Foreign as Self; Self as 'Foreign-Foreign.'" *Journal of Material Culture* 7(3): 273–93.

Kasinitz, Philip, John Mollenkopf, and Mary C. Waters. 2004. *Becoming New Yorkers: Ethnographies of the New Second Generation.* New York: Russell Sage.

Mangru, Brenda, and Pillai Madhu. *Voices of New York: Indo-Guyanese, A LOTE speaking Community in Richmond Hill, NY.* New York: New York University [Online article; retrieved 7/20/09.] http://www.nyu.edu/classes/blake.map2001/indo.html.

Mars, P. 2001. "Ethnic Politics, Mediation, and Conflict Resolution: The Guyana experience." *Journal of Peace Research* 38: 353–72.

Massey, Douglas S. 1995. "The New Immigration and Ethnicity in the United States." *Population & Development Review* 21: 631–52.

Misir, Prem, ed. 2006. *Cultural Identity and Creolization in National Unity: The Multiethnic Caribbean*. Lanham, MD: University Press of America.

Moore, Brian L. 1995. *Cultural Power, Resistance, and Pluralism: Colonial Guyana, 1838–1900*. Montreal; Buffalo: McGill-Queen's University Press; Barbados: Press University of the West Indies.

Nettles, Kimberly D. 1995. "Home Work: An Examination of the Sexual Division of Labor in the Urban Households of the East Indian and African Guyanese." *Journal of Comparative Family Studies* 26: 427.

Peake, Linda, and Alissa Trotz. 1999. *Gender, Ethnicity and Place: Women and Identities in Guyana*. London: Routledge.

Persaud, Farah. 2008. "Immigration and Women's Empowerment: Indo-Caribbeans in New York City." *Honors College Theses*. Paper 77. [Online article; retrieved 7/31/09.] http://digitalcommons.pace.edu/honorscollege_theses/77.

Plaza, Dwaine. 2006. "The Construction of a Segmented Hybrid Identity Among One-and-a-Half-Generation and Second-Generation Indo-Caribbean and African Caribbean Canadians." *Identity* 6: 207–29.

Premdas, Ralph R. 1995. "Racism and Anti-Racism in the Caribbean." In *Racism and Anti-Racism in World Perspective,* edited by B. P. Bowser, 241–60. Thousand Oaks, CA: Sage Publications.

Rabe, Stephen G. 2005. *U.S. Intervention in British Guiana: A Cold War Story*. University of North Carolina Press: Chapel Hill, NC.

Ramraj, Robert. 2003. *Guyana: Population, Environment, Economic Activities*. Greensboro, NC: Battleground Printing and Publishing.

Roopnarine, Lomarsh. 2001. "Indo-Guyanese Migration: From Plantation to Metropolis." *Immigrants & Minorities* 20: 1–25.

Roopnarine, Lomarsh. 2005. "Indo-Caribbean Intra-Island Migration: Not So Marginalized!" *Social and Economic Studies* 52: 107–36.

Roopnarine, Lomarsh. 2006. "Indo-Caribbean Social Identity." *Caribbean Quarterly* 52: 1–10.

Tanikella, Leela. 2009. "Voices from Home and Abroad: New York City's Indo-Caribbean Media." *International Journal of Cultural Studies* 12(2): 167–85.

Trotz, D. A. 2005. "Rethinking Caribbean Transnational Connections: Conceptual Itineraries." *Global Networks: A Journal of Transnational Affairs* 6: 41–59.

U.S. Department of Homeland Security, U.S. Citizenship and Immigration Service, Refugee, Asylum, and Parole System. "Yearbook of Immigration Statistics: 2008." Washington, D.C.: Department of Homeland Security. [Online article; retrieved 7/20/09.] http://www.dhs.gov/files/statistics/publications/yearbook.shtm.

U.S. Department of State. "Human Right Report: Guyana. 2008." Washington, D.C. [Online article; retrieved 7/20/09.] http://www.state.gov/g/drl/rls/hrrpt/2008/wha/119162.htm.

Vertovec, Steven. 2004. "Migrant Transnationalism and Modes of Transformation." *International Migration Review* 38: 970–1001.

Warikoo, Natasha. 2003. "The Importance of Social Context: Gendered Ethnic Identities among 1.5 and Second Generation Indo-Caribbeans." In *Conference Papers—American Sociological Association,* 1–21. American Sociological Association. [Online article; retrieved 5/25/11.] http://www.allacademic.com/meta/p107867_index.html.

Warikoo, Natasha. 2005. "Gender and Ethnic Identity among Second-generation Indo-Caribbeans." *Ethnic & Racial Studies* 28: 803–31.

Waters, Mary C. 1990. *Ethnic Options: Choosing Identities in America.* Berkeley: University of California Press.

Waters, Mary C. 2002. *The Changing Face of Home: The Transnational Lives of the Second Generation.* New York: Russell Sage Foundation

Further Reading

Abraham, Sara. 2007. *Labour and the Multiracial Project in the Caribbean: It History and Its Promise.* Lanham, MD: Lexington Books.

Covers political developments in Trinidad and Tobago and Guyana with focus on social movements and class formation.

Coolies: How Britain Reinvented Slavery. BBC Documentary Film, 2005.

Details British practice of indentured labor, which transported over 1 million Indian workers were around the world to replace African slaves.

Khandelwal, Madhulika S. 2002. *Becoming American, Being Indian: An Immigrant Community in New York City.* Cornell University Press.

Examines the development of identity and community among Indians living in Queens and Manhattan.

Moore, Brian L. 1995. *Cultural Power, Resistance, and Pluralism : Colonial Guyana, 1838–1900.* Montreal; Buffalo: McGill-Queen's University Press; Barbados: Press University of the West Indies.

Historical text focused on Guyana after the abolition of slavery examining the multiracial colonial society.

New York City's Department of City Planning. 2000. *The Newest New Yorkers: Briefing Booklet, Immigrant New York in the New Millennium.* [Online; retrieved 5/25/11.] http://www.nyc.gov/html/dcp/pdf/census/nny_briefing_booklet.pdf

Detailed demographic and socioeconomic profile of New York City's 2.9-million foreign-born residents and their distribution throughout the city's five boroughs.

Rabe, Stephen G. 2005. *U.S. Intervention in British Guiana: A Cold War Story.* Chapel Hill: University of North Carolina Press.

Account of the U.S. covert intervention in British Guiana between 1953 and 1969.

Ramraj, Robert. 2003. *Guyana: Population, Environment, Economic Activities.* Greensboro, NC: Battleground Printing and Publishing.

A scholarly study of aspects of the country of Guyana.

Haitian Immigrants

by Bertin M. Louis Jr.

Introduction

On January 12, 2010, a 7.0 earthquake devastated Port-au-Prince, Leogane, and other parts of Haiti. This natural disaster claimed more than 300,000 lives, according to the Haitian government, this catastrophe claimed more than 300,000 lives and left more than 1 million Haitians homeless. As Americans watched horrifying images of devastation, death, and destruction, Haitian Americans in Miami, Fort Lauderdale, and West Palm Beach, Florida; Brooklyn, Queens, and Staten Island, New York; and Chicago, Illinois, tried to contact their loved ones. Many people around the world wondered whether Haiti, with its history, political corruption, and geography was doomed to permanent poverty, governmental inefficiency, and misery. But other Haitian Americans returned to their homeland determined to contribute to earthquake relief and begin the long process of rebuilding and reshaping Haiti—a Haiti with a sustainable future. Many of those same Haitian Americans are glad that they are American citizens and can use their status in the United States as a way to help rebuild Haiti. This Haitian presence in the United States is not due to a recent migratory phenomenon, which occurred during a larger wave of immigration to the United States from Africa, Asia, and Latin America in the 1960s, 1970s, and 1980s; Haitian presence is part of a larger trend that dates back to the inception of the United States as a country.

Although many Haitians left their home country during periods of intense political and economic turmoil, they have persevered and flourished in the United States despite encounters with prejudice and racism. Haitian Americans have overcome these obstacles by leaning on varied aspects of their culture that make them a distinct ethnic group in the United States. Haitian Americans have gained employment in all sectors of American society and created institutions that connect them to each other across the United States as well as to their kin in their homeland. Haitians also wield significant political power in cities like Boston and Miami due to their strong civic and electoral participation. As President Obama mentioned in a 2009 statement about the significance of Haitian Flag Day (May 18), Haitian Americans contribute to the economic, social, cultural, scientific, and academic fabric of the United States (White House 2009). Haitian Americans are also involved in shaping the future of Haiti through contributions to their kin and through social and political organizations that attempt to stem the crisis that predated the 2010 earthquake.

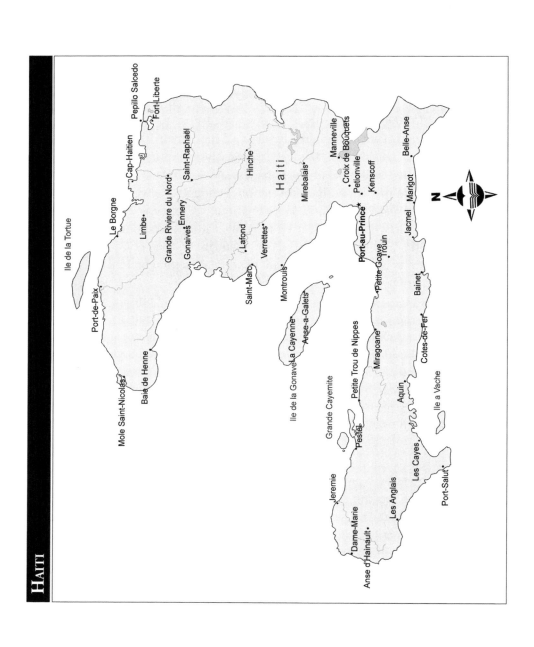

As the 21st century continues, the relationship between Haiti and the United States will be largely determined by the Haitian government, in cooperation with NGOs (non-governmental organizations), to execute some important programs that will help rebuild Haiti in the aftermath of the earthquake. Additionally, Haiti will also need the assistance of the United States and the international community in rebuilding efforts, and the cooperation and expertise of Haitian Americans in the execution and support of programs designed to address critical infrastructural issues such as electricity, health care, and housing. Indeed, it is the hope of Haitians in the United States that the nation of Haiti will be rebuilt, and Haitians, regardless of geographical location, will obtain respect, dignity, and justice among the other nations of the world.

Chronology

1779   Freedmen from the French colony of Saint Domingue (colonial Haiti) fight at the Siege of Savannah.

1779   Jean Baptiste Pointe DuSable migrates from Saint Domingue and founds the city of Chicago.

1804   Haitian independence occurs as the result of a series of victories by slaves revolting against the French colonial powers.

1822   Haiti invades the Spanish colony of Santo Domingo (today's Dominican Republic) and unifies the island under Haitian rule.

1838   France recognizes Haiti's independence after ignoring its independence since 1804.

1862   President Abraham Lincoln grants Haiti formal diplomatic recognition.

1889   Frederick Douglass is appointed U.S. minister and consul general to Haiti.

1915   Haiti is invaded and occupied by U.S. Marines.

1934   The 19-year U.S. occupation of Haiti ends.

1957   Francois "Papa Doc" Duvalier is elected president of Haiti.

1971   Francois Duvalier dies and is succeeded by his son, Jean-Claude "Baby Doc" Duvalier.

1986   Baby Doc flees Haiti on February 7 in an American chartered jet and takes up exile in France.

1990   Jean-Bertrand Aristide is elected president of Haiti in mid-December.

1991	Jean-Bertrand Aristide is deposed in a military coup d'état in late September. Aristide goes into exile in the United States.
1994	Aristide is restored to office of the presidency following a multinational military intervention in September sanctioned by the United Nations and led by the United States.
1996	Aristide completes his five-year term in office on February 7 and is succeeded by Rene Préval, who was elected in December 1995.
1999–2000	Haitian Americans are elected to state legislatures in Florida and Massachusetts and to key municipal posts in south Florida.
2001	Aristide is elected president of Haiti for the second time and succeeds Préval.
2004	Haitians around the world celebrate Haiti's 200th anniversary of independence.
2004	In early February, Aristide is coerced into leaving Haiti after an armed insurgency erupts in the port city of Gonaïves.
2006	René Préval is elected president of Haiti in May as part of new political party called Lespwa (Hope).
2010	An earthquake of 7.0 magnitude destroys parts of Haiti, claims over 300,000 lives, and leaves more than a million Haitians homeless.

Background

Geography of Haiti

Haitians come from Hispaniola, an island in the Caribbean. The island of Hispaniola is the second-largest island in the Caribbean, after Cuba, and has an area of 29,418 square miles. Present-day Haiti occupies the western third of the island of Hispaniola. Haiti covers 10,695 square miles, roughly the size of the state of Maryland. The other two-thirds of the island is the Dominican Republic. To the north, Haiti is bounded by the Atlantic Ocean; to the south, the Caribbean Sea; to the east, the Dominican Republic; and to the west is the Windward Passage, which separates Haiti from the island nation of Cuba. There are also two small islands that are a part of Haiti. La Gonâve is the larger of these two islands and is located in the west. The island of La Tortue is in the north.

The terrain of Haiti is covered with rugged mountains, small coastal plains, and river valleys. Haiti also has a large east-central elevated plateau. Haiti's climate is warm and semiarid throughout the year, but there is also high humidity in many of Haiti's coastal areas. The CIA *Factbook* notes as of October 2010 that there are approximately 9.6 million inhabitants in the country of Haiti.

History of Haiti

Haiti is derived from the word *Ayti*, which means "mountainous" and comes from the language of the indigenous people of the island. On December 5, 1492, Christopher Columbus encountered the Tainos, a branch of the Amerindian people called Arawaks. Columbus called the island Hispaniola (meaning "Little Spain"). Hispaniola's Taino population ranged between 300,000 to 1 million people. While Columbus consolidated the first permanent European settlement in the Americas, Tainos were enslaved and forced to cultivate crops and prospect and extract gold from rivers, streams, and mines. Enslaved Tainos were forced to convert to Catholicism and were subject to physical and psychological violence. In response to their enslavement, many Tainos committed suicide, rebelled, and escaped to the mountains of the island they called Quisqueya. The Tainos also had no natural immunity against diseases carried by Europeans, such as smallpox, tuberculosis, typhus, and influenza. Consequently, by the middle of the 16th century, only a few hundred indigenous people remained on the entire island.

After the indigenous population of Hispaniola was decimated, the Spanish brought in Africans, who were considered stronger workers than indigenous people, to replenish their labor supply. Africans were used as the next source of forced labor in Hispaniola and arrived on the island as early as 1501. Soon after their arrival, enslaved Africans and indentured servants were used throughout the colony to work on plantations. After time, the Spanish shifted their attention to their gold- and silver-rich colonies of Cuba, Mexico, and Peru so much so that by the end of the 16th century large tracts of land in the western part of Hispaniola had been abandoned and taken over by European marauders. Many of them were of French origin and began to settle and cultivate vacant lands. In 1697, the Treaty of Ryswick ceded to France the western third of the island, later known as the French colony of Saint Domingue.

In the 1780s, Saint Domingue was an object of international renown and in the words of one scholar, it was "the most fruitful and pleasant of Europe's Caribbean colonies" (Geggus 1982, 12). At that time, Saint Domingue was also referred to as "the pearl of the Antilles" because of the wealth it generated for European planters and the French merchant bourgeoisie. The plantations produced coffee, sugar, tobacco, and indigo. At one point in its history, Saint Domingue produced about two-fifths of the world's sugar and over half of the world's coffee.

Africans who survived the rigors of the passage from Africa to Saint Domingue were sold as chattel destined for life as slaves. Once they reached a plantation, West Africans from diverse tribes, such as Aradas, Congos, Bambaras, and Ibos, were assigned slave tutors who showed them how to perform different tasks necessary for the production of commodities that would eventually be consumed in Europe and throughout the world. *Le Code Noir* (The Black Code) prescribed baptism and instruction in the Catholic religion for all enslaved Africans and deemed assemblies of enslaved Africans for purposes other than Catholic worship as illegal (Simpson 1945).

The disciplining of Africans to turn them into plantation laborers came in the forms of psychological and physical violence. It was not uncommon for planters and overseers, for example, to:

> Hang a slave by the ears, mutilate a leg, pull teeth out, gash open one's side and pour melted lard into the incision, or mutilate genital organs. Still others used the torture of live burial, whereby the slave, in the presence of the rest of the slaves who were forced to bear witness, was made to dig his own grave . . . Women had their sexual parts burned by a smoldering log; others had hot wax splattered over hands, arms, and backs, or boiling cane syrup poured over their heads. (Dupuy 1989, 39)

The physical brutality and mutilation of African peoples on plantations in Saint Domingue was an important part of the process that made them slaves. Without these violent mechanisms of labor control, it would have been extremely difficult for the interests of commodity production to coerce Africans into their roles as plantation laborers. Africans' positions as slaves within sugar plantations were concretized by poor housing, diets that underfed and undernourished them, and the rule of the planters to control and restrict slave behavior.

This whole complex, which was performed with the intention to extract the greatest amount of labor from slaves, had deleterious effects on Saint Domingue's slave population. In her study of the Saint Domingue revolution, Carolyn Fick used Hilliard d'Auberteuil's observations of Saint Domingue at that time to illustrate the deadly consequences of slave labor in this French colony. Hilliard d'Auberteuil noted during the years from 1680 to 1776 over 800,000 Africans had been imported from Africa to Saint Domingue. By the end of that period there were only 290,000 Africans in Saint Domingue (Fick 1990, 26). These figures demonstrate that Africans were not reproducing themselves quickly enough in Saint Domingue as a result of the effects of the process of slave-making and the physical demands of plantation labor. Over one-third of the Africans brought over to Saint Domingue usually died off in the first few years as a result of arduous labor processes and the accompanying violence that maintained them (26).

Besides death and the production of commodities for world consumption, a religion was created on the plantations of Saint Domingue between 1750 and 1790 as the result of the combination of French authority, the culture of the indigenous people of Hispaniola, and the enslavement of assorted Africans on plantations in Saint Domingue: Vodou. *Vodou* is the Fongbe (Benin) term for "spirit" or "god." Some scholars view Vodou as only "a genre of ritual music and dance performed in honor of a category of spirit" and tend not to view Vodou as a belief system (Richman 2005). Others view Vodou to stand for all African-derived religious practices in Haiti (Olmos and Paravisini-Gebert 2003, 102). Most scholars of Vodou would agree that it is the most maligned and misunderstood of all African-inspired religions in the Americas and one of the most complex religions in the region. Vodou liturgy and rituals revolve around a pantheon of spirits known as *lwa* (Olmos and Paravisini-Gebert 2003, 102). *Lwa* represent a fusion of African and Creole gods, the spirits of deified ancestors, and syncretized manifestations of Catholic saints, and they can be thought of as supernatural beings that possess its adherents (Richman 2005).

Vodou served an important role in the eventual struggle for liberation that transformed Saint Domingue into Haiti. As one author writes, Haiti could not have become an independent nation as early as the nineteenth century without Vodou because its "rituals provided the spirit of kinship that fueled the slaves' revolts against their colonial masters" (Desmangles 1992, 6). An example of how Vodou provided a spirit of kinship among enslaved Africans in Saint Domingue was the Bwa Kayiman Vodou Congress led by Boukman, a Maroon born in Jamaica who escaped from a plantation near Morne Rouge. C.L.R. James (1963) notes the importance of this historical moment in a stirring narrative that has also been noted by other scholars of Haiti:

> On the night of the 22nd (August 1791) a tropical storm raged, with lightning and gusts of wind and heavy showers of rain. Carrying torches to light their way, the leaders of the revolt met in an open space in the thick forests of the Morne Rouge, a mountain overlooking Le Cap. There Boukman gave the last instructions and, after Vodou incantations and the sucking of the blood of a stuck pig, he stimulated his followers by a prayer spoken in creole, which, like so much spoken on such occasions, has remained. "The god who created the sun which gives us light, who rouses the waves and rules the storm, though hidden in the clouds, he watches us. He sees all that the white man does. The god of the white man inspires us with crime, but our god calls upon us to do good works. Our god who is good to us orders us to revenge out wrongs. He will direct our arms and aid us. Throw away the symbol of the god of the whites who has caused us to weep, and listen to the voices of liberty, which speaks in the hearts of us all." (87)

Six days later, led by Boukman, slaves of the Turpin plantation indiscriminately massacred every white man, woman, and child they could (Simpson 1945). This began a general insurrection, which led to the Haitian Revolution, the first successful slave revolt in the Western Hemisphere that extended the "rights of Man"—liberty, equality, and brotherhood—beyond French males to the emancipated black and mulatto peoples of Haiti.

As some scholars note, there were a number of reasons why the Haitian Revolution was a success. "The French Revolution weakened and divided the French in France and in Saint Domingue; the conflicts between free mulattoes and whites intensified; and Britain and Spain, the other colonial powers of the time, intervened to further their own interests. But above all else it was the role played by blacks that made the Haitian Revolution successful. During the war, the slaves defeated local whites, the forces of the French Crown, a Spanish and a British invasion and the massive expeditionary force sent by Napoleon Bonaparte" (Arthur and Dash 1999, 19–20). Toussaint Louverture rose to become the leader of the black armies and deserves credit for many of the military victories that led to the freeing of black slaves. Through the course of the Haitian Revolution, Toussaint united rebellious slaves into an efficient fighting force, invented guerilla warfare, and skillfully exploited the rivalries between all the other main players in the conflict (20).

In 1802, Toussaint was taken prisoner by the French forces sent by Napoleon Bonaparte to restore slavery and French rule in Saint Domingue. "When he was put aboard a ship that would take him to his death in a dungeon in France, Toussaint uttered these prophetic words, 'In overthrowing me, you have cut down only the tree of liberty in Saint Domingue. It will spring up again from the roots for they are numerous and deep'" (Arthur and Dash 1999, 20). Less than a year later, Jean-Jacques Dessalines united the black and mulatto forces and started a campaign against the French. In a decisive battle during the Haitian Revolution, Dessalines and his forces defeated the French at the Battle of Vertières. As a result, the last French regiments withdrew from the island. The Haitian Revolution ended with independence declared on January 1, 1804, and the world's first black republic used the Taino term *Ayti* (or Haiti, meaning "mountainous") as the name for a new nation of slaves who emancipated themselves.

After the Haitian Revolution, Jean-Jacques Dessalines, governor-general-for-life and later emperor of Haiti, ordered the slaughter of the remaining French on the island. After he consolidated his power, Dessalines was faced with the task of building a new nation in the aftermath of a violent revolution that had decimated the country. "The colonial powers operating within the region were openly hostile to the world's first black republic, and for several decades there was a constant threat of invasion. The plantations, on which the economic prosperity of the French colony had been based, were in ruins, and many towns had been razed to the ground" (Arthur and Dash 1999, 45). In addition to capital and labor shortages, many of the white planters fled the country, and war and disease reduced the population on the island to about a third of its original size.

Among the Haitians who survived the revolution, two distinct and separate views of what the new society was going to look like divided the fledgling nation along color lines and the ownership of land. The mulattoes, fair-skinned blacks of mixed African, European, and indigenous descent, were a small but powerful minority that consisted of free men and property owners before the revolution. They planned on inheriting the power and wealth of the defeated French colonists. The black ex-slaves, who formed the majority of the country, resisted the plantation system and hoped to farm their own land.

"Under Dessalines a large portion of cultivated land was brought under state control, and he planned to continue with Toussaint's attempts to revive large-scale agriculture as a way to sustain the nascent nation. But less than three years into his leadership, Dessalines was assassinated (October 17th, 1806) as the result of a power struggle which was linked to ownership of agricultural land and tensions between blacks and mulattoes" (Arthur and Dash 1999, 45).

After the assassination of Dessalines, Haiti split into two separate entities. Henri Christophe was Dessalines's successor and controlled blacks in the north. Alexandre Pétion controlled the mulattoes in the west and the south of Haiti. Christophe crowned himself king and created a black nobility. Using military force to resuscitate the plantation system and an export economy based on sugar and coffee, Christophe instituted a type of feudalism in the north in which military and state officers ran plantations. "This militarized agriculture generated large surpluses and the revenue was used to fortify Christophe's army and build extensive fortifications in case of another French invasion. The most spectacular fortification built during Christophe's reign was La Citadelle of La Ferrière (The Citadel)" (Arthur and Dash 1999, 46). Many men and women died building the Citadel due to a deadly admixture of forced labor, insufficient diets, exhaustion, and the toll of forcing stones and other heavy materials up the sides of a steep mountain. In 1820, Christophe, physically weakened by a catastrophic stroke, committed suicide as the result of an uprising against his forced labor policy.

After the death of Christophe, Jean-Pierre Boyer, Pétion's successor, brought the two parts of Haiti together as one country. As a way to remove the threat of foreign invasion, Boyer annexed the eastern part of the island of Hispaniola in 1822. The occupation of the eastern part of the island lasted until 1844, when an independent Dominican Republic was established. Boyer continued Pétion's practice of allocating small parcels of land to members of the Haitian military and peasantry. Haiti was isolated economically and politically by the international community at the time, especially by the United States and France. So as an attempt to integrate Haiti into a larger world economy and to gain political recognition as a sovereign nation, Boyer began payment of 90 million gold francs, a massive indemnity that compensated French planters who made the lives of enslaved Africans hell.

Overall, the socioeconomic legacy of the Haitian Revolution left the country in complete ruins. The agrarian system was nonfunctional, and the country was divided between the army and the peasants and between a mulatto and a black elite. "Since the mid-nineteenth century, Haitian politics has been dominated by the struggle between groups within the country's small elite for control of the state apparatus through control of the presidency" (Arthur and Dash 1999, 47). These dynamics were reflected throughout 19th century and 20th century Haiti (Zéphir 2004, 43). This is illustrated by the fact that only two rulers managed to complete their terms in office between 1843 and 1915 (Arthur and Dash 1999, 47). During this period in Haitian history there were 22 heads of state; 14 of which were overthrown.

"Up until 1915, the minority mulatto elite continued to exercise power while paying lip service to the political aspirations of the small number of black elite families and high-ranking black army officers. The 'politique de doublure (government of the understudy)' system saw black presidents in power but controlled and manipulated by mulatto politicians masking a continuing and deep-seated social antipathy between mulatto and black elites" (Arthur and Dash 1999, 47).

"The acute political and economic instability of Haiti, particularly during 1911 and 1915 when six presidents succeeded one another in office, motivated the United States to invade Haiti" (Zéphir 2004, 45). The Haitian elite borrowed heavily from foreign powers such as particularly the United States, Germany, and France. American investors were eagerly looking for ways to have the monopoly of investments in the country. Also, after the establishment of the Monroe Doctrine, and later the Roosevelt Corollary, gaining absolute control of the Caribbean region became a fundamental principle of U.S. foreign policy. So both financial interests and strategic factors weighed heavily in the U.S. decision to occupy Haiti, and on July 29, 1915, U.S. Marines landed in the Haitian capital of Port-au-Prince, and a 19-year U.S. occupation began.

The U.S occupation of Haiti from 1915 to 1934 reignited deep-seated resentment of foreign occupation and reunited both sides of the divided Haitian elite in a nationalist movement, albeit temporarily. Once the Marines departed, old tensions between the two groups reappeared. "Those who favored the mulatto hegemony were opposed by those who championed a redistribution of economic and political power. This latter tendency was bolstered by an emerging black middle class of schoolteachers, clerks, civil servants and small businessmen" (Arthur and Dash 1999, 47–48). Also as a result of the occupation, administrative, economic, and political power was centralized in Port-au-Prince (the capital) and the influence of elite groups in coastal towns decreased. "As part of this process, the Haitian military was reorganized and became increasingly linked and involved with political affairs in the capital" (Arthur and Dash 1999, 48). An example of this involvement is the ousting of presidents Lescot (1946) and Estimé (1950) by the Haitian military.

In 1957, François Duvalier won a general election and became president of Haiti. Duvalier was a physician who was part of a group of black middle-class intellectuals known as *noiristes*. "Noiristes mingled literary and ethnological interests, promoting the idea of Haiti's essentially African identity and championing the black majority against the Europeanized elite" (Ferguson 1987, 33). Initially considered little more than a tool of the military, "Papa Doc," as he became known, soon proved that he had his own political goals and methods that helped him maintain political power in Haiti.

"François Duvalier, president for life of Haiti from 1957 to 1971, had his political opponents and their supporters arrested or driven into exile. Then, to guard against threats of military coups, Papa Doc transferred or replaced senior officers, and placed elite units under his direct command. The army leadership, François Duvalier's own cabinet and inner circle were regularly purged" (Arthur and Dash 1999, 48). As a counterbalance to the Haitian military, Papa Doc created an irregular force of armed men called Tonton Macoutes. "The Tonton Macoutes became synonymous with François Duvalier's type of state terrorism" (Ferguson 1987, 40).

The Tonton Macoutes were Duvalier loyalists who provided information and detected subversion in every sphere of Haitian society. The tactics they used to maintain Papa Doc's repressive regime included bullying, extortion, and murder

President François Duvalier is inaugurated "president for life," June 22, 1964, in Haiti. (AP Photo)

(Ferguson 1987, 40). Under François Duvalier's regime, "trade unions were dismantled, progressive Catholic priests were expelled, newspapers were closed down and even the Boy Scouts were disbanded" (Arthur and Dash 1999, 48).

Papa Doc's 14-year-long dictatorship relied on extreme violence in order to maintain rule and probably claimed the lives of more than tens of thousands of Haitians. To complete his ascension, Duvalier proclaimed himself president-for-life with the power to designate his successor. The public treasury was siphoned and foreign aid diverted to pay off supporters, Macoutes, and high-ranking administrators. As the result of his regime, Haiti slid deeper into social and economic ruin and created a brain-drain that began during his regime and has continued unabated. "Between 30,000 and 60,000 people were killed by state terrorism during this period" (Ferguson 1987, 57).

"When François Duvalier died in 1971, the disabling of all serious opposition, and the tacit endorsement of important power-brokers such as the United States, the military high command and much of the business community, ensured that power was transferred smoothly to his 19-year-old son, Jean-Claude. Under the new leader, dubbed 'Baby Doc' by the foreign media, the ruthless repression of internal dissent, both real and imagined, continued" (Arthur and Dash 1999, 49).

Jean-Claude's regime (1971–1986) was described as a "kleptocracy"—a state in which those in power exploit national resources and steal. Indeed, the process of stealing state revenues by those in the Duvalier regime reached new heights. "Hundreds of millions of dollars were stolen by Jean-Claude and his small circle of associates" (Arthur and Dash 1999, 49).

In addition to maintaining a kleptocracy started by his father, Baby Doc encouraged offshore assembly industry under the guise of economic liberalization, which began towards the end of his father's reign and accelerated the downward slide of Haiti becoming the poorest country in the Western Hemisphere. At the end of Papa Doc's tenure as Haitian head of state, offshore assembly for U.S. corporations and markets began. "In the assembly industry, materials produced in a well-to-do country are exported to a poor country to be assembled by the comparatively cheap and 'disciplined' labor there" (Farmer 1994, 115).

This form of business did little to arrest an economy in free fall, and Haiti continued to sink deeper into debt. During Baby Doc's tenure, a widening gap between the urban and rural areas forced Haitians living in the countryside to migrate to Port-au-Prince in search of jobs at factories. While Jean-Claude and members of his circle grew fabulously rich, the majority of Haitians slipped deeper into poverty. The percentage of the population living in extreme poverty rose from 48 percent in 1976 to 81 percent in 1985. Under the Duvaliers, Haiti became the poorest country in the Western Hemisphere; a description that accompanies contemporary media descriptions of Haiti. In other words, we can clearly see the connection between the Duvalier brand of state repression of the Haitian people, Duvalierist embezzlement of foreign aid and taxes, and how that contributed to creating extreme poverty in Haiti. During his continuation of his father's dictatorship, Jean-Claude alienated important supporters among the old-guard noiristes and the black middle class by shifting his power base towards younger mulatto merchants and technocrats. "The alliance between the Mulatto and the new regime was sealed in May 1980 when Jean-Claude Duvalier married Michèle Bennett, daughter of a wealthy speculator" (Zéphir 2004, 50). As the regime faltered and an internal and external opposition movement grew, the U.S. and the Haitian military withdrew their support for Jean-Claude's rule and Jean-Claude left Haiti aboard an American-chartered jet in February 1986.

After Baby Doc's departure, a four-year period in Haitian history known as "Duvalierism without Duvalier" ensued. Consisting of a series of military juntas headed by senior officers, this period was characterized by attempts to secure the former order in the face of challenges from the poor majority and a section of the elite (Arthur and Dash 1999, 49). During this time period, opposition grew between the masses seeking retribution against former Duvalierists and Tonton Macoutes. From 1986 to 1988, the hope for democracy in Haiti was crushed: in July 1987, peasant activists were massacred, and in November 1988, hundreds of voters waited to cast their ballots at the voting polls. After the fall of Jean-Claude, the elite were pushing for reforms to modernize the Haitian state. Part of these reforms, which were backed by the United States and international finance institutions, included a proposed transition to electoral democracy but the Duvalierists violently resisted changes to the political system. By 1990, internationally monitored democratic elections were held in Haiti and the late entry of the charismatic liberation theology priest, Jean-Bertrand Aristide, and the subsequent voter registration of tens of thousands of previously unregistered peasants and urban poor, threw a wrench in the plans of the Haitian elite. Aristide, the presidential candidate for the Lavalas party, won an overwhelming majority of the vote (Arthur and Dash 1999, 50).

Jean-Bertrand Aristide's victory in the 1990 elections represented the first serious challenge to the status quo and the reforms proposed by the Aristide government were enough to upset most sections of the elite (Arthur and Dash 1999, 50). For example, large landowners were disturbed by presidential rhetoric about agrarian reform. Industrialists were vexed by discussion of a proposed increase in the national minimum wage. The Haitian military, the institution that at many times in Haitian history was responsible for overthrowing numerous heads of state, was distressed by proposals that would separate the police from the army. Duvalierists were upset with talk of disbanding the section chief system and reform of corrupt state institutions. The Lavalas movement also threatened the conservative hierarchy of the Catholic Church and traditional politicians. These fears, manifested in elite and powerful sectors in Haitian society, manifested in a coup d'état that toppled Aristide.

"Less than eight months after taking office, Aristide was overthrown by a military coup d'état which was rumored to have been financed by leading elite families" (Arthur and Dash 1999, 51). Aristide fled to the United States. The Haitian military and a resurgent Macoute sector carried out an intense and violent campaign of repression for the next three years against the popular organizations that had flourished since the fall of Baby Doc and had formed the foundation of the Lavalas movement. The international community supported an embargo, which did not weaken the military junta but exacerbated poverty among the poorest sectors of Haitian society. Subsequently, emigration from Haiti to other countries in the region, most notably the United States, intensified.

Through assistance from the United Nations and the presidency of Bill Clinton, elected president of the United States in 1992, an agreement known as the Governors Island Accord was put together to solve the Haitian impasse. The accord stipulated that Aristide was to return to Haiti on October 30, 1993, accompanied by a United Nations peacekeeping force. Due to rising violence with the impending return of Aristide to Haiti, the Clinton administration issued a resolution in July 1994 authorizing a direct American military intervention in Haiti. The U.S. occupation was scheduled to begin on September 19, 1994. General Raoul Cédras, the head of the Haitian military junta, agreed to relinquish power in October 1994. Under the protection of the U.S. military, President Aristide returned to Haiti to finish his term, which expired on February 7, 1996. René Préval was elected the next president of Haiti, and then Aristide was re-elected in 2001 for a second term as president until February 2006.

During his second term as president, Jean-Bertrand Aristide's administration was cut short by two years. Aristide was coerced into leaving Haiti after an armed insurgency erupted in the port city of Gonaïves in early February 2004 (Dupuy 2005, 187). Gerald Latortue became the head of an interim government, and members and supporters of Aristide's Lavalas party were summarily imprisoned and executed. René Préval was elected president of Haiti in May 2006 as part of new political party called Lespwa (Hope).

Causes and Waves of Migration

Although Haitians are part of the wave of recent immigration to the United States in the 20th century, the Haitian presence in the United States is not a recent migratory phenomenon but part of a larger trend which dates back to the 18th century. We can view this history of Haitian immigration to the United States as an uninterrupted stream with high, low, and dormant periods (Laguerre 1998, 2). The peak periods of Haitian immigration to the United States roughly correspond to the following: the Haitian revolutionary era and aftermath (1791–1810); the period of American occupation of Haiti (1915–1934); the Duvalier and immediate post-Duvalier era (1957–1994); and the times of stringent economic crisis and political unrest during the Aristide presidencies, military juntas, and Préval presidencies (1994–2009).

Early Immigration

The early migration of Haitians to the United States consisted of different sectors of colonial Haitian society (1791–1803) who fled the island colony of Saint Domingue during revolutionary unrest, including French colonists, the slaves of French colonists, and free people of color. Some of these Haitian ancestors contributed to the revolutionary struggle of the United States during the 18th century. For example, 750 soldiers from Saint Domingue (Colonial Haiti) fought alongside American patriots against the British at the Siege of Savannah, in Georgia, on October 9, 1779. Currently, there is a monument in Savannah, Georgia, that commemorates Haitian involvement in the American War of Independence.

Another example of how early Haitian immigration to the United States in the 18th century contributed to the social fabric of the United States is the life of Jean Baptiste Pointe DuSable. In 1779, Jean Baptiste Pointe DuSable migrated from the French colony of Saint Domingue and founded the city of Chicago. DuSable was born around 1745, and his birth was traced to the city of St. Marc, Haiti. He was born a free man, the son of a French sea captain and a Haitian slave. When he was young, DuSable's father sent him to France for his education. It is reported that DuSable traveled with his father on his merchant ships and was injured aboard a ship on a voyage to New Orleans. However, when DuSable arrived there, he discovered that the city had been taken over by the Spanish and that he was in danger of enslavement. A local chapter of the French Jesuits hid him until he was well enough to travel on his own. He left New Orleans and headed north via the Mississippi River. Along the way he came in contact with French fur trappers and land speculators. DuSable settled in what is now known as Peoria, Illinois, and sold furs and bought large tracts of land. He became a wealthy businessman and headed north toward the Great Lakes and established his home, and a thriving trading post, on the bank of the Chicago River (Zéphir 2004, 12).

Later Waves of Immigration

After the 18th and 19th centuries, Haitian immigration to the United States was low until the second half of the 20th century. During the U.S. occupation of Haiti (1915–1934), a group of Haitian immigrants from the urban areas of Haiti migrated to the United States. "The Immigration and Naturalization Service began separately recording Haitian immigration in 1932; for the period of 1932–1940, it recorded

191 Haitian immigrants, and it recorded 911 between 1941 and 1950. From 1951 to 1960, 4,442 more Haitians were recorded" (Zéphir 2004, 17). However, as a result of the 1965 Immigration Act, which allowed the legal admission of hundreds of thousands of new immigrants per year beyond quotas, Haitian immigration to the United States increased dramatically. "From 1932 through 2000, a total of 414,401 Haitians immigrated legally to the United States" (Zéphir 2004, 17).

Papa Doc's regime caused massive numbers of people from all sectors of Haitian society to leave the country. Based on the Immigration and Naturalization Service's (INS's) statistical yearbooks, over 40,000 Haitians legally migrated to the United States (40,011) from 1960 to 1971, and over 138,000 (138,157) were admitted to the United States on temporary visas during the same time period.

During Baby Doc's regime, the political and economic situation of Haiti worsened. Legal immigration of Haitians to the United States, therefore, increased steadily for most of Jean-Claude's dictatorship. According to the Statistical Yearbooks of the INS, nearly 108,000 Haitians (107,818) migrated to the United States legally between 1972 and 1986. During this same time period, the INS reports that close to 625,000 Haitians (624,803) were admitted to the United States on temporary visas. The INS also reports that there are gaps in their record of nonimmigrant data for Haitians between 1980 and 1982, when, according to estimates by reporters and scholars, the highest number of undocumented Haitian immigrants came to the United States (INS Statistical Yearbook 2000).

It must be noted that a substantial number of Haitians migrated to the United States illegally during Baby Doc's dictatorship. Illegal Haitian migration to the United States coincided with the Duvalier dictatorship, especially during Jean-Claude Duvalier's reign (1971–1986). Many Haitians who visited the United States during this period overstayed their visas with the hope that they could legalize their status one day. One scholar of Haitian history notes that one of the most striking features of Jean-Claude's time in power was the process of escape and voluntary exile of Haitians, many of whom were determined to reach the United States for the prospects of work and food (Ferguson 1987, 63). This process began in 1972. Many of these Haitians, peasants who were desperate to leave a cycle of drought and famine, were persuaded to sell their family smallholdings and any other possessions in return for a place on a boat bound for Miami. In 1981 it was estimated that there were at least 50 or 60 such boats operating from Haiti's north coast, where cities such as Port-de-Paix and Cap Haitian are. These migrants were dubbed Haitian "boat people" in the media.

The departure of Jean-Claude Duvalier from Haiti in 1986 led to more political and social chaos, as opposition grew between the masses seeking retribution against former Duvalierists and Tonton Macoutes. The brutal domination and oppression of Haitians during this time period is reflected in the elevated number of Haitians who migrated to the United States. In 1988, for example, the INS reported that 34,806 Haitians legally migrated to the United States and that 94,819 nonim-migrants were admitted on temporary visas.

Another difficult year in Haitian history was 1991, the year that the democrati-cally elected president, Jean-Bertrand Aristide, was overthrown by a military coup. Fearing for their lives, many of Aristide's supporters fled the country. The INS records for 1991 reflect this migration pattern: 47,527 Haitians were admitted to the United States as immigrants while another 73,994 were admitted on temporary visas. As one scholar tells us, "let us remember a CNN report indicating that 67,000 boat people were intercepted during the same year" (Zéphir 2004, 71).

Demographic Profile

Size and Composition of Community

Census figures provide the best estimates of the Haitian population in the United States. According to the American Community Survey of the 2000 U.S. Census, which is compiled from census data, there were 694,123 Haitian-born blacks in the United States as of 2005.

Age and Family Structure

Out of this population of 694,123 Haitians in the United States, the median age, as of 2005, was 28.4 years old; 10.4 percent were under 5 years old; 22.1 percent were 5 to 17 years old.; 11.9 percent were 18 to 24 years old; 15.2 percent were 25 to 34 years old; 13.8 percent were 35 to 44 years old; 14 percent were 45 to 54 years old; 7.1 percent were 55 to 64 years old; 3.7 percent were 65 to 74 years old; and those 75 years or old comprised 1.8 percent.

Educational Attainment

According to the American Community Survey from 2005, approximately 386,000 of the 694,000 Haitians in the United States are 25 years or older. From that popula-tion, 23.1 percent has less than a high school education, and 30.3 percent are high school graduates (or the equivalency of a high school diploma); 28.5 percent of this population has some college or associate's degree, and 13 percent has a bachelor's degree; and 5.1 percent of the population of Haitians in the United States 25 years or older has a graduate or professional degree.

Occupation and Income Patterns

According to the American Community Survey of 2005, out of the civilian pop-ulation 16 years and older among Haitians in the United States (approximately

326,000), approximately 36.6 percent were employed in service positions; 22.6 percent were employed in sales and office occupations; 21 percent were employed in management, professional, and related occupations; and 14.7 percent worked production, transportation, and material moving jobs. The remaining Haitians were employed in construction-related occupations and farming, fishing, and forestry occupations (5.1%).

As of 2005, the median Haitian household income in the United States was approximately $40,000. In 2005, 45 percent of Haitians owned their own home as opposed to 55 percent of Haitians who rented.

Health Issues

In Haiti, health is directly tied to one's economic status. Haitians are exposed to numerous infectious diseases that accompany poverty and malnutrition such as infantile tetanus, tuberculosis, the HIV virus, and malaria. In the late 1970s, tuberculosis was allegedly endemic among Haitians; in the early 1980s, the Center for Disease Control (CDC) identified Haitians as one of the primary groups at risk for AIDS, along with homosexuals, hemophiliacs, and intravenous drug abusers. In spite of the removal of Haitians from that list, the Food and Drug Administration (FDA) in the late 1980s officially refused to accept the donation of blood from individuals of Haitian descent (Stepick 1998, 2).

Regardless of the stigma attached to Haitians, when Haitians migrate to the United States, they tend to become more affluent and their access to health care improves along with the quality of health care they receive. But even though the average lifespan of Haitians increases when they live in the United States, there are still diseases that affect their collective health. Bertin M. Louis, M.D., former chief of nephrology at Maimonides Medical Center of Brooklyn, New York, who has worked closely with the Haitian community of New York City, notes that the some of the diseases that afflict Haitians in the United States are hypertension (high blood pressure), diabetes mellitus (type 2 diabetes), and hyperlipidemia (high cholesterol).

Adjustment and Adaptation

Family, Culture, and Life-Cycle Rituals

"Families are the foundation for social networks that provide both material and emotional support, everything from temporary housing and food to how to find a job and get into school" (Stepick 1998, 16). When Haitian immigrants first arrive in the United States, they usually take temporary residence in the home of a relative (Stepick 1998, 17). These families, then, do not only consist of a mother, father, and children but at many times include grandparents, uncles and aunts, cousins, god-children, and sometimes non-relatives from one's hometown. These additional relatives temporarily reside with a relative and can move from household to household while working different jobs until they are able to rent or buy their own home.

Birth/Baptism, Coming of Age, Marriage, and Funerals

In Haiti, the rites of passage that mark the lives of Haitians, such as baptism, marriage, and funerals, vary according to religious affiliation and whether they live in urban areas or in the Haitian countryside. A look at the Catholic and Protestant traditions of Haiti offers us a glimpse into the diversity of rituals associated with important milestones in human life.

The majority of Haitians are Catholic. Haitian Catholics usually baptize their children a few months after birth in a ceremony at a Catholic church. At the age of seven years, young Haitian boys and girls are *komune* (receive communion). At the age of 13, young girls and boys are *konfirme* (consummated in the Catholic Church).

Father Ferry Brutus waves incense over the coffin during a funeral service at the Notre Dame D'Haiti Catholic Church in the Little Haiti neighborhood of Miami, April 21, 2007. (AP Photo/ Lynne Sladky)

With regard to engagements and marriages, Haitian men ask Haitian women for their hand in marriage. It is traditional for Haitian men to ask permission from the family of the woman they intend to marry. In many cases, many Haitians do not have enough money associated with a large wedding. In this case, many Haitian women and men enter into common-law marriage, which is known as *plasaj*.

The wedding ceremony is similar to what occurs in the United States. The groom wears a tuxedo and the bride wears an ornate white dress. As in the United States, the father of the bride gives the daughter away. After the wedding, the best man and the maid (or matron) of honor are consulted by the husband and wife when moments of marital discord occur within the marriage.

Haitian funerals vary according to local traditions and religious affiliations. Wakes for people in the Haitian countryside are very animated. People entertain themselves by playing dominoes, singing, and telling flattering and honorific stories (*bay blag*) about the deceased. At the actual funeral in the Haitian countryside, the body of the deceased is carried on the shoulders of four males who sing and engage in a choreographed walk that is almost dance like. At some points during this animated funeral march, the corpse is transferred to another group of four men who continue with the body in a similar animated manner. People at the funeral are also served *tafia* (strong Haitian rum) after the body is interred.

The behavior we find at funerals for Haitian Protestants varies according to one's religious affiliation and stands in stark contrast to funerals in the Haitian countryside. At funerals for traditional Haitian Baptists, for example, the ceremony tends to be very sedate and reserved. Crying and screaming are viewed as inappropriate outbursts. However, at some Pentecostal and Charismatic Haitian funerals, funeral attendees are expected to faint, cry, and scream openly.

Families and Changing Gender Relations

In a book about the relationship between Haitian Americans and Haiti, Dr. Georges Fouron, professor of education and Africana studies at Stony Brook University in Long Island, New York, wrote about the relationship he had growing up in Haiti with his mother. When he was a child, his mother was physically and emotionally abusive towards him. But when he moved to the United States and earned his PhD in education, his mother tried to reclaim him as her son. When Dr. Fouron brought his mother to the United States, her reaction to living in New York revealed something to him about gender relations in Haiti and how they can change when a Haitian woman moves to the United States. According to Dr. Fouron, his mother was totally transformed in New York. She lived with him, then his brother, found a job as a home health aide and earned her own income. One day, Dr. Fouron's mother told him "This [the United States] is my country now. I will never return to Haiti" (Glick Schiller and Fouron 2001, 131).

The revelation that Dr. Fouron made with regard to gender in Haiti and the Haitian diaspora is that his mother's violent behavior towards him was due to her social condition. In other words, Dr. Fouron's mother beat him because of her gender position (the fact that she was a woman in a repressive, patriarchal society) in a hierarchy that reinforces the exploitative class system of contemporary Haiti (Glick Schiller and Fouron 2001, 132). The restrictions placed on the mobility of Dr. Fouron's mother were lifted when she migrated from Haiti to the United States and gained economic independence.

Unlike Dr. Fouron's mother, other Haitian American women remain invested in Haiti although they are U.S. citizens. Glick Schiller and Fouron use the example of a Haitian American woman named Yvette to demonstrate that not all Haitian women in the United States reject Haiti. Yvette is obligated to take care of siblings, nieces, and nephews in Haiti whom she hardly knows (Glick Schiller and Fouron 2001, 143). Yet Yvette's skin had become gray from working overtime to pay the debts she had incurred sending money to Haiti. She told Dr. Fouron, "My body is like Haiti. It is tired and without hope" (144).

Using the examples of these two Haitian women in the United States, we can see that there are contradictory results to the migration of Haitian women to the United States. Dr. Fouron's mother considered herself to be independent and associated her life in Haiti with a lack of freedom and autonomy outside of marriage. The obligations that Yvette must meet for her siblings, nieces, and nephews were physically taxing, taking a toll on her health.

Retaining a Sense of National Culture and Identity

Haitian Americans retain a sense of national culture and identity through various practices, institutions, and through the maintenance of certain cultural traditions. Remittances from Haitian Americans to kin in Haiti sustain familial obligations. Hometown associations (groups that contribute to the upkeep and development of their towns and cities of birth) allow Haitians to position themselves in the United States as an ethnic group distinct from African Americans while reifying their identities as Haitian nationals. Haitian American service organizations and community centers throughout the United States serve as important institutions that diffuse Haitian culture and values, aid in the integration of new immigrants, and educated and defend members of its ethnic community. Religious practices help to maintain a Haitian identity that is distinct from other nationalities and ethnicities in the United States. The continued use of Haitian Creole by first- and second-generation Haitian Americans ensures the continued use of the language of the Haitian masses for future generations. The celebration of national holidays such as Haitian Independence Day, the preparation and consumption of Haitian cuisine, and the performance and support of Haitian artists and musicians also ensures that Haitians in the United States can celebrate their culture.

Continued Links to Country of Origin: Remittances and Hometown Associations

An important way that Haitian Americans are linked to Haiti is through the practice of sending remittances, which is the act of migrants sending money back to the place of their origin. In the 1990s, Haitians sent approximately $250 million to $350 million to Haiti per year in the form of remittances (Catanese 1999, 118).

Many Haitian families have become transnational in nature. In other words, the families extend from one nation-state (the United States) to another (Haiti). Haitian families living in south Florida, for example, are linked to their kin in Haiti and are morally obligated to send their relatives money, clothes, and food. Many in Haiti, in the face of unemployment and poverty, are economically dependent on their overseas kin. Family members support and assist each other, both financially and emotionally. In addition to the economic dependence that Haitians have on Haitians in the United States, families also plan and finance the immigration of other family members. "Haitians in the United States are also expected to help with the future immigration of others, establishing a chain of immigrants" (Stepick 1998, 15).

Numerous Haitian Americans also belong to hometown associations. Examples of Haitian hometown association activities are digging water wells in a Haitian village or building a school for children in Haiti. According to Pierre-Louis (2006), Haitian hometown associations emerged from the efforts of exile leaders in the 1980s to establish institutions in a foreign land and as an alternative form of organizing by immigrants who did not want to engage in open political activities against the Duvalier regime (27). Hometown associations allow Haitians to position themselves in the United States as an ethnic group distinct from African Americans, support the democratization process in Haiti, and address humanitarian crises there (Pierre-Louis 2006, 19). The Haitian Hometown Association Resource Group (http://haitirg.org/), formed in March 2008 to strengthen community development and alleviate poverty in Haiti; they partnered with the worldwide Vincentian Family, DePaul University, and Fonkoze (http://www.fonkoze.org/) to create Zafèn (https://www.zafen.org/), a new initiative that provides interest-free microloans to Haitians. Specifically, Zafèn enables lenders and donors to finance small- and medium-sized Haitian businesses.

In addition to the material contributions that hometown associations make to Haiti, Haitian immigrants who face discrimination in the United States can always fall back on their homeland to maintain their culture and to ascertain their identities (Pierre-Louis 2006, 12). Emigrants who leave their homelands do not simply assimilate into a new, dominant culture but rather renegotiate their identities in relation to familial obligations, discrimination, and the culture that cultivated them. Involvement in their homeland culture helps Haitians maintain their ethnic identity.

Social Organizations Based on National/Ethnic Background

Using the example of Haitians in New York, we can see that Haitians have formed several service organizations and community centers that are critical to the diffusion of Haitian culture and values. In New York City, the best known of these institutions is the Haitian Centers Council, established in 1982 and based in Brooklyn, which maintains eight centers throughout the New York metropolitan area. "Four are located in Brooklyn (the Flatbush Haitian center known as Brooklyn); one in Queens (the Haitian American United for Progress Community Center, or HAUP); one in Manhattan (the Haitian Neighborhood Service Center); one in Spring Valley (Rockland County); and the other also within the Greater New York metropolitan area" (Zéphir 2004, 94). These organizations centers focus on job training, immigration, refugee assistance, and employment.

Based in Brooklyn, Dwa Fanm (Women's Rights) is an organization that is committed to the rights of Haitian women and girls. "Another important agency that serves New York's Haitian community is the National Coalition for Haitian Rights (NCHR), which deals with matters of immigration, welfare and legal rights of Haitian immigrants. NCHR is also involved in fighting for Haitian boat people in detention centers and raises awareness about human rights abuses for Haitians living in other parts of the diaspora (stopping abuses against Haitians living in the Dominican Republic, for example)" (Zéphir 2004, 94).

Religion

As one author correctly notes, Haitians are very religious people (Stepick 1998, 85). Most Haitians in the United States practice three major religions, all of which have roots in Haiti: Vodou, Catholicism, and Protestantism. Vodou, one of the most maligned and misunderstood of the African-derived religions in the Western Hemisphere, combines aspects of Roman Catholic, African, and indigenous religions. Its origins represent the hybrid nature of Haitian culture. Rituals of the religion involve reciting prayers in French and Creole, being possessed by *lwa* (spirits), singing, and dancing.

Many Haitians who enter the United States are Roman Catholic. Slaves in colonial Haiti (Saint Domingue) were baptized and instructed in the Catholic religion (Simpson 1945). After Haitian independence in 1804, Catholicism became the religion of the Haitian state. Many Haitians living in the United States are practicing and nominal Catholics.

The roots of Protestantism in Haiti can be traced as early as 1816, when Stephen Grellet and John Hancock, from the United States, visited Haiti for a meeting with Alexandre Pétion, the Haitian ruler at that time. Protestantism among Haitians in its diaspora scattered in the Caribbean (Brodwin 2003) and the United States (Richman 2005) is rising, and we are beginning to see Haitian Protestants outnumber

Reverend Dr. Soliny Védrine

In the United States, Protestantism is growing exponentially as a form of religious affiliation for Haitian Americans. An example of this growth can be seen in the work of one of Boston's most dedicated community members, Reverend Dr. Soliny Védrine. Dr. Védrine is the head pastor of Boston Missionary Baptist Church, a Haitian Baptist Church founded in 1973. He is the director of Haitian Ministries International at Emmanuel Gospel Center in Boston and a cofounder of a Haitian Evangelical International Crusade, which occurs annually in New Providence, Bahamas. As part of Vision Globale de Protestantisme dans le Milieu Haïtien (Global Vision of Protestantism in the Haitian Context), Dr Védrine also coordinates efforts to spread Protestantism among Haitians in Haiti and its diaspora within North America and the Caribbean (including the Bahamas, the Dominican Republic, and St. Martin).

Born in Lazile, Haiti, Dr. Védrine moved to Boston in 1972 with his wife Emmeline after they had lived in New York City. On March 15, 1973, Dr. Védrine and his wife were able to use an American church building to start a Haitian church group. This church became the Boston Missionary Baptist Church. Their congregation met in that church for almost eight years. Then they bought an old funeral home and the congregation called that home for 11 years. Then, the

Reverend Dr. Soliny Védrine and wife Emmeline. (Courtesy of Kloe York)

funeral home was demolished and then the first Haitian church to be erected in New England was built for a cost of $1.2 million. At the time of an interview in 2004, Dr. Védrine stated that Boston Missionary Baptist Church had a congregation of about 600 at-large Haitian members and about 200 young Haitians who attended church regularly (Védrine 2004).

As part of his ministry, Dr. Védrine assists Haitians who are need in the United States, the Bahamas, the Dominican Republic, Haiti, and St. Martin. In each of these countries, Dr. Védrine brings Haitian pastors together for a program that includes preaching, medical work, and counseling for young people of Haitian descent and community leaders. Dr. Védrine also brings groups of Haitians in the United States to Haiti two or three times a year to finish construction on church buildings and clinics. Dr. Védrine will return to Haiti in summer 2010 to assist in relief and rebuilding.

Catholic Haitians in some locales. In a recent article about the spread of evangelism in Haitian American communities in New York City, Haitian Protestant churches (which were estimated to be more than 100) have grown to outnumber Catholic churches (Ng 2006). Although Protestants may not be the new religious majority among Haitians in New York City, the number of Haitians who attend Haitian Protestant churches is rising and that there may eventually be a new religious majority among Haitians in the New York City area.

Overall, the religious needs of Haitian Americans are met by several Catholic and Protestant churches as well as Vodou practitioners.

Language Issues

Haiti can best be described as a nation predominantly composed of two linguistic communities: a minority French bilingual elite and a monolingual Creole-speaking majority. In their study of language debates over Creole in Haiti, Schieffelin and Doucet (1994) remark that Haitian French used to be viewed as the high prestige form of language while Haitian Creole (Kreyòl) was considered the low prestige form (178). While Haitians of earlier generations still view French as a high prestige form of language among themselves, Kreyòl (Haitian Creole) has become the language of choice among the majority of Haitian Americans and a strong symbol of Haitian heritage. Haitian Creole was formed on the plantations of Saint Domingue and became a common language that linguistically united disparate Africans.

Haitian Creole was an unwritten language until recently. There have been different ways of representing the spoken language of Haitian Creole over the years. In the 1980s, an orthographic system was established to represent Haitian Creole that is currently used among Haitian educators in the United States and is taught in Haiti. Each letter in the current Haitian Creole orthographic system only has one sound. Consonants are sounded as they are in English, every vowel is pronounced separately, and all the letters are pronounced in a word. For example, the word "activity" in English is pronounced "ak-tee-vee-tay" and written in Haitian Creole this way: *aktivite*. There are nasalized sounds in Haitian Creole, as well, like *an* in *mouvman* ("movement"), *en* in *genyen* ("to win, to beat"), and *on* like *milyon* ("million"). An additional sound in Haitian Creole, *en*, is not found in English. *En* is nasalized and is similar to the sound in the word *envy*. We find an example of that sound in the word *gouvenen* ("to govern, to direct"). *Ch* in Haitian Creole is pronounced like words beginning in "sh" in English like *shower*. An example of a *ch* word is *chita* ("sit").

National/Regional-Language Press and Other Media

Along with restaurants, Haitians have established barber and beauty shops, music stores, and money transfer stores in major American cities such as Boston, New York City, and Miami. Haitians have also established their own community media—newspapers, radio, and television—that keeps them informed of daily events in the Haitian diaspora and in the homeland. Major Haitian newspapers produced in New York, for example, include the *Haitian Times, Haïti Observateur,* and *Haïti Progrès,* all located in Brooklyn. "In New York City's Haitian community, for example, there are five radio stations which function on a 24-hour basis: Radio Triomphe Internationale, Radio Soleil, Radio Lakay, Radio Tropicale, and Radyo Pa Nou. Also, *Haiti Dyaspo* and *La Lanterne Haïtienne* are widely watched news magazine programs" (Zéphir 2004, 93). Another source of Haitian news and information, in the greater Boston area, is the *Boston Haitian Reporter,* established in 2000 by William Dorcena.

Celebration of National Holidays

Two of the most important holidays that Haitian Americans celebrate are Haitian Independence Day (January 1) and Haitian Flag Day (May 18). Haitian Americans take great pride in Haitian Independence Day and visit each other to celebrate. It is also customary for many Haitian Americans to make a squash-based soup called *joumou,* which they share with company. It is said that the newly freed slaves who fought in the Haitian Revolution ate soup *joumou* on Independence Day as an act of defiance because the French did not allow slaves to eat the soup.

In Haitian communities across America, thousands of Haitian Americans celebrate Haitian Flag Day (May 18) at concerts, festivals, and parades. On May 18, 1803, in the city of Archaie, not far from Port-au-Prince, Dessalines, the leader of the blacks, and Pétion, the leader of the mulattoes, agreed on an official flag, with blue and red bands placed vertically. Haiti's first flag was sewn by Catherine

Flon. "On Independence Day, however, the flag was modified again. The blue and the red bands were placed horizontally this time, with the blue band on top of the red band" (Fobrum 2002). Haiti used this flag until 1964, when François Duvalier used a vertical black and red flag and added a modified version of the arms of the republic. On February 25, 1986, after Jean-Claude Duvalier fled Haiti and the Duvalier regime fell apart, the Haitian people in its vast majority requested that the red and blue flag be brought back. The red and blue flag remains the official flag of Haiti.

Foodways

Haitian cuisine is a mixture of African, French, and Caribbean influences. *Djiri kole* (literally "rice mixed with beans") is a staple of the Haitian diet (as is rice and beans throughout the Caribbean). Haitians, however, have numerous unique versions of beans and rice, such as adding pigeon peas, *djon djon* (tiny black mushrooms), and green peas. Haitians also make chicken, goat, and beef in sauces that many times have a tomato paste base (*sòs Kreyòl*). Other Haitian specialties are *banan pèze* (fried plantains), *griyo* (fried pork), *pate* (Haitian pastries filled with fish, chicken,

A large Haitian flag flutters in the wind as revelers and floats pass by during the Haitian Day Parade in Brooklyn, New York, on May 30, 2004. The third annual parade also commemorates 200 years of the Caribbean nation's independence. (AP Photo/Dean Cox)

or spiced beef), and *lambi* (conch). We find many Haitians throughout the United States dining on these Haitian delicacies. Many Haitians in the United States also enjoy *akasan,* a drink made of cinnamon, evaporated milk, flour, corn starch, star anise, and vanilla extract; and many imbibe Rhum Barbancourt, a rum produced in Haiti since 1862. In celebration of Haitian independence, Haitians in the United States commonly eat soup *joumou* (pumpkin soup), which is made with squash and is offered to guests who drop by to offer their best wishes for the upcoming year. Variations of soup *joumou* contain vegetables, beef, turkey, and thin pasta like macaroni and vermicelli.

Music, Arts, and Entertainment

Haiti has a longstanding tradition of artistic expression that is internationally recognized. Some of the prominent Haitian artists of the 20th century are Vodouist painter Hector Hyppolite and Georges Liautaud. The Galerie d'Art Nader, which opened in Port-au-Prince in 1966, has the finest collection of Haitian paintings in Haiti available for purchase, consequently contributing to the dissemination of Haitian art, as it receives hundreds of visitors and customers from around the world. "The Milwaukee Art Museum, in Milwaukee, Wisconsin, is home to the largest collection of Haitian art in the world. This collection of Haitian art classics, named the Flagg collection, was originally purchased by the late multimillionaire Richard Flagg (and his wife, Erna) at the urging of his friend, Monsignor Alfred Voegeli, the Episcopalian Bishop of Haiti who was from Milwaukee" (Zéphir 2004, 63). The collection was donated to the Milwaukee Art Museum upon Richard Flagg's death.

Music is also another form of artistic expression that has brought increased visibility to Haitians. One popular form of Haitian music with deep roots in Haiti's peasant class and is used in Vodou ceremonies is *Rara. Rara* bands perform in the streets of Haiti at various times when there are particular political events that incite grassroots movements. However, the established tradition of the *Rara* festival is during the Lent season, right after Carnival up until Easter Sunday. In the mid-1950s, another form of Haitian music called *Konpa* developed. *Konpa* is influenced by merengue, which is from the Dominican Republic. *Konpa* dominated the Haitian music scene with artists like Nemours Jean-Baptiste and Weber Sicot. Tabou Combo—which was formed in Haiti and relocated to New York when the political situation worsened in the late 1970s–and Miami-based T-Vice are two bands illustrative of this type of music. *Mizik Rasin* (roots music) developed in the late 1970s among Haitians. This musical form came about as the result of the interest of returning to Haitian folk forms such as Vodou and *Rara* musical traditions. The group Boukman Eksperyans (named after Boukman who presided over the Vodou ceremony that ignited the Haitian Revolution) started in 1978; they used their music to speak out against the abuses of the Duvalier regime and allied themselves with the struggles of the Haitian masses (Zéphir 2004, 64).

Integration and Impact on U.S. Society and Culture

Intergroup Relations

Haitians in the United States have established ties to other Haitians through extended families and institutions. Many Haitians are concentrated along the Eastern seaboard of the United States in cities such as Boston; New York; Washington, D.C.; and Miami. Haitians frequently visit their relatives who live in each of these cities as well as kin who live within the greater metropolitan areas of the major cities that Haitians live in. For example, there are an estimated 25,000 Haitians in the greater Washington, D.C., metropolitan area, which includes Silver Spring, Langley Park, and Hyattsville, Maryland. Many of them have relatives in the greater New York metropolitan area, and they visit each other frequently by car.

The institutions created by Haitians in the United States also provide ample opportunities for Haitians to congregate based on a shared ethnic identity. In the Washington, D.C., area, for example, Dr. Joseph Baptiste, responded to the coup d'état in Haiti in 1991 by founding the National Organization for the Advancement of Haitians (NOAH). NOAH is a nonprofit organization for social policy and economic development and allows Haitians from the Washington, D.C., area to interact and connect with Haitians living in other parts of the United States with the shared goal of the betterment of Haiti (http://www.noahhaiti.org).

Since its inception, NOAH has responded to emergencies in Haiti including natural disasters such as the earthquake of January 2010. NOAH members set up water pumps for over 5,000 Haitians living in tent cities and delivered thousands of meals to people who had been affected by the quake. Additionally, NOAH has an earthquake action plan, which includes a medical action plan including triage, consultation, emergency interventions, and specialized medicine.

Political Associations and Organizations

Since their migration to the United States, Haitians have created numerous professional organizations that help them maintain their ethnic identity, promote their interests, and continue links with their ancestral homeland. An example of a vibrant Haitian organization that helps Haitian Americans maintain their ethnic identity, assists members of the Haitian immigrant community, and continue links with Haiti is the AMHE, Association des Medecines Haïtiens à l'Étranger (the Associations of Haitian Physicians Abroad). According to the organization's Web site, the AMHE was founded in August 1972 by a group of Haitian physicians determined to mark their presence as a growing ethnic entity in the United States, foster professional alliances, promote the health and interests of the Haitian immigrant community at large, and contribute to the health care needs of Haitians through medical student training and donations (www.amhe.org). Since the January 12, 2010, earthquake, countless members of the AMHE, as well as other Haitian Americans who work in health care, have returned to Haiti to contribute their medical expertise and care for Haitians who need medical attention for compound fractures, amputations, and mental illness.

Civic and Electoral Participation

In the major American cities we find Haitians (Boston, Chicago, Miami, and New York, for example), Haitians have made an impact with regard to representing members of their community. Haitians also do this through increased electoral participation as a strategy in the shaping of their communities. The example of Haitian civic and electoral participation in Boston demonstrates this commitment.

Haitian organizations emerged in the Boston area in the 1980s to serve the population. Examples of these organizations are AFAB, or Asosyasyon Fanm Ayisyenn Boston (Association of Haitian Women in Boston); the Haitian-American Public Health Initiative (HAPHI); the Haitian American Public Health Initiative; Haitian-Americans United; and the Haitian Multi-Service Center. These organizations mobilize their resources and experience to assist newcomers to Boston's Haitian community.

According to one author, Haitians in Boston have also had a strong voice in U.S. politics since 1999, when Democrat Marie St. Fleur was elected as state house representative from the Fifth Suffolk District, representing Dorchester and part of Roxbury. Marie St. Fleur campaigned as the "girl from the neighborhood" and gained numerous votes from Haitians, who are overwhelmingly represented in her district.

Public Policies and Political Representation

Although Haitians have positively contributed to the creation of the United States and the communities which they live in, Haitians are continually stigmatized by negative stereotypes, especially in the latter 20th century. Indeed, no other American immigrant group in the 1970s and 1980s endured more prejudice and suffered more discrimination than Haitians (Stepick 1998, 2). For example, Haitians have the highest disapproval for political asylum requests of any national group. They have been disproportionately incarcerated in comparison to other nationalities seeking political asylum requests, and Haitians were identified as health risks for tuberculosis and AIDS during the 1970s and 1980s. As a result of this climate of discrimination, advocacy organizations that were disappointed that Haitians were not one of the nationalities benefiting from the Nicaraguan Adjustment and Central American Relief Act put tremendous political pressure on the U.S. Congress to pass some type of benefit to the estimated 50,000 Haitian refugees living in the United States in 1988. Applicants eligible for permanent residence in the United States included those who (a) were living continuously in the United States since December 31, 1995; (b) were either orphaned or abandoned after entering the United States; (c) were determined to have a credible fear of persecution if returned to Haiti, (d) had applied for asylum before December 31, 1995; or (e) had previously been paroled into the United States by U.S. authorities for emergent reasons or reasons deemed to be in the national interest.

The Second and Later Generations

Second-generation Haitian Americans are more numerous and heterogeneous that the first generation of Haitians that migrated to the United States. According to one scholar, the greater number of children of Haitian immigrants tends to fall within two broad categories: "(1) those who were born in the United States, who have always lived in this country and may or may not have had a chance to visit Haiti; and (2) those born in Haiti who came to the United States at an early age (usually before adolescence) and are schooled in the United States, and who may not have spent any time or significant amount of time in Haiti since their relocation" (Zéphir 2004, 129). They are fluent in English and some may have an active or passive knowledge of Haitian Creole (French in rare instances).

Ethnic Identity: Degrees of Haitianness

Second-generation Haitian Americans can be divided into three broad categories with some overlap: "(1) those who display a strong form of Haitianness; (2) those who display a weaker form of Haitianness; and (3) those who have absolutely nothing to do with Haiti, the undercovers" (Zéphir 2004, 130).

"Haitianness is demonstrated mostly through an intense involvement in the Haitian diasporic community and an interest in Haitian matters in the United States and Haiti. Haitianness can also be expressed by a preference for the label 'Haitian' as a self ethnic descriptor, an acknowledgement of one's birthplace of Haiti and parents' birthplace, length of residency in Haiti or repeated trips to Haiti, and a high level of fluency in Haitian Creole" (Zéphir 2004, 130–31). They speak Haitian Creole without the use of a lot of English to express their thoughts and are active in Haitian clubs and organizations. Second-generation Haitian Americans who exhibit a strong form of Haitianness also feel that it is their responsibility to educate Haitian American youth and the general public about Haiti. They defend Haiti from some

Youth Profile

A Haitian Star on the U.S. Men's National Soccer Team

Jozy Altidore (Josmer Volmy Altidore) is a 19-year-old forward for the U.S. Men's National Soccer Team and a soccer prodigy of Haitian descent. He was born on November 6, 1989, in Livingston, New Jersey, to Joseph and Giselle Altidore, who were both born in Haiti. Jozy has made a huge impact on the U.S. Men's National Soccer team although he has only been on the team for a relatively short time. He was the youngest player to score for the United States in a match with Mexico's team. He also became the youngest United States player to score a hat trick, putting in all three goals in a 3–0 win over Trinidad and Tobago in April 2009.

Jozy began his professional soccer career at the age of 16, when he was drafted by the MetroStars (now known as the New York Red Bulls) of Major League Soccer (MLS). Altidore had to miss most of his first season away from the MetroStars, however, while he worked toward his high school diploma in Florida. He made his first MLS appearance on September 9, 2006, as a substitute in the 81st minute.

Although Jozy Altidore is an American and a prominent member of the U.S. Men's National Team, he is also aware and proud of his Haitian roots. He counts his parents, Joseph and Giselle, as his role models, and in November 2006, Jozy went to Haiti along with his Red Bull teammates, Seth Stammler and Haitian-American soccer player Jerrod Laventure, as part of a six-day service trip for Yélé Haiti, the charitable organization of Wyclef Jean, the Grammy award–winning artist of Haitian descent.

Source: http://en.wikipedia.org/wiki/Jozy_Altidore—cite_note-6#cite_note-6.

of the negative accusations the country receives in the media. An example of a second-generation Haitian American who fits this description is Wyclef Jean, who is arguably the most prominent Haitian living in the United States. Wyclef Jean is an award-winning musician and producer, and he is a Haitian Goodwill Ambassador. He created a foundation called Yélé Haiti, which supports projects that improve the education of Haitian youth, the health of Haitians, the Haitian environment, and community development in Haiti. Since the 2010 earthquake Wyclef Jean, his wife Claudinette, and Yélé Haiti have distributed clothes, medical supplies, and over 80,000 hot meals across Haiti. Yélé Haiti also distributed tents to Haitians rendered homeless by the earthquake and has enacted a plan to augment Haiti's agricultural production through a farming community outside of Port-au-Prince in Croix-des-Bouquets. Finally, Yélé Haiti plans to build permanent housing for communities destroyed by the earthquake.

Daphne Dorlean (left) and Albertha Roundtree, both from Shadowlawn Elementary School in the Little Haiti section of Miami, dance a Haitian *compas* dance as part of Haitian heritage celebrations in Miami, May 17, 2002. (AP Photo/Marta Lavandier)

"Second generation Haitian Americans who are positioned at the weaker end of the Haitianness axis define themselves as Haitian Americans" (Zéphir 2004, 133). There are various factors that explain this choice of identification. For example, the fact that some Haitian Americans were born in the United States, or lived in the United States since a young age, has given them a thorough knowledge of American and African American culture that surpasses their knowledge of Haitian culture. Also, their lack of a foreign accent may prevent them from sounding like other Haitians who speak accented English. They may like elements from Haitian culture such as cuisine and music, but they are less involved with Haitian diasporic matters, as well as those of Haiti. Haitian Americans who display this weaker form of Haitianness stand in stark contrast to those Americans of Haitian descent who cover up their ethnic heritage to deal with the reality of ethnic prejudice that is pervasive in the United States. One author refers to people of Haitian descent such as this as an undercover (130).

Educational Attainment

The assistance of state and city agencies that have attended to the specific cultural needs of Haitians has facilitated the education of second-generation Haitian

Youth Profile

American Idol Finalist and Model

(Courtesy of Willis Roberts)

Joanne Borgella is a singer of Haitian descent who was a finalist on season 7 of American Idol in 2008. She is also a plus-size model represented by Wilhelmina Models, one of the largest and most successful model management companies in the world. Joanne was born in Oyster Bay, Long Island, on May 29, 1982, to Joel Borgella MD and Paule Danielle Ford, who are both from Haiti. Her parents are the founders of Radio Tropicale, the first international Haitian radio station. Dr. Joel Borgella was also a presidential candidate in Haiti's 2006 presidential elections.

Joanne's big break in the entertainment industry occurred in 2005 when Joanne earned one of the coveted spots on the Oxygen Channel's groundbreaking special created by Mo'Nique of *Queens of Comedy* and *The Parkers* fame, entitled "Mo'Nique's Fat Chance." Joanne took the competition very seriously, and ended up victorious, winning the title of Miss F.A.T. (which stands for "*F*abulous *A*nd *T*hick").

Joanne is represented by Wilhelmina 10/20 division in New York, Miami, and Los Angeles. Ms. Borgella is currently the face of Ashley Stewart, a nationwide plus-size retailer for urban women; Wal-Mart; and Macy's. She is also currently one of the faces of Proctor & Gamble's new campaign for African American women called "My Black is Beautiful," which celebrates the diverse collective beauty of African American women and encourages black women to define and promote their own beauty standard. As the result of her modeling career, Joanne has been featured in African American magazines such as *Essence* and *Jet*. Joanne has also been the face of Torrid and Kohl's department store and was featured in ads in *Seventeen* and *In Style* magazine.

Joanne is also very proud of her Haitian roots. She has performed at numerous Haitian charity events as a special guest and has also donated food, gifts, and clothing to Gonaïves, Haiti, which was ravaged by numerous tropical storms and hurricanes in 2008.

Americans. In New York City, for example, "the large number of Haitian students attending public schools compelled the board of education to hire Haitian teachers and guidance counselors who could address the needs of Haitian students. Many of these Haitian teachers are used in bilingual education programs (Haitian Creole and English) that are designed to help Haitian children with limited English proficiency" (Zéphir 2004, 95). Programs such as these have helped many second-generation Haitian Americans to integrate into American educational systems and achieve at very high levels. Many second-generation Haitian Americans, whether they were born in Haiti and moved to the United States or were born in the United States, have done well in American schools and have gone on to obtain advanced American university degrees, which have secured them employment as doctors, engineers, nurses, lawyers, professors, and business owners.

Issues in Relations between the United States and Haiti

Forecasts for the 21st Century: Hope for Post-Earthquake Haiti

More than 200 years ago, the ancestors of Haitian Americans fought a revolution in which they defeated colonial powers that tried to reinstitute chattel slavery. The main lesson the Haitian Revolution taught the world is that black people (people of African descent) are human beings with the right to live dignified lives (Louis 2010). The Haitian Revolution was also supposed to allow Haitians to lead dignified lives, but as the January 12, 2010, earthquake in Haiti demonstrated, the majority of Haitians are still struggling to lead dignified lives.

Haitian Americans reacted immediately to this unimaginable cataclysm in numerous ways. For example, Haitian Americas rushed to Port-au-Prince, the capital of Haiti, and Leogane, the epicenter of the earthquake, to lend their expertise for Haitians trapped under rubble and injured by debris. Anesthesiologist Billy Ford, pediatric surgeon Henri Ford, and internist Jean Ford, Haitian brothers who migrated to the United States, all went back to Haiti after the earthquake and helped with medical treatment in Port-au-Prince. Andia Augustin, a doctoral candidate in French at Washington University in St. Louis, interrupted her studies and served as a translator for a medical team from Tennessee that provided medical care to Haitians injured in the earthquake. Guerda Nicolas used her expertise in psychology to help inform well-meaning relief organizations, missionary groups, and other groups with disaster counseling skills that American treatments for mental illness needs to integrate Haitian culture, Haitian folk medicine, and Haitian coping mechanisms (such as singing, dancing, praying, and receiving comfort from one's minister) as ways to treat depression and posttraumatic stress disorder (PTSD) in Haiti.

The cataclysm of January 12, 2010, overshadowed some of the good news that was coming out of Haiti with regard to its difficult past. Specifically, there was cause for hope for Haiti among Haitian Americans because the Obama administration took steps before the earthquake to ensure a brighter future for Haiti. For example, in 2009 President Obama appointed former president Bill Clinton as a special U.S. envoy to Haiti. One of the responsibilities for the former president was to see that international donors converted their collective pledge of $353 million into viable aid for Haiti. Since that appointment, former president Clinton visited Haiti in July 2009 to raise awareness about reconstruction efforts in Gonaïves, a battered seaside city that was nearly destroyed in 2008 by a series of tropical storms. During that visit, special envoy Clinton said the Haitian government and its international backers hoped to create 150,000 to 200,000 jobs in Haiti over the next two years. Many of those jobs were supposed to come from projects to rebuild roads and shore up erosion-prone hillsides (Katz 2009a). Before the earthquake, Haiti benefited from the presence of 9,000 United Nations peacekeeping troops, which helped with security matters. In addition, the U.S. Congress granted Haiti access to the American textiles market, allowing for the duty-free sale of Haitian textiles in the United States for a decade (as part of the Hope II Trade legislation). This policy added 12,000 jobs to Haiti.

There were other areas of improvement that gave Haiti hope. Recently three international organizations (the Inter-American Monetary Fund, the International Monetary Fund, and the World Bank) canceled $1.2 billion of Haiti's debt on June 30, 2009, freeing up approximately $50 million per year for spending to reduce poverty over the next 10 to 15 years (Katz 2009b). A significant portion of the debt dates back to loans that lined the pockets of Haiti's dictators, especially François and Jean-Claude Duvalier. Before January 12, 2010, Haiti's government embarked on a focused action plan to safeguard the gains already achieved and ensure that the country continues on a path towards economic security. This included job creation and infrastructural improvement, which was supposed to attract more foreign investment to Haiti.

Since the earthquake, the international community, the U.S. government, and the Haitian diaspora (Haitian Americans) have helped to rebuild Haiti in different ways. The main contribution made by the international community to the rebuilding of Haiti is external debt relief. After the earthquake, Venezuela announced that it would cancel nearly $300 million in Haitian debt. Haiti owes Taiwan $88 million. On May 29, 2010, Taiwan announced that the Taiwanese government would shoulder the Haitian interest payments for five years as Haiti recovers from the earthquake. France promised €230 million (approximately $400 million) towards Haitian earthquake relief. Numerous telethons in the United States (HOPE FOR HAITI NOW telethon; S.O.S.—Saving Ourselves: Help for Haiti) raised millions of dollars for Haitian earthquake relief. On March 22, 2010, the Inter-American Development Bank agreed to forgive $479 million of Haiti's debt. Additionally, the IADB will provide Haiti with $2 billion in loans over the next 10 years. And on May 28,

2010, the World Bank agreed to cancel approximately $36 million of Haitian debt. The World Bank also made $479 million in grants to support post-earthquake Haitian recovery and development through June 2011. Finally on March 31, 2010, over 150 countries pledged over $5.3 billion over the next 18 months to help rebuild Haiti.

In addition to providing military and medical assistance in Haiti since January 12, 2010, the Obama administration granted temporary protected status to undocumented Haitians living in the United States. Temporary protected status protects undocumented Haitians from deportation for 18 months and allows them to continue to work in the United States. This special immigration status was extended to approximately 100,000 Haitians and 30,000 Haitians who were ordered to be deported. The protection status only applies to Haitians who were in the United States before January 12, 2010 (Wu 2010). President Obama also donated part of his Nobel Peace Prize Award to the Clinton Bush Haiti Fund. The Clinton Bush Haiti Fund distributes essential medical equipment to critically injured Haitians, creates clinics, and delivers relief supplies, including water purification tablets, hygiene kits, mosquito nets, and temporary latrines (http://www.clintonbushhaitifund.org/).

The Haitian diaspora in the United States responded immediately to the earthquake as it has during past crises. In addition to Haitian American hometown associations and professional associations that went to Haiti to help with earthquake relief, Haitian Americans have contributed to rebuilding post-earthquake Haiti. Maurice Bonhomme and Jean Cayemitte, who work jobs as security guards and in the kitchen of an upscale French restaurant in Chicago, Illinois, returned to Petite Goave, Haiti, which was devastated by the earthquake (Lazar 2010). Between the two of them, Jean and Maurice raised enough money to get 500 tents to Petit Goave and are rebuilding a grammar school that they supported with their own money before the earthquake. Jean and Maurice's story is an example of the power of Haitian Americans in rebuilding Haiti. According to a 2008 World Bank study, émigrés remittances made up roughly 30 percent of Haiti's GDP (Lazar 2010). As the result of the earthquake, it would be safe to assume that Haitian Americans are sending even more money.

Haiti was the first nation to articulate a general principle of common, unqualified equality for all of its citizens. The fundamental concept of a common humanity also ran deeply through the early Haitian constitutions. This belief is what connects Haitians with other people around the world, as was highlighted by U.S. President Barack Obama in a speech he delivered in the aftermath of the earthquake. In the coming months and years, Haitians will continue to struggle to live dignified lives in the midst of destroyed homes, deceased family and friends, infrastructural challenges, and possible waves of infectious diseases that could claim additional lives. But if most of the international aid that was pledged to Haiti is donated, if infrastructural improvements occur in Haiti, and if Haitian Americans continue to help rebuild Haiti, there may be reason for hope in post-earthquake Haiti.

Appendix I: Migration Statistics

Table 134 Persons obtaining legal permanent resident status by region and country of birth: Fiscal years 2000 to 2009

Region and country of birth	2000	2001	2002	2003	2004	2005	2006	2007	2008	2009
Total	841,002	1,058,902	1,059,356	703,542	957,883	1,122,257	1,266,129	1,052,415	1,107,126	1,130,818
Haiti	22,337	27,031	20,213	12,293	14,191	14,524	22,226	30,405	26,007	24,280

Source: U.S. Department of Homeland Security. Office of Immigration Statistics. 2010. Adapted from Table 3.

Table 135 Persons naturalized by region/country of birth and selected characteristics (2003–2008). Region/country: Haiti

Year	Naturalized U.S. citizens from Haiti
2003	7,247
2004	8,215
2005	9,740
2006	15,979
2007	11,552
2008	21,229
Total	73,962

Source: U.S. Department of Homeland Security, U.S. Citizenship and Immigration Service (USCIS), *Yearbook of Immigration Statistics*.

Table 136 Nonimmigrant admissions by region and country of residence (Haiti): Fiscal years 1999 to 2008

Year	Nonimmigrant admissions from Haiti to the United States
1999	75,210
2000	76,185
2001	72,418
2002	68,725
2003	66,675
2004	70,187
2005	76,092
2006	62,650
2007	89,990
2008	103,784
Total	761,916

Source: U.S. Department of Homeland Security, U.S. Citizenship and Immigration Service (USCIS), *Yearbook of Immigration Statistics*. Nonimmigrant Admissions (Table 27d).

Table 137 Individuals from Haiti granted asylum total: 1999 to 2008

Year	Individuals from Haiti granted asylum in the United States
1999	406
2000	985
2001	1,595
2002	1,478
2003	1,732
2004	2,313
2005	2,936
2006	2,995
2007	1,648
2008	1,237
Total	17,325

Source: U.S. Department of Homeland Security, U.S. Citizenship and Immigration Service (USCIS), *Yearbook of Immigration Statistics*. Individuals Granted Asylum by Region and Country of Nationality: Fiscal Years 1999 to 2008 (Tables 17d and 19d).

Appendix II: Demographics/Census Statistics

Census figures provide the best estimates of the Haitian population in the United States. According to the American Community Survey, which is compiled from Census data, there were 694,123 Haitian-born blacks in the United States as of 2005.

Table 138 shows the leading states in the United States where those Haitians obtaining legal permanent residence in 2009 lived. Chief among them are Florida, New York, New Jersey, and Massachusetts.

Table 138 Persons obtaining legal permanent resident status during fiscal year 2009. Leading States of Residence; Region/Country: Haiti

Characteristic	Total	Male	Female
Total	24,280	10,845	13,435
California	103	57	46
Colorado	20	8	12
Connecticut	519	251	268
Florida	13,403	5,957	7,446
Georgia	333	157	176
Illinois	142	61	81
Maryland	288	126	162
Massachusetts	1,948	840	1,108
Michigan	41	19	22
Minnesota	17	11	6
Nevada	20	7	13
New Jersey	1,775	789	986
New York	4,229	1,876	2,353
North Carolina	55	24	31
Ohio	37	16	21
Pennsylvania	406	180	226
Texas	82	38	44
Virginia	82	39	43
Washington	44	20	24
Other	736	369	367

Source: Adapted from U.S. Department of Homeland Security. Profiles on Legal Permanent Residents: 2009.

Appendix III: Notable Haitian Americans

A few notable Haitian Americans include the following individuals:

Marleine Bastien is a social worker and founder and executive director of Fanm Ayisyen nan Miami (Haitian Women of Miami), which is also known as FANM (the Haitian Creole word for "woman"). She was born in Haiti in 1959 and immigrated to the United States in 1981.

Edwidge Danticat was born in Haiti in 1969. She is arguably the most prominent Haitian American writer. Edwidge migrated to the United States in 1981 and earned a bachelor of arts degree in French translation and literature from Columbia University's Barnard College in 1990 and earned an MFA degree in creative writing in 1993. She is a prolific writer who has published more than 40 essays and short stories and several novels that have garnered acclaim such as *Breath, Eyes, Memory* (1994), chosen by the Oprah Winfrey book club in 1998; and *Krik Krak* (1995), which was a finalist for the National Book Award. She is also very involved in the Haitian community, regularly organizing cultural programs and speaking to Haitian children and teenagers at public schools.

Marie St. Fleur is a Massachusetts state house representative who served Dorchester for 11 years but now serves as Boston Mayor Thomas Menino's chief of advocacy and strategic investment, which oversees many education, immigration, and antipoverty programs, according to the *Boston Globe* (April 24, 2010). She was born in Haiti in 1962 and immigrated to the United States in 1969. While attending the University of Massachusetts at Amherst she earned a BA in political science in 1984. In 1987 she earned her law degree after attending Boston College Law School. She has worked extensively in aiding the Haitian immigrant population in Boston, especially after the Haiti earthquake in 2010.

Henri R. Ford, M.D., is vice president and chief of surgery of Children's Hospital in Los Angeles, California, as well as vice-dean of medical education, professor, and vice chair for clinical affairs in the department of surgery and at the Keck School of Medicine of the University of Southern California. He received his BA in public and international affairs, cum laude, from Princeton University in 1980 and his MD from Harvard Medical School in 1984. Dr. Ford did his internship (1984–1985) and residency (1985–1987; 1989–1991) in general surgery at New York Hospital Cornell Medical College. He completed a research fellowship in immunology (1987–1989) in the department of surgery at the University of Pittsburgh and a clinical fellowship (1991–1993) in pediatric surgery at Children's Hospital of Pittsburgh.

Abner Louima currently lives in Miami, where he is an advocate for Haitian refugees. In 1997, Louima was brutally attacked in one of the most outrageous cases of police brutality against black men, and Haitians. Louima was beaten and sodomized with a plunger handle by New York Police Department officers. As the result of this incident a series of trials occurred from 1999 to 2002. The four New York City police officers involved included Justin Volpe, who pleaded guilty to sodomizing Louima and who was sentenced to 30 years in prison. One other officer served five years in prison. Two others were fired from the New York Police Department and were not tried again after having their convictions overturned. On July 12, 2001, Abner Louima accepted a settlement of $8.7 million from the City of New York and the police union after he filed a civil suit.

Glossary

Brain drain: An out-migration of a country's technical and intellectual professionals (such as doctors, engineers, lawyers, teachers, and nurses).

Kleptocracy: A state in which those in power exploit national resources and steal.

Lavalas: Haitian Creole for a flood that washes everything away.

Lwa: Spirits; associated with the practice of Vodou.

Tonton Macoute: Name of a traditional bogeyman in Haiti. Also a Duvalier loyalist who provided information and detected subversion in every sphere of Haitian society through bullying, extortion, and murder.

References

Arthur, Charles, and Michael Dash, eds. 1999. *Libète: A Haiti Anthology.* Kingston, Jamaica: Ian Randle Publishers.

Catanese, Anthony. 1999. *Haitians: Migration and Diaspora.* Boulder, CO: Westview Press.

Central Intelligence Agency World Factbook. [Online information; retrieved 08/07/09.] https://www.cia.gov/library/publications/the-world-factbook/geos/ha.html.

Desmangles, Leslie. 1992. *The Faces of the Gods: Vodou and Roman Catholicism in Haiti.* Chapel Hill: University of North Carolina Press.

Dupuy, Alex. 1989. *Haiti in the World Economy: Class, Race and Underdevelopment since 1700.* Boulder, CO: Westview Press.

Dupuy, Alex. 2005. "From Jean-Bertrand Aristide to Gerard Latortue: The Unending Crisis of Democratization in Haiti." *Journal of Latin American Anthropology* 10(1): 186–205.

Farmer, Paul. 1994. *The Uses of Haiti.* Monroe, ME: Common Courage Press.

Ferguson, James. 1987. *Papa Doc, Baby Doc: Haiti and the Duvaliers.* New York: Basil Blackwell.

Fick, Carolyn. 1990. *The Making of Haiti: The Saint-Domingue Revolution from Below.* Knoxville: University of Tennessee Press.

Fobrum, Carl. 2002. "Haitian Flag Day Speech." [Online information; retrieved 6/2/09.] http://www.webster.edu/~corbetre/haiti-archive/msg11939.html.

Geggus, David. 1982. *Slavery, War and Revolution: The British Occupation of Saint-Domingue, 1793–1798.* New York: Oxford University Press.

Glick Schiller, Nina, and Georges Fouron. 2001. *Georges Woke Up Laughing: Long-Distance Nationalism and the Search for Home.* Durham, NC: Duke University Press.

Immigration and Naturalization Service. 2000. Statistical Yearbook.

James, C.L.R. 1963. *The Black Jacobins: Toussaint L'Ouverture and the San Domingo Revolution.* New York: Random House.

Katz, Jonathan. 2009a. "Clinton Draws Crowds on First Visit as Envoy." [Online article; retrieved 8/7/09.] www.bostonhaitian.com/BHR%207-09web.pdf.

Katz, Jonathan. 2009b. "1.2 Billion in Debts Canceled to Help Haiti." [Online article; retrieved 8/7/09.] www.bostonhaitian.com/BHR%207-09web.pdf.

Laguerre, Michel. 1998. *Diasporic Citizenship: Haitian Americans in Transnational America.* New York: St. Martin's Press.

Lazar, Elizabeth. 2010. "The Return of Jean and Maurice: How the Diaspora Will Rebuild Haiti." [Online article; retrieved 6/3/10.] http://www.newint.org/features/web-exclusive/2010/05/12/haiti-diaspora/.

Louis, Jr., Bertin M. 2010. "Haiti's Pact with the Devil (Some Haitians Believe This Too)?" [Online essay; retrieved 6/3/09.] http://blogs.ssrc.org/tif/2010/02/18/haitis-pact-with-the-devil-some-haitians-believe-this-too/.

Ng, Alicia. 2006. "Evangelism Spreads Throughout Haitian Communities" [Online article; retrieved 6/23/09.] news.newamericamedia.org/news/view_article.html?article_id=764 eab64c5229a37356b9faf052bc638.

Olmos, Margarite, and Lizabeth Paravisini-Gebert. 2003. *Creole Religions of the Caribbean: An Introduction from Vodou and Santeria to Obeah and Espiritismo.* New York: New York University Press.

Pierre-Louis, François. 2006. *Haitians in New York City: Transnationalism and Hometown Associations.* Gainesville: University of Florida Press.

Richman, Karen. 2005. "The Protestant Ethic and the Dis-Spirit of Vodou." In *Immigrant Faiths: Transforming Religious Life in America,* edited by Karen I. Leonard, 165–85. Walnut Creek, CA: AltaMira Press.

Schieffelin, Bambi, and Rachelle Charlier Doucet. 1994. "The 'Real' Haitian Creole: Ideology, Metalinguistics and Orthographic Choice." *American Ethnologist* 21(1): 176–200.

Simpson, George E. 1945. "The Belief System of Haitian Vodoun." *American Anthropologist* 47(1): 35–59.

Stepick, Alex. 1998. *Pride Against Prejudice: Haitians in the United States.* Needham Heights: Allyn & Bacon.

Védrine, Soliny. 2004. *Life History Interview* with Bertin M. Louis, Jr. Boston, MA.

White House, 2010. "Remarks by the President on Rescue Efforts in Haiti." [Online information; retrieved 6/3/10.] http://www.whitehouse.gov/the-press-office/remarks-president-rescue-efforts-haiti.

White House. 2009. "Statement of President Barack Obama on Haitian Flag Day." [Online information; retrieved 6/3/09.] www.whitehouse.gov/the_press_office/Statement-of-President-Barack-Obama-on-Haitian-Flag-Day/.

Wu, Scott. 2010. "Temporary Protected Status for Haitians in the US for 18 Months." [Online information; retrieved 6/3/10.] http://www.nowpublic.com/world/temporary-protected-status-haitians-us-18-months.

Zéphir, Flore. 2004. *The Haitian Americans.* Westport, CT: Greenwood Press.

Further Reading

Farmer, Paul. 1994. *The Uses of Haiti*. Monroe, ME: Common Courage Press.

The Uses of Haiti uses the quest for human dignity of the majority of Haitian society (the Haitian poor) as a critical lens to analyze Haitian history. By reviewing the actions of nations, such as France and the United States, and particular actors in Haitian history, such as Toussaint Louverture, the Haitian upper class, the Haitian military, François and Jean-Claude Duvalier, Farmer's goal is to reveal the structural issues (structural adjustment programs, an indemnity the Boyer administration paid France in the 19th century so that France would not invade Haiti, and the Duvalier kleptocracy) to answer why poverty and underdevelopment are persistent in Haiti.

Glick Schiller, Nina, and Georges Fouron. 2001. *Georges Woke Up Laughing: Long-Distance Nationalism and the Search for Home*. Durham, NC: Duke University Press.

Georges Woke Up Laughing is a superb ethnography that uses research in the United States and Haiti to demonstrate the continued ties between Haitians living in the United States and their homeland. Using the experiences and family history of Dr. Georges Fouron, a professor of education and Africana studies at Stony Brook University who is of Haitian descent, the text takes readers from the United States to Haiti to analyze gender, nationalism, and the relationship between later generations of Haitian Americans and Haiti.

Pamphile, Leon. 2001. *Haitians and African Americans: A Heritage of Tragedy and Hope*. Gainesville: University of Florida Press.

Haitians and African Americans is an informative text that demonstrates the long historical relationship between Haitians and African Americans. This book deals with the shared heritage of slavery for both groups and how the paths of African Americans and Haitians have crossed repeatedly in their dual quest for freedom from human bondage and equality. For example, this book recognizes some of important contributions made to American society by Haitians like the founding of Chicago by the Haitian Jean Baptiste Point du Sable. In addition, the text notes the African American political support of Haiti and Haitians especially during the Haitian boat crisis of the late 20th century.

Zéphir, Flore. 2004. *The Haitian Americans*. Westport, CT: Greenwood Press.

The Haitian Americans is the premier resource about the Haitian presence in the United States. The author provides a detailed history of Haiti, a history of Haitians in the United States, statistics about Haitian migration to the United States, information about established and growing Haitian communities across the United States, and short biographies about prominent Haitian Americans who contribute to the fabric of American society.

Honduran Immigrants

by Suyapa G. Portillo Villeda

Introduction

Honduran immigrants are a small but growing community in the United States. Earlier waves of migration from Honduras date back to the early half of the 20th century. Many Honduran intellectuals arrived in New York and other cities, but migration by employees of the banana companies to New Orleans was the most prominent influx of Hondurans. Several major U.S. companies operated banana businesses in the North Coast of the country for the last 100 years. The Tela Railroad Company and the Truxillo Railroad Company, both subsidiaries of the United Fruit Company, began to operate there in 1912. The Standard Fruit and Steamship Company (began under the Vaccaro Brothers) operated business that purchased from local growers and resold bananas in the United States. For much of the 20th century Honduras was derogatorily referred to as the "Banana Republic," a term used by United States citizens to refer to Honduras. The term is understood to mean not only that the main export of the country was bananas but also to mean that the banana companies controlled politics in the country. Nowadays, the country's number one exported commodity is not bananas but people. Honduran society is complex and diverse, and this can be seen in the migratory networks of immigrants that come to the United States. Most of the 20th century has been a complex time for political affairs in Honduras. A series of military and political dictatorships stifled the development of national infrastructure and national industry. Honduras has also been a site of geopolitical interest by the United States. In the 1980s, the contras operated in Honduras to curtail the Nicaraguan and Salvadoran liberation forces (Lapper 1985, 84). Millions of dollars from the administration of Ronald Reagan supported military forces and training of the contras, the counterrevolutionary forces. Very little of this funding was invested in Honduran society and education. Today, Honduras is one of the poorest countries in Latin America. The infant mortality rate reported by the Honduran government in 2009 is of 25.82 deaths per 1,000 live births. Although all Hondurans, also known as *catrachos,* enjoy a publicly funded education in Honduras, many do not make it all the way to high school, having to work to support their families; 76.2 percent of the population over 15 years of age can read and write.

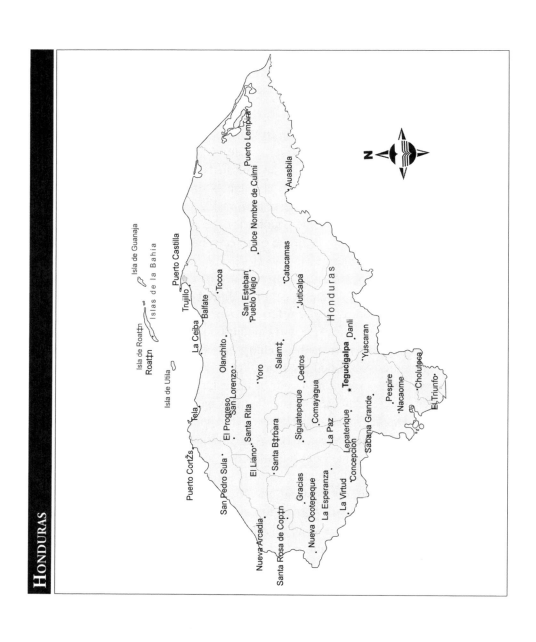

Chronology

5th to 9th century	Mayan Empire in Copán.
pre-1500	Honduras is inhabited by Lencas, Tolupanes, Pech, Tawah-kas, Chortís.
1502	Christopher Columbus lands in Trujillo on his fourth voyage.
1524	Hernán Cortés sends an expedition to Honduras, founding the North Coast towns of Puerto Caballos (Puerto Cortés) and Trujillo.
	Pedro de Alvarado leads an expedition to Honduras, founding San Pedro Sula.
1537	Governor Francisco de Montejano founds the city of Comayagua.
1797	Garifuna peoples arrive in Honduran Bay Islands and Roatán.
1821	The Central American Federation gains independence from Spain.
1839	Honduras becomes an independent republic.
1907	Sam Zemurray forms the Cuyamel Fruit Company in Honduras.
1911–1912	Zemurray, of the Cuyamel Fruit, attempts to oust President Davila because he was not favoring his company. The United States steps in to negotiate the situation.
	President Bonilla favors Zemurray's company by giving him more concessions. U.S. invasion helps to secure U.S. control in the region.
1912	United Fruit Company is established in Honduras via the Tela and the Trujillo Railroad Company; land concessions are given by the Honduran government to build a railroad.
1929	United Fruit Company purchases Cuyamel Fruit Company; Zemurray is the largest shareholder and becomes general manager.
1932	Tiburcio Carias Andino takes the presidency and remains in power as a dictator for 16 years; his regime represses workers attempting to organize unions and Liberal party members.

1949	Tiburcio Carias Andino dictatorship ends.
1954	Workers of the United Fruit Company lead the Great Banana Strike of 1954, a national general strike.
	Bilateral military training agreement is signed with the United States.
1955	Sindicato de Trabajadores de la Tela Railroad Company (SITRATERCO) is formed by United Fruit Company. Workers at the end of the strike.
1957	Ramon Villeda Morales takes the presidency in a power sharing government with the military.
	Ministry of Labor and the Ministry of Social Security is formed.
1961	Agrarian Reform Program is introduced.
1963	Ramon Villeda Morales is ousted by a military coup led by military colonel Osvaldo López Arellano.
1969	"Soccer War" with El Salvador begins and lasts four days. Discrimination and exodus of Salvadoran citizens of Honduras begins.
1972–1978	The period of "Military Reformism" begins.
1974	Hurricane Fifi leaves 12,000 dead and 150,000 homeless.
1977	Worker-owned banana cooperative Las Isletas is invaded and destroyed by Honduran soldiers who arrive in Standard Fruit railroad cars.
1979	U.S. President Jimmy Carter strengthens ties to Honduras after the fall of Somoza in Nicaragua.
1980	Constitutional assembly elections. Treaty signed with El Salvador.
	Economic crisis hits all the Central American nations.
	U.S. military presence in Honduras begins for the purpose of funding the contras.
1981	President Suazo Cordova becomes first democratically elected president in 20 years.
	Military advisors arrive in Honduras.
1982	Constituent assembly ends in approval of the 14th Constitution.

Reagan's administration pledges 50 percent more military aid to Honduras.

Four clandestine cemeteries full of bodies of activists found during the contra war.

Strikes and land occupations are declared "subversive acts" in new decree.

In June, Honduran army begins to cooperate with the United States in joint operations with the Salvadoran army against Farabundo Martí National Liberation Front (FMLN).

In July, joint-U.S.-Honduran military operations along Nicaraguan border.

In November, *Newsweek* reveals that U.S. Ambassador Negroponte in control of contra operations against Nicaragua.

1983   U.S. training base opens at Puerto Castillo.

1984   Sixty thousand demonstrators in Tegucigalpa and 40,000 in San Pedro Sula protest U.S. presence in Honduras.

Kissinger Commission recommends $8 billion developmental aid to Central America and increased military assistance to Honduras, El Salvador, and Guatemala.

1998   Hurricane Mitch hits Central America, killing 7,000; 8,300 are missing.

United States agrees to extend temporary protected status (TPS) to Honduran immigrants after Hurricane Mitch.

2009   President Manuel Zelaya Rosales is kidnapped and taken to Costa Rica in what is recognized by most of the international community as a political military coup d'état.

During the coup, thousands of Hondurans protested in the streets of Tegucigalpa and San Pedro Sula.

In November, illegal elections are held and President Pepe Lobo is elected by less than 40 percent of the population.

2010   By January, human rights organizations report 4,000 human rights violations and over 3,300 civil rights violations committed during the coup d'état.

The National Front of Popular Resistance (FNRP) continues to fight for a national constitutional assembly to redraft the constitution in Honduras.

Background

Geography of Honduras

Honduras has a diverse geography of valleys and mountains. Most of its land mass, 80 percent, is comprised of mountains. The mainland territory is 69,593 square miles in size. The territory has access to both the Caribbean Sea, with a coastline extending 457 miles, and the Pacific Ocean, with a coastline extending 95 miles along the Gulf of Fonseca. Honduras has an extensive border with Nicaragua, extending 573 miles along the southeast. On the southwest, Honduras and El Salvador share a 213-mile border. On the west, Honduras and Guatemala share a 159-mile border. Although Honduras has several islands and islets off its Caribbean Coast, the most important ones are the Islas de la Bahía (Bay Islands), comprised of Roatán, a large island about 31 miles long and 3 miles wide, and the smaller islands of Utila and Guanaja (Merrill 1995). Other islands are the Santanilla Islands (Swan Islands), where the United States and Honduras maintain a meteorological station in the Caribbean. Smaller keys, islets in the Caribbean, are Barbareta, Morat, Santa Elena, Cayos Zapotillos and Cayos Cochinos, the latter used for military exercises. In the Gulf of Fonseca, there are three islands: Tiger Island, Zacate Grande, and Exposición.

The waterways and lakes in Honduras are extensive, though not all navigable. The rivers that end in the North Coast beaches have been an important source of water for the banana industry, for both local and foreign growers and companies. One of Honduras' most important and largest rivers is the Río Patuca. Other rivers include the Río Grande to the south, the Río Coco bordering Nicaragua, the Río Lempa and the Río Guascarán on the border with El Salvador. Rivers are an important part of the life and work for farmers and workers in the North Coast region, where there are several rivers, the Río Ulúa, the Río Chamelecón, and the Río Aguán. The Río Plátano runs through the Río Plátano Biosphere Reserve. The largest lake is the Lake of Yojoa, at one time a water route between the coast and the capital in the center of the country.

Honduras' mountainous regions connect to the mountainous regions in Guatemala, from the western part of Honduras to the eastern side, to Nicaragua's mountainous region. Deep valleys cut through the Honduran mountains and have been key for the large agricultural economy and the export economies. Mountainous regions have challenged the creation of roads and transportation routes. Roads were not officially built until 1957. Before there were paved highways, there was a system of dirt roads known as the Camino Real, linking the Central American territories during the colonial period.

For most of the 20th century, the majority of the country has relied on subsistence farming despite booming periods of export by foreign-owned banana, coffee, and sugar companies. The North Coast of Honduras was developed in the

20th century for the export of bananas by the foreign-owned companies. As the colonial rule matured, Honduras remained an mostly unexplored hinterland, yet it was an important source of mining. In the 17th and 18th centuries, the exploitation of mines continued. Toward the end of the 18th century, cattle ranching developed as important industry.

History of Honduras

The region that is now Honduras was a region within the great Mayan empire up until 900 c.e. The Nahualt also had competing influence in the region. The Spanish found smaller tribes living in Honduras, as opposed to a huge empire comparable to the great empires of Mexico and Peru. Although Christopher Columbus landed in the Gulf of Honduras in 1502, on his fourth voyage, it was not until 1524 that an expedition set out to explore the Central American isthmus. A second expedition, led by a captain in the Pedrarías Dávila army named Francisco Hernández de Córdoba, set out from Panama to the north of the isthmus at the same time (Perez-Brignoli 1989, 34–35). But it was the expedition led by Hernán Cortés from Mexico that arrived first. Cortés founded Puerto Caballos (current-day Puerto Cortés) and Trujillo (35). One of Hernán Cortés lieutenants, Pedro de Alvarado, led a bloody expedition into Guatemala and later into Honduras founding San Pedro Sula and Gracias in 1524. Another expedition led by Governor Francisco de Montejano founded the city of Comayagua in 1537 (36).

Indigenous peoples in Honduras revolted and challenged the Spanish incursions. Their resistance was debilitated not only by weapons but also by disease carried by the Spanish. The decimation of indigenous populations was extensive, believed to have been to disease, hard labor, and destruction of their habitat. Indigenous peoples were forced to work in the mines exploited for the Spanish crown as well as local farms and haciendas kept by the Spanish. At the same time, Christianization contributed to the pacification of the rebelling indigenous groups. Manuel de Jesus Subirana, a Spanish missionary, managed to move the Honduran government to give the indigenous communities communal land titles between 1862 and 1864 (Rivas 1993, 29). The Spanish began to import Africans as slaves to labor in the plantations of the Caribbean and Honduras. By the 18th century, the African population had surpassed one million in Central America (Perez-Brignoli 1989, 52).

Honduras has a relatively short history of nationhood, winning independence alongside other Central American nations in 1821. From 1821 to 1839, Honduran-born liberator Francisco Morazán fought many wars to maintain the Central American isthmus united as a federation. Honduran itself experienced many civil wars and changes of regime between 1821 and 1876 (Lapper 1985, 19). By 1876 Liberal reformers Marco Aurelio Soto and Ramon Rosa were influencing politics and life in Honduras. They were known as Liberal reformers because they felt that the only way to advance Honduras was through the development of an export economy, which they believed required a national railroad (d'Ans 1997, 128–31; Meza 1991, ix). While other Latin American nations invested in the development of infrastructure and the development of rails in public-private partnerships, this process was ill-fated for Hondurans. First, Hondurans contracted with the British to build a railroad, but the money would be squandered, and Honduras was left with debt and without the promised railroad (d'Ans 1997, 106–7). Then Honduran presidents conceded land grants to banana companies in exchange for the building of railroads (145–47). These land grants produced rail, but only from banana plantations to the port cities and never linked the major cities or capital city to the rest of the country.

The banana companies began to operate in the early 20th century. Among the main companies were the Cuyamel Fruit Company founded in 1907 (later incorporated into the Tela Railroad Company); the Vaccaro Brothers (later consolidated into the Standard Fruit and Steamship Company); and the Tela Railroad Company and the Truxillo Railroad Company (subsidiaries of the United Fruit Company). The United Fruit Company was created in 1899 and was the first company to create the process of vertical integration. The process of vertical integration demanded that the company control every step of production from planting and processing to shipping and distribution, affording the company complete control over the banana industry. Soon the United Fruit subsidiaries were buying and sometimes forcibly taking the land of small national banana producers. When they could not take the land, they financially broke local banana growers by not buying their product or by preventing them from transporting their product to the ports for sale (d'Ans 1997, 142–43).

Local society in the first half of the 20th century was marked by infighting between two national parties, the Liberal Party and the Nationalist Party. In 1933, Tiburcio Carias Andino came to power and remained in dictatorial rule until 1949. His reign was marked by an iron-fisted rule with power centralized in Tegucigalpa, the capital. Liberal party members were constantly persecuted and worker movements were repressed. Carias Andino was a friend to the banana companies, and in this period, there were many more land concessions and powers granted to the banana companies by his presidency (Lapper 1985, 54). The United States embassy remained a watchdog on behalf of the banana companies and intervened for them with the Honduran government. By the end of World War II, the United States was no longer openly supporting dictatorships in Latin America. The McCarthy era in the United States, however, did influence relationships with Latin America and particularly Honduras. In order to prevent communism, the banana companies and U.S. embassy went to great lengths to repress workers' efforts to organize unions.

Manipulation of electoral politics and instability continued to plague Honduras throughout the 20th century. When Tiburcio Carias Andino stepped down, his handpicked successor was Juan Manuel Galvez, also a Nationalist Party member and former lawyer to the Tela Railroad Company (of the United Fruit Company). Free elections were held and won by Ramon Villeda Morales, a Liberal Party member, in 1954. He was perceived to be a threat and was prevented from taking power until 1957 in a power sharing government with the military (Dunkerly 1988, 527–28, 535). Villeda Morales would be removed in a coup d'état in 1962; the coup consolidated a set of military regimes that would last until 1982.

In the 1920s and 1930s, the Honduran government, in collaboration with the U.S. embassy and U.S. companies, openly persecuted and incarcerated workers and activists perceived to be communist. In the late 1940s and 1950s, the U.S. embassy and the banana companies used the coercion and infiltration of labor movements as "prevention" measures against communism. Through the Inter-American Regional Organization of Labor (ORIT) and the American Institute for Free Labor Development (AIFLD) (Lapper 1985, 40), the U.S. embassy was able to influence and track organizers of the growing labor movement. A key event of the evolution of the labor movement was the 1954 banana strike, which became a national general strike. During the 69 days of the strike, 25,000 Tela Railroad workers and Standard Fruit workers stopped work demanding better wages and working conditions. The strike reverberated to other industries, foreign and national. This single event marked the emergence of the organized labor movement, the right to organize, and the creation of the Ministry of Labor and the adoption of the Labor Code of 1957.

Workers in Honduras unload the first shipment of bananas since ending their two-month strike against the Standard Fruit Company, September 3, 1954. The strike spread to other industries and eventually became a national general strike. It marked the beginning of the labor movement in Honduras. (AP Photo)

Women had been fighting for suffrage since the early 1920s, but the women's right to vote was not signed into law until 1957. While this was a project of elite and middle-class women, mostly led by educated teachers and wives of politicians, it also had dramatic effect on working-class women's lives by enabling their potential participation in electoral campaigns. Women in general were taken more seriously by political parties as voting members of civil society.

Although the official history claims that Hondurans come from a Mayan and indo-Hispanic past, Honduras is a society with many indigenous peoples. Honduras, in fact, is not a mestizo nation but rather a multiracial and ethnically diverse society with varied expressions of those identities. The following indigenous groups make up part of the Honduran society of today: the Chortís and the Lencas originating in the west and southwest of the country; the Tolupanes in the central region; the Pech in the eastern region, the Misquitos (Miskitos) in the very eastern region bordering Nicaragua; the Gariganu (plural for Garifuna) and the Isleños (Islanders) in the North Coast and Bay Islands (Rivas 1993, 22). The Central American isthmus, and Honduras in particular, is a racially and ethnic diverse region. In the early 20th century, as the nation began to consolidate, there was a prioritization of an ethnic and racial claim of an Indo-Hispanic past eliding the African and Indo-Caribbean past (Andersen 2009, 78–79; Euraque 2003, 230–31).

The Garifuna people attribute their heritage and language to the Caribs and the Arawak peoples who intermixed with escaped slaves of African descent in the Caribbean (Suazo 1997, 18, 23). The Caribbean island of Saint Vincent became the refuge for many escaped slaves and indigenous people rebelling against colonial rule. But this shared land was site of much conflict as indigenous peoples fought against British rule. In bitter rebellion against the British, the Garifuna people were led by Satuyé (also known as Chatoyer), a fierce leader who fought incessantly and was killed by a British soldier. In 1796, after the murder of Satuyé, the British began to look for suitable places to exile the bellicose Garifuna from the island of Saint Vincent (142). The British authorities ordered the Gariganu be exiled to the Bay Island of Roatán, which was under British control (now part of Honduras). The 2,248 Garifuna prisoners were forced into several ships. The voyage set out from Saint Vincent to the Bay Islands of Honduras on March 11, 1797, landing on the island of Roatán on April 12, 1797. One ship with 289 Gariganu on board was captured by the Spanish and forced to land in the port of Trujillo on the mainland of Honduras (Suazo 1997 150–51; Euraque 2003, 91). Of the 2,248 Gariganu on board during departure from Saint Vincent, 2,026 made it to either Port Royal in Roatán or Trujillo on the Honduran mainland. The Garifuna people, however, are not confined to the Honduran territory. Garifuna communities are found in Belize, Honduras, and Nicaragua.

The Garifuna community is a vibrant community inhabiting 11 major villages in the North Coast of Honduras (Andersen 2009, 23). The small hamlets have been the home to Gariganu since the late 1700s. Historically, the Garifuna community is associated with the banana companies because they live in proximity to the ports and banana plantations. Gariganu experienced racial and labor discrimination by the banana companies where they sought work as stevedores or dock workers. The Honduran government has also not been very inclusive. In the 1926, in a debate over the national coin, the government declared itself a mestizo nation, claiming an Indo-Hispanic past, thereby eradicating the history and contributions of black and Garifuna people in the construction of the nation (Euraque 2003, 231; Andersen 2009, 78).

To this day the Garifuna people are marginalized in Honduran society despite their large role in the North Coast labor and cultural history. The villages still rely on fishing and self-subsistence farming. The remaining Garifuna communities in Honduras are facing land evictions, a non-bilingual educational system that threatens their culture, and poor living and economic conditions in most of the villages, many of which lack paved roads and local development. Hotel resort builders and local elite have set their eyes on the Garifuna villages, seeking to turn the pristine local beaches into resorts and tourist havens. A major source of income for the villages is remittances from the heightened migration to favorite destination cities of New York, Los Angeles, and Houston in the United States.

For much of the 1980s, the United States had its interests on Honduras. First, as a strategically important geopolitical location for the war against the liberation armed movements of the Farabundo Martí National Liberation Front (FMLN) in El Salvador, the Sandinista National Liberation Front (FSLN) in Nicaragua, and the Guatemalan National Revolutionary Unity (URNG) in Guatemala. Secondly, the United States has remained vigilant of its business interests. The banana companies continue to operate in the North Coast. There is also a growing export processing zone (known as *parques industriales* or *maquiladoras*) to Hondurans, which produce garments at half the price of those produced in other parts of Latin America. In 2003, a free-trade agreement was signed between the United States and all of the Central American nations further making labor and production laws more flexible in the country. Foreign-owned manufacturers were exempt from paying taxes to the government for up to 15 years. Droves of young women migrated to the North Coast as well as sectors outside of Tegucigalpa looking for work in these export processing zones. The export processing zones are manufacturing operations for assembly and sometimes dyeing of garments. Manufacturers do not own the land in which their factories are located, and the materials are imported from the United States. The export processing zones break government-established labor codes and do not allow unionization. According to watchdog groups, workers perceived to be unionizing are fired and often blacklisted, unable to get a job in the same industrial park (CDM Proyecto Mujer y Maquila 2007).

In 2009, President Manuel Zelaya was ousted in a politico-military coup. President Zelaya was attempting to hold a mid-year ballot survey on June 29, 2009 (known as the *cuarta urna,* fourth ballot box), in which Honduran citizen would be able to vote on whether or not to have a fourth ballot box in the November 2009 elections. In Honduras, during national elections, you typically have three ballot boxes at every voting booth, one to deposit the presidential vote, a second to vote for legislative representatives, and a third for the mayoral vote; in this case, the proposed fourth ballot box was be used to deposit the vote that sought to make possible a constitutional convention. The constitutional convention would bring together delegates and citizens to redraft the current constitution. The Honduran constitution was drafted in 1982, during the period of the Cold War. The constitutional assembly would rewrite the constitution in a process that would address issues that affect current present-day populations. President Zelaya's proposed vote was threatening to the military, Liberal party elites, and business owners, who in collusion, took over the government. The Honduran Supreme Court accused Zelaya of wanting to redraft the constitution to prolong his presidency and remain in power for various other terms (in Honduras a president can only serve one term). Civil society protested and challenged the militarization of Honduran society. The Frente Nacional de Resistencia Popular (FRNP), a peaceful, civil movement that aims at address the illegal coup and push for the constitutional assembly, was born out this situation. Despite international outcry and the sustained illegal and unconstitutional coup, elections were held by those in power in Honduras on November 2009, electing nationalist leader, Porfirio "Pepe" Lobo to the presidency.

Causes and Waves of Migration

Honduran migration to the United States is best described as a series of migrations. Each wave has distinct historical roots and push pull factors. The following time periods are approximations of the Honduran migration waves: the first wave occurred from the early 1900s to 1963; the second wave, from 1963 to 1970s; the third wave, in the 1980s, during the civil wars in Central America; and the fourth wave runs from the 1990s through the present.

First Wave: Early Immigration

The first migration, occurring in the early 1900s to 1963, was marked by travel related to banana industry work and recreation travel by elites, artists, and writers to New York. These elite writers and thinkers were cultural ambassadors who came sponsored by institutions or corporations. The only way for any Honduran to travel to the United States was aboard the steamships of the United Fruit Company's White Fleet, company steamships that dominated the Caribbean seas. Hondurans' long history of migration to the United States dates back to the early 1900s and coincides with the United Fruit Company and Standard Fruit Company's development of the banana export economy. Honduran poets, elected officials, and local businessmen also travelled to New Orleans for work related to the fruit companies (Chinchilla and Hamilton 2001, 24–25); company employees were known as *empleados de confianza,* trusted employees. Although working-class migration has been sparsely documented throughout history, we know that many stevedores and dock and ship workers also worked on board of White Fleet as *embarcados,* ship workers. The North Coast's historical significance as a port of entry for different people and ideas about modernity inspired working-class Hondurans to seek opportunities in the North Coast, and many eventually migrated to the United States. The banana companies presence and their domination of local and national politics influenced migration to and from the North Coast. Internal migration created the conditions for international migration to the United States and other countries.

Waves of Migration up to the 1965 Immigration Act

The Second Migration, occurring from 1963 into the 1970s, began after the 1963 coup d'état, when dictator Oswaldo Lopez Arellano ousted Ramon Villeda Morales from the presidency, a power struggle that left Liberal party members and workers in jail or without work. The second migrations are characterized by male political exiles leaving the country during a politically unstable period, a continued migration by company *empleados de confianza* for work or pleasure, and a small but significant migration of women to work in the service industries. The Liberal party activists left Honduras, some to work in the United States and others to nearby countries to work for low wages. Many of these exiles were teachers and local activists; many were also working-class railroad workers and technicians and other laborers who worked for the fruit companies in the North Coast and had been disenfranchised because of their allegiance to the Liberal party. The second wave of migration points to the diversity and challenges of migration and exodus. State violence made it hard for local Liberal party activists and leftists to remain, but it also made it near impossible to leave; workers devised creative clandestine paths to exit the country and re-enter whenever necessary. The ousting of Ramon Villeda Morales formed a class of dissidents and disillusioned Liberal party members who fled Lopez Arellano's military regime.

The small Honduran community of the second-wave migrants provided a support network for other immigrants. One of the ways in which this small community may have been obscured was that in larger working-class Los Angeles, Hondurans were confused for Mexicans (Argueta 2007). The second wave was made up mostly of men, who often migrated for shorter periods due to political exile. There were also a growing number of women migrants to the United States who tended to remain in the settlement country to work in the service industry.

Immigration Act of 1965 and Succeeding Legislation

The third period of Honduran migration to the United States, during the 1980s, is marked by the carnage created by the wars in neighboring Guatemala and El Salvador. Hondurans migrated in large numbers during this period, but this migration was overshadowed by the large Salvadoran and Guatemalan migrations. The Sanctuary Movement of the 1980s was concerned with helping Salvadorans and Guatemalans obtain asylum and refuge from torture and brutality. True horror stories about the poor treatment and abuse of refugees by the contras and Honduran authorities were ubiquitous. Honduras was then seen by local activists of the Sanctuary Movement as complicit in the U.S.-backed campaign, and many believed their migration stories had perhaps been obfuscated. The reality is that Hondurans also had organized revolutionary movements during the 1980s. These movements, though small and localized, supported many of the organized movements of nearby El Salvador and Nicaragua (Hamilton and Stoltz Chinchilla 1991).

The interethnic exchange between Hondurans and Salvadorans can be attributed in part to the legacy of Honduran and Salvadoran tensions since the 1969 Soccer War; the role of Honduras in then 1980s; and later territorial disputes over border regions and access to the Pacific Ocean. These state disputes had great impact on the local citizens and residents of border towns—as well as on Salvadoran migrants in the North Coast. Honduran authorities' deported Salvadorans, in some cases violently, from the country without their belongings. Historical memory of events such as these are not easily erased and continue to create challenges in the relations among Central Americans; many immigrants may be descendants of people expelled from Honduras.

Economic instability intensified as the banana companies began to threaten union stability and militancy with violence and massive firings. Workers' livelihoods were threatened as well as their lives in the North Coast. A reluctance to confront this paradox of state-supported repression and worker resistance of the period further obscures Hondurans and their history of migration. Migration during the 1980s was difficult. People made their way however they could, riding on buses or on top of trains, or paying *coyotes* (who help bring people across the border) to smuggle them into the country (Escobar 2007). Honduran migrants sought out *coyotes* to bring them from Honduras directly to the Tijuana border (Velasquez 2007; Rodriguez 2007; Escobar 2007). Some of these experiences mirror those of other Central American immigrants of the time, but it is valuable to consider the distinct characteristics of Honduran immigrants.

Honduran migrants, mostly economic migrants but also some fearing the political destabilization, migrated alongside Salvadorans and Guatemalans, traveled north and found a niche within the already existing Central American and Mexican communities in cities such as Los Angeles and New York. This generation of immigrants struggled side-by-side with Salvadoran and Guatemalan and Mexican undocumented immigrants, as none had access to any form of legalization.

In 1986, the U.S. government passed the Immigration Reform and Control Act (IRCA), which imposed employer sanctions for hiring undocumented workers. This period was a formative one for Honduran immigrants who arrived then, many of whom became active in the immigrant rights movement and in their labor unions, including those for janitors, garment workers, and domestic workers. The shared space with other Central Americans and Mexican undocumented immigrants created an opportunity for coalition building, but, at the same time, it marginalized Honduran voices due to their limited numbers compared to the large Mexican and Salvadoran populations. The shared work and living experiences, IRCA, and the constant deportations brought Hondurans to work collectively (Rodriguez 2007). These migrants were able to enter into Central American networks being formed at the time even though Hondurans were still lower in numbers. Hondurans learned to work under larger umbrella groups.

Honduran Migration: 1990s to Present

The most recent Honduran migration to the United States, occurring from the 1990s to the present, is marked by growing instability created by natural disasters, the closing of banana plantations, the loss of stable union jobs in the North Coast, and neoliberal policies that have made it hard for subsistence farmers. At the same time, due to the decline of the banana industry, the North Coast has become the prime area for the development and proliferation of the export processing zones that employ many young women and men from the interior. This period is marked by significant migration to the United States, Mexico, and Spain. According to Honduran newspaper *La Prensa* (2006), one Honduran leaves the country every five minutes. The forms of migration are brutal, with men and women leaving the country with little money, expecting to work en route, and hopping trains for undetected and free passage.

The well-known tragedy of Hurricane Mitch, which devastated Honduras, prompted the United States to pass the temporary protection status (TPS) policy, which answered Honduran advocates' original requests to be included in the Nicaraguan and Central American Relief Act (NACARA), a program for asylees or potential asylees left out during the 1980s—mainly Guatemalans and Salvadorans and also controversially Nicaraguans. While Hondurans did not gain entry into NACARA (and all the benefits and resources this program provided), they gained TPS, which is essentially a one-year renewable work permit that allows Hondurans to work legally, process their taxes, and open bank accounts in the United States. While a step in the right direction for Honduran immigrants—many still failed to file taxes in time for fear of being deported. To this day 78,000 to 80,000 Hondurans are registered with the TPS program (Rodriguez 2007; Migration Policy Institute 2006), and every two years there is a long and drawn-out struggle to petition for its continuance and expansion, even though it was meant to be a temporary program.

It is this set of circumstances that prompted the organization of HULA (Hondurans United in Los Angeles), taking the example of other Central American and Mexican groups to organize around immigration reform and services. Other organizations sprung up throughout the country in places like New York, Florida, Washington, and New Orleans (especially post Hurricane Mitch), among others. Another great accomplishment of Honduran groups occurred on October 19, 2007, when after lobbying for many years, this date was designated as the Día del Hondureño(a) (Day of the Honduran), voted in by the 14 city council representatives in the city of Los Angeles, a historically important city for Central American immigrants. The collective work with other Central American and broader immigrant coalitions continues—the stage is set to demand that the 78,000 Honduran *tepesianos* (TPS recipients) be made eligible for residency status.

Hurricane Mitch

Hurricanes have been a part of Honduras history as its largest land area faces the Caribbean Sea. The North Coast residents and banana companies have been affected by hurricanes. The companies themselves have even used these natural disasters as excuses to close banana plantations. Such was the case when a 1954 Hurricane destroyed most of the Tela Railroad Company plantations; the Tela Railroad used this natural disaster to lay off union supporters. In 1974 Hurricane Fifi devastated the region again with similar circumstances. Once again in 1998, Hurricane Mitch destroyed most of the plantations and killed over 7,000 people in Honduras. Hurricane Mitch, a category five hurricane, affected all of Central America and the Caribbean. It devastated Honduras, destroying 80 percent of the banana fields and leaving thousands dead or orphaned. The hurricane washed away 25 small villages and leveled 70 percent of the infrastructure in its first days; roads, bridges, and telecommunications were unusable for months after. Although international relief poured in via religious groups and other organizations, the neediest places were hard to reach. After the hurricane, many more perished from illness and lack of food. This tragic natural disaster struck Central America and leveled the islands and the North Coast of Honduras—the regions once owned by the largest banana exporters in the world—Chiquita Bananas (formerly United Fruit company) and Dole (formerly Standard Fruit Company). This region is now Honduras' largest immigrant sending regions. In 2005, another devastating natural disaster, Hurricane Gamma, caused floods and plantation closures. When the banana plantations are damaged, the banana companies either close the plantation and do not re-open or they sell the plantation to the workers or to local growers. Moving production out of the country and closing production centers for months at a time limits the earning ability for North Coast workers, both men and women, forcing them to migrate north for work.

After Hurricane Mitch, U.S. immigration policy changed to include Hondurans in the TPS program; this change increased Honduran applicants to the program. While immediate relief and temporary aid alleviated dire conditions, longer term changes to address the fundamental causes of economic hardship and migration were elusive in the disaster response.

Demographic Profile

Size and Composition of Community

Hondurans have been fairly "invisible" in the United States due to their relatively small documented population size. According to data from the American Community Survey 2006–2008 (three-year estimates), there are 543,274 Hondurans in the United States. The largest numbers of the Honduran population are spread out in three regions, the South, the Northeast, and the West. In the South, in the states of Florida, Texas, and Louisiana there are 286,000 Hondurans (Pew Hispanic Center 2009). In the West, there are 93,000 Hondurans, with California boasting 69,000 Hondurans (Pew Hispanic Center 2009). Of the total Honduran population of 543,274 (American Community Survey [ACS] 2006–2008), 383,962 were not born in the United States. Of those Hondurans not born in the United States, 41.2 percent entered the country in the year 2000 or later, while 34.2 percent entered between 1990 and 1999, and 24.6 percent entered the United States before 1990.

According to figures held by the Honduran Consulate in Los Angeles, in 2007, there were 350,000 Hondurans in Southern California, including Los Angeles County and surrounding counties of Orange, San Fernando, and San Bernardino (Rodriguez 2007). This number is a significantly higher number than the 2000 Census data of 69,000 Hondurans in Los Angeles. This apparent discrepancy elucidates census undercount of undocumented immigrants. Other reasons for the discrepancy may be that Hondurans have intermarried and are not self-identified. The dispute over the Honduran consulate number of 350,000 reveals not only the potential inaccurate count of undocumented Hondurans in Southern California but also the inaccuracy of counts at time of exit in Honduras; many immigrants may not make it all the way to the United States. Many Hondurans overstay their visas, and there are just as many crossing the border via the *coyote* rings that span from home towns in Honduras to U.S. cities.

Age and Family Structure

According to recent estimates, the population is younger than the overall population with a median age of 28.7 (ACS 2006–2008). Leah Schmalzbauer identified in her study (2004) that Honduran immigrants on the East Coast are transnational families in which "productive labor occurs in the host country and reproductive labor in the home country" (1317). Being transnational migrants, Hondurans sustain social familial and care-giving relations in the country of origin and the region of settlement (1319). Schmalzbauer claims that migration is a "response to structural inequalities that make it impossible for families to sustain them" (1319). The Honduran family, in the country of origin, usually has a member of the family working in the United States. The family member or members sends money home in remittances that average about $242 dollars a month (1325). The family structure of Hondurans can best be described as that of a transnational family, with one or two members of the family in the United States and the rest of the family members back in Honduras. Many migrants create alternate lives and families in the United States, but connection to family in the home country via remittances continues.

Educational Attainment

Of the Honduran population that is 25 years and over in the United States, 49.3 percent (of 322,629) have not attained a high school diploma. Of the population of Hondurans that are five years and older, 91.9 percent (of 485,349) speak a language other than English. And 62.3 percent (of 485,349) of Honduran Americans over five years of age speak English less than "very well." Of 126,998 Hondurans enrolled in school at the time of the survey analysis, 46.6 percent were enrolled in elementary school (grades 1–8), 6.8 percent were enrolled in preschool, 6.4 percent were enrolled in kindergarten; 22.9 percent were enrolled in high school; and 17.3 percent were enrolled in college or graduate school. While the educational attainment is low when compared to other Latino populations, the numbers also demonstrates the relative youth of the recent immigrant population.

Economic Attainment, Occupation and Income Patterns

Of the 405,523 Honduran Americans that are 16 years and older, 282,673 participate in the labor force (ACS 2006–2008). Of the 282,673 who reported an occupation, 29.3 percent have service occupations and 28.6 percent work in construction, extraction, maintenance, and repair occupations. This is gendered with men predominantly employed in construction; of 173,170 employed males 16 years and older, 45.6 percent of them are employed in construction, extraction, maintenance, and repair jobs. Of the 109,503 employed women over 16 years old, 47.2 percent are employed in service occupations. Of the 282,673 employed Hondurans over the age of 16 years old, 86.5 percent work for private industry and are salary employees. Of 142,029 Hondurans who reported income, according to the American Community Survey analysis, the median household income is $38,662 a year (with 2008 inflation adjusted dollars). Perhaps the most striking statistic is the 22.4 percent poverty rate in Honduran households. There are 27.3 percent households living in poverty with children under 18 years of age. Of the households living in poverty, 41.4 percent of them are female-headed households with no husband present; 47.7 percent of those households are living with children under 18 years old.

Adjustment and Adaptation

Immigrants from different periods of migration have different levels of involvement in the current immigration movement and reflect different levels of integration into U.S. society. The immigrants from the 1960s tend to be more acculturated; their incorporation may have happened in the 1960s and 1970s, when it was perceived as easier to legalize. The very recent wave of immigrants on the other hand are still at the margins of society and the immigrant rights movement—facing the everyday uncertainty of the current immigration climate and the threat of *redadas,* or deportation raid stings. Visibility is contingent on each immigrant period's particular relationship with immigration status, acculturation to U.S. society, the size and history of the migration trajectory, and degree of involvement in the immigrant rights movement. Undocumented migration has as much to do with exit factors as it does with pull conditions and information flows from the new country. Tropes about life in the United States are deployed in a variety of ways depending on the time of arrival of the family member or friend. Immigrants that arrived during the Central American exodus of the 1980s, alongside Guatemalan and Salvadorans, tend to be more involved and participate in activism networks established by Central Americans and other Chicano and Mexican groups.

Family, Culture, and Life-Cycle Rituals

Hondurans for the most part identify as Catholic, with a Protestant minority. Honduran communities celebrate baptisms commonly within a year of the birth of the child. This is an opportunity for the child to have a *padrino* (godfather) and *madrina* (godmother), who would care for them in case of their parent's death. The baptism is a great opportunity for Hondurans to reunite the family and have a big party. Confirmation, another Catholic rite of passage, is also celebrated, and the *madrina* and *padrino* are also chosen in this ritual. Slowly, the child is supposed to develop a network of family to support them throughout life. Birthdays, weddings, and *quinciañeras* (sweet 15 parties and coming-of-age rituals for women) are also celebrated and a good opportunity for family gatherings. Funerals are also important; they involve the viewing of the body, the funeral procession, and the nine-day prayer ritual (*novena/novenario*), which is attended by every family member immediately after burial.

Garifuna people have more elaborate rituals that reflect syncretism between Catholic and Afro-Caribbean traditions. One important ritual to immigrants is known as the Dügü, or feasting of the dead. During this ceremony a family who is going through a tough period, a death or illness, asks their ancestors for advice and then throws a feast to appease them. The ancestors are seen as oracles in the Dügü ceremony. The family members ask the ancestors to tell them why sadness has befallen the family and ask for a feast to make better times come to the family. The Dügü lasts for two or four days. This Dügü practice continues among Garifuna immigrants in the United States, where instead of disrupting the ritual, it is re-conceptualized within a larger tradition of the African diasporic religion (Andersen 2009, 47).

Celebration of National Holidays

Hondurans celebrate Independence Day on September 15. The Garifuna community celebrate the arrival of their people to Honduras every April 12 with festivals and cultural events. Catholic Hondurans celebrate Christmas, New Year's Eve, and New Year's Day, and on February 3, they celebrate the day of the Virgin of Suyapa on February 3. In Los Angeles and New York, local Catholic churches, such as the Saint Thomas parish in Pico Union in Los Angeles, celebrate masses to Central American saints, particularly the Virgin of Suyapa. There is a growing evangelical movement of Christian churches and missionaries in Honduras and in the United States; although exact figures are not available, this community's power is growing.

Foodways

Honduran cuisine is varied and depends on regional and ethnic traditions of cuisine, but some commonalities exist within each region. Beans, rice, tortillas, cheese, *mantequilla* (Honduran sour cream), eggs, and fried plantains are the typical *cena* (dinner plate). Soups are an important part of Honduran food fare: beef soup, chicken soup, *mondongo* soup (stomach-wall soup made with coconut milk), and conch and fish soups. Other Honduran favorites such as *baleadas* (a flour tortilla folded over beans and *mantequilla*) can be found in local Central American restaurants. The similarities with Salvadoran cooking are also evident, and many Hondurans use Salvadoran products to make their favorite meals, such as the frozen *loroco* and *chipilín* flower brought from El Salvador to make Honduran *ticucos* (small tamales) or *pastelitos* (fried beef pastries). Overall, a diverse cooking fare comes alive in new ways with the use of Mexican and Salvadoran products to recreate traditional favorites. Christmas and New Year's are common times for *nacatamales* (tamales), made from cornmeal and pork or chicken, green olives, and raisins. Garifuna celebrations usually demand *kassave*, a tortilla-like patty made from pounded cassava root (*yuca*) plant. Seafood such as soups made of *caracol* (conch) and fish soups are very rich staples of the Garifuna celebrations. Rice cooked in coconut milk and served with beans is a typical North Coast and Bay Island dish known as "rice-n-beans." Coconut bread is also found in Garifuna celebrations.

Music, Arts, and Entertainment

Honduran Garifuna music was extremely popular in dance clubs in Latin America and the Caribbean and United States throughout the 1990s. The sound that is most associated with Honduras is *punta* music. *Punta* is a traditional dance of courting for Gariganu in Central America. Traditional Garifuna dances are not well known in the United States, but in cities like New York and Los Angeles they are performed for special holidays around Independence Day and Garifuna festivals. Local bands began to incorporate Garifuna beats, made popular by local radio, with *merengue* and reggae sounds. Another piece of music associated with Honduras and Central America is what was originally called *playero* music in the late 1990s, now referred to as *reguetón*. Hondurans also enjoy tropical variations of *merengue* and *salsa*. Mexican *boleros* and *ranchera* music is also extremely popular among Hondurans both in Honduras and in the United States.

Integration and Impact on U.S. Society and Culture

Paths toward Citizenship

Hondurans are able to retain their Honduran citizenship when becoming citizens in the host country. This means that they are able still to participate in civic life in Honduras, retaining the right to vote in Honduran presidential elections. Many Hondurans, however, are not becoming U.S. citizens, as the most common but limited way to legalize their status in the United States is via the TPS program. An estimated 374,000 Central American are on TPS status; it is estimated that 80,000 of them are Hondurans (Migration Policy Institute 2006). Although immigrant Honduran organizations dedicate themselves to helping Hondurans process TPS, they also help by advocating and insisting that government authorities grant residency status to these Hondurans. Their reasoning is that many Hondurans pay the fees to file TPS every year, and for many years, they file taxes and report their stay to the government. Their lawful behavior should at least be rewarded with a path to legalization. Few Hondurans have gained permanent residency when compared to the rest of Latinos in the nation.

The most common scenario Hondurans face is to live and work with undocumented status facing entrapment and detention by Homeland Security. The entrapment and deportation scenario for Hondurans is grim in the United States. Rates of deportation have increased drastically since 2000. In 2000, 4,768 people were deported to Honduras; by 2005, the rates of Honduran deportees had climbed to 15,572; by 2008, the numbers were at a staggering figure of 28,851; and by 2009 Homeland Security reported 19,959 Honduran deportees (Department of Homeland Security 2009). The Honduran government has entered into a "expedited Honduran removals" agreement with U.S. Homeland Security so that Honduran nationals facing deportation will only be held 15 days. This process involves video teleconferencing to advise detainees in order to issue them proper travel documents (Department of Homeland Security 2005). The Honduran government encourages Hondurans in the United States to apply for TPS. Many who arrived before 2001, however, may not be eligible for TPS, as this temporary program is hardly a catch-all response to the massive Honduran migration.

For the recent and growing Honduran community, the process of naturalization and permanent residency is only possible through intermarriage and family petition. According to the U.S. American Community Survey, 159,312 Hondurans were born in the United States. There are 383,962 foreign born; 78,459 of those foreign born have become naturalized U.S. citizens; and 305,503 foreign born are not U.S. citizens. The Honduran community, as evidenced by these numbers, is in a precarious situation in terms of their paths to naturalization.

Forging a New American Political Identity

As we begin to scrutinize the presence and participation of the Honduran immigrant community in the United States, we see a small group dispersed within the larger Central American population. Hondurans living in the United States have only recently (post 1998) begun to claim a political identity, one that is informed by transnational politics and based on their historical memory of the home country. Whether it is demographics, intermarriage to other groups, or the limitations of racialized and gendered informal networks, the Honduran American community has been challenged in finding a voice and an identity within the predominantly Mexican and Salvadoran communities, the recognized representatives of the Latino community in the media and local politics. Los Angeles has been one of the major recipients of immigrants from the North Coast of Honduras, but a Honduran immigrant identity has been slow to emerge within a community dominated by other Central American groups, mainly Salvadorans and Guatemalans. Arriving in the United States, Hondurans came into existing Central American networks often obfuscating a larger Honduran political identity. The sharing of space among Central Americans and other recent immigrants, however, clearly set the framework for a strong network that supported recent immigrants by helping people find jobs and obtain immigration assistance; recruiting and guiding them toward local social and cultural groups and support organizations. The interactions with other Central Americans has been positive in that eventually Hondurans were able set up their own networks based on these earlier experiences in other communities where they worked to build greater local and political power.

The Honduran immigrant political identity is now differentiating from the larger umbrella of the Central American political identity and from the Mexican immigrant and Mexican American political identity. Having learned the ropes from Salvadorans, Guatemalans, and Mexicans on how to build immigrant rights groups and hometown associations, Hondurans have devised useful tactics to challenge the U.S. government and Honduran government to pay attention to the plight of the migration trajectory of Hondurans. A remaining need may be for the established Central American groups to contend with the acknowledgement and incorporation of racial and ethnic realities of Garifuna and indigenous Hondurans.

Political Associations and Organizations

In 1997 Honduran organizers, as part of HULA, lobbied for TPS alongside Salvadoran activists in CARECEN (Central American Resource Center) but were stalled in their efforts until 1998, when Hurricane Mitch devastated Honduras. In the aftermath of Hurricane Mitch, the Clinton administration granted the inclusion of

Orlando Cruz, from Honduras, carries a picture of the Statue of Liberty during a gathering of immigrants and supporters in a Washington, D.C., park to highlight their demand for legalization, May 1, 2006. (AP Photo/Manuel Balce Ceneta)

Honduran immigrants in the TPS program in 1998. Hondurans in Los Angeles attended meetings at CARECEN to learn about the required paperwork, but many still feared exposure as undocumented immigrants. Nevertheless, enough acquired TPS status that it has given Hondurans more of a presence within the local Los Angeles multiethnic immigrant rights and organizing community. The energy and interest generated helped Honduran activists and CARECEN organizers begin to conceive of a newly organized Honduran group. Sponsoring organizations, such as CARECEN, and hometown associations created the infrastructure for the development of leadership among Honduran activists.

Hondurans in Los Angeles witnessed the Honduran government changing its attitude toward the diaspora in the United States during the 1990s. The change in attitude and policies in the consulates towards immigrants has been fueled by two growing areas of concern in the home country: remittances and gang violence. The Honduran embassy and consulates did not get involved in local immigrant issues; the consulates in particular saw themselves as providers of documentation. This demonstrated the Honduran government's relative lack of involvement in the earlier years in the situation of immigration. Honduran immigrant advocates claim that the Honduran government began to care and get involved when immigrant remittances were the largest source of income (GDP) for the country (Rodriguez 2007; Velasquez 2007).

Immigrant remittances to Honduras put immigrants in the United States on the map for local and state governments in Honduras. For the first time embassies and consulates were pulled into local debates on immigration in the big U.S. cities. Although advocacy in the United States is limited, organized groups have been able to press the consulate on their level of active involvement.

The Second and Later Generations

Ethnic Identity

Of the 543,274 total Honduran population, 383,962 are foreign born and identify as Hondurans. Hondurans born in the United States consider themselves Honduran American. Hondurans see themselves as ethnically mestizo or may identify more ambiguously as Latinos or Hispanic. Garifuna people (also known as Gariganu when speaking in plural) self identify as Garifuna people from Honduras. Spanish is the main language spoken at home. Garifuna and black Hondurans, however, come into networks of other Garifuna multinational communities—possibly filtering into the U.S. racial binary of black and white. In the case of the Garifuna community in Los Angeles, their ethnoracial background serves as the network into which Garifuna people arrive in Los Angeles. In response to questions about Garifuna community, the organized Honduran groups, mostly mestizo, report that it is mostly during Independence Day celebrations or cultural festivals that they collaborate and that the immigration situations may be different in terms of language, access to legalization, and trajectory of migration; their push factors may also be different given the economic and political exclusion of Gariganu and black workers in the home country. Another reason cited for not working together is that Gariganu come into local L.A. networks based on similar cultural knowledge, language, and social political networks. They do not come just from Honduras; many are from Belize, Guatemala, and Nicaragua. Garifuna culture practices and ethnoracial background unite these immigrants above nationality. Traditionally, Garifuna people have been migrants to the East Coast or New Orleans, but the community may be more established in Los Angeles than previously documented. Collective organizing with mestizos from Honduras is not charted, but it is evident that the Gariganu groups from Belize, Guatemala, Honduras, and Nicaragua have formed organizations and networks that remain separate from the larger mestizo Honduran immigrant community and vice versa.

Educational Attainment

Second-generation Hondurans in general have lower educational attainment than most Latinos in the nation. Of 322,629 individuals over 25 years old, only 25.6 percent have earned a high school degree or equivalency and 49.3 percent have not earned a high school degree; 25.1 percent of individuals older than 25 years of age

---

A Young Honduran Comes to Los Angeles

Marina Argueta, now residing in northeast Los Angeles, came to the United States in the 1960s when her husband, who belonged to the Liberal party, saw that his career was over due to the coup d'état and dictatorship of Oswaldo Lopez Arellano in 1962 and he lost his job (Argueta 2007). The political situation resulted in her migration to the United States. She heard from a friend that she could find work and success in Los Angeles. Marina Argueta heard about Los Angeles being a good place to work from her network of friends, other Honduran women. These Honduran women helped her get a job and rent an apartment in the Rampart and Beverly area of Los Angeles. She brought two of her daughters and later the rest of her family. Although the clearest and fastest option was to work, like most of her friends, as a live-in maid in a house, Marina was lucky and ended up getting a job in a tent-making garment factory that was unionized in east Los Angeles. She rarely returns to Honduras; Hondurans and other Latinos in Los Angeles became her community and home.

Jonadad Luque, a Honduran immigrant, reads to his daughter in their home in Nashville, Tennessee, July 10, 2007. (AP Photo/Mark Humphrey)

have continued on to higher education; 14.5 percent have obtained an associate's degree or some college; 8.0 percent have obtained a bachelor's degree; and 2.6 percent have earned a graduate or professional degree. Of individuals 5 years and older (total Hondurans that are 5 years and older is 485,349), 91.1 percent of Hondurans speak Spanish as a primary language in the household. Of the 126,998 Hondurans enrolled in school, the majority, 46.6 percent, are enrolled in high school (grades 9–12); and 17.3 percent of Hondurans are enrolled in higher education, college or graduate school.

Cultural Identification

The later generations of Hondurans are developing pride in their heritage. The Honduran immigrant organizations, such as HULA and AHLA (Alianza Hondureña de Los Angeles) in Los Angeles, also have cultural events that allow the younger generations to learn about their cultural heritage. The Garifuna Heritage Foundation (GAHFU), in Los Angeles and New York, hold language and drumming classes for the younger generations on Saturdays. During the Independence Day parades and Garifuna celebrations, the younger generations participate in cultural dances and parade activities, exhibiting involvement in cultural activities and pride.

Issues in Relations between the United States and Honduras

Forecasts for the 21st Century

According to the *Centro de Atención al Migrante Retornado (CARM)* in Tegucigalpa, 500 Hondurans migrate daily to the United States. Many get deported in Mexico; it is estimated that 24,000 Hondurans are deported from Mexico (*La Tribuna* 2010). The voyage north through Mexico is treacherous, and many immigrants are mauled when they jump off and on the trains or are robbed by gangs.

The following years will show an increased migration from Honduras due to economic and politically unstable conditions. The 2009 coup d'état in Honduras has created an unstable situation in Honduras. Because the coup created an unmitigated crisis, many people lost jobs and others were fired and many others were exiled. Human rights violations are increasing while Washington and the U.S. embassy claim there is democracy. The incongruity will be most apparent in the migration and exiled population growth.

There is no commitment from Washington toward a comprehensive immigration reform in the next few years. Immigrants from Honduras will continue arriving and will continue to be deported as the TPS program is not applicable to all. Many of the local Honduran immigrant organizations and hometown groups sided with political parties during the coup d'état. Many of them, such as HULA and AHLA, actually aligned with the Honduran elite interests that supported the coup. As migrants from the economic and political fallout of the 2009 coup arrive as immigrants in the United States, new organizations will have to be created, ones that speak clearly and honestly about the connection between human rights violations in Honduras and human rights violations against immigrants in the United States. New organizations will also have to engage more directly in organizing around a comprehensive immigration reform instead of merely providing services during the application deadlines for TPS.

Appendix I: Migration Statistics

The U.S. Department of Homeland Security maintains a tally of deportees and country of origin. Using this data we can get an approximation as to how many Hondurans leave Honduras and come to the United States. Keep in mind that many Hondurans who leave may not make it to the United States. Table 139 shows U.S. legal permanent resident status for those born in Honduras, for the years 2000–2009.

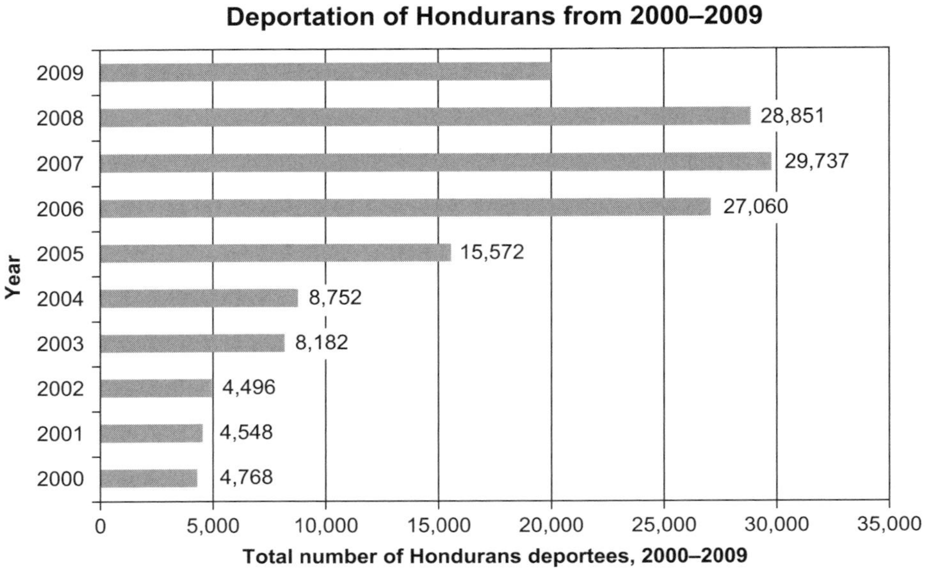

Deportation of Hondurans from 2000–2009

Figure 17   Deportation of Hondurans, 2000–2009.
Source: U.S. Department of Homeland Security, 2000–2009.

Table 139 Persons obtaining legal permanent resident status by region and country of birth: Fiscal years 2000 to 2009

Region and country of birth	2000	2001	2002	2003	2004	2005	2006	2007	2008	2009
Total	841,002	1,058,902	1,059,356	703,542	957,883	1,122,257	1,266,129	1,052,415	1,107,126	1,130,818
Honduras	5,917	6,571	6,435	4,645	5,508	7,012	8,177	7,646	6,540	6,404

Source: U.S. Department of Homeland Security. Office of Immigration Statistics. 2010. Adapted from Table 3.

Appendix II: Demographics/Census Statistics

Hondurans self-identify in the 10-year census survey. The American Community Survey issues reports on Hondurans, and other groups, every one to three years. The Pew Hispanic Institute also analyzes the American Community Survey Data for Hondurans.

Table 140 General statistics of Hondurans in the United States

Description	Figures
Total population	543,274
Total population: Male	52.5%
Total population: Female	47.50%
Foreign born	383,962
Employed over 16 years of age	282,673
Employed male	173,170
Employed female	109,503
Median age (years)	28.7
Household population	148,029
Average household size	4.12, owners (renters 3.53)

Source: U.S. Census Bureau American Community Survey, 2006–2009, three-year estimates.

Table 141 Social and economic characteristics of Hondurans in the United States

Description	Figure
Total population over 25 years old	322,629
High school graduate or higher	25.6%
Less than high school diploma	49.3%
Speak a language other than English	91.9% (of 485,349, over 5 years old)
Poverty rate for families	22.4%
Female householder, no husband, children under 18 years	47.7%

Source: U.S. Census Bureau American Community Survey, 2006–2009, three-year estimates.

Table 142 Persons obtaining legal permanent resident status during fiscal year 2009.
Leading States of Residence: Region/Country: Honduras

Characteristic	Total	Male	Female
Total	6,404	2,766	3,638
Arizona	74	39	35
California	798	332	466
Colorado	39	17	22
Connecticut	53	25	28
Florida	1,381	538	843
Georgia	130	59	71
Illinois	134	56	78
Maryland	171	84	87
Massachusetts	170	78	92
Minnesota	34	21	13
Nevada	55	16	39
New Jersey	404	182	222
New York	718	312	406
North Carolina	187	83	104
Ohio	31	16	15
Pennsylvania	57	32	25
Texas	818	370	448
Virginia	273	123	150
Washington	51	28	23
Other	826	355	471

Source: Adapted from U.S. Department of Homeland Security. Profiles on Legal Permanent Residents: 2009.

Appendix III: Notable Honduran Americans

Dario Euraque is a Honduran historian and professor at Trinity College in Connecticut. In 2006, he was named director of the Honduran Institute of Anthropology and History (IHAH). Dr. Euraque was ousted by the coup d'état in Honduras in 2009. His written works focus on ethnicity, race, class, and identity in Honduras. He is a prolific writer in both English and Spanish; his well-known work is *Reinterpreting the Banana Republic Region and State in Honduras, 1870–1972* (University of North Carolina Press, 1996).

America Ferrera is an actress born in Los Angeles, California, on April 18, 1984. She is the daughter of Honduran parents who migrated in the mid-1970s. Her mother was a housekeeping staff director in a hotel in Los Angeles. She is best known for her role in the television series *Ugly Betty* on the ABC network.

Carlos Mencia was born on October 22, 1967, in San Pedro Sula, Honduras, the 16th of 18 children. He immigrated to the United States with his parents early in his childhood. Mencia grew up living alternately in East Los Angeles and Honduras, and attended high school in Los Angeles. He attended California State University Los Angeles. He began his comedian career by performing at the major Los Angeles comedy clubs. He is now an established comedian in both Latino and United States mainstream media.

Glossary

Baleadas: A fast food often purchased in the street; made with a flour tortilla folded over beans and Honduran *mantequilla* (sour cream). May contain more ingredients depending on the locale where it is made.

Catrachas/os: Of Honduran descent; Hondurans.

Campeños/campeñas: Hondurans that live in the North Coast of Honduras and work in the banana fields or for the foreign-owned banana companies.

Dügü: A Garifuna ritual known as the feast for ancestors; it is performed when illness, death, or bad luck befall a family; ancestors are consulted and the celebration lasts two to four days.

References

Amaya Amador, Ramon. 1987. *Prisión Verde*. Tegucigalpa, Honduras: Editorial Universitaria.

American Community Survey. 2006–2008. [Online information; retrieved on 8/16/10.] http://www.census.gov/acs/www/.

Anderson, Mark. 2009. *Black and Indigenous Garifuna Activism and Consumer Culture in Honduras*. Minneapolis: University of Minnesota Press.

Argueta, Marina. 2007. Immigrant and merchant in banana plantations of the United Fruit Company. Interviewed in Los Angeles, California.

Arias, Arturo. 2003."Central American-Americans: Invisibility, Power and Representation in the US Latino World." *Latino Studies* 1: 168–87.

Barahona, Marvin. 2002. *Evolución Histórica De La Identidad Nacional*. Tegucigalpa: Editorial Guaymuras.

Barahona, Marvin. 2004. *El Silencio Quedó Atrás Testimonio De La Huelga Bananera De 1954*. Tegucigalpa, Honduras: Editorial Guaymuras.

Barahona, Marvin. 2005. *Honduras En El Siglo 20 Una Sintesis Histórica.* Tegucigalpa, Honduras: Editorial Guaymuras.

Barahona, Marvin. 1989. *La Hegemonia De Los Estados Unidos En Honduras (1907–1932).* Tegucigalpa, Honduras: Centro de Documentación de Honduras.

Barahona, Marvin. 2001. *Memorias De Un Comunista Rigoberto Padilla Rush*, Talanquera. Tegucigalpa, Honduras: Editorial Guaymuras.

CDM Proyecto Mujer y Maquila. 2007. "Violación de las garantías constitucionales de libertad de petición y asociación: Represión y listas negras en las empresas maquiladoras de Honduras." [Online information; retrieved 8/20/10.] http://www.derechosdelamujer.org/.

d'Ans, André-Marcel. 1997. *Honduras Emergencia Dificil De Una Nacion, De Un Estado.* Paris: KARTHALA.

Delgado, Hector L. 1993. *New Immigrants, Old Unions Organizing Undocumented Workers in Los Angeles.* Philadelphia: Temple University Press.

"Department of Homeland Security Introduces New Procedure to Expedite Honduran Removals." 2005. Press Release, April 19. [Online information; retrieved 8/20/01.] http://www.dhs.gov/xnews/releases/press_release_0660.shtm

Department of Homeland Security. 2009. [Online information; retrieved 8/20/10.] http://www.dhs.gov/files/statistics/immigration.shtm.

Dunkerley, James. 1988. *Power in the Isthmus A Political History of Modern Central America.* New York: Verso.

Escobar, Julio. 2007. Member of Honduran United in Los Angeles (HULA). Interviewed in Los Angeles, September 23.

Euraque, Dario A. 1993. "San Pedro Sula Actual Capital Industrial De Honduras: Entre Villorio Colonial y Emporio Bananero, 1536–1936." *Mesoámerica* 26: 217–52.

Euraque, Dario A. 1998. "The Banana Enclave, Nationalism, and Mestizaje in Honduras, 1910s–1930s." In *Identity and Struggle at the Margins of the Nation State the Laboring Peoples of Central America and the Hispanic Caribbean*, edited by Aviva Chomsky and Aldo Lauria-Santiago, 169–95. Durham: Duke University Press.

Euraque, Dario A. 2003. "The Threat of Blackness to the Mestizo Nation: Race and Ethnicity in the Honduran Banana Economy, 1920s–1930s." In *Bananan Wars Power Production and History in the Americas*, edited by Steve Striffler and Mark Moberg, 229–49. Durham, NC: Duke University Press.

Euraque, Dario A. 2004. *Conversaciones Historicas Con El Mestizaje Y Su Identidad Nacional En Honduras.* San Pedro Sula, Honduras: Centro Editorial.

Euraque, Dario A. 2007. "Free Pardos and Mulattoes Vanquish Indians Cultural Civility and Conquest and Modernity in Honduras." In *Beyond Slavery the Mulilayered Legacy of Africans in Latin America and the Caribbean*, edited by Darién J. Davies, 81–105. New York: Rowan & Littlefield.

ERIC-SJ (Equipo de Reflexión Investigación y Comunicación de la Compañía de Jesús en Honduras). 2004. "El uso de las remesas y su impacto en las familias de la colonia Berlin en el Municipio de El Progreso en el departamento de Yoro, Honduras (un estudio de Caso)." 25. El Progreso, Yoro: ERIC-SJ.

Hamilton, Nora, and Norma Stoltz Chinchilla. 1991. "Central American Migration: A Framework for Analysis." *Latin American Research Review* 26(1): 75–110.

Hamilton, Nora, and Norma Stoltz Chinchilla. 2001. *Seeking Community in a Global City Guatemalans and Salvadorans in Los Angeles*. Philadelphia: Temple University Press.

Lapper, Richard. 1985. *Honduras State for Sale*, edited by Latin American Bureau. London: Latin American Bureau.

Menjivar, Cecilia. 2000. *Fragmented Ties Salvadoran Immigrant Networks in America*. Berkeley: University of California Press.

Merrill, Tim, ed. 1995. *Honduras: A Country Study*. Washington: GPO for the Library of Congress. [Online information; retrieved 8/20/10.] http://countrystudies.us/honduras/.

Meza, Victor. 1991. *Historia Del Movimiento Obrero Hondureño*. Tegucigalpa, Honduras: Centro de Documentación de Honduras (CEDOH).

Migration Policy Institute. 2006. "The Central American Foreign Born in the United States." [Online information; retrieved 8/22/10.] http://www.migrationpolicy.org/.

Perez-Brignoli, Hector. 1989. *A Brief History of Central America*, translated by Ricardo B. Sawrey. Berkeley: University of California Press.

Pew Hispanic Center. 2009. "Hispanics of Honduran Origin in the United States, 2007." [Online information; retrieved 8/16/2010.] http://pewhispanic.org//files/factsheets/55.pdf.

Rivas, Ramón D. 1993. *Pueblos Indígenas y Garífuna de Honduras (Una Caracterización)*. Tegucigalpa, Honduras: Editorial Guaymuras.

Rodriguez, Cecilia. 2007. President of Alianza Hondureña de Los Angeles (AHLA). Interviewed in Los Angeles, California, August 10.

Suazo, E. Salvador. 1997. *Los Deportados De San Vicente*. Tegucigalpa: Editorial Guaymuras.

Velasquez, Leoncio. 2007. President of Honduran United in Los Angeles (HULA). Interviewed in Los Angeles, California, September 1.

Further Reading

Amaya Amador, Ramon. 1987. *Prisión Verde*. Tegucigalpa, Honduras: Editorial Universitaria.

Prisión Verde is a classic novel in which Amador describes life in the banana fields and living quarters of the banana companies. This novel examines the challenges of local growers in the North Coast as they faced competition with large U.S.-owned companies. Amador details the loss of land and the shifting of power relations in the North Coast between local growers, workers, and the foreign-owned companies. The text has not been translated to English.

Anderson, Mark. 2009. *Black and Indigenous Garifuna Activism and Consumer Culture in Honduras*. Minneapolis: University of Minnesota Press.

In this incisive study of Honduran Garifuna culture and Garifuna immigrants in the United States, Anderson explores indigeneity and blackness, which have historically been understood as contradictory identities. Anderson's analysis of indigeneity and blackness, tradition and modernity, nativism, diaspora, and multiculturalism asserts that the Garifuna make a powerful claim on indigeneity as a cultural identity. Andersen's rich use of ethnography also provides a good history of contemporary youth culture, consumerism, and local activism.

Benjamin, Medea, ed. 1989. *Don't Be Afraid, Gringo: A Honduran Woman Speaks from the Heart: The Story of Elvia Alvarado*. New York: Harper Perennial.

This short but powerful book details the life of Elvia Alvarado, a *campesina* (farm worker) organizer, in her own words. The oral history, edited by Benjamin, is an ethnography of Alvarado's life and traces her involvement in social movements, and her life as a woman, mother, and wife. The book introduces a discussion of social movements in Honduras during a period of the Cold War in the 1980s. The book also provides an analysis of gender relations in *campesina* life and in social movements.

England, Sarah. 2006. *Afro Central Americans in New York City: Garifuna Tales of Transnational Movements in Racialized Space*. Gainesville: University Press of Florida.

England uses ethnography to trace the lives and struggles of Gariganu in New York. The book explores the Gariganu's negotiation of identities (nationality, gender, race, ethnicity, and class, etc.) necessary for survival and the relations of these identities to social movements. England points out that the Garifuna people's history of migration is important to Garifuna culture, as their history involves migration first to Central America and then to the United States. This history of migration and transnationality informs the Garifuna communities and creates various avenues to engage in social movements as a community and as individuals.

Euraque, Dario. 1996. *Reinterpreting the Banana Republic Region and State in Honduras, 1870–1972*. Chapel Hill: University of North Carolina Press.

Euraque provides an economic history of San Pedro Sula, Honduras, the North Coast city lauded as the industrial capital of the country. Euraque traces the history of the North Coast's capitalist economic structure, labor and labor relations, and local and national bipartisan political dynamics. Euraque demonstrates the agency of Honduran government officials, local business elites, and the labor movement in determining Honduran history, along with the foreign-owned banana companies.

Frank, Dana. 2005. *Women Transforming the Banana Unions of Latin America*. Cambridge, MA: South End Press.

Frank writes about the formation of women's committees within the largest banana union in Honduras, SITRATERCO (Tela Railroad Company Union) and the work of the coordinating body COSIBAH (Coordinating Body of the Banana Unions in Honduras). She traces the development of the women's committees, the programs of these committees, leadership development, and the various roles of women in the current banana unions.

Hamilton, Nora, and Norma Stoltz Chinchilla. 1991. "Central American Migration: A Framework for Analysis." *Latin American Research Review* 26(1): 75–110.

This essay provides scholars, researchers, and students of Central American migration a good starting point in understanding the key issues facing Central Americans in the United States. Hamilton and Chinchilla provide a framework for understanding Central American migration as a result of political repression, aggravated by economic underdevelopment. The authors take into account historical and contemporary reasons for migration to present an interesting analysis of Central American migration, immigrant networks, and settlement. The essay analyzes the series of politically repressive governments and conditions and the economic neoliberal free-trade laws and underdevelopment in Central America that have made survival a challenge, and thus, migration an important outlet.

Johnson, Paul Christopher. 2007. *Diaspora Conversions: Black Carib Religion and the Recovery of Africa*. Berkeley: University of California Press.

Johnson explores Garifuna religiosity, the historical memory of religion among Garifuna, and the ways in which these are passed down and maintained after migration. Using ethnographic research, Johnson demonstrates how immigrant Garifuna communities change and adapt their religious beliefs in the new environment by using their memory of their religion to envision and create a new version of the religion. The Garifuna diaspora, he claims, re-conceptualizes their religion and the historical memory of religion to one that is more in line with an African diasporic religion. Johnson also provides a good history of the Garifuna past, their present, and their migration story.

El Libertador. http://www.ellibertador.hn/.

El Libertador is a monthly Spanish-language newspaper publication. It is a progressive news source that reflects the national Honduran reality. It is also a source of news in the country and analyses of everyday events. Although it is a monthly publication, it is updated daily online and provides sharp and critical analyses of Honduran issues as they occur.

Perez-Brignoli, Hector. 1989. *A Brief History of Central America*. Translated by R. B. Sawrey. Berkeley: University of California Press.

This now classic text translated from Spanish to English provides a sweeping history of Central America from the period of colonization to the 1980s. Perez-Brignoli traces the history of the various Central American nations individually and in relation to each other. The intra-Central American nations' history includes an analysis of shared borders and debates of nationhood and sovereignty in the modern era. It is an easy and clear read, full of important facts.

Schmalzbauer, Leah. 2004. "Searching for Wages and Mothering from Afar: The Case of Honduran Transnational Families." *Journal of Marriage and Family* 66(5): 1317–31.

In this essay Schmalzbauer traces the story of a Honduran transnational immigrant community in a suburb of Boston. In her research she traces Honduran immigrants' ongoing social relations in the country of origin, demonstrating that immigrants in the United States maintain a transnational relationship to the home country. In the home country, she documents the ways in which extended family members take over mothering and care-taking roles for children who are left behind by migrant mothers.

Indian (Asian Indian) Immigrants

by Karen Isaksen Leonard

Introduction

This essay focuses primarily on immigrants to the United States from post-1947 India, utilizing the census category of Asian Indian that best captures the Indian immigrant and ancestry population in the United States. There are striking differences between the Asian Indian immigrants who came before and after 1965, when the U.S. Immigration and Naturalization Act redressed the historic discrimination against Asians. The contrasts between the "old" and "new" (post-1965) Asian Indian immigrants are many, and most of the new immigrants are part of a highly cosmopolitan and well-placed immigrant population. Indian immigrants cluster in high-income professions and are very important to the American economy.

Chronology

1900–1910	The number of Indian immigrants rises from 200 to about 2,000, including mostly Punjabi farmers migrating to California.
1913	Alien Land Laws are enacted in California to prevent "aliens ineligible to citizenship" from owning or leasing agricultural land.
1917	"Barred Zone" act prevents most immigration from Asia.
1920–1921	Alien Land Laws strengthened.
1923	U.S. Supreme Court Thind decision makes Asian Indians ineligible for U.S. citizenship.
1924	National Origins Quota Act sets immigration quota for India at 105 per year.
1946	Luce Celler Bill makes citizenship by naturalization available to Asian Indians.
1947	Indian and Pakistani independence from British India.
1956	Dalip Singh Saund elected to the U.S. Congress from the Imperial Valley, California.

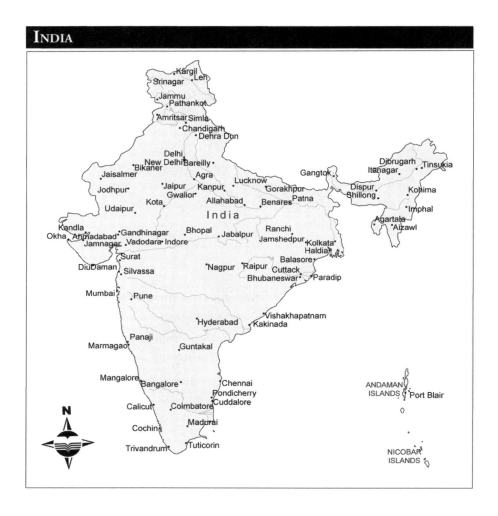

1965	Immigration and Naturalization Act gives preference to Asian immigrants with needed skills.
2003	The government of India begins working on an Overseas Citizenship of India (OCI) category, which becomes operational in December 2005. This is not quite dual citizenship, which is not allowed in the Indian Constitution.
2005	India's Lok Sabha, the lower house of parliament, introduces a bill for the compulsory registration of all marriages.
2007	India's Supreme Court rules that the marriages of couples belonging to all religions and communities in India, in the states and union territories, must be registered (it was ordered in 2006 that rules had to be framed to carry out compulsory registration of all marriages).
2011	Hindus were the second most affluent religious group in the U.S., with 65% of households surveyed by a Pew Forum on Religion and Public Life making more than $75,000 per year.

Background

Geography of India

Historically, the designation "India" was used to include the entire South Asian subcontinent. The Hindu Kush, Karakoram, and Himalayan mountains in the north prevent easy travel to Central Asia, Tibet, and China, and the Vindhya mountains in central India divide the northern Gangetic plain from central India and the coastal plains of southeastern India. Seaports along the western edge of the subcontinent connected historical India to the Persian Gulf, Middle East, and East Africa, while the Indus river system in the northwest and the Khyber and other passes through the mountain ranges along today's Pakistan/Afghanistan border connected India to Afghanistan, Iran, Turkey, and Central Asia. Wheat in the north and rice in the south are the staple crops. India's 19 or so vernacular languages also reflect the north/south difference, with Indo-Aryan (a branch of Indo-European) languages spoken in the north and Dravidian languages in the south; there are also tribal languages spoken by populations in the far northeast and extending down through central India's hills and forests. Modern states within both India and Pakistan have been formed along linguistic lines.

History of India

India's history is long and complex, and controversies centered on language, religion, and state policies concerning them are many. The earliest civilization in the Indian subcontinent, the Indus Valley civilization, is generally dated from 3000 to 1700 B.C.E. This extensive series of urban centers and villages was based on the five rivers (called *panch ab,* meaning five waters, the Indus and its tributaries), a territory now divided between Pakistan's Punjab state and India's Punjab and Haryana states. The rediscovery of this civilization in the 1920s raised more questions than it answered, upsetting the then-prevalent "Aryan invasion" theory crediting Indo-Aryan language bearers from Central Asia and eastern Europe with initiating settled civilization in the Gangetic valley and writing down the sacred Sanskrit texts, the Vedas, transmitted orally by the priestly Brahmans for some one thousand years. But the Indus Valley civilization not only predated these postulated Aryans but had reached a level that Sanskritic civilization did not attain until at least 600 B.C.E.

This early society was stable, highly centralized, and literate, but its pictographic script has not yet been deciphered; the script cannot be assigned conclusively to either the Indo-Aryan or Dravidian (South Indian) language families. The ending of the Indus Valley civilization is as mysterious as its origin, for scholars can point to no obvious cause for its decline. Issues centered on this earliest civilization continue to fuel political controversies with both linguistic and religious implications.

The three great religions of South Asia—Hinduism, Jainism, and Buddhism— arose in the Gangetic valley in the sixth century B.C.E., a time of urbanization, political conflict, and social instability. The institution of caste developed within Hinduism; caste ranks people according on their standing in the four varnas or social orders and their performance of dharma or caste-ordained duty. The four varnas were the Brahmans or priests, Kshatriyas or warriors, Vaishyas or merchant financiers, and Sudras or peasants and artisans (the Untouchables fell below these). While one explanation of the caste system stressed occupational complementarity, another stressed relative purity and pollution: the Brahmans were at the top because they were considered to be the purest, pure enough to intercede with the gods on behalf of others. They knew Sanskrit, avoided intoxicating foods such as meat and liquor, and neither took food from nor ate with members of lower castes; they arranged their children's marriages at an early age to guard against mixed-caste progeny and prohibited divorce and widow remarriage. Women, Sudras, and Untouchables were prohibited from studying the Vedas. The Untouchables were at the bottom because they worked with and ate polluting substances: their jobs included disposing of human excrement, washing dirty clothing (even menstrual cloths), cutting off and disposing of body hairs, delivering babies and cleaning up the blood of childbirth, disposing of dead human and animal bodies, making leather products from animal skins, and so on. Women ranked below men in all castes because they could not prevent the bodily production of polluting substances, such as menstrual blood and the blood of childbirth.

The caste system explained and justified socioeconomic inequality in the world, yet individuals could look to the future with hope because one could achieve liberation after a series of increasingly higher births and rebirths. This fundamental assumption of inequality by birth also underlay Hinduism's conceptual openness to many ways of achieving salvation. In early Hinduism or Brahmanism, the emphasis was upon knowledge (*jnana*) and ritual actions (*karma*), paths to salvation best followed by higher caste men who could study the Sanskrit texts and carry out rituals and actions in the world. But over the centuries, a third *bhakti* path of devotion or faith reached out to all people. The *bhakti* movements, led by charismatic founders all over India beginning in the seventh century in the south, focused primarily on forms of Vishnu or Shiva and used the vernacular languages; they recognized the differential capacities of persons of various castes, genders, and stages of the life cycle and engaged ordinary people, women, and members of the low and Untouchable castes, in new kinds of devotional worship in temples and home settings without Brahman intermediaries.

Whether early kingdoms were ruled by Hindus, Buddhists, or Jains, South Asian rulers traditionally showed tolerance for, even encouraged, all forms of religion. The royal role was that of patron of and mediator among religions. Important changes concerned the replacement of Sanskrit by Persian and then English as the language of rule and imperial power, as Muslim and Christian rulers came to power in India, but many argue that this tradition of tolerance continued (although this contention is controversial).

A major new religion and civilization entered the subcontinent with Arab traders along the western coast from the eighth century. Turkish and Afghan warriors came through the Khyber pass from 1000 C.E. to rule parts of northern India for brief periods, while in the southern or Deccan plateau, Shia Muslim rulers of Iranian ancestry established several sultanates. In the 16th century, Babur, a young warrior from Central Asia descended from two world conquerors, the Turk Timur (Tamerlane in English) and the Mongol Genghis Khan, swept down into the north Indian plains and founded the Mughal empire in 1526. His grandson Akbar began ruling in 1556, followed by Akbar's son Jehangir, grandson Shah Jahan, and great grandson Aurangzeb, whose rule ended in 1707. The Mughals employed many Muslim immigrants from Iran, Turkey, and Central Asia and also recruited heavily from the indigenous population. Persian, the courtly language most esteemed throughout the growing Muslim world, became India's new central administrative language, and all aspiring officials learned it, including many Hindus. Preceding Mughal rule, the Deccani sultanates had begun patronizing a new vernacular language, Dakhni or Urdu, the language of the (military) camp. Most often written in the Arabic or Persian script, Urdu's grammar was based on that of the Indo-Aryan vernaculars, but much of its vocabulary came from Persian. Urdu became the lingua franca throughout the Mughal empire.

Mughal rule was followed by British rule. By the early 18th century, the Mughal power in Delhi declined and European seaborne trade brought private European companies to India's coasts. In 1757, the British East India Company took Calcutta and was confirmed by the Mughal emperor in Delhi as Diwan, or revenue minister of Bengal. British rule spread, and at first the continuities between Mughal and British rule were striking: Persian remained the administrative language until 1833.

However, after an unsuccessful uprising against the company in 1857, the British Crown stepped in and India became a colony of Great Britain. Some princely or native states were left unannexed, so the subcontinent was a patchwork of British direct rule and princely rule. British migration to India was minuscule compared to earlier Muslim migrations, and the Christian religion made little headway there compared to Islam. Yet the impact of colonial rule deepened as English became the language of administration, and education in English produced increasing numbers of Western-educated Indians who wanted a devolution of power and eventual independence for India. The Indian National Congress was founded in 1885, and the nationalist movement developed under the leadership of Mohandas Karamchand Gandhi and Jawaharlal Nehru. Unfortunately the Muslim League and its leaders, notably Muhamed Ali Jinnah, became alienated from the Congress and argued that Hindus and Muslims were two nations, not one. The League pushed successfully for a Muslim state and the partition of India into India and Pakistan when Britain granted independence in 1947. The partition was accompanied by bloodshed and mass migrations in the subcontinent as new political boundaries were established and new national languages set, Hindi for India and Urdu for Pakistan.

Mohandas Gandhi, with All-India Congress's president Jawaharlal Nehru, at a meeting of the India Congress in Bombay in 1946. (Library of Congress)

Causes and Waves of Migration

Early Immigration

The "old" immigrants from British India constituted a relatively homogeneous group; they came to the United States at the end of the 19th and the beginning of the 20th century in relatively small numbers. The first migrants were almost all men and from only one part of India, the Punjab province along the northwestern frontier where the Punjabi language was spoken by Sikhs, Hindus, and Muslims. From farming backgrounds, most of these men settled in California in the early 1900s and worked in agriculture and strove to become citizens, acquire land and status, and establish families in the United States. Yet the pioneer farmers encountered discriminatory laws, laws that effectively ended immigration in 1917 and affected their rights to gain citizenship, hold agricultural land, and marry whom they chose. Federal policies and laws included the 1917 Barred Zone Act, which barred most Asians from legal immigration; the 1924 National Origins Quota Act, which set a quota of only 105 immigrants per year from India; and the 1923 U.S. Supreme Court Thind decision, which declared Indians to be Caucasians but not "white" and therefore ineligible for U.S. citizenship. State policies and laws included California's Alien Land Laws of 1913, 1920, and 1921, which prohibited noncitizens from owning and leasing agricultural land (and these were copied by other states) and various state antimiscegenation laws that prohibited marriages between people of different races.

Immigrant Culture/Early Issues of Assimilation and Separation

Despite the many legal constraints, many Punjabi pioneer immigrants, called "Hindus" by others (simply meaning "people from Hindustan" or India), stayed on. The laws against miscegenation encouraged most of them to marry women of Mexican ancestry: the Punjabi men and Mexican women looked racially similar to the county clerks issuing marriage licenses. The bi-ethnic couples produced many children, children with names like Maria Jesusita Singh, Jose Akbar Khan, and Carmelita Chand. These "Mexican-Hindu" children, mostly Catholic and bilingual in English and Spanish, called themselves Hindus and were extremely proud of their Indian heritage. Post-1965 Indian immigrants were usually unable to imagine the conditions in which the pioneers lived and found it hard to acknowledge these descendants of the Punjabi pioneers (most of whom were actually Sikhs) as "Hindus" or Indians.

Later Waves of Immigration: Up to 1965 Immigration Act

Asian Indian immigration opened up again after passage of the Luce-Celler Bill in 1946. The result of successful lobbying by Indian immigrants in the United States, the bill gave Asian Indians the right to become naturalized U.S. citizens and use the quota of 105 per year set by the 1924 National Origins Quota Act (because of the Supreme Court Thind decision in 1923, this quota had been used only by whites born in India). Then, in 1947, Great Britain's Indian empire gave way to the independent nations of India, Pakistan, Sri Lanka, and Burma. Once they took American citizenship, the pioneers could revisit their places of origin and sponsor relatives as immigrants, and their pride in their newly independent nations was an impetus to such reconnections. These political changes at the national level in both the United States and India made it possible for the old immigrants to reestablish connections with their homeland and for limited numbers of new immigrants to come.

Immigration Act of 1965 and Succeeding Legislation

An even greater spur to new migration came with the 1965 U.S. Immigration and Naturalization Act. The legislation vastly increased the numbers of immigrants from Asia and set preferences that favored two types of immigrants, skilled professionals and the relatives of earlier immigrants. The new Asian Indian immigrants are strikingly diverse: they come from all of India's states and speak many languages (India has some 19 major vernacular languages, and the political structure was realigned in 1956 so that internal state boundaries would reflect linguistic ones). In the United States, the most numerous regional groups are Gujaratis, Punjabis, and Malayalis, from the states of Gujarat, Punjab, and Kerala, respectively. The post-1965 immigrants are not rural people but predominantly urban, highly educated professionals. Unlike the bachelor pioneers, they typically migrate in family units, women and children accompanying the men. Adherents of many religions have migrated, Hindus, Muslims, Buddhists, Christians, Sikhs, Jains, and Parsis (or Zoroastrians), and many so-called traditional caste and community categories still have significance in the lives of the immigrants, particularly for purposes of marriage.

Through IRCA to the Present

While IRCA had no major impact upon the Asian Indian immigrants, changes on the international scene have produced ups and downs for them. The early 21st century, with an American and world economic crisis deepening in 2008–2009, has changed the patterns of migration for both education and jobs again. Fewer Indian students are applying to American graduate schools, although on the whole India continues to send high numbers of students to the United States (from 2001 to 2007 India was the leading place of origin for international students enrolled in American colleges and universities). Graduate school applicants from India had increased in 2006–2007 by 26 percent but increased only 2 percent in 2007–2008 and declined 9 percent in 2008–2009, according to the Council for Graduate Schools (Springer

2009a, A4); the decline seems related to better prospects for career advancement in India and the global economy's impact on students' ability to borrow money and come to the United States. Furthermore, foreign students graduating from American universities and colleges with science and engineering degrees are leaving the United States to pursue jobs opportunities in their home countries, Indians among them. In contrast to past trends, only 6 percent of the Indian students interviewed in October 2006 in a study conducted by the Ewing Marion Kauffman Foundation said they wanted to stay in the United States permanently (Springer 2009b, A44). This economic loss to the United States has prompted a bill in the U.S. House of Representatives to grant direct permanent residency to foreign students obtaining a PhD in science, technology, engineering, and mathematics in the United States. India and the United States formed, in 2009, a joint working group to focus on institutional linkages in the fields of secondary, higher, and vocational education; cooperation in this knowledge-driven era is deemed essential to both countries.

Demographic Profile

Size and Composition of Community

The 2000 Census showed the population of Asian Indians had more than doubled since 1990, reaching almost 1.7 million and taking Asian Indians to third place among Asian American groups (the Chinese numbered 2.4 million and Filipinos 1.8 million). California again led the states with the largest number of Asian Indians, followed by New York, New Jersey, Texas, and Illinois, and Indians are now the largest Asian group in 19 states. By 2006, according to the American Community Survey of the Census Bureau (Springer 2007a), another 800,000 Indian Americans had been added, so the Indian American population reached nearly 2.5 million.

Age and Family Structure

In terms of household characteristics and family stability, the immigrants from India led the foreign born in the 1990 Census in percent of population married and were at the bottom in percent of those separated and divorced. The most common household size was four. In the 2000 Census, immigrants from India continued to be among the highest of the foreign-born men and women in percent of population married and among the lowest of such men and women separated and divorced. There were slightly more men than women, 53.9 percent to 46.1 percent. Fertility was low, with 59 percent of Indian immigrant women having only one to two children and only 9 percent having more than three children. Indian Americans were and are typically not clustered in residential areas but dispersed; when Indian ethnic enclaves are mentioned, they are usually shopping enclaves, featuring businesses and not residences.

Educational Attainment

In the 1990 Census, Asian Indians had the highest percentage with a bachelor's degree or higher and the highest percentage in managerial and professional fields of any foreign-born group. Again in 2000, Asian Indians had the highest percentage of foreign-born Americans with a bachelor's degree or higher and were among the highest percentages in managerial and professional fields. In both the 1990 and 2000 censuses, over 70 percent of Indian Americans were bilingual, using English and also a "heritage language."

Economic Attainment: Occupation and Income Patterns

The first wave of post-1965 immigrants set high socioeconomic standards, as evident in the 1990 Census: those immigrants born in India had the highest median household income, family income, and per capita income of any foreign-born group at that time. Also, in the 1990 Census, Asian Indians had the highest percentage in managerial and professional fields of any foreign-born group. The Asian Indians arriving since the mid-1980s brought the averages and medians down slightly, many of them coming in under the Family Reunification Act and not as well qualified as the earlier professional immigrants. There were recessions in the U.S. economy, and Indians arriving after 1985 showed a much lower percentage in managerial and professional jobs, a much lower median income, and a much higher unemployment rate. By the mid-1990s the percentage of South Asian families in poverty was high, putting those born in India 12th on the lists of both families in poverty and individuals in poverty. The U.S. Immigration Act of 1990 reversed the slight downward trend by sharply increasing the numbers of highly skilled immigrants from India (and Asia generally) at the expense of unskilled workers and nonemployed immigrants (parents and spouses of citizens). In the 2000 Census, immigrants born in India had the third-highest median household income (behind only South Africans and Britishers), the second-highest median family income (behind South Africans), and the second-highest median per capita income (behind Britishers) of the foreign-born groups. Again in 2000, Asian Indians held among the highest percentages in managerial and professional fields.

Indian immigration to the United States continues to be high in the early 21st century, as the United States experiences a great surge in immigration (one in five residents is a recent immigrant or a close relative of one). Some 60,000 to 70,000 Indians enter the United States each year, many of them highly skilled workers on H-1B temporary visas that are good for up to six years. Many have become permanent residents or American citizens. In 2008, Indians cornered 38 percent of the H1-B visas, and they also accounted for the maximum number of people entering the United States on L-1 visas, primarily used for intra-company transferees. The H1-B visa proportion is down from the late 1990s, when Indians accounted for almost half of all such visas and India became the world's fourth-largest economy; the so-called brain drain worked to India's advantage, as remittances increased. The high socioeconomic profile of the immigrants in America has helped make India the top receiver of migrant remittances in the world: Indians overseas remitted a total of $27 billion to India in 2007, with the United States being the main remittance source ("India Top Receiver" 2008).

The profile of foreign-born Indians in the United States in the Census Bureau's American Community Survey of 2007 showed very significant contributions to the American economy and society. In the United States, foreign-born workers (17,553,000) constituted 17 percent of all workers, and the India-born 746,200 workers were in third place, behind those born in Mexico, 5,286,400, and the Philippines, 848,800. But Asian Indians ranked first in high-income occupations, some 40 percent of them in four occupational categories: 30 percent of all computer software developers were foreign born, and Indians dominated this group with 125,300 workers (Chinese, next, numbered only 39,200); and 16.8 percent of all foreign-born Indians were computer software developers. Of all doctors in the United States, 29 percent were foreign-born, and Indians led this category, with 40,000 doctors (Filipinos, next, numbered 12,800); 5.4 percent of all foreign-born Indians were doctors. Of engineers and architects, 20 percent were foreign-born, Indians leading with 46,500 (Chinese, next, numbered 30,300); 6.2 percent of all foreign-born Indians were engineers and architects. And 19 percent of all scientists and quantitative analysts were foreign-born, Indians again leading with 81,400 (Chinese, next, numbered 52,500); 10.9 percent of all foreign-born Indians were scientists and quantitative analysts.

Indian doctors are a particularly large and important group, and many gained visas by serving in America's rural areas. About 25 percent of doctors in the United States are international medical graduates, or IMGs, and Indians are the largest single group, about 20 percent of that. In 1999, 26,000 of America's 600,000 doctors, or 4 percent, were of Indian origin. By 2007, 40,000 of 677,600 doctors in the United States were Indians, an increase from 4 percent to 6 percent of doctors in America. The largest ethnic body of doctors in the United States is the American Association of Physicians from India. These impressive figures continue in the second generation: in 1999, 1 of every 10 freshmen in U.S. medical colleges was an Indian American, showing that the second generation is heavily invested in medical careers; it is estimated that nearly half of these students are children of doctors or related to doctors. There are also are the Association of Indian Pharmacists in America and the Indo-American Physicians and Dentists Political Association.

Another cluster of Indian Americans works in the hospitality industry in America, with more than 55 percent of the "economy lodging sector" (motels) owned by Indian immigrants from all over the world. They helped form, in 1985, what became the Indo American Hospitality Association and, in 1989, the Asian American Hotel Owners Association (AAHOA). These groups merged in 1994 as AAHOA and have over 9,000 members owning 22,000 hotels and motels in 2009. Most of the AAHOA officers, as well as the hotel and motel owners and managers, have last names of Patel and are of Gujarati ancestry. The movement of Patels into the motel business, not their traditional occupation in India, started in San Francisco even before the new immigration spurred by the 1965 immigration act.

Indian immigrants also cluster in the Silicon Valley Internet-based economy, along with Chinese engineers and entrepreneurs. In 1998, 7 percent of the 774 companies in the valley were run by Indian Americans; the percentage of companies run by Indian and Chinese doubled from 1984 to 1999, to 25 percent. The high-tech firms there employed 58,000 workers in 1999 and accounted for over $17 billion in sales in 1998. The region's scientific workforce was over 30 percent immigrants, again with the Chinese and Indians dominating. The Sunnyvale Hindu temple, one of the largest in California when it opened in 1994, was outgrown by 2001 as its membership grew from 380 families to 4,800. The tech market crashed in 2000, however, and while the setbacks were considerable, a 2007 survey showed Indians in a very good position again (Springer 2007a).

Continuing patterns evidenced in the 1990 and 2000 censuses, India-born people led the United States in education and median income in 2006, according to the Census Bureau's 2007 American Community Survey, a nationwide sample survey. A very high percentage of people born in India, 74 percent, had a bachelor's degree or higher, more than people born in any other foreign country and more than natives. Median household income in 2006 for people born in India was $91,115, compared to $46,881 for the total foreign-born population, $51,249 for the native population, and $50,740 for the total population. The next highest foreign-born high income populations were those from Australia, South Africa, and the Philippines.

Health Statistics and Issues

With respect to health, Asian Indians all over the globe are stricken by cardiovascular disease disproportionately; in the United States they suffer at a rate three to four times that of the general population. Their rates of diabetes, hypertension, and the metabolic syndrome are also higher than those of many other ethnic and immigrant groups. Puzzlingly, conventional cardiovascular risk factors do not explain the high rates of heart disease, and research is underway on Asian Indian diets, traditions, and cultural beliefs about health.

Adjustment and Adaptation

Families and Changing Gender Relations

Asian Indians are settling into the United States in ways unanticipated only a few decades ago. With the achievement of dual citizenship options in 2003, more of the migrants are becoming U.S. citizens, and family dynamics are adjusting transnationally. Elderly parents are being brought from India to join their adult children in the United States, but too often they feel isolated from their old friends and former lives and find themselves stuck in the suburbs without access to shops or other people, serving as babysitters, phone answerers, perhaps even cooks, for their children. Clubs have been started for the aging parents in the United States. Even a few old-age homes (although this was initially thought unnecessary) and "temple tours" like those back in India that take seniors to various new Hindu temples are being established in the United States. When no relatives are there to help, servants cannot be afforded, and with Indian immigrant parents both working, other solutions are being found. One innovative company in California was started by a middle-aged mother of two to offer maids, nannies, chauffeurs, and cooks to Indian Americans. Gita Patel's most popular service is the "Cook & Clean" team, featuring an Indian cook and a person who cleans.

Gender issues loom large in Indian American life, with some communities strongly upholding patriarchy and gender complementarity (different male and female roles) in family and community, perceiving the dominant American values of gender equality and freedom of sexual expression as serious threats to ordered social life. Some fear American individualism, interpreted not as a moral ideal but as egoism that could lead to family and societal breakdown. Whether certain practices are religiously required or simply matters of culture can be vigorously debated, and gendered and generational tensions are shared to some extent by all Indian immigrants as they worry about emerging "problems" involving their children and whether these should be attributed to cultural and religious values brought from the homeland or to those of the host society.

Just as the early Punjabi immigrants and their descendants redefined themselves, their families, and their work relationships, the post-1965 Indian immigrants are also defining and experiencing family and work relationships in new ways in the United States, and first-generation women often play key roles in these changes. Charged with embodying and transmitting "tradition," many women are revising tradition as they contribute to the material prosperity of the family and become active agents of change in public as well as private life. Indian women making desirable, often necessary, contributions to family earnings are being empowered within the family. Women make more decisions about spending than do their mothers-in-law back home, and they make more decisions than do their visiting or even co-residing mothers-in-law in the United States. Parents come to visit or live with their immigrant daughters as well as their sons.

The fact of Indian women working in the United States has different consequences from the fact of women working in India, where immediate and extended family members and servants can help diffuse responsibilities within a broad support network. Perhaps the consequences are more far-reaching for those women working in ethnic businesses, for an ethnic economy is almost by definition a gendered economy. Family businesses use women's labor power as a cheap resource, keeping labor costs and wages low. It is also a new resource for many of the Indian immigrants, since women running groceries or restaurants in the United States would not have done this back in India. But the changes go beyond bringing women into family businesses, for even when family histories show a continuity of entrepreneurial activity, important changes in gender roles occur within the families. A study done in Los Angeles found that not all of the Indian women engaged in managing and working in ethnic business enterprises were doing so in their own family businesses. The model was not that of a mom-and-pop store, where both husband and wife worked in the store with the man clearly in charge. Instead, the characteristic pattern found husbands holding other full-time jobs while their wives opened and ran groceries, restaurants, or boutiques. Research on Gujarati motel owners also found women taking important roles in the business, while their men sometimes worked elsewhere. This marks a departure from employment patterns back in India, where private businesses, including family businesses, rarely employ women as managers and clerks.

Indian American women participate prominently in public life, in activities ranging from political groups addressing themselves to the Indian and American governments to local vernacular and sectarian cultural and religious associations. They are providing support for battered South Asian women, educating them about physical and mental health issues, and working on legal issues connected with marriage, divorce, and migration. Women's organizations actively addressing issues of domestic violence include Apne Ghar in Chicago, Sakhi in New York, Narika in Berkeley, and Manavi in New Jersey. President Obama appointed two Indian American women in 2009 to a faith-based advisory council, part of the White House Office of Faith-based and Neighborhood Partnerships: Eboo S. Patel, founder and executive director of Interfaith Youth Core in Chicago, and Anju Bhargava, a Hindu woman priest who is also president of the New Jersey–based Asian Indian Women of America. In 2009, President Obama also appointed Farah Pandith, of Kashmiri origin, as a special Muslim representative for outreach to Muslims around the world.

Retaining a Sense of National Culture and Identity

Continued Links to India

Despite the many measures of economic success, post-1965 Indian immigrants did not immediately become American citizens, partly because many thought of themselves as economic migrants who would return one day and partly because India did not permit dual citizenship until very recently. Many migrants have family networks, financial interests, and political commitments that span two or more nations. As the population grew, Indian Americans formed many linguistic associations, ethnic organizations, and religious sectarian or guru-centered groups, many of them reproducing divisions important back in India and continuing to link Indians to India. For example, the Telugu Association of North America is dominated by members of the Kamma caste, while their rivals in the countryside of Andhra Pradesh (the Telugu-speaking state in South India), members of the Reddy caste, have formed the American Telugu Association; these organizations are transnational.

Transnationalism is evident in all aspects of Indian American life, strengthening and revitalizing Indian culture in America but also infusing American culture into India. Retaining Indian culture and identity became easier for first-generation immigrants when India's TV channels began invading the U.S. market in the 1990s. At the same time, a soap opera (*Mausam*, or "Seasons") produced by nonresident Indians (NRIs) for the Indian TV market became successful there. Indian musicians and religious figures tour North America and Indian American artists flock to Chennai (Madras) for the Carnatic music concert season. On the Hollywood/Bollywood front, the triumph of the film *Slumdog Millionaire* internationally and in the 2009 American Academy Awards exemplifies the global scale of movie-making (the director was British, the music director was Indian, and most actors were Indian). In the spring of 2009, the Motion Picture Association of America opened its first office in India, serving as an advocate of American movies, videos, and television but also working against piracy by reducing market restrictions and taxes and strengthening intellectual property rights in the Indian law and courts.

Social Organizations Based on National/Ethnic Background

Organizations seemingly based on occupation, like those of doctors, hospitality industry people, and software programmers are often old-boy and old-girl networks and emphasize social goals as well. Indians have formed a plethora of language- and caste-based organizations in the United States. Many religious organizations, as discussed in the following section, combine new and old immigrants from diverse countries in interesting ways.

Religion

The religious arena was an important site of change for the Indian immigrants even in the early 20th century and it is arguably even more important today. The early immigrants met together in houses, rented halls, or buildings purchased and adapted for purposes of worship. Sikh, Muslim, and Hindu, almost all had adopted practices characteristic of American churches such as sitting on chairs, leaving one's shoes on, and seating men and women together as families. Now reversals are occurring as the post-1965 immigrants, larger in terms of both numbers and resources, build traditionally designed religious institutions and introduce "more authentic" practices from India. For example, the Punjabi pioneers had introduced chairs in their Stockton Sikh temple, shoes did not have to be taken off or heads covered, men and women sat together, and the *prasad* (consecrated sweets) was served on paper plates and eaten with utensils. The new Sikh immigrants, however, have removed the chairs, required shoe removal and head coverings, and instituted gendered seating, and they serve *prasad* on the hand to be eaten with fingers, as done in Indian *gurdwaras* or temples.

Madame Pandit (sister of Jawaharlal Nehru and India's first prime minister to the United Nations) solicits funds at the Sikh temple in Stockton, California, about 1946. The first new East Indian women are in the front row. (Courtesy of Isabel Singh Garcia)

Another early development was the arrival of charismatic Indian teachers who recruited non-Asian Americans into their religious movements. Swami Vivekananda's impressive appearance at the World Parliament of Religions in Chicago in 1893 inaugurated the Vedanta Society in the United States, although he did not stay to lead it. An early Muslim Sufi teacher and musician, Hazrat Inayat Khan, from India, founded the Sufi Order in the West in 1912. Attracting American followers in the early decades of the 20th century were Swami Paramahansa Yogananda, who taught Kriya Yoga and founded the Self Realization Fellowship in the 1920s, and Jiddu Krishnamurti, whose background in the Theosophical movement led him to stress self-reliance and inner reflection in his spiritual teachings.

In the late 1960s, Indian religious figures could immigrate more easily and the American "counterculture generation" was receptive to their teachings. Yogi Bhajan, teaching Kundalini Yoga, founded Sikh Dharma in the West. His Los Angeles Sikh temple helped move Sikhism from a Punjabi religion to a world religion by being the first *gurdwara* to have non-Punjabi Sikhs (sometimes called *gora* or white Sikhs) conduct the Sikh initiation ceremony. Maharishi Mahesh Yogi founded the Transcendental Meditation movement, which now has about one hundred centers in North America and a university in Iowa. A Vaishnavite *sanyasi* Srila Prabhupada was sent from Calcutta to bring Krishna's message to the West and founded ISKCON, or the International Society for Krishna Consciousness (the Hare Krishnas), in New York in 1966. ISKCON has not only gone back to India and founded temples there, but perhaps 50 percent of the U.S. followers are now of Indian origin.

Religious preachers traveling to the United States from India in the 21st century address themselves to primarily Indian immigrant followers. Swami Chinmayananda, one of India's most popular spiritual leaders, died in 1993 in San Diego, California, on one of the extensive overseas lecturing tours he had undertaken to establish missions and youth camps in the United States. Sikh congregations raise money to bring Punjabi preachers and hymn-singing groups for tours in North America, and Muslim groups also sponsor many visitors. All of these relatively new religions in the United States sponsor the immigration of "religious workers" to staff their institutions. While these Hindu priests, Sikh *granthis,* and Muslim *moulvis* are acceptable to first-generation congregation members, they are less satisfactory for members of the second generation, since they often do not speak English well and are not at home in the American environment.

Sikh *gurdwaras,* Hindu and Jain temples, South Asian mosques, and Parsi fire temples are being built all over America, fueled by the relative prosperity of the post-1965 immigrants and the ease of securing the necessary materials, as well as the craftsmen, artisans, and religious specialists to put them together. Earlier Hindu temples, Sikh *gurdwaras,* and Muslim mosques tended to be older buildings taken over by immigrants, but now they are being newly constructed, and inconspicuous structures designed to blend in have given way to strong statements of pride and "authenticity." Congregations that can afford it try to faithfully reproduce Indian structures in outer details. Sometimes municipal governments force changes in design: a Hindu temple in Norwalk, in southern California, had to adopt a Spanish mission style of architecture before its congregation got permission to build. Workmen and building materials can be brought from India, and the buildings are situated according to traditional preferences. For example, Hindu temples should be placed near water and mountains, such placements evoking home and recreating it in the new context. The first big Los Angeles Hindu temple was located in the Malibu hills near the ocean in 1984, modeled after the Tirupati Vaisnava temple in Andhra Pradesh devoted to a South Indian form of Vishnu. Craftsmen, materials, and continuing institutional ties help this temple reproduce that particular devotional tradition, but it has recruited north Indian members, installing new images that appeal to them as well. This broadening of appeal was partly inspired by the need to pay the mortgage. Similar innovations broaden other congregations: a Hindu Unity temple in Dallas has 11 deities from different regional and sectarian traditions and a Shiva/Vishnu temple in Livermore east of San Francisco has both a *shikhara* and a *gopuram,* central towers typical of north and south Indian temples, respectively.

Temples and mosques present themselves differently in the United States than in the homeland. Often they are parts of "center" complexes or have enhanced roles as educational institutions; they are not just places of worship. Thus many mosques have shops with books and pamphlets about Islam. Some changes involve gender roles. At the Los Angeles Malibu Hindu temple, well-dressed Indian women sit at the doorway and give out pamphlets to all visitors. It is they, not the three South Indian priests (brought from India and not well-versed in English), who explain Hindu beliefs and rituals to casual visitors. Hindu temples in the United States have become the site of congregational worship and cultural as well as religious activities. In the Malibu temple basement, *bharatnatyam* (South Indian classical dance) performances are held, as professional Indian female dance teachers present their students' *arangetrams,* or debuts. Temples in India were once the sites of *bharatnatyam,* and in the diaspora, temples and *bharatnatyam* are being reunited. Though held in "traditional" temple settings, the social aspects of such dance performances can be enhanced by a meal served in the interval or afterward, and many temples are being designed with internal non-sacred spaces that encourage recreational activities.

Not only worship centers but Hindu and Islamic schools and institutes and producers of textbooks and TV shows suited for youngsters in the United States are springing up all over America. Sophisticated programs have been developed for computerized learning of the relevant languages and texts (particularly Sanskrit and Arabic; and the Bhagavad Gita and the Quran). Teaching materials of all sorts are available; for example, a Harvard project put lectures and information concerning South Asian religions on CD-ROM. Transnational religious networks circulate new media, videos, CDs, and DVDs throughout the Indian diaspora (like the TV series of the Indian epics, the *Ramayana* and the *Mahabharata,* produced by India's national television, Doordarshan, in the 1990s). The Internet gives easy access to some religious sites in India as well, allowing devotees to worship and make offerings from the United States.

For Indian Hindus, Sikhs, Muslims, Christians, Parsis, and possibly even Jains, changes from homeland practices are occurring in American religious spaces as congregants from different linguistic, caste, and sectarian backgrounds in India and elsewhere are brought together. Interactions between immigrant and indigenous American followers of the religions from the Indian subcontinent are more important for some communities than others. Looking first at the Sikhs and Hindus, one sees that these are primarily immigrant communities still strongly oriented toward India, but they are also flourishing in the United States. North American converts to Sikhism and Hinduism—members of Yogi Bhajan's Sikh Dharma, the Ramakrishna Mission, the Transcendental Meditation movement, and the Hare Krishnas—form very small parts of the two communities. The American followers of Sikhism and Hinduism (and Islam) often differ strikingly from the Indian immigrants, and, depending on the interpreter, their beliefs and practices can be considered dangerously hybrid or more "authentic (text-based)" than those of the immigrants.

The Punjabi Sikh immigrant community in the United States sees itself as a diaspora community, and many of its members also recast the "old Hindus," or the pioneer Punjabi immigrants to North America, as "the Sikh diaspora." The Indian Sikhs have a public profile marked by sharp, public disagreements over their place in India and the nature and extent of Sikh religious authority. Sikh minority status everywhere (they constitute some 2% of India's population) and specific grievances in India exploded in the 1980s in demands for a Sikh homeland, or Khalistan ("land of the pure," a Sikh state), by many North American Sikhs. Particularly after Indira Gandhi's government sent the Indian Army into Amritsar's Golden Temple to rout militant secessionists in 1984, damaging the holy shrine, Sikhs all over the world who had discarded the turban and beards adopted these outward markers again, enhancing their identity as Sikhs. The assassination of Indira Gandhi by two of her bodyguards, who were Sikhs, a few months later sent shock waves worldwide, with some outspoken Sikhs in America defending Gandhi's killing while several thousand Sikhs in India were being slaughtered by their fellow citizens in retaliation for it. The head of the governing body in Amritsar tried to extend his influence over Sikhs outside India, and Sikh *gurdwaras* all over the United States saw takeovers or takeover attempts by Khalistani Sikhs. The Punjabi Sikhs are famous for rivalry and fighting in their *gurdwaras* outside India (this is not unknown in Hindu temples in the United States either). As Sikh militancy and orthodoxy has increased, the use of the external markers—the wearing of turbans or the carrying of *kirpans,* or swords—has sometimes been contested in American courts. Can Sikhs wear turbans when a job requires safety helmets, and can Sikh youngsters carry *kirpans,* knives which are usually small and symbolic but have been known to inflict damage, on school playgrounds? Sikhs have traditionally resisted outside authority from beyond their immediate community, but now Sikhs sometimes invoke outside authorities, including American courts and religious figures in the Punjab, to achieve religious or political control over American Sikh congregations.

The decline of the Khalistan movement by the end of the 20th century has facilitated a closer integration of the Punjabi immigrant Sikhs with the small group of predominantly white American converts and that, along with converging second-generation conceptions of Sikhism as a world religion, has had impacts back in the Punjab. The Sikh Dharma group has become active in India, setting up a school in Amritsar and sending its children to learn Punjabi culture. Meanwhile, pressure for the gender equity promised by Sikhism has increased, partly because of convert Sikh expectations. Sikh Dharma women reportedly won the right for all Sikh women to perform certain previously male-only duties in the Golden Temple in Amritsar (Sikhism's most holy site), but in practice this has not yet been honored.

Hindus are the largest of the post-1965 Indian religious groups in the United States and constitute an overwhelmingly immigrant religious population, with Hindu politics in the United States focused primarily on goals in India. Some Hindu sectarian or caste groups in India do extend authority over members overseas, and Hindu religious specialists recruited from India staff the new temples in America. There are parallels to the Sikh court cases involving contested leadership of particular Hindu temples, but such cases are not part of a national or transnational pattern contesting the nature and extent of religious authority exercised from India. Hindu and Hindu-related associations are forming federations and coordinating religious, cultural, and political events.

As in India, Hindu beliefs and practices are extremely diverse and religious authority is decentralized. Hinduism has not been promoted as a universal or world religion and does not seek converts. Nevertheless, it has had a major impact on American popular culture through yoga and "new age" meditation movements, ones so hybrid that they are no longer recognizably religious or Indian in nature. Some Hindus in America are seeking to unify and standardize Hinduism, focusing on the second generation, but efforts to build one unified Hindu community in the United States appear insignificant. The religious beliefs and practices designated as Hinduism have relied primarily on family- and caste-based rituals, and new temples in the United States were financed, at least initially, by particular regional and sectarian groups. Some of the many linguistic, regional, caste, occupational, and educational (old-boy and old-girl) associations to which Hindus in the United

States belong crosscut religious boundaries, but others reinforce sectarian or caste boundaries, regulating marriages and conduct in the diaspora as in the homeland. However, new congregations and temples in the United States are combining deities, architectural styles, and language groups seldom combined in India.

While changes in beliefs and practices are occurring among American Hindus, it is hard to generalize. Hindus in the United States deal in many ways with the increased demands on their time and the loss of family priests and other religious specialists available in the Indian context. Temples and temple priests have assumed increased importance, with temples often offering language and music classes. Daily rituals can be contracted, shortened on weekdays and lengthened on weekends, or they can be combined, with both morning and evening rituals performed in the evenings. Rituals can be temporarily suspended, perhaps by students in dormitories, and resumed upon return to the parental home. Ritual responsibility can be delegated to only one family member, perhaps an elderly mother, who performs religious observances on behalf of the entire family. Families can postpone all rituals to weekends, or they can rotate the observance of holiday rituals among a number of families, simplifying observances for any one family. Since the sacred fire altar cannot be used in many settings, incense or candles can be substituted. Hindus must make places in their American-designed homes for *puja* rooms or shrines, converting kitchen cupboards, closets, or studies into worship centers.

Beliefs as well as practices are being adapted to the new setting. Hinduism has many sources of religious authority and first-generation Hindu immigrants generally accept numerous and diverse sources and follow a multiplicity of rituals and social practices. However, for second-generation Hindus being raised in the United States, such diffuseness is confusing. Growing up in a predominantly Christian context and knowing little about the conflict and diversity that has characterized the history of Christianity, the children of Hindu immigrants want to be presented with one easy set of beliefs and texts, analogous to Christianity and Islam (or so they think). To achieve this, the parents tend to emphasize beliefs only, not socio-religious practices—not the caste system, village society, gendered practices, or daily interactions with fellow citizens of other religious backgrounds. They present their children with a static belief system floating through time, an ideal system unresponsive to changing economic, political, and social forces—such a religion does not exist (although many other believers view their respective religions in the same way). Thus, at a time when scholars are recognizing the constructed nature of "Hinduism," the distortion and inaccuracy involved in treating it as an organized whole, Hindus themselves are constructing or reconstructing it in ways that simplify and unify it. Some forces in Hinduism are busy producing the kind of Hindu beliefs the second generation is seeking. A major effort to standardize and inculcate Hinduism abroad is being made by the Vishwa Hindu Parishad (VHP, or World Hindu Assembly) of America. In India, the parent organization is part of the militant Hindu political movement. In 1993, in Washington, D.C., the VHP held a major conference, which was ostensibly a centenary celebration of Vivekananda's 1893 address to Chicago's World Parliament of Religions but also a celebration of the demolition of the Babri Masjid (a mosque erected in the 16th century by order of the first Mughal emperor Babur, allegedly on the site of an earlier temple to the Hindu god Ram) only a few months earlier in India. This conference fueled the Hindu right in America. Despite its extreme political agenda, Hindu parents in the United States have flocked to join the VHP, seeing it as a way to formalize religious classes for their children and affirm their Hindu identity and Indianness.

The growth of the VHP in America is one indication of the threat to the secular nature of the Indian state coming from Hindus in the United States. Both within India and transnationally, this contemporary insistence on the privileged position of Hinduism in Indian national culture leads to a narrowed and more rigid view of Indian civilization. Thus, despite centuries of presence in South Asia and many measures that show significant integration into Indian civilization, Muslims, Christians, Jews, and Parsis are being recast in the minds of some Hindu immigrants and their children as "alien" to India. Second-generation youth of Hindu background studying Indian history may ask why they have to learn about Islam and Muslims, no longer seen by them (or their parents) as important in India. Add to this situation a new generation of young academics and writers from India or of Indian background, people who are rewriting colonial and postcolonial interpretations of Indian history and culture, and you have active debates on American campuses today.

Buddhist and Muslim immigrants from India are extremely diverse in terms of national origin, class, language, and race and ethnicity. In both cases, there are significant American-born components. Buddhists from India are a very small proportion of American Buddhists. While monks from India's neighbor, Sri Lanka, with their high English-language educational attainments and the backing of well-off Sri Lankan immigrants, have been conspicuous in Buddhist institution-building and interfaith efforts, Buddhists from India are primarily Dalits or Untouchables. They are mobilizing in the United States to help their caste-fellows back in India, where a small-scale conversion movement of Dalits to Buddhism is underway. An international journal, *Dalit,* was published for about 10 years in the United States at the end of the 20th century, disseminating information about issues in India and soliciting funds for education and uplift projects. There are other international Dalit journals and Web sites, many with Christian or Buddhist orientations.

Particularly among Muslims, there are efforts to unify believers across the many internal boundaries. Muslims from India are only a part, but a large and very important part, of America's emerging Muslim community. The earliest Muslims in the United States were African Americans, and they are still about a third of the American Muslim population. Interestingly, it was Ahmadiyya missionaries from British India (the Ahmadi movement was founded in the Punjab in the late 19th-century) who helped the African American Muslim movements in the early 20th century by bringing an English translation of the Quran in 1920, publishing the first English-language Muslim magazine in the United States, and telling America's black Muslims about the five pillars of Islam, thus heading them toward mainstream Sunni teachings.

After the 1965 Immigration and Naturalization Act, new Muslim immigrants came from many countries. The post-1965 Indian Muslim immigrants rank high in terms of educational and socioeconomic status, and South Asian Muslim men, by the 1990s, began to share the national political leadership of American Muslims with earlier Arab Muslim immigrants. Many first-generation Indian Muslims are working to expand the basic definition of America's civic religion, the Judeo-Christian tradition, to the Abrahamic (Judeo-Christian-Muslim) tradition. American Muslims also write about the compatibility between Islam and democracy, and here the long experience of Indian Muslims with democratic politics in India qualifies them well for leadership positions.

An American Islam is being constituted, and many Indian (and Pakistani) Muslims are contributing to it. Without long-standing communities and mosques, Indian Muslims in America teach Islam through texts, ones that are intended to convey universal teachings but often reflect the relocation and reorientation of the teachers. Thus a textbook for Islamic education produced in Orange County, California, authored by South Asian Muslim Americans, explains *zakat* (charity) thus: "Some have a lot and some have none. We live in America, the richest country in the world. We live in big houses, drive good cars, wear good clothes and play with the best toys. . . . We should also look at the other people here or in other countries who have nothing" (Ali 1991, 67).

After September 11, 2001, Indian Muslims have had to battle against the stereotyping of Muslims as terrorists. They work with other Muslims, but American Muslims follow divergent beliefs and practices rooted in many countries and many sectarian traditions (the dominant Sunnis, the various Shiites, etc.). Leading scholars of *fiqh,* or Islamic jurisprudence, agree that Muslim mobilization in the United States involves the development of *fiqh* in a new context rather than transnational applications of *fiqh* from various homelands. Gender issues are prominent in American Muslim community discourses. Patriarchy and gender complementarity (different male and female roles) in family and community are generally upheld, although a vigorous "gender jihad" is underway, led by American Muslim women of African American, South Asian, and Arab backgrounds. Asra Nomani, an Indian Muslim feminist, has been prominent in this effort.

Indian Christians in the United States are also very internally diverse, representing communities ranging from Latin and Syrian Catholics to Jacobite, Mar Thomite, Nestorian, and many post-Reformation Protestant denominations. Contrasting with the pattern of male-led family migrations from India, Christian nurses from Kerala led the way for their communities, with interesting gender reversals in some areas of family life. Indian Christians have sometimes joined mainstream American Christian congregations and sometimes retained their ethnic or national origin identities. Like Muslims from India, Indian Christians have asked for help not only from co-religionists but from other Indian immigrants as anti-Christian attitudes and actions in India have threatened their ancestral communities.

In the United States, the Parsis or Zoroastrians from India and Pakistan find themselves confronting Zoroastrians from Iran. Both populations are doing extremely well economically, and the Indian Gujarati- and English-speaking Parsi immigrants are working hard with the Persian-speaking Iranian immigrants to build an integrated North American community of Zarthustis, the name upon which they have agreed. Zarthustis from Iran and India, worship together but are conscious of the national and linguistic differences. Marital and religious ties are international, with the funders of the Westminster center/temple in Southern California also funding temples in Chicago, Toronto, Canada, and Sydney, Australia. A journal, *Fezana,* published in the Chicago area includes North American and international news.

The Zarthustis, whose religion traditionally prohibited conversion, are dealing with new issues raised in the diaspora. The Zoroastrian or Zarthusti centers being built in North America's major cities include fire temples, but a gas flame replaces the ever-burning sacred fire, which is prohibited by U.S. fire regulations. Funeral rituals are carried out fully, but there are no "towers of silence" on which to place the bodies for disposal by flesh-eating birds, so most Parsis choose cremation. The Indian Parsis are providing trained priests to American congregations even where they are outnumbered by Iranians (in Los Angeles, for example), because the religion has been weakened in Iran, and the priests in India and America are no longer always in agreement. The priests in India refuse to marry Parsi women to non-Parsi grooms, and they refuse to baptize the children of mixed marriages. But in North America, such practices are becoming accepted as concern grows about the declining numbers in the community. The new Zarthustrian religious centers in the United States are also cultural centers, intended to strengthen second-generation attendance and encourage marriages among the young people. Intermarriages and baptisms of "mixed" children raise the possibility of conversion, at least in the United States.

The Jains also have a Federation of Jain Associations in North America, and their challenge is to establish their religion as distinct from Hinduism and transmit it to the second generation. A small minority community similar to the Indian Parsis but without co-believers from elsewhere, they often represent and transmit an Indian ethnic identity, and members of the second generation may be marrying non-Jains far more than in India. The Jains are a predominantly lay community in the United States, one which uses its considerable resources to build temples that serve cultural as well as religious purposes.

The religious landscape has changed from earlier decades, when immigrants from any one background were fewer and Indians of all religious backgrounds participated in nation-based meetings and associations. In the case of the so-called Mexican Hindus in California, Sikh, Muslim, or Hindu traditions may not have been transmitted in much detail, but there was recognition of and respect for religious differences. The many post-1965 Indian immigrants bring numerous, very specialized religious traditions, but the diversity is confusing to the second generation. In India, a whole range of societal beliefs and practices is readily observable and provides a rich context for religious and cultural learning. Children can see how religions function in extended families, in subcastes and castes, in neighborhoods and cities, and how religions are implicated in social practices, economic systems, and political movements. Children of Indian descent in America are growing up with less knowledge and less tolerance of the religious commonalities and differences in the homeland, and the simplification and standardization of these many strands into just a few major religious categories is taking place not only in an American context but in a politically charged global context.

Language Issues

Indian Americans, while often multilingual (especially the first-generation immigrants), most often qualified for post-1965 immigration because of professional skills, so English is a language in which they are comfortable. Indeed, they are often outstanding (notice the many Indian American youth winning spelling bees), and they are contributing much to the growing field of Asian American and general immigration literature.

National/Regional Language Press and Other Media

Reflecting the competence of Indian immigrants in English, almost all of the Indian American ethnic press is in English and it is growing, with new journals and magazines attempting to capture the second-generation readership. *India-West, India Abroad, India Journal,* and others cover news from India and regional events of interest to Indian Americans. *India Currents,* started in 1987 and based in San Francisco, specializes in cultural events and has won many media awards over the years. *India-West* started a glossy popular magazine aimed at younger Indian Americans, *India Life and Style,* in 2004 and shifted it from a print to an online publication in spring of 2007. The 2001 feature film *American Desi* (about American-born confused *desis,* or countrymen [ABCDs]) and other such films cater to the young Indian American crowd. Events like a Masala Cruise from Los Angeles to Ensenada,

Mexico, featuring Indian cuisine, Dandia (Gujarati folk dance) on the Deck, Bhangra (Punjabi folk dance) by the Sea, Bollywood Fever Show, and so on, attract members of the second generation with full-page color ads in the ethnic press.

Celebration of National Holidays

Celebrations mark India's Independence Day, August 15, and Republic Day, January 26; other festivals and cultural performances based on the Indian national holiday calendar occur throughout the year in most U.S. cities. Their timings are sometimes adjusted to coincide with American holidays.

Foodways

Indian women are the front line in families' changing food habits, and their ideas about food and Indian ethnic identity emerge in many arenas. Indian women who manage ethnic grocery stores serve as cultural consultants for other immigrants and also for non-South Asian shoppers; they help diverse customers to formulate ideas about what is Indian or South Asian food, and they provide many other goods and services including cookbooks along with the foodstuffs, audio and video cassettes, clothing, and even supplies for religious rituals. They stock ready-made and fast foods for other South Asian working wives and for the many students who have no time or ability to prepare meals for themselves. Typically, snacks and sweets from several regional cuisines are sold side-by-side, the variety surpassing that available in almost any city in India itself. Just as it was for the early immigrants, food is at the core of identity construction for the new immigrants as well, and the domain of food and its preparation is strongly gendered. The Hispanic wives of the Punjabi pioneers had learned to prepare some Punjabi dishes, a task central to their "Hindu" identity. Two restaurants run by Punjabi Mexican sons from the Imperial Valley, El Ranchero in Yuba City and Pancho's in Selma, feature chicken curry and *roti* in addition to full Mexican menus. More recent immigrant women from India shape ideas about the homeland as they prepare meals at home, patronize restaurants, and play hostess to guests from all over the world. They adjust recipes and menus and must also cater to their own children, who typically adopt a taste for more American foods than do their parents. (Thus mothers are charged both with enculturation of their children in Indian ways and with catering to their changing, Americanized tastes.) Indian couples and families have begun to dine out, too, often in South Asian restaurants that had been patronized primarily by non-South Asians and that are now adapting themselves to broader clienteles.

There is a growing market for Indian restaurant food among both Americans and South Asian immigrants. Some Indian restaurants aim for affluent customers, but others are moderately priced, and many have gone into the catering business. Large

El Ranchero Restaurant in Yuba City, California, owned by Ali Rasul, who was born in the Imperial Valley. (Photo by Karen Leonard)

upscale hotels sometimes seek convention and wedding business by advertising that they can offer Indian food. Tandoori and Mughlai cuisine is most common, but a few South Indian and vegetarian restaurants are springing up. Transnationalism shows up in the restaurant trade too, as great restaurant chains from India come to United States. This might happen because of an owner's migration. For example, Kapal Dev Kapoor, the man who founded Delhi's Embassy restaurant in 1948 and began the first automated ice cream plant in India in 1957 (Kwality ice cream), came to Los Angeles in 1977 and introduced excellent Mughlai and *tandoori* cuisine to Southern California by taking over the Akbar restaurant in Marina del Rey. Dasaprakash, a South Indian vegetarian restaurant chain in India, has a branch in California that helps set the standard for such food in the United States.

Music, Arts, and Entertainment

The availability of Indian culture in the United States has increased dramatically, providing many resources for the construction of immigrant identities and strongly influencing the host society as well. In earlier decades, "Hindu" recreational activities were few: visits with other Punjabi-fathered families, going to the Stockton *gurdwara* and to wrestling matches and political speeches. The pioneer Punjabi farmers had to persuade Indian students from colleges in nearby cities to come out and give amateur performances in the small farm towns of California and Arizona

Indian Weddings

An Indian wedding economy has developed in the last two decades in North America. *Pandits*, *moulvis*, *granthis*, and priests are available to perform the various ceremonies throughout the United States. The strictly religious ceremonies themselves usually last one or two hours but are preceded and followed by other rituals and festivities. Despite astrological forecasts in some cases, for convenience they are increasingly scheduled on weekends just prior to a noon or evening meal. Some performers of marriages now use English-language texts, complete with explanations of text and rituals, while others reproduce the ceremonies of the homeland as closely as possible.

(Courtesy of Neha Vora)

Providers of goods and services for Indian weddings are springing up all over America, even offering horses or elephants for the bridegroom's procession. An Indo-Pak Bridal Expo is held regularly in Buena Park, California. Like the first one in 1989, billed as showing "everything needed for an authentic wedding," the expo is complete with fashion shows and the displays of more than 80 Indian and American mainstream vendors. Ads for horoscope-matching services ("Astro Scan USA"), wedding *puja* (Hindu worship) items, wedding catering, flower decorations, Indian-style disposable plates, wedding jewelry, and the like have joined other ads in the pages of the ethnic newspapers.

in the 1950s, putting the students up in their own homes. Hindi movies from India began to be screened soon after 1965, in movie theaters central to new South Asian immigrants, but with the coming of VCRs around 1980 the moviegoers retreated to home settings. Now, the new Indian immigrants sponsor and attend cultural performances and other popular recreational activities that are almost as accessible as back in the homeland, and there are many "fusion" or crossover arts and activities.

All over the United States Indian organizations sponsor concerts by local and visiting artists. These are sponsored by established organizations or by private entrepreneurs, like ethnic grocery store owners or other businessmen. Events are advertised in the South Asian ethnic newspapers and by flyers distributed in grocery stores and religious centers. The mainstream press may also give advance notice and review the performance when a really big name performer comes to town. Depending upon the sponsor and audience, these performances may run on "Indian" time, meaning that they start late (and later than scheduled) and continue far into the night, or they may be more attuned to American timings, starting when scheduled and ending at a "sensible" hour.

Indian classical music and dance play major roles in winning a place for Indian culture in the North American scene: Indian dance academies offer classical Bharatnatyam and regional folk dances like Punjabi *bhangra* and Gujarati *garba raas* or *dandiya*, along with dances from Hindi films and "hip-hop bhangra." Ali Akbar Khan (d. 2009), master of the *sarod,* founded the Ali Akbar College of Music, which became a northern California Bay Area institution. Claiming descent from the lineage founded by Tansen, the renowned court musician of the Mughal emperor, Ali Akbar Khan taught many Euro-American students, as do other permanently settled Indian artists providing instruction in Indian music and dance all over the United States. The master sitarist Ravi Shankar settled down in Southern California; his daughter Anoushka has also become world famous as a sitarist, while her half-sister, Shankar's daughter Norah Jones, is a Grammy Award–winning singer and songwriter. For Ravi Shankar's 75th birthday in 1995, the Music Circle of Southern California sponsored an 11-hour concert in his honor, held in a Los Angeles college auditorium and featuring outstanding instrumentalists and vocalists. An Indian restaurant provided tea and food during the breaks, and the celebration drew a majority of non-South Asians.

While the American public may be somewhat more familiar with North Indian Mughlai music (Ravi Shankar on *sitar,* Ali Akbar Khan on *sarod,* and Zakir Hussain on *tabla*) than the Carnatic or South Indian music, both vocal and instrumental Carnatic music is developing equally well in the United States. Cleveland, Ohio, hosts an annual Easter weekend of Carnatic music, which is the biggest assemblage of Carnatic musicians outside of India. This is the Thyagaraja festival, celebrating the great composer of the 18th century. Begun in 1977 by a small group in a church basement, the festival has grown to a four-day event with an audience of over 3,000, and it is now officially recognized by the state of Ohio. In other centers of Carnatic music activity, great teaching and performing lineages from India are continuing in the United States, and young Indian American Carnatic vocalists and instrumentalists can trace their ancestries back to famous disciples of Thyagaraja in India; some of them now tour in India.

It is the South Indian *bharatnatyam* dance that has become best known in the United States. Originally practiced in South India by girls given to temples for dancing and perhaps for prostitution, *bharatnatyam* has become highly respected and is still strongly connected to Carnatic music and devotional Hindu themes. Among the outstanding schools established in the United States is the Kalanjali school run by K.P. Kunhiraman, from the Kalakshetra dance school in Madras, and his American wife Katherine, from the Bharata Kalanjali school in Madras; they began their Berkeley dance school in 1975 and have several branches. At the Padmini Institute of Fine Arts in New Jersey, Padmini, a former Indian movie star, teaches students *bharatnatyam,* also at several locations. American museums and funding agencies have become sources of support for Indian classical dance.

For those Indian American daughters who study Indian classical dance with female professional teachers in the United States, the controlled sexuality and formal beauty of the performances convey new meanings in America. *Bharatnatyam* performance has been analyzed as "a marker of ethnic and feminine identity," an opportunity for lavish public display of eligible daughters in an Indian cultural, even spiritual, setting. Not only Indian Americans looking for roots in the United States, but Euro-Americans, other Asian Americans, and Hispanic Americans, South Asian Christians, and Muslims as well as Hindus, now study classical Indian dance. In one *arangetran* (debut) of two Muslim girls, sisters from Pakistan, the opening and closing numbers were *qawwalis,* Sufi devotional songs made famous by Pakistan's Nusrat Fateh Ali Khan and choreographed by the *bharatnatyam* teacher for her students. Dance traditions from North India also are taught in the United States, including not only the *kathak* dance, patronized by the Mughals, but also the slightly less respectable *mujra* dance, associated with courtesans and old-style weddings of the Indo-Muslim nobility.

Not only classical and courtly art forms but folk ones and especially Hindi film dances are being taught in the United States. On this more popular level, cultural performances typical of Indian celebrations and festivals feature teenage Indian American girls dancing in public in alluring costumes. The Hindi film dances are erotic and provocative. Indian American girls do not simply reproduce the film dances as they see them on video but reinterpret them, competing with other daughters of the community. Acceptable displays of adolescent beauty and skill in a coeducational setting, these dances performances meet with parental approval because they are Indian, "ethnic," and "traditional." Exuberant popular folk dances, especially Punjabi and Gujarati ones, similarly evidence an expanded public role for young Indian American women in community events. Second-generation Punjabi girls are performing the *bhangra,* the more flamboyant male form of Punjabi dance, rather than the tamer *giddha* traditionally danced by women in the Punjab. At the Gujarati festival programs, youngsters dance the *garba raas* in colorful costumes.

Music and dance performances may dominate the Indian American cultural scene, but *mushairas,* evenings of Urdu poetry that typically feature both local and visiting international poets, and vernacular language theater performances are also popular. An excellent command of the language is needed to appreciate these compositions, and many associations sponsor *mushairas,* some of them branches of Indian, Pakistani, or international associations, such as Bazm-i-Urdu, Aiwan-i-Urdu, or Urdu Markaz International. These poetry societies bring together not only Indians and Pakistanis but also Afghans, Bangladeshis, and others who may speak and appreciate Urdu. Indian language theater is barely visible in the United States, but Gujaratis are a large enough group to support local and transnational productions; some Gujarati directors and playwrights shift back and forth between Bombay, California, London, and New York.

Indian Americans pioneering in many arenas draw upon their cultural heritage. Their training and their specific knowledge and cultural references may be originally Indian but they use these things in new ways and for American or international audiences. The pioneer movie stars Kabir Bedi and Persis Khambatta acted in both Hollywood and Bollywood (Bombay) films, and Kavi Raj acted regularly in TV's *St. Elsewhere.* Parminder Nagra, London-reared star of *Bend It Like Beckham,* joined the regular cast of *ER.* Kal Pen, who starred in two *Harold and Kumar* films and the TV show *House,* took a job with President Obama, joining his administration's Office of Public Liaison in 2009. There are many artists, mostly painters and mostly in New York, of Indian origin, and a well-known curator and scholar of Indian art (Pratapaditya Pal at the Los Angeles County Museum of Art). There are world-famous cultural figures from India whom Americans want to claim, people who did or do maintain residences, travel, and work in the United States very frequently: Zubin Mehta and his father Mehli Mehta, conductors originally from Bombay; Ismail Merchant, the independent filmmaker, also from Bombay; Shabana Azmi, Indian actress and political activist; Ravi Shankar, sitar virtuoso; and Salman Rushdie, the noted author born in Bombay now resident of New York.

Many younger Indian immigrants and members of the second generation are highlighting their bicultural heritages as they move into mainstream American culture. There are those in the entertainment and media industries, older filmmakers like Amin Chaudhri, Krishna Shah, Ashok Amrit Raj, and Jagmohan Mundhra, and younger ones like Mira Nair, M. Night Shyamalan, Radha Bharadwaj, and Deepa Mehta whose films are being distributed by major Hollywood studios. Less-established directors of Indian ancestry are showing in film festivals and museum series. There are news reporters and anchors, the best example in the early 20th century being Fareed Zakaria from Bombay, editor of *Newsweek International,* host of a weekly hour-long TV program on foreign affairs, and author of a best-selling book, *The Post-American World.* Doctors Deepak Chopra and Sanjay Gupta appear frequently as TV guests and commentators. On the lighter side, the Indian grocer Apu is one regular animated character on the cartoon *The Simpsons,* and the actor/writer Aasif Mandvi appears regularly on Jon Stewart's *Daily Show.* These media figures come from very different backgrounds, but all are working with bicultural perspectives in one way or another.

Indian American authors are highlighting cultural and multicultural themes. The list is long and includes many award winners and book club nominees. Names like Meena Alexander, Agha Shahid Ali, Chitra Banerjee Divakaruni, Amitav Ghosh, Minal Hajratwala, Jhumpa Lahiri, Gita Mehta, Ved Mehta, Bharati Mukherjee, A. K. Ramanujan, Raja Rao, and Vikram Seth are widely known. With solid careers as doctors, Atul Gawande and Abraham Verghese have also distinguished themselves as authors. Sexuality is a major theme in a powerful new writings by predominantly young women of Indian descent in America, not only heterosexual feelings and activities but lesbian ones as well.

Genuinely new hybrid or fusion cultural productions abound, especially in the domains of music and food, where new combinations of instruments, rhythms, ingredients, and methods lead to innovative sounds or tastes, where there is a self-conscious combination of cultural elements from different traditions. Often the fusion producers are second-generation Indian immigrants, but not always—they can be first-generation immigrants, or they can be American business people. Dance, music, food, and restaurants are the big areas for fusion. Some Indian dance academies offer more classes on regional folk dances and dances from popular Hindi movies than on classical *bharatnatyam* and blend the styles in choreographed performances. Indian dance is also crossing over and inspiring American dance leaders, lending its instrumental music, its vocals, and its costumes.

At the "high culture" end, examples of fusion music in the United States include Carnatic violin virtuosos L. Subramaniam and L. Shankar playing with Western musicians, or *ragas* (North Indian instrumental music) and *ghazals* (Urdu love songs, poems) combining Western instruments, for example the saxophone, and voice. These experiments and interactions are often truly transnational and not just American, and they include such striking examples as Pakistan's *qawwali* singer Nusrat Fateh Ali Khan doing the sound track on the Hollywood film *Dead Man Walking*. Among the younger "popular culture" crowd, and taking the lead from the Punjabi British hit singer Apache Indian, it is *bhangra* rock or reggae that rules: it is a loud, vibrant dance music combining Punjabi peasant stock with Caribbean reggae, British rock, and black American rap. Dance parties throb to this music, now adding elements of hip-hop, chutney, and jungle. Weddings are occasions where music and dance frequently mix cultures: if the wedding guests include Punjabis, they may insist on dancing the boisterous *bhangra* at even the most dignified of Indian weddings. For that matter, American rock music is being played at more and more Indian weddings, as the young people demand it.

The United States has become a major market for producers of Indian clothing in India. Exhibitions and sales of Indian women's and men's clothing are held in hotels or private homes, and the styles available in Little India shopping centers around the United States often come straight from Bombay or Delhi. Famous boutiques from India's biggest cities send annual displays to American centers of the Indian diaspora like Los Angeles, Austin, Dallas, Chicago, New York, and

Indianapolis. Stores from India are even opening outlets in the United States to sell saris and the *salwar-kameez* outfits originally typical of the Punjab.

Fusion cuisine is another new trend, being pioneered in New York. *Chutney Mary* in Manhattan mixed *desi* flavors with Mexican, Italian, and Thai cuisine; Floyd Cardoz, chef at Tabla, infuses haute cuisine with flavors from Goa, his family's home state. Vegetarian burritos, tacos, quesadillas, and nachos are natural candidates for crossover cuisine as well. In Indian restaurants, the trend is to use less oil and fewer spices, and there is a spate of Indian cookbooks tailored to American tastes, including popular ones by Ismail Merchant, Bharti Kirchner, Julie Sahni, Yamuni Devi, and Madhur Jaffrey. Padma Lakshmi not only wrote a cookbook but is the TV host of *Top Chef.* Indian restaurants offer amazing combinations of food, cultural performances, and ambience. (These kinds of changes are occurring back in India too, but with American clientele a major factor in the United States, the changes are faster and more attuned to non-Indian tastes.) Advertisements in the ethnic press tout Chinese Islamic and Thai Islamic restaurants, where all meats are *halal.* There are also *halal* Mexican restaurants and an Indian restaurant featuring Hindi karaoke. The *Westin Bonaventure,* perhaps Los Angeles' most prestigious hotel, offers banquet facilities with Indian cuisine, that is, full-service catering by two of the finest local Pakistani and Indian restaurants.

A miscellaneous set of enthusiasms and practices reflects the mixing of different cultural traditions, if not true fusion. This would include things like yoga and Ayurvedic medicine, now attractive and available options for recreation and health. Then there are the Indian entrants to beauty pageants and Miss India beauty pageants, well captured in a 1997 film, *Miss India Georgia.* Here the "showcasing of daughters" analysis applied to *bharatnatyam* seems relevant, and the prize monies can be used for higher education (for medical school, perhaps).

Integration and Impact on U.S. Society and Culture

Paths toward Citizenship

Naturalization

Taking U.S. citizenship is one way of dealing with the complex and changing U.S. immigration law and regulations, but at first many post-1965 migrants planned to take their expertise back to the home countries, having promised their parents they would return. Practical reasons for retaining Indian citizenship had to do with the holding of property and bank accounts in India and the nonnecessity of getting visas to visit there. About half of those migrating from India from 1977 to 1991 became naturalized U.S. citizens, although they had to give up their Indian citizenship to do so then. The 2000 Census showed 37.7 percent of Indian immigrants as naturalized citizens, slightly lower than previously because over 50 percent had come only since 1990. In the Census Bureau's American Community Survey of 2007, 44.4 percent of those born in India had been naturalized, lower than for Vietnamese, Filipino, and Chinese immigrants (74%, 64%, and 58% respectively); the lower rate is no doubt explained by the impossibility, still, of dual citizenship and the very recent arrival of more than half of the immigrant population.

Indian families are now strongly rooted in the United States, and the first generation realizes that it will not be easy to take the children "back home." Many immigrants have finally told their parents they will not be returning and are instead bringing their parents to the United States, at least for the annual visits required to maintain their status as permanent residents. And as more and more immigrants bring their siblings and other relatives, whole families are shifting permanently to the United States, so there is less reason to return to India. Citizenship status expedites family reunification, since citizens are preferred over permanent residents when it comes to bringing relatives. There are also federal estate tax benefits for citizens with respect to foreign estate taxes and marital deductions. Finally, citizens are in a much stronger position than noncitizens to challenge existing laws and practices, mobilize public opinion, and initiate new laws, and, of course, to influence U.S. policies towards the homeland.

Dual Citizenship

Indian Americans, termed NRIs or non-resident Indians by India, continually pressured India to change its policy and allow dual citizenship (Pakistan allowed it), but India's leaders initially encouraged its NRIs to become American citizens and work for themselves and India through the U.S. political system. India finally developed an overseas citizen of India (OCI) category, close to dual citizenship, in 2003.

Forging a New American Political Identity

Political Associations and Organizations

Participation in American political life was a goal for the early Asian Indian immigrants and has become one for the newcomers. Political mobilization began with militant anti-British Ghadar party the early Punjabi immigrants formed in California in 1913, but this effort was very short-lived, ended by internal conflicts based on regional origins in the Punjab and U.S. government persecution. Instead, Punjabi farmers focused their strongest and most sustained political efforts on gaining access to American citizenship, working with other Indians across the United States in a lobbying campaign that succeeded in 1946 with the passage of the Luce Celler Bill. Many old-timers became citizens then and helped elect Dalip Singh Saund from California's Imperial Valley in 1956, the first congressman from India. They also supported Indian nationalist leaders who visited California to raise money for the Congress party in the 1940s, but most Punjabis in California were taken by surprise by the partition of British India in 1947 into India and Pakistan.

Other political mobilization was based in early decades on issues like crimes against Indians, discrimination against Indians in higher education and business, and problems with municipal regulations of various sorts. Indian merchants fought to achieve "minority" business preference status and many fight now to name a business area "Little India." Indian American organizations show a progression over time from the individual-level adaptations made by the first migrants to early organizations based on national origin (India, Pakistan) or ecumenical religious categories (incorporating Indians into various Christian churches or Muslim mosques).

Civic and Electoral Participation

After Dalip Singh Saund's 1956 election to Congress, decades passed before the post-1965 immigrants mobilized for electoral participation. Among the national-level organizations based on Indian ancestry, the four leading ones were the Association of Indians in America, the National Federation of Indian Associations (NFIA), the Indian American Forum for Political Education (IAFPE), and the National Association of Americans of Indian Descent. These competing national federations reflected not only rivalry among leaders but uncertainty over the best term for the community—Asian Indian is the census term, while Indian American and Indo-American are the other leading contenders. However, in 2001, four major organizations did form the umbrella Indian American National Foundation (IANF). The four were the NFIA, the IAFPE, the American Association of Physicians of Indian Origin (AAPI), and the Asian American Hotel Owners Association (AAHOA). The chair position was to rotate among the four groups while the new umbrella organization focused its efforts on both the U.S. Congress and the Indian Embassy. This effort has not been successful: the AAHOA withdrew and the NFIA suffers from internal conflict, one faction suing the other from time to time.

Indian Americans are active in both Democratic and Republican party political funding and campaigning. In 2004, Bobby Jindal, a Republican and a Catholic (since his high school conversion) of Indian descent, won a congressional seat from Louisiana's first district (becoming the second congressman from India). In 2007, Jindal was elected governor of Louisiana, the first Indian American governor and the youngest governor at that time. Others of Indian descent have been winning seats in state legislatures and becoming the "first Indian American" to hold particular positions. Examples include Kalpana Chawla, astronaut, member of NASA space rocket crew in 1997; Anuradha Bhagwati, daughter of economists Jagdish Bhagwati and Padma Desai, who became a U.S. Marine officer in 2000; and Kamala Harris, of mixed Asian Indian and African American descent, elected San Francisco's first female district attorney in 2003 (and the first DA in the United States of South Asian descent; she was reelected in 2007).

Louisiana congressional candidate Bobby Jindal (left) talks with a constituent at Dot's Diner in Jefferson, Louisiana, October 18, 2004. Jindal, a Republican, later became governor of Louisiana. He is the son of immigrants from India. (AP Photo/Bill Haber)

Public Policies and Political Representation

Indian Americans have led in the formation of international associations, with Global Organization of Peoples of Indian Origin (GOPIO) being the best known. Formed in 1989 in New York and with numerous chapters around the world, it puts out a monthly newsletter and holds annual conventions in India. GOPIO works closely with the government of India. Pressure from GOPIO helped spur the Indian government to set up a separate Ministry for Overseas Indian Affairs for NRIs. A major purpose of that ministry was to facilitate investments in India by overseas Indians. GOPIO also pushed for a persons of Indian origin (PIO) card, a card made available in 1999 that provided PIOs like NRIs exemption from visa requirements and other economic and educational benefits. Most notably, GOPIO pushed for dual citizenship and came close to achieving that with the OCI category in 2003.

In the late 20th century, Indian American businessmen, leaders in innovative enterprises, rose above local and regional interests to build a powerful economic network with international political potential. Indian businessmen in the United States founded the Indus Entrepreneurs (TiE) in the Silicon Valley in 1992, a South Asian organization that expanded rapidly and has chapters in 12 countries. These successful entrepreneurs, corporate executives, and senior professionals number more than 11,000 and work to foster entrepreneurship globally through mentoring, networking, and education. TiE hosts many events, and best known is its annual

TiEcon, the largest professional and networking conference for entrepreneurs. It has branches for women and youth and, notably, works across political boundaries in South Asia. Its charter members are 17 transnational Indian businessmen and innovators, including, based in the United States, Arun Sarin of Airtouch, Vodafone, and Verizon Wireless; C. K. Prahalad, professor of business at the Ross School, University of Michigan, and author of books on corporate strategy; Kanwal Rekhi of Excelan/Novell, Inventus Capital Partners, and CyberMedia; Victor Menezes of Citicorp and New Silk Route Partners; and Vinod Khosla of Sun Microsystems and Khosla Ventures.

Political issues continue to focus on race, class, gender, and generational issues in the United States. Leftist or liberal Indian American activists invoke African American and immigrant Indian history to argue eloquently against conservative religious and racist forces among the post-1965 immigrants and attack Asian American "model minority" status as a false stereotype that conceals sharp class differences among Indian Americans. Young Indian Americans, most of them members of the second generation, have worked for gay and lesbian rights. Urvashi Vaid, who came to the United States as a girl in the 1960s, became a lawyer, writer, and executive director of the National Gay and Lesbian Task Force from the late 1980s to 1991, the first woman of color and first Indian American in the position. Parvez Sharma, based in New York, filmed *A Jihad for Love* in 12 countries, focusing on the lives of gay and lesbian Muslims struggling to reconcile their sexual orientation with their faith. SATRANG (in California) formed in 1997 to serve the South Asian lesbian, bisexual, gay, transgender, intersex, queer, and questioning (LBGTIQ) people. It has gained support from more general community organizations like the South Asian Network (SAN) in Southern California to commemorate the annual National Coming Out Day, and the two organizations produced the first-ever South Asian LBGTIQ Needs Assessment report in 2007. The decision by Delhi's High Court in India in July 2009 to decriminalize homosexuality was welcomed in America by such groups (although the decision is only the first step, as other jurisdictions in India must also repeal portions of the Indian Penal Code that treat consensual gay sex between adults as a crime).

Coalition-building with other groups, such as Asian Americans and/or Muslim Americans, is a promising political strategy. Among Asian Americans, Indians or rather South Asians have moved from being the fourth-largest group, after the Chinese, Filipinos, and Southeast Asians, to third largest, overtaking the Southeast Asians. The South Asian group includes immigrants from India, Pakistan, Bangladesh, Sri Lanka, Nepal, Bhutan, the Maldive Islands, Afghanistan, and even Indian-origin people from Fiji and the West Indies. Also drawing on a very broad membership are the Islamic or Muslim coalitions. Islam either already is or will soon be the second-largest religious group in the United States, and Indian Muslims are among the intellectual and political leaders of Muslim Americans.

After September 11, 2001, Indians (and South Asians) of all religions have found much of the American public unable to distinguish among them. Turban-wearing Sikhs have been singled out as possible terrorists, and they have mobilized, separately as well as with various Muslim groups, to fight media scapegoating, harassment, and attacks based on a generalized fear of terrorism. National Sikh organizations like Sikh Mediawatch and Resource Task Force (SMART), founded in Washington, D.C., in 1996, focus on old issues (issues like wearing the *kirpan* or the turban in various situations continue to crop up) and new 9/11–related issues. A New York-based national coalition, United Sikhs, formed in 1999, has also taken on political issues affecting Sikhs in the United States and internationally.

Religious issues have become more important in the 21st century. Hindu groups mobilize to protest products or events that seem disrespectful of their religion, such as a Sony PlayStation video game called *Hanuman: Boy Warrior,* pictures of Hindu gods and goddesses on the inside of toilet seat covers, or the use of Hindu chants and symbols in performances and CDs by pop artists like Madonna. A Hindu Students Council formed in 1990 and has a network of chapters on campuses across America, presenting events and talks on Hinduism (they include Jainism and Buddhism within Hinduism). Muslim student unions on many campuses include Indian Muslims, and these groups present informative programs and particularly ones combating negative stereotypes. Writing and teaching in North America about Sikhism has also come under scrutiny, not so much by students as by self-proclaimed orthodox Sikhs based in North America. Their challenges have been particularly sharp to young Sikh scholars placed in North American universities, scholars who, in the view of the nonscholar believers, are falsely alleging that the Sikh religion has changed over time in various ways. Scholars teaching Hinduism and Islam on campuses have also come under attack, especially if they are not Hindu or Muslim by birth or belief, and sometimes if they are not "orthodox enough" Hindus or Muslims.

Indian Americans want their culture and heritage taught in America's higher educational institutions. South Asian studies have long been offered at many top universities, and research in India has been promoted by the American Institute of Indian Studies (AIIS) based at the University of Chicago. The institute was established in 1961 by a group of American scholars involved in programs of Indian studies at leading American universities. Wealthy Indian Americans have begun endowing chairs for scholars of India at American universities: chairs have been established so far for Indian studies generally, Indian history, Tamil studies, and Bengali studies. Chairs for the study of a religion have been more controversial, particularly in the case of Sikh studies. These chairs usually involve a matching contribution from the university, and agreements between the relevant community and the university are carefully negotiated.

Return Migration

In the early 21st century, Indian immigrants have begun to return to India, and this represents an economic loss for the United States. While some NRIs responded to India's 1991 economic liberalization by returning to India, reportedly they often returned to the United States in frustration. But in the early 21st century, returnees are finding living conditions in India much improved. A study found that as many as 100,000 Indians will return to India in the next three to five years, moves that will boost India's economy and undermine technological innovations in America. Even on the marriage market, where Indian men living in the United States at the end of the 20th century were very popular bridegroom choices by the families of young women in India, the tide is turning as parents in India fear the effects of the recession. India's economy is also slowing down, but the situation there is not so bad as in the United States in 2009–2010, and parents and prospective brides both see better opportunities and more livable situations if bridegrooms live in India.

Some older immigrants, concerned that their children will "lose" their culture and perhaps feeling that they themselves cannot ever be more than second-class citizens of the United States, are returning to India upon retirement. Complexes are being built in India for returning senior citizens, and Social Security payments can be sent to India after 10 years of employment. Their return presents a considerable problem to their children who were born or brought up largely in America. Again parents and children may be living on different continents, but travel is faster and perhaps more affordable in the 21st century than it once was.

The Second and Later Generations

Many conference sessions, public talks, and private conversations are devoted to worrying about the children of Indian descent being raised in the United States. Parental ambitions are high with respect to the economic success of their offspring: children are encouraged to undertake higher education and professional training, particularly in medicine and engineering. Parents also stress the retention of the culture from home rather than the adoption of American culture. This places the children in a difficult position, since they are inevitably products of their American cultural context and are comfortable in that context in ways that their parents are not. When I asked a grandmother in Hyderabad, India, if her grandchildren in Texas were in any way Hyderabadi, she replied despairingly, "Hyderabadi? They're not even Indian," and then cried as she told how her granddaughter asked her to wear some other clothing, not a sari, when accompanying her to school.

Neha Vora, Anthropologist

Neha Vora, whose parents migrated to the United States from India in 1970, was born and raised in suburban New Jersey, where she enjoyed a vibrant Indian cultural life among the Gujarati community of the tristate area but also faced prejudice from schoolmates and teachers in her mostly Caucasian hometown. Always interested in bridging her personal experiences as a South Asian American with her academic pursuits, she researched her South Asian peers in college at Wesleyan University and went on to earn a MA in women's studies from San Francisco State University, where she studied the dynamics of gender and ethnicity among Bay Area South Asian communities. As a PhD student in anthropology at UC Irvine, she conducted fieldwork among the large Indian migrant community in Dubai. Her work at every stage has centered on the dynamics of belonging and exclusion among South Asian migrant communities. She is currently an assistant professor of anthropology and women's studies at Texas A&M University and continues to work on South Asian diasporas in the Middle East. In 2003, Neha married a Korean American software developer in a mixed Indian and Korean ceremony in her New Jersey hometown. She is currently working on her book manuscript and enjoying living among the large Indian community of the greater Houston area.

Ethnic Identity

The experience of growing up in America has not been a uniform one because so much depends upon the local demographic mix and the specific context. Some youngsters of Indian descent go through a cycle of early identification with American culture and then, later, identification with Indian culture, and even after they become more interested in their heritage, these young people do not necessarily see themselves as part of a larger community of Indian Americans. Others remain closely tied to their parents' ethnic or religious communities and aspire to maintain close relationships with those communities as adults. But, Gauri Bhat asserted (1992), what young Indo-Americans had in common was their parents: "parents who are overinvolved, overworried, overprotective. Parents who have an opinion on every minor life decision, who make demands, impose guilt, withhold approval. . . . As children of immigrants, the promise we fulfill is our parents' own promise, long-deferred and transmuted now into the stuff of American dreams (and nightmares). So we must become respectable, make money, buy a house, bear children. . . . My parents' love supports me and enfolds me, but sometimes also weighs me down" (1–6).

Educational Attainment

Statistical data is lacking but the impression that young Indian Americans are doing very well is overwhelming. They are a force in Asian American organizations and activities, overtaking representatives of groups that arrived earlier from more diverse class backgrounds. While parental pressure pushes youth toward careers as doctors, engineers, or professors, young Indian Americans are choosing to enter a wide range of careers. A South Asian Bar Association has many chapters nationwide, and young Indian Americans are moving conspicuously into the creative and performing arts.

Cultural Identification

The second generation's difference, its participation in American culture in all its contemporary diversity and intensity, is borne out in many ways. In campus youth conferences, discussion topics always include interracial marriage, South Asian coalition-building, hip-hop culture, homosexuality, premarital sex, and violence against women, as well as identity formation, discrimination in corporate America, and racism. Young Indian Americans, be they working class, middle class, or upper class, are forging confident new identities in communities across America.

Members of the first generation of post-1965 immigrants, however, may perceive a "youth problem." This concern often stems from religious leaders and organizations, both Hindu and Muslim, and it is ostensibly about the continuity of family, caste, and community religious traditions. Just as clearly, it is about sexuality and marriage, in particular about parental arrangement of marriages and parental control of family life. Indian American parents often oppose dating on the grounds that it inevitably leads to having sex or to date rape; this view prevailed in a survey of post-1965 Indian immigrants carried out in 1990. It is the young women of Indian background, not the young men, who are of most concern because it is their behavior that can damage a family's or community's reputation through pregnancy or an undesirable marriage. The strategy of nondisclosure, not telling one's parents about the significant choices one is making in life, is common. Priya Agarwal's 1991 book about the second generation, *Passage from India: Post 1965 Indian Immigrants and Their Children,* highlighted poor communication between parents and children, and more than half the young people in her survey preferred to date without telling their parents.

Gender and generational differences become magnified when it comes to that very important life event, marriage. Because of parental opposition to dating and "love-marriages," the children of the immigrants are usually put into an either/or situation. They must trust their parents to arrange their marriages or they must trust themselves. The stakes are high, for one knows of many marriages made by Indian parents for their children that have not worked out. Divorce is now a distinct possibility, and the frequently transglobal marriage and family networks add international legal complications to the emotional costs of divorce for Indian Americans.

Most members of the second generation in the United States seem to be entering arranged or semi-arranged marriages. Although they increasingly have a say about the choice of spouse and even about the actual wedding arrangements, marriages continue to be at least partially arranged by family elders. Arrangements made by parents can bridge national boundaries to continue family, caste, or religious preferences. Adherents of all religions place matrimonial advertisements in ethnic newspapers, usually specifying or indirectly indicating preferences for caste, sect, and regional origin. Sometimes endogamy (marriage within) is redefined, by occupation (there are many couples where both man and wife are doctors) or "ethnicity" (this may simply mean nationality, as in Indian or Pakistani, or language, as in Punjabi- or Gujarati-speakers). Preferences for particular professions or for possession of a green card or U.S. citizenship are frequently included. Characteristically, parents or older siblings place these ads, although men and especially divorced or widowed men place their own ads, and an exchange of information and photographs follows. Matrimonial services are springing up within the United States, and on the Internet. These arranged or semi-arranged marriages still tend to emphasize the parents' interests. In the worst cases, arranged marriages are strategies to assist individuals who want to migrate to the United States, but few families risk their children's happiness to that extent.

Perceptions of social distance and national difference concern those who manage the transnational marriage networks. People are quite conscious of the different contexts in which second-generation Indians abroad are being raised; they recognize that young people raised in America and young people raised in India will have different expectations, ones that pose risks to the marriage. Marriages between cousins (practiced primarily by Muslims), marriages essentially within family cultures, can overcome these differences, some say. Others stress that girls raised in India can adjust themselves, so the preference is to bring brides from India. But girls there worry about marrying boys raised in the United States, who may already have girlfriends, and young women in India know of friends who have married, migrated, and found themselves in second place. And Indians say that it is easier to make marriages between India and Great Britain than between India and the United States. Because the standard of life in England is lower and Indians are more segregated there, it is more like India, whereas in the United States the higher standard of life and greater integration with Americans means a wider gulf between the two ways of life. Also, the second generation in the United States is said to be Americanizing more rapidly than the second generation in Britain is becoming British, so marriages between India and Britain seemingly have a better chance of success.

The public and highly celebratory nature of Indian weddings helps reconcile young people to some degree of marriage arrangement. The ideal marriage is a large, lavish, and very public display of the two families and their resources, representing major parental investments. Often now young people get to meet the proposed spouse or spouses and exercise a veto power. If one does not go along with the choice of spouse made by one's parents, or if one marries against one's parents' wishes, there will be no wonderful wedding, no beautiful photo album, no four- or six-hour video—basically, no parental approval of or investment in the marriage, and that is something no one likes to forfeit. But, alternatively, the young people are quite aware of the problems that can arise after the arranged marriage has been carried out, after the money has been spent on dowry and wedding and honeymoon and house. They know that all marriages do not work out and they know that divorce is an option for them. If the child has trusted the parents and gone through with a recommended marriage, in exchange parents may now support the child, their love for a child triumphing over the lifelong commitment to a marriage however badly made, which was more traditional in South India.

Indian weddings illustrate the changing gender and generational balances of power in Indian American families and communities. Decisions are many and the financial costs are usually high. Hindu and Muslim weddings require several days and involve rituals and dinners at homes, public wedding halls, gardens, or hotels. Many types of traditional clothing, foods, decorations, flowers, and other paraphernalia are involved. The dowry can include not only clothing and jewelry but a house, a car, major home furnishings, and even a boy's continuing educational expenses. The guests may number from 300 to 1,300, some of them flown from India or other diasporic sites and put up in local hotels. Until quite recently, the preferred locations for marriages were back in Indian cities, partly because they were major sources of brides for the transnational marriage networks and partly because many, perhaps most, of one's relatives and friends still resided there. Weddings were also held in India because of the availability of the necessary supplies and the cheaper costs there, but the balance is now tipping towards holding weddings in the United States.

Weddings held in the United States do present some problems, particularly to communities that practice forms of gender segregation. The spatial arrangements in American hotels, community halls, or other hired meeting places where weddings are often held are not gendered. In the "function halls" of India or the outdoor tented pavilions of Pakistan, built-in *purdah* (seclusion of women) arrangements are typical. In the United States, *purdah* has to be enforced by those attending, and Indian immigrant men sometimes try to manage the space. Women had their own spaces and their own ceremonies in the set-ups in India, but they are making space for themselves at weddings in the West. At an Indian Muslim wedding in a Los Angeles hotel, men designated a rear section of the large room, a raised area with a railing around it, as the women's place to sit. However, the women were not satisfied to be so far from the platform where the *nikah* (the marriage ceremony, the signing of the contract) was to take place, and they immediately filtered down into the general seating area, taking over the very front rows. Later, as the wedding guests entered the banquet room on another floor, Mexican American waiters tried to seat all the women on one side of the room and all the men on the other, as they had been ordered to do. But one of the first parties to enter was led by a young wife brought up in the United States. She insisted upon sitting at a central table "as a family, family style," and this example was followed by many of the other guests. Thus, a member of the second generation successfully posed "family values" against gender segregation, suggesting a fruitful avenue for negotiation of traditions.

Many issues centered on the making and unmaking of marriages for and by members of the second generation of Indians in the United States remain to be worked out. The trend, however, is for Indian parents to listen and find a middle way, helping their children to meet others of similar backgrounds and encouraging them to talk to potential spouses at length about family issues before deciding to marry. Most parents are not ready to trust love marriages, seeing the high rate of divorce in the United States and attributing it to the way of making marriages, but they are ready to take the best elements from both systems, balancing attraction, sensibilities, and family guidance, to strengthen their families in the West.

Indian American young people are slowly but surely forging new identities for themselves and envisioning new kinds of marriages and families. Just one small but visible change began in the 1990s, signaled by a 1994 photograph in *India-West*: one looked directly into the eyes of a happy young bride seated next to her groom with a dazzling smile on her face. Before this, and back in India still, almost all brides, whether in person, on video, or in photo albums, look down modestly and often are covered with a veil of one sort or another. And the contrast found explicit and amusing confirmation in an account given by an Indian American of her trip to India for her Indian cousin's wedding.

> I had a blast like everyone else, except maybe the bride. . . . [who] wore a very distressed look throughout. . . . During the obligatory picture-taking sessions with the 700-plus guests, she did not look up or smile once. I had to bribe her with a 5-Star chocolate to smile when taking a picture with us. Afterwards, she whispered that I would get her in trouble. . . . Even though she was happy about the beginning of her new life, [she] had to act, at the least, modest. But wouldn't it be really neat if Indian women weren't made to feel they had to act in such a way and actually enjoy the most important day of their lives with some overt tranquility and merriment. . . . just like the bridegroom? (Singh 1995, 59)

Issues in Relations between the United States and India

Forecasts for the 21st Century

U.S.–Indian relations can be discussed at the national level, looking at foreign-relations issues, or at the level of Indian immigrants and their relations with their homeland. A significant development was the signing on August 1, 2008, of the Indo–U.S. civilian nuclear agreement, or the Indo–U.S. nuclear deal. Developed from a joint statement of President George W. Bush and Prime Minister Manmohan Singh in 2005, this bilateral accord on civil nuclear cooperation marks a high point in U.S.–Indian relations. India agreed to separate its civil and military nuclear facilities and place its civil facilities under International Atomic Energy Agency safeguards, while the United States agreed to work toward full civil nuclear cooperation with India. The deal required amendments to American law and agreements within India between civil and military authorities, and it had to pass the U.S. Congress and India's Parliament.

President Obama and Prime Minister Manmohan Singh have met and emphasized their shared values: democracy, pluralism, and the rule of law. In addition to implementation of the Indo-U.S. nuclear deal, the two countries are implementing a 10-year defense agreement calling for expanding bilateral security cooperation, and they have engaged in combined military exercises. Major U.S. arms sales to India are underway. The U.S. Congress has an India caucus that is the largest country-specific one, recognizing the importance of the Indian American community as constituents. The United States favors India-Pakistan peace talks and recognizes the continuing problem of Kashmir and cross-border terrorists. India and the United States are interested in economic partnerships; the United States views India as a lucrative market and site for foreign investment and thus favors increasing liberalization of India's economy. Interests in stopping the global warming process and the spread of HIV/AIDS also link the two countries. Even America's premier mainstream conservation organization, the Sierra Club, has begun forging working relationships with "Green Groups" in India, awarding amounts of about $41,000 each to Ecosphere Spiti in Himachal Pradesh and Barefoot College in Rajasthan in 2009.

Looking at Indian immigrants, it is clear that they are increasingly transnational in very real ways, ones that connect American interests to those of India at an individual level and in ways that produce incremental changes. For example, Indian doctors settled overseas are seeking permission to practice medicine in India. Licensing issues have prevented Indian doctors settled abroad (including those from the United Kingdom, where Indians constitute more than a third of all physicians) from working in India. Doctors from India have started or are trying to start health care projects in various Indian states, but despite memorandums of agreement, bureaucratic obstacles often have slowed or prevented the initiation of projects. The Overseas Indian Affairs Ministry is considering granting permission to overseas doctors to come back to India for short- or long-term practice. In a related development, chief executives and clinical leaders of nearly 75 percent of America's drug companies see the interests of U.S. and Indian biotech and pharmaceutical industries converging, as U.S. companies seek partnerships with Indian academics and industry leaders.

Charitable projects link Indian Americans to their homeland. The American Association of Physicians of Indian Origin established clinics in the 1990s in the Punjab, Maharashtra, Tamil Nadu, Karnataka, Gujarat, Orissa, Andhra Pradesh, and Uttar Pradesh. The Association of Indian Muslims of America (AIM) set up a polytechnic for Muslim women in Delhi in 1996, one of many such efforts linking Indian Muslim immigrants to their homeland; another major funder of Muslim projects is the Indian Muslim Relief Committee, a committee of the Islamic Society of North America. Other efforts are more narrowly based on "old boys" associations, like the MediCity project in Hyderabad initiated by the Osmania Medical Graduates Association.

In the early 21st century, the post-1965 immigrants from India are beginning to honor the experiences of the Punjabi pioneers and their Punjabi-Mexican families, experiences that emphasized the flexibility of ethnic identity and of culture. They and their families are participating in the construction of new and changing identities in the American and global arenas. Time and place are very important components here, as changes in the historical context have powerful consequences for individual, family, and community identity. The turnabouts in U.S. citizenship and immigration policies in the 1940s and 1960s had dramatic consequences for Punjabi Mexican family life in California. For the "old" immigrants, the possibilities opened up by the 1940s access to U.S. citizenship and the sponsorship of relatives from India endangered the inheritance rights of some spouses and children in the United States, while also changing the pool of potential spouses for both first- and second-generation "Hindus." Similarly, access to overseas citizenship rights and the rapidly changing global economy and society in the early 21st century are having dramatic consequences for the much larger and more diverse population of Indian American immigrants today.

Appendix I: Migration Statistics

Table 143 Indian Immigrants to the United States by year of admission

1946–1964	6,319
1965	582
1966	2,458
1967	4,642
1968	4,682
1969	5,963
1970	10,114
1971	14,317
1972	16,929
1973	13,128
1974	12,795
1975	15,785
1976	17,500
1977	23,208
1978	20,772
1979	19.717
1980	22,607
1981	21,522
1982	21,738
1983	25,451
1984	24,964
1985	26,026
1986	26,277
1987	27,803
1988	26,268
1989	31,175
1990	30,667
1991	45,064
1992	36,755
1993	40,121
1994	34,921
1995	34,748
1996	44,859
1997	38,071
1998	36,482
1999	30,237
2000	42,046
2001	70,290
2002	71,105
2003	50,372

Sources: Adapted from Minocha (1987), and *Statistical Yearbooks of the Immigration and Naturalization Service*, 1988 and 1994: Washington, D.C., U.S. Government Printing Office, 1989 and 1995, and *The 2003 Yearbook of Immigration Statistics*, published by Homeland Security, September 2004. After that, the categories have changed and total immigration figures are no longer available in this *Yearbook.*

Table 144 Persons obtaining legal permanent resident status by region and country of birth: Fiscal years 2000 to 2009

	2000	2001	2002	2003	2004	2005	2006	2007	2008	2009
Total	841,002	1,058,902	1,059,356	703,542	957,883	1,122,257	1,266,129	1,052,415	1,107,126	1,130,818
India	41,903	70,032	70,823	50,228	70,151	84,680	61,369	65,353	63,352	57,304

Source: U.S. Department of Homeland Security. Office of Immigration Statistics. 2010. Adapted from Table 3.

Appendix II: Demographics/Census Statistics

Table 145 Asian Indians living in the United States, according to U.S. census data

1910	2,544
1920	2,544
1930	3,130
1940	2,405
1950	2,398
1960	8,746
1970	13,149
1980	387,223
1990	815,477
2000	1,678,765

Note: In 1980, "Asian Indian" became the official census designation. Before that, this population was termed or counted as "Hindu" (1920, 1930), included under "other Asian" (1940), or could be determined by subtracting whites born in India from the total born in India (1910).

Table 146 Asian Indians by major states of residence, 2000

State	Total
California	360,392
New York	296,056
New Jersey	180,957
Texas	142,689
Illinois	133,978
Florida	84,527
Pennsylvania	62,616
Michigan	60,236
Maryland	55,245
Virginia	54,781

Source: Lai and Arguelles (2003, 52).

Table 147 Persons obtaining legal permanent resident status during fiscal year 2009 region/country: India

	Total	Male	Female
Total	57,304	28,185	29,119
Leading states of residence			
Arizona	553	255	298
California	12,826	6,313	6,513
Colorado	322	154	168
Connecticut	866	420	446
Florida	1,675	837	838
Georgia	1,856	909	947
Illinois	3,946	1,922	2,024
Maryland	1,518	750	768
Massachusetts	1,666	828	838
Michigan	1,294	620	674
Minnesota	596	303	293
New Jersey	7,080	3,423	3,657
New York	4,410	2,184	2,226
North Carolina	1,026	506	520
Ohio	1,101	546	555
Pennsylvania	2,142	1,056	1,086
Texas	4,716	2,306	2,410
Virginia	1,944	920	1,024
Washington	1,670	841	829
Other	6,097	3,092	3,005

Source: U.S. Department of Homeland Security.

Table 148 Asian Indian American occupations, 2000, percentages

Category	Asian Indian	Asian	All workers
Management, professional, related	59.5	44.6	33.6
Service	7.	14.1	14.9
Sales/office	21.4	24.0	26.7
Farming, fishing, forestry	0.6	0.3	0.4
Construction, extraction, maintenance	2.1	3.6	9.4
Production, transportation, material moving	9.4	13.4	14.6

Source: U.S. Census Bureau (2004, 14).

Table 149 Asian Indian American educational attainment, 2000, percentages

Category	Asian Indian	Asian	All workers
Less than high school	13.3	19.6	19.6
High school graduate	13.3	15.8	28.6
Some college, associate's degree	12.5	20.5	27.4
Bachelor's degree or more	63.9	44.1	24.4

Source: U.S. Census Bureau (2004, 12).

Appendix III: Notable Indian Americans

Ashok Amritraj was born in Madras. Amritraj became a tennis star and moved to the United States in the 1970s; he is now a Hollywood producer of over 809 films and chairman and CEO of Hyde Park Entertainment.

Subrahmanyan Chandrasekhar (October 19, 1910–August 21, 1995) was an astrophysicist and educator who moved from Cambridge in the United Kingdom to the University of Chicago in the mid-1930s; he won the Nobel Prize in Physics in 1983 for his study of white dwarfs that laid the groundwork for the discovery of black holes.

Dr. Deepak Chopra (ca. 1947–) was born in Delhi. A graduate of the All-India Institute of Medical Sciences, Chopra came to the United States in 1970; he was chief of staff of a Boston-area hospital but resigned in 1985 to write books and promote Ayurveda, an Indian system of holistic healing.

Dr. Sanjay Gupta (October 23, 1968–) was born in the United States. He is a neurosurgeon and media personality, best known as CNN's chief medical correspondent and host of the weekend health program *House Call with Dr. Sanjay Gupta*.

Zakir Hussain (March 9, 1951–) was born in Mumbai; his father is the *tabla* player Ustad Alla Rakha. A child music prodigy, he began touring at the age of 12 and has a base in San Francisco. He plays the *tabla* and teaches students, composes music, acts in films, and collaborates with a variety of musicians on fusion musical projects.

Bobby Jindal (June 10, 1971–) was born in the United States. His political career began with his election in 2004 and reelection in 2006 to the House of Representatives from Louisiana. He won the governorship of Louisiana in the fall of 2007, becoming at 36 the youngest current governor in the United States.

Ali Akbar Khan (April 14, 1922–June 18, 2009) was born in Bengal. The son of the classical Hindustani musician Allauddin Khan, Ali Akbar plays the *sarod*. Following careers in India and Canada, he moved to the United States and founded the Ali Akbar College of Music in Marin County, California, in 1967, training students in Indian music and dance.

Har Gobind Khorana (January 9, 1922–) was born in India. He began teaching molecular chemistry at the University of Wisconsin in 1960 and in 1971, at MIT; he shared the Nobel Prize in Medicine in 1968 and was awarded the U.S. National Medal of Science in 1987.

Ved Prakash Mehta (March 21, 1934–), was born in Lahore, India (now Pakistan). Mehta studied at the Arkansas School for the Blind in Little Rock, Arkansas, eventually becoming an American citizen (in 1975), a staff writer for the *New Yorker*, an author of many books, and a filmmaker.

Indra Nooyi (October 28, 1955–) was born in Chennai (Madras). She began her career in India but earned an MA at Yale in 1978 and has worked in the United States since then; in 2006, she became CEO and in 2007 chair of PepsiCo, one of the world's leading food and beverage companies.

Dalip Singh Saund (1899–1973) was born in India's Punjab province. Saund attended the University of California, Berkeley, and earned a PhD in mathematics in 1924; he farmed in Southern California and was elected to the House of Representatives in 1956 and reelected twice (a stroke in 1962 forced his retirement).

Gayatri Chakravorti Spivak (February 24, 1942–), Calcutta-born, earned an MA and a PhD in comparative literature at Cornell University in the 1960s. She teaches at Columbia University; her writings on French poststructuralism, modernism, and feminist issues have made her an influential educator in the interdisciplinary field of cultural studies.

Fareed Zakaria (January 20, 1964–) was born in Mumbai, India. Zakaria attended Yale for his BA and Harvard for his PhD in political science; he became managing editor of *Foreign Affairs,* then in 2000, editor of *Newsweek International,* and, after numerous publications and news analyst TV appearances, in 2008, he began hosting a weekly TV show on CNN, *Fareed Zakaria Global Public Square.*

Glossary

Arangetram: Debut performance of a *Bharatnatyam* dancer.

Bhangra: Punjabi folk dance.

Bharatnatyam: South Indian classical dance.

Bollywood: The Indian film industry based in Bombay (now Mumbai).

Fiqh: Islamic jurisprudence.

Garba raas: Gujarati folk dance.

Granthi: Sikh priest.

Gurdwara: Sikh temple.

Masala: Mixture of spices.

Moulvi: Muslim cleric.

Mughlai: Relating to the Mughal empire, to Indo-Muslim culture.

Mushaira: Evening of Urdu poetry.

Nikah: Muslim wedding ceremony.

Prasad: Blessed food or offering distributed after Hindu worship.

Puja: Hindu worship.

Purdah: Seclusion of women.

References

Abraham, Margaret. 2000. *Speaking the Unspeakable: Marital Violence among South Asian Immigrants in the United States.* New Brunswick, NJ: Rutgers University Press.

Abramovitch, Ilana. 1988. "Flushing Bharata-Natyam: Indian Dancers in Queens, N.Y." Paper presented at the Conference on South Asia, University of Wisconsin, Madison, WI, Nov. 4–6.

Agarwal, Priya. 1991. *Passage from India: Post 1965 Indian Immigrants and Their Children.* Palos Verdes, CA: Yuvati Publications.

Aiyar, V. Shankar. 1999. "The Dream That Died." *India Today International,* February 8, 36.

Ali, Faiz-u-Nisa A. 1991. *The Path of Islam Book 3*, 3rd ed. Tustin, CA: International Islamic Educational Institute.

Anand, Shefali. 2009. "Ineligible Bachelors: Indian Men Living in U.S. Strike Out," April 6. [Online article retrieved 04/09.] http://online.wsj.com/article/SB123896998996190775.html.

Anand, Tania. 1993. "Gift-Wrapping Hindutva." *India Today*, August 31, 48c–d.

Arora, C. K. 2001. "United State." *India Today International*, April 23.

"Asian Indian Seniors Assoc. Hosts Temple Tour." 1997. *India-West*, January 24.

Balagopal, Sudha Sethu. 1994. "Sound of Music." *India Today*, December 31, 64k.

Barrier, N. Gerald. 2001. "Gurdwaras in the U.S.: Governance, Authority, and Legal Issues." *Understanding Sikhism* 4 (1): 31–41.

Basu, Kaushik. 2000. "Immigration Check." *India Today International,* May 29, 38.

Bhat, Gauri. 1992. "Tending the Flame: Thoughts on Being Indian-American." *COSAW* [Committee on South Asian Women] *Bulletin* 7 (3–4): 1–6.

Bhaumik, Saba Naqvi. 1999. "Privileges at a Price." *India Today International*, April 12, 24c.

Boxall, Bettina. 2001. "Asian Indian Remake Silicon Valley." *LA Times*, July 6.

Clothey, Fred. 1983. *Rhythm and Intent*. Madras: Blackie and Sons.

"Despite Economy, Upswing in U.S.-India Drug Partnerships." *India-West*, July 3, A31.

Dusenbery, Verne A. 1999. " 'Nation' or 'World Religion'? Master Narratives of Sikh Identity." In *Sikh Identity: Continuity and Change,* edited by Pashaura Singh and N. Gerald Barrier, 127–44. New Delhi: Manohar.

Eck, Diana, ed. 1997. *On Common Ground: World Religions in America* (CD-ROM). New York: Columbia University Press.

Fenton, John Y. 1988. *Transplanting Religious Traditions: Asian Indians in America*. New York: Praeger.

Fenton, John Y. 1995. *South Asian Religions in the Americas: An Annotated Bibliography of Immigrant Religious Traditions*. Westport, CT: Greenwood Press.

George, Sheba Mariam. 2005. *When Women Come First: Gender and Class in Transnational Migration*. Berkeley: University of California Press.

Ghei, Kiren. 1988. "Hindi Popular Cinema and the Indian American Teenage Dance Experience." Paper presented at the Conference on South Asia, University of Wisconsin, Madison, WI, Nov. 4–6.

Hansen, Kathryn. 1999. "Singing for the Sadguru: Tyagaraja Festivals in North America." In *The Expanding Landscape: South Asians and the Diaspora,* edited by Carla Petievich, 103–21. Chicago: American Institute of Indian Studies.

"India, U.S. Form Joint Working Group For Cooperation in Education." 2009. *India Journal*, June 19, A23.

"India Top Receiver of $27 Billion Remittances." 2008. *India Journal*, March 28, B1.

"Indians Corner 38 Per Cent of H1-B Visas in 2008: U.S." 2009. *India Journal*, April 17, A8.

Jain, Neela, and Benjamin Forest. 2007. "From Religion to Ethnicity: The Identity of Immigrant and Second Generation Indian Jains in the United States." In *Sociology of Diaspora: A Reader*, vol 2, edited by Ajaya Kumar Sahoo and Brij Maharaj, 816–44. New Delhi: Rawat Publications.

Jain, Usha R. 1989[1964]. *The Gujaratis of San Francisco*. New York: AMS Press.

Kang, K. Connie, and Robin Fields. 2001. "Asian Population in U.S. Surges, but Unevenly." *Los Angeles Times*, May 15, A16.

Karthik, Prabha. 1998. "Gita Patel Re-Opens Domestic Service Company." *India Journal*, November 27, B3.

La Brack, Bruce. 1988. *The Sikhs of Northern California 1904–1975: A Socio-Historical Study*. New York: AMS Press.

Lai, Eric, and Dennis Arguelles. 2003. *The New Face of Asian Pacific America: Numbers, Diversity and Change in the 21st Century*. San Francisco: Asian Week.

Leonard, Karen Isaksen. 1992. *Making Ethnic Choices: California's Punjabi Mexican Americans*. Philadelphia: Temple University Press.

Leonard, Karen Isaksen. 1997. *The South Asian Americans.* Westport, CT: Greenwood Press.

Leonard, Karen Isaksen. 1999. "Second Generation Sikhs in America." In *Sikh Identity: Continuity and Change,* edited by Pashaura Singh and N. Gerald Barrier, 275–97. New Delhi: Manohar.

Leonard, Karen Isaksen. 2002. "South Asian Leadership of American Muslims." In *Muslims in the West: From Sojourners to Citizens,* edited by Yvonne Haddad, 233–49. Oxford: Oxford University Press.

Leonard, Karen Isaksen. 2003. *Muslims in the United States: The State of Research.* New York: Russell Sage.

Leonard, Karen, and Chandra Sekhar Tibrewal. 1993. "Asian Indians in Southern California: Occupations and Ethnicity." In *Comparative Immigration and Entrepreneurship: Culture, Capital and Ethnic Networks,* edited by Parminder Bhachu and Ivan Light, 141–62. New Brunswick, NJ: Transaction.

Lessinger, Johanna. 1995. *From the Ganges to the Hudson: Indian Immigrants in New York City.* Boston: Allyn and Bacon.

Mazumdar, Shampa. 1995. "Sacred Spaces: Socio-Spatial Adaptations of Hindu Migrants." Ph.D. diss., Northeastern University, Boston.

Melwani, Lavina. 1994. "Migratory Montage." *India Today*, December 15, 60d–f.

Melwani, Lavina. 1997a. "Following Their Hearts." *India Today*, May 15, 52c–d.

Melwani, Lavina. 1997b. "East Storms West." *India Today*, January, 56f–g.

Melwani, Lavina. 2001. "Diaspora Spreads." *India Today International*, July 2, 36c.

Minocha, Urmilla. 1987. "South Asian Immigrants: Trends and Impacts on the Sending and Receiving Societies." In *Pacific Bridges: The New Immigration from Asia and the Pacific Islands,* edited by James T. Fawcett and Benjamin V. Carino, 347–74. New York: Center for Migration Studies.

Murarka, Ramesh P. 1998. "India's T.V. Channels Begin Invasion of U.S. Market." *India-West*, June 26, B1, 10–12.

Potts, Michel W. 2007. "SAN Joins Satrang in Support of South Asian Gays." *India-West*, October 26, A16.

Potts, Michel W. 2009. "NRI Doctors May Get Permission to Practice in India." *India-West*, January 16, A29.

Rajagopal, Arvind. 1994. "Disarticulating Exilic Nationalism: Indian Immigrants in the U.S." Paper presented at the American Anthropological Association Conference, November 30–December 4.

Ramesh, Jairam. 2000. "India Ahead of Germany." *India Today International,* May 29, 35.

"Remade in America." 2009. *New York Times* (National), March 15, 16 [Online article retrieved 06/09.] www.nytimes.com/interactive/2009/04/07us/20090407-immigration-occupation.html.

Saxenain, Anna-Lee. 1999. "Silicon Valley's New Immigrant Entrepreneurs." Public Policy Institute of California study.

Shankar, Shalini. 2008. *Desi Land: Teen Culture, Class, and Success in Silicon Valley.* Durham, NC: Duke University Press.

Shanker, Meenakshi. 1994. "The Annual Pilgrimage." *India Today*, April 30, 44i.

Shekhara, G.C. 1997. "Migratory Musicians." *India Today*, January 31, 48d.

Singh, Mona. 1995. "Oh Darling, Yeh Hai India." *India-West*, February 3, 59.

Sohrabji, Sunita. 2009. "Immigrant Exodus Means Huge Loss for U.S." *India-West*, March 6, B1–2.

Springer, Richard. 1998. "India Airs Soap Opera—With an NRI Twist." *India-West*, June 19, C1–2.

Springer, Richard. 1999. "Indians Prospering in Silicon Valley: Study." *India-West*, July 9, A1, 32.

Springer, Richard. 2001. "Calif. Has Most U.S. Indians." *India-West*, May 25, A1.

Springer, Richard. 2007a. "Indian Population In U.S. Nearly 2.5-M." *India-West*, October 5, A1, 4, 16.

Springer, Richard. 2007b. "India Again Sends Most Foreign Students to U.S." *India-West*, November 23, A14.

Springer, Richard. 2009a. "Fewer Indian Students Applying to U.S. Graduate Schools." *India-West*, April 17, A4.

Springer, Richard. 2009b. "Foreign Students Leaving U.S." *India-West*, March 27, A44.

Springer, Richard. 2009c. "India-Born Lead U.S. in Education, Median Income." *India-West*, February 27, A18.

Springer, Richard. 2009d. "Less Indian Students Coming to U.S. for Graduate Studies." *India Journal*, April 17, A18.

Springer, Richard. 2009e. "Bill Would Give Foreign Ph.D.s Permanent Status." *India-West*, April 17, A4.

Springer, Richard. 2009f. "Sierra Club Awards Rs. 50 Lakh to Green Groups in India." *India-West,* July 3, A12.

Sundaram. Viji. 1994. "Nurturing Their Passion of Bharatnatyam in the West." *India-West*, July 15, C49, 68.

Swapan, Ashfaque. 2009. "Darwin's 200th Anniversary." *India-West*, March 13, A10.

Thakar, Suvarna. 1982. "The Quality of Life of Asian Indian Women in the Motel Industry." *South Asia Bulletin* 2: 68–73.

Thakkar, Rahesh. 1992. "Transfer of Culture through Arts: The South Asian Experience in North America." In *Ethnicity, Identity, and Migration,* edited by Milton Israel and N.K. Wagle, 217–37. Toronto: Center for South Asian Studies, University of Toronto.

Trivedi, Niraj. 1997. "NRIs Want Indian Ministry Set Up For Overseas Indians." *India-West*, August 15.

Tsering, Lisa. 2009. "Hollywood's Motion Picture Association Opens First India Office." *India-West,* March 5, C1, C6.

U.S. Census Bureau. 2004. *We the People: Asians in the United States.* Washington, DC: U.S. Department of Commerce.

Varadarajan, Tunku. 1998. "Pat for Patels." *India Today International*, November 23, 24i.

Venkatachari, K.K.A. 1992. "Transmission and Transformation of Rituals." In *A Sacred Thread: Modern Transmission of Hindu Traditions in India and Abroad,* edited by Raymond Brady Williams, 177–90. Chambersburg, PA: Anima.

Williams, Raymond. 1988. *Religions of Immigrants from India and Pakistan: New Threads in the American Tapestry.* New York: Cambridge University Press.

Williams, Raymond, ed. 1992. *A Sacred Thread: Modern Transmission of Hindu Traditions in India and Abroad.* Chambersburg, PA: Anima.

Further Reading

Bhardwaj, Surinder M., and N. Madhusudana Rao. 1990. "Asian Indians in the United States: A Geographic Appraisal," In *South Asians Overseas: Migration and Ethnicity*, edited by Colin Clarke, Ceri Peach, and Steven Vertovec, 197–218. New York: Cambridge University Press.

This is good on settlement patterns.

Dasgupta, Shamita Das. 1998. *A Patchwork Shawl: Chronicles of South Asian Women in America* New Brunswick, NJ: Rutgers University Press.

This gives personal voices.

Eck, Diana. 2001. *A New Religious America: How a "Christian Country" Has Now Become the World's Most Religiously Diverse Nation.* San Francisco: Harper Collins.

Read for a broad overview of religions from India in America.

Gopinath, Gayatri. 2005. *Impossible Desires: Queer Diasporas and South Asian Public Cultures* Durham, NC: Duke University Press.

This is a pioneering work on emergent population and issues.

Gupta, Sangeeta R. 1999. *Emerging Voices: South Asian American Women Redefine Self, Family, and Community.* New Delhi: Sage Publications.

This gives personal voices.

Kerns, Roshni Rustomji. 1995. *Living in America: Poetry and Fiction by South Asian American Writers.* San Francisco: Westview Press, 1995)

This is a representative selection of new writers on the American scene.

Koshy, Susan. 1998. "Category Crisis: South Asian Americans and Questions of Race and Ethnicity." *Diaspora* 7: 285–320.

This discusses racial placement of Asian Indians.

Lessinger, Johanna. 2003. "Indian Immigrants in the United States: The Emergence of a Transnational Population." In *Culture and Economy in the Indian Diaspora*, edited by Bhikhu Parekh, Gurharpal Singh, and Steven Vertovec, 165–82. New York: Routledge.

An excellent survey of the relationship between India's prestigious state-funded technical universities (Indian Institutes of Technology or IITs) and their NRI (non-resident Indian) graduates in the United States; the NRI alumni are pressing to restructure the institutions in India more along the lines of mixed science and entrepreneurship prevalent in the United States. The Indian side is outraged by the idea of restructuring their state-funded universities.

Maira, Sunaina Marr. 2002. *Desis in the House: Indian American Youth Culture in New York City* Philadelphia: Temple University Press.

This is a pioneering work on second-generation Indian Americans.

Mukherji, Dhan Gopal. 1923. *Caste and Outcast.* Stanford: Stanford University Press. Republished in 2002.

The early immigrant experience is evoked here.

Prashad, Vijay. 2000. *The Karma of Brown Folk.* Minneapolis: University of Minnesota Press.

This is an oft-cited work on racial placement of Asian Indians.

Sahay, Anjali. 2007. "Indian Diaspora in the United States and Brain Gain: Remittances, Return and Network Approaches." In *Sociology of Diaspora: A Reader*, edited by Ajaya Kumar Sahoo and Brij Maharaj, vol 2, 940–74. New Delhi: Rawat Publications.

There is lots of good economic information in this piece.

The Women of South Asian Descent Collective. 1993. *Our Feet Walk the Sky: Women of the South Asian Diaspora.* San Francisco: Aunt Lute Books.

This is a pioneering work on women's personal experiences.

Indonesian Immigrants

by Jennifer Cho

Introduction

Indonesia is one of the most diverse countries in the world. The national motto of Indonesia is *Bhinneka Tunggal Ika,* which is generally translated as "Unity in Diversity." The source of the motto was the 14th-century Javanese poem, *Kakawin Sutasoma*, written by Mpu Tantular in the 14th century (*The Jakarta Post* 2000). The poem and its message of religious tolerance continue to inspire Indonesians who stage contemporary performances of the text, most recently in Bali. The motto readily applies to a country with 17,508 islands, over 300 ethnic groups, and religious traditions in Buddhism, Hinduism, Islam, Protestantism, Catholicism, animism, and local customs. With an estimated 240.3 million people, Indonesia is ranked fourth in total population behind China, India, and the United States (Vaughan 2009). Over 86 percent of Indonesia's population is Muslim, which is higher than any other country. Yet Indonesian Americans are only the 14th-largest Asian American ethnic group in the United States (U.S. Census 2000).

Chronology

600s	The Buddhist kingdom of Srivijaya rises to prominence across the Malay peninsula.
1200s	The Muslim communities of Perlak and Pasai are established in Indonesia.
1293	The Hindu kingdom of Majapahit is founded by Raden Wijaya.
1602	The Dutch East Indies Company (VOC) is formed as a consolidation of separate Dutch companies trading in Indonesia. Dutch colonial rule lasts from the 17th century to 1945.
1799	The VOC shuts down due to bankruptcy.
1800	The Dutch East Indies is established as a state colony of the Netherlands.

INDONESIA

Banda
Aceh
Lhokseumawe
Langsa
Manggeng Binjai Medan
Balige
Labuhanbilik
Padangsidempuan
Duri
Kotahopan Pakanbaru
Singkawang
Bangkinang
Bukittinggi
Mempawah
Airhadji
Padang
Palembang
Banjarmasin
Ketapang
Sambas
Sangau
Pontianak
Sandae
Nangpinoh Samarinda
Sampit
Bandjermasin
Tandjungselor
Tandjungredeb
Ujungpandang

Manado

Indonesia

Lunjuk-besar
Kupang

Jakarta
Bandung Garut
Semarang Pati
Kebumen
Surabaya
Malang

Manokwari

Jayapura

N

1801	The United States establishes consular relations in Batavia (now Jakarta).
1908	The founding of Budi Utono indicates the rise of the nationalist movement.
1928	The Youth Pledge is read at the Second All Indonesia Youth Conference on October 28. The pledge declares one country (Indonesia) and one language (Indonesian).
1942	Japan invades the Dutch East Indies and defeats the Dutch.
1945	Japan surrenders. The Republic of Indonesia declares independence from the Netherlands with Sukarno as its first president.
1947	The Dutch launch the first of two military actions to reclaim Indonesia as a colony.
1949	The Dutch government officially recognizes Indonesian independence after pressure from the United Nations and transfers sovereignty on December 27. The United States formalizes diplomatic relations with Indonesia on December 28.
1953	The U.S. Refugee Relief Act admits 7,831 Indo-Europeans to the United States. Small numbers of Indonesian students attend high schools and colleges in the United States.
1965	The Immigration and Nationality Act (also called the Hart-Cellar Act) is passed in the United States, which raises immigrant quotas from Asian countries. The murder of six generals during the September 30 Movement unleashes a wave of violence to purge Indonesia of communists. An estimated 500,000 are killed, including scores of ethnic Chinese.
1968	Suharto replaces Sukarno as president. Sukarno is placed under house arrest until his death in 1970.
1997	The Asian economic crisis devalues the Indonesian rupiah.
1998	Amid protests, Suharto's presidency ends and B. J. Habibie becomes president.
	The May 9 riots result in the mass murders and rapes of Chinese Indonesians, who apply for asylum in the United States.
2004	Bambang Yudhoyono is elected president in the first direct presidential voter elections. A tsunami kills an estimated 170,000; Indonesian Americans send aid to victims.

2005	The Netherlands recognizes de facto independence of Indonesia as August 17, 1945.
2009	Inauguration of Barack Obama as the 44th president of the United States. His stepfather is Indonesian-born Lolo Soetoro. Secretary of State Hillary Clinton visits Indonesia in February. Yudhoyono is re-elected to a second term as president.
2010	U.S. President Barack Obama is scheduled to visit Indonesia.

Background

Geography of Indonesia

Indonesia is an archipelagic country that consists of approximately 17,508 islands (6,000 inhabited). With a total land mass of 1,125,657 square miles, Indonesia borders Malaysia, Brunei, Papua New Guinea, and East Timor, in close proximity to Australia (The World Factbook 2009). Indonesia's largest islands are Sumatra, Sulawesi, and Java; the islands of New Guinea and Borneo are partitioned into territories claimed by other countries. New Guinea is the world's second-largest island and is divided into Papua New Guinea to the east and the Indonesian provinces of West Papua and Papua to the west. West Papua was formerly known as West Irian Jaya until the name was changed in 2007 (Radio New Zealand International 2007). Borneo is the world's third-largest island and is separated into regions claimed by Indonesia, Malaysia, and Brunei (Cunningham 1997). In English, Kalimantan refers to the Indonesian part of Borneo; in Indonesian, the term specifies the whole island (Encyclopedia Britannica 2008). The capital city of Jakarta is located on Java, the country's most populous island.

Indonesia's wet and dry seasons are characteristic of its tropical climate. The equator runs directly through the country, notably along the islands of Sumatra, Kalimantan, and Sulawesi. Heavy rainfall during the monsoon seasons often results in flooding. There are four monsoons from each compass direction—summer monsoons from the east and south, and winter monsoons from the west and north. Temperatures are hot and humid at sea level, with some cooling in the mountains. Indonesia is prone to earthquakes and volcanic activity because it lies at the intersection of several tectonic plates. The majority of the country's estimated 130 active volcanoes are situated between the islands of Java and Sumatra. The most famous volcanic explosion occurred in Krakatoa on August 26 and 27, 1883. From 2004 to 2009, several natural disasters occurred in Indonesia that resulted in scores of deaths and widespread homelessness. On December 26,

2004, a tsunami triggered by a 9.1 magnitude earthquake killed over 122,000 people (Vaughan 2009).

The official language of Indonesia is Bahasa Indonesia ("the language of Indonesia"), which is a standardized form of Malay. In English, the official language is known simply as Indonesian. Over 250 living languages and dialects are spoken in Indonesia (Suharno 2007). The largest ethnic group in Indonesia is the Javanese, who comprise 41.6 percent of a population that includes more than 300 ethnic groups (Suharno 2007). Other ethnic groups include the Sundanese (15.41%), Malay (3.45%), Madurese (3.37%), Balinese (1.51%), Batak (3.02%), Minangkabau (2.72%), and Betawi (2.51%) (Suryadinata, Arifin, and Ananta 2003). Chinese Indonesians comprise less than 4 percent of the total population.

History of Indonesia

Indonesia encompasses a rich diversity of cultural, religious, and ethnolinguistic traditions that present ongoing challenges in governing the country. Waves of migrations from Southeast Asia, Taiwan, China, India, the Middle East, and Europe have made an indelible impact on Indonesia's history and population. The human skull cap of "Java Man" (*Homo erectus*), discovered by Eugène Dubois in Trinil, Java, in 1891, offers evidence that Indonesia was inhabited over 500,000 years ago. Most Indonesians are believed to be descended from Austronesians who migrated to the archipelago by 2000 B.C.E. as well as Austromelanesians who arrived even earlier (Brown 2003; Drakeley 2005). The Austronesians are credited with introducing agricultural methods such as dry-rice farming and shifting cultivation, which supported larger settlements of people (Drakeley 2005).

During the fourth century, certain regions of the archipelago were undergoing an "Indianization" from exposure to Hinduism and Buddhism (Cribb and Kahin 2004). In the seventh century, the Buddhist maritime kingdom of Srivijaya rose to prominence on the island of Sumatra and dominated the Sunda and Malacca straits until its decline. Construction on the Buddhist monument Borobudur began around the ninth century near present-day Magelang, Java. The ruler Airlangga (991–1046 C.E.) divided Mataram between his two sons. In Central Java, the Hindu-Buddhist kingdom of Mataram was founded in the 8th century and co-existed with Srivijaya until the two empires went to war in the 11th century. A second incarnation of Mataram emerged in the 1570s as a Muslim state. Ethnic Chinese settlements in Indonesia date back to the 10th century (Cribb and Kahin 2004). By the 16th century, the Indonesian archipelago had evolved into a major force in international trade. The region's vast network of sea lanes and river routes facilitated migration and the exchange of goods and ideas, especially religions.

The rise of Islam loosely coincided with the time period of the great Hindu-Javanese kingdom of Majapahit (1293–1527 C.E.). Although the exact dates for

Islam's first conversion in the archipelago are unknown, Marco Polo wrote that the state of Perlak in Sumatra was a Muslim community in 1292 (Brown 2003). As Islam spread across the coastal areas, Muslim traders also appeared in Majapahit. The reign of Hayum Wuruk (also called Rajasanagara, r. 1350–1389 C.E.) and his chief minister, Gajah Mada, was deemed the "golden age" of Majapahit because of the political, commercial, and cultural achievements made during this period (Cribb and Kahin 2004). Through conquest of its neighboring territories, Majapahit set a precedent for conceptualizing the scope of Indonesia's present-day boundaries (Ricklefs 2008).

Trade influenced Islam's expansion across the archipelago (Brown 2003). Muslim traders from India, the Middle East, and China arrived in coastal areas to meet the exploding demand for Indonesian spices. Conversion to Islam was a spiritual decision as well as a strategic means of maintaining trade contacts. Aceh, Banten, and Pasisir in Java became Muslim in the 16th century; Minangkabau and Central Java followed in the 17th century (Cribb and Kahin 2004). Hinduism was largely on the decline except in Bali, which remains Hindu to this day. By the time the Europeans arrived in the 16th century, Islam had replaced Hinduism as the main religion in Java and Sumatra.

The first Europeans to arrive at the archipelago were the Portuguese. Although an earlier Catholic presence had existed in Java, Sumatra, and Kalimantan, the Portuguese were primarily responsible for spreading Catholicism throughout the islands after capturing Malacca in 1511. The objective of the Portuguese was to dominate trade in the region, so they built ports, trading posts, and missions to that end. East Timor became a Portuguese colony from 1702 until 1975, when it was invaded by Indonesia. Other European powers who followed Portugal to the archipelago included England, Spain, and the Netherlands.

The Netherlands ultimately prevailed in Indonesia, mostly because the Dutch expended the most resources toward establishing a monopoly over the region while the rest of Europe shifted its attention to other pursuits. In 1596, the first Dutch fleet reached Java with four ships and 249 men (Brown 2003). A few years later, various Dutch trading companies consolidated into the Vereenigde Oost-Indische Compagnie (VOC). The English names for the VOC include the United East Indies Company, the Dutch East Indies Company, the Dutch East India Company, and the United East India Company (Cribb and Kahin 2004). The VOC was a joint-stock company that ran from 1602 to 1799, when it went bankrupt. Governor General Jan Pieterszoon Coen founded the VOC's main headquarters in Jayakarta, which was renamed Batavia by the Dutch (Cribb and Kahin 2004). After the VOC collapsed, the Dutch government took control of VOC lands, assets, and debt. The territory became a Dutch state colony called the Netherlands Indies. Batavia remained the capital of the Netherlands Indies until World War II; the city's name was changed to Jakarta after the declaration of Indonesian independence in 1945.

Under VOC rule, the Chinese evolved into a limited economic class as farmers, tax collection agents, sellers of opium, and more (Cribb and Kahin 2004). *Peranakan* ("native born") Chinese had already been assimilating to Malay customs since the 10th century. Both Chinese and Dutch men intermarried with *pribumi* indigenous women; these unions resulted in new generations of Chinese Indonesian or Eurasian descendants. The Chinese were excluded from politics by the Dutch, who became suspicious of a possible Chinese rebellion in the 18th century. Tensions exploded during the Chinese War of 1740–1741, in which an estimated 10,000 Chinese were massacred by the Dutch in Batavia (Brown 2003). The 19th century brought a new wave of Chinese immigrants who migrated to Kalimantan, Bangka, and East Sumatra (Cribb and Kahin 2004). Newly arrived Chinese who maintain cultural links to China were referred to as *totoks* (Cribb and Kahin 2004). The Agrarian Law of 1870, passed during the Liberal Period (1870–1900), prevented Chinese and Europeans from owning land. But the law granted long-term land leases to foreigners, especially corporations that commercialized agriculture to an industrial scale.

Resistance to the Dutch dates back to Mataram's attacks on Batavia in the 1620s, but the Netherlands continued to dominate the archipelago for over three centuries. The Java War of 1825–1830 was the last rebellion against the Dutch government until World War II. Led by Javanese prince Pangeran Diponegro, the Java War resulted in an estimated 250,000 indigenous deaths (Cribb and Kahin 2004). Within an international context of change, the early 20th century gave rise to a nationalist movement for an independent Indonesia. Revolutions in China and Russia instituted new governments while India and the Philippines struggled against their colonizers. The Dutch government instituted the Ethical Policy to civilize the "brown Dutchmen" by providing a Western education to *inlanders,* as Indonesians were called (Drakeley 2005). The Dutch caste system imposed a racial hierarchy in which *inlanders* were the lowest class (Drakeley 2005). Young nationalist leaders believed in education as a means of liberation from colonial rule. The shared experiences of Dutch colonialism brought people of different ethnic and religious backgrounds together in a collective struggle for independence.

A precursor to the nationalist movement occurred in 1908 with the establishment of Budi Utono, an organization that advocated on behalf of Javanese identity and culture. Early nationalist parties included the Indische Partij (Indies Party), founded around 1911–1912, which advocated for equality on behalf of individuals born in the Indies. Partai Komunis Indonesia (PKI) emerged in 1920 and became the first Communist party in Southeast Asia (Cribb and Kahin 2004). In 1928, Sukarno founded the Partai Nasional Indonesia (PNI) with members from the Perserikatan Nasional Indonesia (Indonesian Nationalist Union). (Cribb and Kahin 2004). Students were instrumental as leaders in the nationalist movement, which coalesced with the reading of the Youth Pledge at the Second All Indonesia Youth Congress on October 28, 1928. The Youth Pledge called for one nation (Indonesia) and one language (Indonesian) (Drakeley 2005). Malay was chosen as the official national language of the new Indonesia because of its common usage in trade and its non-geographical affiliation.

The three most prominent nationalist leaders were Sukarno (1901–1970), Mohammad Hatta (1902–1980), and Sutan Sjahrir (1909–1966). They were all arrested and exiled by the Dutch but were released after the invasion of Indonesia by Japan. In 1942, Japanese forces landed in Borneo, Sumatra, and Java and swiftly defeated the Dutch. Japan occupied Indonesia for the remainder of World War II until its surrender in 1945. Indonesia declared its independence from the Netherlands on August 17, 1945. However, the Dutch government tried to reclaim its colony by force until it bowed to international pressure and officially transferred sovereignty on December 27, 1949 (Drakeley 2005). Sukarno became the first president of Indonesia, with Mohammad Hatta as vice president and Sjahrir as prime minister.

Supporters of Indonesian president Sukarno hold a banner bearing his portrait at a rally in Macassar, Indonesia, 1962. A leader of Indonesia's independence movement, Sukarno's secular model of government was opposed by traditional ethnic and religious groups and helped create political societal rifts in the young nation during the 1950s and 1960s. (Library of Congress)

The democracy of Indonesia is based on five principles known as *Pancasila*. The *Garuda Pancasila* is the national coat of arms and represents each principle on a shield borne by the golden Garuda, a birdlike creature in Hindu mythology. The shield defends Indonesia and bears five emblems: (1) a golden star, which denotes belief in one God; (2) the golden chain of humanity that links together successive generations (circular links for women, squares for men); (3) the banyan tree of Indonesian unity; (4) the *banteng* (wild buffalo), which calls for Indonesian democracy by discussion and consensus; and (5) rice and cotton sprigs, which symbolize social justice for all (Mirpuri and Cooper 2002). In its talons, the Garuda carries a scroll with the national motto, *Bhinneka Tunggal Ika*. The five principles were read by Sukarno, the first president of Indonesia, during a speech on June 1, 1945, that elucidated the future of Indonesia as an independent country. The United States established diplomatic relations with Indonesia in 1949. In 1950, Indonesia joined the United Nations as its 60th member.

In 1963, Sukarno declared himself president-for-life (Cribb and Kahin 2004). His presidency was marked by corruption and growing tensions between the army and the PKI, whose membership surged in the 1960s. Sukarno's downfall was triggered in 1965 by an attempted coup during the September 30 Movement, in which six generals were killed by army soldiers with the help of PKI youth (Brown 2003). General Suharto (1921–2008) and his forces crushed the coup and blamed the PKI. Over the next six months, hundreds of thousands of PKI members, suspected Communists, Chinese, and other civilians were murdered during the Massacre of 1965–1966. Suharto became acting president of Indonesia in 1967 and then president in 1968. Sukarno was placed under house arrest and died in 1970.

Dubbed the "New Order," the Suharto years (1966–1998) resulted in significant economic growth for Indonesia, followed by financial catastrophe, rioting, and Suharto's resignation. In 1997, the Asian economic crisis resulted in the rapid devaluation of the Indonesian rupiah and paved the political climate that led to Suharto's downfall. Confidence in Suharto's presidency deteriorated as he and his family were widely criticized for corruption. Widespread student protests called for *reformasi* ("reform") and Suharto's resignation.

In May 1998, shooting deaths of four students by army troops launched massive rioting across the country. Resentment against the Chinese, a historically persecuted group in Indonesia, culminated during this time. The economic success of Chinese Indonesians made them an easy scapegoat during periods of unrest. During the May 9 tragedy, the Chinese became targets of outraged mobs who committed murders, rapes, looting, and arson against Chinese Indonesians. The attacks on Chinese Indonesians resulted in international condemnations of Indonesia and politicized Chinese Indonesians abroad to become involved in politics. Suharto resigned on May 21, 1998, and his vice president, B. J. Habibie, became Indonesia's third president.

Abdurrahman Wahid was elected as the fourth president with Megawati Sukarnoputri as vice president. When Wahid was ousted in 2001, Sukarnoputri became the fifth president. In the country's first direct presidential election, Sukarnoputri lost to Susilo Bambang Yudhoyono, who was re-elected to a second term in 2009.

Causes and Waves of Migration

Early Immigration

Recent efforts to understand the history of early Indonesian immigration have been spearheaded by the Embassy of Indonesia in Washington, D.C., which began conducting oral histories of Indonesians who arrived in the United States before World War II. Retired embassy employee Abdullah Balbed (2006) wrote the article, "Indonesians in America," which states that a small number of Indonesian immigrants likely arrived with Dutch settlers as domestic servants or farm laborers. Other Indonesians worked as seamen for Dutch ships and arrived in the United States in port cities such as New York or Baltimore (Balbed 2006). Prior to the Indonesian declaration of independence on August 17, 1945, immigrants from the region declared the Dutch East Indies as their birthplace or last residence and traveled with Dutch passports. Foreign exchange between the United States and the Dutch East Indies primarily occurred in the fields of diplomacy, business, trade, missionary work, and education. Cultural exchanges between the United States and Indonesia also occurred before World War II. For example, Balinese dancer Devi Dja brought a dance troupe and gamelan orchestra to the United States in 1939. Dja was unable to return to Indonesia due to World War II, so she settled in the United States and became a citizen in 1954.

During the years between Indonesia's proclamation of independence in 1945 to the official transfer of sovereignty by the Dutch on December 27, 1949, Indonesian passports were not recognized by other governments (Abdullah Balbed, interview with the author, December 8, 2009). Indonesians traveling outside the country were issued *laisser passer* travel documents by the United Nations, which was established on October 24, 1945. Indonesian seamen continued to arrive in the United States after World War II. On January 2, 1946, the *Jan Steen* ship arrived at the port of New York City with over 50 Indonesians listed as crew members. These Indonesians had joined the *Jan Steen* at the cities of Liverpool, Manchester, Cardiff, and Amsterdam before disembarking in New York City less than a month later. By the 1950s, a growing number of Indonesians arrived in the United States to study and explore the country. Medical faculty from the University of Indonesia received scholarships from the International Cooperation Administration (ICA, later USAID) to attend the University of California at Berkeley (Yang 1995). The ICA also facilitated an exchange program for faculty from the Bandung Institute of

Technology to attend the University of Kentucky and vice versa (Yang 1995). The Immigration and Nationality Act of 1965 (Hart-Cellar Act) ended the exclusion of Asian immigrants that had been set forth by the Immigration Act of 1924.

Immigrant Culture/Early Issues of Assimilation

After Indonesian independence, the United States granted entry to refugees from Indonesia and the Netherlands. The terms *Indo* and *Indische* have been used to describe individuals with mixed European and Indonesian ancestry. The status of Indos has been mostly at the periphery of Dutch colonial society in Indonesia because they were not completely accepted by full-blooded Dutch citizens or native Indonesians. After the declaration of Indonesian independence in 1945, thousands of Indos fled for the Netherlands, where they encountered resentment and suspicion from the host society (Kwik 1989).

Dutch Indonesian author Greta Kwik (1989) published a comprehensive ethnography of the Indo community in Southern California in the 1970s. Her research reveals the process of assimilation undergone by Indos in both the Netherlands and the United States. Kwik describes how the immigration of Indos to the United States was greatly facilitated by American churches such as the Catholic Relief Service and the Church World Service, who matched sponsors with an Indo family or individual. Citing reasons such as cold weather, discrimination by the Dutch, and lack of socioeconomic opportunities, these Indo refugees began migrating to the United States under laws passed by Congress after World War II (see following table). Sponsors played an important role in easing the assimilation process for the new arrivals to American culture. Indo immigrants often settled near their sponsors, who introduced them to their social circles, churches, and local service organizations; and even found jobs for the adults (Kwik 1989).

Discrimination against Chinese Indonesians resulted in migration from Indonesia to Europe or the United States in the 1950s and 1960s. Chinese Indonesians did not fare well under Suharto's New Order policies, which banned the Guomingdang,

Indo immigration to the United States

Act/year	Number of immigrants
Refugee Relief Act of 1953	7,831
Refugee-Escapee Act of 1957	582
Act of September 2, 1958	12,544 (estimated)
World Refugee Year Law of 1960	12,544 (estimated)
1962–1973	30,000

Source: Kwik (1989, 69–70).

Chinese organizations, the use of Chinese characters, and the celebration of Chinese holidays (Cribb and Kahin 2004). Chinese Indonesian Kong Oei left Indonesia with his family in 1955 to avoid persecution by the Indonesian government. Through a business connection, Oei's father was able to gain Dutch citizenship, which allowed him to move his family to the Netherlands. The Oei family immigrated to the United States in 1961.

Later Waves of Immigration

Out of a total of 25,002 foreign-born Indonesians counted by the 1990 Census, only 9,344 arrived in the United States before 1980 and 15,653 arrived between 1980 and 1990. These figures are considerably smaller than the number of Indo immigrants who arrived before 1980, most likely because the 1990 Census did not allow respondents to mark more than one ethnic group. An estimated 20,000 Chinese Indonesians applied for asylum in the United States as a result of the May 1998 riots in Indonesia with 7,359 cases approved and 5,848 denied (Sukmana 2009). By 2000, the Indonesian population in the United States had doubled to 63,073 Indonesians alone or in combination with another ethnic group. By 2005, this number grew by over 30 percent to an estimated 81,587 Indonesians alone or in any combination (U.S. Census 2005).

Despite the growth in the Indonesian American community, a major Indonesian ethnic enclave has yet to take root in the United States. Southern California has the largest demographic of Indonesians and Chinese Indonesians in the United States, but residents are scattered throughout various cities. The Indo community in the 1970s did not evolve into a recognizable "Indotown," because sponsors of Indo refugees did not live in one centralized location. Yet Indonesian community leaders remain hopeful that an enclave will emerge. In 1994, the *Los Angeles Times* reported that a promising cluster of Indonesian businesses opened in Hollywood, but those have now closed down (Brown 1994). Two Indonesian businesses in the Palms neighborhood of Los Angeles, Simpang Asia and Indonesian Café, are popular social magnets for Indonesians, Indonesian Americans, and Chinese Indonesians in Southern California.

Demographic Profile

Size and Composition of Community

Although Indonesia is the fourth most populated country in the world, Indonesians are only the 14th-largest Asian ethnic group in the United States (U.S. Census 2000). The 2000 Census counted 63,073 Indonesians, which includes individuals who identified as Indonesian alone (39,757) or as Indonesian in combination with one or more ethnic groups. The 1990 Census counted 30,085 Indonesians but did not differentiate between Indonesians alone or Indonesians in combination with another ethnic group (U.S. Census 1990). The 2000 Census questionnaire provided boxes to write-up two race categories but did not specify the non-Indonesian categories. The Indonesian alone population was 39,757 in 2000; 52,267 in 2004; 63,609 in 2005; 66,431 in 2006; and an estimated 61,384 in 2008 (U.S. Census 2005, 2006, 2007).

California has the largest population of Indonesians alone and Indonesians in any combination with other races (14,785 in 1990 and 29,710 in 2000). In 1990, there were 6,490 Indonesians in Los Angeles County and 13,065 in Southern California overall. According to the 1990 Census, counties with Indonesian populations in California were San Bernardino County (1,609), Orange County (1,395), Santa Clara County (742), San Diego County (643), San Mateo County (587), San Francisco County (562), Ventura County (250), Alameda County (189), Monterey County (97), and Kern County (96). By 2000, there were 10,899 Indonesians in Los Angeles County—of which 6,648 were identified as Indonesian alone and the rest were listed as Indonesian in combination with one or more ethnic groups. Overall, the states of California, New York, and Texas have the largest Indonesian communities.

The 2000 Census also reported 72,550 individuals who were born in Indonesia and reside in the United States. This number includes individuals who were born in Indonesia but are not of Indonesian descent—including 9,930 people categorized as "white alone" and 365 who are "Hispanic or Latino (of any race)."

Age and Family Structure

The following data on the age and family structure of Indonesians is drawn from the 2006 American Community Survey (ACS), published by the U.S. Census, which counted 66,431 Indonesians alone (not in combination with other ethnic groups). According to ACS, there are a higher percentage of Indonesian females (53%) than males (47%) in the United States. The median age of Indonesians is 33.1 years, which is lower than the national median age of 36.4 years. Most Indonesians fall between the ages of 35 to 64 years (25,633), which is only slightly larger than the second-largest age group of 18- to 34-year-olds (24,108). Out of 13,063 Indonesian children in the United States, 7.8 percent are under five years old. Since Indonesian immigration is primarily a post–World War II phenomenon, the number of Indonesians who are ages 65 and older (3,627) is much smaller than other Asian ethnic groups. Approximately 43.6 percent of Indonesian grandparents are also responsible for taking care of their grandchildren.

The average Indonesian household size in the United States is 3.06, which is slightly larger than the average Indonesian household size in Los Angeles County (3.0), but smaller than the average household size in Indonesia (4.5). In terms of marital status, 61.2 percent of Indonesians are married, 29.9 percent are single, 5.3 percent are divorced, 2.1 percent are widowed, and 1.6 percent are separated (margin of error: +/–0.1%). The majority of the 21,323 Indonesian households in the United States are families (74.7%). There are more male non-family households (15%) than female non-family households (10.3%), but there are more females living alone (8.2%) than males living alone (7.6%).

Educational Attainment

The United States is a prime destination for Indonesian and Chinese Indonesian students at all levels of study. Among the 1990 Indonesian population ages 25 and over in the United States, approximately 41.6 percent (7,902 persons) had a bachelor's degree or higher (U.S. Census 1990). In 2000, that number grew to 42.7 percent (15,699 persons) of Indonesians alone or in any combination (U.S. Census 2000). High school graduation rates are even higher; 92.4 percent of Indonesians ages 25 and over (17,548 persons) finished high school by1990, and 91.5 percent (33,641 Indonesians alone or in any combination) finished high school by 2000. In 2005, 31.6 percent of Indonesians in the United States spoke English only at home; 68.4 percent spoke a language other than English; and 31.1 percent spoke English less than very well (U.S. Census 2005).

During the 1950s, the American Field Service (AFS) began to sponsor a foreign exchange program in which Indonesian and Dutch high school students lived with a host family in the United States for one school year. Biographical details of Indonesian high schoolers were recorded in yearbooks across the country. In 1961, Indonesian student Hendrati Insijah enrolled at Gettysburg High School in Pennsylvania for one term. In 1963, El Camino High School in California dedicated a yearbook page to Soetoro, an Indonesian exchange student who was excited to learn about American student government and sports such as baseball and football. Nineteen-year-old Muslim student Soemarja Toen Moerdijat was a senior at Fort Morgan High School in Colorado from 1962 to 1963. She was the third-youngest child in a family of five siblings and her father worked in the Surahaja municipal office as chief of accounting. While visiting Jakarta in 2009, Secretary of State Hillary Clinton announced plans to expand educational opportunities for Indonesians and Americans by increasing the number of Indonesian students in the United States, opening a Peace Corps branch in Indonesia, and providing Fulbright fellowships for Americans to Indonesia.

American scholars have conducted research in Southeast Asia as early as the 1870s. In 1947, Yale opened the first Southeast Asian studies program in the United States. The University of California at Berkeley (UCB) began offering courses in Indonesian language in 1942 and later established its Center for Southeast Asian Studies in 1960. The UCLA Center for Southeast Asian Studies was founded in 1999 and formed a consortium with the UCB program in 2000. In 2008, UCLA established the Indonesian Studies Program through a grant from scholar and film-maker Robert Lemelson and held the first UCLA Indonesian Studies Graduate Student Conference in 2009.

Economic Attainment

U.S. Census Bureau data from the years 1990, 2000, and 2006 reveals a steady rate of growth in the economic attainment of Indonesians in the United States. According to the 1990 Census, there were 14,972 Indonesians ages 16 and over in the labor force, including 6,387 women. The median household income was $28,597 and the per capita income was $12,559. The majority of Indonesians worked in technical, sales, and administrative support occupations (4,667); managerial and professional specialty occupations (4,609); service occupations (2,012); and precision production, craft, and repair occupations (1,383). Popular industries included manufacturing (2,458); retail trade (2,231); health services (1,522); education (1,234); finance, insurance, and real estate (1,296); personal, entertainment, and recreation services (906); business and repair services (756); and transportation (603). The unemployment rate was 5.2 percent, or 778 persons.

The 2000 U.S. Census provided statistics in two categories: Indonesians alone and Indonesians alone or in combination with other ethnic groups. Out of a population of 39,757 Indonesians alone, 19,561 individuals were employed in the work force and earned a per capita income of $18,932. The median household income was $38,175, which was lower than the median family income of $47,038. About 1,353 Indonesian families and 7,650 individuals lived below the poverty level.

For Indonesians alone or in combination with other ethnic groups: 31,433 were in the labor force; the per capita income was $18,819; and the median household income was $39,839, which was also lower than the median family income of $48,083. A higher number lived below poverty level: 1,953 families and 11,254 individuals.

From 1989 to 2006, the median household income for Indonesians doubled from $28,597 to $57,594. The 2006 data is based on the U.S. Census Bureau's American Community Survey of the Indonesian alone community. The per capita income was $22,380, which was lower than national per capital income of $25,267, but over 78 percent higher than the 1989 per capita income for Indonesians. Approximately 34,458 Indonesians ages 16 and over were employed in the civilian labor force, with a higher number of working males (18,550) than females (15,908). This represents a 130 percent increase in the total number of Indonesians in the labor force from 1989 to 2006. The unemployment rate for Indonesians was 4.4 percent, which was lower than the 1990 rate of (5.2%) and the national unemployment rate of 4.6 percent in 2006. Most Indonesians worked in management or professional occupations (39.4%), including law, dentistry, and engineering. Service occupations were the second-highest category (25.4%); and sales and office jobs employ the third-highest number of Indonesians (23.7%). Indonesians also served in the military, but in lower numbers than other Asian ethnic groups. The 1990 Census counted 106 Indonesians in the armed forces (including six women); by 2006, this figure remained steady at 0.2 percent of the total Indonesian alone population (about 108 persons). ACS 2006 provided the following breakdown of industries that employed Indonesians in the United States.

Health Statistics and Issues

In the 1970s and 1980s, health care activists and advocacy groups began organizing to improve health care services for Asian Pacific Americans. Language and cultural barriers were often obstacles that prevented first-generation Asian Americans from finding and receiving quality health care. Founded in 1986, the Asian Pacific Health Care Venture (APHCV) in Los Angeles offered a full range of health care services to patients in 12 Asian languages, including Indonesian. As the Indonesian population grew in Southern California from the 1990s to the present, APHCV distributed outreach and educational materials translated in Indonesian to raise awareness about preventive health care and its services. Based on data from its annual reports,

Employment of Indonesians in the United States

Industry	Percentage
Arts, entertainment, recreation, accommodation, food services	22.5
Educational services, health care, social assistance	17.7
Manufacturing	13.4
Retail trade	9.9
Professional, scientific, management, administrative, waste management services	8.7
Transportation, warehousing, utilities	5.6
Public administration	5.2
Finance, insurance, real estate, rental, and leasing	5.2
Wholesale trade	4.1
Information	2.7
Construction	1.8
Agriculture, forestry, fishing, hunting, mining	0.7
Other services	5.2

Source: U.S. Census 2006 American Community Survey.
Note: Data available for the 2006 population of 66,431 Indonesians in the "alone" category.

APHCV provided health care to 44 Indonesians in 1999–2000; 146 in 2000–2001; 65 in 2001–2002; 121 in 2002–2003; 152 in 2003–2004; and 104 in 2005.

The 2007 Indonesian Community Needs Assessment Summary Report (IC-NASR) surveyed health care issues among Christian and Muslim Indonesians in Montgomery County, Maryland, who immigrated in the 1980s and early 1990s. Participants indicated that diet-related health issues such as diabetes, obesity, and high cholesterol affect the Indonesian community due to an intake of fattening American and Indonesian foods (Maryland Asian American Health Solutions 2007). The National Diabetes Education Program published "The 4 Steps to Control Your Diabetes for Life" in Indonesian to combat diabetes within the community.

Other health concerns among Indonesians are heart disease, hypertension, arthritis, and stroke. After Chandra Sutanti, who is Chinese Indonesian, suffered from a stroke in 2000 and entered a nursing home to recover in Bellevue, Washington, she encountered a language and cultural barrier between herself and the staff (Ho 2002). The growing Asian senior population and increased demand for services resulted in the establishment of Legacy House by the Seattle Chinatown International District Preservation Development Authority in 1998. Legacy House is an assisted-living facility that caters to the pan-Asian, low-income population in the greater Seattle area. By 2002, Sutanti had moved into Legacy House and was enjoying Asian cuisine and nightly games of Bingo with her new multicultural friends.

ICNASR also identified the need to raise awareness within the Indonesian community about preventive care and screenings. Many Indonesian immigrants cannot afford health insurance and only go to the doctor for emergency cases. To educate the community about health care issues, Indonesian-language periodicals such as *Kabari News* include articles on diet, health, and beauty. Through its Web site and print publication, *Kabari News* also informs its readers about free or reduced-cost public health clinics in California. In Southern California, Indonesian and Chinese Indonesian consumers rely on Sam's Nutrition Center in Monterey Park to purchase traditional medicines imported from Indonesia.

Adjustment and Adaptation

Family, Culture, and Life-Cycle Rituals

Indonesian wedding traditions depend on a variety of factors, including the ethnicity, region of origin, and religion of the bride and groom. For example, a Hindu Balinese wedding will involve different customs than a Javanese Muslim or West Sumatran wedding. Toba Batak people maintain wedding rituals such as the traditional *tortor* dance and the gift of a bridal dowry (Cunningham 2009). If cost is not a factor, then an Indonesian couple may prefer to get married in Indonesia to receive their parents' blessing. A few common practices among Indonesian weddings in the United States include performances of gamelan music, traditional Indonesian dances, and the serving of Indonesian foods.

Indonesian Christian weddings in the United States usually take place in a church with the reception held at a local restaurant. If the couple's first language is Indonesian, then the pastor will perform the service in Indonesian. If the couple is Chinese Indonesian, they may hold a wedding banquet at a Chinese restaurant. To celebrate the arrival of a child, family and friends often throw a baby shower for the mother. The practice of baptism depends on the church. At Temple City CBC in California, children are not baptized at birth because the church wants the individual, not the parents or pastor, to decide if he or she wants to be baptized.

Indonesian Muslims in the United States perform life-cycle rituals with the help of Islamic community networks that are usually based around an urban center. In New York City, Indonesian Muslim weddings take place at a local mosque, such as Masjid Al-Hikmah in Queens. Masjid Al-Hikmah provides wedding services to Muslims from all over the world; a licensed imam conducts the wedding ceremony and adheres to Islamic teachings for the completion of the marriage contract. The wedding reception, called the *walima,* will also be held in a local mosque if space allows.

To celebrate the birth of a child, Indonesian Muslims follow the *aqiqah* custom of slaughtering an animal and donating the meat to the needy. One animal is sacrificed for a girl and two animals are sacrificed for a boy; the practice is done at a halal butcher. In Indonesia, Muslim boys are circumcised a few years after birth; in the United States, this practice is done during infancy to alleviate the cost of surgery and the physical pain associated with the procedure.

Funerary traditions vary according to the religion, ethnicity, and country of origin of the deceased. Many Indonesian immigrants prefer to be buried in Indonesia. If the family of the deceased wishes to send the corpse back to Indonesia, they may seek the assistance of the Embassy of Indonesia. The embassy has a staff member who will accompany the corpse on the plane. Indonesian Christians generally hold a memorial service at their community church and arrange for burial at a local cemetery. Balinese Hindus cremate their dead, whereas cremation is strictly forbidden for Muslims. If an Indonesian Muslim dies in the United States, the family or community will come together to purchase a plot for the deceased at either an Islamic cemetery or the Islamic section of a local cemetery. Indonesian Muslims follow the practice of washing the body, usually within 24 hours of death. Mosques such as Masjid Al-Hikmah will host a *tahlilan,* a prayer service for the deceased that includes readings from the Qur'an.

Retaining a Sense of National Culture and Identity

Indonesian culture and identity are preserved and expressed through a variety of activities throughout the United States. The Consulate General of the Republic of

Indonesia in Los Angeles (KJRI-LA) sponsors several events to bring Southern California's Indonesian community together and to raise awareness of Indonesian arts and culture to the public. The Indonesian Consulate Dance Troupe performs regularly at official, social, and cultural events in Los Angeles. KJRI-LA holds monthly screenings of Indonesian films and sponsored the first-ever Indonesian Film Festival in the United States in 2009. KJRI-LA also allows Indonesian citizens living in America to vote in the national election. Voting for *Pemilu 2009* occurred on July 8, 2009, with Indonesians throughout Southern California commuting to the consulate to cast their votes.

Social Organizations

The growing population of Indonesian Americans corresponds to an increasing number of social organizations throughout the United States. The Indonesian-American Association (Ikatan Keluarga Indonesia, also known as "IKI" and the Indonesian Community Association) was founded on March 2, 1952, by a group of Indonesians in Washington, D.C. (www.indonesianamerican.org). The history of IKI was written by Abdullah Balbed (2006), who states that the goal of the association was to promote community and networking among a growing group of Indonesians, most of whom were either students or employees of organizations such as the Embassy of Indonesia, the World Bank, the International Monetary Fund, or Voice of America. IKI provided valuable services to newly arriving Indonesians, such as instructions job placement and housing assistance, instructions on social security card and driver's license procedures, and referrals to schools for English classes. Today, IKI plays an important role in uniting the evolving Indonesian community through events such as the annual Indonesian Independence Day celebration, voting for elections (*pemilu*) in Indonesia, and the Miss Indonesia pageant held in Washington, D.C. IKI also publishes a bilingual monthly newsletter called *Warta Iki* that keeps readers informed of Indonesian news and cultural events in the Washington, D.C.; Maryland; and Virginia metropolitan area. Another national organization is the Society for Indonesian-Americans, which was established in 2001 with the mission of building community and promoting awareness of Indonesian American culture.

A small number of clubs catered to Indos (short for Indo-Europeans). Avio was a Dutch club that organized dances, card games, sports contests, and other activities for its members, who numbered 18,000 in Southern California (Kwik 1989). The IMI (Ikatan Masjarakat Indonesia) was a community center with a membership of 250 Indos (Kwik 1989). De Soos was founded in 1963 as a club for Indos only and had a membership of around 200 (Kwik 1989; Cunningham 2009). Indos in California were often members of more than one club.

Indonesian youth in the United States are highly prolific in creating social networks through schools and the Internet. Established on December 24, 1961,

PERMIAS stands for Persatuan Mahasiswa Indonesia di Amerika Serikat, which means Organization of Indonesian Students in the United States (Abdullah Balbed, interview with the author, December 8, 2009). PERMIAS is also known as the Indonesian Student Association. There are branches in several cities and universities such as Oregon State, Virginia Tech, Louisiana State, and Texas A&M. PERMIAS LA includes Indonesian youth and students from Southern California colleges and universities such as the University of Southern California, UCLA, California State University at Northridge, Santa Monica College, among others.

Other Indonesian American organizations can be found in almost every state. The Indonesian American Association organizes several events for the community in Arizona. The Indonesian American Society of Florida celebrates Indonesian Independence Day every year. The Indonesian American Association of the Carolinas was founded in 2005. The Minnesota Indonesia Society and the Indonesian Performing Arts Association of Minnesota promote awareness about the arts and culture of Indonesia. Dharma Wanita of Chicago brings together Indonesian wives of civil officials for cultural activities and socializing. Organizations based on regional or ethnic affiliations include: (a) MAESA, which brings together Minahasa people from North Sulawesi (Cunningham 2009); (b) the Batak Community of California Club (Ikatan Masyarakat Batak di California), which dates back to the 1980s; (c) Minahasa NY, a group of Manadonese around New York City; and (d) Krama Bali, a Los Angeles–based organization of Balinese established around 2008. Many social groups are based in churches that offer services and activities throughout the week for adults and youth.

Religion

A significant number of Indonesians in the United States are Protestant or Catholic. In 2009, *Spirit Indonesian Magazine* listed 152 Indonesian churches and fellowships in 18 states and Washington, D.C., with 99 in California alone ("Daftar Gereja" 2009). The first two Indonesian churches in Southern California were the Indonesian-American Seventh-Day Adventist Church and the First Indonesian Baptist Church (Cunningham 2009). With roots dating back to 1971, the Indonesian-Dutch Seventh Day Adventist Church was formally established on February 10, 1973. In 1986, the church changed its name to the Indonesian-American Seventh Day Adventist Church after moving to its present location in Asuza, California.

Pastor John Lim arrived in the United States to attend seminary in Kansas City, Missouri, in 1971. In 1976, he migrated to Los Angeles and started a Bible study for Indonesian Christians in spaces rented from churches. The First Indonesian Baptist Church was founded in October 1980 with a congregation of 66 members. In 1983, the church moved to its current location in Monrovia, California, and raised enough funds to purchase the building. Today, there are First Indonesian Baptist churches in Houston, New York, and California.

Although Indonesia is the largest Muslim country in the world, Indonesian Muslims are a small minority within the overall Muslim American community (Widjanarko 2006). With roots dating back to the early 1980s, the Indonesian Muslim Community, Inc. (IMCI) was founded on December 22, 1989, in New York City (Masjid Al-Hikmah n.d.). After years of fundraising, IMCI bought a warehouse in Queens, New York, on the symbolic date of August 17, 1945, which was the 50th anniversary of Indonesian independence. The mosque was named Masjid Al-Hikmah ("Wisdom Mosque"), inspired by a passage in the Qur'an. With an estimated 600,000–800,000 Muslims in New York City, both Indonesian and non-Indonesian Muslims worship at the mosque and participate in its activities (Widjanarko 2006). Masjid Al-Hikmah offers Saturday school classes, Islamic gatherings called *pengajian,* and social services for the community. According to the Web site of Masjid Al-Hikmah, the mosque also provides space for weddings, prayers for the deceased, interfaith dialogues, and community bazaars. The prayer room holds about 450 individuals; as many as 2,000 Indonesian Muslims mark the end of Ramadan, Idul Fitri. Indeed, the prayer is held two or three times during the day to accommodate the crowd that fills the prayer room and parking lot to capacity.

The Indonesian Consulate General in Los Angeles (KJRI-LA) has worship rooms for Muslims on the third floor and for Christians on the second floor. The consulate also holds public prayer ceremonies in its parking lot to observe Idul Adha (Feast of Sacrifice) and Idul Fitri (end of Ramadan). Every autumn, Idul Fitri attracts hundreds of Muslims to KJRI-LA for morning prayers and a day of socializing.

Language Issues

Indonesian is a form of Malay that was chosen by nationalists as the official language of Indonesia on October 28, 1928 (Cribb and Kahin 2004). Malay had been widely spoken throughout Indonesia's history and was selected as Bahasa Indonesia ("the language of Indonesia") because it has no regional association. Indonesian belongs to the Austronesian language family, which includes an estimated 1,000 languages such as Javanese, Tagalog, Samoan, Maori, and Malay (Bengtson 2007). Unlike Chinese or Thai, Indonesian is written in the Roman alphabet and is not a tonal language. Indonesian does not use verb conjugations, and its vocabulary contains words borrowed from Arabic, Dutch, English, Sanskrit, and regional languages such as Javanese or Balinese (Quinn 2001). Dutch was spoken among the colonial population and a minority of Indonesians. Mixed-race Indos spoke a hybrid dialect of Dutch and Malay called Petjoh (Kwik 1989). When Japan occupied Indonesia from 1942 to 1945, Indonesians were forced to learn Japanese.

First-generation Indonesians in the United States tend to speak Indonesian and one or more regional dialects or languages such as Balinese or Javanese. Language retention among the children and grandchildren of first-generation Indonesian immigrants varies greatly due to a variety of factors (Wijaya 2006). In recent years, the

Indonesian Muslims mark the end of Ramadan, *Idul Fitr*, at the Indonesian Consulate of Los Angeles, September 20, 2009. (Courtesy of Jennifer Cho)

study of Indonesian in the United States has benefited from the growing number of classes in schools and other institutions. Indonesian language classes are available at universities such as UCLA, Yale, Cornell, University of Hawaii-Honolulu, University of California at Berkeley, University of Wisconsin–Madison, University of Texas–Austin, Arizona State University, and University of Michigan–Ann Arbor. The Embassy of Indonesia in Washington, D.C., also offers Indonesian classes to the public.

National/Regional-Language Press and Other Media

American academic interest in Indonesia began in the 19th century. Accordingly, the first American publications about Indonesia focused on the country itself. In April 1966, Cornell University released *Indonesia Journal,* a semi-annual publication of academic articles about the history, politics, society, and culture of Indonesia. In 1969, the *Indonesian Letter* was published by the Asia Letter, Ltd. and included articles on politics, economics, and sociology in Indonesia (Yang 1995).

During the 1980s, the Indonesian population in Southern California became large enough to sustain Indonesian-language publications. In 1988, Emile Mailangkay founded the *Indonesian Journal,* a monthly magazine based in Fontana, California. *Indonesian Journal* was preceded by *Pelita,* also published by Mailangkay (Cunningham 2009). In addition to being the chair of MAESA, Mailangkay also published the *1994–1995 Indonesian Business Directory U.S.A.,* which lists over 370 Indonesian business entities. In 1996, K.E. Sianipar established *Actual Indonesian News,* a biweekly newspaper based in Loma Linda, California (Cunningham 2009).

Published in Glendora, California, *Indonesia Media* was established in 1998 by Chinese Indonesians in wake of the May 9, 1998, riots in Indonesia. Alex Yee is the president and Dr. Ibrahim Irawan is executive editor and manager of day-to-day operations. Irawan and his wife immigrated to the United States in 1985, where they pursued advanced degrees in dentistry. Irawan's family had a long legacy of medical service and activism throughout Asia. His grandfather, Chen Lung Kit, had been a colleague of Sun Yat-Sen during the 1911 revolution in China. In addition to *Indonesia Media,* Irawan is the vice president of the Indonesian Chinese American Association (ICAA) and a board member of the Arcadia Chinese Association. Irawan believes that the tragedy of May 9, 1998, was a wake-up call for Chinese Indonesians to get involved with politics and journalism. With the support of the Chinese Indonesian and Indonesian community in Southern California, the circulation of *Indonesia Media* quickly grew to 530,000 and it expanded from a monthly publication to a biweekly release in 2004.

With offices in San Francisco, Los Angeles, and Jakarta, *Kabari* magazine published its first issue in 2008 with the English motto: "Bridging the World for Indonesians." It has a circulation of 15,200 issues in the United States and 10,000 in Indonesia. The Web site for Kabari (www.kabarinews.com) features blogs and articles about Indonesian culture and immigration issues. Another free publication called *Spirit Indonesian Magazine* is based in Rowland Heights, California.

Los Angeles–based Bhinneka Indonesia TV (BITV) premiered on Channel 18 KSCI-TV in 2007 but was unable to continue its television programming past 2008. It continues to produce content via its Web site (www.bhinnekatv.com) and posts updates on the Twitter for audiences to follow. The show hopes to earn enough revenue to resume broadcasting in the future.

A small number of Indonesian radio stations exist online. Voice of America Indonesia broadcasts news in Indonesia at http://www.voanews.com/indonesian. Indosound (www.indosound.com) is an online radio station that plays Indonesian music 24/7 and is used by the Indonesian consulate in Los Angeles to disseminate information. Based in Jefferson City, Missouri, the Indonesian Muslim Society in America (IMSA) was founded in December 1998 and sponsors an online radio station called Radio IMSA.

Celebration of National Holidays

The Indonesian calendar encompasses several holidays that reflect the country's history and diversity. The Independence Day of the Republic of Indonesia is celebrated on August 17, with events at Indonesian consulates general in Los Angeles, New York, Chicago, San Francisco, Houston, and the Embassy of Indonesia in Washington, D.C. Indonesian Independence Day is marked by an official flag-raising ceremony and reception. Indonesian students dressed in white march to the flagpole and raise the red and white flag, which is accompanied by the singing of the national anthem.

The Indonesian calendar observes Muslim, Christian, Hindu, and Buddhist religious holidays. Indonesian Muslims celebrate the birthday and ascension of Muhammad; Idul Fitri, marking the end of Ramadan; Idul Adha, the Festival of Sacrifice; and Islamic New Year. Christian holidays include Good Friday, Christmas, and Easter. Called Nyepi, the Hindu New Year occurs in March, and the birthday of the Buddha, Waisak 2553, occurs in May. In 2000, President Wahid allowed Chinese Indonesians to celebrate Chinese New Year, which became a national holiday in Indonesia in 2003.

Foodways

Indonesian cuisine reflects an array of regional tastes and international influences. The "spice islands" of Maluku were a leading supplier of cloves, nutmeg, and mace (Drakeley 2005). Black pepper was initially imported from India but then was cultivated by Sumaterans as a top export (Brown 2003). Rice is the mainstay of the Indonesian diet. Cooked rice (*nasi*) accompanies a variety of dishes such as *nasi goreng* (fried rice) or *nasi bungkus* (rice wrapped in banana leaves). Noodles are tossed with other ingredients to make favorites such as *bihun goreng* (stir-fried rice noodles), *mie tek tek* (street-style egg noodles with vegetables and chicken), and more. Like their Southeast Asian neighbors, Indonesians use coconut milk and curries in creative ways. Sweet coconut curry is combined with jackfruit, chicken, tofu, and eggs to make *gudeg*. The Minangkabau are known for their *beef rendang,* a ceremonial dish in which chunks of beef are simmered in coconut milk and spices for over an hour.

During the 1970s, a growing demand for Indonesian groceries led to the establishment of restaurants and stores throughout the United States. Today, shoppers have a variety of choices for finding Indonesian food and groceries in Southern California. Every Saturday, the Indonesian Food Fair (*Pondok Kaki Lima* in Indonesian) is held in the parking lot of the Duarte Inn, which is run by Chinese Indonesians. Indonesian groceries are sold at popular stores such as Simpang Asia in West Los Angeles, Sam's Nutrition Center in Monterey Park, Tip Top Mart in San Gabriel, and Asian grocery stores such as 99 Ranch Market, Ai Hoa Market, A

Grocery Warehouse, India Sweets & Spices, and Bangkok Market. Food festivals around the country include the Indonesian Food Bazaar, which occurs regularly in the parking lot of the al-Hikmah mosque in Astoria, Queens.

Music, Arts, and Entertainment

Indonesian music and dance classes are offered throughout the United States. Gamelan is the most recognized type of Indonesian traditional music and is popular among students and musicians who comprise approximately 110 school-based or independent orchestras in the United States (Benary et al. 2006). The term *gamelan* describes an orchestra or ensemble of instruments that usually consist of metallophones, drums, cymbals, xylophones, gongs, gong-chimes, and flutes. Gamelan music may be accompanied by singers, dancers, or puppet shows such as *wayang*. Styles of gamelan vary by region; Balinese gamelan is generally faster in tempo and brighter in sound than Javanese gamelan.

Indonesian traditional dances are also performed throughout the United States. Balinese dancer Devi Dja was a pioneering force in educating the world about Indonesian dance and music. On November 6, 1939, a review of "Devi Dja and her Bali-Java Dancers" appeared in *Time* magazine after their sold-out performance at the Guild Theater in Manhattan ("Music" 1939). New generations of dancers continue to perform and promote Indonesian dance to the public. In 1995, the dance company Harsanari was founded in San Francisco to provide lessons and stage performances of Indonesian dance. In Los Angeles, the Indonesian Consulate Traditional Dance Troupe holds weekly practices and performs throughout Southern California several times a year. In 2009, University of Minnesota students presented "Rite of Fall" by Indonesian choreographer Sardono Kusomo.

In art history, Indonesian textile arts have been the subject of recent exhibitions in the United States. From September 2008 to 2009, the Los Angeles County Museum of Art presented "Five Centuries of Indonesian Textiles: Selections from the Mary Hunt Kahlenburg Collection." This exhibition featured 90 selections from guest curator Kahlenburg's collection. Ann Dunham, the mother of 44th U.S. President Barack Obama, was an avid collector of Indonesian batik clothing. An exhibition of Dunham's batik collection traveled to Chicago, Los Angeles, San Francisco, Houston, New York, and Washington, D.C., in 2009. The batik collection is administered by Maya Soetoro-Ng, Obama's half-sister, who was born in Jakarta in 1970. Soetoro-Ng's father and Obama's stepfather, Lolo Soetoro, was born in Indonesia in 1936 and died in 1987.

Indonesian martial arts are collectively known as *pencak silat* and have a growing following in the United States. Regional styles have their own names, such as Pencak Silat Harimau Minangkabau or Pencak Silat Mande Muda. In the United States, classes and groups such as the Texas Association of Pencak Silat have been organized to promote the learning of Indonesian martial arts.

Integration and Impact on U.S. Society and Culture

Paths toward Citizenship

Out of 30,085 Indonesians reported by the 1990 Census, 6,044 were naturalized citizens of the United States and 18,958 were not citizens. About 20 percent or 5,083 persons identifying as Indonesian were born in the United States. According to the 2000 Census, less than half of the total population of Indonesians became U.S. citizens (26,695), with the majority having arrived before 1980 (16,860). The majority of non-citizens arrived in the United States between 1990 and 2000 (33,535). This suggests that the road to citizenship is a long process for Indonesians, who, like other immigrant groups, must wait for many years before becoming citizens.

From 1997 to 2006, approximately 11,972 Indonesians became U.S. citizens. In 2005, the American Community Survey counted 81,587 Indonesians alone or in any combination living in the United States; 26,279 were native born; 18,396 were naturalized U.S. citizens; and 36,912 were not citizens. The percentage of Indonesian women obtaining citizenship in 2005 was higher than males (57.6% females and 42.4% males). In 2006, there were 15,371 naturalized citizens and 34,578 non-citizens who identified as Indonesian alone. Indonesian-speaking lawyers cater to the Indonesian community by offering assistance in immigration, citizenship, asylum, removal or deportation, work visas, and other issues. Media outlets such as *Indonesia Media* and *Kabari News* provide the latest information on immigration, deportation, and citizenship matters.

In the years 2008–2009, Indonesians in Southern California have expressed that obtaining U.S. citizenship is not a priority because the economic recession has prevented many from achieving long-term financial stability. Indonesian law prohibits dual citizenship for adults, but children born after 2006 are eligible for dual citizenship. However, Indonesians living in the United States who do not renew their passports at an Indonesian consulate risk losing their Indonesian citizenship.

Intergroup Relations

With over 300 ethnic groups comprising the total population and centuries of trade with other countries, Indonesia presents a fascinating case study in intergroup relations. Before independence, Indonesia consisted of separate kingdoms delineated along ethnic, religious, and regional lines. Intermarriage between *pribumi* ("native Indonesians") and non-Indonesians parallels the history of Indonesia itself. *Peranakan* ("native born") refers to the descendants of Chinese and Indonesian parents, namely 15th-century ethnic Chinese traders who had children with Indonesian wives or concubines. During the colonial period, mixed marriages between Europeans and Indonesians gave rise to generations of multiracial Indo-Europeans, also called *Indos* or *indische*. In 1608, Dutch soldiers were allowed to marry native women (Kwik 1989). A *stamboel* is a type of play that reflects the problems that arise between an Indo married to a Dutch spouse. After Indonesian independence, a high-profile marriage occurred between Sukarno and his Japanese wife, Naoko Nemoto, who was 19 years old when she met the Indonesian leader. Nemoto, known informally as "Madame Dewi" (shorter version of her married name Ratna Sari Dewi Sukarno), gave birth to one daughter, Kartika Sukarno.

Interracial marriage among first and later generations of Indonesians in the United States has become increasingly common. From 1946 to 1952, Balinese dancer Devi Dja was married to Creek-Pawnee artist Acee Blue Eagle (also known as Alexander C. McIntosh). By the 1970s, 72 percent of Indos married outside of their group (Kwik 1989). In 2000, approximately 37 percent of Indonesians in the United States reported two or more ethnic groups (U.S. Census 2000). Although *gado gado* is widely known as an Indonesian salad with an eclectic combination of ingredients, the term is also used colloquially to describe an interracial couple. Setiawan and Jill Onggo run a business called Gado Gado Home Gallery in Atlanta, Georgia. The name reflects the variety of Indonesian handcrafted furniture sold in their store as well as their diverse backgrounds (Setiawan is from Sumatra; Jill is from Buffalo, New York, and is of Polish descent). The Web site www.indousa-couples.com was founded by an interracial couple in the United States to provide a forum for couples to talk and build community with other Indonesians married to non-Indonesians.

Forging a New American Political Identity

Indonesia gained a higher worldwide profile during the presidential campaign of 44th U.S. president Barack Obama, who lived for a time in Indonesia with his mother, Ann Soetoro. Both Obama and Secretary of State Hillary Clinton have called for greater cooperation and understanding between the people and governments of the United States and Indonesia. Earthquakes and tsunamis led to fund-raising efforts by Indonesian Americans in the United States to aid victims of the natural disasters. The May 1998 riots in Indonesia served as a wake-up call for Chinese Indonesians in the United States to become more politically active. In August 1998, Chinese Indonesians organized a protest in front of the Indonesian Consulate in Los Angeles that drew over 3,000 people and gained national media coverage.

On August 17, 2009, California Governor Arnold Schwarzenegger commemorated Indonesian Independence Day with a speech that celebrated the contributions and diversity of Indonesian Americans. San Francisco Mayor Gavin Newsom joined the governor in praising the Indonesian community by declaring August 17 Indonesian Heritage Day.

Return Immigration

Many non-naturalized Indonesians who are currently studying or working in the United States have expressed a desire to return to Indonesia sometime in the future. Increasing economic opportunities in Indonesia have encouraged Indonesian students to pursue college degrees in the United States with the goal of putting them to use in their homeland. After the 9/11 attacks on the World Trade Center, Indonesian nationals were required to register with the U.S. Department of Homeland Security. Those whose papers were not in order were deported. Approximately 487 Indonesians were deported in 2006 (U.S. Department of Homeland Security 2006).

The Second and Later Generations

Like other immigrant groups, second and later generations of Indonesian Americans are more assimilated to American culture than their parents. Language retention depends on whether the parents speak Indonesian and/or a local dialect with their children. In the social organization Krama Bali, parents speak Balinese to their children; as a result, the children understand Balinese better than Indonesian. Since many Indonesian American children communicate in a mixture of Indonesian and English, a child's listening skills tend to be stronger than speaking or writing in Indonesian.

Interest in Indonesian culture among second and later generations of Indonesian Americans tends to be stronger in areas where there is a sizeable Indonesian community. Schools and universities such as UCLA that promote Indonesian cultural days as an annual activity play an important role in facilitating and reinforcing Indonesian American identity. At the 2009 UCLA Indonesian Cultural Night, students produced a play that examined Indonesian American identity among first- and second-generation families. The Indonesian Bruin Students Association at UCLA features first and later generations of Indonesians who proudly displayed various aspects of Indonesian culture, including fashion, pinisi ships, art and woodwork, and a slideshow of facts about the country. The term "1.5 generation" describes individuals who migrated to a new country as children. The 1.5 generation of Indonesians have shown a stronger predilection for learning and retaining their native language by speaking with their parents or taking classes, when available.

Churches, mosques, social networking, and media are vital in reinforcing Indonesian cultural heritage among first, 1.5, second, and future generations of Indonesian Americans and Chinese Indonesians. Depending on their congregation, Indonesian churches may offer services in Indonesian, English, and Chinese. For their 2009 Christmas performance, the Temple City Christian Bible Church in California presented *The Kingdom,* a play that featured a cast of Chinese Indonesians who spoke Indonesian. A multicultural audience listened to audio headsets that translated the play into Mandarin and English. Another young leader in the community is Bryant Irawan, a second-generation Chinese Indonesian who has already authored over 30 articles for the magazine *Indonesia Media*. The son of Dr. Irawan, managing editor of *Indonesia Media*, 16-year-old Bryant founded CUTE (Cultural Unification Through Education), a volunteer organization of high school students that provides services throughout Southern California.

Issues in Relations between the United States and Indonesia

The United States has a vested interest in building and maintaining positive foreign relations with Indonesia. Since the end of Suharto's rule in 1998, Indonesia has undergone a rapid transformation from an autocratic nation to the world's third-largest democracy. The *reformasi* ("reform") era of Indonesia bore fruit in the country's first direct presidential election in 2004, in which voter turnout was an estimated 75 percent. Indonesian President Susilo Bambang Yudhoyono welcomed former Secretary of State Condoleezza Rice in March 2007 and 43rd U.S. President George

Indonesian children march in the Muslim Day Parade in New York City, September 2004. (Ethel Wolvovitz/The Image Works)

Youth Profile

A Young Indonesian Actress

Tania Gunadi was born in Bandung, Indonesia. As a youth, she was a carefree girl who preferred to spend her days at the roller rink instead of school. Her life changed during her teenager years when she won the green card lottery and was allowed to immigrate to the United States. She joined her older sister and brother in Southern California and got a job working full-time at a local Pizza Hut. Her big break came when her friend asked her to join her on an audition for a Disneyland commercial and she booked the part. The producer liked her work and hired her for two more Disneyland commercials. It was then that Tania discovered her calling in life—to become an actor.

After signing with an agent, Tania booked roles on *It's Always Sunny in Philadelphia, Boston Public, Go Figure,* and several other productions. Although she was not the best student in high school, she became serious about her career and trained with acting coaches to hone her craft. Her hard work paid off when she landed her biggest role to date as a series regular on the Disney Channel's *Aaron Stone*. While shooting *Aaron Stone* in Canada, Tania also found time to volunteer at a local animal shelter. She is passionate about animal rescue and donates her time to the cause when her schedule permits.

Tania is devoted to her family and connects with them often. Tania's brother and sister both live in San Gabriel, California. Her parents, who are Chinese Indonesian, remain in Bandung. Tania speaks Indonesian, Sundanese, a bit of Mandarin, and English. Her mother fondly tells her that she has become "Americanized." Tania jokingly says that she sometimes craves peanut butter and jelly instead of fried rice. Yet, she is ecstatic to see Indonesian culture in Southern California—on the weekends, she occasionally visits the Indonesian Food Bazaar in Duarte or shops at Simpang Asia. She often encounters people who know little about Indonesia aside from Java coffee or the island of Bali—as a result, she has become a sort of informal cultural ambassador in Hollywood.

In 2009, Tania became a United States citizen. It was a tough decision that required several years of thought, but Tania ultimately concluded that it was the best choice for her. Indeed, Tania's rapid rise to success typifies the American Dream. She advises youth to listen to their hearts and work hard—because in America, all things are possible.

W. Bush in November 2007. Both American leaders called for a higher degree of partnership between the two countries, especially in fighting the war on terror.

The election of 44th U.S. President Barack Obama further raised Indonesia's profile on the world stage. Obama's family ties in Indonesia focused media attention on a country that few Americans were familiar with prior to the election. During her visit to Indonesia in February 2009, Secretary of State Hillary Clinton praised Indonesia as an example of how Islam, democracy, and women's rights can co-exist in one country (Vaughan 2009). As the largest Muslim country in the world, Indonesia plays a crucial role in fostering communication and bridging the gap in understanding between the United States and other Muslim countries.

The geographical position of Indonesia also plays a critical role in the economic, trade, and security interests of the United States. The sea lanes of the Strait of Malacca, the Sunda Strait, the Makassar Strait, the Ombai Straight, and local waterways provide routes for international shipping and U.S. military vessels that travel between the Pacific and Indian Oceans. These routes are vulnerable targets for piracy and terrorist activities. In terms of energy, Indonesia is a major resource for natural gas and has an estimated petroleum reserve of 9.7 billion barrels; the exportation of energy across these sea routes must be safeguarded. The United States and Indonesia have also launched talks about environmental issues, notably on illegal logging (Vaughan 2009).

Appendix I: Migration Statistics

Table 150 Persons obtaining legal permanent resident status by region and country of birth: Fiscal years 2000 to 2009

Region and country of birth	2000	2001	2002	2003	2004	2005	2006	2007	2008	2009
Total	841,002	1,058,902	1,059,356	703,542	957,883	1,122,257	1,266,129	1,052,415	1,107,126	1,130,818
Indonesia	1,767	2,525	2,418	1,805	2,419	3,924	4,868	3,716	3,606	3,679

Source: U.S. Department of Homeland Security. Office of Immigration Statistics. 2010. Adapted from Table 3.

Table 151 Indonesian refugees admitted

Year	Total
1998	N/A
1999	26
2000	14
2001	5
2002	18
2003	17
2004	5
2005	6
2006	10

Source: U.S. Department of Homeland Security. U.S. Citizenship and Immigration Service (USCIS). *Yearbook of Immigration Statistics: 2008*. Table 14, p. 40.

Table 152 Individuals granted asylum affirmatively by region and country of nationality: Indonesia

Year	Applications granted
1998	15[a]
1999	1,543
2000	937
2001	616
2002	479
2003	211
2004	104
2005	95
2006	428
2007	566
2008	385

Source: U.S. Department of Homeland Security, U.S. Citizenship and Immigration Service (USCIS), *Yearbook of Immigration Statistics: 2008*. Table 17, p. 45.
[a] U.S. Department of Homeland Security, U.S. Citizenship and Immigration Service (USCIS), *Yearbook of Immigration Statistics: 1998*. Table 29, p. 103.

Table 153 Naturalizations of Indonesians 1998 to 2008

Year	Naturalizations
1998	609[a]
1999	1,459
2000	2,480
2001	1,242
2002	1,003
2003	963
2004	1,131
2005	1,234
2006	1,287
2007	1,213
2008	1,832

Source: U.S. Department of Homeland Security, U.S. Citizenship and Immigration Service (USCIS), *Yearbook of Immigration Statistics: 2008*. Table 21, p. 54.
[a] U.S. Department of Homeland Security, U.S. Citizenship and Immigration Service (USCIS), *Yearbook of Immigration Statistics: 1998*. Table 53, p. 189.

Table 154 Nonimmigrant admissions (I-94 only): Indonesia 1999–2008

Year	Total
1999	72,394
2000	86,938
2001	86,660
2002	59,609
2003	53,895
2004	62,517
2005	68,218
2006	71,345
2007	75,497
2008	76,828

Source: U.S. Department of Homeland Security, U.S. Citizenship and Immigration Service (USCIS), *Yearbook of Immigration Statistics: 2008*. Table 27, p. 72.

Appendix II: Demographics/Census Statistics

Table 155 Population of Indonesians alone 2000–2007

Year	Total
2007	61,384 (est.)
2006	66,431
2005	63,609
2004	52,267
2001–2003	N/A
2000	39,757

Source: 2000 U.S. Census; 2007 American Community Survey 1-Year Estimates; 2006 American Community Survey; 2005 American Community Survey; 2004 American Community Survey.

Table 156 2000 U.S. Census statistics

Demographic characteristics	Indonesians alone	Indonesians alone or in any combination
Total population	39,757	63,073
Male	19,287	30,789
Female	20,470	32,284
Median age	30	29
Under 5 years	2,348	4,656
18 years and over	32,646	48,916
65 years and over	1,761	3,018
Household population	38,905	61,733
Group quarters population	852	1,340
Average household size	3	3
Average family size	3	3
Occupied housing units	13,173	20,300
Owner-occupied housing units	5,016	8,605
Renter-occupied housing units	8,157	11,695

Source: Fact Sheet Census 2000 Demographic Profile Highlights, Population Group: Indonesian alone and Indonesian alone or in any combination (www.factfinder.census.gov).

Table 157 Persons obtaining legal permanent resident status by region and country of birth: Indonesia, 1997 to 2006

Year	Total
1997	905
1998	1,017
1999	1,186
2000	1,767
2001	2,525
2002	2,418
2003	1,805
2004	2,419
2005	3,924
2006	4,869

Source: U.S. Department of Homeland Security, *Yearbook of Immigration Statistics: 2006*, Washington, D.C.: U.S. Department of Homeland Security, Office of Immigration Statistics, 2007, Table 3, p. 13.

Table 158 Persons naturalized by region and country of birth: Indonesia, 1997 to 2006

Year	Total
1997	570
1998	603
1999	1,459
2000	2,480
2001	1,242
2002	1,003
2003	963
2004	1,131
2005	1,234
2006	1,287

Source: U.S. Department of Homeland Security, *Yearbook of Immigration Statistics: 2006*, Washington, D.C.: U.S. Department of Homeland Security, Office of Immigration Statistics, 2007, Table 21, p. 54.

Table 159 Persons obtaining legal permanent resident status during fiscal year 2009 leading states of residence: Region/country: Indonesia

Characteristic	Total	Male	Female
Total	3,679	1,322	2,357
Arizona	59	14	45
California	1,522	583	939
Colorado	83	29	54
Florida	67	18	49
Georgia	98	33	65
Hawaii	31	9	22
Illinois	75	30	45
Maryland	79	24	55
Massachusetts	45	16	29
Michigan	31	10	21
Minnesota	38	16	22
Nevada	43	17	26
New Jersey	105	36	69
New York	329	117	212
North Carolina	27	7	20
Ohio	53	19	34
Pennsylvania	157	62	95
Texas	190	67	123
Virginia	80	24	56
Washington	191	72	119
Other	376	119	257

Source: Adapted from U.S. Department of Homeland Security. Profiles on Legal Permanent Residents: 2009. State of Residence, Stbk 15. 2010.

Appendix III: Notable Indonesian Americans

Michelle Branch is a singer-songwriter of Dutch Indonesian, French, and Irish heritage. Her maternal grandmother was born in East Java in Indonesia. She has been nominated for five Grammy Awards, three MTV Video Music Awards, and three CMA Awards. In 2003, she won a Grammy Award for Best Pop Collaboration with Santana for the song, "The Game of Love."

Devi Dja (1914–1989) was a Balinese dancer who performed all over the world with her troupe, Devi Dja and her Bali-Java Dancers with Native Gamelan Orchestra. She arrived in the United States in 1939, stayed because of the war and later became a citizen in 1954. As a dancer or choreographer, she worked on films such as *Road to Singapore*, *The Moon and Sixpence*, *Road to Morocco*, *The Picture of Dorian Gray*, *Three Came Home*, and *Road to Bali*. She was buried under the name Ibu Devi Dja Assan with her nickname "The Pavlova of the Orient" on her gravestone.

Mark-Paul Gosselaar is an actor whose mother is Indonesian and father is Dutch. Gosselaar was born in Panorama City, California, and rose to fame as a teenager on NBC's *Saved by the Bell*. He later joined the cast of the television series *NYPD Blue* as Detective John Clark.

Tania Gunadi is an actor who was born in Bandung, Indonesia. She was a series regular on the Disney Channel drama series *Aaron Stone*. She has also appeared in *Boston Public*, *It's Always Sunny in Philadelphia,* and *Even Stevens*.

Tony Gunawan is an Olympic champion in doubles badminton. He relocated from Indonesia to play for the United States.

Maya Soetoro-Ng is a writer, teacher, activist, and the half-sister of 44th U.S. president, Barack Obama. Her father is Indonesian-born Lolo Soetoro and her mother is Ann Dunham. Born in Jakarta, she attended Barnard College and New York University, and she received her PhD from the University of Hawaii at Manoa. In 2003, she married Konrad Ng, who was born in Canada to Malaysian Chinese parents. Soetoro-Ng spoke at the 2008 Democratic National Convention on behalf of Obama.

Cindy Suriyani (Mei Xian Qiu) is a Chinese Indonesian artist based in Los Angeles, California. Born in Pekalongan, Java, she was given a Chinese name, Indonesian name, American name, and a Catholic name as a means of protection.

Armand Van Helden is an internationally renowned DJ and record producer whose father is Dutch Indonesian. He was born in Boston, Massachusetts.

Glossary

Adat: Local customary law.

Aqiqah: The sacrifice of an animal on the seventh day of a newborn.

Bahasa: Bahasa Indonesia is the national language of Indonesia.

Bhinneka Tunggal Ika: The national motto of Indonesia, translated as "unity in diversity."

Budi Utono: an organization founded by medical students in 1908 that called for the reawakening of Javanese culture through education.

Gado gado: An Indonesian vegetable dish and a colloquial phrase to describe an interracial couple.

Gamelan: Traditional music of Indonesia that consists of an ensemble of musicians.

Garuda: Birdlike creature in Hindu mythology.

Imam: A Muslim religious leader.

Indische Partij: Early nationalist party that called for equality for those who were born in the Indies.

Kakawin Sutasoma: A Javanese poem written by Mpu Tantalar in the 15th century that was the source of Indonesia's national motto.

Pancasila: Five principles that describe the philosophy behind Indonesia's government.

Pemilu: The Indonesian word for election.

Penchak silat: Indonesian martial arts.

Pengajian: A gathering of Indonesians to recite from the Qur'an and discuss Islam.

Peranakan: Mixed race descendants of Indonesian and ethnic Chinese parents.

Pribumi: Term that describes one who is native or indigenous to Indonesia.

Reformasi: Reform movement in Indonesia begun by students in 1997 and culminating in the resignation of Suharto in 1998.

Tahlilan: A prayer for the deceased.

VOC: Abbreviation for Dutch company Vereenigde Oost-Indische Compagnie, or United East Indies Company. Also known as the Dutch East Indies Company.

Walima: An Islamic wedding ceremony.

Wayang: Traditional Indonesian dramatic arts. *Wayang kulit* utilizes shadow puppets.

References

"Arja Dance Tells of the Need to Love and Respect. " 2009. *The Jakarta Post.* [Online article retrieved on 6/30/09.] www.thejakartapost.com/news/2000/05/25/arja-dance-tells-need-love-and-respect.html.

Benary, Barbara, Jody Diamond, Richard North, and Marc Hoffman. 2006. "Gamelan Groups in the U.S.A." [Online information; retrieved on 4/03/11.] http://www.gamelan.org/directories/directoryusa.html.

Asian Pacific American Legal Center. 2004. *The Diverse Face of Asian and Pacific Islanders in Los Angeles County,* pamphlet.

Balbed, Abdullah. 2006. "Indonesians in America" [Online information retrieved on 7/1/09.] http://indoeduculture.org/index.php?option=com_content&task=view&id=35&It emid=1.

Bengtson, John D. 2008. *Linguistic Fossils: Studies in Historical Linguistics and Paleolinguistics.* Calgary: Theophania Publishing.

Brown, Colin. 2003. *A Short History of Indonesia: The Unlikely Nation?* Crows Nest, N.S.W.: Allen & Unwin.

Brown, Scott Shibuya. 1994. "Indonesian Culture Takes Root in Hollywood Community: Shops Are Flourishing on Sunset Boulevard, Catering to the More Than 20,000 Island Immigrants in L.A." *Los Angeles Times*, October 2, 1.

Central Intelligence Agency. 2009. *The World Factbook 2009.* "Indonesia." [Online article retrieved; 05/31/09.] www.cia.gov/library/publications/the-world-factbook/geos/id.html.

Cribb, Robert, and Audrey Kahin. 2004. *Historical Dictionary of Indonesia.* Lanham, MD: Scarecrow Press.

Cunningham, Clark. 2009. "Unity and Diversity among Indonesian Migrants to the United States." In *Emerging Voices: Experiences of Underrepresented Asian Americans*, edited by Huping Ling, 90–125. New York: Rutgers University Press.

"Daftar Gereja di USA." 2009. *Spirit Indonesian Magazine*, April, 46–47.

Drakeley, Steven. 2005. *The History of Indonesia.* Westport, CT: Greenwood Press.

Encyclopedia Britannica. 2008. "Kalimantan." [Online article; retrieved 07/02/09.] http://www.britannica.com/EBchecked/topic/310183/Kalimantan.

Ho, Vanessa. 2002. "The Number of Elderly Asians in America is Rising, and, in a Break with Tradition, Fewer are Living with their Children; Culture Shift Strains Social Services." *Seattle Post-Intelligencer*, April 3.

Kwik, Greta. 1989. *The Indos in Southern California.* New York: AMS Press.

Maryland Asian American Health Solutions. 2007. "In Focus: A Summary of the Asian American Community Group Reports, Indonesian Community Needs Assessment Summary Report," University of Maryland College Park School of Public Health. [Online article; retrieved on 04/1/2011.] http://www.maahs.umd.edu/Reports.html.

Masjid Al-Hikmah New York City. "Beginning." [Online article; retrieved on 07/31/09] http://www.masjidalhikmahnewyork.org/index.php?option=com_content&view=articl e&id=46&Itemid=54&lang=en.

Mirpuri, Gouri, and Robert Cooper. 2002. *Indonesia.* New York: Benchmark Books.

"Music: Old Ladies from Bali." 1939. *Time Magazine,* November 6.

Quinn, George. 2001. *The Learner's Dictionary of Today's Indonesian.* Sydney: Allen & Unwin.

Radio New Zealand International. 2007. "Papuan Province Changes Name from West Irian Jaya to West Papua." February 7. [Online article; retrieved on 07/07/09]. www.rnzi.com/pages/news.php?op=read&id=29965.

Ricklefs, M. C. 2008. *A History of Modern Indonesia Since c. 1200.* Stanford, CA: Stanford University Press.

Suharno. 2007. "Forthcoming: The 2010 Indonesian Population and Housing Census." The 23rd Population Census Conference, April 16–18, Christchurch, New Zealand.

Sukmana, Damai. 2009. "Game of Chance: Chinese Indonesians Play Asylum Roulette in the United States." [Online article; retrieved on 07/30/09.] http://insideindonesia.org/content/view/1164/47/.

Suryadinata, Leo, Evi Nurvidya Arifin, and Aris Ananta. 2003. *Indonesia's Population: Ethnicity and Religion in a Changing Political Landscape.* Singapore: Institute of Southeast Asian Studies.

U.S. Census Bureau. 1990. "Table 1: General Characteristics of Selected Asian and Pacific Islander Groups by Nativity, Citizenship, and Year of Entry: 1990." Washington, D.C.

U.S. Census Bureau. 2000. "Census 2000 Demographic Profile Highlights: Indonesian Alone or in Any Combination." Washington, D.C.

U.S. Census Bureau. 2005. "S0201. Selected Population Profile in the United States. Indonesian Alone or in Any Combination." American Community Survey. Washington, D.C.

U.S. Census Bureau. 2006. "S0201. Selected Population Profile in the United States. Indonesian Alone." American Community Survey 1-Year Estimates. Washington, D.C.

U.S. Census Bureau. 2007. "B02006. Asian Alone by Selected Groups." American Community Survey. Washington, D.C.

U.S. Department of Homeland Security. 2008. U.S. Citizenship and Immigration Service (USCIS), Refugee, Asylum, and Parole System (RAPS). *Yearbook of Immigration Statistics* 2008. Washington, D.C.: Department of Homeland Security.

Vaughn, Bruce. 2009. "Indonesia: Domestic Politics, Strategic Dynamics, and American Interests." Congressional Research Service, Washington, D.C.

Widjanarko, Putut. 2006. "Indonesian Muslims in New York City: A Transnational Community in the Making?" Presented at the Muslim Peace Building and Interfaith Dialogue Conference, April 28–29, American University, Washington, D.C., organized by Salam Institute for Peace and Justice.

Wijaya, Juliana. 2006. "Indonesian Heritage Learners' Profiles: A Preliminary Study of Indonesian Heritage Language Learners at UCLA." *Journal of Southeast Asian Language Teaching* 12(2): 1–14.

Yang, Eveline. 1995. "Indonesian Americans." In *The Asian-American Almanac: A Reference Work on Asians in the United States,* edited by Susan B. Gall and Irene Natividad, 91–98. Detroit: Gale Research.

Further Reading

Consulate General of Republic of Indonesia—Los Angeles. www.kjri-la.net.

> This bilingual Web site offers up-to-date information on Indonesian news and immigration. It also posts upcoming Indonesian cultural events and activities sponsored by the consulate.

Cunningham, Clark. 2009. "Unity and Diversity among Indonesian Migrants to the United States." In *Emerging Voices: Experiences of Underrepresented Asian Americans*, edited by Huping Ling, 90–125. New York: Rutgers University Press.

> Cunningham is a distinguished scholar on Indonesia and Indonesian Americans. His article is an excellent resource, particularly on Indonesian Americans in Southern California.

Embassy of Indonesia. www.embassyofindonesia.org.

> The embassy recently launched the Indonesian Embassy Channel on its Web site, which is a series of videos about Indonesian news and culture. The Web site also features news articles and information about upcoming events in Indonesia and the United States.

Ikatan Keluarga Indonesia—Indonesian American Association. www.indonesianamerican.org.

> The Indonesian American Association was established in 1952. The Web site provides information about the Indonesian American community and archival issues of its newsletter, *Warta Iki*.

Indonesian American Association. www.indonesianamericanassociation.org.

> This Web site focuses on the Indonesian American community in Arizona.

Indonesian Education and Cultural Center. www.indoeduculture.org.

> This Web site contains invaluable articles on Indonesian American history. It is sponsored by the Embassy of Indonesia and the Ministry of Education, Republic of Indonesia.

The United States-Indonesia Society. www.usindo.org.

> The United States-Indonesia Society publishes academic reports and articles on politics, politics, public policy, economics, history, and culture affecting both countries.

Yang, Eveline. 2008. "Indonesian Americans." *Every Culture*. http://www.everyculture.com/multi/Ha-La/Indonesian-Americans.html.

> Yang's article is a comprehensive overview of Indonesian American history.

Iranian Immigrants

by Maboud Ansari

Introduction

Iranian migration to the United States is a recent political phenomenon. It began 55 years ago with the study abroad of young Iranians. They came to the United States in the 1950s, often as temporary residents (students and interns), but eventually changed their status to permanent residents. However, it was the Iranian Revolution of 1979 that was both organizationally and culturally crucial to the making of the Iranian community in the United States. Prior to the revolution, though there were Iranians living in the United States, the Iranian immigrant community had not yet developed.

With regards to the making of the Iranian community in America, it is suggested that the dialectically interrelated Islamization of Iranian society and anti-Iranian and anti-Islamic sentiments in America not only transferred the already available marginal situation to a much larger group of postrevolutionary immigrants and refugees, but also reinforced the development of a new community of Iranian Americans. This is a new kind of ethnic community, one of the highest-status foreign-born groups in the United States. It is a new, nonterritorial community based on non-traditional foundations found in an urban, bureaucratized America and manifests peculiarities derived predominantly from the middle class and highly trained professionals. Iranians brought not only the riches of the Persian culture, one of the oldest and most colorful heritages of humankind, but also a considerable amount of wealth. Of all recent immigrant groups, Iranians have made one of the greatest investments in America. However, Iranian pride does not just stem from what they were, but rather from what they have been able to achieve in the United States.

Today, as the nation of Iran is passing through crucial historical moments, Iranian Americans are making their own history. Much of this history-making contains the best of both world adaptations. In doing so, Iranian Americans borrow heavily from their host society as well as from the resurrected imagery, symbolism, and cultural heritage of ancient Persia. In this state, even as the Iranian American community continues to accommodate to the American context, it rummages the distant past to self-consciously maintain and/or recreate its ethnic identity or "Iranianness." Thus, the ethnic identity of this community, as modified by its American experience, is not simply Iranian but is something that is grounded more in Iranian nationalism and secular ideas.

Chronology

1500 B.C.E.	The Persians migrate to the Iranian plateau from Central Asia.
550–530 B.C.E.	The Achaemenid dynasty establishes the first Persian Empire, which is the world's first religiously tolerant empire and consists of a multitude of different languages, religions and cultures.
334 B.C.E.	Alexander the Great invades Persia.
224–642	Sasanian dynasty, a golden era of city building and grand art.
662–1258	The Muslim-Arab occupation of the Iranian region. Persia is brought under Arab rule, but Persians remain a cultural force in the emerging Muslim world, becoming Islamized but remaining Iranians.
1220s	The Mongols invade Iran.
1501–1736	Safavid dynasty and the revival of religious-national spirit; Shia Islam begins, which coincides with major cultural contact between Persia and the West.
1795–1925	Qajar dynasty. Following the humiliating defeat by Russia in 1813, the process of study abroad begins, because this humiliation results in a realization that Iran's weakness is due to its technologically backward army. Thus the first group of young Iranians is sent abroad to study military arts and techniques.
1908	The discovery of oil reserves in Iran.
1909	The constitutional revolution and establishment of Iran's first parliament.
1921	Reza Khan (1888–1944) and modern times of Iran. Reza Khan executes a coup d'état and establishes the Pahlavi dynasty.
1941	Abdication of Reza Shah in favor of Mohammad Reza Shah Pahlavi.
1951	Premiership of Mohammad Mosaddeq (1880–1967) begins.
1953	The CIA-backed overthrow of Iran's elected and popular prime minister, Mohammad Mosaddeq, arguably a crucial point in Iran–U.S. relations.
1979	The shah, Mohammad Reza Pahlavi, flees Iran and Iran becomes officially the Islamic Republic of Iran.
1979	The hostage crisis. On November 4, 1979, 52 American diplomats are taken hostage and subsequently held for 444 days in

Iran. Diplomatic relations with the United States become severed and remain so until the present.

2002   President Bush in his State of the Union address in January 2002 classifies Iran as a member of the "Axis of Evil."

2009   The fallout from the Iranian election (on June 12) has been the most sustained challenge to the Iranian government since the 1979 revolution. It has also been a turning point in the political life of Iranian Americans.

Background

Geography and Ethnic Diversity

Iran is situated in southwestern Asia and is bounded in the north by the Caspian Sea, Azarbaijan, and Turkmenistan; to the west by Turkey and Iraq; to the east by Pakistan; and to the south by the Persian Gulf and the Indian Ocean. However, historically, the Persian cultural and even political sphere was much wider than the present national boundaries.

With an area of 635,932 square miles, Iran ranks 16th in size among the countries of the world. However, by European standards, Iran is a very large country. It is about three times the size of England and Northern Ireland. By American standards, it is about one-fifth the size of the continental United States, or slightly larger than the combined areas of California, Arizona, Nevada, Oregon, Washington, and Idaho. In comparison with one state, Iran is six times the size of Colorado.

Iran, like the United States, is a multilingual and diverse society. The national (official) language of Iran is Farsi, known in English as Persian. In addition to Persian, other languages and dialects, such as Azeri, Kurdish, Blouch, Luri, and Arabic are spoken in various parts of the country.

The Persian language is also the main language in Afghanistan (referred to there as Dari) and in Tajikestan (referred to as Tajik). Persian, Dari, and Tajik are essentially a single language despite numerous differences in specialized vocabularies and spoken dialects. Historically, the Persian language was, for several centuries, the chief literary and administrative language of a large part of central, western, and southern Asia, including northern India. Currently, the Persian language is the national language of a combined population of more than 150 million people. Moreover, it is the community language of as many as 6 million more who are part of Iranian, Afghan, and Tajik diasporas.

The Iranian languages, of which the Persian branch is the most important, belong to the Indo-European family. As a language of written literature, Persian, in one or another form, had been used at least 1,200 years before the rise of Islam. However, after the Islamic conversion of Persia (637 C.E.), the Persian language (Pahlavi) was replaced by Arabic as a written language, though it continued in oral use and eventually emerged as what is now called New Persian. Moreover, many Arabic words were introduced into the Persian language and became an integrated part of the language in the same way that words of Latin origin have been absorbed into English. In the English language today, we use a number of Persian words, such as *bazaar, balcony, jasmine, jungle, lilac, orange, paradise, pajamas, shawl,* and *spinach,* to name a few. What is remarkable about the Persian language is that for over a thousand years it has shown a remarkable continuity: "the Persian of the tenth century C.E. presents no greater problem to a modern Persian than Shakespeare does to an Englishman today" (Morgan 1987).

Demography and Religious Groups

The Iranian population increased dramatically during the latter half of the 20th century, reaching about 72 million by 2008. More than two-thirds of the Iranian population is under the age of 30.

The vast majority of Iranians are Muslims, mostly of the Shia branch, which is the official religion and to which about 89 percent of Iranians belong. Shia Islam distinguishes the Iranian nation from the mainstream Sunni world. Since 1501, Shiism has been the official religion of Iran. Therefore, the Islamic religious identity has, over the centuries, even before the Islamic revolution of 1979, melded with the Iranian national identity. The most important cultural developments in Islam, in the area of medicine, mathematics, astronomy, philosophy, chemistry, music, literature, and theology resulted from the contributions of Iranian thinkers and scientists who wrote in Arabic, the lingua franca of the time.

About 9 percent of Iranians belong to the Sunni branch of Islam, mainly Kurds and Iran's Balochi. The remaining 2 percent are non-Muslim religious minorities, including Zoroastrians, Jews, Christians, and Bahais. Historically, Iran has been the home of the largest and oldest Jewish community in the Muslim Middle East. All religious minorities, except the Bahais, are officially recognized and protected and have reserved seats in the Iranian Majlis (parliament).

Iran, or Persia as it was known in the West for most of its history, is regarded by historians to be one of the world's oldest civilizations. Iranians have always called their country Iran, while Westerners, using a Greek term, often referred to it as Persia. Iranians define their Iranianness, in part, in terms of history. The recorded history of the country itself spans some 2,500 years. When the Arabs conquered Persia in the seventh century C.E., 1,200 years had already passed since the establishment of the first Persian Empire. At this time, the Zoroastrian religion was the official faith of Iranians. The prophet Zoroaster (born in the second millennium before Christ—1767 B.C.E.) was one of the first prophets to introduce the concepts of monotheism and duality of good and evil. He believed that human salvation in life and the afterlife could only be ensured through "Good Thoughts, Good Words, and Good Deeds." Many concepts of the Zoroastrian faith have influenced many religions, including Judaism, Christianity, and Islam. Nowhere is Iran's cultural heritage and contribution to human civilization more apparent than in the precepts of the ancient native religion of Zoroastrianism.

Are Iran and Persia truly synonymous? The short answer is no. The term *Persia* derives from an ancient Hellenized form, Persis, the name of one province in the southwest of the country. Parsa is the name of the Iranian tribe that founded the Persian Empire in 550 B.C., the most extensive empire that the world had yet seen. The empire once included what are today's Iraq, Pakistan, Afghanistan, Turkmenistan, Uzbekistan, Tajikistan, Turkey, Jordan, Cyprus, Syria, Lebanon, Israel, Egypt, and the Caucasus region. Cyrus "the Great" (known to Iranians as Kourosh), was the first king of the Achaemenid dynasty, who introduced the Declaration of Human Rights. This declaration (a clay cylinder) is housed at the British Museum in London, and a replica is displayed at the United Nations in New York City. Cyrus freed the Jews from their Babylonian captivity and permitted them to return to Jerusalem and rebuild their temple, which may be why he is referred to in the Book of Isaiah as the Shepherd of the Lord. In 1935, the government of Iran declared that the term *Iran* had to be used even by foreigners in all official correspondences when referring to the country. However, since World War II, the words *Iran* and *Persia* have been used interchangeably to identify the same country.

The history of Iran throughout the two and a half millennia displays an unusual degree of continuity and homogeneity of a distinctive culture, despite enormous diversity and periodic upheaval of the societal and community life. "In the light of Iran's ethnic and linguistic diversity, as well as invasions and all the changes in rulers and political boundaries, a sense of Persian consciousness, of Iranianness (Iraniyat) remains throughout the country's history" (Morgan 1987).

Modern History

Iranian society experienced two revolutions in the 20th century. The discontent with the Qajar Dynasty's despotic rule and corruption (1786–1925) led to the constitutional revolution in 1906 and the establishment of Iran's first parliament. The constitutional aspirations for the rule of law was flawed and brought about political instability. In 1921, through a coup, Reza Khan (an Iranian officer of the Persian Cossak Brigade), with some help from British military officers, abolished the Qajar Dynasty and made himself shah, thus establishing the Pahlavi dynasty and ruling as Reza Shah for almost 16 years. It was in the first decade of Reza Shah's time that the foundation for modern industry was laid, security was reestablished in the state, and the army was reorganized. Reza Shah also reformed the educational system and secularized it.

Moreover, Tehran University was established, and faculties of law, medicine, literature, science, and technical schools were opened. This period (1921–1931) was a decade of growing dictatorship. In 1941, Reza Shah was forced to abdicate in favor of his son, Muhammad Reza Pahlavi, who came to power at the age of 22. In 1951, Dr. Mohammad Mosaddeq was elected prime minister. He nationalized Iran's oil reserves. The nationalization of Iranian oil became symbolic for a popular movement to rid the country of British interference in Iran's politics. Eventually the American and British governments managed to stage the coup d'état of August 1953.

From the mid-1960s until late 1979, Iranian power was concentrated entirely in the Shah's hands, and the explosion of the oil revenues greatly strengthened the state vis-à-vis the public. "The total absence of freedom coupled with Western, especially American, support for the Shah convinced the public that he was no more than a puppet who was implementing the policies of American imperialism. This led to very strong feelings against both the Shah and the West" (Katouzian and Shahidi 2008). Therefore, in 1978 the Shah's opponents of all political affiliations were united and gave rise to a revolutionary movement that brought about the 1979 revolution and the fall of the Pahlavi dynasty. After 2,500 years of monarchy, Iran's government was changed to an Islamic republic.

An effigy of the deposed shah of Iran is burned during a demonstration outside the United States Embassy in Tehran in late 1979. Iran's Islamic Revolution of that year began as an uprising against Shah Mohammad Reza Pahlavi, whose autocratic rule and ties to the West were extremely unpopular in his country. (AP/Wide World Photos)

Causes and Waves of Migration

The Pattern of Iranian Emigration

Emigration from Iran to the United States is a recent phenomenon, developed within the last 30 years, and it is situated within the larger context of U.S.–Iran relations. It became significant only in the early 1980s and occurred during three phases. The first phase started in the 1950s and lasted until 1977. During this period, Iranians often came as sojourners and temporary migrants (students and interns), who eventually changed their status and became a community of nonreturnee professionals. During the peak period of immigration from other countries to the United States (1842–1903), only 130 Iranian nationals were known to have immigrated. However, starting in 1945, emigration from Iran rose steadily and in 1966 reached 12,624 per year. The number of nonimmigrants (visitors, students, and interns) increased drastically from an annual average of about 1,400 in the 1950s to 6,000 in the 1960s, reaching the highest figure of 98,018 in 1977. According to the Institute of International Education, more Iranian students were enrolled in U.S. institutions of higher education at this time than students from any other country. However, during the same period, a total of only 34,855 Iranian immigrants were admitted, and 8,877 became naturalized U.S. citizens.

It is particularly notable that the pattern of Iranian migration during this period did not involve "chain migration"; it was basically individuals, and not the migration of whole families. For the most part, it involved professional groups such as physicians, dentists, scientists, engineers, and so on. From a different perspective, it was a problem of "brain drain," that is, the migration of highly professional and technical young Iranians to the United States. The Iranian immigrant was usually a student immigrant—a sojourner who had not arrived in this country with the intention of becoming a permanent resident. However, the Iranian migration of physicians (interns and residents), for instance, was not essentially an "overflow" of excess talent at home. In the 1970s, an acute shortage of doctors in rural areas of Iran led the government there to hire several hundred Pakistani physicians to work in the countryside. In 1973, there was only one doctor for every 4,000 Iranians (the ratio in the United States during that same year was one doctor for every 600 people). At the time, the yearly cost of medical education in Iran was $40,000 to $700,000. The supreme irony was that the Iranian government, through migration of its American-trained physicians, used to pay $700,000 annually in "foreign aid" to the United States.

The majority of these immigrant professionals had voluntarily chosen migration as an outlet for their general alienation from the sociopolitical system in Iran (Ansari 1988). The migration of these educated Iranians also involved a process of becoming immigrants while they were studying abroad. Few Iranian professionals had immigrant status upon arrival—most were admitted as students or as visitors.

Once living in the United States as permanent residents, they perceived their return to Iran as involving three major dimensions of political, social, and professional marginality.

The second phase of Iranian migration began immediately before and after the Iranian revolution of 1979 and became significant in the early 1980s. The 1979 revolution and the 1980–1988 war with Iraq transformed Iran's class structure, politically, socially, and economically. As the revolution ousted the Pahlavi dynasty, displaced the ruling elite directly associated with it, and established itself as an Islamic republic, it drastically changed the pattern and nature of Iranian emigration to the United States. In addition to the revolution, the eight years of the Iran–Iraq war during the 1980s was also another factor that forced many of the best-educated and most wealthy families into exile in the United States and other countries. By 1990, the number of Iranian immigrants had steadily increased to a peak of almost 25,000. More recent Department of Homeland Security statistics show that these trends have continued in the years 2000–2009.

The arrival of the postrevolutionary political refugees and immigrants opened an entirely new chapter in the short history of Iranians in the United States. Never before in Iran's long history had so many people involuntarily had to leave their country. What was once basically a problem of "brain drain" during the Pahlavi regime was now predominantly an involuntary emigration of a relatively large number of middle- and upper-class families, including the movement of a considerable amount of wealth (in liquidated assets). There are no data available about the capital flight, but the estimate is in the range of $30 to $40 billion. Through all these waves of emigration, the United States was and still is the most favored destination of the Iranians. Iranians benefited more from the U.S. political asylum laws than any other nationality. According to Immigration and Naturalization Service (INS) statistics, in the period from October 1981 through February 1985, more Iranians (11,055) were being granted asylum than any other nationality. In addition, from 1990 to 2008, 6,255 Iranian refugees were granted asylum (see Table 160).

The new pattern of Iranian emigration is complex in quality, motivation, and quantity. In terms of quality, it is heterogeneous in social class, education, occupations, political orientations, and age distribution. As far as religious affiliation, this wave of emigration includes higher proportions of such Iranian religious minorities as Sunnis (Kurds and Turkmen), Zoroastrians, Christians (Armenian and Assyrians), Jews, and Bahais. In terms of political orientation, it includes sympathizers with the old regime (monarchists) and postrevolutionary alienated intellectuals (both Marxist and non-Marxist activists). In terms of motivation, a combination of political, social, religious, and professional marginality has produced a "vocabulary of motive" for emigration of postrevolutionary immigrants to the United States.

Therefore, the immigration of Iranians as a voluntary action contains some essentially involuntary factors (Ansari 1992). In other words, immigrants and refugees have managed to escape the compound crisis of being disenchanted intellectuals, individuals disillusioned with the Islamic republic, rejected Western-trained professionals, and the powerless affluent. Whether for political, economic, or religious reasons, Iranian immigrants and the self-exiled came to the United States to seek a better life, particularly for their children. However, they came not to stay, but to return home when and if the political situation would permit. Gradually, they decided to stay permanently but still maintained the hope of the eventual return home. Uprooted and transplanted, each wave of Iranian immigrants has undergone dramatic social, economic, and cultural transitions from their traditional native culture. Through hard work, perseverance, and education, Iranian immigrants have managed to become an ethnic community and to prosper in American society. Given the heterogeneity of Iranian American communities in terms of ethnic origin, religious affiliations (Iranian Armenian, Jewish Iranian, Zoroastrian Iranian, and others), generation, length of time in the United States, immigration status, language ability, and socioeconomic status, it was only a matter of time before Iranian Americans became an ethnic community and started using their growing financial clout to gain political power.

The third phase of Iranian immigration started in 1995 and continues to the present. This phase comprises an increasing number of elderly (65 and over) middle-class Iranians, as well as young Iranian men who fled military service during the Iran–Iraq war. These elderly Iranian immigrants are those who arrived in America as aging parents to join their adult children or their siblings, who, as naturalized

---

Tehranjeles

Tehranjeles is a blend of Tehran, the capital of Iran, and Los Angeles.

Iranians everywhere call Tehranjeles their largest exile community. Neon signs in Persian decorate the windows of the Westwood Iranian American stores in Los Angeles. Products labeled in Persian and English reflect the dual identity of most consumers.

"The exile community of at least 500,000 Iranians has carved out a distinctive subculture here. At the Encino Town Center, two of six movie screens show Iranian movies."* The Community has Iranian Republican clubs, Iranian Rotary clubs, Iranian banks, over 35 media outlets (TV, radio, and newspaper), Iranian bookstores, and Persian restaurants. The neighborhood, also called Little Persia, has the largest Persian bookstore outside of Iran. On March 16, 2010, Jimmy Delshad was reelected as the Mayor of Beverly Hills.

Like Iranians anywhere, Los Angeles Iranians are rich or poor, Muslim, Jewish, Baha'i, Christian, or Zoroastrian, secular or religious, conservative or leftist, highly educated or less so. Most are Shiite Muslims, but in West Los Angeles, the Jewish Iranians are the most cohesive, connected through synagogues, marriages, and jobs.

---

*Neil MacFarquhar, "Exiled in Tehranjeles Are Split on Iran," *New York Times,* May 9, 2006.

citizens, had filed for them to be admitted as permanent residents. The elderly immigrants arrive here at the age of retirement and often travel back and forth regularly between Iran and the United States. This phenomenon, of the Iranian elderly going back and forth between their homeland and their adopted country, was almost inconceivable 20 years ago.

Foreign Education and the Problem of Dual Marginality

What is striking is that Iranians' contact with the West since the early eighteenth century has had a paradoxical dual character: on the one hand, a high degree of acculturation of Western ideas and values; on the other hand, an ongoing resentment, both open and silent (symbolic reaction) toward the West. It is this historical character that greatly influenced the forming of a peculiar social type, such as the familiar stranger, in contemporary Iranian society. The familiar stranger (*ashena-i-biganeh*) is the cultural hybrid whose divided identification stems mostly from his foreign education and also from oversocialization abroad.

The concept of dual marginality has been developed to explain the situation in which some immigrants find themselves. Those Iranians that came to this country initially as sojourners, with strong feelings of belonging at home, and a firm conviction of returning, are subject to the experience of dual marginality. That is, they find themselves estranged from both the host and the home society. The concept of dual marginality is considered here as having two major components: native and alien marginality. Each culture produces a dual pattern of partial identification and divided loyalty for the individual. Thus, the dually marginal person is an involuntary immigrant who is representative of marginality at home and abroad. The dually marginal person in the restricted sense is an unintended immigrant who is not a fully integrated member of either society, home or host. Both situations, at home and abroad, contain for this person some elements of uncertainty, nonbelongingness, and insecurity. As a sojourner who has become an uncertain immigrant, the person is caught between two conflicting reference groups in two different cultural settings. The immigrant remains an uncertain, undecided immigrant in conflict about whether to adhere to American cultural patterns and settle there or to embrace those of his own country and return home. As long as he remains an undecided immigrant, his situation may be characterized as one of dual marginality, with a feeling of not belonging to either society. While he has a feeling of being a marginal person at home, he experiences marginality in the United States as well. When he starts to psychologically organize himself as a permanent resident in this country, he is then a marginal person.

A concrete example of dual marginality is that of the Iranian professional immigrants who were living in the United States prior to the 1979 revolution. During the revolutionary period, some returned to Iran and some settled permanently in the United States. Those returned professionals found themselves in a situation of political, social, and professional marginality and were forced to immigrate to the United States.

Demographic Profile

Size

The Iranian migration is essentially the migration of middle-class and highly trained professionals. It also contains a selective contingent of American-trained professionals who left Iran and retuned to the United States. The broadest definition of Iranian Americans includes all persons descended from Iranian stock: immigrants from Iran or those born in America of fully Iranian or mixed ancestry. At the present time, Iranian immigrants are disproportionately immigrants themselves or the children of immigrants rather than descendants of earlier generations of "hyphenated" Americans.

In terms of quantity, estimates of the size of the Iranian American population vary from 500,000 to one million. The 2000 Census measured a U.S. population of 281.4 million, including 338,000 who reported an Iranian ancestry. According to the Census, Iranians are less than one percent of the total foreign-born U.S. population. It is possible that the census figure is an undercount, because the information on ancestry was collected on the "long form" of the census questionnaire, which was sent to approximately one-sixth of all households. Ancestry refers to ethnic origin, descent, "roots," heritage, or place of birth of the person or the person's ancestors. Despite persistent claims by some Iranian community activists that their population in the United States is over two million, a fair approximation in 2009 is about half a million. Regardless of the exact number, more Iranians live in the United States today than in any other country in the world except Iran.

What is most significant about the Iranian community is its continuing growth. In less than three decades, Iranians in the United States have grown from a scattered, marginal, ambivalent, and undecided immigrant group (123,000 in 1980)—a community without a community—into a new ethnic community of over 338,000 (2000 Census). At the present time, Iranians are one of the fastest-growing ethnic groups in the United States. The population doubled from 123,000 in 1980 to 285,000 in 1990, primarily through immigration. With the current rate of influx, the Iranian population in the United States is expected to triple by 2020.

Composition of the Community

According to the 2000 Census, about 60 percent of the total Iranian population resided in California, particularly in Los Angeles, where they live within a spatially bounded area called "Tehranjeles" or "Iranjeles." Los Angeles became a favorite destination of many Iranian immigrants and refugees after the 1979 revolution. Despite the major settlement of Iranian Americans on the West Coast, a greater proportion lives in the Northeast and the South. Other large enclaves are in New York, Texas, and the Washington, D.C., metropolitan area. The initial geographic distribution of Iranians in the United States shows the importance of universities and colleges in attracting Iranian students. By the late 1970s, their most pronounced concentrations were in southern California, New York, New Jersey, Texas, and Massachusetts. In the last decade, a few new Iranian American communities have developed in the southern states, such as Miami, Florida and Atlanta, Georgia.

Despite their initial intention of being temporary immigrants and exiles, Iranians in the United States are today mostly American citizens or permanent residents. According to the Department of Homeland Security, from 1999 to 2008, approximately 130,310 Iranian immigrants obtained U.S. citizenship (see Table 161). Those Iranian immigrants who are not American citizens are permanent residents who have not been in the United States long enough to apply for American citizenship. It seems that almost 30 years of exile are homeland enough. In other words, like most exiles, Iranians have realized that they cannot go home. That is, there is no "home" to go back to, or it is changed beyond recognition. However, many of the self-exiled Iranians still dream of returning home and getting back what they lost, and though others have started new businesses and new lives, they remain saddened by their losses in Iran.

Educational and Economic Attainments

From the very beginning, the Iranian immigrants differed from other arrivals by their high educational and professional achievements. They belong to a generation of upwardly mobile, secularized cosmopolitans. Unlike the "tired and poor," uneducated traditional refugees, Iranian immigrants are urban professionals, entrepreneurs, and often bilingual. According to the 2000 Census, 57 percent of foreign-born Iranians have a college degree or higher, a rate twice as high as that among all foreign-born people (see Figure 18). Currently, many of the best universities and colleges have a disproportionately large number of Iranian American students. A combination of former college students and political elites and professionals of high socioeconomic status, including exiles, make Iranian Americans one of the country's wealthiest and most educated immigrant populations.

The Iranian experience in the United States from the start has included ethnic pride. However, the immigrants' Iranian pride does not just come from what they were, but rather from what they have been able to achieve in the United States. An occupational profile of Iranians in the United States shows that they rank very high in the percentage of the population working in professional occupations, coming just after Asian Indians. About 50 percent of all working Iranian Americans are in professional and managerial occupations, greater than any other group in the United States. By comparison, 30 percent of all foreign-born people hold white-collar occupations such as physicians, engineers, accountants, and supervisors. Iranian Americans also have the smallest proportion of its members in low-status jobs. Today, American-trained professionals such as physicians, college professors, scientists, dentists, lawyers, engineers, nurses, and managers comprise the largest occupational segment of Iranian Americans. In the last 10 years, an increasing number of Iranian Americans have become college presidents, college deans, CEOs in corporate America, senior executives at Fortune 500 companies, top scientists in NASA, executives in the Silicon Valley, and even a deputy assistant to the president. A median income of approximately $59,000 makes Iranian American one of the highest-status ethnic groups in the United States (see Figure 19).

While Iranians can be found in a variety of occupations, one striking aspect is their self-employment rate of 22 percent, making them one of the most entrepreneurial ethnic groups in the United States. It is estimated that Iranians are among the top 25 immigrant groups with the highest self-employment rate. There is growing evidence that such a high rate of self-employment has played an important role in the economic adaptation of the newly arrived Iranian immigrants in the United States. "In Los Angeles, the percentage of Iranians in self-employment is about fifty nine percent. Similarly, close to fifty six percent of working Iranian men and women in Dallas are self-employed and run some kind of business" (Mobasher 2006). These family owned businesses are found in both cities and suburbs and, with the exception of Iranian grocery stores, most of the Iranian businesses are oriented toward the larger market of the American society. Iranian businesses today go far beyond the traditional Persian carpet, garment, and jewelry outlets (Ansari 2005).

As discussed earlier, Iranian emigration has not only been one of scientists, professionals, and entrepreneurs, but also one of a considerable amount of capital. Of all recent immigrant groups, Iranians have made the greatest investments in America. Herein lies the supreme irony of the closing decade of America's post–World War II imperial claim over Iran—Iran's loss of talent and capital turned out to be America's gain. In other words, the Iranian revolution with all of its anti-American sentiments turned out to be a success for America.

Iranian immigration also brought one of the most significant waves of affluent families to come to the United States. Regarding those super-rich Iranians or "money refugees," there is no success like exile. They are today most likely naturalized Americans and have established themselves as wealthy real estate developers, bankers, and successful businesspeople in corporate America. Wherever Iranian American entrepreneurs have concentrated, they have injected new dynamism into local and national economies. Particularly in Los Angeles and New York City, their economic influence far outweighs their numbers.

This success, however, is qualified by the initial downward mobility of some exiles and the discrimination Iranians as a whole face in the labor market. Not all Iranians who fled the country were part of an affluent group. Among the educated

Iranians were a large number of refugees who were unable to follow their own line of training. For example, the entry of former army officers into the American occupational structure has been marked by downward mobility and some disappointments. These Iranian immigrants are well educated by Iranian standards, but after a lifetime of military careers they have had no choice but to drive cabs or manage their own small stores or restaurants. Iranian immigrants who were confronted with downward mobility (like the leading character in the recent movie *House of Sand and Fog*) experienced more than other Iranians the psychological pains of the loss of status and dislocation. Even today, not all Iranian Americans have affluent lifestyles. In 1994, over 12,500 Iranian immigrants received Supplemental Security Income benefits. However, during the same year, noncitizen Iranian elderly make up the smallest group of immigrants receiving Supplemental Security Income.

Adjustment and Adaptation

New Community Structure

Historically, Iranians were not only open to other cultures, but often freely adapted to other cultural systems they found useful. In fact, an eclectic cultural elasticity has been said to be one of the key defining characteristics of the Iranian spirit. Iranian Americans today are incredibly diverse. The differences are not only generational, although that is part of the story. In fact, what makes the Iranian Americans yet more intriguing, aside from their remarkable achievements, is the complexity of the community itself. Because each wave of immigrants came from differing circumstances, their adjustment to their new environment is also the story of their adjustment to each group that came before them. An additional layer of diversity can also be attributed to the various other Iranian immigrants that came to the United States from Iranian communities in countries such as Canada, France, England, and Sweden.

The Iranian revolution of 1979 and its aftermath (including eight years of the Iraq–Iran war) were both culturally and organizationally crucial to the making of the Iranian community in the United States. Prior to the revolution, the Iranian immigrant community had not yet developed. It is suggested that the dialectically interrelated Islamization of Iran and anti-Islamic and anti-Iranian sentiment in America not only transferred the already available marginal situation to a much larger group of postrevolutionary immigrants, but also reinforced the development of a new community of Iranian Americans. Starting in 1980, Iranians gradually formed cultural organizations in several states. No organization, secular or religious, represents all Iranian Americans. However, today over 100 regional, cultural, religious, and professional Iranian American organizations and foundations exist in the United States.

The Iranian American community is a new nonterritorial community based on nontraditional foundations found in an urban, bureaucratized America; it manifests peculiarities derived from the predominantly professional origin and business class of the immigrants. In other words, Iranian Americans live with no distinguishable pattern of common locale. In some areas such as Los Angeles, there is a heavy concentration but no "Little Iran" similar to Chinatown, Little Italy, or Little Cuba in Miami. The Iranians arrived in this country at a time when the host society had already undergone a rapid urbanization process and the disintegration of distinctively ethnic institutions. Moreover, the Iranians' pattern of migration, along with their social conditions, were hardly conducive to the formation of a collective settlement. Since cultural assimilation goes hand-in-hand with education and economic advancement, Iranian immigrants have had no difficult time integrating into American society.

Family Structure

The Iranian family in the United States is fundamentally different than the traditional family in Iran. In terms of structure, it is a nuclear family; a married man and woman living with their two or three children. Emigration as individual families has separated the Iranian American families from their own extended families. In some cases, the extended families are scattered throughout the United States, Europe, Australia, and Iran.

The Iranian American family is decidedly child-centered, and its patriarchal and authoritarian character is already undermined in the new environment. There is also some evidence that among young Iranian American couples, the institutionalization of equalitarian norms has already taken place, particularly in the area of child rearing. Unlike in Iran, where the extended family, older siblings, and neighbors play a significant role in child rearing, in the United States parents chiefly play that role. The Iranian mother is the child's most important socializer, and it is from her that the child receives the most affection and, in most cases, unconditional love. In the absence of older people at home, such as grandmothers, the Iranian mother depends heavily on experts for guidance regarding character training.

The majority of first-generation Iranian parents express a strong desire to cultivate the positive aspects of their culture. However, because of cultural conflict, most second-generation Iranians have grown up alien to the culture of their parents. They have their own subculture, which contains a new set of values and new ways of thinking.

Iranians are emotionally expressive people regardless of sex. Both men and women show their tears, anger, and affection easily. Kissing and hugging as ways of greeting are common between both men and women but are less socially acceptable between a man and a woman.

Today, the second generation of Iranians receives an early socialization that involves a great amount of social-psychological absorption of the most subtle

American middle-class values, training, and behavioral patterns. Their level of income, professional status, and assimilating tendencies allow Iranian American families to provide their children with a middle- and upper-class way of life.

However, generational change has already brought about cultural conflict and tensions between parents and their children. Today many Iranian American parents are seriously challenged in their efforts to accommodate the values of two different worlds. Moreover, they experience a cultural divide with their children, because they have no frame of reference for their children's high school and, in some cases, collegiate experience. This situation reflects modernity and tradition at a cultural crossroads. Growing up in America and being heavily influenced by the larger society, members of the second generation desire greater freedom to determine their own destinies. Second-generation Iranians will be shaped by the American social context rather than their parents' memories of Iran or their cultural expectations. While they acknowledge their parents' willingness to offer sufficient love and financial support, they complain that their parents are unprepared to understand the second generation's way of life.

Within the Iranian American family, elderly immigrants experience a degree of loneliness and isolation. It seems that the social-psychological problems of these late-life immigrants are due to a lack of social connections, and having traditional values that sometimes conflict with those of their assimilated children.

In terms of family values, the Iranian American family emphasizes Iranianness, respect for elders, friendship, hospitality, obligation, loyalty, and respect toward the family above all else. Other values include an unquestionable thirst for education, which goes back to the very roots of their cultural heritage, as they reserve the highest respect for those who are superior to them in knowledge and wisdom. Friendship, hospitality, politeness, and courtesy are specific cultural behaviors to which Iranians attach special importance.

In a major survey of Iranian Americans (Ansari 2006), in response to the question of "what qualities are important in the Iranian part of your identity?" the following categories were considered important for the participants: Iranian family, Persian language, Now-Ruz (the Persian New Year celebration), Persian food, love of poetry, politeness, hospitality, respect for elders, and courtesy. In the same survey, second-generation Iranian Americans identify "parental love and care" as the one Iranian family value that they are most proud to pass on to their children.

Iranians have their own set of manners and etiquette, which are rooted in their culture. One of these unique cultural traits is *ta'arof*. *Ta'arof* derives from an Arabic root denoting knowledge and acquaintance. As a form of behavior, *ta'arof* dictates formalized expressions of respect, kindness, and genuine feelings of hospitality. Through *ta'arof*, Iranians manage the impression they give to others. *Ta'arof* is practiced particularly at the time of meeting, departure, and paying the bill at a restaurant.

National Culture and Identity

Ethnic identity in a new country is maintained in various ways. Iranian Americans, like many other past and present immigrant groups, have established institutions and foundations to preserve their cultural heritage, strengthen their ethnic identity, and keep them cohesive as a community. The Iranian American community has encompassed a variety of organizations since its inception. These organizations serve a variety of functions. Some are cultural and others are educational, charitable, religious, and political. Over the last 30 years, Iranian Americans have developed an impressive array of cultural programs. The Persian cultural centers, better known to the Iranian American community as *kanoons* or *anjomans*, are the earliest forms of community-based organizations for Iranians in the United States. The Iranian American community, particularly during the 1980s, witnessed a remarkable flowering of an essentially Persian character, as renovated cultural symbols and institutions provided channels for expressing their ethnic identity. They constituted the functional equivalent of the myths, values, and familiarities in which the traditional immigrant identity and community was grounded. The strongest supporters of these organizations have been the first-generation Iranians. Today, almost no major American city lacks its quota of Iranian American cultural associations.

Among communal activities sponsored by Iranian cultural centers are celebrations of national festivals. From ancient times, Iranians have celebrated three national festivals, which play a significant role in the Iranian national consciousness. These celebrations are Now-Ruz, Mehregan, and Sadeh. Of all these festivals, Now-Ruz has had the greatest impact on the Iranian ethnic consciousness, because it reflects the core of Iranianness.

Now-Ruz (pronounced no-ruze, meaning new day), the Persian New Year festival, is the greatest of the Persian feasts. It is celebrated on the first day of spring (March 21), the vernal equinox, and is deeply ingrained in the social structure of Iranian society and institutionalized in all of the Iranian religious groups. Now-Ruz has a long history—when the Pilgrims celebrated their first Thanksgiving in the United States, it had already been around for more than 2,000 years. Now-Ruz originated in pre-Islamic Iran and is celebrated today by over 300 million people throughout central Asia, the Caucasus, northwestern China, and in parts of the Middle East, the Balkans, and South Asia. The secret power behind Now-Ruz's appeal to such a diversity of cultures has to do with the fact that it is a spring-time ritual that celebrates the relationship between humans and nature.

For Iranians, Now-Ruz is a 13-day celebration anticipated all year. Preparations begin weeks ahead with spring cleaning, cooking, and buying new clothes and arrangement of the Sofreh Haftsin. Haftsin is traditionally a table beautifully decorated with flowers, typically hyacinth and daffodils, and with seven items that begin with the Persian letter "S." These include "Sabzeh (wheat sprouts) for rebirth, Seeb (apple) for health and beauty, Seer (garlic) for health and medicine, Serkeh (vinegar) for age and patience, Samanu (a custard pudding) for affluence, Somagh (sumac) for sunrise and Senjid (oleaster fruit) for love" (Rahni 2007). Among Now-Ruz traditions is Charshanbeh Souri, which is the last Wednesday of the outgoing year. It is celebrated by jumping over a bonfire while declaring "take away my yellow complexion and give me your red glow of health." The festivities continue until the 13th day of the new year, which is called Sizdah Bedar. On the morning of this day, Iranians plan an outdoor picnic.

Since the early 1980s, Now-Ruz has been institutionalized among Iranians in the United States. It remains the most culturally distinctive institution for Iranian Americans and is celebrated with great extravagance. A telling sign of the growing cohesion and national consciousness among Iranian Americans is the number of new Now-Ruz public ceremonies in city halls and museums, where usually a sizable number of non-Iranians are among the guests. In the last few years, there have been Now-Ruz celebrations in the White House, New York City's Mayor Bloomberg's residence, Gracie Mansion, city halls in Los Angeles and San Francisco, the Metropolitan Museum of New York, and the Smithsonian Institution.

The 2009 Now-Ruz was particularly important, because President Obama released a special message to the people and the government of Iran. President Obama's message went significantly beyond the standard practice of U.S. presidents delivering statements in celebration of Now-Ruz. President Obama stated that "a common humanity binds us together despite three decades of strained relations. We know that you are a great civilization and your accomplishments have earned the respect of the U.S. and the world." Acknowledging the contributions of Iranian Americans, he stated, "Here in the U.S., our own communities have been enhanced by the contributions of Iranian Americans."

In addition to Now-Ruz, there are other cultural systems that provide institutional support for Iranians to adjust and at the same time maintain their cultural identities in the United States. These institutional support systems include the Persian media, Shab-I-Shehr (poetry reading night), Persian language programs, religious centers, *hanegah* (Sufi centers), Persian food, Persian music, the Internet, and, as of 2004, the Persian parade in New York City.

The Persian parade is held every year along 15 blocks of Madison Avenue in New York City. Iranian Americans of all ethnic backgrounds walk side-by-side and display native costumes ride floats to celebrate the richness and diversity of the Persian culture in exile. As the most spectacular Persian festival in America, the Persian parade has more effectively than any other festival attracted the new generation of Iranian Americans to their Iranian cultural heritage. As the only publicly visible Iranian American ceremony, the annual Persian parade has created an atmosphere of national identity, particularly for the second-generation Iranians.

The Persian media in the Iranian American community have grown rapidly since 2000. Today, Iranians in the United States are an ethnic group with a large number of TV satellite stations. There are 30 TV and 5 radio stations broadcasting in

Dressed in Iranian festival garb, Nelly Sayaidi, 15, of North Haven, Connecticut (left), walks down New York's Madison Avenue as she and others participate in the Persian Day Parade, March 19, 2006. (AP Photo/Tina Fineberg)

the Persian language from Los Angeles to Iran, Europe, and a few other countries where Iranian immigrants live. The satellite TV programs have become an emotional outlet for a large number of Iranians in exile. In addition to the TV and radio programs, there are over 20 newspapers and magazines published in several states where there are large concentrations of Iranian Americans. Today, the Persian media are an active component of the Iranian American community and have helped Iranian Americans preserve their cultural heritage and remain in constant contact with Iranians in Iran and in the diaspora.

The electronic community is another new feature of the larger Iranian American community. The Internet over the past decade has slowly become the public space in which Iranian Americans engage in a most influential dialogue. Today, regardless of where young Iranians physically reside, the Internet has enabled them to be able to exchange ideas and experience a sense of solidarity with other Iranians. The Internet, Facebook, Twitter, and other social media have become important means of association among the nationally and internationally scattered Iranian diaspora.

Religion

Iran is a primarily Shia Muslim country, a fact reflected in the Iranian immigrant population in the United States. However, Iranian Americans are not homogeneous in terms of religious affiliations. There are Muslims, Jews, Zoroastrians, Christians, and Bahais. Even though the majority of Iranian Americans are Shia Muslim, initially they had no interest in establishing their own mosques. As a whole, they have maintained a secular rather than religious outlook and also consider "Iran's theocratic regime" as the main cause of their involuntary emigration (Bozorgmehr 1998). Therefore, unlike many other immigrant groups, the religious institution was not there to serve as an anchor in the Iranian Muslim immigrants' early years of adjustment. The Iranian Shia Muslims are also a diverse mixture of relatively secular and moderate Shias. A survey of Iranian Americans in New Jersey in 2005 indicates that Iranian American Shias are less religiously observant or "mosque going" than other Shia groups in America. However, since the early 1990s, a remarkable religious cohesiveness has developed among a devout segment of Iranian American Muslims. Yet, except in a few states, the Iranian mosque is not yet a visible symbol of Iranian American presence at the community level.

Language

Although coming from a non–English speaking country, knowledge of English among Iranian immigrants is impressive and is undoubtedly related to their exposure to Western education. Nevertheless, like many of the other newly arrived immigrant groups, they prefer to use their own native language.

More than 80 percent of Iranian American households in the United States communicate in both English and Persian. About 20 percent communicate only in English. The preference of Iranian Americans to speak Persian amongst themselves

Hossein Hejdazi, program director and talk show host at KIRN-AM, a Farsi-language radio station, poses at the console at his studio in Los Angeles, June 14, 2007. (AP Photo/Reed Saxon)

indicates a renewed pride in their own cultural heritage as a response to the threat to their cultural identity posed by the Islamization of Iran and as an ironic by-product of successful integration—assimilation breeds nostalgia.

Most Iranian Americans are bilingual. Some even speak other languages, such as French and German, but the majority of the second-generation Iranian Americans speak only English, except for some occasional Persian words or terms of affection. Another novel development that serves to mark a sense of Persian identity and community is the establishment of Persian language programs in every area in which Iranian Americans reside. It seems that the phenomenon of language loyalty found in some other immigrant groups has also prevailed among Iranian Americans. This renewed interest in teaching Persian to children who live in a cultural milieu that contains no significant elements of their own cultural heritage, a sense of ethnic identity, does seem to develop at an early age. Iranian Americans are fiercely proud of the continuity and stability of their language, and much debate persists about why and how Iranian parents should speak mostly, if not all, Persian at home.

Foodways

Food habits are among the most persistent of all cultural patterns. Iranian food is diverse and reflects the diversity of Iranian society. Iranian immigrants have brought their Iranian cuisine to the United States, and it has quickly become one of the most popular ethnic foods in the country. Iranians in the United States, particularly the first generation, are extremely in love with their own native cuisines. Persian food is considered by many to be one of the most balanced and satisfying diets in the world. It is not surprising then that Iranian grocery stores and restaurants specializing in Iranian food products were among the first Iranian-owned businesses to open in Los Angeles, where a large number of Iranians have settled. The number of Iranian restaurants in America has doubled in the last 10 years. Iranian restaurants have been successful in comparison to other restaurants in the United States serving the ethnic cuisine of the most recent immigrants.

Nearly all Iranian dishes are accompanied by rice, which is made with saffron to add color and flavor. Vegetables (including raw onions and greens, or *sabzi*) and fresh fruits are also an essential part of Iranian cuisine. *Chelo kabab, khoresht sabzi,* and *fesenjan* are the most favored dishes among Iranians. Younger Iranian Americans, who are born and raised in the United States, typically have the most diverse food habits, including the usual attraction to popular American fast foods. However, most Iranian Americans still prefer Iranian food most of all.

Music and the Arts

Another integrating feature of the Iranian American community is Persian music. Iran has a great musical tradition, closely linked to poetry and mysticism. Yet, after the 1979 revolution, the Iranian government banned music, viewing it as a means of promoting the "decadent" culture of the West. At the present time, only certain types of music are allowed in Iran, and anyone caught in possession of nonpermitted music, such as pop music tapes and CDs, is treated as a criminal. However, the musical heritage that Iranian immigrants brought with them to the United States is rich and diverse. As a medium of subcultural expression, traditional Persian music reinforces a sense of ethnic identity and group consciousness among Iranian immigrants.

The forced emigration of Iranian musicians and singers added another important communal focus for Iranians in the United States. Today, there are several centers whose purpose is to promote Iranian traditional music. In the absence of physical proximity, these cultural institutions provide the primary component of Iranian identity, and, like poetry reading nights, respond to the immigrants' psychological needs.

The Iranian community's sphere of interest in the arts is growing, as evidenced by the two to three exhibits in New York City that occur every several months. Today, Iranian American artists, whose art works are inspired by Persian epics and landscapes, find their American home at major galleries in New York and Los Angeles.

Integration and Impact on U.S. Society and Culture

Intergroup Relations

Generally, Iranian Americans are not strangers in their new environment. Throughout their period of studentship or internship, they have familiarized themselves with the larger society. That is, they have become immigrants in this country. Iranian immigrants who have had an American education enjoy a greater opportunity for social contact with Americans. As a group of professionals, Iranian Americans have regular face-to-face contact with out-group individuals. However, most of these relations are based on secondary contacts, in which they are related by a single role relationship. However, those Iranian Americans who have married non-Iranians and achieved marital assimilation have an extended relationship with the host group. Based on a recent survey taken in New Jersey in 2005, there are a relatively high number of marriages between Iranians and non-Iranians. It is estimated that almost 50 percent of marriages between 1995 and 2007 are intercultural marriages. This figure shows that a large percentage of second-generation Iranians are structurally assimilated individuals.

Forging a New American Political Identity

After over two decades of largely abstaining from organized political activity, Iranian Americans are beginning to seek a voice in American political affairs. In the last 10 years, Iranian branches of the two major political parties have been established. In 2003, two prominent Iranian Americans ran in the recall election for governor of California. A few years earlier, another Iranian American was a GOP candidate for Maryland's Senate seat. In 2005, the first Iranian American woman ran for a seat in Congress from Oregon. Politically, Iranian Americans are still one of the least organized ethnic groups, but one of the potentially most powerful. Even in the areas with high concentrations of Iranian immigrants, like Los Angeles, Iranian American candidates have so far had little success in uniting the Iranian vote behind them.

However, there are indications that Iranian Americans have come of age in terms of political participation and community empowerment. The election and reelection of an Iranian American as the mayor of Beverly Hills (2007) symbolizes the growing influence of the Iranian community of that area. By some accounts, Iranians comprise as much as 15 to 20 percent of Beverly Hills's 35,000 residents, which is also a telling sign of the fact that the Iranian community is growing and integrating with the broader mainstream population.

The year 2008 was indisputably the Iranian American community's coming of political age. For the first time, a significant number of prominent Iranian Americans became actively involved in fundraising efforts for political candidates. There was also a large scale of community participation in the U.S. presidential election. For example, in New York and New Jersey, second-generation Iranians were visibly active, not only in voting in favor of their own candidates, but also in volunteering as campaign workers, poll watchers, and election judges.

The most significant political development has been the establishment of the Iranian American Political Action Committee (IAPAC). The goal of IAPAC is to insure that Iranian Americans have an influential voice and presence in the American electoral and legislative process. Today, the leading Iranian American political group is the Public Affairs Alliance of Iranian Americans (PAAIA). It seeks to achieve its mission through three major areas of activity: community-building, image-building and influence-building. The PAAIA is a new public affairs organization that seeks to represent the interests of the Iranian American community with U.S. policy makers, the media, and the American public. The PAAIA has produced an even greater momentum among the second generation of Iranian Americans. It is likely that during the next decade, the bipartisan nature of these political organizations will play a major role in the empowerment of the Iranian American community.

The Second and Later Generations

Ethnic Identity

Children born in America to Iranian or Iranian American parents, or those who are brought to America young enough to receive their early socialization here, may be considered second-generation Iranian Americans. Currently, a profound demographic change is taking place in the Iranian American community. With regard to the generational change, in 2000 only 20 percent of the Iranians in the United States were American-born, while based on a New Jersey survey of Iranians in 2007, the American-born were estimated at 55 percent. In addition, there are about 10 percent who are considered one-and-a-half generation Iranians. They are generally the Iranian-born who came to America in their early teens and have become bicultural through school and work. Most members of the second generation of Iranian Americans are today of school age or older.

As a whole, the younger generation of Iranian Americans does not share the same historical and cultural context as the older generation. Therefore, for some, being Iranian American is not a fixed state of being, something given to them by their parents. For this group, arguments on cultural authenticity or inauthenticity have no intellectual merit. The younger generation is decidedly American in their outlook, values, and attitudes. Even though they have a sensibility that is uniquely Iranian American and have a renewed pride in their cultural heritage, for the most part they think of Iran as simply the country from which their parents came.

There is a fair amount of evidence that a sense of Iranianness or Persian pride exists at the forefront of most of the Iranian American second generation's collective consciousness. Regarding ethnic self-identification, the second-generation respondents to the New Jersey survey in 2005 were asked, "How do you think of yourself?" Only 10 percent of the sample stated that they were American, and 20 percent said they were Iranian or Persian. The majority of the sample (70 percent) identified themselves as Iranian Americans, Persian Americans, or American Iranians. Obviously, these finding are suggestive of a significant degree of ethnic identification or Iranianness among the second generation of Iranian Americans. However, in an earlier study in 1988, only about 30 percent of the same age group identified themselves as Iranian Americans. It seems that many of the second generation have come all the way from shame to pride. During the hostage crisis, a large number of second-generation Iranian Americans found themselves subjected to negative comments and reactions because of their ethnic background and were therefore less likely to assert themselves as Iranian Americans. In the New Jersey survey in 2005, in response to the question of "who am I?," most acknowledged stages of change in their attitudes toward Iran, from the age of 12 when they denied their origins to the age of 13 when they began to feel a sense of pride in attending Persian classes and having coethnic friends and peers and sensing a double strength in their two cultures. Empirical evidence indicates that for a large number of young Iranian Americans, the college years have had significant power in shaping their Iranian American identities. In fact, it is during the college years that, through involvement in Persian clubs, young Iranian Americans rediscover their roots and heritage and begin to feel comfortable about embracing their hyphenated identity.

Youth Profile

Proud to be an Iranian American: Two Cultures Becoming One

This profile is by Pardis, a young Iranian American woman, on first realizing what it means to be an Iranian American.

It's all I thought it was going to be; just a visit. Just a visit that was going to make me miss school for a month. Little did I know then as a 13-year-old Iranian American that this visit was going to be a great turning point in my life.

I was born in America but I lived in Iran until I finished first grade. That's when my family left Iran to go to the "Land of Opportunity"—America. I hadn't gone back to Iran until this trip. Because of the experiences I had during this visit in Iran, my expectations of myself changed drastically, and my perception of Iran and its wonderful people changed as well.

(Courtesy of Esmat Ansari)

One of the most important experiences I had was when I went outside and walked among everyday Iranians. It was very hard for me to believe that even though the government had set such strict rules for them, the people still managed to be high-spirited, optimistic, and grateful.

On the airplane ride on the way back home, my mother was talking about her mother, who had passed away while we were in the United States. That is when I fully appreciated the sacrifices that she and my father had made just so my brother and I could have better educational opportunities.

Before this trip, I hadn't been exactly proud of being Iranian, thanks to the "objective" Western media at that time.However, I now found myself filled with nothing but pride and respect for my heritage. After this trip when people asked me who I was, without hesitating, I always said Iranian American.

Like all immigrant groups, Iranian Americans feel torn between their parents' traditions and their American culture. However, it seems that the length of residency, place of residency, the media's image of Iran and Iranians, family context, school location, and population size all influence patterns of ethnic identification (Iranianness). Findings indicate that those second-generation Iranian Americans who were adolescents at the time of the 1979 revolution felt the greatest ambivalence about their identity. The age group over 40, who were too young to have had an independent life in Iran but too old to feel completely at home in America, are the social type who experienced a situation of dual marginality. While there are unifying features that make an Iranian identity possible, various religious subgroups living in the United States also display distinct features that make broad generalizations about Iranian Americans problematic.

The main reason for such a high degree of ethnic revivalism among the younger generation is that in the last 15 years, through a process of reverse assimilation, they have become increasingly reintegrated into the Iranian communities in the United States. Their expression of Iranianness is evident in their voluntary participation in Now-Ruz celebrations, the annual Persian parade in New York City, political demonstrations (solidarity with other Iranian people), enrollment in Persian language classes at their colleges or universities, willingness to visit and revisit Iran, writing and publishing of memoirs, construction of and interest in Web sites on Iran and Iranian culture, organization and involvement in annual conferences such as Iranian Alliances Across the Borders (IAAB), creation of summer camps (Ayandeh camp for young Iranian Americans), and creation of Persian music bands and artistic works with Persian influences.

However, the assimilation (called Americanization by Iranian parents) that the first generation of Iranians in the United States had feared is well underway. Yet, what the Iranian parents had not foreseen was that this assimilation is not a straight-line process. It is a process of reverse assimilation, meaning that while their children become fully assimilated, they are also reclaiming their Iranianness. The second generation of Iranian Americans have not only reclaimed their cultural heritage, but also have come to recreate an ethnic identity that is both Iranian and American. Unlike the second generation of the earlier immigrants in America, for whom assimilation was the goal, for the second generation of Iranian Americans who are already fully assimilated, the goal is to keep alive the consciousness of their Persian heritage in the process of integration. In other words, for the second generation of Iranian Americans, the process of assimilation and maintenance of symbolic ethnicity go hand-in-hand. A more tolerant and pluralistic America, as well as the new era of globalization, notably the diffusion of personal computers around the world, including Iran, have allowed children of high-status immigrants like Iranians to have an experience of reverse assimilation (Bozorgmehr 1988). Additionally, those who identify themselves as Iranian American view their hyphenated identity as a positive one. In the past, Iranian immigrants might have underplayed their ethnic background to succeed. Today, however, the children and grandchildren of Iranian immigrants celebrate their ethnicity.

Another interesting phenomenon has been the changing nature of Iranianness. The change has been from traditional Iranianness (being Iranian), in which proficiency in the Persian language is a necessity, to symbolic Iranianness (feeling Iranian), which is characteristic of the American-born generation of Iranian Americans, though the distinctions are not absolute. The symbolic Iranians conceive of their hyphenated identity as a choice, expressed in terms of pride in their Persian heritage and strong feelings toward the people and culture of Iran. However, this attachment or sense of belongingness is different from the attachment of the earlier generation. The American-born generation keeps a distance from the sentimental attachment their parents have with their homeland. What is evident is that a new definition of Iranianness is emerging from second-generation Iranian Americans. In this new definition, proficiency in the Persian language and observation of Persian mannerisms are not necessarily determining factors. As one respondent in the 2005 New Jersey survey stated, "For us, the Persian language, while very important, does not occupy as high of a place as it does for our parents." However, an overwhelming number of the second-generation respondents said that they would insist that their children preserve their Persian heritage. They are Iranian in their own terms. For the second generation of Iranian Americans, their ethnic community does not exist in a fixed or identifiable location. It is a form of consciousness, a widely variable set of loyalties and personal identities. For those immigrant children who have no actual memories of Iran, a constructed memory of what Iran means is the basis for their identity. Almost three decades after the making of the Iranian American community, a new generation of Iranians is growing in numbers and asserting itself as a hyphenated new ethnic category. The second generation of Iranian Americans will continue to be shaped by their American social context rather than their parents' memories of Iran or their cultural expectations.

Educational Attainment

Second-generation Iranian Americans have demonstrated a strong commitment to pursuing higher education. According to the New Jersey survey in 2006, almost 99 percent of high school graduates in the survey finished at least four years of college. Currently, many of the best universities and colleges have a disproportionately large number of Iranian Americans. These students are pursuing more diverse majors and professional interests than the generation before them. While the first generation of Iranian Americans traditionally felt most comfortable entering fields of medicine and technology, the second generation is now more independently pursuing careers in the social sciences, law, liberal arts, media, and communication, in addition to the traditional sciences.

Empirical observations (through multiyear New Jersey surveys) indicate that almost all of the one-and-a-half generation and second generation of Iranians have "made it," in the sense that they have gained admission to highly selective institutions of higher education. They are the most highly educated and most advantaged in their cohort of the new immigrant group. Thus, many will be at the core of the future Iranian American elite. Among the younger generation of Iranian Americans, the one-and-a-half generation has been highly successful in obtaining the highest degrees and professional positions in American society. Today, they are partners at prestigious law firms, physicians with distinctions, young professors, senior executives at Fortune 500 companies, professional athletes, a founder of Google, an eBay inventor, philanthropists, editors, senior correspondents, and chief economists, to name a few. This success has been achieved despite three decades of antagonistic relationships between the Iranian and American governments. Based on a recent media report, young Iranian American professionals have outstripped most other recent immigrants in occupational achievements and education.

Issues in Relations between the United States and Iran

Anti-Iranian Reaction in America

Few ethnic out-group relations in the United States have had a more positive beginning than that which characterized the experience of the Iranian immigrants from 1950 to 1979. Prior to November 4, 1979, when a group of radical students took over the American Embassy in Tehran, Iran and America were close friends. America's attitude toward Iranians in America was positive, resulting primarily from the medical and educational services of Iranian immigrants in the United States. From 1950 to 1979, an estimated 800,000 to 850,000 Americans had visited or lived in Iran, whether as teachers, health care workers, Peace Corps volunteers, scholars, or diplomats. These Americans returning from Iran had often expressed their admiration for the Iranian people. During the same period, Iranian people also had a positive and even welcoming attitude toward America and Americans. Iranians saw America as a liberating force whose influence would protect Iran from its traditional enemies (Britain and the former Soviet Union).

However, Iranian attitudes toward America changed dramatically after the American role in the overthrow of Dr. Muhammad Mosaddeq (in August 1953) and the restoration of the shah. U.S. foreign policy, not the American people, created a strong undercurrent of anti-Americanism among Iranians. This anti-Americanism was increasingly intensified by America's close relationship with the shah, whom the Iranian intelligentsia considered a despotic client of the United States. It was actually during the antimonarchial revolutionary movement of 1978–1979, with its sharp anti-American edge, that Iranian anti-Americanism reached its apex, as demonstrated by the hostage crisis of 1979. During the hostage crisis, Iran and Iranians were consistently in the headlines, and this provoked a considerable amount of anti-Iranian immigrant sentiment among Americans, a prejudice almost nonexistent prior to that time.

The hostage crisis was primarily provoked by the actions of the radical Islamists in Iran. It brought about a new era in Iranian American relations—an era still dominated by hatred, distrust, violence, and the most adverse consequences for Iranian Americans. During the entire 14 months of the crisis, "Death to America" became increasingly intertwined in the ritualistic chants of the religious masses in Tehran, Iran. Thus, a wave of anti-Iranian sentiment swept across America, and the hatred of Iranians grew fast and deep among Americans. A Harris Poll taken in February 1987 showed that a majority of Americans named only one country as "the enemy," which was Iran.

Another major event that fueled the anti-Iranian, anti-Muslim feeling in the United States was the publication of *Not without My Daughter* in 1984. This book, and especially its 1991 movie adaptation, were met with angry reaction from Iranian Americans offended by what they considered a biased depiction of their culture. The movie was also criticized as an utter artistic failure for its reliance on cultural stereotypes. Caryn James of *The New York Times*, in a review, stated that the movie exploited the stereotype of the demonic Iranian. Iranians generally thought that the movie portrayed them as mean, rude, brutal, and uncivilized.

Consequently, in a manner reminiscent of the experience of Japanese Americans in the 1940s, Iranians residing in the United States became the immediate targets of American anger and frustration. Paradoxically, Iranian immigrants and the political refugees who allied themselves with Americans against the extremist religious government in Iran felt that Americans resented them and unfairly blamed them for the hostage crisis. The anti-Iranian reaction was so widespread that it forced many Iranian Americans to either change their names or misrepresent their ethnic identity, because one's Iranian identity was a stigma to be hidden or evaded as much as possible. To avoid potential confrontations and differential treatment, most Iranian Americans started to call themselves Persian Americans.

Anti-Iranian reactions and negative characterization had a damaging effect on the psyche of Iranians, and particularly their children. The psychological damage done to second-generation Iranians, possibly irreversible, was evident when Iranian American children began to display feelings of inferiority and insecurity. This negative characterization of Iranian and Islamic culture was again reinforced following the tragedy of September 11, 2001. Despite the Iranian Americans' high rate of citizenship at the time and their remarkable contributions toward building a better American society, Iranian Americans yet again became victims of defamation, negative media stereotyping, and discrimination. Widely-used phrases such as "Iran or Iranians supporting terrorism" and "Iranian behavior" by the American media and even American officials created an atmosphere in which Iranian Americans became victims of unjustifiable harassment and restriction. In December 2003, the Iranian community in Los Angeles was outraged when men from some Muslim countries including Iran were ordered to register with the Immigration and Naturalization Service. Reportedly, several hundred Iranians residing in Los Angeles, including many Iranian Jews, were detained on visa violations. Most were eventually released, but Iranian Americans came "to realize that the strategy of passing as non-Iranians or disassociating themselves from the Iranian regime does not protect them against hostility in the United States" (Bozorgmehr 2007).

According to PAAIA, nearly half of the Iranian Americans surveyed in 2008 by ZAGBY International have themselves experienced or personally know another Iranian American who has experienced discrimination because of his or her ethnicity or country of origin. The most common types of discrimination reported are being stopped at the airport, employment or business discrimination, social discrimination, racial profiling, and discrimination at the hands of immigration officials. To increase awareness of the rise in discrimination against the Iranian American community, Congress member Martin Meehan, a member of the House Judiciary Committee, on July 1, 2005, introduced a House resolution condemning bigotry, violence, and discrimination against Iranian Americans.

However, it is important to note that the estrangement and animosity was always between the governments of Iran and the United States due to their foreign policies. Despite three decades of estrangement between the two governments, from the hostage-taking to the "Axis of Evil" and more recently the depiction of Iran as the "nuclear pariah," the dominant orientation of the Iranians (particularly the generation of the revolution, who grew up after 1979 and account for more than two-thirds of Iran's population), has been one of respect and admiration for the United States and its people. Iranians living under the repressive regime that had long demonized the United States as the "Great Satan" and presented it as a scapegoat for all of Iran's troubles called America the "fortune land." In fact, Iranian have remained the most pro-American people in the Muslim world. After the tragedy of September 11, Iranian people were the only people in Islamic society that held a candlelight vigil as an act of solidarity with the American people. Moreover, in the United States, the Iranian community was among the very first ethnic groups that condemned the terrorist act and showed its support by contributing to the World Trade Center Relief Fund. The Iranian American community of New York had a one-page advertisement on the first page of *The New York Times* expressing profound sadness and condemning the attacks as a vicious criminal act. However, despite Iranians' love for America, they are frustrated with or even angry about U.S. policy toward their country, which they tend to see as unjustly threatening and hostile.

In the words of President Obama, "common humanities" bind the two people together. The fact that Iranians have had a special place in their hearts for American core values at least in part reflects the common grounds between the two cultures.

Sa'di, a poet of Iran, probably better than anyone, captured the spirit behind the cultural affinity of Iranians for American values. He wrote, "We are all one by one by creation, bound together at limbs in a body, should one part ache, the rest would suffer as well." Former Supreme Court Justice William O. Douglas once stated that "Persians are spiritually close kin to Americans." More recently, former Secretary of State Madeleine K. Albright has acknowledged this common ground by saying that "both are idealistic, proud, family-oriented, spiritually aware and fiercely opposed to foreign domination."

Iranian Americans and Home Politics

Historically, Iranian immigrants as a group have lacked a united political front regarding politics in Iran. However, the self-exiled Iranians throughout these years have maintained a "mission" orientation—a national commitment toward an eventual return to Iran. Having remained divided and disillusioned, this mission orientation did not function as an organizational element in the Iranian diaspora in the United States. However, in the last few years, the situation of disengagement from politics in Iran has changed to a certain degree. Since 1999, as the student uprisings in Iran have received more international attention, Iranians in the United States, regardless of political orientation, have come together as a national group and have become an outpost of the democratic movement in Iran.

Three generations of Iranian Americans celebrate Now-Ruz (Persian New Year), around the Haftsin table, with lights, flowers and sweets in Milburn, New Jersey, March 2010. (Courtesy of Alireza Tarighian)

As of June 2009, this situation drastically changed, and an unprecedented wave of citizen activism was born within Iranian American communities throughout the nation. As a reaction to the violent crackdown against protesters in Iran, Iranian American communities organized rallies and demonstrations, and the community, once again similar to the anti-shah demonstration of the late 1970s, became an active outpost for the Iranian democratic movement in Iran. This unexpected political activism is a telling sign that Iranian Americans' main concern is still the politics of Iran, the very political situation that pushed them to emigrate in the first place. The large majority of Iranian Americans, based on a recent letter-writing campaign to Congress, do not, however, support confrontational approaches in how the United States should deal with the political situation in Iran. Likewise, Iranians are overwhelmingly in favor of Iran normalizing relations with the United States but oppose any level of military action against their homeland, where they still possess family and cultural ties.

Forecasts for the 21st Century

The most remarkable achievement of the last century for Iranian immigrants has been the making of the Iranian community in America. As the 21st century progresses, qualitative and quantitative developments of the Iranian American community, at least in part, will be determined by political changes in Iran. If and when

---

To "Go Iranian" Means to Protest

"Finally, a positive image of Iranians as proud, patriotic, courageous and pro-democracy people." According to a recent blog entry posted on the Huffington Post by a New York City high school teacher, "Iran" has now become a verb. Below is the text of the blog entry:

The word Iran has become a verb
For any Iranians:
I teach at a NYC high school, and recently one student stood up to our very intimidating principal, (something that almost never happens). When he did not get permission for what he intended another student said, "Let's go Iranian on him." By that he means organize a protest. And so now they "Iran" anything they want to change. So it has become a verb now and to "Iran" the situation is to stand up to authority, well at least here in this corner of the universe. And it is a huge bonus for me because I cannot usually get them to even pay attention to another part of the world. Point being, even these students who get very small amounts of news equate "Iranian" with bravery and I completely agree, and wish I had that kind of intestinal fortitude.

major democratic changes take place in Iran, there is most likely going to be a degree of reemigration of Iranian Americans to Iran. Those who will return home will share the wealth of their experiences, and thus, Iran will harvest the fruits of its diaspora.

The 21st century will also provide an opportunity for history to catch up with the long-term magnitude of Iranians' contributions to America. Regarding the Iranian American community, second-generation Iranian Americans are likely to become increasingly more politically involved and to have a forceful voice in the American electoral and legislative process.

Appendix I: Migration Statistics

Table 160 Asylum applications granted to Iranian nationals 1999 to 2008

Year	
1999	1,004
2000	1,057
2001	1,119
2002	908
2003	536
2004	405
2005	285
2006	254
2007	279
2008	408

Source: U.S. Department of State, Bureau of Population, Refugees, and Migration (PRM), Worldwide Refugee Admissions Processing System (WRAPS).

Table 161 Naturalizations of Iranian nationals 1999 to 2008

Year	Number of Iranian Naturalizations
1999	18,205
2000	19,171
2001	13,834
2002	11,773
2003	10,782
2004	11,781
2005	11,031
2006	11,363
2007	10,557
2008	11,813

Source: U.S. Department of State, Bureau of Population, Refugees, and Migration (PRM), Worldwide Refugee Admissions Processing System (WRAPS).

Table 162 Persons obtaining legal permanent resident status by region and country of birth: Fiscal years 2000 to 2009

Region and Country of Birth	2000	2001	2002	2003	2004	2005	2006	2007	2008	2009
Total	841,002	1,058,902	1,059,356	703,542	957,883	1,122,257	1,266,129	1,052,415	1,107,126	1,130,818
Iran	8,487	10,425	12,960	7,230	10,434	13,887	13,947	10,460	13,852	18,553

Source: U.S. Department of Homeland Security. Office of Immigration Statistics. 2010. Adapted from Table 3

Appendix II: Demographics/Census Statistics

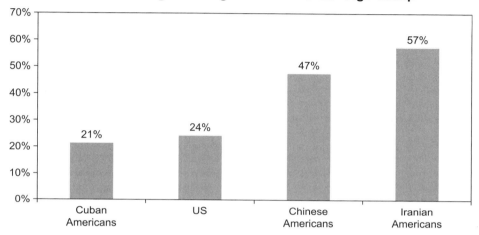

Figure 18 Bachelor's degree or higher, percentage of 25+ age group.
Source: 2000 U.S. Census.

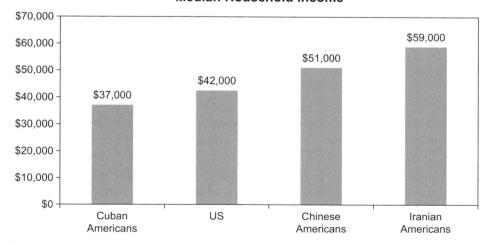

Figure 19 Median household income.
Source: 2000 U.S. Census.

Table 163 Persons obtaining legal permanent resident status during fiscal year 2009, leading states of residence: Region/country: Iran

Characteristic	Total	Male	Female
Total	18,553	9,002	9,551
Arizona	279	146	133
California	11,227	5,420	5,807
Colorado	124	62	62
Florida	310	143	167
Georgia	333	166	167
Illinois	322	167	155
Maryland	531	256	275
Massachusetts	208	92	116
Michigan	105	51	54
Minnesota	99	50	49
Nevada	171	96	75
New Jersey	198	98	100
New York	495	245	250
North Carolina	164	78	86
Ohio	133	61	72
Pennsylvania	120	62	58
Texas	1,481	741	740
Virginia	658	311	347
Washington	371	186	185
Other	1,224	571	653

Source: Adapted from U.S. Department of Homeland Security. Profiles on Legal Permanent Residents: 2009.

Appendix III: Notable Iranian Americans

Although Iranians are a comparatively small group, their contributions to science, business, education, and government are perhaps equal to that of the larger ethnic groups in the United States.

Christiane Amanpour has been an international correspondent for 18 years and is currently working for CNN. She has reported on many major crises from around the world, including Iraq, Afghanistan, Iran, Israel, Pakistan, Somalia, Rwanda, the Balkans, and the United States during Hurricane Katrina.

Anousheh Ansari became famous for being the first female private space explorer. A successful entrepreneur, Ansari is the fourth private explorer to visit space and the first astronaut of Iranian descent.

Reza Badiyi is one of the most prolific television directors in America, having directed more hours of TV programming than any other person.

Dr. Hamid Biglari is currently a vice-chairman and a Senior Leadership Committee member of Citicorp, the main operating arm of Citigroup, a $60 billion revenue business with operations in over 100 countries.

Nariman Farvardin is currently president at Stevens Institute of Technology, Hoboken, New Jersey. Formerly Senior Vice President for Academic Affairs and Provost at the University of Maryland, College Park. Farvardin holds a PhD degree in Electrical Engineering from Rensselaer Polytechnic Institute.

Dr. Akbar Ghahary is the owner of several international patents (in polymers and advanced composites) and currently the CEO and chairman of the board of Safas Corporation, an equity partner with General Electric Capital Corporation.

Mahin Khatamee founded Banou Inc., an Iranian American women's organization, in late 1980s. Based in New Jersey, Banou is a nonprofit, nonpolitical, and nonreligious charitable organization that strives to promote Iranian culture within the Iranian American community.

Omid Kordestani served as the senior vice president for Worldwide Sales and Field Operations of Google until April 2009.

Dr. Firouz Naderi is the associate director of NASA's Jet Propulsion Laboratory (JPL). He led programs that included the successful landing of the Mars Exploration Rovers, Spirit, and Opportunity.

Azar Nafisi is the best-seller author of *Reading Lolita in Tehran* and most recently *Things I've Been Silent About: Memories.*

Shirin Neshat is a contemporary visual artist who lives in New York. She is known primarily for her work in film, video, and photography.

Pierre Omidyar is the inventor of eBay and has been named one of the top 15 people "Who Make America Great" by *Newsweek*. He is currently a full-time philanthropist and founder of Family Foundation, a $10 billion foundation to "help people tap into their own power."

Atoosa Rubenstein served as the editor-in-chief of *Seventeen* magazine. She was also the founding editor of CosmoGIRL! and is currently the founder of Big Momma Productions, Inc., and Atoosa.com.

Glossary

Ashena-i-biganeh: Familiar stranger.

Now-Ruz: New year.

Sofreh Haftsin: A table decorated with seven items all starting with the letter "s."

Ta'arof: Iranian etiquette.

References

Ansari, Abdolmaboud. 1988. *The Iranian Immigrants in the U.S.: A Case Study of Dual Marginality*. New York: Associated Faculty Press.

Ansari, Maboud. 1992. *The Making of the Iranian Community in America.* New York: Pardis Press.

Ansari, Maboud. 2005. "From Immigrant to Ethnic: Iranian Americans." *Mirase Iran* 39(Spring): 28–31.

Ansari, Maboud. 2006. "Iranian American Identify." *Iran Times* 115: 10–12.

Bozorgmehr, M., ed. 1998. "Iranians in America." *Iranian Studies* 31(Spring): 3–95.

Bozorgmehr, Mahdi. 2007. "Iranian Immigrants." In *The New Americans,* edited by Mary Waters and Reed Veda, 150–95. Cambridge, MA.

Bozorgmehr, Mahdi, and G. Sabagh. 1988. "High Status Immigrants: A Statistical Profile of Iranians in the U.S." *Iranian Studies* 21: 4–34.

Katouzian, Homa, and Hossein Shahidi. 2008. *Iran in the 21st Century: Political, Economic and Conflict*. New York: Routledge.

Mobasher, Mohsen. 2006. "Migration and Entrepreneurship: Iranian Ethnic Economy in the U.S." In *Handbook of Research on Ethnic Minority Entrepreneurship,* edited by Dana Lee-paul, 297–306. Cheltenham, UK: Edward Elgar.

Morgan, David. 1987. *Medieval Persia 1040–1797*. Essex, England: Pearson.

Rahni, Davood N. 2007. "The Fourth Annual Persian Parade in New York City Draws Huge Enthusiastic Crowd." March 27. Payvand.com. [Online article accessed 3/27/07.] http://www.payvand.com/news/07/mar/1327.html.

Further Reading

Abrahamian, Ervand. 2009. *A History of Modern Iran*. Cambridge, MA: Cambridge University Press.

Abrahamian traces Iran's modern history in the 20th century, through the discovery of oil, imperial actions, the Pahlavis' rule, and the revolution and birth of the Islamic Republic in 1979.

Abrahamian, Ervand. 1982. *Iran Between Two Revolutions*. Princeton, NJ: Princeton University Press.

Abrahamian discusses Iranian society and politics during the period between the constitutional revolution of 1905–1909 and the Islamic revolution of 1977–1979.

Bill, James, A. 1988. *Eagle and Lion: The Tragedy of American-Iranian Relations*. New Haven, CT: Yale University Press.

Bill provides a thorough analysis of the American–Iran connection from its beginning in 1835.

Dabashi, Hamid. 1992. *Theology of Discontent: The Ideological Foundation of the Islamic Revolution in Iran*. New York: New York University Press.

Dabashi examines the ideological foundations of the Islamic revolution, with particular attention to the most notable and enduring consequences for radical Islamic revivalism in the entire Muslim world.

Dollafar, Arlene. 1994. "Iranian Women as Immigrant Entrepreneurs." *Gender and Society* 8: 541–61.

Dollafar illustrates how ethnic resources are gender specific, and that there is differential access to these resources in the ethnic economy, by examining two case studies of women's entrepreneurial endeavors in family-run businesses and in home-operated businesses.

Hanassab, Shideh. 1987. "Acculturation and Young Iranian Women: Attitudes Toward Sex Role and Intimate Relationships." *Journal of Psychology* 127: 565–71.

Hanassab's study examines the acculturation of Iranian women into the American culture of Los Angeles, California, their attitude toward the role of women, and their attitude toward intimate relationships.

Hillmann, Michael C. 1990. *Iranian Culture: A Persianist View*. New York: University Press of America.

Hillmann focuses on leading Persian authors and classic literary works in attempting to discern enduring cultural features and values.

Karim, Perssis, and Mehdi M. Khorrami, eds. 1999. *A World Between: Poems, Stories and Essays by Iranian Americans*. New York: George Braziller.

Karim and Khorrami's anthology includes stories, essays, and poems by more than 30 first-and second-generation Iranian Americans, set against the backdrop of the Islamic revolution in Iran and refugee life in America.

Katouzian, Homa. 2003. *Iranian History and Politics: The Dialectic of State and Society*. New York: Routedge.

Katouzian elaborates on his theory of arbitrary state and society in Iran, and its applications to Iranian history and politics, both modern and traditional.

Kelley, Ron, and Jonathan Friedlander, eds. 1993. *Iranjeles: Iranians in Los Angeles*. Berkeley, CA: University of California Press.

Kelley and Friedlander explore Iranian life and activities in the metropolitan Los Angeles area.

Kinzer, Stephen. 2005. *All the Shah's Men: An American Coup and the Roots of Middle East Terror*. New York: John Wiley and Sons.

Kinzer reconstructs the CIA's 1953 overthrow of the elected leader of Iran, Mohammad Mossadegh.

Mackey, Sandra. 1996. *The Iranians: Persia, Islam and the Soul of a Nation*. New York: The Penguin Group.

Mackey chronicles the history of the Iranian people, from the "glory days" of Persia to the overthrow of Mohammed Reza Shah and the rise of the Ayatollah Khomeini.

Milani, Farzaneh. 1992. *Veils and Words: The Emerging Voices of Iranian Women Writers*. Syracuse, NY: Syracuse University Press.

Milani illustrates that in Iran the 19th-century movement to unveil was closely linked to women's emergence as literary figures.

Nafisi, Azar. 2002. *Reading Lolita in Tehran*. New York: Random House.

Nafisi's memoir chronicles the true story of young women in the Islamic Republic of Iran who met in secret each week to read and discuss forbidden Western classics.

Pinault, David. 1992. *The Shiites: Ritual and Popular Piety in a Muslim Community*. New York: St. Martin's Press.

Pinault provides an overview of the history, beliefs, practices, and various sects of Shiite Islam, with particular emphasis on the Shi'ites in Hyderabad, India.

Sabagh, Georges, and Mehdi Bozorgmehr. 1987. "Are the Characteristics of Exiles Different from Immigrants?" *Sociology and Social Research* 10(January): 75–95.

Sabagh and Bozorgmehr examine the demographic, religious, and socioeconomic differences between immigrants and political refugees or exiles from Iran in Los Angeles, California.

Takeyh, Ray. 1990. *Hidden Iran: Paradox and Power in the Islamic Republic*. Chicago: University of Illinois Press.

Takeyh critically examines American–Iranian relations since the 1979 revolution.

Tavakoli-Targhi, Mohamad. 2001. *Refashioning Iran: Orientalism, Occidentalism and Historiography*. New York: Palgrave.

Tavakoli-Targhi argues for a radical rewriting of Iranian history, with profound implications for Islamic debates on gender.

Wright, Robin. 1989. *In the Name of God: The Khomeini Decades*. New York: Simon and Schuster.

Wright tells the story of the first decade of Khomeini's Islamic revolution and explains Iran's position in the Middle East, distinguished by its history, ethnic identity, and religious character.

Zonis, Marvin. 1991. *Majestic Failure: The Fall of the Shah*. Chicago: University of Chicago Press.

Zonis addresses four basic elements of the shah's psychological character (belief in divine protection, identification with other powerful people, sharing the strength of others, belief in the adoration of the Iranian people) and documents his deterioration, which began with the discovery of his cancer.

Iraqi Immigrants

by Mary C. Sengstock

Introduction

Iraqis represent one of America's smallest ethnic groups, numbering less than 300,000 persons. Iraqis have been coming to the United States since the early 1900s, prior to the establishment of Iraq as an independent nation. Throughout its highly varied history, Iraq has been home to a wide variety of peoples. In today's world, this translates into widely disparate religious and linguistic groups. Immigration from Iraq has varied throughout the past century, depending on conditions in the country of origin, as well as changes in American immigration laws. Consequently, Iraqi-Americans do not form a single cultural entity, being divided along religious, linguistic, and historical dimensions. All of these issues will be detailed in the following discussion.

Chronology

B.C.E	Mesopotamia settled in Tigris and Euphrates valleys; occupied by Akkadians, Sumerians, Chaldeans, Assyrians, Babylonians, and Jews.
First century C.E.	Most residents of the area converted to Christianity, establishing Christian churches.
Seventh century C.E.	Conversion of most residents of the area to Islam.
	Karbala battle and formation of the Shi'a sect of Islam.
16th and 17th centuries	Occupation of the area by the Ottoman Empire.
19th century	British colonialism, including Protestant missionary activity, in area.
ca. 1910	Earliest immigrants from Iraq arrive in United States; most are Christians and a few are Jews.
1914	Hostilities in area involving local, British, and Ottoman forces.

IRAQ

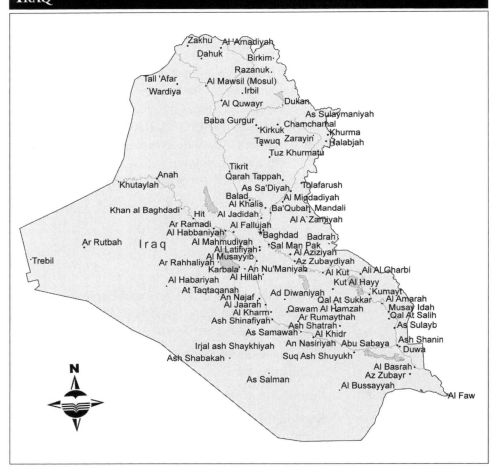

1918	British protectorate over the area; Iraq's population approximately three million, primarily Muslims, and including a portion of Kurdistan; Christians and Jews involved in British colonial government.
1921	Passage of legislation in the United States establishing the quota system, and limiting the number of Iraqi immigrants admitted to 100 per year; preference for relatives of citizens limits the immigration primarily to Christians.
1932	Iraq established as an independent nation by League of Nations.
1939–1945	World War II.
1948	Establishment of the nation of Israel, generating animosity against Jews in Iraq, and leading many to emigrate, mainly to Israel, but also to United States; diminished hopes of Kurds for an independent homeland; rise of the Ba'th Party in Syria, with influence in Iraq and other Arab nations; student visas also became available in the United States, increasing the number of young Iraqi immigrants, most Christian.
1965	Passage of the Immigration Act permits more Iraqis to enter United States.
1968	Saddam Hussein assumes control of Iraq; new immigration law in United States, allowing more immigrants from Iraq.
1973	Kurdish uprising in Iraq, causing continued ethnic unrest.
1980	War between Iraq and Iran, generating further ethnic hostilities between Sunnis/Shiites and Iraqis/Kurds; Muslims vs. Christians and Jews; impetus for increased emigration by Christians and Shiite Muslims.
1990	Iraqi forces invade Kuwait; United States and Western powers intervene on behalf of Kuwait, forcing Iraq to withdraw; continued ethnic hostilities in Iraq; sanctions against Iraq impede reconstruction; further impetus for immigration, and producing many refugees; major influx of Iraqi Shiites into United States begins; U.S. Census shows 44,916 Iraqi immigrants living in United States.

2000	U.S. Census shows 89,892 Iraqi immigrants living in United States.
2003	U.S. invasion of Iraq and fall of Saddam Hussein's government; U.S. occupation of Iraq; more refugees and increased impetus for immigration, primarily of Christians and Shiite Muslims.
2009	Iraqi Chaldeans estimate their population at 150,000; entire Iraqi-American population estimated at 245,000 to 265,000.
2010	United States ends major military involvement in Iraq.

Background

Geography of Iraq

Modern-day Iraq occupies the site of ancient Mesopotamia, a name that means "land between two rivers": the Tigris and Euphrates. The name *Iraq* similarly refers to the river location. This area has often been viewed as the "cradle of civilization," in which the earliest cultures leading to Western civilization developed. Iraq is bounded by Syria and Jordan on the west, Turkey on the north, Iran on the east, and Saudi-Arabia and Kuwait on the south.

In the pre-Christian era, it was home to a wide variety of cultural groups, including the Akkadians, Sumerians, Chaldeans, Assyrians, and Babylonians. Major cities included Ur, Babylon, Assur, and Nineveh. Ruins of these early settlements have been uncovered throughout Iraq. Jews also lived in Mesopotamia from pre-Christian times, a result of their capture by the Babylonians. Small communities of these cultural groups have continued to live in what is now Iraq since these early times. Throughout most of its history, the area has largely been a collection of tribal and familial connections. Beginning in the seventh century, most of them were loosely associated with the religion of Islam and the Arabic language and culture. Others, however, were remnants from the Jewish, Christian, and numerous smaller religious sects, all of which have remained there in varying numbers into the 20th century, often in isolated regions (Roux 1992).

History of Iraq

Mesopotamia became part of the Ottoman Empire in the 16th and 17th centuries, with the Ottomans eventually controlling three provinces of modern Iraq, focused around the cities of Mosul, Baghdad, and Basra. The culture was predominantly based on Arabic and Muslim traditions, but with considerable village and tribal influences. There were also small pockets of other cultural and religious groups, including Christians (Assyrians, Chaldeans, and Protestants), Mandeans (followers of John the Baptist), and Jews. This segment of the Ottoman Empire was the focus of hostilities with the British, beginning in 1914, and ending with a League of Nations Mandate, which gave the British control over the area in 1918. There were also constant disputes between Iraq, Great Britain, and other nations over the rights to Iraq's oil reserves. The Babylonian Jewish community traces its origins to the earliest days of Jewish history. The Prophet Abraham came from Ur in what is now southern Iraq, and the Jewish community of Baghdad traces its origin to the exile of Jews from ancient Israel, first by the Assyrians (around 721 B.C.E.), and later by the Babylonians (in 597 and 586 B.C.E.) (Roux 1992). Jews reportedly have continued to live in Iraq from that time until the 20th century (Shohet 1999).

At the time of the British Mandate, it was estimated that Iraq had a population of approximately three million. Over half were Shiite Muslims; about 20 percent were Kurds, who lived in the northern province of Mosul. Kurds spoke Kurdish rather than Arabic, had a distinct culture, and were part of a larger population, which was divided among Iraq, Turkey, Iran, and several other countries. Sunni Muslims were a minority but constituted the majority of the army and government officials. Less than 10 percent of the population consisted of Jews, Christians, Turks, and other minorities. The Iraqi Jewish community reportedly had approximately 250,000 members. The Kurdish population consisted primarily of Muslims, with a few Christians and Jews. This British period was characterized by attempts on the part of the various subgroups to ensure their representation in the government, both during the British era and in the independent Iraq that was to follow. Some of the religious minorities played a role in British government agencies, leading to distrust on the part of the majority Muslims (Tripp 2007).

The League of Nations recognized Iraqi independence in 1932, at which time the Hashemite monarchy was established. However, British influence remained strong, and minority Sunni Muslims had more influence than the majority Shiites, leading to continued resentment, unrest, and attempts to overthrow the government. In addition to the religious sectarianism, nationalistic issues were involved. A desire for unity among the various Arab nations was growing. Most Iraqis resented the continued control of the British. The powerful Sunnis distrusted the Shiites because of their presumed ties to non-Arabic Muslim nations, particularly neighboring Iran. Jews and Christians were distrusted because of their long-standing ties to the British (Tripp 2007).

World War II and its aftermath exacerbated the situation. Israel was established as an independent nation, further fueling the Pan-Arab movement and raising questions about the loyalty of Iraq's Jewish community, which then numbered slightly over 100,000 members. They were suspected of collaborating with Zionists and

Israel; all but a few thousand were forced to leave Iraq. Soviet Russia's desire for southern expansion threatened Iraq's newfound independence and suggested the need for connections with other nations in the region. Sunnis sought ties to other Arab nations, particularly Egypt. The pan-Arab movement also diminished the hopes of Iraqi Kurds for a unified Kurdistan.

The Ba'th Party, which had its origins in Syria, began to exercise an influence in Iraq during this period. The party was largely dominated by Iraq's President, Ahmad al-Bakr, and his relative, Saddam Hussein. Ba'thists attempted to bring together the many conflicting perspectives within the nation: Iraqi nationalism, pan-Arabism, and the numerous ethnic and religious divisions. In 1968, Saddam Hussein assumed control, solidifying his own personal control of the Ba'th Party and the government. His rise to power was facilitated by the burgeoning wealth of Iraq's oil reserves. He attempted to use his personal identity to forge a link among Iraq's diverse ethnic groups and with its historical ties to ancient Mesopotamia. Again, this was largely a minority party, with most of its leadership drawn from a Sunni region of northern Iraq; however, members of several groups were included within his government. Some Iraqi immigrants claim that this period was one of interethnic and interreligious cordiality, and intergroup conflicts were rare (Tripp 2007).

Kurdish dissatisfaction came to a head in 1973, with a Kurdish revolt in northern Iraq. Again, Kurds had hopes for greater autonomy, which were dashed when

Iraqi president Saddam Hussein waves to cheering crowds during a visit to the holy Muslim shrines in Samara on August 9, 1988. (AP/Wide World Photos)

Iraq and Iran came to terms on an exchange of territory. Many Kurds were forced to relocate from their traditional villages in the north to largely Shiite areas in the south. Resistance of the Shiites remained strong and was brutally suppressed, leading many to escape to Iran, which became the scene of the next confrontation between the two countries in 1980. With the outbreak of new hostilities with Iran, the Ba'th Party began a campaign to purge those seen as enemies, reviving and intensifying old ethnic hostilities: Sunni/Shi'a, and Iraqi/Kurd. Conflicts developed over which Islamic traditions should dominate in controlling the economy and political structure. The majority Shiites were particularly targeted, due to their perceived association with neighboring Iran (Tripp 2007).

By the mid-1980s, Iraq, with the assistance of the United States, Great Britain, and other Western powers, was experiencing success on the Iranian front. Again, Iraq's many ethnic divisions played a role. The Iraqi army included large numbers of ethnic minorities who could not be depended upon to support the Hussein government. Kurdish areas again became the scene of unrest. Hussein viewed the Gulf as a means to solidify his power, leading to the invasion of Kuwait. This move did not have the desired success, and the Iraqi withdrawal from Kuwait generated uprisings among the disaffected populations of adjoining southern Iraq, where Shiites were a majority.

To a considerable degree, this marked the beginning of the end for the Hussein regime. The UN Security Council was determined to prevent Iraq from taking similar aggressive actions in the future. Any substance that could conceivably be used in the production of weapons was placed under embargo, a measure that inflicted severe hardships on the people of Iraq. It became impossible to rebuild Iraq's infrastructure, including its supply of electricity and safe water. Food shortages and disease followed quickly, and medical supplies were in short supply, further fomenting unrest among the Iraqi people. Finally, continued suspicion about Iraq's weapons stockpile led to an invasion by the United States and its allies in March 2003, culminating in the fall of Hussein's government (Ricks 2007). With the Ba'thist government at an end, the old divisions that had plagued Iraq again came to the fore, greatly complicating the establishment of a new governmental structure, and forcing the U.S. government into its extended occupation of Iraq. The military aspect of this involvement was terminated under President Barak Obama in 2010.

Clearly, the divisions that plague Iraq at the present time have their origin in these long-standing historical disputes among various economic, ethnic, and cultural divisions in Iraqi society. They have also served as the impetus for members of these groups to emigrate from Iraq in the hope of finding a better life elsewhere. Hence, migration from Iraq can include persons from the various religious and cultural groups, depending upon the varying conditions in Iraq for each group at different times. Furthermore, the location and nature of the communities they establish after leaving Iraq also differ significantly. In the following discussion, distinctions will be made among three groups of Iraqi-Americans, based on whether their religious preference is Christian, Muslim, or Jewish (Tripp 2007).

Causes and Waves of Migration

Early Immigration

The earliest known immigration from Iraq to the United States occurred in the first two decades of the 20th century, during the final years of Ottoman control of Mesopotamia, and prior to the establishment of Iraq as a separate entity. At that time, the religion of Islam and the Arabic language predominated in the area, and groups that differed were more likely to emigrate. Christian Iraqis, feeling pressure from the surrounding Muslim society, were particularly likely to migrate. Their contact with the British government also made them aware of the advantages of living in a predominantly Christian society. Iraqi Chaldeans are an example. They began coming to the United States around 1910, with about a dozen members in the early 1920s, when the quota system of immigration control was introduced (Sengstock 1999, 2005). Iraq received the minimum quota (100 per year), slowing community growth. Iraqi immigrants to the United States in the earliest years of the 20th century included persons of Jewish descent. Approximately 20 Iraqi Jewish families came to the United States in the first decade. The breakup of the Ottoman Empire resulted in the migration of approximately 60 more members, with another 70 families coming with the outbreak of World War II in 1939.

Most early Christian immigrants made a distinct effort to maintain their identity as Middle Eastern Christians. Both Christians and Jews took great pride in their origins from Mesopotamia, the cradle of civilization. Neither group viewed themselves as Iraqis or Arabs. Return to Iraq was not a goal; rather, they expended considerable effort to bring relatives to the United States and expand their communities here. The American quota system, with its emphasis on reuniting families, assisted in this goal.

Later Waves of Immigration

Following World War II, the United States made student visas available; young Iraqi Christians took advantage of the program to attend school. In contrast, Muslims found Iraqi society more congenial and few sought to emigrate. Furthermore, the 1920s quota system was designed to ensure that new immigrants reflected, as closely as possible, the population already established in the United States, giving preference to persons with relatives already here and giving Iraqi Christians an advantage. Muslim Iraqis who came for educational purposes tended to complete their degrees and return to Iraq, as was expected under the program; Christians used the program to obtain entry into the country, after which they married citizens or obtained employment, enabling them to remain in the United States. The 1948 establishment of the state of Israel brought about major hostilities against Jews in Iraq and other Arabic countries and caused the exodus of the majority of Jews. Most were relocated to Israel, but some came to the United States. By the time of the U.S. invasion of Iraq in 2003, Jews remaining in Iraq numbered less than a dozen.

Immigration Act of 1965 and Succeeding Legislation

The Immigration Act of 1965 marked a change in the character of Iraqi immigration by making it possible for more Iraqis to obtain visas. While accurate numbers are difficult to obtain, agencies that work with American Middle Eastern communities report receiving dramatically more requests for assistance from Iraqi immigrants, both Muslim and Christian. Because Sunnis were more powerful in Iraq, Shiites were more likely to emigrate. Iraqi Christians continued to immigrate in substantial numbers, leading to a remarkable increase in community size (exceeding 100,000 by 2000).

As noted previously, the greatest wave of migration from Iraq occurred as a result of the hostilities between Iraq and Iran in the 1980s, and the wars involving the United States that followed. As conditions in Iraq became unbearable, residents from all religious and ethnic backgrounds sought to leave. Many went to nearby countries, mainly Syrian and Jordan (Lobe 2007). Others came to the United States as refugees; upon arrival, most were in need of assistance, since some fled with little more than the clothes on their backs (Brown 2008; Wiswell 2007). Agencies within the Muslim, Chaldean, and Assyrian communities are often called upon to provide this assistance. Jews who left Iraq during this period were more likely to go to Israel; those who came to the United States generally sought assistance from Jewish agencies, such as the Hebrew Immigrant Aid Society, rather than from agencies in the Iraqi communities.

The Sunni tradition predominates throughout the Muslim world, including the leadership of Iraq. Some Sunnis had come to the United States in the 1960s and 1970s, mainly for education. Iraqi Shiites are an anomaly within the Middle East. They are distrusted by Sunni Iraqis because of their association with predominantly Shiite Iran. Iranians, however, associate them with the Arab language and culture. During the war with Iran, Saddam Hussein questioned their loyalty and they were the target of vicious attacks, leading many to flee. Many Iraqi emigrants had planned to return to Iraq; with the growing unrest in Iraq, however, most were fearful of returning and remained in the United States.

Through IRCA to the Present

The major influx of Iraqi Shiites to the United States began following the war over Kuwait in 1990. Many Shiites living near the Kuwait border supported the Allied attack against Saddam Hussein, hoping the Allies would aid them in loosening Hussein's grip on their region. However, Allied forces failed to provide support, leaving them defenseless when Iraqi troops pursued them. When these hopes were dashed, thousands fled to the desert, eventually being relocated in Saudi Arabian refugee camps by United Nations workers. The situation deteriorated with sanctions against Iraq in the 1990s and the Gulf War in early 2003. It is estimated that 1 million Iraqis have been killed, and another 4.5 million displaced by bombings and kidnappings as a result of the Gulf War (Tirman 2009). They fled to nearby nations, the largest numbers going to Syria (800,000), Jordan (700,000), and Egypt (80,000) (Lobe 2007). Many nations have given them refugee status, granted to persons who can prove a reasonable threat of danger in their homeland. The United States was expected to admit an estimated 17,000 Iraqi refugees by the end of 2009; the United States also grants special status to Iraqis who assisted U.S. forces as advisers or translators. However, humanitarian experts contended the United States had a responsibility to admit far more (Baltimore Sun Staff 2009; Brown 2008; International Rescue Committee 2009; Tate 2009).

The Plight of Iraqi Refugees

The plight of Iraqi refugees is vividly demonstrated by the stories they bring. Ibrahim is a Christian who arrived with his wife, Asho, and their five sons (Wiswell 2007). In Saddam Hussein's Iraq, the threat of jail or worse was always present. Ibrahim was in jail for three years, suspected of opposing the Iraqi government. He is missing two fingers, due to injuries received when a guard smashed his hand. His sister, a teacher, was jailed and beaten for refusing to raise the grades of a student whose relatives were government officials. She was killed in 2004 by anti-Christian rebels. Another relative had been jailed and beaten when she was only 15. The family fled to the Turkish border. During the flight, two teenaged sons were also jailed; the family feared they had been killed. Eventually they were freed and made it back to their family in Turkey. The boys reported sleeping on the floor, with no blankets and only bread to eat. Another refugee escaped with her three teenaged daughters. Her husband was not able to escape and remains in Iraq. She tells of a sister-in-law, kidnapped from a boarding school in Baghdad, who was held for two weeks until the family could raise money for her ransom. Although she was Christian, her kidnappers threatened to kill her if they ever saw her with her head uncovered; she continued to wear the veil out of fear for her life (Bardazzi 2009).

Muslim Iraqis report similar atrocities. In the aftermath of the invasion of Kuwait, Shiite Muslims near the Kuwait border rose up against the Hussain government. When the United States and allied forces allowed Hussain to remain in power, providing fuel for his planes and tanks, these weapons were used against the Shiites. Many tried to reach the Saudi Arabian border. Government forces attacked them as they fled. One man reported seeing the body of a woman, lying in the carnage, her infant still nursing at her breast. Another saw a friend, in tears, sitting amid the bombs, bodies, and dirt. He urged his friend to flee. However, the friend said the man lying dead was his cousin and insisted he must remain with the body, which was already half eaten by dogs.

Refugee life had its own share of problems. Hundreds met death in Saudi Arabian refugee camps, which held over 30,000 Shiites. Dead bodies were kept in a refrigerator. An observer reported to an official that one of the bodies was still alive. The official raised his gun and fired, then ordered the body placed in the refrigerator with the others. In the north, Ibrahim's family fled to Turkey, where they lived in a small, damp apartment. They spent much of their time indoors, fearful of being identified and returned to Iraq. Those who were able to find work found that illegal aliens like themselves were paid less than Turkish nationals.

About life in America, Ibrahim says, "For the first time in our lives we feel like a human being. Everything is so clean, people treat us nice, and everything is legal" (Wiswell 2007).

Iraqi refugees include members of all social and religious groups. Among Muslims, there have been three major waves of immigrants during the last quarter of the 20th century and into the 21st century. Before 1980, most Muslims coming to the United States were educated Sunnis. During the Hussein regime, most were Shiites, currently the largest group of Iraqi Muslim immigrants; most came from rural southern Iraq, largely under the control of tribal leaders and relatively isolated from outside influences. Following the fall of Saddam Hussein, changes in the political structure forced Sunni Muslims to emigrate from Iraq, as Shiites showed resentment for their role in Hussein's government (Lobe 2007). Adjustment to American society varies among these groups, with the urban, educated Sunnis adjusting more easily. Iraqi refugee problems cross religious lines, however. Most Jews had already left Iraq prior to the Gulf War. But Christians of all religions suffered greatly as a result of the Gulf War; they were associated, in the minds of Muslim Iraqis, with the Western Christian invaders, which caused them to leave (Bardazzi 2009). Christian leaders have complained that the suffering of Iraqi Christians has been ignored by both sides in the Gulf conflict (Kohn 2008).

Unlike other immigrants, refugees usually migrate virtually penniless, greatly straining the community's ability to provide assistance (Brown 2008). Indeed, local politicians have complained publicly about the refugee program, noting the difficulty a refugee influx creates in local communities, particularly during times of economic distress. In response, federal refugee programs attempt to minimize the local impact by directing refugees to widely varying parts of the country. This approach can be counterproductive, however, since areas without an Arabic-speaking population are less able to provide adaptive assistance. The Detroit area, particularly the suburb of Dearborn, is well known for its large Arabic community, and many refugees gravitate to this area where Arabic speakers and refugee assistance are available, together with services such as medical evaluations, employment assistance, and help with necessities such as food or household goods (Abraham 2000; Leonard 2003).

However, the magnitude of the influx places great stress on community resources. One Detroit area agency, assigned to handle refugee mental health problems, dealt with 2,500 refugees in 2008; they were told to expect 4,000 in 2009. In 1997, the Dearborn school district enrolled over 800 Iraqi students; like most immigrant children, they needed assistance with English, but they also had health problems from their refugee experience. Refugees of all ages suffer from health problems and posttraumatic stress disorder (PTSD), due to months or years in a war zone and refugee camps, and exposure to chemical agents, contaminated water, and communicable diseases. Those with chronic conditions, such as diabetes, may not have received treatment for months. Refugees bring these conditions with them to their new environments.

Demographic Profile

Size and Composition of Community

In 2000 the U.S. Census Bureau counted 89,892 immigrants from Iraq living in the United States, more than double the number enumerated in the 1990 census (44,916). Iraqis still represented less than one percent of immigrants to the United States. Due to conditions in Iraq, immigration has increased recently, and approximately one-third of Iraqi immigrants hold refugee status. In 2000, Iraqi immigrants were concentrated primarily in three states: Michigan (31,927); California (20,532); and Illinois (9,634) (see Table 164). Other states with over 2,000 Iraqi immigrants at that time were Tennessee, Texas, New York, and Arizona. Most of Michigan's Iraqi immigrants were in Detroit, with 30,569. Chicago had 9,513; San Diego, 7,507; Los Angeles, 5,499. Phoenix, Arizona, Nashville, Tennessee, and Washington, D.C., each had more than 1,700 Iraqi immigrants (see Table 165). As a result of the wars in Iraq, immigration into the United States increased dramatically since the mid-1990s, from less than 2,000 per year in 1989 through 1991, to more than 4,000 in 1992, and over 5,000 per year in 1994–1996 (see Table 166) (Grieco 2003). According to the U.S. Department of Homeland Security, this dramatic increase continued into the 21st century. In fiscal year 2009, 12,110 received legal permanent resident status. The number of Iraqis granted permanent residence in 2009 was well over double the number allowed just nine years earlier (see Table 167). This very likely represents an attempt on the part of the U.S. government to assist refugees from the Iraq War. Upon arrival, the major destinations of those migrants continued to be the states that already had the largest concentrations of Iraqi immigrants: Michigan (2,691) and California (2,768) (see Table 168).

Most ethnic populations remain intact in further generations after immigration. Hence, a complete picture of Iraqi communities includes persons of Iraqi ancestry, as well as those born in Iraq. Census data present serious difficulties in estimating the size of the population by ancestry. This inadequacy derives from problems inherent in census data collection methods. Ancestry questions do not distinguish immigrants from subsequent generations, nor are they likely to generate a response from persons who no longer identify with their countries of origin. Even those who identify strongly with their homelands may not respond, due to suspicion about

Iraqi refugee Rawaa Bahoo laughs with her children Marvin (left), Maryana, and Maryam, in Farmington Hills, Michigan, August 21, 2009. Family ties and cultural support from the region's large Middle Eastern community continues to draw new refugees despite a depressed economy. (AP Photo/Paul Sancya)

data-collection programs and fear of reprisals. Consequently, nonresponse issues create a persistent undercount of ethnic ancestry. Some data collection problems are unique to Iraq. Some Iraqis prefer to identify with the general "Arab" category, and non-Muslim Iraqis are reluctant to claim Iraqi ancestry. Iraqi Jews and Kurds are also unlikely to claim Iraqi descent. Iraqi Christians, who identify as Assyrians, Chaldeans, or Syriac, were granted a new category in the 2000 census and are not included in either the Iraqi or the Arab category.

The 2000 Census listed a total of 37,714 persons claiming Iraqi ancestry; most of these are likely to be Muslims (see Table 169). An additional 82,154 persons identified themselves as being of "Assyrian/Chaldean/Syriac" ancestry. Most, but not all, probably originate from Iraq. Hence these Christian Iraqis are double the size of the Muslim Iraqi group. While they may not identify as Iraqis, it is clear they retain many ties with Iraq. Their immigration papers, or those of their ancestors, list Iraq as the country of origin. Many maintain contact and send remittances to relatives remaining in Iraq. If they were to commit crimes in the United States, they might be deported to Iraq. Hence Iraqi Christians, Jews, and other non-Muslims should be included among the Iraqi ancestry group. Since they identify more with their religious and linguistic orientations than with the nation of Iraq, once these immigrants arrive in the United States, their settlement patterns also vary, depending on their religious preference and linguistic orientation.

Community estimates are an alternate source for the enumeration of ethnic community size. In 2009, the Chaldean community of Detroit estimated its numbers at 150,000 members. Iraqi Christians in other states probably constitute another 30,000 to 50,000 persons, for a total of 180,000 to 200,000 Iraqi Christians. Based on the total of 37,714 persons claiming Iraqi ancestry in the 2000 census, Iraqi Muslims probably number at least another 50,000 by 2009. The Iraqi American Jewish community is estimated at 15,000. Hence the total Iraqi American population is approximately 245,000 to 265,000 (see Table 169). In general, Christian Iraqis are concentrated primarily in Michigan, Illinois, Arizona, and California; Muslim Iraqis in Michigan; and Jewish Iraqis in New York and California (Schopmeyer 2000; Sengstock 1999, 2005; Shohet 1999).

Muslim immigrants into the United States have come from a wide variety of nations, primarily southern Asia (India, Iran, Pakistan, Bangladesh, and Afghanistan) and the Arab world (Lebanon, Syria, Palestine, Egypt, Jordan, and Morocco). Iraqi Muslims are relative newcomers. Iraqi Kurds should be included here as well, since most are Muslim, with a few Christians and Jews. However, Kurds come from Iran and Turkey as well as Iraq. There is a community of Iraqi Kurds in the San Diego area, while Iranian Kurds are in Los Angeles. Most Kurds support the concept of an independent Kurdistan and tend not to identify as Iraqis. The most accurate estimates of Iraqi Jews come from Jewish agencies; one estimates their total number at over 15,000. Most live in New York and Los Angeles, both of which have organizations for Iraqi Jews; smaller concentrations are in Connecticut, Florida, Massachusetts, and New Jersey. The American Babylonian Jewish community is considered the largest outside of Israel (Shoket 1999).

Age and Family Structure

Iraqi American community make-up varies depending upon the religious and cultural background of the immigrants. Groups that began immigrating in the early years of the 20th century now have a substantial number of older members, some of them immigrants, and others the descendants of the earliest immigrants. This is true of Iraqi Jews and Christians. Muslim Iraqis, who began their immigration following the 1965 change in immigration law, or as refugees from the Iraqi wars, tend to be younger populations, with fewer aged members.

All of these groups reflect, to a considerable extent, an overall family pattern prevalent in the Arab Middle East. This pattern is characterized by a strong commitment to long-term marriages, intense patriarchal authority, and an emphasis on modesty for women. Men are expected to be the head of the house. Women are valued for the number of children that are born to them and are expected to remain in the home rather than be employed. Marriage within most Iraqi groups is largely an extended family matter. Prior to the last half of the 20th century, many marriages were arranged, often preferring marriages within the patriarchal lineage. Even today, families attempt to exert a substantial influence over their children's marital choices. Iraqi ethnic communities often sponsor youth groups and other social events to encourage their young people to socialize with each other only under the watchful eyes of the older members of the extended family and community.

The authority of the father and the father's lineage continues to remain strong, with wives and children expected to conform to the father's expectations. Demands for female modesty are particularly strong. Girls are expected to remain virgins until they marry, and this represents a major influence on the family's honor. Hence boys may be permitted a considerable degree of freedom to participate in social activities and dating prior to marriage, but girls are expected to remain close to home. These traditions are rigorously kept among the most religious Muslims; Christian and Jewish Iraqi Americans, and less religious Muslims, are less likely to do so.

Educational and Economic Attainment

Iraqi Americans tend to exhibit the educational patterns typical of many immigrant groups, with the earlier arrivals being relatively uneducated, while their children and grandchildren are more likely to gain a higher education. Hence Christian and Jewish Iraqi Americans represent a more educated population; recently arrived Muslim Iraqis tend to be less educated.

The earliest Iraqis in the United States tended to follow the occupational patterns of other Middle Easterners, such as the Syrians and Lebanese. In the earliest years, most Christian Iraqis were engaged in small business enterprises. Detroit's first Chaldeans became extremely adept in the retail grocery business. By the late 20th century, there were over 1,000 retail grocery stores in the Detroit area owned and operated by Chaldeans. Some Chaldeans also established subsidiary businesses, such as wholesale food companies and suppliers to retail stores. Chaldeans also became adept at real estate sales and development. Their success in these businesses led them to maintain these occupations for several decades, rather than seeking advanced education. This began to change in the second half of the 20th century, when student visas and the 1965 Immigration Law produced more persons with higher education. By the 1990s, many Chaldeans had college educations and had moved into the professions, including law, business, teaching, and the medical fields. Assyrian Christians in other communities have a similar record of educational and professional advancements, and pride in their accomplishments.

With the influx of Iraqi refugees, the economic structure of these communities has experienced considerable change. Refugees come with few resources and need more assistance upon arrival (International Rescue Committee 2009). Many recent arrivals

Rae Alzaweny sorts produce in the Iraq Market grocery store in Dearborn, Michigan, May 1, 2003. Alzaweny is an Iraqi immigrant and owner of the store, which caters to the largely Middle Eastern community of Dearborn. (AP Photo/Paul Sancya)

are Shiite Muslims and are concentrated in lower income and nonprofessional occupations, particularly factory work and operating gas stations and convenience stores. Little data are available on Jewish Iraqis, but they have largely joined the larger Jewish community and exhibit similar income and occupational patterns.

Health Statistics and Issues

Health statistics are rarely available on a group as small as Iraqis. In general, Iraqis who have been in the United States longer have good health care, while those with lower income often lack health care and have poorer health. They also tend to be accepting of the health care they receive, even though it may be lacking in several respects. Recent arrivals come with the health problems of the refugee camps. Some Middle Eastern cultural patterns are also conductive to poor health outcomes (Sengstock 1996). For example, smoking is a widely accepted behavior in this population, leading to smoking-related health problems. Detroit area health institutions have attempted to deal with these problems in the Arabic-speaking communities as a whole.

Adjustment and Adaptation

Family, Culture, and Life-Cycle Patterns

Family patterns have exhibited considerable change in some Iraqi communities, particularly the sizeable Christian population. Many communities have diverged from the traditional patriarchal structure. Family patterns also exhibit great divergence along religious lines.

Iraqis generally follow the customs specified for their particular religious preference for the birth of a child. The Chaldean or Assyrian churches are the central focus for most activities of Christian Iraqis. Children are brought there for baptism, which generally follows Christian tradition, with the exception that it would be conducted in the Aramaic language. Similarly, Iraqi Jews follow Jewish religious tradition requiring circumcision for male children shortly after birth. Among Muslims, circumcision is also practiced; in the Middle East, this is often done later, when the child is six to eight years old; in America, it is usually done at birth, with a home celebration following. Muslims also recite a call to prayer at the time of birth, to accustom the child to his/her responsibility as a devout Muslim. The Muslim child's head is also shaved, accompanied by the slaughtering of two goats (one for a girl) to celebrate the birth.

For Christians, a confirmation ceremony often takes place when the child has completed a course of study in the religion, usually between 9 and 14 years of age.

Some Christians also hold a major celebration when the child receives the Eucharist for the first time, giving a party similar to a wedding celebration. Muslim tradition requires that the child begin studying the Quran at the age of four years, four months, and four days; this event is marked by a ceremony, with another ceremony taking place a few years later, once the child has succeeded in reading the entire Quran. Jews hold a traditional Bar or Bat Mitzvah ceremony when the child reaches the age of 13, with the child reciting from the Torah.

Iraqi Christian marriages generally occur in the families' religious denomination. Many of these rituals have been altered from the original form in Iraq a century ago, where marriages were conducted in the village, beginning with a procession from the bride's home to that of the groom. Following the patriarchal customs of the Middle East, the groom's family played a major role. Brides of old dressed in the village's traditional colorful dress. Today's Iraqi Christian weddings tend to follow local Christian traditions, with the exception that the ceremony is usually in Aramaic. Chaldean brides wear an elaborate white gown, have numerous bridesmaids and groomsmen, and host a reception for several hundred guests, with alcoholic beverages, music, and dancing. Chaldean tradition does not acknowledge the Muslim prohibition against the consumption of alcohol, although other Christian groups may not agree. Many Iraqis still retain a major role for the groom's family, which often pays for the celebration (Sengstock 1999, 2005).

In Muslim tradition, marriage tends to be a cultural rather than a religious ceremony and often involves a family agreement, in addition to consent from the bride and groom (Patheos 2009). Grooms are expected to provide their brides with a dower, a gift of money or jewelry, which becomes her property; without this, the marriage may not take place. The bride's family also provides her with a dowry to bring to the marriage; often this is a gift of a business or home for the young couple. Christian Iraqis have also been known to follow the dowry custom (Sengstock 1999, 2005). Again, Iraqi Jews tend to follow general Jewish customs, such as marrying under a chuppah (canopy).

Death rituals also have a religious character. Chaldean funerals are similar to those of other Catholics, with the exception that they are generally conducted in Aramaic. Like other Chaldean rituals, they exhibit a boisterous exuberance that may surprise the typical American observer, with loud singing and chanting. Muslim tradition requires dying persons to repent their sins and repeat the first pillar of Islam (belief in Allah). Family members should gather around and join in the prayers, especially if the dying person is unable to do so. After death, the body must be washed, wrapped in a white shroud, and buried as soon as possible, with the body facing Mecca (Patheos 2009). Gifts of money or food are given to the poor in memory of the deceased. Jews also bury the dead soon after death and follow general Jewish custom.

Among Christian Iraqis, gender relations have largely been adapted to the American environment. Choice of a marriage partner is an example. In the Chaldean community, the groom, and later the bride, gradually received the right to voice an opinion, or even decline a proposed marriage partner, although young Iraqi Chaldeans still give greater weight to family opinion in their marital choices than the typical American couple. Gender relations have changed in other respects as well. In the mid-20th century, seating in Chaldean churches was usually segregated by sex; this was rarely the case at century's end. Today's Chaldean women often obtain a college education and have professional positions. Many girls still complain, however, that Chaldean families prefer male children over females, and girls often have more household responsibilities than their brothers. In the area of gender relations, Muslim women are expected to keep themselves covered; at its extreme, they wear a long dress that covers from head to toe. Less traditional Muslim women may wear the hijab, covering only the head, or even no head covering at all (Barazangi 1996; Cainkar 1996; Haddad and Smith 1996; Sengstock 1999, 2005).

Retaining a Sense of National Culture and Identity

Both Assyrians and Chaldeans have made extensive efforts to retain a sense of their unique identity as descendants of the people of ancient Mesopotamia and Babylonia, speakers of the ancient Aramaic language, and among the earliest converts to the Christian religion. They have done this mainly through their churches, by attempting to continue the Assyrian rituals handed down from their Apostolic founders, and by urging their children and grandchildren to learn the Aramaic/Assyrian language. This too has taken place largely through the churches and community centers, many of which offer language programs for both children and adults. It must be emphasized that this identity is to be distinguished from identification with the nation of Iraq or the Arab world. Few Chaldeans or Assyrians think of themselves in this manner, an issue that irritates, even angers, their fellow Iraqi immigrants, who seek to present a broadly based, unified front in influencing national and pan-Arabic issues in their homeland as well as the United States. Assyrians and Chaldeans, however, generally believe that Iraqi and Arab movements have placed them at a distinct disadvantage and seek fairer treatment in Iraq for persons of their heritage. Iraqi Christians also disagree among themselves over identity, with Chaldeans preferring their religious identity, while Assyrians identify linguistically (Sengstock 1999, 2005).

Both Christian and Muslim Iraqis maintain close ties to their homeland, mainly through connections with relatives in Iraq. These ties are used to provide assistance to their families in the difficult conditions of 21st-century Iraq. This contact is often at a high level, involving frequent communication by phone or e-mail, sending remittances back to family members, and attempting to obtain visas for relatives to immigrate. These activities involve not only recent immigrants, but also second- and third-generation members. Since there are few Jews left in Iraq, Iraqi Jews tend to have few ties to their country of origin.

Social Organizations Based on National/Ethnic Background

The Iraqi Chaldean community has a highly developed social structure: two Chaldean dioceses, several churches, and numerous community organizations, including a business association, women's charitable group, and youth groups, to name but a few. They are also in the process of establishing a Chaldean Cultural Center, including a museum to display their history and culture and maintain archival records. Other Iraqi Christian groups also have well-established organizations, including churches and organizations to promote the Assyrian language. There have also been some recent attempts on the part of varying Assyrian and Chaldean religious leaders to form a united effort on behalf of the Christian minority suffering in Iraq.

Both Christian and Muslim agencies provide community assistance, particularly to refugees. Dearborn's Muslim community has the Arab Community Center for Economic and Social Service (ACCESS), and the Karbala Islamic Education Center. Chaldeans, residing in northern Detroit and bordering Oakland and Macomb counties, provide services through the Chaldean Ladies of Charity and Chaldean Federation of America. The Arab and Chaldean Social Services Council attempts to serve clients from both religious communities. Refugee assistance is often funded by the federal government, but federal assistance is limited, and many refugees were led to expect more extensive aid.

Shiite Muslims established the Islamic Center of America in Dearborn in 1963, with a new building opening in 2005; this center is mainly attended by Lebanese. Although Iraqi Shiites may also attend, many prefer the Karbala Education Center of America, established specifically for them in 1995. The center's name is significant, since it commemorates the revered Shiite birthplace and shrine (Walbridge and Aziz 2000). Both centers have also developed museums to highlight Islamic religion, history, and culture. While Iraqi Jews associate with the larger Jewish community, they also have a Web site and newsletter to maintain their connection to Iraqi Jewry.

Religion

Religion is one of the dominant cultural institutions in the Middle East. This was the case when the earliest immigrants left Iraq, and it continues in the United States This is true even for second- and third-generation Iraqis. Because of the critical role of religion, the Christian communities tend to establish separate institutions for the different denominations. For example, Turlock, California, has churches for those who follow the ancient Assyrian Christian faith, as well as for the Chaldean rite and for Assyrian Protestants (Sengstock 1999). In this community, pride in being Assyrian and speaking Aramaic are the major unifying mechanisms.

Iraqi Christians take pride in the fact that their Christian tradition originates from the earliest days of Christianity; they claim to have been converted to Christianity by St. Thomas, the Apostle of Jesus, during his missionary journeys. From the outset, this area was the site of numerous disputes within the Christian community. Nestorius, a local bishop, had a dispute with the Western Church in the 400s C.E., resulting in the establishment of a separate church, usually termed the Assyrian Church. About 1,000 years later, some members of this group joined the church in Rome, leading to the establishment of a separate "rite" of the Roman Catholic Church, the Chaldean rite (Sengstock 1999, 2005). During the 19th century, British missionary activities resulted in the conversion of some residents of this area to Protestantism. Consequently, Christians of northern Iraq adhere to a wide variety of religious denominations, some of which can be found in other parts of the Middle East as well. The two major divisions of Iraqi Christians in the United States focus on these two dimensions. Chaldeans belong to the Catholic Church, while followers of Nestorius and Protestants consider themselves "Assyrians" or "Syriac."

Little research has been conducted as yet on Iraqi Muslims in the United States. However, previous research on other Muslim communities provides a basis for analyzing the direction they are likely to take. Regardless of nationality, Muslims follow the religious traditions of Islam, established in what is now Saudi Arabia by the Prophet Muhammad in the early seventh century C.E. Muslim tradition is based on five core elements, called the pillars of Islam. The first is to have faith in Allah, the one God, and his Prophet, Muhammad; the other four are the obligation to pray five times each day, give alms (*zakat*), fast during the month of Ramadan, and make a pilgrimage (*haj*) to the holy city of Mecca if finances allow. The religious center for Muslims is the mosque, but the obligation is to pray daily, not necessarily in a common center. Muslims revere Friday as the holy day.

Also critical to an understanding of Islam is *shari'a,* the law of Islam as drawn from the Quran, and from *sunnah* (the Prophet's practices). These are applied to all aspects of social behavior, including marriage, family life, the economic sphere, and the manner in which society as a whole should be organized. Islamic religious leaders frequently issue opinions (known as *fatwah*), concerning the proper application of Islamic traditions. Early in the development of Islam, a dispute occurred regarding the appropriate leaders to impart Mohammed's message. The earliest leaders were elected caliphs. One of the later candidates was Husain, grandson of Mohammed. Prior to his election, Husain and members of his family were killed in a battle that occurred in the city of Karbala in southern Iraq. Followers of Husain revered him and viewed him to be a martyr, leading to the development of the Shi'a sect. Karbala subsequently became a major Shiite shrine and is venerated as the birthplace of the Shi'a sect. A permanent split between the Sunni and Shi'a divisions resulted from this event, and different legal perspectives are taken by the two factions. Members of one group commonly do not accept the opinions issued by leaders from the other sect.

This division is not rigid. Even in the Middle East, some Sunni and Shi'a followers interact regularly and may intermarry. Furthermore, Muslims may choose to attend a mosque of either sect. This pattern had prevailed within Iraq for several decades in the mid-20th century. These divisions are important for understanding the manner in which Muslim immigrants from different national and religious divisions interact within the U.S. context after immigration. Other issues also play a role, including cultural differences among immigrants. These include language variation, differences in cuisine, and urban–rural variations. The Arabic language has numerous dialects, which vary by national origin, making religious services uncomfortable for persons of a different nationality.

In all these respects, recent Iraqi Muslim immigrants, most of them Shiites, represent a new category in the American Muslim community. In Dearborn, several mosques had been established by both Sunni and Shiite Muslims prior to the arrival of the Iraqis. The majority of Dearborn's Shiites were Lebanese, and variations exist between the cultures of the two countries, including different Arabic dialects and variation in traditional foods. Furthermore, Iraqi Shiites are more rural, resulting in a more conservative pattern of religion and culture, as compared with Lebanese Shiites and Iraqi Sunnis, both of whom are more urbanized and assimilate more easily. Since Iraqi Shiites may not be comfortable with the patterns of Muslims who preceded them, some developed their own mosques and other organizations.

It is important to note that the mosque is not equivalent to a Christian church, which is often used for social gatherings such as weddings. Mosques are centers for prayer and should not be used for such nonreligious activities. They are also primarily gathering places for men. Women either do not go to the mosque or must enter by a separate door or congregate in a separate area. Muslim marriages are family matters and are usually conducted in the home. In America, many marriage ceremonies have been moved to the mosque, but associated social events are usually held separately. Muslim communities often resolve these issues by developing a communal center, with an area for prayer equivalent to a mosque, and a separate area for social gatherings and educational activities. Both Sunnis and Shiites have developed such centers in the United States.

Traditions of the Jewish community in Baghdad were distinctly different from those of European Jewish communities, the origin of most American Jews. European Jews follow the Ashkenazic tradition, which originated in Germany. In contrast, Iraqi Jews follow the Sephardic traditions, common throughout Asia,

Imam Husaini leads a group of Iraqi immigrants in prayer at the Karbala Islamic Center in Dearborn, Michigan. (Courtesy of MaryCay Sengstock)

Northern Africa, and Spain. These distinctions are not primarily religious in character but refer to various cultural traditions. For the most part, however, Iraqi Jews have been incorporated into the larger American Jewish community.

Language Issues and the Media

Most Iraqis in the United States are Christians from the province of Mosul, in northern Iraq near the ancient city of Nineveh. They speak Aramaic rather than Arabic. Hence they differ from Iraqis as a whole in both religion and language. While Christian Iraqis are divided by religion, the one characteristic they share is their ancestral linguistic heritage. Recent Christian immigrants are more likely to know Arabic, but many still value the Aramaic heritage. Iraqi Christian churches often hold services in Arabic or English, to accommodate the needs and preferences of recent immigrants, or for second- or third-generation descendants who know only English. Muslims, on the other hand, speak Arabic. The few Kurdish Iraqis prefer to speak their traditional Kurdish, rather than Arabic. Iraqi Jews are generally integrated into the Jewish community, where English is generally spoken.

Efforts to perpetuate their linguistic and religious identity have taken numerous forms in the Assyrian and Chaldean communities. The Assyrian linguistic heritage is highlighted in a publication entitled *Nineveh*, published by the Assyrian Foundation of America; the title pays homage to the ancient Mesopotamian city by that name. Members of Detroit's Chaldean community publish a monthly newspaper, *The Chaldean News*. Iraqi Jewish congregations in New York and Los Angeles have developed newsletters to assist Iraqi Jews in maintaining their identity and contact with each other.

Celebration of National Holidays

Iraqi holidays are not generally celebrated. However, religious holy days and religious festivals related to each group's religious preference are celebrated. Christians recognize the traditional Christian observances (Christmas, Lent, Easter), which they commemorate in ways similar to those in their homeland. Religious ceremonies are conducted in Aramaic, and some traditions, such as the Chaldeans' Lenten fast, tend to be more rigorous than in the American Catholic Church. Iraqi Muslims observe the annual Ramadan fast and the traditional Muslim feasts. In particular, Shiite Muslims commemorate the Karbala battle, which is viewed as the birth of the Shi'a sect.

With regard to American holidays, some Iraqis have adapted their food patterns to American customs. For example, Thanksgiving is celebrated in Chaldean households, much as it would be in typically American households, with the traditional turkey dinner. Side dishes, however, are likely to include a combination of American and Chaldean foods.

Foodways

Iraqi Americans have maintained many original food patterns. The Middle Eastern style of food preparation tends to be shared by both Christian and Muslim Iraqis. Both groups eat a great deal of lamb, rice, and pita bread; they also share a taste for dishes such as falafel (fried chickpea balls), hummus (a dip made from chickpeas), shish kebab (cubes of meat and vegetables grilled on a skewer), dolma (stuffed grape leaves), kibbeh (a ground meat and bulghur wheat dish), and pastries such as baklava (Najor 1981). Jewish Iraqis are likely to follow the food patterns of other American Jews, including keeping kosher for those who follow the Orthodox or Conservative tradition.

Islamic law also governs food patterns, including a prohibition against eating pork, abstention from alcohol, and use of only *hallal* meats, which have been slaughtered in a ritually specified manner. Muslims are also required to fast during the holy month of Ramadan, which is determined by the lunar calendar and can occur at various times throughout the year. This fast is particularly rigorous, requiring the observer to abstain from all food and drink during daylight hours, and partake of a ritual meal after sundown. The requirement can cause problems for the devout Muslim in a non-Muslim society, where work or school schedules require their presence throughout the fasting period. Christian Iraqis do not follow these restrictions.

Music, Arts, and Entertainment

Christian Iraqi Americans are just beginning to establish themselves in the world of arts and entertainment. Some actors and musicians are finding their way into the media, particularly at the local level, but also, to a limited extent, in the national media. Recently arrived Muslim Iraqis are less likely to have moved into these areas. To some degree, they are still limited by the prohibitions against secular entertainment prevalent in Shiite Muslim tradition.

Integration and Impact on U.S. Society and Culture

Christian Iraqis tend to be more assimilated into American life than Muslim Iraqis. This is due, in part, to their longer period of time in the United States. It is also a reflection of the fact that Christians may find it easier to adjust to a Christian society than Muslims. Followers of Islam are more likely to settle in areas with immigrants from other Islamic nations. Since the differences between Iraqi Jews and other Jews are cultural rather than religious, Iraqi Jews have merged into the broader Jewish community upon their arrival in the United States.

The plight of Iraqi Muslims, particularly Shiites, is also complicated by the fact that some do not, as yet, consider themselves to be permanent immigrants. Like most ethnic communities, Iraqis are greatly influenced by factors in the homeland. Each upheaval in Iraq has an impact upon them. Unlike the Christians and many Sunnis, some Iraqi Shiites are still committed to Iraqi society and hold a dream that conditions will improve, enabling them to return to a more peaceful Iraq. In many ways they resemble the Palestinian community, which is distressed by the absence of a Palestinian state and still longs for a homeland. As long as the dream of a new Iraq remains alive, some are likely to resist acculturation and attempt to retain as much of Iraqi Shiite culture as possible.

Paths toward Citizenship

Attaining citizenship has long been a goal among Iraqi Christians, because it enables them to sponsor the immigration of their relatives. Most Iraqi Christians seem committed to the goal of recreating a new homeland for their Assyrian or Chaldean heritage in North America. Some Shiite Muslims hope for a change in Iraq, such that they could return to their homeland. As they adapt and have children born in America, they will feel more tied to American society, as their predecessors did before them, and seek citizenship. The number of Iraqis seeking citizenship has increased in recent years (see Table 170).

Dual citizenship was generally not a major goal among most Christian Iraqis. However, when the Iraqi elections were held in January 2009, many Iraqi Americans, both Christian and Muslim, took advantage of the opportunity to vote.

The earliest Iraqi immigrants tended to remain within their group and had little relations with outsiders. This was particularly true of Chaldeans, whose population was large enough to be relatively self-sufficient. Other Christian communities, as well as Iraqis Jews, were often forced to move outside the ethnic group. Recently, most Christian and Jewish Iraqis are becoming quite integrated into American life and are developing positive relations outside the ethnic circle. Muslim Iraqis, having come more recently, are less integrated into American society but are becoming integrated into the American Muslim community as a whole.

It is difficult to view Iraqi Americans as a political entity due to their religious divisions. Instead, they constitute a minimum of three separate entities, although efforts to unite the groups around a common cause have developed around the problems in Iraq since 1990.

Iraqi Americans who choose to become active in American politics do so through normal political parties and pressure groups. There have been some recent efforts on the part of Christian Iraqis to work together to influence American government policy with reference to Iraq and Iraqi refugees. Some Iraqi Muslims have also been involved in such actions. These actions have involved community leaders, including religious leaders. Only rarely do Muslim and Christian groups work together.

Iraqi Americans have worked through existing political organizations more often than developing their own. In the last few decades of the 20th century, Iraqi Americans have begun to express interest in the political structure. Some have run for political office, often successfully. Upon occasion, Iraqi Americans attend or hold political rallies for political candidates.

Political issues of most interest to Iraqi Americans focus on conditions in Iraq during the periods of war. On domestic issues, some Iraqi Chaldeans, as devout Catholics, have become involved with the antiabortion movement. Muslims are particularly concerned about freedom of religion, a matter of particular concern for them in a society that is not based on Islamic law; the United States is one of the few nations Muslims consider to be hospitable to the free practice of their religion.

Christian and Jewish Iraqi Americans exhibit little interest in returning to Iraq. Shiite Muslims may be interested in returning but are unlikely to do so under current conditions.

The Second and Later Generations

Ethnic Identity

Detroit's Chaldean community constitutes the largest and earliest community of Iraqis in the United States. It now includes third-, fourth-, and even fifth-generation descendents, as well as persons of non-Chaldean ancestry married into the community. Most Christian Iraqi immigrants adapt rapidly to American society. They learn English quickly and obtain employment, often within the ethnic community. Descendants of the immigrants often obtain higher education and move into non-ethnic occupations (Sengstock 1999, 2005).

Second-generation Shiite Iraqis tend to be less influenced by conditions in their parents' homeland. They are more influenced by conditions in the United States and the community leadership they encounter. American-born Iraqi Muslims are obtaining an American education and moving into professional careers. Gradually, the divisions of their parents' homeland have less influence. As they attend school and participate in community settings, they encounter Muslims from other nationalities and religious sects who have already adapted to America. Consequently, old world identity factors begin to decrease in importance. The newer generation becomes less likely to identify as Iraqi or Lebanese, Sunni or Shiite, and is more likely to cross nationality and sectarian divisions for religious services, friendships, even marriage. Community leaders recognize that an identity as "American Muslim" is being developed, and Iraqi Muslims, both Shiites and Sunnis, are gradually becoming part of that broader identity.

Educational Attainment and Cultural Identification

Christian and Jewish Iraqi Americans of the second and subsequent generations are likely to be college-educated. This is also true of the few Sunni Iraqis. As the second generation of Shiite Iraqis grows up, many aim for higher education as well.

Cultural identification among Iraqi Americans depends largely on religion. Most Christian and Jewish Iraqis identify with ancient Mesopotamia and the Assyrian, Chaldean, and Babylonian cultures, rather than with modern Iraq. If one reads their publications or visits their churches and community centers, one is likely to see Babylonian representations, such as the Lion of Babylon, Gates of Ishtar, or Hanging Gardens, rather than symbols of Iraq and the Arab world, all of which are associated with the Muslim tradition. Muslims, on the other hand, generally identify with Iraq, Islam, and the Arab world.

Youth Profile

Active in Community Service

Andrew Bashi was born in Detroit, Michigan, in 1987; his parents are Chaldean immigrants from Iraq. Like many Chaldean youth, Andrew was educated in Catholic schools, attending St. Hugo grade school and the University of Detroit Jesuit High School. From a young age, he was interested in conditions in his parents' homeland. He recalls being teased in grade school because of the actions of Saddam Hussein in Iraq. He empathized with family members remaining in Iraq. After high school, Andrew attended Oakland University, in Rochester Hills, Michigan, receiving a Bachelor of Arts degree in International Relations in 2009, with a concentration in the Middle East and North Africa. He also took classes in both the Arabic and Aramaic languages and received numerous honors and scholarships.

Throughout his college years, Andrew was active in community service activities, including assisting elderly deaf families in New Orleans following Hurricane Katrina, and building homes for Mexican laborers in Texas. He has also developed social programs for Iraqi refugees coming into the United States, with particular emphasis on assisting Iraqi youth in adjusting to life in America, and becoming responsible and successful in their new lives. Andrew has also been active in numerous organizations representing the various dimensions of Iraqi identity, including the Syriac community in New Jersey, Assyrians in Chicago, Chaldeans in Detroit, and numerous Arab American organizations. He plans to attend Loyola University School of Law in Chicago to prepare for a career in public interest law.

Issues in Relations between the United States and Iraq

Until recently, Iraqi Christians were relatively uninvolved in American politics. The democratic process is largely foreign to Iraqis. This is changing as a result of two major circumstances. One is the increasing number of second, third, and successive generation community members, who are more knowledgeable about American government and the political process. This has led to increased political involvement, including a number of persons running for and being elected to political offices. Involvement in the political sphere also received considerable stimulus from the deteriorating situation in Iraq, where the basic necessities of life, such as food, clean water, and sanitary facilities, are scarce or nonexistent. Iraqi American Christians are particularly concerned about the plight of Christians in Iraq: churches have been bombed, and priests and bishops kidnapped and killed; many Iraqi-Americans have lost relatives to the violence.

These tragedies have led the heretofore nonpolitical Assyrians and Chaldeans to become politically active. This activity has taken the form of articles in their publications, Web sites, and contacts with their political representatives in the federal government. This tragedy has even generated contacts between clergy and members of different Iraqi Christian groups, which previously had little experience working together. Efforts have been made to provide direct assistance to the homeland. Lack of confidence in either Iraqi or U.S. government agencies lead Iraqi Americans to hire their own agents to carry relief supplies directly to friends and relatives. At the same time, most Iraqi Christians have little hope that their efforts will be of much use to those suffering in the Mesopotamia they consider their ancestral home.

Forecasts for the 21st Century

With the continued unrest in Iraq, Iraqi Americans are likely to continue to bring their relatives to the United States. Consequently, they are also likely to continue their ties to Iraq and their attempts to influence public policy both in Iraq and the United States. They may begin to work together with other Iraqi Americans across religious lines, although the internal divisions among the different linguistic groups and denominations are likely to remain strong. Most Iraqi Christians and Jews already consider themselves Americans, though they maintain a nostalgic commitment to their Mesopotamian roots and attempt to aid relatives and friends still in Iraq. Shiite Muslims are unlikely to achieve their goal of returning to Iraq, since the violence is unlikely to subside to a significant degree. Over time, they too are likely to become established and have American-born children and grandchildren; they will adjust to American culture and develop community resources similar to those their predecessors established in previous generations.

Appendix I: Migration Statistics

Table 164 U.S. states with largest population of Iraqi-born (2000 Census: Total U.S. = 89,892)

States	No. of Iraqi Foreign-Born in State	Percent of Total Foreign-Born in State
Michigan	31,927	6.10
California	20,532	0.23
Illinois	9,634	0.63
Tennessee	2,766	1.74
Texas	2,752	0.09
New York	2,721	0.07
Arizona	2,456	0.37

Table 165 U.S. cities with largest population of Iraqi-born (2000 Census)

Cities	No. of Iraqi Foreign-Born in City	Percent of Total Foreign-Born in City
Detroit, MI	30,569	9.12
Chicago, IL	9,513	0.67
San Diego, CA	7,507	1.24
Los Angeles, CA	5,499	0.16
Phoenix, Mesa, AZ	2,343	0.51
Nashville, TN	2,143	3.72
Washington, DC	1,797	0.22

Table 166 Immigrants from Iraq admitted to United States annually from 1989 to 2001

1989: 1,516	1996: 5,481
1990: 1,756	1997: 3,244
1991: 1,494	1998: 2,220
1992: 4,111	1999: 3,372
1993: 4,072	2000: 5,134
1994: 6,025	2001: 4,985
1995: 5,596	Total (1989–2001): 49,006

Table 167 Iraqis obtaining legal permanent resident status by country of birth, as compared with the overall total: Fiscal years 2000 to 2009

Region and Country of Birth	2000	2001	2002	2003	2004	2005	2006	2007	2008	2009
Total	841,002	1,058,902	1,059,356	703,542	957,883	1,122,257	1,266,129	1,052,415	1,107,126	1,130,818
Iraq	5,087	4,965	5,174	2,450	3,494	4,077	4,337	3,765	4,795	12,110

Source: U.S. Department of Homeland Security. Office of Immigration Statistics. 2010. Adapted from Table 3.

Appendix II: Demographics/Census Statistics

Table 168 Iraqis obtaining legal permanent resident status during fiscal year 2009 by leading states of residence

Characteristic	Total	Male	Female
Total	12,110	6,206	5,904
Arizona	751	369	382
California	2,768	1,425	1,343
Colorado	150	89	61
Connecticut	71	44	27
Florida	175	84	91
Georgia	217	97	120
Illinois	760	360	400
Maryland	127	62	65
Massachusetts	139	69	70
Michigan	2,691	1,309	1,382
Minnesota	68	34	34
New Jersey	91	47	44
New York	289	151	138
North Carolina	177	96	81
Ohio	153	79	74
Pennsylvania	231	124	107
Texas	813	451	362
Virginia	559	295	264
Washington	244	125	119

Source: Adapted from U.S. Department of Homeland Security. Profiles on Legal Permanent Residents: 2009.

Table 169 Religious groups in the Iraqi American population as reported by U.S. Census data and community estimates

Ancestry Category	Census 2000 (Ancestry Only)	Community Estimates (Immigrant + Ancestry)
Iraqi (probably Muslim)	37,714	50,000
Chaldean	(not enumerated)	150,000
Assyrian/Syriac	(not enumerated)	30,000–50,000
Assyrian/Chaldean/Syriac	82,154	(180,000–200,000)
Jewish	(not enumerated)	15,000
Totals	119,868	245,000–265,000

Note: Census data on the Iraqi population is inaccurate; hence most scholars make use of community population estimates, which have limitations as well. This table provides both sets of data for the reader's information.

Table 170 Iraqi immigrants becoming U.S. citizens annually from 1994 to 2001

1994	1,808
1995	1,609
1996	2,309
1997	1,621
1998	2,033
1999	3,230
2000	5,217
2001	3,451

Appendix III: Notable Iraqi Americans

Dr. Nathima Atchoo is an obstetrician/gynecologist who practices through the Gary Burnstein Community Health Clinic in Pontiac, Michigan. She frequently traveled to the Middle East to treat refugees and received the "Chaldean Humanitarian of the Year" award in 2009 from the Chaldean Federation of Michigan. The Burnstein Clinic named her an "Esteemed Woman of Michigan" in 2010. (http://www.garyburnsteinclinic.org/EsteemedWomen.html)

Dr. Hind Rassam Culhane is cochair of the Social and Behavioral Sciences Division, Mercy College, Dobbs Ferry, New York.

Wadie P. Deddeh is a former senator of the California State Assembly.

Imam Husham al-Husainy is director of the Karbalaa Education Center of America, Dearborn, Michigan.

Mar Sarhad Jammo is bishop of the Chaldean Church in the Western United States, St. Peter's Chaldean Catholic Cathedral, El Cajon, California.

Mar Ibrahim Ibrahim is bishop of the Chaldean Church in Eastern North America, Mother of God Church, Southfield, Michigan.

Joseph Kassab is executive director of the Chaldean Federation of America and leader of refugee assistance programs.

Dr. Majid Khadduri (1909–2007) was the founder of the Graduate Middle East Studies Program, Johns Hopkins University, Baltimore, Maryland.

Imam Hassan al-Qazwini is Imam of the Islamic Center of America, Dearborn, Michigan. According to his Web site, he has worked to "depict a genuine representation of Islam and Muslims. He has thus far spoken at over a hundred churches, colleges and universities about the genuine and authentic teachings of Islam, thereby dispelling the common misconceptions about Muslims in America" (http://alqazwini.org/qazwini_org/).

Ahmed Qusai al-Taayie is a sergeant in the U.S. Army and a linguist. He was kidnapped in Iraq on October 23, 2006. There have been demands for ransom on his behalf, as well as reports that he has been killed, the most recent in February, 2010. He remains the only member of the American military still listed as missing in Iraq.

Heather Raffo is a playwright and actress who has presented her works off-Broadway and on tour. In her plays and acting she attempts to introduce American audiences to what it means to be an Iraqi woman. (http://www. heatherraffo.com/9parts.html).

Alia Martine Shawkat is an actress who has been in several films, most recently playing an Arab American teenager in *Amreeka*. She also played in *State of Grace*, for the Fox Family channel, and in *Arrested Development*, on Fox Network, the role for which she is probably best known. (http://www.starglimpse.com/celebs/pages/alia_shawkat/alia_shawkat.shtml)

Glossary

Baklava: A sweet Middle Eastern pastry.

Ba'th: Political party in Iraq and the Arab world.

Bulghur: Cracked wheat, used in Middle Eastern cuisine.

Cailiph: A religious leader in early Islam.

Dolma: Stuffed grape leaves.

Falafel: Fried chickpea balls.

Fatwah: Religious opinions issued by Islamic leaders.

Karbala: Shiite religious shrine in southern Iraq.

Kibbeh: A ground meat and wheat dish.

Haj: Pilgrimage to Mecca.

Hallal: Meat that has been processed according to Islamic ritual requirements.

Hijab: A veil covering the head, worn by Muslim women.

Hummus: A dip made from chickpeas.

Quran: Islamic holy book.

Rite: A cultural subgroup of the Roman Catholic Church with a unique ritual.

Shari'a: Religious law of Islam.

Shi'a, Shiite: The largest denomination of Islam in Iraq.

Sunnah: Practices of the Prophet Muhammad.

Sunni: The largest denomination of Islam in the Middle East.

Zakat: Alms required under Islamic law.

References

Abraham, Nabeel. 2000. "Arab Detroit's 'American' Mosque." In *Arab Detroit: From Margin to Mainstream,* edited by Nabeel Abraham and Andrew Shryock, 279–309. Detroit, MI: Wayne State University Press.

Baltimore Sun Staff. 2009. "Iraqi Refugee Timeline." *Baltimore Sun,* December 18. [Online article retrieved 6/18/09.] http://www.orlandosentinel.com/services/newspaper/printedition/bal-iraqirefugeetimeline,0,4242845.story?page=1.

Barazangi, Nimat Hafez. 1996. "Parents and Youth." In *Family and Gender Among American Muslims,* edited by Barbara C. Aswad and Barbara Bilge, 129–42. Philadelphia, PA: Temple University Press.

Bardazzi, Marco. 2009. "The Diaspora of the Christians /1 That Corner of Iraq in Detroit." Oasis Center. [Online article retrieved 7/18/09.] http://www.oasiscenter.eu/en/node/2590.

Brown, Matthew Hay. 2008. "U.S. Slow to Meet Needs, Refugees Say." *Baltimore Sun,* December 29. [Online article retrieved 6/18/09.] http://www.orlandosentinel.com/services/newspaper/printedition/bal-te.refugee29dec29,0,83186.story.

Cainkar, Louise. 1996. "Immigrant Palestinian Women Evaluate Their Lives." In *Family and Gender Among American Muslims,* edited by Barbara C. Aswad and Barbara Bilge, 41–58. Philadelphia, PA: Temple University Press.

Grieco, Elizabeth. 2003. "Iraqi Immigrants in the United States." Migration Policy Institute. [Online article retrieved 6/18/09.] http://www.migrationinformation.org/USfocus/print.cfm?ID=113.

Haddad, Yvonne Y., and Jane I. Smith. 1996. "Islamic Values among American Muslims." In *Family and Gender Among American Muslims,* edited by Barbara C. Aswad and Barbara Bilge, 19–40. Philadelphia, PA: Temple University Press.

International Rescue Committee. 2009. "Iraqi Refugees in the United States: In Dire Straits." [Online article retrieved 6/20/09.] http://www.theirc.org/special-report/iraqi-refugee-crisis.html.

Kohn, Joe. 2008. "Chaldean Bishop Ibrahim N. Ibrahim: 'No One Is Defending Us'." *Catholic Online.* [Online article retrieved 6/3/09.] http://www.catholic.org/international/international_story.php?id=27184.

Leonard, Karen I. 2003. *Muslims in the United States.* New York: Russell Sage.

Lobe, Jim. 2007. "Iraq Exodus Fuels Rise in Refugees, Displaced." Inter Press Service, July 11. [Online article retrieved 6/18/09.] http://www.globalpolicy.org/component/content/article/167-attack/35667.html.

Najor, Julia. 1981. *Babylonian Cuisine: Chaldean Cookbook from The Middle East.* Detroit, MI: Nationalbooks, International.

Patheos. 2009. "Islam Rites and Ceremonies." [Online article retrieved 8/23/09.] http://www.patheos.com/Library/Islam/Ritual-Worship-Devotion-Symbolism/Rites-and-Ceremonies.html.

Ricks, Thomas E. 2007. *Fiasco: The American Military Adventure in Iraq.* New York: Penguin Books.

Roux, Georges. 1992. *Ancient Iraq,* 3rd ed. New York: Penguin Books.

Schopmeyer, Kim. 2000. "A Demographic Portrait of Arab Detroit." In *Arab Detroit: From Margin to Mainstream,* edited by Nabeel Abraham and Andrew Shryock, 61–92. Detroit, MI: Wayne State University Press.

Sengstock, M.C. 1996. "Care of the Elderly within Muslim Families." In *Family and Gender Among American Muslims,* edited by Barbara C. Aswad and Barbara Bilge, 271–97. Philadelphia, PA: Temple University Press.

Sengstock, M.C. 1999. *Chaldean-Americans: Changing Conceptions of Ethnic Identity.* Staten Island, NY: Center for Migration Studies.

Sengstock, M.C. 2005. *Chaldeans in Michigan.* East Lansing: Michigan State University Press.

Shohet, Maurice. 1999. *Iraqi Jews.* New York: Congregation Bene Naharayim. [Online article retrieved 6/1/09.] http://www.iraqijews.org/.

Tate, Deborah. 2009. "US Senate Panel Considers Plight of Iraqi Refugees." *Voice of America News,* March 31. [Online article retrieved 6/18/09.] http://sz104.ev.mail.net/service/home/'/US%20Senate%2oPanel%20Considers%20Plight%20of%20Refugees.htm?auth=co&loc.

Tirman, John. 2009. "Iraq's Shocking Human Toll: About 1Million Killed, 4.5 Million Displaced, 1–2 Million Widows, 5 Million Orphans." *Alternet,* February 2. [Online article retrieved 6/18/09.] http://www.alternet.org/world/123818/iraq%27s_shocking_human_toll%3A_about_1_million_killed%2C_4.5_million_displaced%2C_1–2_million_widows%2C_5_million_orphans/.

Tripp, Charles. 2007. *A History of Iraq,* 3rd ed. Cambridge, UK: Cambridge University Press.

Walbridge, Linda S., and T.M. Aziz. 2000. "After Karbala: Iraqi Refugees in Detroit." In *Arab Detroit: From Margin to Mainstream,* edited by Nabeel Abraham and Andrew Shryock, 321–42. Detroit, MI: Wayne State University Press.

Wiswell, Joyce. 2007. "A New Life: First Iraqi Refugees Arrive." *Chaldean News,* September 1. [Online article retrieved 8/26/09.] http://www.chaldeannews.com/index.cfm?articleid=718.

Further Reading

Abraham, Nabeel, and Andrew Shryock, eds. 2000. *Arab Detroit: From Margin to Mainstream.* Detroit, MI: Wayne State University Press.

A series of research reports on the Muslim communities in the Detroit Metropolitan Area, which is the major concentration of Middle Eastern immigrants in the United States.

"About Nineveh and Assyrians, Who Are We?" [Online article retrieved 8/26/09.] http://www.nineveh.com.

This Web site is dedicated to the interests and concerns of persons, many of them Iraqis, who identify as Assyrians. Attention is paid to the controversies about identity patterns of persons of Assyrian backgrounds. Available in several languages to serve the needs of Assyrians in various parts of the globe.

"Assyrian/Chaldean/Syriac-Americans." [Online article retrieved 8/26/09.] http://www.answers.com/topic/assyrians-in-the-united-states.

A Web site associated with Wikipedia and Answers.com, providing information on Christians from the Middle East who identify as Assyrian, Chaldean, or Syriac; many of these are from Iraq.

Assyrian Community. [Online information retrieved 8/26/09.] http://www.assyrian4all.net.

A Web site to bring Assyrian and Chaldean Christians together. Provides an opportunity for them to meet others, post pictures, obtain information, and the like. Some text is in Aramaic.

Assyrian Voice. [Online information retrieved 8/26/09.] http://www.assyrianvoice.net.

A Web site to enable persons who identify as Assyrians to maintain contact with each other, and obtain information on religion, history, sports, celebrities, and the like.

Aswad, Barbara C., and Barbara Bilge, eds. 1996. *Family and Gender Among American Muslims*. Philadelphia, PA: Temple University Press.

A collection of essays about family patterns in American Muslim communities from several Middle Eastern and Asian nations.

Chaldean American Chamber of Commerce. [Online information retrieved 8/26/09.] http://www.chaldeanchamber.com.

This Web site is sponsored by the business association of Detroit's Chaldean community. It serves as an information and communication mechanism for the extensive Chaldean business community.

Chaldean Federation. [Online information retrieved 7/16/09.] http://chaldeanfederation.org.

This Web site was established by the federation of Chaldean organizations throughout the United States. It reports issues of concern to the community, particularly relating to the conditions of Christians in Iraq, and Iraqi Christian refugees in the Middle East and the United States.

The Chaldean News. Farmington Hills, MI.

A monthly newsletter published by the Chaldean community of Metropolitan Detroit. Provides information on activities of the local community, as well as reports and commentary on international status of Chaldeans.

Christian Assyrians of Iraq. [Online information retrieved 8/26/09.] http://www.christiansofiraq.com/sympo.html.

This Web site is devoted to providing the international community with information on conditions experienced by Assyrian Christians from Iraq. It contains reports from common news sources.

Hebrew Immigrant Aid Society. [Online information retrieved 7/16/09.] http://www.hias.org.

This Web site is devoted to the welfare of Jewish refugees throughout the world. It provides assistance and a source of communication. This group has provided considerable assistance to Iraqi Jews.

Marr, Phebe. 2004. *The Modern History of Iraq,* 2nd ed. Boulder, CO: Westview Press.

A detailed description and analysis of modern Iraqi history, from the British Mandate in 1920 to the early stages of the 2003 Iraq War.

Miller, John, and Aaron Kenedi, eds. 2002. *Inside Iraq.* New York: Marlowe & Co.

A series of journalistic essays on conditions in Iraq leading up to the 2003 war in Iraq.

Nineveh.

This quarterly publication of the Assyrian Foundation of America provides information on Assyrian-speaking communities in the United States, primarily those that identify as Assyrian or Syriac.

Perry, Bryon. 2008. *The Chaldeans.* West Bloomfield, MI: Chaldean Cultural Center.

An elegantly illustrated volume of essays about history, representatives, and events in the Chaldean Community of Metropolitan Detroit.

Suleiman, Michael, ed. 1999. *Arabs in America: Building a New Future.* Philadelphia, PA: Temple University Press.

A series of essays analyzing the status of Arabs in the United States and Canada, and their views on various aspects of life in North America.

Zinda Magazine—Periodical For The International Assyrian Community. [Online information retrieved 8/26/09.] http://www.zindamagazine.com.

Zinda is a weekly online magazine that promotes the use of the Assyrian language.